Writing with POWER

Contributing Author
Joyce Senn

Senior Consultants
Constance Weaver
Peter Smagorinsky

Language

Composition

21st Century Skills

Perfection Learning®

Editorial

Editorial Director	Carol Francis
Executive Editor	Jim Strickler
Editorial Team	Gay Russell-Dempsey, Terry Ofner, Kate Winzenburg, Sue Thies, Andrea Stark, Paula Reece

Design

Art Director	Randy Messer
Design Team	Tobi Cunningham, Deborah Bell, Emily Greazel, Mike Aspengren, Jane Wonderlin, Dea Marks, Lori Zircher, Jill Kimpston
Illustration/Diagrams	Mike Aspengren, Sue Cornelison
Image Research	Anjanette Houghtaling

Joyce Senn taught both middle and high school before putting her experience and love of language to work in her distinguished career as educational consultant and author. Specializing in grammar, Senn was a pioneer in textbook publishing in her use of themed activities, helping to provide a context for once-isolated grammar, usage, and mechanics practice. Senn's other publications include the acclaimed children's reference book *Quotations for Kids* (Millbrook Press, 1999) and *Information Literacy: Educating Children for the 21st Century* (with Patricia Breivik, National Education Association, 2nd Ed., 1998).

Special thanks to Joan McElroy, Ph.D., for contributions to the research strand of *Writing with Power*, and to David Kulieke, English instructor and consultant, for his review of the grammar, usage, and mechanics chapters.

All rights reserved. No part of this book may be used or reproduced, stored in a retrieval system or transmitted by any means electronic, mechanical, photocopying, recording, or otherwise, without written permission from the publisher.

Printed in the United States of America

Copyright © 2011
by Perfection Learning® Corporation
1000 North Second Avenue
P.O. Box 500
Logan, Iowa 51546-0500
Tel: 1-800-831-4190 • Fax: 1-800-543-2745
perfectionlearning.com

2 3 4 5 6 7 WC 16 15 14 13 12
ISBN 13: 978-1-61563-626-6
ISBN 10: 1-61563-626-9

Senior Consultants

Peter Smagorinsky wrote the activities that form the project-centered "structured process approach" to teaching writing at the heart of the composition units of *Writing with Power*. A high school English teacher for fourteen years, Smagorinsky has also taught in the English Education programs at the University of Oklahoma (1990-1998) and University of Georgia (1998-present). In addition to numerous articles, he has published books through Heinemann (*Teaching English by Design*, 2007, and *The Dynamics of Writing Instruction: A Structured Process Approach for the Composition Teacher in the Middle and High School,* with Larry Johannessen, Elizabeth Kahn, and Thomas McCann, 2010); through Teacher's College Press (*Research on Composition: Multiple Perspectives on Two Decades of Change*, ed., 2006); through Cambridge University Press (*Vygotskian Perspectives on Literacy Research: Constructing Meaning through Collaborative Inquiry*, with Carol D. Lee, 2000; and through the National Council of Teachers of English (NCTE) Press (*Standards in Practice, Grades 9–12,* 1996). For NCTE, he also chaired the Research Forum, co-edited *Research in the Teaching of English*, co-chaired the Assembly for Research, chaired the Standing Committee on Research, chaired the Research Foundation, and served as President of the National Conference on Research in Language and Literacy.

Constance Weaver developed the "power" concept and features for *Writing with Power,* identifying strategies for using grammatical options to add power to writing and thinking as well as developing the "Power Rules," beginning with ten "must know" conventions for success in school and the workplace and expanding into features more relevant for advanced writers. Weaver has shaped English education for more than thirty years, illuminating the relationship between grammar and writing and providing practical, effective teaching guidance, from her earliest works on the subject, the best-selling *Grammar for Teachers* (NCTE, 1979) and the widely acclaimed *Teaching Grammar in Context* (Boynton/Cook, 1996), to her most recent *Grammar Plan Book* (Heinemann, 2007) and *Grammar to Enrich and Enhance Writing* (with Jonathan Bush, Heinemann, 2008). She has also long been a leader in literacy and reading. Her book *Reading Process and Practice* (Heinemann, 1988) is authoritative in its field. In 1996, Weaver was honored by the Michigan Council of Teachers of English with the Charles C. Fries award for outstanding leadership in English education. Weaver is the Heckert Professor of Reading and Writing at Miami University, Oxford, Ohio, and Professor Emerita of English at Western Michigan University, Kalamazoo.

National Advisory Panel

Writing with Power was developed under the guidance of outstanding educators—teachers, curriculum specialists, and supervisors—whose experience helped ensure that the program design was implemented in a practical, engaging way for every classroom.

Middle School

DeVeria A. Berry
Curriculum Specialist
Frank T. Simpson-Waverly School
Hartford Public School
Hartford, Connecticut

Marylou Curley-Flores
Curriculum Specialist
Reading/EnglishLanguage Arts
Curriculum and Instruction
San Antonio Independent School District
San Antonio, Texas

Karen Guajardo
Curriculum Specialist
Reading/English Language Arts
Curriculum and Instruction
San Antonio Independent School District
San Antonio, Texas

Tina DelGiodice
English Teacher/Staff Developer (retired)
Jersey City Public Schools
Jersey City, New Jersey

Julie Hines-Lyman
Curriculum Coach
Agassiz Elementary School
Chicago Public Schools
Chicago, Illinois

Marcia W. Punsalan
Language Arts Department Chair
Clay High School
Oregon City Schools
Oregon, Ohio

Melanie Pogue Semore
Director of Upper School
Harding Academy
Memphis, Tennessee

High School

Nathan H. Busse
English Language Arts Teacher
Fox Tech High School
San Antonio Independent School DIstrict
San Antonio, Texas

Joyce Griggs
Instructional Specialist
Peoria Unified School District
Peoria, Arizona

Jill Haltom
English Language Arts/Reading Director
Coppell Independent School District
Coppell, Texas

Linda M. Moore, M.Ed.
English Instructor
Coppell High School
Coppell Independent School District
Coppell, Texas

Debora Stonich
Secondary English Curriculum Specialist
Humanities Teacher
Lovejoy Independent School District
Lovejoy High School
Allen, Texas

Student Contributors

Writing with Power proudly and gratefully presents the work of the following students, whose writing samples—from effective opening sentences to in-depth literary analyses—show so clearly the power of writing.

**From Lucyle Collins Middle School
Fort Worth, Texas**
Marbella Maldonado
Victor Ramirez

**From Evanston Township High School
Evanston, Illinois**
Morgan Nicholls

**From Canton South High School
Canton, Ohio**
Griffin Burns
Cody Collins
Marti Doerschuk
Reanna Eckroad
Erica Gallon
Lindsay Kerr
Elise Miller
Katie Smith
Natalie Volpe

Contents in Brief

Unit 1 — Style and Structure of Writing — 2

1. A Community of Writers — 4
2. Using Words Powerfully — 34
3. Writing with Sentence Variety — 60
4. Writing Well-Structured Paragraphs — 82
5. Writing Effective Compositions — 100

Unit 2 — Purposes of Writing — 124

6. Personal Writing — 126
7. Descriptive Writing — 150
8. Creative Writing — 174
9. Expository Writing — 210
10. Writing to Persuade — 240
11. Writing About Literature — 266

Unit 3 — Research and Report Writing — 300

12. Research: Planning and Gathering Information — 302
    Research Companion — *322*
13. Research: Synthesizing, Organizing, and Presenting — 340

Guide to 21st Century School and Workplace Skills — 362

Unit 4 Grammar — 474

14	The Sentence	476
15	Nouns and Pronouns	502
16	Verbs	520
17	Adjectives and Adverbs	536
18	Other Parts of Speech and Review	558
19	Complements	578
20	Phrases	598
21	Verbals and Verbal Phrases	616
22	Clauses	636
23	Sentence Fragments and Run-ons	660

Unit 5 Usage — 676

24	Using Verbs	678
25	Using Pronouns	708
26	Subject and Verb Agreement	738
27	Using Adjectives and Adverbs	766

Unit 6 Mechanics — 800

28	Capital Letters	802
29	End Marks and Commas	828
30	Italics and Quotation Marks	858
31	Other Punctuation	878
32	Spelling Correctly	906

Language QuickGuide	934
Glossary	960
Index	983

COMPOSITION

UNIT 1 Style and Structure of Writing 2

1 A Community of Writers 4

Writing with Power 5
  1 The Six Traits 5
  2 The Power of Language 7
  3 The Power Rules 8
  4 Writing in the 21st Century 12

Collaborating Through the Writing Process 13
  1 Prewriting: Getting Started 13
    Collaboration in Action: Prewriting 17
  2 Prewriting: From Ideas to a Plan 18
  3 Drafting 21
  4 Revising 22

Using a Six-Trait Rubric 23
  Collaboration in Action: Revising 25
  5 Editing and Publishing 28

Timed Writing: On Your Own 33

2 Using Words Powerfully 34

Writing Project: The Way I See It *Imaginative* 34
Developing Your Style and Voice 38
Varieties of the English Language 39
  1 Dialects and Standard American English 39
  2 Nonstandard American English 40

Choosing Vivid Words 42
  1 Denotations and Connotations 42
    In the Media: Advertising 43

	2 Using Specific Words	44
	3 Finding Synonyms	46
	4 Appealing to the Senses	47

⚡ *The Power of Language:*
Adverbs and Prepositional Phrases — 51

    Think Critically: Elaborating — 54

    The Language of Power: Run-on Sentences — 55

  5 Tired Words — 56

Using a Word Choice Rubric — 57

Writing Lab — 58

3 Writing with Sentence Variety — 60

Writing Project: Facing Fear
Personal Narrative — 60

Writing Varied Sentences — 64

  1 Sentence Combining with Specific Details — 64

⚡ *The Power of Language:* Appositives — 67

  2 Combining Sentence Parts — 68

    The Language of Power: Agreement — 69

  3 Creating Compound Sentences — 70

    Think Critically: Seeing Relationships — 72

  4 Varying Sentence Beginnings — 73

    In the Media: Television Nightly News — 74

Writing Concise Sentences — 75

  1 Rambling Sentences — 75

  2 Repetition — 77

Using a Fluency Rubric — 79

Writing Lab — 80

COMPOSITION

4 Writing Well-Structured Paragraphs — 82
Writing Project: Powerful Memories *Memoir* — 82
Paragraph Structure — 86
- 1 Topic Sentence — 87
  - Think Critically: Generalizing — 89
- 2 Supporting Sentences — 91
⚡ **The Power of Language:** Semicolons — 93
- 3 Concluding Sentences — 94
  - The Language of Power: Sound-Alikes — 96
  - In the Media: Magazines, Internet, Newspapers — 97

Writing Lab — 98

5 Writing Effective Compositions — 100
Writing Project: Lives Worth Remembering *Biography* — 100
Composition Writing: Prewriting — 104
- 1 Choosing and Limiting a Subject — 104
- 2 Listing Supporting Details — 106
- 3 Developing the Main Idea — 107
- 4 Arranging Details — 109
  - Think Critically: Ordering — 110
⚡ **The Power of Language:** Phrases — 112
Composition Writing: Drafting — 113
- 1 Drafting the Introduction — 114
- 2 Drafting the Body — 115
- 3 Drafting the Conclusion — 116
  - In the Media: News Styles — 117

Composition Writing: Revising — 118

Composition Writing: Editing		120
The Language of Power: Possessive Nouns		120
Composition Writing: Publishing		121
Writing Lab		122

Unit 2 Purposes of Writing 124

6 Personal Writing 126

Writing Project: Small Acts
Personal Narrative 126

Personal Narrative Structure: Analyzing 129

Personal Narrative Writing: Prewriting 130
 1 Reflecting on an Experience 130
 2 First-Person and Third-Person Narratives 132
 3 Organizational Strategy 133
   Think Critically: Recalling 134

Personal Narrative Writing: Drafting 135
 1 Introduction 135
 2 Transitions 137
⚡ **The Power of Language:** *Adverbs* 138
 3 Adding Specific Details: Zoom In 139
 4 Conclusion 140

Personal Narrative Writing: Revising 141
 1 Checking for Development of Ideas 141
 2 Checking for Unity, Clarity, and Style 142
   In the Media: Television Talk Shows 144

Personal Narrative Writing: Editing 145
   The Language of Power: Pronouns 145

COMPOSITION

Using a Six-Trait Rubric: Personal Narratives	146
Personal Narrative Writing: Publishing	147
Writing Lab	148

7 Descriptive Writing — 150

Writing Project:
The Comfort of the Ordinary *Description* — 150

Elements of Descriptive Writing — 157

1. Structure in Descriptive Writing — 157
2. Specific Details and Sensory Words — 159
   Think Critically: Visualizing — *161*
3. Spatial Order and Transitions — 162

⚡ **The Power of Language:** *Parallelism* — 164

4. Logical Order — 165
   In the Media: Classified Advertisement — *166*
5. The Six Traits — 167
   The Language of Power: Verb Tense — *169*

Writing Lab — 170

Descriptive Writing Workshops — 172

1. Describing an Object — 172
2. Describing a Person — 173

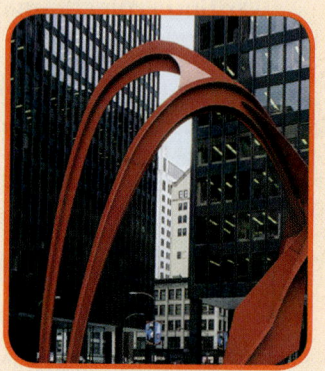

8 Creative Writing — 174

Writing Project: Wishes Denied
Imaginative Story — 174

Analyzing a Story — 181

Writing a Short Story: Prewriting — 184

1. Building an Engaging Plot — 184
2. Sketching Interesting Characters — 185
   Think Critically: Imagining — *186*

3	Creating a Believable Setting	187
4	Ordering and Pacing Events	188

⚡ **The Power of Language:** *Participial Phrases* — 189

Writing a Short Story: Drafting — 190
Writing a Short Story: Revising — 193
Writing a Short Story: Editing and Publishing — 194
    The Language of Power: Past Tense — *194*

Using a Six-Trait Rubric: Stories — 195
Writing a Play — 196
    In the Media: Movies and Plays — *202*

Writing a Poem — 204
Writing Lab — 208

9 Expository Writing — 210

Writing Project: Welcome to My World
Expository — 210

Developing Your Expository Writing Skills — 219
  1 Paragraph and Essay Structure — 219
    In the Media: News Lead-ins — *222*
  2 Methods of Development — 223

⚡ **The Power of Language:** *Strong Verbs* — 224
    Think Critically: Analyzing — *226*
  3 Logical Order and Transitions — 227

Using a Six-Trait Rubric: Expository Writing — 232
Expository Presentations — 233
Writing Lab — 234
Expository Writing Workshops — 236
  1 Explaining Symbols — 236
    The Language of Power: Past Tense — *238*
  2 Giving Directions — 238

COMPOSITION

10 Writing to Persuade — 240
Writing Project: Words into Deeds
Persuasive — 240
Developing Your Skills of Persuasion — 247
1 Structure — 247
2 Facts and Opinions — 249
   In the Media: Opinions and Advertising — 251
3 Other Points of View — 252
   *Think Critically:
   Evaluating Counter-Arguments* — 253
4 Order of Importance and Transitions — 254

⚡ **The Power of Language:** *Say It Again* — 256
Persuasive Writing: Checklist — 257
   The Language of Power: Negatives — 258
Using a Six-Trait Rubric: Persuasive Writing — 259
Writing Lab — 260
Persuasive Writing Workshops — 262
1 Persuading with Examples — 262
2 Persuading with Facts — 264
3 Persuading with Reasons — 265

11 Writing About Literature — 266
Writing Project: Character Analysis
Interpretive Response — 266
Structure of a Literary Analysis — 273
Responding to Literature — 274
1 Responding from Personal Experience — 274
2 Responding from Literary Knowledge — 276

⚡ **The Power of Language:** *Adjectives* — 278
Writing a Character Analysis: Prewriting — 279
1 Choosing a Subject Related to Character — 279

2	Developing a Thesis	281
3	Gathering Evidence	282
4	Organizing Your Details	285

Writing a Character Analysis: Drafting — 286
    In The Media: Evaluating Performances — *289*

Writing a Character Analysis: Revising — 290

Writing a Character Analysis: Editing — 291
    The Language of Power: Of v. Have — *291*

Using a Six-Trait Rubric: Interpretive Response — 292

Writing a Character Analysis: Publishing — 293

Writing a Book Report — 294
    Think Critically: Summarizing — *295*

Writing Lab — 298

UNIT 3 — Research and Report Writing — 300

12 Research: Planning and Gathering Information — 302

Writing Project:
Don't Let Me Be Misunderstood
Research Report — 302

Writing a Research Report: Planning — 308
  1 Structure of a Report — 308
  2 Choosing and Limiting a Subject — 309
  3 Developing Research Questions — 311

Writing a Research Report:
Gathering Information — 312
  1 Finding Sources — 312
    In the Media: Documentary — *314*

COMPOSITION

2 Evaluating Sources	315
Writing a Research Report: Taking Notes	318
Writing Lab	320
Research Companion	322
1 Library Arrangement	322
2 Print and Nonprint Reference Materials	329
3 Using the Internet for Research	337

13 Research: Synthesizing, Organizing, and Presenting — 340

Writing Project: Don't Let Me Be Misunderstood *Research Report* — 340

Writing a Research Report: Synthesizing — 341

Writing a Research Report: Organizing — 342
  1 Organizing Your Notes — 342
    Think Critically: Classifying — *343*
  2 Outlining — 344

⚡ **The Power of Language:** *Fluency* — *346*

Writing a Research Report: Drafting — 347
  1 Drafting the Introduction — 347
  2 Drafting the Body — 349
  3 Drafting the Conclusion — 351
  4 Including Visuals — 352
  5 Citing Sources — 353

Writing a Research Report: Revising — 356

Writing a Research Report: Editing — 357
    The Language of Power: Fragments — *357*

Using a Six-Trait Rubric: Research Reports — 358

Writing a Research Report: Publishing — 359

Writing Lab — 360

Guide to 21st Century School and Workplace Skills — 362

Part I Critical Thinking and Problem Solving for Academic Success — 364

Essential Skills — 364
- Critical Thinking — 364
- Developing Solutions — 365

A. Learning Study Skills — 366
- Developing Effective Study Skills — 367
  - Adjusting Reading Rate to Purpose — 367
  - Taking Notes — 369

B. Taking Standardized Tests — 372
- Strategies for Taking Standardized Tests — 372
  - Vocabulary Tests — 373
  - Analogies — 375
  - Sentence-Completion Tests — 378
  - Reading Comprehension Tests — 380
  - Tests of Standard Written English — 384

C. Taking Essay Tests — 391
- Kinds of Essay Questions — 391
- Writing an Effective Essay Answer — 395
- Timed Writing — 398

Part II Communication and Collaboration — 400

Essential Skills — 400
- Communication — 400

xvii

Composition

Collaboration	401
A. Vocabulary	402
The Growth of the English Language	402
Origins	402
Spelling	404
Pronunciation	404
Meaning	405
Developing Your Dictionary Skills	405
Word Location	405
Information in an Entry	407
Expanding Your Vocabulary	411
Context Clues	411
Base Words, Prefixes, and Suffixes	412
Synonyms	415
Antonyms	416
B. Letters and Forms	418
Real-World Communication	418
Communicating for a Purpose	418
Using Technology to Communicate	418
The Purpose and Format of Letters	419
Writing Personal Letters	419
Writing Business Letters	424
Completing Business Forms	430
C. Directions and Speeches	432
Developing Your Informal Speaking Skills	432
Giving Directions	433
Participating in Group Discussions	434
Developing Your Formal Speaking Skills	435
Preparing Your Speech	435

Practicing Your Speech	439
Delivering Your Speech	439
Developing Your Listening Skills	440
Listening to Enjoy and Appreciate	440
Listening for Information and Taking Notes	441
Listening Critically	443
Listening to Evaluate	445

Part III Media and Technology — 447

Essential Skills — 447
- Information Literacy — 447
- Media Literacy — 448
- Technology Literacy — 448

A. Electronic Publishing — 449
- Desktop Publishing — 449
- Nonprint Media—Audio and Video — 456
- Publishing on the Web — 462

B. Using the Internet — 464
- How Does the Internet Work? — 464
- Communicating on the Internet — 469
  - Using E-mail — 469
  - Other Online Communication — 471

GRAMMAR

Unit 4 Grammar — 474

14 The Sentence — 476
The Sentence: Pretests — 476
- **A Sentence** — 478
- *When You Speak and Write:* Slang vs. Complete Sentences — *478*
- **Complete and Simple Subjects** — 479
  - Complete Subjects — 479
  - Simple Subjects — 480
- **Complete and Simple Predicates** — 481
  - Complete Predicates — 481
  - Simple Predicates, or Verbs — 482
  - Verb Phrases — 484
  - Interrupted Verb Phrases — 485
- **Different Positions of Subjects** — 487
  - Understood Subjects — 488
- ⚡ **Power Your Writing:** Let It Flow — *489*
- **Compound Subjects and Verbs** — 490
  - Compound Subjects — 490
  - Compound Verbs — 491
- **Kinds of Sentences** — 493
- **Sentence Diagraming** — 495
  - Diagraming Subjects and Verbs — 495
- **Chapter Review** — 497
- **The Sentence: Posttest** — 499
- **Writer's Corner** — 500

15 Nouns and Pronouns — 502
Nouns and Pronouns: Pretests — 502
Nouns — 504
When You Write: Specific, Concrete Nouns — 505
   Compound Nouns — 506
   Common and Proper Nouns — 507
Pronouns — 509
   Pronoun Antecedents — 509
   Personal Pronouns — 510
   Reflexive and Intensive Pronouns — 510
   Indefinite Pronouns — 512
   Demonstrative and Interrogative Pronouns — 512
   Relative Pronouns — 513
Chapter Review — 515
Nouns and Pronouns: Posttest — 517
Writer's Corner — 518

16 Verbs — 520
Verbs: Pretests — 520
Action Verbs — 522
Transitive and Intransitive Verbs — 524
⚡ *Power Your Writing:* Getting into the Action — 525
   Helping Verbs — 526
   Linking Verbs — 528
     Additional Linking Verbs — 528
     Linking Verb or Action Verb? — 529
Chapter Review — 531
Verbs: Posttest — 533
Writer's Corner — 534

GRAMMAR

17 Adjectives and Adverbs — 536
Adjectives and Adverbs: Pretests — 536
Adjectives — 538
When You Write: Specific Adjectives — *538*
   Different Positions of Adjectives — 540
   Articles — 541
   Proper Adjectives — 541
   Adjective or Noun? — 543
   Adjective or Pronoun? — 544
⚡ *Power Your Writing:* Adjectives Come Lately — 546
Adverbs — 547
   Adverbs That Modify Verbs — 548
   Adverbs That Modify Adjectives and Other Adverbs — 549
Sentence Diagraming — 551
   Diagraming Adjectives and Adverbs — 551
Chapter Review — 553
Adjectives and Adverbs: Posttest — 555
Writer's Corner — 556

18 Other Parts of Speech and Review — 558
Other Parts of Speech and Review: Pretests — 558
Prepositions — 560
   Prepositional Phrases — 561
   Preposition or Adverb? — 563
⚡ *Power Your Writing:* Fine Points — 565
Conjunctions and Interjections — 566
   Conjunctions — 566

Conjunctive Adverbs	567
Transitions	568
When You Write: Using Transitions	*569*
Interjections	569
Parts of Speech Review	570
Chapter Review	573
Other Parts of Speech and Review: Posttest	575
Writer's Corner	576

19 Complements

	578
Complements: Pretests	578
Kinds of Complements	580
Direct and Indirect Objects	581
When You Write: Prepositional Phrases	*582*
Predicate Nominatives and Predicate Adjectives	584
Sentence Patterns	588
Sentence Diagraming	590
Diagraming Complements	590
Chapter Review	593
Complements: Posttest	595
Writer's Corner	596

20 Phrases

	598
Phrases: Pretests	598
Prepositional Phrases	600
Adjectival Phrases	601
Adverbial Phrases	604
Appositives and Appositive Phrases	607

GRAMMAR

When You Write: Appositive Phrases	607
Sentence Diagraming	609
Diagraming Phrases	609
Chapter Review	611
Phrases: Posttest	613
Writer's Corner	614

21 Verbals and Verbal Phrases — 616

Verbals and Verbal Phrases: Pretests	616
Participles and Participial Phrases	618
Participles	618
Participial Phrases	621
When You Write: Participial Phrases	622
⚡ **Power Your Writing:** Getting Into the Action	623
Infinitives and Infinitive Phrases	626
Infinitive Phrases	627
Parallelism with Verbals	628
Sentence Diagraming	629
Diagraming Verbals and Verbal Phrases	629

xxiv

Chapter Review	631
Verbals and Verbal Phrases: Posttest	633
Writer's Corner	634

22 Clauses 636

Clauses: Pretests	636
Independent and Subordinate Clauses	638
Uses of Subordinate Clauses	640
Adverbial Clauses	640
Adjectival Clauses	643
Kinds of Sentences	647
Simple and Compound Sentences	647
Complex Sentences	650
When You Write: Sentence Variety	*650*
Sentence Diagraming	653
Diagraming Sentences	653
Chapter Review	655
Clauses: Posttest	657
Writer's Corner	658

23 Sentence Fragments and Run-ons 660

Sentence Fragments and Run-ons: Pretests	660
Sentence Fragments	662
When You Write: Fragments in Fiction	*662*
Phrase Fragments	664
Clause Fragments	666
Ways to Correct Clause Fragments	666
When You Write: Fragments in Dialogue	*666*

Grammar

Run-on Sentences	668
Ways to Correct Run-on Sentences	669
Chapter Review	671
Sentence Fragments and Run-ons: Posttest	673
Writer's Corner	674

Unit 5 Usage — 697

24 Using Verbs — 678

Using Verbs: Pretests	678
The Principal Parts of Verbs	680
Regular Verbs	680
Irregular Verbs	682
When You Speak: Irregular Verbs	*685*
Six Problem Verbs	689
⚡ **Power Your Writing:** ReVerberate	*692*
Verb Tense	693
Uses of the Tenses	693
Verb Conjugation	694
Shifts in Tense	698
When You Write: Verb Tense	*699*
Progressive Verb Forms	700
Emphatic Verb Forms	702
When You Write: Emphatic Verb Forms	*702*
Chapter Review	703
Using Verbs: Posttest	705
Writer's Corner	706

25 Using Pronouns — 708

Using Pronouns: Pretests — 708
The Cases of Personal Pronouns — 710
    The Nominative Case — 711
    The Objective Case — 716
When You Write and Speak: Using Between — 718
Pronoun Problem: *Who* or *Whom*? — 724
Pronouns and Their Antecedents — 726
    Indefinite Pronouns as Antecedents — 728
Unclear, Missing, or Confusing Antecedents — 730
    Unclear Antecedents — 730
    Missing Antecedents — 731
    Confusing Antecedents — 732
Chapter Review — 733
Using Pronouns: Posttest — 735
Writer's Corner — 736

GRAMMAR

26 Subject and Verb Agreement — 738

Subject and Verb Agreement: Pretests — 738

Agreement of Subjects and Verbs — 740
- Number — 740
- Singular and Plural Subjects — 742

Common Agreement Problems — 745
- Verb Phrases — 745
- *Doesn't* or *Don't*? — 746
- Interrupting Words — 748
- Inverted Order — 749

⚡ **Power Your Writing:** Who or What? — 751

Other Agreement Problems — 752
- Compound Subjects — 752
- Collective Nouns — 754

Agreement Problems with Pronouns — 756
- *You* and *I* as Subjects — 756

When You Write: Authentic Dialogue — 756
- Indefinite Pronouns — 758

Chapter Review — 761

Subject and Verb Agreement: Posttest — 763

Writer's Corner — 764

27 Using Adjectives and Adverbs — 766

Using Adjectives and Adverbs: Pretests — 766

Comparison of Adjectives and Adverbs — 768
- Regular Comparison — 769
- Irregular Comparison — 771

Problems with Modifiers	774
Other and **Else**	774
When You Speak or Write: Logical Comparisons	775
Double Comparisons	776
Double Negatives	777
Power Your Writing: Scene Setters	778
Good or **Well?**	779
Chapter Review	781
Using Adjectives and Adverbs: Posttest	783
Writer's Corner	784
A Writer's Glossary of Usage	786
When You Speak and Write: All ready *vs.* Already	787
When You Use Technology: Spell Check	788
When You Speak and Write: Using In	791
When You Speak and Write: This *and* That	796

Unit 6 Mechanics   800

28 Capital Letters   802

Capital Letters: Pretests	802
Rules of Capital Letters	804
First Words	804
When You Write: Capitalization in Poetry	805
The Pronoun *I*	806
Proper Nouns	807
Other Uses of Capital Letters	816
Proper Adjectives	816
Titles	817

Grammar

Chapter Review	823
Capital Letters: Posttest	825
Writer's Corner	826

29 End Marks and Commas — 828

End Marks and Commas: Pretests	828
End Marks	830
Other Uses of Periods	831
Commas That Separate	835
Items in a Series	835
When You Write: Parallelism	*836*
Adjectives Before a Noun	837
Compound Sentences	839
Introductory Structures	841
Commonly Used Commas	843
When You Write: Using Commas	*844*
Commas That Enclose	846
Direct Address	846
Parenthetical Expressions	847
Appositives	848
Nonrestrictive and Restrictive Elements	850
Chapter Review	853
End Marks and Commas: Posttest	855
Writer's Corner	856

30 Italics and Quotation Marks — 858

Italics and Quotation Marks: Pretests	858
Italics (Underlining)	860
Italics with Titles	860

Quotation Marks	863
Quotation Marks with Titles	863
Quotation Marks with Direct Quotations	864
Capital Letters with Direct Quotations	866
Commas with Direct Quotations	867
End Marks with Direct Quotations	868
Other Uses of Quotation Marks	870
Chapter Review	873
Italics and Quotation Marks: Posttest	875
Writer's Corner	876

31 Other Punctuation — 878

Other Punctuation: Pretests	878
Apostrophes	880
Apostrophes to Show Possession	880
Apostrophes with Contractions	886
When You Write: Using Apostrophes	*886*
Apostrophes with Certain Plurals	888
Semicolons	890
Semicolons with Compound Sentences	890
When You Write: Using Semicolons	*890*
Semicolons to Avoid Confusion	892
When You Write: Long Sentences	*892*
⚡ **Power Your Writing:** *Catch and Release*	893
Colons	894
Hyphens	897
Other Uses of Hyphens	898
Chapter Review	901
Other Punctuation: Posttest	903
Writer's Corner	904

Grammar

32 Spelling Correctly 906
- **Spelling Correctly: Pretests** 906
- **Strategies for Learning to Spell** 908
- **Spelling Strategies** 909
- *When You Write:* Spelling Correctly *910*
- **Spelling Patterns** 911
- **Plurals** 914
- **Prefixes and Suffixes** 922
- **Words to Master** 929
- **Chapter Review** 930
- **Spelling Correctly: Posttest** 931
- **Writer's Corner** 932

Language QuickGuide 934

Glossary 960

Index 983

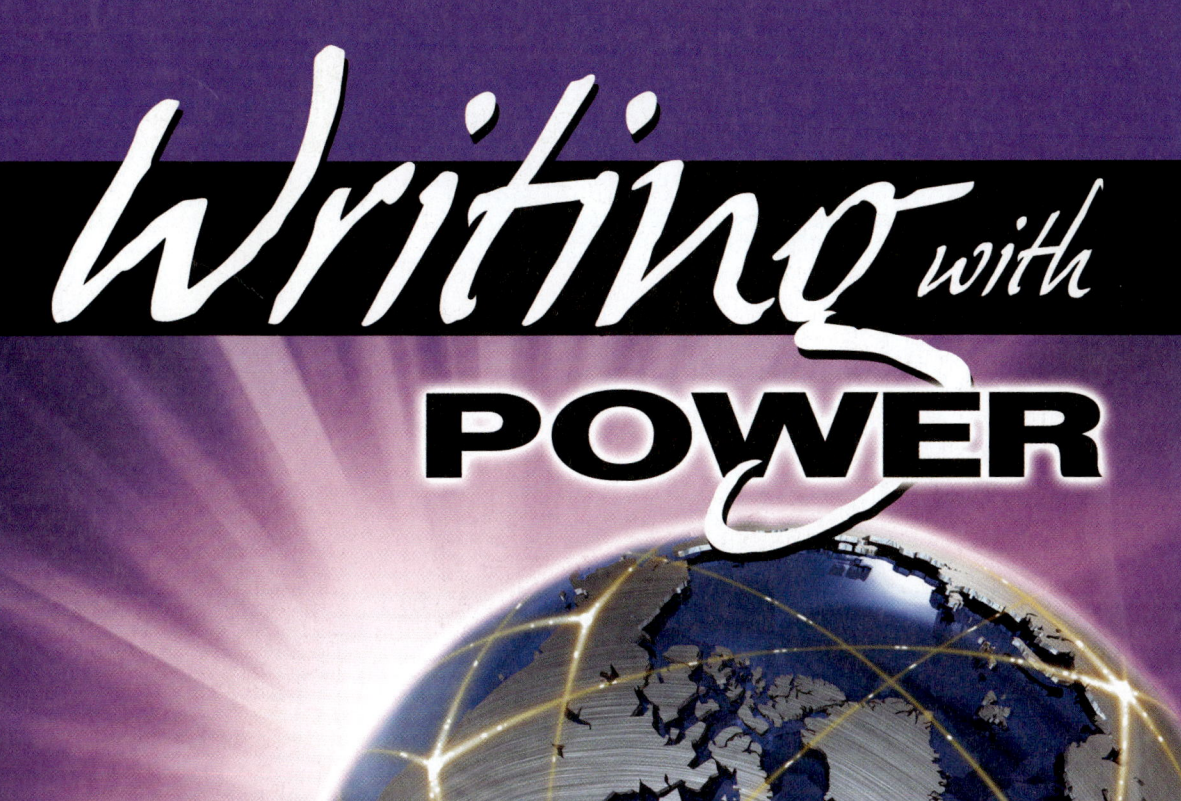

Writing with POWER

Language

Composition

21st Century Skills

Perfection Learning®

Unit 1
Style and Structure of Writing

Chapter 1	A Community of Writers	4
Chapter 2	Using Words Powerfully	34
Chapter 3	Writing with Sentence Variety	60
Chapter 4	Writing Well-Structured Paragraphs	82
Chapter 5	Writing Effective Compositions	100

If you have ever done Japanese paper folding, you probably know that when you make your first fold, it's hard to imagine the finished product growing out of it. Yet without that first fold, graceful cranes or magnificent dragons could never come into being. In the same way, when you first begin to put your thoughts on paper, you may not be able to see where they might lead. Little by little, with each new sentence you write, your creation comes into sharper focus. This unit will introduce the styles and structures you can use to express your thoughts effectively in writing. It will also help you appreciate your presence in a community of writers and how you can learn from one another.

Get it down. Take chances. It may be bad, but it's the only way you can do anything really good. — William Faulkner

CHAPTER 1

A Community of Writers

The title of this program is *Writing with Power.* What do you think it means to write with power? What is different about the writing you do as a young person coming of age in the 21st century compared with the writing of your parents' generation? This chapter will answer those questions and lay the foundation for the writing instruction and activities presented in future chapters.

Writing with Power

You read all kinds of texts every day. Usually, you can tell when one has been written with power. Such writing usually:

- demonstrates the **six traits** of good writing
- uses **language in varied, interesting ways** to show relationships and provide details
- follows the **conventions** appropriate for the purpose, occasion, audience, and genre

This program will help you to write with power and enable you to accomplish your goals through your writing.

 The Six Traits

IDEAS

Strong writing is characterized by a clear idea, message, or theme. To this basis, writers add appropriate details that help explain or support their message in a lively way. Powerful writing helps you focus your thinking so that your readers can easily understand what you are trying to say.

ORGANIZATION

Well-organized writing typically has a clear beginning, middle, and ending. Well-organized writers present details in a logical order. You can make your logic clear to your readers by using the kinds of transitional words and phrases listed in the chart below.

WRITING PURPOSE	ORGANIZATIONAL PATTERNS	COMMON TRANSITIONS
Expository (to explain or inform)	Order of importance	*First, next, most important*
	Comparison/contrast	*Similarly, in contrast, on the other hand*
	Cause/effect	*As a result, for that reason, because*
Narrative (to tell a real or imaginary story)	Chronological (time) order	*First, yesterday, the next day, last year, next, until*
Descriptive	Spatial (location) order	*At the top, near the middle, to the right, on the other side, next to, behind*
Persuasive	Order of importance	*The most important, equally important, in addition, also, in fact*

Voice

Voice is the quality that gives your readers the impression that you have a unique personality and message. It suggests your personal and individual way of expressing ideas. Make sure the voice you use meets the expectations for the situation. For example, a fan letter to a favorite musician and a letter to your school's principal recommending a change in school rules require two very different voices. The following chart identifies appropriate voices for different writing occasions.

WRITING PURPOSE	WHAT THE WRITER'S VOICE SHOULD CONVEY
Expository and persuasive writing	Genuine interest in the subject, often including personal insights about why the subject is important to the writer and what the reader might expect to gain from it; respect for differing viewpoints; confidence without being conceited
Descriptive and narrative writing	A genuine, not phony, personality; often some personal statements that show a willingness to trust readers with ideas you may be sensitive about

Word Choice

You can capture your readers' attention by using specific, lively, precise, and natural-sounding language. Such word choice involves using active voice verbs (page 224), precise nouns and modifiers (pages 278 and 538), and colorful and figurative language appropriate to the situation. (You will learn more about word choice in Chapter 2.)

Sentence Fluency

In writing that meets readers' expectations, sentences flow smoothly into one another, creating **internal coherence.** Readers also expect a text to have **external coherence,** a smooth, logical flow from one paragraph to the next. To achieve this flow, writers employ transitions, repeated words, and pronouns that refer back to an earlier word. These devices enable sentences to be seamlessly connected to one another.

Sentence fluency also depends on using a variety of sentence types, such as simple, compound, and complex sentences. (You will learn more about sentence fluency and variety in Chapter 3.)

Conventions

Good writing is generally free of problems with spelling, capitalization, punctuation, and appropriate words. Paragraph breaks occur in appropriate locations, and sentences follow rules for grammar and usage. Writing that includes these qualities can make a strong positive impression on readers. Writing that does not may disappoint and confuse your readers and undercut the impression you are trying to make on your readers. (You will learn more about some of the most important conventions on pages 8–10.)

2 The Power of Language

Speakers and writers can produce a seemingly endless number of sentences because there are so many words and sentence structures to draw from. Simple pictures can communicate an idea such as "DeQuan started the lawnmower," but language can add detail, meaning, subtlety, and feeling to that idea in seemingly endless ways: "DeQuan got out the mower, praying that it would come to life when he pulled the starter cord. He pulled once, and the mower gave a bored cough. He pulled again, and this time it spun the engine a few times, just to taunt him. DeQuan got on his game face, let out a mighty bellow, and pulled. The mower giggled at this effort. DeQuan paced up and down the driveway. He positioned himself in his starting position and then noticed that he'd forgotten to adjust the choke. He moved it a few notches, pulled on the cord, and the mower roared to life."

Fluent writers generate their power through their careful use of language. For this reason, each composition chapter in this program includes a warm-up activity called "The Power of Language." These activities help you learn how to create interesting and varied patterns in your writing to help you express your thoughts in persuasive ways. Most of these language strategies have two names. The first identifies the language concept. The second name, after the colon, reflects its purpose or function. The "Power of Language" strategies in this book are:

- Adverbs and Prepositional Phrases: Scene Setters, page 51
- Appositives: Who or What? page 67
- Semicolons: Catch and Release, page 93
- Phrases: Scene Setters, page 112
- Adverbs: Fine Points, page 138
- Parallelism: The Power of 3s, page 164
- Participial Phrases: Getting into the Action, page 189
- Strong Verbs: In Living Color, page 224
- Repetition: Say It Again, page 256
- Adjectives: Modifiers Come Lately, page 278
- Fluency: Let It Flow, page 346

Using these strategies will help you transform your writing from "DeQuan started the lawnmower" to a myriad of detailed, interesting, and original expressions, giving your language significant *power*.

③ The Power Rules

Your use of language can help you get what you want out of life. Your language usage—the words you use, the structure of your sentences, the rules you follow—is one way you show you belong to a social group. In casual speech and writing, you use language from home, community, and peer interactions. You might have learned to say, "I don't have anything," or you might have learned to say "I ain't got none." The language you use usually follows the form of the people you spend time with or hope to spend time with. This kind of speech is the language of power among the people you choose to spend your time with, so you use it comfortably and confidently.

However, your everyday speech is often not the language of power in other situations where "Standard English"—the language often used in workplaces—is the norm. Its conventions may be quite different from the speech you use with your family, friends, or other social group. However, if you hope to succeed in school, the job market, or college, you benefit from using the language of power that people use in those settings. The speech conventions you follow are thus not absolutely right or wrong. Rather, they depend on the people you are with and their expectations for speech or writing.

Language experts have found that certain grammatical errors create more negative impressions than others. Since these errors can have a great influence on your future success, you should learn how to edit your writing so that it meets the standards for formal occasions. The list below identifies ten of the most important conventions to master, the Power Rules. Check to see if you have followed the Power Rules whenever you edit.

EDITING FOR MAINSTREAM CONVENTIONS: THE POWER RULES

1. Use only one negative form for a single negative idea. (See pages 258 and 777.)

Before Editing	After Editing
We *didn't* do *nothing* last night.	We *didn't* do *anything* last night.
I *didn't* have *nothing* to eat.	I *didn't* have *anything* to eat.

2. Use mainstream past-tense forms of regular and irregular verbs. (See pages 680–688.)
   You might try to recite and memorize the parts of the most common irregular verbs.

Before Editing	After Editing
I already *eat* the cheesecake.	I already *ate* the cheesecake.
Chester *come* to my house yesterday.	Chester *came* to my house yesterday.
We *brang* the salad to the potluck.	We *brought* the salad to the potluck.
You should have *went* to the game!	You should have *gone* to the game!

3. **Use verbs that agree with the subject.** (See pages 740–760.)

Before Editing	After Editing
It *don't* make a difference. Bruno always *study* for the test. The cat and the dog *gets* along well. Either the frogs or the Princess *marry* the king. Neither Hank nor his friends *feels* terrible about the accident.	It *doesn't* make a difference. Bruno always *studies* for the test. The cat and the dog *get* along well. Either the frogs or the Princess *marries* the king. Neither Hank nor his friends *feel* terrible about the accident.

4. **Use subject forms of pronouns in subject position. Use object forms of pronouns in object position.** (See pages 712–719.)

Before Editing	After Editing
Her and her mom look alike. *Him* and his brothers live in different houses. Marie wants to start a business with Frank and *I*.	*She* and her mom look alike. *He* and his brothers live in different houses. Marie wants to start a business with Frank and *me*.

5. **Use standard ways to make nouns possessive.** (See pages 880–883.)

Before Editing	After Editing
Where is the *rabbit* foot? Where are all the *kings* men? Buffy repainted the *houses* exterior. The *trees* leaves are starting to fall. The *soldiers* rifles all shot in unison.	Where is the *rabbit's* foot? Where are all the *king's* men? Buffy repainted the *house's* exterior. The *trees'* leaves are starting to fall. The *soldiers'* rifles all shot in unison.

6. **Use a consistent verb tense except when a change is clearly necessary.** (See page 698.)

Before Editing	After Editing
The rooster *crows* when the sun *rose*. When the show ended, he *stands* up and cheered.	The rooster *crows* when the sun *rises*. When the show ended, he *stood* up and cheered.

7. **Use sentence fragments only the way professional writers do, after the sentence they refer to and usually to emphasize a point. Fix all sentence fragments that occur before the sentence they refer to and ones that occur in the middle of a sentence.** (See pages 662–667.)

Before Editing	After Editing
One day. The cat let me pet her. Trying to sail is hard. *During a typhoon.* So we try to avoid it. I let my plants die. *The reason being that* I forgot to water them.	*One day* the cat let me pet her. Trying to sail *during a typhoon is hard,* so we try to avoid it. I let my plants die *because* I forgot to water them.

Writing with Power

8. **Use the best conjunction and/or punctuation for the meaning when connecting two sentences. Revise run-on sentences.** (See pages 668–669.)

Before Editing	After Editing
We dropped by the elementary school we visited with our favorite teacher.	*When* we dropped by the elementary school, we visited with our favorite teacher.
The private saluted improperly, the sergeant told him to do 50 pushups.	*After* the private saluted improperly, the sergeant told him to do 50 pushups.
I adjusted the speakers, they sounded better.	I adjusted the speakers, *and* they sounded better.

9. **Use the contraction *'ve* (not *of*) when the correct word is *have*, or use the full word *have*. Use *supposed* instead of *suppose* and *used* instead of *use* when appropriate.** (See pages 291, 790, 794, and 796.)

Before Editing	After Editing
They should *of* turned left instead of right.	They should *have* turned left instead of right.
We might *of* added the ingredients in the wrong order.	We might *have* added the ingredients in the wrong order.
The car could *of* started if we'd had the key.	The car could *have* started if we'd had the key.
We were *suppose* to read chapter 6 for homework.	We were *supposed* to read chapter 6 for homework.
Pedro *use* to live on a farm.	Pedro *used* to live on a farm.

10. **For sound-alikes and certain words that sound almost alike, choose the word with your intended meaning.** (See pages 291 and 736.)

Before Editing	After Editing
I am going *too* save money for a rainy day. (*too* means "also" or "in addition")	I am going *to* save money for a rainy day. (*to* is part of the infinitive of the verb *save*)
I will shoot *to* free throws. (*to* means "in the direction of")	I will shoot *two* free throws. (*two* is a number)
Was that *you're* meal I ate? (*you're* is a contraction of *you are*)	Was that *your* meal I ate? (*your* is the possessive form of *you*)
They're commute is very long. (*they're* is a contraction of *they are*)	*Their* commute is very long. (*their* is the possessive form of *they*)
Let's have a seat over *their*. (*their* is the possessive form of *they*)	Let's have a seat over *there*. (*there* means "in that place")
Its a great day to be alive! (*its* is the possessive form of *it is*)	*It's* a great day to be alive! (*it's* is a contraction of *it is*)

Writers often use the following proofreading symbols to indicate where they need to make changes when they edit. These symbols help writers to know where their writing should be revised so that it follows the Power Rules.

PROOFREADING SYMBOLS

Symbol	Meaning	Example
∧	insert	We went on a ∧fantastic journey.
∧,	insert comma	Meg enjoys hiking, skiing∧ and skating.
⊙	insert period	Gary took the bus to Atlanta⊙
ꝰ	delete	Refer back ꝰ to your notes.
¶	new paragraph	¶ Finally Balboa saw the Pacific.
no ¶	no paragraph	no ¶ The dachshund trotted away.
...	let it stand	I appreciated her sincere honesty.
#	add space	She will be#back in a moment.
⌒	close up	The airplane waited on the run⌒way.
tr	transpose	They only have two dollars left.
≡	capital letter	We later moved to the ≡south.
/	lowercase letter	His favorite subject was /Science.
ⓢⓟ	spell out	I ate ⓢⓟ2 oranges.
ⱽ" ⱽ"	insert quotes	ⱽ"I hope you can join us,ⱽ" said my brother.
= ∧	insert hyphen	I attended a school=∧related event.
ⱽ'	insert apostrophe	The ravenous dog ate the catⱽ's food.
⟲→	move copy	I usually (on Fridays) go to the movies.

Learning Tip

Write the following sentence on a piece of paper, just as it's written here:

  Emily, the girl who sits next to me seems alittle concieted.

Add proofreading symbols to show corrections. Compare your work with a partner's. Did you find the same errors and mark them the same way?

Writing with Power 11

4 Writing in the 21st Century

You are probably an expert in 21st century writing. If you are like most teenagers, you send about 100 text messages every day. You spend at least an hour a day on the Internet, often on a social networking Web site. You blog to share your opinions and respond to other people's blogs and social networking sites and are aware of the conventions for these occasions. You upload photos, videos, and other images, and viewers often respond to them. You "talk" with friends in chat rooms and with instant messaging software, often carrying on multiple conversations at once.

You also write in school. You write papers for English, reports in social studies, film summaries in science, and you answer essay questions on tests. Outside school, you may write poems that you share with friends, keep a journal or diary, make shopping lists, and keep records of things you collect.

THE RIGHT KIND OF WRITING?

With all these kinds of writing, what is the "right" way to write? There is no single way to write that is "right" for every occasion. The right way to write is the way that's appropriate for the situation, your reasons for writing, and the expectations of your readers. In other words, writing should be "in tune" with what is appropriate for the situation.

GLOBAL INTERACTIONS

Technology makes it possible for you to stay connected with others. It has helped people stay in touch with one another. Life today has a global character: Many goods sold in the U.S. are made in China, and you can buy music recorded in South Africa almost as easily as you can buy music recorded in Los Angeles.

Those who live in this connected world benefit from **creative thinking** and the ability to **work creatively and cooperatively with others,** including those from different cultures. Life in the 21st century—with its many challenges—also requires **critical thinking** with logical reasoning and effective **problem solving.** You will need to know how to communicate and to use **technology** to find and evaluate information. Writing can contribute to all of those skills and prepare you to live a satisfying life in the 21st century.

> **Learning Tip**
>
> For one day, keep a log of how many times you write and under what circumstances. Include text messaging. Compare your log to those of your classmates, looking for patterns.

Collaborating Through the Writing Process

When you think of writing, do you picture a solitary person with a wastebasket full of crumpled up drafts? Of course, some parts of the writing process can be done only by a lone writer. Picture, though, how most people write. Many film and television scripts are coauthored and are continually revised throughout filming by the director and actors who bring the words to life. When people are writing important memos, letters, or other texts, they often ask friends or colleagues to read them over for suggestions. Writing does have some solitary stages, but it is nonetheless a social act. For the writing in this program, you and your classmates will create and participate in a **community of writers** and work in **collaboration** throughout the writing process, often in groups of three to four students.

1 Prewriting: Getting Started

STRATEGIES FOR FINDING A SUBJECT

Your first goal during prewriting is to think of a worthwhile subject. Much of what you write will come from your own interests.

Taking an Inventory of Your Personal Interests Make lists of what you like, things you know about, even things you want to know more about. You may discover new things about yourself.

Personal Interest Inventory	
Subjects I know a lot about	
Hobbies	
Unusual experiences I have had	

Keeping a Journal Journal writing will also help you discover ideas. You can write about anything you want in your journal: the day's events, your worries, your hopes and dreams for the future. Your journal should be a place where you always feel free to write about what interests you. As you record thoughts, be sure to write in your journal every day and date each entry.

Reading, Interviewing, Discussing Use the strategies on the next page to develop ideas for subjects. In each case, take notes to remember the ideas that surfaced.

 **Strategies for Thinking of Subjects**

- Do some background reading on broad topics that interest you. If you are interested in computers, for example, find some recent articles to read. Check the library or the Internet.
- Interview someone who knows more about a subject than you do.
- Discuss possible subjects with classmates, friends, and/or family to find new ways of looking at a subject.

Keeping a Learning Log A Learning Log is a section of your journal where you can write down ideas or information about math, science, history, health, or any other subject that interests you. You can use it to capture what you know about a subject and what you still need or want to learn about it. You can record your writing progress there.

CHOOSING AND LIMITING A SUBJECT

A good way to find a subject is to review everything you have written to see if any ideas or subjects appear more than once. As you read the following guidelines for choosing a good subject, remember that the most important guideline is your genuine interest in exploring a subject more fully in writing.

 Guidelines for Choosing a Subject

- Choose a subject that genuinely interests you.
- Choose a subject that will interest your readers.
- Choose a subject that you know something about or can research with reasonable effort.

Avoid choosing general topics, such as "sports" or "current events." Such subjects are too broad and often result in compositions that are poorly organized and over-generalized. Your next step is to limit your subject to one you can cover in the time and space you have.

Guidelines for Limiting a Subject

- Limit your subject to one person or example that represents the subject.
- Limit your subject to a specific time or place.
- Limit your subject to a specific event.
- Limit your subject to a specific condition, purpose, or procedure.

CONSIDERING YOUR PURPOSE, OCCASION, AUDIENCE, AND GENRE

Much of the writing you encounter has been written for a specific audience and purpose. For example, a political speechwriter may compose a speech intended to convince legislators to pass a law. Here are some purposes for writing and appropriate types of writing for each purpose.

WRITING PURPOSES	POSSIBLE FORMS
Expository to **explain** or **inform;** to focus on your subject matter and audience	**Factual writing** scientific essay, research paper, business letter, summary, descriptive essay, historical narrative, news story
Creative (literary) to **create;** to focus on making imaginative use of language and ideas	**Entertaining writing** short story, novel, play, poem, dialogue
Persuasive to **persuade;** to focus on changing your readers' minds or getting them to act in a certain way	**Convincing writing** letter to the editor, persuasive essay, movie or book review, critical essay (literary analysis), advertisement
Self-expressive to **express** and **reflect** on your thoughts and feelings	**Personal writing** journal entry, personal narrative, reflective essay, personal letter

Once you have determined your purpose and the type of writing, you can begin to gather details that are appropriate to your purpose. If your purpose is to create a story, for example, you might develop your subject with events and descriptions. If your purpose is to persuade the reader to buy a product, you could gather together facts, examples, and reasons why the reader should buy the product.

Occasion is your motivation for composing—the factor that prompts you to communicate. Occasion usually can be stated well using one of the following sentences.

- I feel a need to write for my own satisfaction.
- I have been asked to write this by [name a person].
- I want to write an entry for [name a publication].
- I want to enter a writing contest.

Understanding the needs of your **audience**—the people who will be reading your work—will also help you choose the best details for your composition. Ask yourself the following questions.

Audience Profile Questions

- Are my readers adults, teens, or children?
- What do they already know about my subject?
- What opinions or attitudes are they likely to have about my subject?
- What terms, if any, might I need to define for my readers?

For most of the writing you do in school, your teacher and classmates will be your audience. From time to time, though, you might want to write for a different audience: a friend, a relative, a newspaper editor. Always ask yourself questions about your audience to understand how best to address audience needs.

The **genre,** or form of writing, you choose will also shape your subject. (See the chart on the previous page for a listing of common forms or genres of writing.) Each genre has several characteristics that make it different from the others. Your readers expect these characteristics to be present when they read. If you are reading a recipe in a cookbook, for example, you expect that there will be a list of ingredients, an oven temperature, a servings number, and directions. If you open a cookbook and you find instead that the book consists of one long article on the subject of cooking with various foods, you wouldn't know what to make of it, even though it is still about cooking. In the same way, if you apply for a job in a bread bakery by creating a video commercial for yourself, the bakery owner may not know what to make of you.

Collaboration in Action

Prewriting

Tyler, Peri, and Alejandra are in a writing group together. It's their first writing activity of the year. Each of them is supposed to come up with a topic and choose the purpose and audience for a composition. Here's how their discussion might go:

Tyler: Man, I'm stumped. What are you guys writing about?

Alejandra: I don't know yet either.

Peri: We're supposed to write about stuff we like. I'm writing about baby birds. There's a nest right outside my window and it's got baby birds in it.

Alejandra: Yeah? What kind?

Peri: I don't know. Little red birds.

Tyler: You could look them up in a bird book to find out what kind they are, or go online and look for pictures. What do you like about them?

Peri: They're really cute, and I actually worry about them, like I want to take care of them.

Tyler: I guess you don't get to see that kind of thing too often. I think that would be interesting to read.

Peri: I mean, you're right. I'd never seen anything like it before. I was surprised how into it I got. It was almost like, "Okay, what's going to happen today?"

Alejandra: So you could just tell that story then, I think.

Peri: Yeah. I'll start writing and see what happens.

Talking and listening help Peri focus her thoughts and start to get a good subject. After the group finishes talking about her topic, they have a similar conversation about the subjects Tyler and Alejandra will write about.

Collaboration Practice

Meet with a small group for 10 minutes. Use what you have learned to try to come up with a good writing topic for each member.

❷ Prewriting: From Ideas to a Plan

DEVELOPING A SUBJECT

Once you have determined your subject, audience, purpose, and genre, you have formed the frame of your composition. However, you still need to fill in that frame with facts, examples, events, reasons, or descriptions. The following strategies will help you develop details about your subject.

Brainstorming for Details **Brainstorming** means writing down everything that comes to mind when you think of a subject. One idea will lead to another and then to still another. Before long, you will have a list of ideas, such as the following list Peri came up with on the subject of a mother cardinal caring for her young.

MODEL: Brainstorming List

- nest in vine outside window
- saw eggs
- saw tiny birds with heads up waiting to be fed
- mother sat on eggs to hatch them
- mother would feed hungry birds
- babies looked pink and bare

Writing Tip

Do not worry about neatness when you brainstorm. List ideas as quickly as you can write them. You will be able to rearrange, delete, and add later. Try to write as many details as you can.

Clustering One way to think of ideas and details is to make a cluster diagram. When you create a **cluster,** you group related ideas together. These groupings often lead to new ideas. Cluster diagrams also help organize your ideas for the drafting stage of writing.

To begin, write your subject in the middle of a blank sheet of paper and draw a circle around it. This circled subject is like the hub of a wheel. All the ideas that come to mind about that subject become the spokes of the wheel. The circled "spokes" can form new hubs as well.

MODEL: Clustering

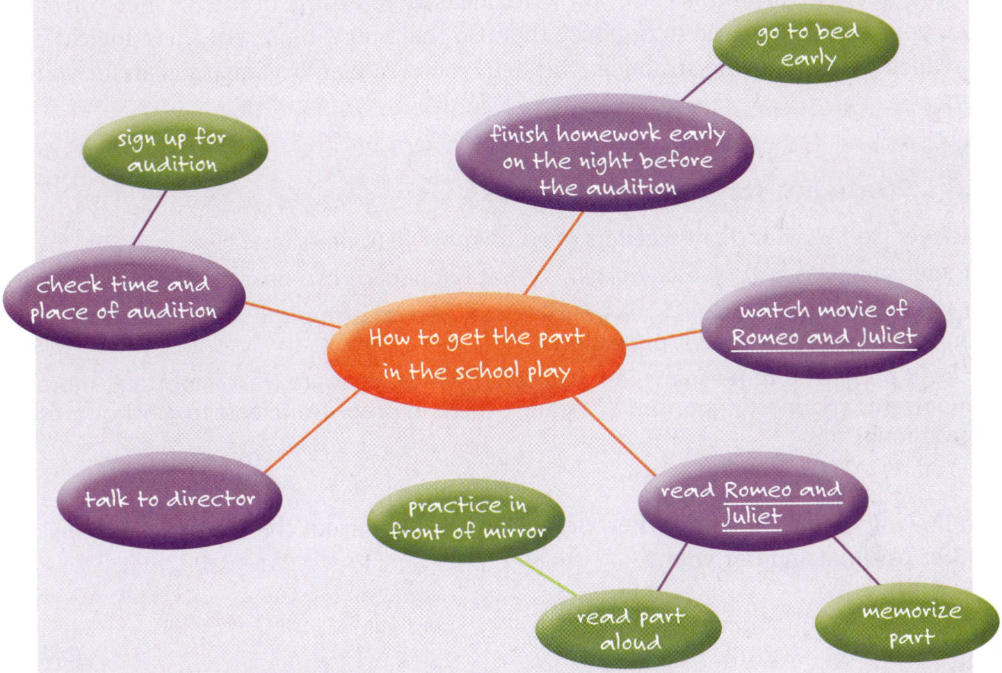

(Cluster diagram centered on "How to get the part in the school play" with branches: sign up for audition; finish homework early on the night before the audition; go to bed early; check time and place of audition; watch movie of Romeo and Juliet; read Romeo and Juliet; memorize part; read part aloud; practice in front of mirror; talk to director)

Inquiring Another way to explore a subject is to ask *who, what, where, when, why,* and *how*. By answering these questions, you should be able to examine your subject completely and develop vivid and precise details. The following model shows how one writer used inquiring to find details on the subject of Internet Web sites. Notice that a number of questions can emerge from each word.

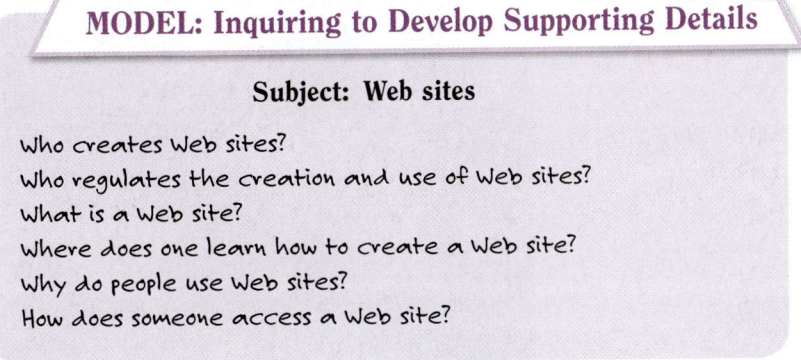

MODEL: Inquiring to Develop Supporting Details

Subject: Web sites

Who creates Web sites?
Who regulates the creation and use of Web sites?
What is a Web site?
Where does one learn how to create a Web site?
Why do people use Web sites?
How does someone access a Web site?

Collaborating Through the Writing Process

ORGANIZING IDEAS

When you freewrite or brainstorm, you write ideas as you think of them. Once you have written your ideas, you need to organize them so that you can present them logically to your readers. The following strategies will help you create an organizing plan for your writing.

Strategies for Organizing Ideas

- Ask yourself, "What do my readers need to know first, next, last?"
- If your subject is a story, ask yourself, "What happened first, next, then, finally?"
- If your purpose is to explain, ask yourself how best to group the details you have chosen to help your reader understand.
- If your purpose is to persuade, ask yourself, "Which ideas are least important, more important, and most important?" Arrange them in order from least to most or most to least important.

The following model shows how Peri organized her ideas from the brainstorming list on a mother cardinal and her young.

MODEL: Organizing Ideas

- First: Mother cardinal made nest in vine outside window.
- Second: I saw eggs.
- Third: Mother cardinal sat on eggs to hatch them.
- Fourth: I saw tiny birds with heads up waiting to be fed.
- Last: Mother fed hungry birds.

 Drafting

During this stage of your writing process, put your ideas down on paper as quickly as you can think of them. Later you can go back and improve your work until it satisfies you. The following strategies will help.

HERE'S HOW Strategies for Drafting

- Write an introduction that will capture the reader's interest.
- Use your organized prewriting notes as a guide, but feel free to include new ideas as they occur to you.
- Write fairly quickly. Do not stop to worry over how a word is spelled or how a phrase sounds. You can always go back and polish your work later.
- Read what you have written aloud. This practice will help you get a "running start" on your next idea and keep your thoughts flowing smoothly.
- Write a conclusion that drives home the main point of your composition.

Peri wrote the first draft below from the notes about how the cardinal cares for her young. Notice that Peri did not take the time to correct mistakes. She can do that work later.

MODEL: Unedited First Draft

A cardinal built a nest in a vine right outside our window. Soon we noticed three eggs in the nest right outside our window. They were visible only when the bird left the nest. It was summertime. She sat on the eggs. To help them hatch. Finally the time came. One morning we seen three little birds with their heads back waiting for food. Their mother returned write a way and fed her babies. As they grow, our family spent more time watching out that window then watching television.

Collaborating Through the Writing Process 21

4 Revising

Following are some strategies you can use to improve your draft.

REVISING STRATEGIES	QUICK FIXES
Check for Clarity and Creativity • Are your ideas interesting, fresh, and original rather than ones that people have heard over and over? • Does the text satisfy its purpose?	• Insert a personal experience or example. • Think of an unlikely comparison between your subject and something else. • Talk with others to get ideas. • Explore your subject from someone else's point of view.
Elaborate by Adding Details • Does your writing seem fully developed? • Are your ideas fully supported? • Have you used details that would help bring a scene or idea to life for a reader?	• Use one of the prewriting strategies on pages 13–17 to come up with lively elaborations. • Get into the action with participial phrases (page 189), tell who or what with appositives (page 67), add fine points (page 138) and/or scene setters (pages 51 and 112). • Show, don't tell. • Take a mental snapshot of a scene and write what you see.
Rearrange Out-of-Order Items • Check the organization of your words, sentences, and ideas. Does one idea lead logically into another? • Can any ideas be combined?	• Use your word processor to rearrange and reorganize your sentences or paragraphs so the reader can easily follow your thoughts. • Use transitions to show the relationships between ideas.
Delete Unnecessary Words or Details • Have you included any details in your draft that do not really relate to your controlling idea?	• Delete, or remove, them. Also delete any extra or unneeded words and repetitive sentences and paragraphs.
Substitute Words and Sentences • Do any parts of your draft seem possibly confusing to a reader? Are any of your words and statements overly general?	• Ask a "test reader" to tell you where you need to provide more or clearer information. • For a dull, general word, find a richer and more vivid synonym.

Using a Six-Trait Rubric

A rubric can help you know how to improve your draft. You can also use it to evaluate the work of your writing partners. Each row focuses on a specific aspect of writing. Each column describes a different level of quality, with the highest quality traits labeled 4.

Ideas	**4** The main idea is clear. Plenty of details such as facts, examples, and anecdotes provide support.	**3** The main idea is clear. There is enough support for the main idea to back it up adequately.	**2** The main idea could be clearer. There are some supporting details, but more details would be helpful.	**1** The main idea statement is missing or unclear. Few examples and facts are provided in support.
Organization	**4** The organization is clear with abundant transitions.	**3** A few ideas seem out of place or transitions are missing.	**2** Many ideas seem out of place and transitions are missing.	**1** The organization is unclear and hard to follow.
Voice	**4** The voice sounds natural, engaging, and unique.	**3** The voice sounds natural and engaging.	**2** The voice sounds mostly natural but is weak.	**1** The voice sounds mostly unnatural and is weak.
Word Choice	**4** Words are specific, powerful, and approriate to the task.	**3** Words are specific and language is appropriate.	**2** Some words are too general and/or misleading.	**1** Most words are overly general and imprecise.
Sentence Fluency	**4** Varied sentences flow smoothly.	**3** Most sentences are varied and flow smoothly.	**2** Some sentences are varied but some are choppy.	**1** Sentences are not varied and are choppy.
Conventions	**4** Punctuation, usage, and spelling are correct. The Power Rules are all followed.	**3** Punctuation, usage, and spelling are mainly correct and Power Rules are all followed.	**2** Some punctuation, usage, and spelling are incorrect but all Power Rules are followed.	**1** There are many errors and at least one failure to follow a Power Rule.

The checklist on the next page is another tool for evaluating and revising your writing.

Evaluation Checklist for Revising

- ✓ Did you clearly state your main idea? (pages 107–108)
- ✓ Does your text have a strong introduction, body, and conclusion? (pages 86–95 and 114–116)
- ✓ Did you support your main idea with enough details? (pages 91–92 and 107–108)
- ✓ Do your details show instead of merely telling what you want to say? (pages 44–53)
- ✓ Did you present your ideas in a logical order? (pages 162–165 and 227–229)
- ✓ Do any of your sentences stray from the main idea? (pages 91–92)
- ✓ Are your ideas clearly explained? (page 5 and 91)
- ✓ Are your words specific? (pages 44–45)
- ✓ Are any words or ideas repeated unnecessarily? (pages 77–78)
- ✓ Are your sentences varied and smoothly connected? (pages 64–65 and 68–71)
- ✓ Is the purpose of your text clear? (page 15)
- ✓ Is your writing suited to your audience? (page 16)
- ✓ Is your writing appropriate for your occasion? (page 15)
- ✓ Does your writing have the usual features associated with the genre you have chosen? (page 16)
- ✓ Is your title effective? (page 116)

CONFERENCING

You have been **conferencing,** meeting with others, throughout the writing process. Conferencing is especially helpful during revising. Be positive and specific and offer praise as well as any suggestions for improvement.

 **Guidelines for Conferencing**

Guidelines for the Writer

- List some questions for your peer. What aspects of your work most concern you?
- Try to be grateful for your critic's honesty rather than being upset or defensive. Keep in mind that the criticism you are getting is well intended.

Guidelines for the Critic

- Read your partner's work carefully. What does the writer promise to do in this text? Does he or she succeed?
- Point out strengths as well as weaknesses. Start your comments by saying something positive like, "Your opening really captured my interest."
- Be specific. Refer to a specific word, sentence, or section when you comment.
- Be sensitive to your partner's feelings. Phrase your criticisms as questions. You might say, "Do you think your details might be stronger if … ?"

A Community of Writers

Collaboration in Action

Revising

Peri's writing group has already discussed Alejandra's and Tyler's drafts. They made notes on their papers about where they could make improvements based on their peers' feedback. Now it is Peri's turn to have her paper discussed:

Peri: So, what do y'all think of what I've got so far?

Tyler: I think you did a good job organizing this. It seems complete. It has a good beginning and then a strong ending.

Peri: Thanks.

Tyler: I did notice, though, that it was kind of choppy in the middle.

Peri: Where?

Tyler: It was summertime. She sat on the eggs. To help them hatch. Finally the time came.

Peri: Okay, when you say it out loud I can hear it.

Tyler: You described what you've seen out the window. I can picture that.

Alejandra: I can too but I think you could use more details.

Tyler: Yeah, that's true. More things so we could picture it even better.

Peri: Like what?

Alejandra: Like a robin's eggs are blue. What do a cardinal's eggs look like?

Peri: They've got spots. I can add that.

Alejandra: Yeah, and what kind of vine?

Peri: Okay, I see what you mean.

Collaboration Practice

Choose a paper you are working on or have completed previously and make two copies, one for each member of your group. Conference with one another to improve your drafts.

Here is a revised version of Peri's composition. For now she is concentrating on her ideas. She will fix the mistakes when she edits.

MODEL: Unedited Revised Draft

Last summer a cardinal built a nest in honeysuckle vine right outside our window. Soon we noticed three speckled egg in the nest right outside our window. they were visible only when the mother cardinal left the nest. During most of the day, she sat on the eggs, warming them with her body to help it hatch. Finally the time came. One morning we seen three little birds with their heads tlited straight back and there beaks wide open waiting for food. Their mother returned write away and fed her tiny help less babies. As they grow, our family spent more time looking out that window then watching television.

26   A Community of Writers

USING FEEDBACK FROM YOUR TEACHER

Your teacher is a member of the community of writers and an excellent collaborator. He or she is probably with you for each stage of the writing process. The chart shows different ways your teacher can provide feedback and how you can use that feedback to improve your writing.

TEACHER FEEDBACK	HOW TO USE FEEDBACK
During prewriting your teacher might: • meet briefly with you to discuss and approve your topic • suggest ways you might gather information and other supporting materials • comment on your organization	**You can use this feedback to improve your work by:** • rethinking if necessary to come up with a sharply focused topic • following the suggestions with an open mind • experimenting with different organizational patterns
During drafting your teacher might: • move from desk to desk to offer suggestions on your process of drafting (for example, continually going back and rereading what you've written) • offer suggestions or concerns about a direction your draft seems to be taking	**You can use this feedback to improve your work by:** • trying out the suggestions, even if they are uncomfortable at first • saving your work and then coming back to it with a fresh eye to try to see the concerns your teacher raised • asking questions if you don't understand your teacher's concerns
During revising your teacher might: • meet with you to go over some issues face to face • make written comments on your work about ideas, organization, and flow	**You can use this feedback to improve your work by:** • making a good effort to change the things you discussed • using the comments as positive guides rather than negative criticisms
During editing your teacher might: • identify errors • offer mini-lessons on challenging points	**You can use this feedback to improve your work by:** • making corrections and adding items to your personalized checklist
During publishing your teacher might: • give you presentation ideas • help you reach your audience	**You can use this feedback to improve your work by:** • gaining confidence in sharing your work with readers and being willing to take risks

Collaborating Through the Writing Process

5 Editing and Publishing

EDITING FOR WORDINESS: EDITING STAR

The Environmental Protection Agency works with makers of consumer products to ensure "energy star" efficiency. Products marked with an energy star are certified to get the same results as others like them but with less power. The less power needed for the job, the more energy-efficient the product is.

You should use word power, like other kinds of energy, efficiently. The fewer words needed to get the job done, the more energy-efficient the writing. Notice how much stronger the efficient version is.

Word Guzzler   Owing to the fact that Kenton had lost his umbrella, he had to go out into the wet rain without any sort of covering to protect himself from getting soaked.

Fuel Efficient   Because Kenton lost his umbrella, he got soaked when he went outside.

Throughout the composition chapters in this book, you will see the language arts version of the energy star logo: the editing star. It will accompany a brief activity that can remind you to cut out wordiness.

USING A GENERAL EDITING CHECKLIST

The best way to use a checklist is to go over your paper several times, each time looking for a different kind of problem. For instance, you might look for spelling errors in one reading and comma errors in the next. You might also want to read your essay backward, word by word. You will find that you are able to spot many errors that you might otherwise miss. The following checklist will help you guard against some common errors.

 Editing Checklist
- ✓ Are your sentences free of errors in grammar and usage?
- ✓ Did you spell each word correctly?
- ✓ Did you use capital letters where needed?
- ✓ Did you punctuate each sentence correctly?
- ✓ Did you indent paragraphs as needed and leave proper margins on each side of the paper?

USING A MANUAL OF STYLE

Your school or library media center may have a style manual, a booklet that explains the conventions the school expects students to follow in written work. If so, make sure you understand the rules for grammar, usage, mechanics, and presentation that your school has. You may wish to consult one of the following style guides or handbooks to review rules for grammar, usage, and mechanics.

- *A Manual for Writers of Research Papers, Theses, and Dissertations.* Kate Turabian. 7th ed., Chicago: University of Chicago Press, 2007.
- *The Chicago Manual of Style: The Essential Guide for Writers, Editors, and Publishers.* 15th ed., Chicago: University of Chicago Press, 2003.
- *MLA Handbook for Writers of Research Papers.* 7th ed. New York: Modern Language Association of America, 2009.

CREATING A PERSONALIZED EDITING CHECKLIST

You may want to reserve an eight-page section at the end of your journal to use as a Personalized Editing Checklist. Here you can record errors that you seem to make over and over. Write one of the following headings on every other page: Grammar, Usage, Spelling, and Mechanics (capitalization and punctuation). Use these pages to record your errors. See the index in this book to find the pages on which each problem is addressed. Write the page numbers in your journal next to the error, with examples of the corrected problem. Add to this checklist and refer to it when you edit your work.

PROOFREADING

Proofreading means carefully rereading your work and marking corrections in grammar, usage, spelling, and mechanics. Following are useful techniques.

Proofreading Techniques

- Focus on one line at a time.
- Exchange essays with a partner and check each other's work.
- Read your essay backward, word by word.
- Read your essay aloud, very slowly.
- Use a dictionary for spelling and a handbook for grammar, usage, and mechanics.

On the next page you can see how Peri used proofreading symbols to edit a portion of her revised draft.

Last summer a cardinal built a nest in a honeysuckle vine right outside our window. Soon we noticed three speckled eggs in the nest right outside our window. they were visible only when the mother cardinal left the nest. During most of the day, she sat on the eggs, warming them with her body to help them hatch. Finally the time came. One morning we saw three little birds with their heads tilted straight back and their beaks wide open waiting for food. Their mother returned right away and fed her tiny help less babies. As they grew, our family spent more time looking out that window than watching television.

PUBLISHING

Following are just a few ways you could share your writing.

Publishing Options

In School
- Read your work aloud to a small group in your class.
- Display your final draft on a bulletin board in your classroom or school library.
- Read your work aloud to your class or present it in the form of a radio program or video.
- Create a class library and media center to which you submit your work. This library and media center should have a collection of folders or files devoted to different types of student writing and media presentations.
- Create a class anthology to which every student contributes one piece. Use electronic technology to design a small publication. Share your anthology with other classes.
- Submit your work to your school literary magazine, newspaper, or yearbook.

Outside School
- Submit your written work to a newspaper or magazine.
- Share your work with a professional interested in the subject.
- Present your work to an appropriate community group.
- Send a video based on your written work to a local cable television station.
- Create and broadcast a podcast.
- Post your work on your blog or social networking site.
- Enter your work in a local, state, or national writing contest.

Using Standard Manuscript Form The appearance of your text may be almost as important as its content. A marked-up paper with inconsistent margins is difficult to read. A neat, legible paper, however, makes a positive impression on your reader. The section called *Electronic Publishing* on pages 449–463 offers tips for presenting texts effectively.

Many compositions will use standard manuscript form. The chart below shows the guidelines for preparing a composition in standard manuscript form.

Standard Manuscript Form

- Use standard-sized 8½-by-11-inch white paper. Use one side of the paper only.
- If writing by hand, use black or blue ink. If using a word-processing program, use a black ink cartridge or black typewriter ribbon and double-space the lines.
- Leave a 1.25-inch margin at the left and right. The left margin must be even. The right margin should be as even as possible.
- Put your name, the course title, the name of your teacher, and the date in the upper right-hand corner of the first page. Follow your teacher's specific guidelines for headings and margins.
- Center the title of your essay two lines below the date. Do not underline or put quotation marks around your title.
- If using a word-processing program or typing, skip four lines between the title and the first paragraph. If writing by hand, skip two lines.
- If using a word-processing program or typing, indent the first line of each paragraph five spaces. If handwriting, indent the first line of each paragraph one inch.
- Leave a 1-inch margin at the bottom of all pages.
- Starting on page 2, number each page in the upper right-hand corner. Begin the first line one inch from the top. Word-processing programs allow you to insert page numbers.

KEEPING A WRITER'S PORTFOLIO

In addition to publishing your work for others to read, you might want keep a **portfolio**— a collection of your work that represents various types of writing and your progress in them. The guidelines on the next page will help you make the most of your portfolio.

Guidelines for Including Work in Your Portfolio

- Date each piece of writing so that you can see where it fits into your progress.
- Write a brief note to yourself about why you included each piece—what you believe it shows about you as a writer.
- Include unfinished works if they demonstrate something meaningful about you as a writer.

On occasion, you will be asked to take "Time Out to Reflect." Use your written reflections to think about what you have learned, what you want to learn, and how you can continue to grow as a writer.

What are your feelings about writing in collaboration with others? Have you done it before? How do you think the experience of working with your peers might affect your writing?

Timed Writing: On Your Own

There are times in school, such as during testing, when you will not be able to benefit from collaboration. The more you collaborate when you can, however, the less alone you will feel in those situations. You will no doubt be able to remember things your writing partners have said during your group meetings and then use them in your solo writing as well. For example, you might catch yourself writing a word or phrase that your group members thought was overused and too general. Or you might remember that time after time, your group members reminded you to use transitions to connect ideas. Use these memories to help you do your very best on timed writing tasks.

The following chart shows the stages of a timed writing experience. In each, imagine what your writing partners would be saying to help you.

Working Through Timed Writing Tasks

- Begin by understanding the task. Read the prompt carefully. Identify the key words in the directions: they will tell you what kind of writing to produce. Ask yourself what your audience—the examiners—will be looking for, and try to provide it.
- Think about the time you have for the test and make a budget. Leave the most time for drafting, but build in time for planning and revising as well.
- Plan your writing by jotting down ideas, making lists, or using any other format that helps you (such as a cluster diagram). When you have good ideas to work with, arrange them in a logical order.
- Think through how to begin your writing. Begin drafting when you know what your main idea will be and you have ideas for introducing it.
- Use your notes to draft the body of your work.
- Remember what you have learned about strong conclusions and write a good ending to your work.
- Read over your work. If something seems confusing or out of place, fix it.
- Check your work for errors in grammar, usage, mechanics, and spelling. Try to remember the mistakes you have made in the past so that you can avoid them.

Like everything else, writing under time pressure gets easier with practice. Each composition chapter in this book ends with a timed writing activity that you can use to practice.

You can learn more about preparing for timed writing experiences and budgeting time on pages 398–399.

CHAPTER 2

Using Words Powerfully

Effective word choice is the use of specific, lively, natural-sounding language that is appropriate to the communication purpose.

Precise words provide the charge that lights up good writing. In the paragraph below, notice how the colorful words enliven Whitecloud's scene.

MODEL: Vivid Words

In the woods there are tracks of deer and snowshoe rabbits and long streaks where partridges slide to alight. Chipmunks make tiny footprints on the limbs, and one can hear squirrels busy in hollow trees, sorting acorns. Soft lake waves wash the shores, and sunsets burst each evening over the lakes and make them look as if they were afire.

— Thomas S. Whitecloud, "Blue Winds Dancing"

- Vivid sights
- Vivid sounds
- Vivid colors

Writing Project — Imaginative

The Way I See It Use vivid and powerful words to create a scene from an unusual point of view by completing the following project.

Think Through Writing Imagine you are something or someone else entirely. What would it be like to experience the world as a baseball bat? A quilting needle? A stone in a creek bed? A waste bin in an alley? Use your imagination to look at the world from the perspective of an object very different from yourself. What might you observe? How would you feel about what you see? What would the world sound, smell, taste, feel, and look like? Write as much as you can, without worrying about grammar, spelling, and other aspects of form. Let your imagination drive your thinking and writing and take you as far as you can go.

Talk About It In a group of three to five students, discuss what you have written about. How vivid is each writer's description? What details might improve the writing so that readers can imagine themselves seeing the world from this perspective?

Read About It In the following passage, Julia Alvarez talks about a teacher who told her students to "write little stories imagining we were snowflakes, birds, pianos, a stone in the pavement, a star in the sky." Think about what she says she learned about writing by using her imagination and paying attention to details.

MODEL: Memoir

From

Learning English: My New Found Land

Julia Alvarez

When I was 10, we immigrated to New York. How astonishing, a country where everyone spoke English! These people must be smarter, I thought. Maids, waiters, taxi drivers, doormen, bums on the street, garbage-men, all spoke this difficult language. It took some time before I understood that Americans were not necessarily a smarter, superior race. It was as natural for them to learn their mother tongue as it was for a little Dominican baby to learn Spanish. . . .

Soon it wasn't so strange that everyone was speaking in English instead of Spanish. I learned not to hear it as English, but as sense. I no longer strained to understand; I understood. I relaxed in this second language. Only when someone with a heavy Southern or British accent spoke in a movie or when the priest droned his sermon—only then did I experience that little catch of anxiety. I worried that I would not be able to "keep up" with the voice speaking in this second language. I would be like those people from the Bible we had studied in religion class, at the foot of an enormous tower that looked just like the skyscrapers all around me. They had been punished for their pride by being made to speak some slightly different version of the same language so that they didn't understand what anyone was saying.

> Specific nouns help readers picture the kinds of people who seemed to speak English effortlessly.

> The priest "droned" his sermon, not "gave" or "delivered." The specific verb tells the reader that the sound was monotonous, like a drone.

But at the foot of those towering New York skyscrapers, I began to understand more and more—not less and less—English. In sixth grade, I had one of the first of a lucky line of great teachers who began to nurture a love of the language, a love that had been there since childhood of listening closely to words. Sister Bernadette did not make our class interminably[1] diagram sentences from a workbook or learn a catechism[2] of grammar rules. Instead, she asked us to write little stories imagining we were snowflakes, birds, pianos, a stone in the pavement, a star in the sky. What would it feel like to be a flower with roots in the ground? If the clouds could talk, what would they say? She had an expressive, dreamy look that was accentuated by her face being framed in a wimple.[3] Supposing, just supposing . . . My mind would take off, soaring into possibilities: a flower with roots, a star in the sky, a cloud full of sad, sad tears, a piano crying out each time its back was tapped, music only to our ears.

> Big words like "interminably" and "catechism" suggest that Alvarez was probably not writing for an audience of very young readers.

Sister Bernadette stood at the chalkboard. Her chalk was always snapping in two because she wrote with so much energy, her whole habit[4] shaking with the swing of her arm, her hand tap tap tapping on the board. "Here's a simple sentence: *The snow fell.*" Sister Bernadette pointed with her chalk, her eyebrows lifted, her wimple poked up. "But watch what happens if we put an adverb at the beginning and a prepositional phrase at the end: *Gently the snow fell on the bare hills.*"

> This paragraph is filled with words that help the reader see and hear the scene being described.

I thought about the snow. I saw how it might fall on the hills, tapping lightly on the bare branches of trees. Softly it would fall on the cold, cold fields. On toys children had left out in the cold, and on cars and on little birds and on people out late walking on the streets. Sister Bernadette filled the chalkboard with snowy print, on and on, handling and shaping and moving language, scribbling all over the board until English, those little bricks of meaning, those little fixed units and counters,

> "Snowy" is a fresh and vivid way to describe the scribblings of chalk on a board.

---

1 **interminably:** Endlessly.
2 **catechism:** Summary of religious doctrine in the form of questions and answers.
3 **wimple:** A piece of cloth worn around the head, framing the face, by some nuns.
4 **habit:** Distinctive clothing worn my members of a religious order.

36 Using Words Powerfully

> became a charged, fluid mass that carried me in its great fluent waves, rolling and moving onward, to deposit me on the shores of the only homeland. I was no longer a foreigner with no ground to stand on. I had landed in language.
>
> I had come into my English.

Respond in Writing Alvarez closes her essay by saying, "I had come into my English." What is *your* English? Why do you speak the way you do? Think about the ways in which you use the English language and how the conventions you follow affect your ability to communicate with others.

Work Together Discuss with your classmates how writing from an unusual point of view has affected the choice of words and images in your scene.

Small Groups: In your writing group, read one another's scenes. How appropriate is the choice of images and language for the perspective taken? Would a snowflake and a baseball bat come across the same situations and describe them in similar language, or would you need to modify your language to suit the particular experiences that each might have?

Whole Class: Take two contrasting subjects from each writing group (for example, a lone tree on a prairie and a rock at the bottom of the ocean) and explain to the class why they would require a different perspective and different language in order to be believable from that point of view.

Write About It You will write a description from the perspective of an object that is very different from yourself. The following table provides possible ways in which you may write about this topic.

Possible Topics	Possible Audiences	Possible Forms
• a leaf falling from a tree	• other leaves about to fall	• a poem
• a can being kicked along a city street	• kids	• a long warning label on a can
• a speed bump	• car drivers	• a speech
• a jump rope	• athletes	• a user's manual

Developing Your Style and Voice

Your writing **style** is your unique way of expressing your ideas through the words you choose and the sentence patterns you use. As you make choices in your writing and develop your style, you will also be developing your writing voice. (See page 6.) **Voice** is the quality in writing that makes it sound as if there is a real and unique person behind the words.

Think about your speaking voice. You use one voice when you're talking on the phone in your room and another when you're at a sports event. In a similar way, the voice you use for your writing depends on your purpose and audience. A report for science class and a journal entry for English, for example, would call for different voices.

WRITING PURPOSE	WHAT THE WRITER'S VOICE SHOULD CONVEY
To provide information and/or persuade people	Genuine interest in the subject, often including personal insights about why the subject is important to the writer and what the reader might expect to gain from it; respect for differing viewpoints; confidence without conceit
To describe a subject clearly and/or tell a real or imaginary story	A genuine, not phony, personality; often some personal statements that show a willingness to trust readers with ideas you may be sensitive about

No matter what the purpose, however, a writer's voice should be engaging and genuine. The following rubric shows the traits of more (4) and less (1) successful writing voices.

Voice Rubric

4 The voice is engaging throughout. It sounds natural and unique.	3 The voice is engaging almost always. It usually sounds natural and unique.	2 Sometimes the voice doesn't connect with the reader. Parts may not sound natural or unique.	1 The voice does not make a connection with the reader and there's little sense of a unique person.

PROJECT PREP Analyzing *Voice*

With a partner, take turns reading the excerpt from Alvarez's memoir. When you have finished, identify her writing purpose. Then try to describe her writing voice. Based on her writing voice, how do you picture her? Does her voice seem well suited to her purpose? Finally, identify the words and expressions that led you to "hear" Alvarez's voice as you did. Use the above rubric to evaluate it. Summarize your discussion to share with the class.

Varieties of the English Language

Although English is one language, there are variations in the way it is spoken and used. How *you* use English helps shape your writing voice.

① Dialects and Standard American English

Across the United States, people in different regions pronounce certain words in different ways. These different ways of speaking are called **dialects.** For example, New Englanders are said to speak with a twang and Southerners with a drawl.

American English varies among three main regional dialects: Eastern, Southern, and General American. Each of these dialects may contain many subdialects. Dialects can vary in vocabulary, pronunciation, and even grammar. In New York, for instance, people waiting to see a movie stand *on* line, while in Chicago they stand *in* line. Texans might address a group as *y'all* while someone in Pittsburgh, Pennsylvania, might say *yinz*. Dialects add color and richness to the English language.

Standard American English is the most widely used and accepted form of English in the United States, allowing people of different regions to communicate clearly. While other variations of American English may be appropriate in informal conversation and creative writing, Standard English should be used in formal speeches and informative writing. Standard English is also academic language—the English taught in school. It is the English used in newspapers, on radios, and in scholarly works.

> **Writing Tip**
>
> Use **Standard English** when writing for school and for a large general audience.

● **Practice Your Skills**

Identifying Dialects

In a small group, discuss the words you use for common things. For example, what do you call the clumps of dust under furniture? *dust bunnies? death balls?* What do you call the strip of grass between the sidewalk and the street? *parkway? devil's strip?* Do you use the dialect you hear on television news?

PROJECT PREP *Prewriting* **Audience and Form**

In your writing group, identify possible audiences and forms for each student's writing. Also discuss the conventions of each form. A user's manual, for instance, looks and functions in ways different from those of an encyclopedia entry. What do readers expect to find in a piece following the conventions of each selected form?

❷ Nonstandard American English

Nonstandard English is English that does not follow the rules and guidelines of Standard English. It is not incorrect, but simply language that is inappropriate in situations, with audiences, or on occasions where Standard English is expected.

COLLOQUIALISMS

Nonstandard English has a number of informal expressions called **colloquialisms.** These are appropriate for informal writing and conversation but not for formal writing.

An **idiom** is an informal phrase or expression that has a meaning different from what the words suggest in their usual meanings. Since idioms do not mean what they seem to mean, avoid them when writing for a large general audience so you won't be misunderstood.

| Idioms | Leanna became known as a **blue-ribbon** babysitter in the neighborhood. (high-quality) |
| | Carlos was **fed up with** his little sister's nagging. (very tired of) |

SLANG

Slang consists of Nonstandard English expressions that are developed and used by particular groups. Such expressions are highly colorful, exaggerated, and often humorous. Although most slang goes out of fashion quickly, a few slang expressions—such as those that follow—have become a permanent part of the language. Slang is not appropriate for formal writing.

| Slang Expressions | Chelsea got a lot of **props** on the outfits she designed for the cheerleaders. (positive feedback) |
| | Leon wrote a program to protect the club's computer from getting **hacked**. (accessed without permission) |

● **Practice Your Skills**

Identifying Informal Language

Each sentence below contains informal language. Rewrite each sentence using Standard English.

1. You should get a load of Jane's new bicycle.
2. James would leap at the chance to earn extra money.
3. My mom keeps bugging me to clean out the garage.
4. The library has tons of books on dinosaurs.
5. I ain't gonna go to the zoo with them on Saturday.
6. There are lots of things to do at the park.
7. It can be difficult and time-consuming to score a part-time summer job.
8. A rainy summer day can be a bummer.
9. I am going to have to power through my homework tonight in order to get it all done.
10. The band's last song brought the house down.

PROJECT PREP *Revising* **Language Choices**

In your writing group, decide which form of language is appropriate for each writer's piece. Be creative and give a personality to your object. Would a snowflake or washing machine use "ain't" or informal language? For each writer, recommend which form of the English language is appropriate for the perspective, object, and situation adopted.

Varieties of the English Language

Choosing Vivid Words

Writers choose precise, vivid words to communicate exactly what they mean. You can experiment with word choice at any stage of the writing process.

❶ Denotations and Connotations

When you look up a word in a dictionary, you will find its denotative meaning. The **denotation** of a word means the *specific* definition of a word. However, sometimes through usage a word takes on additional meanings; this is the **connotation** of a word. For example, although *headstrong* and *stubborn* have similar denotative meaning, they have a different connotative meaning. *Headstrong* has come to mean "opinionated" while *stubborn* means "unwilling to give in." Be aware of these differences when choosing words in your writing.

● Practice Your Skills

Identifying Denotations and Connotations

Read the following list of words. Each pair shares a denotative meaning. What do you think the connotative meaning is for each word? Why?

1. smart; brainy
2. nosy; curious
3. tall; lanky
4. childish; youthful
5. mature; aged
6. boss; leader
7. economical; cheap
8. picky; selective
9. dark; unlit
10. clown; fool

> **Writing Tip**
>
> The **connotation** of a word can have an emotional impact; as a writer, you should be aware of this impact and use the word with the exact meaning you intend.

PROJECT PREP *Revising* **Using Peer Feedback**

In your writing group, identify the denotations and connotations of key words each writer used. Are they the best possible choices to convey the writer's meaning? Write a new draft of the scene you began earlier, taking into account the suggestions that your writing group partners have made. Choose words with the precise meaning you intend.

42 Using Words Powerfully

In the Media

Advertising

Advertisers take the power of words and use them to convince people to buy products. They do this so well that you may find yourself reaching for a cup of hot chocolate in the middle of a summer day.

Creating ads that have just the right words is not easy. Advertisers gather a whole team of people together to brainstorm and find word combinations that will have an impact. Good advertising teams want you to remember their slogans and to have an automatic response when you hear them. You can probably think of many examples of these slogans, especially for athletic shoes, soft drinks, and even milk. Try to develop a catchy slogan yourself.

Media Activity

Working in teams of three or four students, come up with a slogan to sell that cup of hot chocolate during July. Follow these steps.

- Think of a reason to drink hot chocolate on a warm day. Your reason may be serious or silly, or it may appeal to the emotions of your audience.
- Your slogan should be short and to the point. Do not include ideas or thoughts unless they express just what you want to say.
- Present your slogan to classmates, who will evaluate the slogans to decide which is the most persuasive.

Discuss with your classmates why some slogans are particularly memorable. How does the power of words contribute to their effectiveness?

❷ Using Specific Words

Weak, vague words like those in the following sentence make writing dull and provide little information.

Weak   Near the water stood a tree, some flowers, and a stone.

The sentence springs to life with specific, colorful words.

Specific   Near the waterfall stood a crooked birch, daffodils in bloom, and a boulder the size of a bear.

The chart below shows general and specific words for different parts of speech. When you write, always choose precise nouns, lively verbs, colorful adjectives, and specific adverbs.

	GENERAL	SPECIFIC	
Nouns	road	path	avenue
		lane	boulevard
		trail	highway
		alley	turnpike
Verbs	said	mumbled	boasted
		muttered	demanded
		urged	snapped
		whispered	blurted
Adjectives	big	lofty	bottomless
		thick	towering
		bulky	massive
		roomy	important
Adverbs	slowly	gradually	gently
		cautiously	lazily
		hesitantly	reluctantly
		leisurely	sluggishly

44   Using Words Powerfully

● **Practice Your Skills**

Using Specific Words

In the following fable, twenty general words and phrases have been underlined. Write a specific noun, verb, adjective, or adverb to replace each general word or phrase.

The Grasshopper and the Ants

A grasshopper lived in a (1) place near an anthill. Every day the ants worked (2) without stopping. They built (3) things, and they collected (4) things. They were preparing for winter. The grasshopper, on the other hand, said, "I'd rather (5) have fun."

One day the ants (6) said, "What will you eat and where will you sleep when the (7) bad weather comes in (8) a few months and you have no (9) place to go?"

The grasshopper laughed and said, "I'd rather (10) have fun."

In (11) a few months, the wind brought snow and cold. The ants lived (12) well inside their (13) nice (14) place, but the grasshopper was outside, hungry, and cold.

"Please let me share your (15) warm (16) place," (17) said the grasshopper.

"We (18) were busy while you played," said the ants. "Now you are hungry and cold, but we have food and a (19) nice (20) place. You must learn to plan ahead."

PROJECT PREP *Evaluating* Language Choices

Share your new draft with the members of your writing group. For each writer, focus on the language choices. Are the words as specific as they can be? Are they appropriate for the object, situation, and perspective being described? Suggest ways for the writer to improve the piece through attention to the language choices.

Look back over other things you have written. Do a spot check looking for specific words. Did you find some places where you used a general word when a specific one would do a better job? Make a note for your Learning Log about what you've learned about specific words.

Choosing Vivid Words

③ Finding Synonyms

When you substitute a precise, specific word for a more general one, you are using a synonym. **Synonyms** are words that have the same or similar meanings.

General Word	Ben **saw** his sister in the crowd.
Specific Word	Ben **spotted** his sister in the crowd.

In this sentence, *saw* and *spotted* are synonyms because they have similar meanings. *Spotted*, however, is more precise, and it carries an extra shade of meaning. *Spotted* suggests that Ben noticed his sister suddenly, maybe after looking for her for a while. The more general *saw*, in contrast, gives no extra meaning.

USING A THESAURUS

As you write and revise, you will use synonyms that you already know. At other times, however, you may wish to look up the general word in a print or online reference work called a **thesaurus.** This tool lets you look up synonyms for words you know. You then choose which of the synonyms best conveys the meaning you intend.

● **Practice Your Skills**

Using Synonyms

Revise the following paragraph, substituting more precise synonyms for the underlined words. Write your answers on a separate sheet of paper. Use a thesaurus for at least two words so that you can add new vocabulary.

Jumping Beans

The Mexican jumping bean is (1) <u>famous</u> for its quick, jumping movements. These (2) <u>movements</u> are caused by tiny caterpillars inside the seeds. The caterpillars make the seed (3) <u>move</u> by grasping the web they have made on the inner wall of the seed and (4) <u>snapping</u> their bodies. The (5) <u>movements</u> are believed to (6) <u>scare</u> birds who might otherwise eat the seeds. In this way, the tiny caterpillars (7) <u>protect</u> themselves from harm until they have turned into moths. At that time, they (8) <u>leave</u> the seed through a hole in the seed wall.

PROJECT PREP *Revising* **Second Draft**

Based on the recommendations of your writing group partners, write a second draft of your scene written from the perspective of an object. Feel free to use a thesaurus to help you find words that make your writing come alive for your readers.

④ Appealing to the Senses

You experience the world mainly through your five senses—sight, hearing, touch, smell, and taste. You can share your experiences with readers and create vivid pictures by using words that appeal to the five senses.

SIGHT

Writers try to capture the mood and feeling of a subject by painting a picture with words. Here are some words you can use to help your readers see what you see.

SIGHT WORDS			
Colors	**Movements**	**Shapes**	**Sizes**
beige	twisted	round	tiny
rust	raced	craggy	large
tawny	sauntered	curved	enormous
drab	sped	pointed	deep
scarlet	bent	angled	high
brilliant	jogged	zigzag	minuscule
magenta	stretched	rectangular	gigantic

● **Practice Your Skills**

Describing Sights

Answer each question about the photograph.

1. What colors do you see in this picture?
2. What objects do you see?
3. What shapes do you see?
4. What words describe the movements you see?
5. How would you describe the sizes in this picture?

● **Practice Your Skills**

Writing Sentences with Sight Words

Write five sentences describing the scene in the photograph above. Use the words you thought of in the exercise above to paint a vivid picture of the scene.

Choosing Vivid Words

SOUND

All the details in the following paragraph appeal to the sense of hearing. Notice how well they help you imagine the scene.

MODEL: Sound Words

The glider on the front porch creaked to the slow rhythm of my grandmother's rocking. From all around the farm came the sounds of the crickets in a faster tempo. "*Chick chuck, chick chuck,*" they sang in metallic voices. Every now and then the muffled roar of a distant truck would break the soothing monotony of those summer nights.

- Sound of glider
- Sound of crickets
- Sound of faraway truck

The following words will help you communicate to your reader what you hear. They are grouped according to the category with which we usually associate the sound.

SOUND WORDS

Objects	People	Nature	Animals
clang	moan	drip	purr
ring	murmur	splash	roar
tap	laugh	swish	cluck
bang	sigh	crackle	bark
thump	giggle	thud	hiss
crack	whisper	sizzle	whinny
squish	twitter	rustle	howl
snap	whistle	rumble	quack
spring	sneeze	crash	chirp
crush	mumble	patter	screech

Sometimes mixing the categories—applying a nature sound to a person, for example—can freshen and enliven your image. The sound word *sizzle* in the sentence *His voice sizzled with anger* makes the emotion come alive.

Writing Tip

Before you can write about the sounds in a scene, you must be able to hear or imagine them yourself. Practice listening to whatever is around you. If possible, close your eyes to help you concentrate.

- **Practice Your Skills**

  Describing Sounds

  Try to imagine yourself in the picture below. Then write ten sounds that you might hear from the marching band.

  Writing Sentences with Sound Words

  Write five sentences describing the sounds you might hear in the picture of the marching band. Use the sound words that you listed to bring the picture to life.

Touch

Your sense of touch tells you many things. It can tell you whether something is smooth or rough, hot or cold. It can also tell you about things that your hands themselves cannot touch. When your skin feels clammy, for example, your sense of touch is recording dampness and cold. When your cheeks feel flushed, you may be embarrassed or you might have a fever. All of these sensations come under the sense of touch.

The following words will help you appeal to your reader's sense of touch.

TOUCH WORDS			
silky	furry	windy	gooey
smooth	downy	gusty	oozy
cool	soft	coarse	sticky
gritty	clammy	glassy	frozen
rough	arid	wiry	steamy
grainy	damp	sandy	glossy

Choosing Vivid Words

Notice all of the details of touch in the following paragraph.

MODEL: Touch Words

One warm afternoon, Fern and Avery put on bathing suits and went down to the brook for a swim. Wilbur tagged along at Fern's heels. When she waded in the brook, Wilbur waded in with her. He found the water quite cold—too cold for his liking. So while the children swam and played and splashed water at each other, Wilbur amused himself in the mud along the edge of the brook, where it was warm and moist and delightfully sticky and oozy.

—E. B. White, *Charlotte's Web*

- Feel of sun's warmth
- Feel of cold water
- Feel of splashing
- Feel of mud

● Practice Your Skills

Writing Sentences with Touch Words

Try to imagine yourself in the picture below. Write five sentences describing this scene. Be sure to use words that appeal to the sense of touch.

Describing with Touch Words

Think of a favorite place. It could be a garden, a park bench, your bedroom, or a friend's backyard. Then write five sentences describing that place. Instead of describing its appearance, however, use details that will appeal to your reader's sense of touch.

Using Words Powerfully

The Power of Language

Adverbs and Prepositional Phrases: Scene Setters

In Julia Alavarez's account, Sister Bernadette shows her understanding of the power of language in appealing to readers' senses.

> "Here's a simple sentence: *The snow fell.*" Sister Bernadette pointed with her chalk, her eyebrows lifted, her wimple poked up. "But watch what happens if we put an adverb at the beginning and a prepositional phrase at the end: *Gently the snow fell on the bare hills.*"

Sister Bernadette knew that an adverb—a word that modifies, or describes, a verb, an adjective, or another adverb—would add a meaningful detail to the sentence. Adverbs commonly appear after the word they modify. Placing them before a sentence provides variety and also helps to set the scene.

Common Order	The snow fell gently.
Variation and Scene Setter	Gently the snow fell.

Prepositional phrases at the beginning of a sentence can also set the scene. A prepositional phrase is a group of words made up of a preposition, its object, and any words that describe the object.

Common Order	The snow fell gently on the bare hills.
Variation and Scene Setter	On the bare hills, the snow fell gently.

Try It Yourself

Use the sentences above as models for writing sentences with adverbs and prepositional phrases. Write an example of the common order and variation in order for each. If possible, write sentences on your project topic and include them in your draft. Later, check your draft for places where you can add prepositional phrases or adverbs at the beginning of sentences as scene setters.

Punctuation Tip

Put a comma after a prepositional phrase of four words or more that begins a sentence. An adverb at the beginning of a sentence is sometimes followed by a comma.

SMELL

A smell will sometimes bring back a flood of memories. The following words will appeal to your reader's sense of smell.

SMELL WORDS			
musty	fishy	fragrant	piney
burnt	stale	pungent	smoky
fruity	fresh	moldy	mildewed
stuffy	lemony	sour	floral
sharp	sweet	fresh	minty

● **Practice Your Skills**

Sharpening Your Sense of Smell

Write ten words that describe smells you might experience in the scene pictured below.

Describing with Smell Words

Write five sentences describing the scene in the picture. Use at least two smell words from the list above.

TASTE

The following paragraph was written by Laura Ingalls Wilder about an experience in her childhood. How many different things can you taste as you read?

> **MODEL: Taste Words**
>
> When they had eaten the soft maple candy until they could eat no more of it, then they helped themselves from the long table loaded with pumpkin pies and dried berry pies and cookies and cakes. There was salt-rising bread, too, and cold boiled pork, and pickles. Oo, how sour the pickles were!
>
> —Laura Ingalls Wilder, *Little House in the Big Woods*

Besides naming specific foods, you can also use any of the following taste words to whet your reader's appetite.

TASTE WORDS

spicy	bland	sharp	savory
bitter	caramel	smooth	lumpy
tart	sugary	creamy	chewy
doughy	tender	gooey	moist
sweet	sour	dry	crisp
salty	hot	flakey	sticky
juicy	crunchy	tangy	creamy

• Practice Your Skills

Describing with Taste Words

Write five sentences describing your favorite food. Help your reader really taste it by using precise taste words.

PROJECT PREP   *Revising*   Sense Words

In your writing group, focus on the writer's use of sensory details. How would it taste for a baseball bat to be dropped in the dirt? What is the sound of a snowflake landing? What smells would a rock in a creek bed notice? What would it feel like for a quilting needle to weave through fabric? What colors would a falling leaf notice on the way down? Give each writer suggestions for improving the description through the use of vivid sensory details.

Choosing Vivid Words

Think Critically

Elaborating

You can use your skill in appealing to a reader's senses to flesh out your writing and make it richer in detail. When you add details to your writing, you are **elaborating.**

How do you elaborate? One good way is to take a **mental snapshot** by picturing every possible detail in your subject. Carefully reread what you have written. Then ask yourself the following questions: "What exactly did I mean by that? What specific examples can I think of to show what I meant by that?" Take a mental snapshot to answer those questions. Use the specific details to elaborate on your more general ideas.

Consider the following paragraph. As it stands, it lacks detail, giving the reader little to hold on to.

> Every season has its sights, smells, tastes, and sounds. Autumn has its own special sights. The sights and sounds of winter are different from those of fall. Spring is the time of bright colors. Summer is a time capsule full of happy moments.

Notice how the first two sentences can be elaborated into a whole paragraph by picturing the scene and adding specific details that appeal to the senses.

> Every season has its sights, smells, tastes, and sounds. In the autumn you can see deep brown fields of grass and golden trees. If you listen carefully, you'll hear the far-off roar of football cheers and gentle, rustling leaves. Close your eyes and imagine tasting the favorite fruit of autumn lovers: the crisp tang of a ruby-red apple.

Thinking Practice

Complete the paragraph below by writing specific details that appeal to the senses.

The sights and sounds of winter are different from those of fall. In winter I see (1) ___, (2) ___, and (3) ___. The winter sounds of (4) ___ and (5) ___ are everywhere. The sky looks like (6) ___, and the air feels like (7) ___. Spring is the time of bright colors. The flowers are (8) ___, (9) ___, and (10) ___. The blue sky looks like (11) ___. The breeze feels like (12) ___. The sounds of (13) ___ remind me that summer will soon be here. Summer is a time capsule full of happy moments. It smells like (14) ___ and tastes like (15) ___. The days pass quickly. The signs of autumn return.

Using Words Powerfully

The Language of Power *Run-on Sentences*

Power Rule: Use the best conjunction and/or punctuation for the meaning when connecting two sentences. Revise run-on sentences. (See pages 668–669.)

See It in Action While elaborating adds valuable details, sometimes writers try to put too much information into one sentence. This kind of error is called a run-on or fused sentence—two or more sentences that are written as one. Run-on sentences will confuse your readers. Readers won't be sure where one idea ends and another begins. Here is an example of a run-on sentence:

Run-on sentence   The days pass quickly the signs of autumn return.

The ideas are much clearer if the sentences are separated. One common way to join sentences is to add a comma and the conjunction *and*.

Joined with conjunction   The days pass quickly, and the signs of autumn return.

Another common way to clarify this thought is to create two separate sentences by using a period between them and a capital letter at the beginning of the second sentence.

Set apart with period   The days pass quickly. The signs of autumn return.

Remember It Record this rule and these examples in the Power Rule section of your Personalized Editing Checklist.

Use It Read your draft aloud and listen to how your voice changes when you come to the end of a sentence. Are there places where your voice would naturally go down or pause, but where there are no periods or commas and conjunctions? Decide if these are examples of run-on sentences and add a period or a conjunction to fix any you find.

Choosing Vivid Words

5 Tired Words

A **tired word** is a word that has been so overused that it has been drained of meaning. Take, for example, the word *wonderful*. This word literally means "full of wonder." Now, through overuse, the word means "good."

People often use tired words in speech, calling sunsets "pretty," movies "fabulous," and sweaters "cute." None of these words conveys precise information, however.

● Practice Your Skills

Using Fresh Words

Write five sentences describing the sunset in the photo on this page. Avoid tired words and search for fresh, unusual ways to describe what you see.

Writing Tip

Avoid tired words and your writing will be fresh, precise, and interesting to read.

editing

Make the following sentence more economical by eliminating the words that don't add any meaning and rewriting to include fresh language.

> We stayed at a totally awesome state park where the scenery was wonderful and there were really good things to do.

PROJECT PREP Editing Clarity and Conventions

Prepare a final draft of your writing, incorporating all of the ideas you have developed along the way. Edit your paper to make sure it is as clear as possible and that it follows appropriate conventions of grammar, usage, and mechanics. You may use the Editing Checklist on page 28 as a guide.

Using a Word Choice Rubric

Evaluate your word choice with the following rubric.

4 Words are specific, powerful, and rich in sensory images.	3 Words are specific and some words appeal to the senses.	2 Some words are overly general and/or tired.	1 Most words are overly general and tired.
• I used Standard English if required. • I used Nonstandard English, with colloquialisms, if appropriate. • I used words with connotations that match my intended meaning. • I used fresh, not tired words. • I used words with punch and sparkle that appeal to the senses of sight, sound, touch, smell, and taste.	• I was aware of differences between Standard and Nonstandard English and made reasonable choices. • My word choice conveys my meaning but may not have sparkle and punch. • I used fresh words often. • I made a good effort to use words that appeal to the senses, but now see where I might have done more.	• I was not always aware of differences between Standard and Nonstandard English and made some choices that might confuse a reader. • I still need to work on finding the best, most specific word to give sparkle and punch to my writing. • I used a few tired expressions. • My word choices appealed to only one or two senses.	• I was not aware of differences between Standard and Nonstandard English and made some confusing choices. • Few of my words were as specific and vivid as they need to be. • I used some tired expressions. • My word choices didn't really appeal to the senses.

CHAPTER 2

PROJECT PREP   *Evaluating*   Using a Rubric

Use these strategies according to the rating you give yourself:
4. Keep up the good work!
3. Learn from what you did well: how can you apply that throughout your scene?
2. Work with a peer to get ideas for improving word choice.
1. Work with a peer and read your favorite writer to see how he or she uses words.

When you are satisfied with your text, publish it in your chosen form (see pages 30–31) or in another appropriate medium, such as a Web site or class anthology.

Writing Lab

Project Corner

Get Dramatic
Act It Out

In your writing group, **select one piece and develop it into a play** that you either perform before the class or make into a video and show on screen. (See pages 196–203 for help with script writing and pages 456–461 for help with making videos.)

Get Artistic
Change Perspectives

Using any artistic medium—watercolor, chalk, clay, or colored pencil, for example—**prepare a view of the world from the perspective of the object you have created.** What would it see? For example, if you wrote from the perspective of a twig, what would it see if it were flying above the earth in the mouth of a bird? If you are using multimedia, what would it hear?

Experiment Write a Story

If you were to use your scene as the setting for a story, what might the story be about? What other characters might be in it? **Draft a story** and share it with classmates.

Post It
World-Wide Writing

Find a site where creative writing is hosted and with your teacher's permission **upload your own writing** to include at the Web site.

In the Workplace
Bulletin Board Message

Apply and Assess

1. Your employer provides a break room that contains tables and chairs, a microwave oven, vending machines, and a refrigerator for lunches and leftovers. Unfortunately, people frequently forget the food they have put in the fridge. As a result, the refrigerator is filled with spoiled food. **Write a message** to your fellow employees to be posted on the bulletin board in the break room. Use specific details to vividly describe the mess in the refrigerator. Appeal to all five of the readers' senses: sight, sound, taste, smell, and touch.

In Academic Areas Letter to the Curator

2. You are a composer who writes symphonies for non-traditional orchestras. Your symphonies include parts written for instruments such as garbage can lids, lead pipes, and half-filled soda bottles. They also include recorded noises, such as cat meows and car engines. Next week your latest symphony will premiere for the opening of an important art show at the Museum of Modern Art in New York City. As the orchestra plays, slides of paintings from the show will be projected onto a huge screen behind the musicians. **Write a letter** to the curator of the museum describing the slides that you will project while the music is played. Be sure to use specific nouns, verbs, adjectives, and adverbs in your letter.

Timed Writing Paragraph Revision

3. Seventeen general words and phrases are underlined in the paragraph below from a letter you are sending to your brother, who is away at camp. Replace each with a specific noun, verb, adjective, or adverb to make the details more precise. You have eight minutes.

Several of us were sitting in a part of the restaurant. There was food on the plates in front of us, most of it uneaten, and we were trying to decide what to do. Outside the weather was terrible. First we went to Joe's place. We had some fun there. Then the weather got better so we went out. We did a lot of things. Miriam did one especially funny thing. Then we saw Trudy across the street. She came over and we did some more fun things.

Before You Write Consider the following questions: What is the subject? What is the occasion? Who is the audience? What is the purpose?

After You Write Evaluate your work using the word choice rubric on page 57.

CHAPTER 3

Writing with Sentence Variety

Sentence variety, achieved by varying the structure and length of sentences, keeps writing flowing smoothly, as in the following story about a frightening moment.

STUDENT MODEL: Sentence Variety

> Franklin carefully searched the green spiky bushes where he thought the noise came from. Then, out of the darkness of the bushes, flew what seemed like a purple bat. He held onto it for dear life as the thing took him up into the air. He didn't want to open his eyes because he was afraid of heights. Then suddenly it stopped in midair. Franklin slowly opened his eyes and looked down. "Oh mama!" he said. He was about two hundred feet above the ground. He looked up to what he was holding onto, but now it was holding onto him.
>
> —Victor Ramirez, Lucyle Collins Middle School,
> Fort Worth, Texas

Writing Project — Personal Narrative

Facing Fear Write a story with sentence variety about a time when you were very afraid of something that turned out to be harmless.

Think Through Writing Think of a time you were very afraid and then learned your fear was unfounded. Write about it so that a reader believes you feared a very real threat.

Talk About It In your writing group, discuss the experiences you have written about. Think of ways in which the writer builds a sense of fear and foreboding.

Read About It In the following selection, a young character is alone in the wilderness on a dark night. He fears he will be attacked by a dangerous animal. Think about how the author creates a sense of fear and builds up tension.

MODEL: Fiction

From

Hatchet

Gary Paulsen

At first he thought it was a growl. In the still darkness of the shelter in the middle of the night his eyes came open and he was awake and he thought there was a growl. But it was the wind, a medium wind in the pines had made some sound that brought him up, brought him awake. He sat up and was hit with the smell.

It terrified him. The smell was one of rot, some musty rot that made him think only of graves with cobwebs and dust and old death. His nostrils widened and he opened his eyes wider but he could see nothing. It was too dark, too hard dark with clouds covering even the small light from the stars, and he could not see. But the smell was alive, alive and full and in the shelter. He thought of the bear, thought of Bigfoot and every monster he had ever seen in every fright movie he had ever watched, and his heart hammered in his throat.

Then he heard the slithering. A brushing sound, a slithering brushing sound near his feet—and he kicked out as hard as he could, kicked out and threw the hatchet at the sound, a noise coming from his throat. But the hatchet missed, sailed into the wall where it hit the rocks with a shower of sparks, and his leg was instantly torn with pain, as if a hundred needles had been driven into it. "Unnnngh!"

Now he screamed, with the pain and fear, and skittered on his backside up into the corner of the shelter, breathing through his mouth, straining to see, to hear.

The slithering moved again, he thought toward him at first, and terror took him, stopping his breath. He felt he could see a low dark form, a bulk in the darkness, a shadow that lived, but now it moved away, slithering and scraping it moved away and he saw or thought he saw it go out of the door opening.

> Sentences start in a variety of ways, not always with the subject.

> The short first sentence conveys the boy's fears. The longer sentences in the rest of the paragraph provide variety.

> Conjunctions such as *and* and *but* show how ideas are related.

> The drawn-out sentences help convey the boy's mounting and then retreating fears.

Project and Reading

He lay on his side for a moment, then pulled a rasping breath in and held it, listening for the attacker to return. When it was apparent that the shadow wasn't coming back he felt the calf of his leg, where the pain was centered and spreading to fill the whole leg.

His fingers gingerly touched a group of needles that had been driven through his pants and into the fleshy part of his calf. They were stiff and very sharp on the ends that stuck out, and he knew then what the attacker had been. A porcupine had stumbled into his shelter and when he had kicked it the thing had slapped him with its tail of quills.

> The first sentence in this paragraph begins with the subject, but the second begins with a scene-setting introductory clause.

Respond in Writing Think about Gary Paulsen's account of the boy's encounter with the porcupine. Write informally in response to the following questions: How did Paulsen raise your anticipation that it was a much more terrifying beast? How did you feel as you read his story?

Develop Your Own Ideas Talk with your peers about unfounded fears.

Small Groups: In small groups, discuss your own experiences of fear of a seemingly terrifying threat. Create an organizer like the one below to chart your process of imagining threats.

Fears	Physical Setting and Events	Your Emotions
Why you were in a frame of mind to develop fears		
What happened to cause your fears to increase		
What happened to reveal that your fears were unfounded or misplaced		

Whole Class: Make a master chart of all of the ideas generated by the small groups, and use these ideas for further discussion of how to write about your experience in vivid detail.

Write About It You will next develop your story of an experience of strong but unwarranted fear. Your story might take any of the following forms.

Writing with Sentence Variety

Possible Topics	Possible Audiences	Possible Forms
• fear of a physical threat • fear of a social situation • fear of a bad outcome • fear of another person	• other teenagers in a similar situation • people sitting around a camp fire • counselors who want to understand teenagers better • younger kids who have never experienced similar situations	• an article in a teen magazine • an oral narrative • a story for a Web site that features stories of fear • a written narrative

CHAPTER 3

Project and Reading   63

Writing Varied Sentences

When all of the sentences in a passage sound the same, the writing seems dull and difficult to read. Study the example below.

Lack of Sentence Variety Sailboats rocked in the cove. Bell buoys bobbed up and down. There were flags on the boats. They fluttered in the breeze. Children were on the beach. They called to the sailors. The wind carried their voices.
(The sentences are about the same length and have almost the same structure.)

Add variety to your writing by varying the length and structure of your sentences. Notice that the passage below is more interesting and easier to read.

Sentence Variety Sailboats rocked in the cove, and bell buoys bobbed up and down. The flags on the boats fluttered in the breeze. On the beach children called to the sailors, and the wind carried their voices.

❶ Sentence Combining with Specific Details

One short sentence is clear and forceful. Too many short sentences in a row, however, sound choppy and clipped and are hard to read. Sentence combining is one way to vary the length of your sentences and add interest to your writing.

Specific details help readers picture exactly what you are explaining or describing. Often the details in several separate sentences can be combined to form one longer sentence. Read the following short, choppy sentences.

Writing Tip
Combine short sentences into longer, more interesting ones.

Choppy Sentences
The kite bobbed.
The kite was **huge.**
It bobbed **gently.**
It moved **in the wind.**

Writing with Sentence Variety

These four sentences can be combined into one sentence by adding the descriptive words and a phrase to the first sentence. Notice how the sentence flows and the image becomes easier to picture.

Combined Sentence The **huge** kite **bobbed gently in the wind.**

When you combine sentences to include two or more adjectives in a row, a comma is often needed to separate them. Study the following example.

Choppy Sentences The **long** string tugged against my hand. The string was **thin.**

Combined Sentence The **long, thin** string tugged against my hand.

● Practice Your Skills

Combining with Specific Details

Combine each group of short sentences into one longer one.

1. Popeye is a character. He is in a comic strip. He is strong. He is also odd-looking.
2. He eats spinach. He eats it from the can. He eats it often.
3. This vegetable always gives him strength. It gives him strength immediately. It gives him tremendous strength.
4. Olive Oyl is his girlfriend. She is tall. She is thin.
5. Popeye has adventures. Olive Oyl has adventures with him.
6. Another superhero is a visitor. He is not from Earth. The visitor is powerful. He comes from a distant planet.
7. Superman arrived on Earth after the destruction of the planet Krypton. Superman arrived mysteriously. Krypton is an imaginary planet.
8. He pretends to be a newspaper reporter. The reporter is timid. The reporter is mild-mannered.
9. In this disguise Superman can investigate crimes. His disguise is clever. He investigates crimes openly.
10. At the last moment, the hero stops the criminals. They are dangerous. He stops them effortlessly.

PROJECT PREP Revising *Focus*

1. Your first draft of your personal narrative was written freely, which is a good way to get ideas down on paper. Now stand back from what you have written. What is the focus of your story? Is everything in your draft related directly to your focus? Redraft your story, if necessary, to sharpen the focus on the main event.
2. As you revise, if you notice a string of short, choppy sentences, combine them to create a smoother flow.

The Power of Language

Appositives: Who or What?

Adding details that elaborate on a person, place, or thing that may be unknown to your reader will strengthen your writing. As you draft, you can add such details in the form of appositive phrases. An **appositive** is a noun or pronoun phrase that identifies or adds identifying information to a preceding noun. (See pages 607–608.) In the following sentence from *Hatchet*, for example, Paulsen adds chilling details in two appositive phrases in the middle of the sentence. Notice that they are set off by commas.

Appositive Phrases in the Middle

He felt he could see a low dark form, a bulk in the darkness, a shadow that lived, but now it moved away, slithering and scraping it moved away and he saw or thought he saw it go out of the door opening.

Paulsen also uses an appositive to elaborate on the smells surrounding him. This time it comes at the end of the sentence. Notice that a comma separates the appositive phrase from the rest of the sentence.

Appositive Phrase at the End

The smell was one of rot, some musty rot that made him think only of graves with cobwebs and dust and old death.

Try It Yourself

Try writing one sentence on your project topic with an appositive in the middle and another with an appositive at the end. Use the resulting sentences in your draft if you can, and try creating other similar sentences. You can always add more details with appositives when you revise.

Punctuation Tip

Use **two commas** to enclose an appositive in the **middle of a sentence.**

Use **one comma** to separate an appositive from the rest of the sentence when it appears **at the end.**

② Combining Sentence Parts

Another way to combine sentences is to join equal sentence parts to form compounds. Use *and*, *but*, or *or* to form compound subjects and compound verbs.

Compound Subject
The **fish** was fresh.
The **vegetables** were fresh.
The **fish** and **vegetables** were fresh.

Compound Verb
I **can bake** the chicken.
I **can barbecue** the chicken.
I **can bake** or **barbecue** the chicken.

If you combine three or more subjects and verbs, remember to use commas.

Compound Verb
On our vacation in Wyoming, we **hiked.** We **swam.** We also **canoed.**
On our vacation in Wyoming, we **hiked, swam,** and **canoed.**

● Practice Your Skills

Combining Sentence Parts

Combine each group of sentences, using a compound subject or a compound verb. Use the conjunction *and, but,* or *or.* Use commas where needed.

Example Frank left his locker key at home yesterday. He forgot it again today.

Answer Frank left his locker key at home yesterday **and** forgot it again today.

1. Keisha can have my extra ticket to the concert. Gary can have it.
2. We'll broil the hamburgers in the oven. We'll barbecue them on the grill.
3. José finished his science project on time. He left it at home.
4. Phil and Sarah ran a road race on Saturday. They couldn't finish it.
5. Gerard's surprise party will be on Saturday. My first soccer game will be on Saturday too.
6. Kathy skates during the winter. She runs five miles a day in the spring.
7. Willie was named Rookie of the Year. He became a basketball star.
8. Over the weekend I mowed the lawn. I weeded the garden. I also planted some vegetables.
9. The terrier growled at the visitors. He bared his teeth.
10. Penguins cannot fly. They can swim very well, even in ice-cold water.

The Language of Power   *Agreement*

Power Rule Use verbs that agree with the subject. (See pages 740–760)

See It in Action A verb must agree with its subject in number. If you make two singular subjects into a compound subject, you will need to use the verb form that goes with plural subjects. Think of it as a teeter-totter relationship. In most cases, if the subject has an -*s*, then the verb doesn't. The -*s* can be on either the subject or the verb, but not both.

Singular Subjects	The tent **smells** musty. The sleeping bag **smells** musty.
Compound Subject	The tent and sleeping bag **smell** musty.
Plural Subjects	The stars **look** bright. The planets **look** bright.
Compound Subject	The stars and planets **look** bright.

Remember It Record this rule and example in the Power Rule section of your Personalized Editing Checklist.

Use It Read through your project to make sure the verbs agree with the subjects. In each sentence of your draft, underline the subject, highlight the verb, and then ask yourself if the subject is singular or plural. Choose the correct form of the verb to agree with the subject.

PROJECT PREP   *Evaluating*   Reasons and Consequences

1. In your writing group, share your new draft with your partners and get feedback on whether or not your focus is sufficiently sharp. Take notes and make changes as needed when you can.
2. Then, discuss how effectively each author made clear the reasons for or consequences of the actions in the narrative. For example, why did someone in the story choose a certain action? What consequences do the various actions have?
3. Finally, help each writer find ways to vary sentence structure to add to the story's effect. Make notes of the feedback you receive and revise on your own.

③ Creating Compound Sentences

A simple sentence is a sentence that has one subject and one verb.

Simple Sentences   A **bolt** of lightning **flashed.**
The **tree exploded** into flames.

If two simple sentences contain related ideas, they can be combined to form a **compound** sentence, often with a conjunction such as *and* preceded by a comma.

Compound Sentence   A **bolt** of lightning **flashed, and** the **tree exploded** into flames.

In addition to *and*, the conjunctions *but* and *or* may be used to form compound sentences.

● **Practice Your Skills**

Creating Compound Sentences

Use the conjunctions in parentheses to combine each pair of sentences into one compound sentence. Use commas.

1. Many people dream about outer space. These dreams become a reality for students at Space Camp. (but)
2. Space Camp is located in Huntsville, Alabama, at the Space and Rocket Center. The staff runs programs there from March to September. (and)
3. Students can request information by letter. The staff at Space Camp will send them an application form and brochures. (and)
4. Many students from across the United States apply to Space Camp. Each year only three thousand are accepted. (but)
5. Students in grades five through seven are in the Level I program. Students in grades eight through ten are placed in Level II. (and)

6. The students take imitation flights. Information about previous NASA missions is provided. (and)
7. NASA donates equipment to the program. Real astronauts visit and talk with the campers. (and)
8. After Space Camp some students may want careers as scientists. Perhaps they would like to work for NASA as engineers. (or)
9. Space Camp lasts for only one week. The campers will remember the experience for a lifetime. (but)
10. Three-day programs are now available for adults. Two-week advanced courses are being developed for college students. (and)

PROJECT PREP   Revising   Show, Not Tell

Revise your personal narrative to use concrete images instead of overly general statements. Rather than simply stating an emotion, such as "I was scared," think of ways to describe how you felt in ways that your readers will find vivid. For example:

1. Describe an external physical response, such as, "The boy was shaking so much his glasses slipped down his nose."
2. Describe an internal physical response, such as, "I felt my stomach tighten and twist as I waited for Ms. Henchley to return my test."
3. Describe a mental sensation, such as, "Tara's mind tingled like a freshly poured ginger ale when her mother walked in the door."

Also look for places where you can create a smoother flow. Identify places where you used simple sentences and see if you can combine any into compound sentences.

Writing Varied Sentences

Think Critically

Seeing Relationships

When you combine sentences in your own writing, you need to choose the conjunction—*and*, *but*, or *or*—that makes the relationship clear.

When the ideas expressed are similar or of equal importance, use *and* to combine them.

Similar Ideas	Anthony was elected class president. His twin brother was elected treasurer.
Combined	Anthony was elected class president, **and** his twin brother was elected treasurer.

When the ideas are contrasting, use *but*.

Contrasting Ideas	Dana hit two home runs. Her team still lost the game.
Combined	Dana hit two home runs, **but** her team still lost the game.

When the ideas offer a choice, use *or*.

Choice Between Ideas	I can finish the posters after school today. Nate can finish them on Saturday afternoon.
Combined	I can finish the posters after school today, **or** Nate can finish them on Saturday afternoon.

When you combine sentences, you must use a comma as well as a conjunction.

Thinking Practice

Write three sentences about your day, using *and*, *but*, and *or*.

> **Writing Tip**
>
> When combining simple sentences into compound sentences, let the relationship between the ideas expressed in the two sentences determine which conjunction you use.

4 Varying Sentence Beginnings

Another way to add variety to your sentences is to begin them in different ways. Start some of them with an adverb or a prepositional phrase, for example.

Subject	The **raft** floated slowly down the river.
Adverb	**Slowly** the raft floated down the river.
Subject	A souvenir **banner** hung on the wall.
Prepositional Phrase	**On the wall** hung a souvenir banner.

● **Practice Your Skills**

Varying Sentence Beginnings

Rewrite the following paragraph. Add variety to each sentence by moving either an adverb or a prepositional phrase to the beginning of the sentence.

Hot Spots

Volcanoes have frightened people for centuries. Smoke and steam escape during active times. The liquid rock and gases below the earth's surface gain strength. Liquid rock suddenly pours out. The liquid rock becomes lava after the eruption. The lava slowly chokes the opening. The fiery blasts gradually die down. The liquid rock and gases again begin to build pressure. The sleeping giant will repeat its cycle soon.

● **Practice Your Skills**

Writing Sentence Beginnings

Write a beginning for each sentence. Use the kind of opener in parentheses.

1. * the lights in the house went out. (adverb)
2. * the field was too muddy for the soccer game. (prepositional phrase)
3. * Jim slammed the door to his room. (adverb)
4. * there was bumper-to-bumper traffic. (prepositional phrase)

PROJECT PREP *Evaluating* **Sentence Structure**

In your writing group, read one another's writing with a focus on sentence structure. Mark your manuscript in areas where you could improve your sentence variety.

In the Media

Television Nightly News

When you see images on television, you usually assume that the events are portrayed accurately. Although much of the information on television is certainly reliable, there is always a bias of some kind in determining what images and text to include—or exclude.

All commercial television stations are supported by advertising. Even programs such as the nightly news try to grab a viewer's attention and keep it in order to have better ratings and attract advertisers.

Sound bites (brief statements that capture an idea), compelling graphics, and live coverage of current events are a few of the techniques that television news programs use to interest viewers.

Understanding the different ways in which information is presented in this visual medium can help you evaluate what you see and hear. It may also help you become a better communicator as you try to capture in your writing what television can do so easily—combine powerful images with words.

Media Activity

Watch the local and national news on any television station, and record the programs if possible. What do you notice about the way the stories are presented? How long is each story? Is there a difference between the type of news story on the local news and the type covered on the national news?

Choose a story that interests you and present it in a paragraph, using vivid words to capture any images that may have been used. How does the type of story influence your writing style—that is, your word choice and sentence structure?

Writing Concise Sentences

Gymnasts always watch their weight and trim off extra pounds before a meet. When you write, trim off extra words that add no meaning to your sentences. Try to express your meaning in as few words as possible.

① Rambling Sentences

Overly long sentences are as hard to read as short, choppy ones. In this paragraph, too many ideas are strung together.

Rambling Sentences

Our ball landed on the Marshalls' roof, **and** Ted climbed the tree beside the house **and** jumped onto the roof. He picked up the ball, **but** then he was afraid to climb back down, **and** I got a tall ladder from the house next door, **but** Ted still wouldn't budge. I decided to ask Mr. Marshall to help us. He climbed the ladder, **and** soon Ted was safely on the ground, **and** we smiled with relief, **but** then we realized Ted had left the ball on the roof!

A paragraph is easier to read if you break up rambling sentences by removing some of the conjunctions.

Non-Rambling Sentences

Our ball landed on the Marshalls' roof. Ted climbed the tree beside the house and jumped onto the roof. He picked up the ball, but then he was afraid to climb back down. I got a tall ladder from the house next door, but Ted still wouldn't budge. I decided to ask Mr. Marshall to help us. He climbed the ladder, and soon Ted was safely on the ground. We smiled with relief. Then we realized Ted had left the ball on the roof!

CHAPTER 3

● **Practice Your Skills**

Revising Rambling Sentences

Revise the paragraph to eliminate rambling sentences.

Babe Hauls the Lumber

Paul Bunyan had a mighty blue ox named Babe, and Babe often hauled logs to the lumber camp for Paul, but one rainy morning Babe arrived in camp without the logs. The rain had soaked into the leather straps of the harness, and the straps had been stretching for miles, and the lumber was somewhere back in the forest, but Paul wasn't worried. Soon the sun came out, and the leather straps started to shrink, and in no time at all, the shrinking straps pulled the load of logs right into camp.

PROJECT PREP *Revising* **Building Suspense**

Based on the feedback from your writing group, produce a new draft of your story. Make every effort to use dramatic techniques in order to build a sense of suspense, such as providing clues that lead to one conclusion, only to have the events lead to another. Avoid rambling sentences, since they will drag down the suspense.

② Repetition

Make every word count. Avoid **wordiness,** or unnecessary repetition.

Wordy	Because of the storm, the principal dismissed us at noon and said we could go home. *(Dismissed us* and *said we could go home* mean the same thing.)
Concise	Because of the storm, the principal dismissed us at noon.
Wordy	Tired, the weary travelers returned home. *(Tired* and *weary* mean the same thing.)
Concise	The weary travelers returned home.

● **Practice Your Skills**

Eliminating Repetition

Revise each sentence by taking out words that repeat ideas.

1. She whispered to me quietly.
2. Through the mist, we could see the sight of the runway.
3. Stay in the surrounding area near the school.
4. I looked around in the bakery called Abe's Bakery.
5. I have a tiny little scar on my arm.
6. The teacher has an extra book that he doesn't need.
7. Ron lost more than 50 pounds in weight.
8. Some deadly diseases are fatal.
9. A great big bridge crosses into Canada.
10. They ate every single apple and didn't leave any.

EMPTY EXPRESSIONS

Empty expressions are another kind of wordiness. They add nothing to the meaning of a sentence, and they slow the reader down.

Wordy	As a matter of fact, the bus left an hour ago.
Concise	The bus left an hour ago.
Wordy	Because of the fact that I jumped into the pile of leaves, I had to rake them again.
Concise	Because I jumped into the pile of leaves, I had to rake them again.

Writing Concise Sentences

Following is a list of common empty expressions.

EMPTY EXPRESSIONS		
I think that	the thing that	the reason being
on account of	what I mean is	as a matter of fact
the point is that	there is/there was	because of the fact that

● **Practice Your Skills**

Eliminating Empty Expressions

Revise each sentence by taking out the empty expression.

1. There was a dirt road that led to our house in Montana.
2. As a matter of fact, I'd like to join the swim team.
3. I think that whales are an endangered species.
4. The thing that everyone noticed was how tall he was.
5. There were four long tables set up for the banquet.
6. It is a fact that bikers should wear safety helmets.
7. I stayed after school because of the fact that I had band practice.
8. There was a great wave that came crashing down on the boardwalk.
9. What I mean is I would like to go to the going-away party.
10. The reason that many people visit Yellowstone is to see the geysers.

editing

Rewrite the following sentence to make it as economical as possible.

> At this moment in time it is important to remember that success depends on hard work and persistence.

PROJECT PREP *Revising* **Concise Sentences**

In your writing group, read one another's work with a focus on concise sentences. Mark places in your story where you can trim away unnecessary words. Then revise your story accordingly. Share your work with your teacher and make further changes.

Write about what you learned in this chapter. How can you improve your writing? How has your writing improved so far? Make a note for your portfolio recording your thoughts.

Using a Fluency Rubric

Evaluate your fluency or that of your peers with the following rubric.

4 Sentences are varied in length and structure. Every sentence matters.	3 Sentences are mostly varied in length and structure. A few words and sentences seem unnecessary.	2 Many sentences are the same in length and structure. A number of words and sentences seem unnecessary.	1 Most sentences are the same in length and structure. A number of words and sentences seem unnecessary.
• I combined short, choppy sentences into varied, longer ones. • I used coordinating and subordinating conjunctions to improve the flow and show the relationship of ideas. • I started my sentences in a variety of ways, not always with the subject first. • I avoided rambling sentences, unnecessary repetition, and empty expressions.	• I combined some short, choppy sentences into varied, longer ones, but in a few places there is still some choppiness. • I sometimes used coordinating and subordinating conjunctions to improve the flow and show relationships. • I started most of my sentences in a variety of ways. • I avoided rambling sentences, unnecessary repetition, and empty expressions.	• A few parts of my work flow, but there is still choppiness. • I used a few conjunctions to improve flow and show relationships, but I see now that I could have used more. • Many of my sentences start the same way, with the subject. • A few of my sentences ramble or contain unnecessary information.	• I didn't quite achieve a flow. My writing seems to start and stop. • I didn't often combine ideas into one sentence to improve the flow and show relationships. • Most of my sentences start the same way, with the subject. • Many of my sentences ramble or contain unnecessary information.

> **PROJECT PREP** *Evaluating* **Using a Rubric**
>
> After evaluating your work, make changes as needed to improve it. When you are satisfied, publish it in your chosen form (see pages 30–31 and 63) or in another appropriate medium. You might, for instance, create a classroom anthology of stories that you publish in a bound "book" or post on the Internet.

Writing Lab

Project Corner

Get Dramatic Act It Out

In your writing group, select one story and **produce a short drama** based on its action. Present it to the class. (See pages 196–203 for help with script writing.)

Create a Board Game
Roll the Dice

Create a board game in which players travel along a route similar to that traveled by your story's main character. Design your game so that players must navigate the various perils, pitfalls, and problems encountered on the way to a destination.

Cast and Promote It
Go Indie

Imagine that you are an independent film producer who wants to make a movie out of your story. **Select a director and cast** for the film from the movie stars you know, and **produce a poster** that will be displayed in movie theater lobbies.

Apply and Assess

In the Workplace
Business Memo

1. You are a scientist at a soft drink factory, and recently you noticed that the factory has no paper-recycling program. Your boss is in Switzerland researching soft drinks made from snow. She has asked you to write any questions or concerns in a note, which she will read when she returns. **Write a one-paragraph memo** to your boss explaining why the factory needs a recycling program. Use a variety of sentence structures and beginnings in your note.

For Oral Communication
Presentation

2. You work for an advertising agency. Your boss has asked you to come up with a tagline or catchy slogan for CheezeBreeze, a new cheese spread made by PeopleSnax. Although you think CheezeBreeze tastes bland, you are scheduled to make a speech to your boss about your ideas for selling the product. **Prepare a presentation** for your boss that includes at least two slogans for CheezeBreeze. Read or listen to advertisements in magazines, on TV, on the radio, or on the Internet to help you brainstorm for slogans. With your teacher's permission, you may present the speech to your class.

Timed Writing
Magazine Contest Entry

3. The popular magazine *UmpTeen* is holding a writing contest, and your teacher wants you to enter. If you win the contest, your teacher will throw a class party in your honor! Prewrite some notes on one of *UmpTeen*'s topics—Fashion, Movie Stars, or TV Trivia. Using the notes, draft a one- or two-paragraph article that would interest the magazine's readers. Then revise your draft, combining some of your sentences for variety. Avoid wordiness and use conjunctions to help your writing make sense. Vary your sentence beginnings, and check for concise sentences. You have 25 minutes to complete your work.

Before You Write Consider the following questions: What is the subject? What is the occasion? Who is the audience? What is the purpose?

After You Write Evaluate your work using the fluency rubric on page 79.

CHAPTER 4

Writing Well-Structured Paragraphs

A **paragraph** is a group of related sentences that present and develop one main idea. A paragraph can be as short as a single sentence or it can contain dozens of sentences.

The main idea of a piece of writing is often expressed in the first paragraph. Once you are clear about the central idea of your piece, the writing process should flow fairly easily. The rest of your writing can be organized around the center.

Writing Project

Powerful Memories Create well-structured paragraphs as you write about a childhood event.

Think Through Writing Remember the first time you rode a two-wheeler? You probably felt as though you could take that bike over the moon, like the kids in the film *E.T.* Think of a similar memorable childhood event and write about it in your journal. Describe everything about it—the colors, sounds, tastes, textures, and smells of that event. Go into the greatest detail possible—and don't worry about grammar, spelling, or punctuation just yet.

Talk About It In a group with three others, take turns reading your memory out loud. As you listen to each, try to identify the high point of the event recalled. Also let the author know which details stand out for you. Providing feedback to each author will help him or her know how clearly the message is coming through. Be sure to ask for clarification if you do not understand something your group members say.

Read About It In the following passage from *When I Was Puerto Rican,* Esmeralda Santiago recreates her childhood memories of gathering and eating guavas, a favorite food of her native Puerto Rico.

MODEL: Memoir

From

When I Was Puerto Rican

Esmeralda Santiago

There are guavas at the Shop & Save. I pick one the size of a tennis ball and finger the prickly stem end. It feels familiarly bumpy and firm. The guava is not quite ripe; the skin is still a dark green. I smell it and imagine a pale pink center, the seeds tightly embedded in the flesh.

A ripe guava is yellow, although some varieties have a pink tinge. The skin is thick, firm, and sweet. Its heart is bright pink and almost solid with seeds. The most delicious part of the guava surrounds the tiny seeds. If you don't know how to eat a guava, the seeds end up in the crevices between your teeth.

When you bite into a ripe guava, your teeth must grip the bumpy surface and sink into the thick edible skin without hitting the center. It takes experience to do this, as it's quite tricky to determine how far beyond the skin the seeds begin.

Some years, when the rains have been plentiful and the nights cool, you can bite into a guava and not find many seeds. The guava bushes grow close to the ground, their branches laden with green then yellow fruit that seems to ripen overnight. These guavas are large and juicy, almost seedless, their roundness enticing you to have one more, just one more, because next year the rains may not come.

As children, we didn't always wait for the fruit to ripen. We raided the bushes as soon as the guavas were large enough to bend the branch.

A green guava is sour and hard. You bite into it at its widest point, because it's easier to grasp with your teeth. You hear the skin, meat, and seeds crunching inside your head, while the inside of your mouth explodes in little spurts of sour.

> The first paragraph begins in the present. It sets the scene.

> What do you think is the central idea of this paragraph?

> The author's knowledge of and descriptions of the guava are picturesque and vivid.

> Here, the author switches to a memory from her past.

Project and Reading

You grimace, your eyes water, and your cheeks disappear as your lips purse into a tight O. But you have another and then another, enjoying the crunchy sounds, the acid taste, the gritty texture of the unripe center. At night, your mother makes you drink castor oil,[1] which she says tastes better than a green guava. That's when you know for sure that you're a child and she has stopped being one.

> This paragraph is so descriptive that the reader can almost taste the guava.

I had my last guava the day we left Puerto Rico. It was large and juicy, almost red in the center, and so fragrant that I didn't want to eat it because I would lose the smell. All the way to the airport I scratched at it with my teeth, making little dents in the skin, chewing small pieces with my front teeth, so that I could feel the texture against my tongue, the tiny pink pellets of sweet.

> Here, the reader begins to understand the significance of the guava in the author's life.

Today, I stand before a stack of dark green guavas, each perfectly round and hard, each $1.59. The one in my hand is tempting. It smells faintly of late summer afternoons and hopscotch under the mango tree. But this is autumn in New York, and I'm no longer a child.

> The author is now back in the present.

The guava joins its sisters under the harsh fluorescent lights of the exotic fruit display. I push my cart away, toward the apples and pears of my adulthood, their nearly seedless ripeness predictable and bittersweet.

> How does this paragraph relate to the first one? Why does the author call apples and pears "predictable and bittersweet"?

---

[1] **castor oil:** The oil from castor beans used as an old-fashioned remedy for stomachaches.

Respond in Writing Respond to Esmeralda Santiago's childhood memory of gathering and eating guavas. What details does she provide that make the event compelling? Write at least five details that stand out in your memory.

Develop Your Own Details Work with your classmates to develop ideas to help you as you write about a childhood memory.

Small Groups: In your writing group, use a graphic organizer like the one on the next page to list sensory details you and your writing partners can use to describe your childhood events. List at least five details in each column.

Event				
Sounds	Taste	Touch	Smell	Sight

Whole Class: Share your organizer with the rest of your class to be part of a master chart of all of the ideas generated by the small groups. Refer to this chart for details you can use to describe your childhood event vividly.

Write About It You will next use a narrative form to describe in detail your memorable childhood event. Your writing might take any of the following forms:

Possible Topics
- a favorite family trip
- a memorable party
- an important discovery
- an exciting adventure
- a meaningful encounter

Possible Audiences
- other teenagers
- a good friend
- your parents, guardians, or other significant adult

Possible Forms
- a story for a teen magazine
- a diary entry
- a letter to someone who shared the event with you

Paragraph Structure

Usually paragraphs are part of a longer composition. In those cases, the paragraphs must be knit together into a seamless whole. Sometimes, though, paragraphs stand alone. In those cases, a paragraph needs to be complete in itself. In either case, paragraphs focus on one main idea.

A **paragraph** is a group of related sentences that have one central idea.

Most paragraphs that stand alone have three kinds of sentences: the topic sentence, supporting sentences, and the concluding sentence. Each type of sentence plays an important role in making a paragraph work. Study the chart below.

PARAGRAPH STRUCTURE	
Topic Sentence	states the main idea
Supporting Sentences	expand on the main idea with specific facts, examples, details, or reasons
Concluding Sentence	provides a strong ending

You can see this structure at work in the following paragraph.

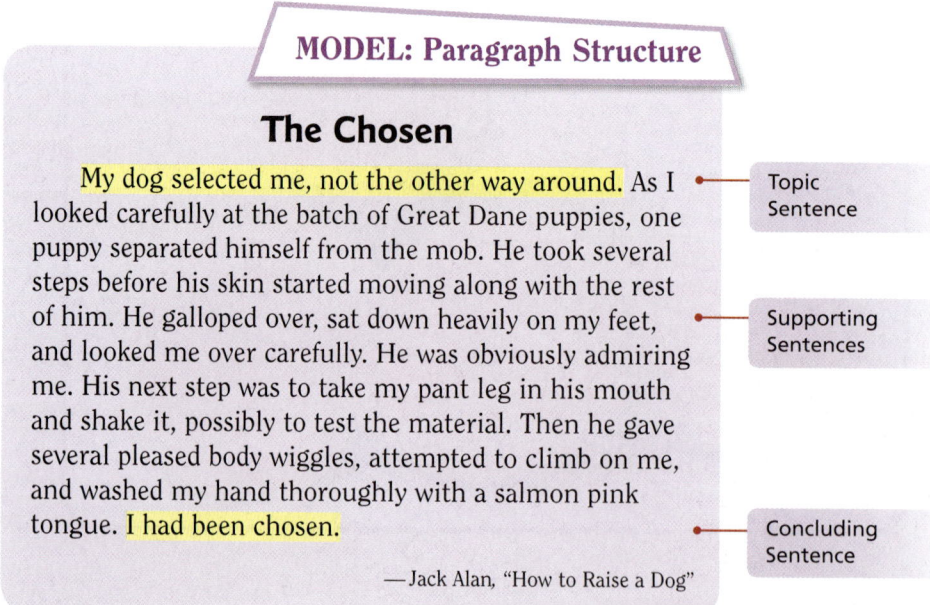

MODEL: Paragraph Structure

The Chosen

<mark>My dog selected me, not the other way around.</mark> As I looked carefully at the batch of Great Dane puppies, one puppy separated himself from the mob. He took several steps before his skin started moving along with the rest of him. He galloped over, sat down heavily on my feet, and looked me over carefully. He was obviously admiring me. His next step was to take my pant leg in his mouth and shake it, possibly to test the material. Then he gave several pleased body wiggles, attempted to climb on me, and washed my hand thoroughly with a salmon pink tongue. <mark>I had been chosen.</mark>

—Jack Alan, "How to Raise a Dog"

- Topic Sentence
- Supporting Sentences
- Concluding Sentence

1 Topic Sentence

The main idea of a paragraph is usually stated by its topic sentence, though in some paragraphs the main idea is implied rather than stated directly. When it is present, it is usually the first sentence. However, it may also be the last sentence of a paragraph or any middle sentence. Wherever it falls in the paragraph, its purpose is the same.

A **topic sentence** states the main idea of the paragraph.

The topic sentence is more general than the other sentences. Notice how the main idea of the following paragraph is expressed in the general statement at the beginning.

MODEL: Topic Sentence

Pelé

<u>The man who made soccer an important sport in the United States is a Brazilian named Pelé.</u> Three times Pelé was on the winning team that Brazil sent to the World Cup in Sweden. When Pelé retired from soccer in 1974, the manager of the New York Cosmos persuaded him to come to New York. Pelé signed a contract to play one hundred games in three years. He made appearances on television and was photographed with famous people. Whenever he played, the stadiums were filled. <u>Wherever he went in the United States, he won friends for himself and for soccer.</u>

— Topic Sentence

— Supporting Sentences

— Concluding Sentence

Paragraph Structure

• **Practice Your Skills**

Identifying the Topic Sentence

Read each paragraph to determine the main idea. Then write the topic sentence from each paragraph.

1. A Real Character

Sherlock Holmes, the fictional British detective, is one of the best-known figures in English literature. Many people used to think he was real. The London post office handled much mail addressed to him at "221B Baker Street." There is even a Sherlock Holmes fan club with members all over the world. The members, who call themselves the Baker Street Irregulars, do research on Holmes's life. When Sherlock died in "The Final Problem," the outcry was so great that Holmes's creator had to bring the famous detective back to life.

2. Edison's Contributions

The first phonograph was invented in 1877. Thomas Edison developed it. Two years later he invented the first lightbulb for home use. Edison improved or invented hundreds of useful machines. The stock ticker, the storage battery, the cement mixer, the dictaphone, and the duplicating machine are only a few. Edison, a man of practical genius, left his mark on many items.

3. Small but Serene

The southern European country of San Marino, all 24 square miles of it, has a population of only 21,000. Its army has a grand total of 180 soldiers. With the exception of its official name, The Most Serene Republic of San Marino, nearly everything about this little country is small.

Think Critically

Generalizing

To write a topic sentence, you use the skill of generalizing. **Generalizing** means forming an overall idea that explains specific facts, examples, or instances.

Suppose, for example, your family signs up for the family swim hour at the local pool. You go on Tuesday. You notice that the pool is fairly empty. On Thursday the pool is also fairly empty. When you go on Saturday, however, the pool is packed. When the pattern repeats itself the following week, your family decides to avoid swimming on Saturday.

By generalizing, you and your family have formed the overall idea that the pool is more crowded on Saturdays. Your generalization explains or clarifies the specific instances that you have experienced. Good generalizations, like good topic sentences, make meaning out of specific details and information.

Thinking Practice

The following chart gives Indian place names. Read each one carefully. Then write a general statement that connects all of the names in a meaningful way.

Susquehanna (river)	means "crooked water"
Merrimack (river)	means "swift water"
Ohio (state)	means "beautiful river"
Massachusetts (state)	means "people of the great hills"
Chicago (city)	means "onion place"
Michigan (state)	means "great water"
Kentucky (state)	means "meadowland"

● **Practice Your Skills**

Choosing Topic Sentences

Read each paragraph and the sentences that follow it. Then choose the best topic sentence for the paragraph.

1. Saving Energy

During the winter months, close outside doors quickly as you go in or out. Cap unused electrical outlets to keep cold air out. Seal the window frames with caulking. Every little bit helps when you're trying to keep warm.

a. A few simple rules will keep your home safer.

b. A few changes can lower your heating bills.

c. The work of a skilled professional can pay for itself.

2. Nature's Sonar

As it travels through the water, a dolphin makes high-pitched sounds. When a sound hits an object, it sends back an echo. By listening carefully to the echoes, the dolphin avoids objects in its path.

a. A dolphin is an amusing mammal.

b. A dolphin can travel tremendous distances.

c. A dolphin uses its eyes *and* its ears to "see."

3. The Dinosaur Dash

A flood in Texas uncovered the tracks of a dinosaur. A scientist studied the tracks and said the dinosaur had been running at nearly 25 miles per hour. Until then scientists believed the top speed of a dinosaur was only about 7 miles per hour. This dinosaur could have beaten the men's Olympic record for the 100-meter dash.

a. Scientists study fossils to learn about the past.

b. The fastest dinosaur on record left tracks in Texas.

c. Some old tracks show that a relative of ancient dinosaurs is still living.

Writing Tip

Make sure your topic sentence expresses the main idea of the paragraph.

PROJECT PREP   Drafting   Topic Sentence

In your writing group, share the main idea you want to convey. For each author, suggest possible ways to express that main idea in a topic sentence. Consider topic, audience, and form (see chart on page 85) so that the topic sentence is appropriate and effective. Note your partners' suggestions and compose your topic sentence.

2 Supporting Sentences

Supporting sentences provide specific details that back up the main idea stated in the topic sentence. The supporting sentences form the body of the paragraph.

Supporting sentences explain or prove the topic sentence with specific details, facts, examples, or reasons.

Most topic sentences raise questions in readers' minds. Consider the following topic sentence.

Topic Sentence   The number of grizzly bears has decreased so seriously that the bears may soon be wiped out.

Readers might be prompted to ask "How many grizzlies are left? What has caused the number of grizzlies to decline? Why is helping grizzly bears an urgent issue?" Supporting sentences answer those questions with specific information.

In the following paragraph, the supporting sentences provide facts to explain the topic sentence. Notice that all the supporting sentences relate directly to the main idea.

Grizzly Bears in Danger

The number of grizzly bears has decreased so seriously that the bears may soon be wiped out. The number of grizzly bears that live in Yellowstone Park dropped 40 percent between the early 1970s and the early 1980s. In colonial times grizzlies west of the Mississippi numbered 50,000. Now about 1,000 remain. Land development has rapidly deprived these bears of places where they can live, roam, and find food. Grizzly bears must be helped soon if they are to be saved.

- Topic Sentence
- Supporting Sentences
- Concluding Sentence

● **Practice Your Skills**

Identifying Supporting Details

Read the list of details under each topic sentence. Then write the letters of the three details that directly support each topic sentence.

1. The Cost of Owning a Horse

Topic Sentence   Owning a horse is expensive.

Details
a. Horses usually cost between $500 and $800.
b. Owners spend as much as six hours a day with their horses.
c. Riding equipment and supplies cost from $500 to $1,000 a year.
d. Horses are mature at the age of five.
e. Veterinary costs usually range from $100 to $300 a year.

2. Cars Threaten Bicycle Riders

Topic Sentence   The greatest threat to bicyclists is from car drivers.

Details
a. Drivers may not see bicyclists.
b. Drivers may open doors and hit bicyclists.
c. Drivers must pass driving tests.
d. Cars may pull out suddenly or slam on their brakes.
e. Some of the cars on the road are new.

Developing Supporting Details

Copy and complete the following cluster diagram. Choose one of the following main ideas and write a supporting detail in each surrounding oval.

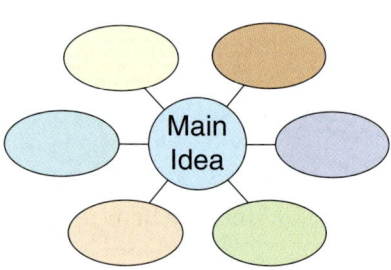

Main Idea

a. Being on time is a good habit.
b. Good study skills will lead to success in school.
c. Technology will change the way people work in the future.
d. Vegetables have an important place in our diets.

PROJECT PREP *Drafting* **Supporting Sentences**

Think back to your early discussion with your writing group about the high point of your event and the most memorable details. Refer to the master chart if you need more ideas and then write a draft of your supporting sentences, keeping your audience in mind.

The Power of Language

Semicolons: Catch and Release

To keep sentences within a paragraph tightly woven, you can use the semicolon. The semicolon, which looks like a comma with a period on top, helps signal a pause in a sentence. If the words before the semicolon catch the idea, the semicolon gets the reader ready for the release of another idea. Look at the following example from *When I Was Puerto Rican* and think about how the semicolon separates each sentence but combines them at the same time.

> The guava is not quite ripe; the skin is still a dark green.

A semicolon works in this sentence because each part is related yet each could stand alone as a single sentence. Santiago could have used two separate sentences or used words between them that told you more about how the sentences are related. For example, she could have written:

> The guava is not quite ripe. If it were ripe, the skin would not still be a dark green.

By using a semicolon, Santiago leaves it up to the reader to supply the words or idea that connects what could be two separate sentences. Through that process, she invites the reader into the act of making meaning. Readers become involved that way.

Try It Yourself

Write two sentences that are related in meaning and join them with a semicolon. Think about the topic of your memoir as you write your sentences. Remember that if you can add a word or phrase that connects the sentences and if each could stand alone, you can use a semicolon between them. Use your sentence in your draft if it fits with your main idea. Later, when you revise your writing, see if there are any other sentences that could be joined with a semicolon.

Punctuation Tip

To connect and/or separate two complete sentences, there are three punctuation marks you can use.
Separate with a period: The comma part joins. The period part separates.
Join with a comma plus *and*: The comma part joins, and the period part separates.
Join and separate with a semicolon: The comma part joins; the period part separates.

③ Concluding Sentences

A stand-alone paragraph without a strong concluding sentence leaves the reader feeling cut off.

A **concluding sentence** adds a strong ending to a paragraph.

Following are several good ways to end a paragraph.

CONCLUDING SENTENCE

A concluding sentence may

- summarize the paragraph.
- state the point of the paragraph or the lesson it conveys.
- restate the main idea using different words.
- add an insight about the main idea.

Avoid using a concluding sentence that doesn't add some meaning to the paragraph. Notice how weak the concluding sentence is in the following paragraph. It simply repeats the words in the topic sentence.

MODEL: Concluding Sentence

Jupiter's Moon

A Chinese astronomer saw one of Jupiter's moons 2,000 years before the astronomer Galileo reported it. An ancient record from 364 B.C. says, "In the year of Chan Yan, Jupiter was very large and bright. A small reddish star was attached to it." This star was most likely the moon called Ganymede.

Weak Conclusion   As you can see, a Chinese astronomer reported one of Jupiter's moons before Galileo did.

The following concluding sentence is also weak. It adds new information that does not relate directly to the paragraph's main idea.

Weak Conclusion   In Greek mythology Ganymede is known as the cupbearer to the gods.

The following sentence would add a strong ending. It adds real meaning that relates directly to the main idea.

Strong Conclusion After 2,400 years, the achievement of this Chinese astronomer is finally being recognized.

Practice Your Skills

Choosing a Concluding Sentence

Read the paragraph below. Choose and write the better concluding sentence. Then write a sentence that tells why you believe your choice is the right one.

> **One Kind of Robot**
>
> Some robots have been around for hundreds of years. One kind is called an android. An android is a machine that looks and acts like a person. Most androids have been used as toys. Chinese emperors had mechanical musicians that entertained them. Japanese homes had dolls that could carry trays and serve tea. One family in Switzerland had a "boy" android that could sit at a writing desk and write messages. Today androids are being used as dental patients. The Japanese have developed a very realistic robotic patient used to train Japanese dentists. The patient can follow verbal instructions from the trainee dentist and has a mouthful of sensors that respond to inept probing, to which she responds, "That hurts."

a. A robot flagman has even been invented to direct traffic.

b. Modern androids, no longer playthings, can help people learn how to save lives.

editing

Trim away the excess from the following concluding sentence.

> So you can see why I think androids can make a difference that is important in our lives.

In your Learning Log, compare the structure of a letter to the structure of a paragraph. In other words, how does the purpose of the salutation, body, and closing of a letter correspond to the purpose of each part of a paragraph?

The Language of Power Sound-Alikes

Power Rule: For sound-alikes and certain words that sound almost alike, choose the word with your intended meaning. (See page 736.)

See It in Action In the passage below, Esmeralda Santiago uses the word *it* in two different ways.

> Green guava is sour and hard. You bite into it at *its* widest point, because *it's* easier to grasp with your teeth.

Learn the difference between *its* and *it's*. In the sentence above, *its* is a possessive pronoun, pointing out an aspect of the guava (*its widest part*). The word *it's* is a contraction of *it is*. When used as a contraction, *it is* always has an apostrophe (*it's easier to grasp*).

Remember It Record this rule and example in the Power Rule section of your Personalized Editing Checklist.

Use It Read your writing over, looking only for *its* and *it's*. Be sure you have used each correctly.

PROJECT PREP Drafting Concluding Sentence

Read through your paragraph to get a fresh feel for the topic sentence and body of supporting sentences. Then add a strong concluding sentence. Share your completed paragraph with your writing group and get feedback. Revise and edit your paragraph using that feedback and your own judgment.

In the Media

Across the Media: Magazines, Internet, Newspapers

At some time far in the future, you might want to understand what Americans at the beginning of the twenty-first century thought was important. How would you go about doing that? One way would be to look at the popular culture of that time through the media: movies, books, television, magazines, newspapers, and the Internet.

What people write about, read about, and watch reflects what they care about. Scanning the front page of several newspapers gives you a good idea of the issues of the day that subscribers of that newspaper probably find most pressing. Examining popular television programs tells you what many television viewers find entertaining. Looking at what is advertised and *how* it is advertised tells you what people might be buying and for what purpose. For example, if you look through a popular magazine, you may notice many advertisements for time-saving food products. Because there are so many of these advertisements, you may conclude that a good number of people aren't cooking from scratch.

Media Activity

Join your classmates in contributing to a time capsule to be opened 1,000 years in the future. Work in three groups: one exploring information gathered from the Internet, one exploring information from a local newspaper, and one exploring magazines devoted to cultural issues. In one sentence sum up what is important about our culture as it is reflected in the medium you explored. Compare your conclusions with those of students exploring different media. Then record your sentences on paper and decorate a time-capsule box you can store them in.

Writing Lab

Project Corner

Speak and Listen Present Your Memoir

Deliver your memoir as a speech. Follow these directions: 1) On a notecard, write your topic sentence. 2) Then create a bulleted list of supporting details you used in your memoir and write this list on a second notecard. 3) Write your concluding sentence on a third notecard. Practice using your notecards to give your speech so that it sounds natural but polished.

Experiment Use a New Form

Rewrite your memoir in a form listed on the chart on page 85 that you did not use. Present your new version to your class, and discuss changes that the different form or genre required.

Get Technical Rearrange Sentences

The Copy, Cut, and Paste functions in the Edit menu of your word processing toolbar allow you to rearrange your sentences easily. Use Copy to create a copy of your paragraph. **Use Cut and Paste to rearrange sentences** in the new copy. Review both old and new versions and decide which makes more sense.

Apply and Assess

In the Workplace
Paragraph for the Librarian

1. You are applying for a volunteer position at the Library of the Comic Arts—a library dedicated to housing collections of old and rare comic books from the twentieth century. The head librarian wants you to write a paragraph explaining why you think you are perfect for the job. **Write a paragraph** describing the kinds of skills you have and why you think you would make a good volunteer at the library. Be sure that your paragraph includes a topic sentence, supporting sentences, and a concluding sentence.

In Academic Areas
Paragraph for a Science Web Site

2. You and seven of your best friends are constructing a Web site dedicated to the eight planets of the solar system—www.earthanditssevenbestfriends.com. Since your friends consider you the most "far out" of the bunch, you have been assigned to write a paragraph about Neptune. Your paragraph will appear when the visitors to the Web site click on the picture of the most "far out" planet. **Write a paragraph for the Web site** providing general information about the planet Neptune. Be sure that your paragraph includes a topic sentence, supporting sentences, and a concluding sentence.

Timed Writing Make Suggestions

3. The director of your local community center wants to start a new program for middle school students. To find out what kinds of classes or activities people your age would enjoy, the director has created a suggestion box. You decide to share your ideas. Write a paragraph describing your suggestions. Include a topic sentence that states the main idea. Use supporting sentences to expand on the main idea with specific facts and details about your new program ideas. Write a concluding sentence to provide a strong ending. You have 20 minutes to complete your work. (See pages 33 and 398–399 for suggestions on budgeting time.)

   Before You Write Consider the following questions: What is the subject? What is the occasion? Who is the audience? What is the purpose?

   After You Write Evaluate your work using the six-trait evaluation form on page 23.

CHAPTER 5

Writing Effective Compositions

A composition presents and develops one main idea in three or more paragraphs.

Compositions can be long or short, serious or humorous. Compositions may cover a wide range of subjects and take many forms.

The following examples show some ways people use compositions in everyday life.

- **A sports reporter writes an article** on the triumph of the local football team.
- **A book reviewer writes an online review** of a popular novel for an Internet bookseller.
- **A student writes an essay about herself** to include in an application for a foreign-exchange program.
- **An actor writes an autobiography** describing his experiences in Hollywood.
- **A politician gives a speech at a rally** just before election day.
- **A popular mystery writer writes an essay** on where she gets ideas for her books.
- **A historian writes a paper** describing newly found letters that shed light on some key events in the life of a 19th-century president.

Writing Project — Biographical Sketch

Lives Worth Remembering Complete the following project by creating a well-structured and effective composition on the life of someone interesting.

Think Through Writing Think of a person living today you think would make the subject of an excellent biography. The person might be famous but might also be someone you know who is not presently well known. Why do you think that people would want to learn more about this person? What events do you know about that would be included in the biography? How could you learn additional information to include? Write informally about this person, highlighting key accomplishments or other activities and giving a sense of why this person would be an interesting subject.

Talk About It In your writing group, discuss the people you have written about. What sorts of qualities do they share that make their lives worth writing about in an interesting biographical sketch?

Read About It In the following biographical sketch of Cleopatra, William A. DeWitt identifies a few key facets of her life and tells why people are still fascinated by her more than 2,000 years after her death. Think about why people still read and talk about Cleopatra and why the subject of your own sketch might be of interest to people well into the future.

MODEL: Biographical Sketch

From *Illustrated Minute Biographies*

Cleopatra

William A. DeWitt

No other woman in history has more successfully used her personal charms to further her political ambitions than Cleopatra. *— What do you expect from the rest of the biography when you read this statement?*

Third daughter of King Ptolemy Auletes, she was born in 69 or 68 B.C. and first came to the Egyptian throne as co-ruler with her younger brother, Ptolemy Dionysus, on her father's death in 51 B.C. Three years later, Ptolemy having conspired to deprive her of regal authority, she was in Syria gathering military forces for an attempt to regain it when Julius Caesar followed Pompey[1] into Egypt. *— This paragraph gives necessary background information.*

The Roman dictator fell quickly and profoundly under Cleopatra's spell. He helped her vanquish the armies of her brother—Ptolemy dying in the war—and afterwards placed her again on the Egyptian throne, with another brother, whom she soon disposed of by poison. *— This sentence supports the main idea statement.*

Legend has it that Caesar's and Cleopatra's union produced a son, Caesarion, whom Octavian later put to death. Certainly, they lived together in Rome from 46 or 45 B.C. till Caesar's assassination in 44 B.C. Then, aware of the Romans' disfavor, she fled back to Egypt. *— The unfolding events are told in chronological, or time, order. Why do they seem to go backward?*

Here Mark Anthony succumbed to her fascination and she used him as she had Caesar. Their long alliance, always unpopular in Rome, led finally to war with *— This sentence also directly supports the main idea.*

---

1 **Pompey:** 106–48 B.C., Roman general and statesman.

Octavian and their historic defeat at Actium (31 B.C.). The following year Octavian landed in Egypt and worked out with Cleopatra the plot that resulted in Anthony's suicide, committed in the mistaken belief that she, too, was taking her life.

Cleopatra then set her cap for[2] Octavian, but the man who was to be Rome's first Emperor (Augustus) proved less susceptible to her wiles[3] than Anthony or Caesar. Learning that he firmly intended taking her to Rome as a captive, Cleopatra played her dramatic last scene, killing herself (according to legend) by the bite of an asp.[4] This was in 30 B.C., and marked the end of the Ptolemies' dynasty, Egypt thereafter becoming a Roman province.

A host of writers, from her time to the present, have found inspiration in the colorful life of the Egyptian queen, among them Plutarch, Shakespeare, Dryden and George Bernard Shaw.

> What is the main idea of this concluding paragraph?

2 **set her cap for:** Pursued.
3 **wiles:** Playful tricks.
4 **asp:** A venomous snake of Egypt.

Respond in Writing According to DeWitt, for what is Cleopatra best remembered? What makes her seem memorable to you, if she is? Note that DeWitt's text is not a complete biography; rather, it introduces readers to Cleopatra by focusing on some fascinating aspects of her life. What three or four aspects might you focus on for readers of your own biographical sketch?

Develop Your Own Categories of Information Work with your classmates to develop ideas that will help you write a biographical sketch.

Small Groups: In your writing group, discuss the sorts of information that you might include in your biographical sketch. What would you as a reader like to know about someone? Develop a list of categories of information you might need for your biographical sketch. A few possibilities are:

- where the person lives, birthplace, and date of birth
- major life events
- key friends, enemies, associates, and family
- why this person should be remembered

Whole Class: Make a master chart of all of the ideas generated by the small groups, and discuss the types of information that would make the sketch interesting for readers.

Write About It You will next write a biographical sketch of a contemporary person. You may choose from any of the following possible topics, audiences, and forms.

Possible Topics	Possible Audiences	Possible Forms
• someone you know personally • someone in your neighborhood, town, or region who deserves a more widespread reputation • a celebrity • a national or international figure who is not a celebrity	• future historians • future readers of a popular magazine • current citizens • the subject's family	• an encyclopedia entry • part of a memoir • a magazine article • a letter to your grandchildren

Composition Writing

The process for writing compositions is similar to the process for writing paragraphs. The first step is to explore your own interests for writing ideas. Compositions written on subjects of real interest to the writer are usually the most effective. To get started, brainstorm a list of things you like in different categories, such as food, music, sports, or hobbies. You can also think about broad subjects that interest you, such as science or history, and list some specific topics about which you could write. These strategies will help you generate ideas for writing.

Remember, though, that you are in a community of writers. Use such strategies as talking with others or interviewing people to help you choose and develop a workable subject.

1 Choosing and Limiting a Subject

Once you have explored your interests for writing ideas, the next step is to choose one subject that suits your purpose and audience.

DETERMINING YOUR PURPOSE AND GENRE

A good composition, like a good paragraph, has a clear purpose. That purpose may be to create a story, poem, or play, to express your thoughts in a diary or journal, to inform or explain, or to persuade. Keeping your writing purpose in mind will help you choose a suitable subject.

DETERMINING YOUR AUDIENCE

A composition must be suited to your audience. In your journal, for example, a composition can be personal and poetic. A composition for science class, on the other hand, needs to be more formal and informative. Sketch out an audience profile chart to help you understand your readers.

LISTING FOCUS POINTS

The final step in developing a good subject is to list several possible focus points that would suit your purpose and audience. **Focus points** are the smaller, more limited topics contained within your general subject. If you had decided to write about gymnastics, for example, you might list the following focus points:

Subject	gymnastics
Purpose and Genre	to explain in a composition
Audience	people who enjoy watching gymnastics but do not know much about it
Focus Points	how women's gymnastics is judged
	movements for the floor exercises
	safety and training equipment
	differences between men's and women's events

Any one of these four focus points would be a suitably limited subject for a short composition.

Steps for Limiting a Composition Subject

- Decide on the purpose of your composition: to create, to express, to inform or explain, or to persuade.
- Think about who your audience (readers) will be.
- List focus points that suit your purpose and audience.
- Choose one focus point as your limited subject.

PROJECT PREP *Prewriting* Limited Subject

1. In your writing group, discuss each writer's subject. Can it be developed with interesting and insightful details? Is it suitably limited? If not, help each author develop a limited subject.

2. Next, make a two-column chart to help you gather information. In the first column, write questions about your subject that you need to answer. In the second column, identify the kinds and locations of sources you can use to find those answers. For example, will you find the information online in a news article or in the library media center at your school in a printed work? When your chart is complete, gather the information you need. Use several sources so you can be sure your information is accurate. Keep notes on paper or on your computer so you have your information handy.

2 Listing Supporting Details

With a clear focus point, you can begin to list the details you will use to support your main idea. Brainstorm with someone, freewrite, cluster, or use any other strategy to stimulate your thinking. Think of as many useful details as possible.

The kinds of supporting details you use will vary according to your writing purpose. The following chart shows the different kinds of details used for different purposes.

SUPPORTING DETAILS IN A COMPOSITION	
Purpose	**Kinds of Details**
to express	sights, sounds and other details that appeal to the senses; thoughts, feelings, reflections
to inform or explain	facts, examples, reasons, steps in a process, and directions
to create	people, places, and events that are real or imagined
to persuade	reasons based on facts that support an opinion

Suppose you had decided to explain how women's gymnastics is judged to people who enjoy gymnastics but do not know much about it. If you brainstormed to come up with details, your notes might appear as follows.

Limited Subject how women's gymnastics is judged

Brainstorming Notes
originality and composition: 2 points
vaulting scored separately
perfect score: 10 points
excellent "general impression" earns maximum of 1 point
difficulty of routine: 5 points
execution: 2 points
variety of easy, medium, and hard movements: 5 points
judging standards set by the Federation of International Gymnastics

PROJECT PREP Brainstorming Developing Details

Make a list of all the supporting details about your subject you have collected. Don't worry about putting them in any order at this point. Talk through your list with your writing group and ask if your group members have any questions they would still like answered about your subject. If there are further questions, gather more information.

❸ Developing the Main Idea

Writing is a continuous learning process. In each stage of the writing process, you discover or clarify more ideas. After brainstorming, for example, you probably have a much clearer understanding of your subject. In fact, by this time you have probably learned or rediscovered enough about your subject to formulate your **main idea statement**—the sentence that expresses the **controlling idea** of your composition.

To formulate your main idea statement, look over all the ideas you have come up with. Is any thought more important than the others as an overall idea? Or do the separate details you came up with add up to some overall idea that you can now express? Asking—and answering—these two questions will lead you to your main idea statement.

The writer who brainstormed about women's gymnastics reviewed her brainstorming notes with these questions in mind. She decided that one of the most important points she had listed was the last one—judging standards are set by the Federation of International Gymnastics. All the other details seemed to fit neatly under this main idea. So she wrote a draft of her main idea statement as follows:

Main Idea   Scoring a women's gymnastic event is a matter of following the guidelines set by the Federation of International Gymnastics.

As the writer continues working, this main idea statement may change somewhat. For now, it will serve as a guide to keep all the other details in the essay anchored to a main idea.

A solid and interesting main idea is worth the time and trouble it may take to formulate it. The best main ideas are those that can be explored in depth and that interest you enough to think creatively and insightfully about them.

Using the idea rubric on the next page, consider whether or not the idea you have for a composition is worthy of earning you a 4.

Composition Writing • Prewriting

Idea Rubric

4 Ideas are presented and developed in depth.	3 Most ideas are presented and developed with insight.	2 Many ideas are not well developed.	1 Most ideas are not well developed.
• I developed each idea thoroughly with specific details. • My presentation of ideas was original. • I made meaningful connections among ideas. • I took some risks to make my writing come to life.	• I developed most ideas thoroughly with specific details. • My presentation of some ideas was thoughtul. • I made some connections among ideas. • I played it safe and did not really put much of myself into the composition.	• I tried to develop ideas but was more general than specific. • I listed rather than developed ideas. • I made few connections among ideas. • I left a few things out but I think my meaning comes across.	• I was more general than specific. • I listed rather than developed ideas. • I did not try to connect ideas. • I left some important things out so my meaning wasn't really clear.

PROJECT PREP *Prewriting* Developing the Main Idea

In your writing group, help each writer develop a main idea. What main idea do all the details gathered about the subject add up to? Help each author develop a main idea that forms a generalization based on the details gathered. Don't worry if the main idea does not relate to every single detail on your list. You don't have to use all the details in your composition.

108   Writing Effective Compositions

 **Arranging Details**

When you brainstorm with someone, you write down ideas in the order they occur to you. Chances are they are not in a logical order. In addition, you may have listed ideas that do not strictly relate to your subject. Now that you've clarified your main idea statement, you can smooth these matters out. First look over your notes and select only those that relate directly to the main idea. Next look for a way to organize your ideas logically. This chart shows some common approaches.

TYPES OF ORDER	
Chronological	Items are arranged in time order.
Spatial	Items are arranged in order of location.
Size or Importance	Items are arranged in order of least to most or most to least important or by size from biggest to smallest or smallest to biggest.
Sequential	Items are arranged in the order in which they must be performed.

If some items do not fit neatly into the order you have chosen, save them for your introduction or conclusion.

Notice how the brainstorming notes about gymnastics have been grouped and logically arranged.

Ideas Saved	judging standards set by the Federation of International gymnastics vaulting scored separately
Largest to Smallest Point Value	perfect score: 10 points
	difficulty of routine: 5 points
	variety of easy, medium, and hard movements: 5 points
	execution: 2 points
	originality and composition: 2 points
	excellent "general impression" earns maximum of 1 point

Composition Writing • Prewriting

Think Critically

Ordering

What makes one method of organizing details "logical" and another "illogical," or hard to follow? The answer lies in the writer's skill in ordering the ideas in his or her composition. **Ordering** means placing in a sequence that makes sense and is guided by a clear principle.

As long as the details in a composition are arranged in some order guided by a principle—even an order not described—chances are they will be logical and easy for a reader to follow.

Thinking Practice

The following notes for an essay are not arranged in any order. Decide how best to arrange them using your skills of ordering. Write them in an orderly list.

Subject puppy discipline

Details DO teach the meaning of *no*.

DON'T use a loud voice, or your pup will be startled.

DO follow correction with praise.

DON'T give your puppy an old shoe to chew on—it will never learn the difference between old clothes and new.

DON'T call your puppy to you to correct him—always go to him.

DO correct your puppy only when you actually catch him in the act of doing something wrong.

DO teach your puppy the command "drop it"—it could save his life.

● **Practice Your Skills**

Arranging Details in Logical Order

The following brainstorming notes are on the subject of the world's highest waterfalls. Two of the items could be used in the introduction or conclusion. Write the two items that do not fit the logical order. Then list the remaining items in logical order.

- Largest falls in the world are Angel Falls in Venezuela.
- North America has the third largest falls, in Yosemite.
- Waterfalls form when water flowing over land meets an abrupt change in the level of the land.
- Angel Falls drops 3,212 feet.
- Tugela Falls in South Africa drops 3,110 feet.
- Yosemite Falls plunges 2,425 feet.
- Because of the erosion power built into them, all waterfalls eventually disappear.

PROJECT PREP *Prewriting* *Ordering in Sequence*

In your writing group, help each author determine the best way to arrange the details. Would chronological order be best or order of importance? Once you have determined the best order for your ideas, arrange them accordingly and check each detail to make sure it fits. Reserve any details that don't fit in case you can use them in the introduction or conclusion of your composition.

The Power of Language

Phrases: Scene Setters

One way to show the order of your ideas is to use phrases that indicate time. In the following sentence from the biographical sketch of Cleopatra, the highlighted phrase shows time and provides added meaning that applies to the entire sentence. Such scene-setting phrases can also indicate place, or they can explain how or why something is said or done.

> A host of writers, from her time to the present, have found inspiration in the colorful life of the Egyptian queen.

This scene-setting information is often most helpful at the beginning of a sentence, before one reads the main part of the sentence.

> From her time to the present, a host of writers have found inspiration in the colorful life of the Egyptian queen.

It can lose its effectiveness when placed at the end of the sentence.

> A host of writers have found inspiration in the colorful life of the Egyptian queen from her time to the present.

Try It Yourself

Write three to five sentences with at least one scene setter each. When you draft your composition, try to put your scene setters first. You can always come back later, if needed, and move other scene setters to the front of their sentences.

> **Punctuation Tip**
>
> If your scene setter at the beginning of a sentence is **four words or more**, put a **comma after it**, though even shorter ones are often followed by a comma, too. If you want your reader to pause, put a comma after your scene setter. (See pages 841–843 on introductory elements.)

Composition Writing

As you work on your draft, use your notes to help you include everything you planned and to help you follow a logical order. Compositions usually contain many facts, but that does not mean they must be dry or boring. You do need to follow a structure in writing compositions, but once you have learned the form, you can be as creative as you like.

As you can see in the following model, a composition has three main parts: an introduction, a body of supporting details, and a conclusion.

MODEL: Composition

The Secrets of Handwriting

When you write, do your letters slant to the right? Do you write in big, bold letters with even lines, or do you write tiny letters that slant backward? ==However you write, you are revealing some aspects of your personality.==

Introduction captures attention and states the main idea.

Highly trained experts have been able to pinpoint some specific links between the slant of handwriting and the writer's personality. According to these experts, people who compose level lines of writing are "on the level" themselves. If a line wanders a little, the writer may be revealing the trait of carelessness. Lines that slant upward often reveal an optimistic person, while downward-slanting lines show moodiness.

Another trait of writing, size, can also reveal hidden qualities. Many people with tiny handwriting tend to be intellectual. Large writing may indicate generosity. Huge writing may mean the person is conceited but generally honest.

The way letters slant is still another indicator of personality. If letters lean far to the left, the writer may be a distrustful person. If they lean far to the right, the writer may be overly sensitive. If they lean only slightly to the right, the writer is likely to be friendly and easygoing.

Supporting paragraphs in the body provide specific information.

In addition to these three points, experts also study the shape of individual letters, spacing between words, and other fine points of writing. ==In the hands of a certified expert, writing samples can be very reliable keys to personality.== Studying your own handwriting can be an interesting and rewarding way to learn more about yourself.

The conclusion provides a strong ending.

Drafting the Introduction

One of the most important features of a strong introduction is a sentence that states the **main idea** of the composition. This sentence can come first, last, or in the middle of your introductory paragraph. Following is the introductory paragraph for the composition on gymnastics. The main idea statement is highlighted. Notice that it has been changed slightly to fit smoothly into the paragraph.

MODEL: Introduction

Anyone who has seen a women's gymnastics match knows the excitement of waiting for the judges' scores. When the numbers finally appear, the crowd usually responds with cheers or groans. In most cases, the scores from the various judges are very close. To a casual observer, the similarity of the scores may seem surprising. <mark>To the judges, however, scoring a gymnastic event is a matter of following the guidelines of the Federation of International Gymnastics.</mark>

In addition to expressing the main idea, an effective introduction has several other qualities. The following guidelines will help you write strong introductions.

 Tips for Writing an Introduction

- Catch the reader's attention with an interesting fact, detail, or incident.
- Give background information if needed.
- Include a statement of the composition's main idea.
- Do not include such empty expressions as "In this essay I will. . . ." or "This essay will be about. . . ."

PROJECT PREP Drafting Introduction

Draft the opening paragraph of your composition and take it to your writing group for feedback. Discuss these questions: Does it capture your attention? Based on the opening paragraph, do you want to continue reading? How might the author jazz up the introduction so that readers will become fascinated and want to continue reading? Help each author introduce the subject in ways that make readers want to continue reading beyond the opening paragraph.

② Drafting the Body

The body of the composition is the longest part. It is where the information, examples, and facts supporting the main idea introduced in the first paragraph appear. As you write the body, try to achieve two goals. Use your notes to write complete, varied sentences—a mix of simple, compound, and complex sentences—with vivid words. Also use transitions as needed to connect your thoughts smoothly.

Notice how the prewriting notes about gymnastics become, with transitions, smooth sentences in the composition body. The transitions are printed in **bold** type.

MODEL: Body

All events except vaulting are scored by the same system. A perfect score is 10 points. **By far the most important** category in that score is "difficulty," which is worth 5 points. If the proper number of difficult movements is included in the routine, the gymnast earns the full 5 points. The **next** category, execution, is worth 2 points. If a gymnast fails to perform a movement properly, she may lose tenths of a point in this category. Originality and composition are **also** worth 2 points. For this category the judges look at how the movements are combined in the routine. The category with the **lowest** point value is "general impression," worth 1 point. In this category judges react to the overall performance of the gymnast.

PROJECT PREP   Drafting   Body

Draft the body of your composition. Then, in your writing group, focus on each author's development of the body paragraphs. Is each paragraph focused on one topic? For the biographical project, does each of these topics include enough information to inform you about the person's life, or is more detail required? Does each paragraph make you want to read on and learn more? Help each author develop each body paragraph so that it contributes to the overall purpose of the composition and stands on its own as an interesting piece of information. Write a revised draft of your composition body based on the discussion in your writing group.

③ Drafting the Conclusion

Some paragraphs may not need concluding sentences. All compositions, however, need a concluding paragraph that sums up the composition and makes clear to the reader that the end has come. A good conclusion often ends with a clincher—a memorable phrase or statement.

The **conclusion** completes the composition and reinforces the main idea.

Read the following conclusion to the composition about gymnastics. Notice how the writer creates tension with the statement "all eyes turn anxiously to the scoreboard."

MODEL: Conclusion

> A perfect 10 is rare. More often, gymnasts will have tenths of points taken off in one or more categories. Most gymnasts know the scoring system so well that they have a good idea of how well they did even before the judges' cards come up. Still, after the final movement or dismount, all eyes turn anxiously to the scoreboard, wondering if the perfect 10 will somehow appear.

Use the guidelines below to write strong conclusions.

Tips for Writing a Conclusion

- Emphasize the main idea without restating it exactly.
- Refer to ideas in the introduction to round out the composition.
- Do not introduce a completely new idea.
- Do not contain empty expressions such as "I have just told you about . . ."

WRITING A TITLE

When you have nearly finished, add a short and catchy title to your composition. It should suggest the main idea of your composition and invite your readers to read on.

PROJECT PREP *Drafting* Conclusion

Draft your conclusion. Then, in your writing group, evaluate the ending. For example, for the biographical sketch, is the person's life neatly summarized? Does the concluding paragraph provide any new insights about the person, based on the events reviewed? Help each author sharpen the conclusion so that it provides an insightful summary and leaves the reader wanting to learn even more.

In the Media

Across the Media: News Styles

Before you started working on your composition, you took time out to think about your audience, purpose, and genre. Writing effectively depends on knowing who will be reading your work, why you are writing it, and what form it will take. In the news media, those factors shape the presentation of the news. The style of a news reporter writing for a national newspaper, for example, will be different from the style of a reporter writing for a radio station. Each reporter is writing for a different medium and addressing a different audience.

- A printed article can be skimmed by the viewer, picked up or put down at any time, or read in one sitting, whereas a report on the radio can only be heard in the moment.
- Television news often shows brief video clips to catch the attention of its channel-surfing audience, while newspapers and magazines might use an interesting picture or a giant headline to grab readers' interest.
- Radio news reports are often short blurbs intended to update commuters driving to and from work.
- Because of time constraints, stories written for broadcast news are shorter, while something written for print may be longer and contain more detail. Television and radio writers both use sound bites (short bits of recorded sounds or videotaped images) to convey information that in a print article would need to be described.

Media Activity

Working in groups of three, brainstorm a list of people currently in the news. Choose one that is likely to be in the news for several days and read about him or her in a newspaper or magazine, watch coverage on television, and listen to coverage on the radio. How is the coverage different in each medium? How is it similar? Which medium presented the story in the greatest depth? Which medium gave the story the least coverage? Write a paragraph describing your findings. Share your work with classmates.

Composition Writing  Revising

The first step in revising is to ask: Does my composition fulfill its purpose, address its audience appropriately, and use the conventions expected in its genre? When you can answer "yes" to those questions, use the checklist below to make other improvements.

 Evaluation Checklist

Checking Your Structure
- ✓ Do you have an interesting introduction that includes a sentence stating the main idea of the composition? (page 114)
- ✓ Do you have a coherent composition in which all your sentences relate to the main idea? (page 115)
- ✓ Are your ideas well organized, with smooth transitions? (pages 109–111 and 115)
- ✓ Do you have a strong conclusion? (page 116)

Checking Your Paragraphs
- ✓ Does the body of your composition contain more than one paragraph? (page 115)
- ✓ Do the sentences in each paragraph relate to the paragraph's main idea? (page 115)

Checking Your Words and Sentences
- ✓ Did you combine related sentences and use a mix of simple, compound, and complex sentences? (pages 64–72)
- ✓ Did you vary the beginnings of your sentences? (page 73)
- ✓ Did you eliminate rambling sentences? (pages 75–76)
- ✓ Are your sentences free of dull and general words? (page 56)
- ✓ Are your words fresh and vivid? (pages 42–57)
- ✓ Have you avoided unnecessary repetition? (pages 77–78)

editing

Keep your writing lean by trimming away unneccessary words, phrases, and sentences. Practice by eliminating the wordiness in the following sentence.

> Few other female rulers in history are as well known as Cleopatra, who became famous during her lifetime and remained famous throughout history and to this day.

You can use the rubric on the following page to evaluate the structure and organization of your composition.

Organization Rubric

4 Ideas progress smoothly and the organizational strategies clarify meaning.	**3** Most ideas progress smoothly and the organizational strategies are clear.	**2** Some ideas progress smoothly but the organizational pattern is not consistent.	**1** Few ideas progress smoothly and there is no clear organization.
• I stated the main idea creatively in the introduction and captured attention. • I used the best organizational pattern to present the supporting paragraphs. • My conclusion was strong and the composition feels complete. • My paragraphs and sentences flowed smoothly from one into another, creating internal and external coherence. • I used transitions to keep the order clear.	• I stated the main idea in the introduction and captured attention. • I used an appropriate organizational pattern to present the supporting paragraphs. • My conclusion helped make the composition feel complete. • Most but not all of my paragraphs and sentences flowed smoothly from one into another. • I used some transitions to keep the order clear.	• I stated the main idea in the introduction but did not capture attention. • I used an appropriate organizational pattern to present the supporting paragraphs but had some things out of order. • My conclusion provided an ending but it did not feel strong. • I repeated some ideas unnecessarily. • I could have used more transitions to keep the order clear.	• I did not state my main idea clearly. • I did not use an organizational pattern. • I did not provide a clear ending. • I repeated some things and also had some things out of order or not related to the topic. • I did not use many transitions so the order was hard to follow.

PROJECT PREP *Revising* **Responding to Feedback**

Based on feedback from your writing group and your evaluation using the rubric above, write a final draft of your composition. In this draft, you can begin editing as you give attention to grammar, spelling, and punctuation so that readers can clearly follow your composition and grasp the points you are trying to make.

Composition Writing — Editing

By the editing stage, you are satisfied with the content and style of your composition. Your main goal now is to polish it. Use the proofreading symbols on page 11 when you edit.

The Language of Power  Possessive Nouns

Power Rule: Use standard ways to make nouns possessive. (See pages 880–883.)

See It in Action To make a singular noun possessive, add an apostrophe and an *-s*. For plural nouns that end in *-s*, show possession by adding an apostrophe after the *-s*. If a plural noun does not end in *-s*, such as *men*, add an *-s* after the apostrophe (men's). The following sentences show correct uses.

> Legend has it that Caesar's and Cleopatra's union produced a son, Caesarion, whom Octavian later put to death. Certainly, they lived together in Rome from 46 or 45 B.C. till Caesar's assassination in 44 B.C. Then, aware of the Romans' disfavor, she fled back to Egypt.

Remember It Record this rule and example in the Power Rule section of your Personalized Editing Checklist.

Use It Read through your composition and find all the possessive nouns. Check each one to make sure you used an apostrophe in the correct place.

PROJECT PREP — Editing — Checking Conventions

Exchange papers with a writing partner and read one another's compositions looking for possible errors, especially those related to the Power Rules, and any other last-minute items that need changing. Based on your partner's feedback, prepare a final polished composition for your readers.

Composition Writing  Publishing

When you prepare to publish your composition, the appearance of it can be almost as important as its content. A paper with uneven margins and words crossed out or crowded together is difficult to read. A neat paper, however, can help you convey your message.

You can learn more about the correct form for a composition on page 31.

ADDING GRAPHICS

A big part of the appearance of a text is its use of graphics. All of the following visual elements could help clarify and enrich compositions.

TYPES OF GRAPHICS FOR COMPOSITIONS		
photographs	timelines	scanned documents
drawings	maps	diagrams
charts	tables	borders and backgrounds

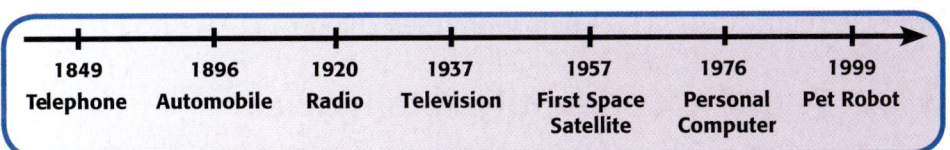

PROJECT PREP *Publishing* Share Your Work

Publish your finished work in the form you chose (see page 103) or through another appropriate medium. For example, for a biographical sketch, you might find a place on the Internet where your subject is featured and contribute your sketch to that Web site. If your topic is not already featured on the Web, think about starting a Web site about it so that others may understand why you find it important.

What types of information can graphics provide that text cannnot? What kinds of information does text do a better job of conveying than graphics? Make a note for your Learning Log about what you've learned about text and graphics.

Writing Lab

Project Corner

Research and Read Brief Biographies

With a partner, **do research on the Internet and in your library** to locate collections of brief biographies. Find three biographies that interest you especially and read them carefully. With your partner, develop a list of traits or features that the three biographies have in common. For example, are they all organized the same way? How much detail do they include? Share your list with the rest of the class and compare notes. Then discuss the extent to which the biographical sketches you wrote share these traits and why. (See pages 322–339 for help with researching.)

Solve Problems Identify Alternatives

With your writing group, discuss any problems the person you wrote about had to face and solve. **Develop a list of alternative solutions** for each person's problem. In light of those, does the choice each person made to solve the problem seem reasonable and appropriate? Discuss what the consequences of the other possible solutions might have been.

Get Technical Create a Multimedia Text

Use computer software to **create an electronic** text that includes sights, sounds, and other features to help bring your person to life for a viewer. (See pages 449–463 for help with creating an electronic text.)

Apply and Assess

In Everyday Life
Informative Composition

1. A new student has come to your school from another country. As you talk with him, you realize that he is very interested in your customs—especially your holidays. **Write a composition** about your favorite holiday to share with your new friend. Tell him about the origins of the holiday and the customs associated with it. Also tell why it is your favorite. Give your composition a strong introduction and develop it with supporting details. Finally, write a solid conclusion for your work. Remember to give your work an interesting title.

In the Workplace Persuasive E-mail

2. A famous talent scout is in your town looking for a young person with a fresh new face who can play a seventh grader in an upcoming movie. Unfortunately for you, the audition appointments are all taken. **Write an e-mail to persuade** the talent scout to make an exception and give you an audition. Tell her why you would make an excellent seventh grader in her movie. Make your introduction attention-grabbing. When writing the body of your work, order your supporting details in a logical order. Be sure to use precise, lively words so that your composition is interesting throughout. (See pages 469–473 for information on composing e-mails.)

Timed Writing Party Planner

3. You own and operate Life of the Party, a well-known party planning service. You are organizing an event for a new client, Poochie, who is a world-famous movie star. She also happens to be a dainty French poodle. Write a composition describing your plan for Poochie's party to be presented to Poochie's owner. Include descriptions of the invitations, menu, decorations, entertainment, and music. You have 25 minutes to complete your work.

Your composition should include an introduction, a body with supporting points, and a conclusion. Use specific details and sensory words to paint a vivid picture of your party plans. Arrange your details in a logical order. Be sure all the parts of your composition work together to form one unified work.

Before You Write Consider the following questions: What is the subject? What is the occasion? Who is the audience? What is the purpose?

After You Write Evaluate your work using the six-trait evaluation form on page 23.

Unit 2

Purposes of Writing

Chapter 6	Personal Writing	126
Chapter 7	Descriptive Writing	150
Chapter 8	Creative Writing	174
Chapter 9	Expository Writing	210
Chapter 10	Writing to Persuade	240
Chapter 11	Writing About Literature	266

Why write? Your writing purpose may be nothing fancier than leaving a note for your brother to feed the fish, or it may be as serious as a letter to a newspaper editor arguing for a new community center where young people can go after school. Each writing purpose—from telling a story to explaining an interesting idea to arguing for a strongly held belief—requires its own set of writing tools. No matter what your purpose, though, if you put your ideas into "some hard phrase, round and solid as a ball" rather than in overly general words and expressions that readers can't hold onto, you will be at least halfway toward accomplishing your purpose.

Put the argument into a concrete shape, into an image, some hard phrase, round and solid as a ball, which [readers or listeners] can see and handle and carry home with them, and the cause is half won. — *Ralph Waldo Emerson*

CHAPTER 6

Personal Writing

Narrative writing tells a real or imaginary story that has a clear beginning, middle, and end. A **personal narrative** is a story based on personal experience.

Here are just a few examples of the ways in which narrative writing is used to relay thoughts, feelings, and events.

- **A refugee from a war-torn country writes daily journal entries** telling about his everyday life during the chaos of war.
- **A firefighter speaks to a group of students** about saving a child from a burning apartment building and relates what the experience means to her.
- **A naturalist keeps a field diary** and records his experience of finding an orphaned wolf cub.
- **A movie actor writes his autobiography** and reflects on his 30-year acting career.
- **Your grandmother writes you a letter** telling you how much your visit meant to her.

Writing Project — Personal Narrative

Small Acts Write a personal narrative about a small act of kindness or love in which you explain why it was important, why it was done, or what its consequences were.

Think Through Writing Write freely about a time when you were on either the receiving or the giving end of a small act of kindess or love. Maybe it was an unexpected apology or a parent's easy forgiveness. Maybe it was a pat on the back or a scrapbook lovingly put together in your honor. Write down as many memories as you can.

Talk About It In your writing group, discuss the writing you have done. What aspects of love have group members focused on?

Read About It In the following passage, author Graham Salisbury describes an occasion in which he witnessed the power of love.

MODEL: Personal Writing

From *Speaking of Journals*

Not Your Normal Beast

Graham Salisbury

Yesterday I was in a huge hurry to get home, driving in slow traffic down by Portland Civic Auditorium. A man was driving in front of me with his wife in the front seat and two teenage sons in the back. Stop, go, stop, go . . . slow, slow, slow! Finally, he stopped in the right-hand turn lane at the corner of a block to let one of his sons out, blocking me and forcing me to wait. I became frustrated, but managed to keep from honking at them. The mother got out and held her seat back for one of the boys to get out. Apparently he was headed for something going on at the Civic. He was young, maybe 14, and off in the big city on his own. To say goodbye to him, his mother put her hand on his cheek and looked into his eyes with the most beautiful, loving look on her face. The moment was so tender it broke my heart down to where it should have been all along. Instantly, all my frustration left me. There is great and wonderful power in such a simple act of love, even to those of us who only manage to observe.

Writing in the first person allows the writer to convey an intimate, personal tone.

These sentences convey a frustrated tone about traffic that many readers will easily relate to.

The concluding sentence contains the main idea of the piece.

Respond in Writing In your journal, write about what you think is the importance of Salisbury's experience. What did it mean to him? What do you think the gesture meant to the boy, and to the mother? What effect did the gesture have on those who observed it?

Develop Your Own Ideas Work with your classmates to develop ideas that will help you write about your experience of a small act of kindness or love.

Small Groups: In your writing group, make a list of things each writer should include in his or her personal narrative. Some items on the list might include:

- The setting of the story
- How you were feeling when the story begins
- Descriptions of the characters

Whole Class: Make a master chart of all of the elements each writing group came up with to include in their personal narratives. Refer to this chart as you are writing your narrative to be sure to include all the distinguishing elements of a personal narrative.

Write About It You will next write a focused narrative in which you tell about a small act of kindness or love. You might focus on why it was important, why it was done, and/or what the consequences of the action were. Your writing might feature any of the following possible topics, audiences, and forms.

Possible Topics and Examples	Possible Audiences	Possible Forms
• a time when someone showed you an unexpected act of kindness • a time when you went out of your way to do something nice for a family member or friend • a small act of friendship between you and a pet or other animal • an act of kindness between you and a stranger	• your family • your friends • other teenagers • other adults who are important to you • yourself	• a blog entry • a memoir or diary entry • a letter • a magazine

128   Personal Writing

Personal Narrative Structure

Whether you are writing a paragraph or an essay, the structure of a narrative is basically the same. Each part moves the story along.

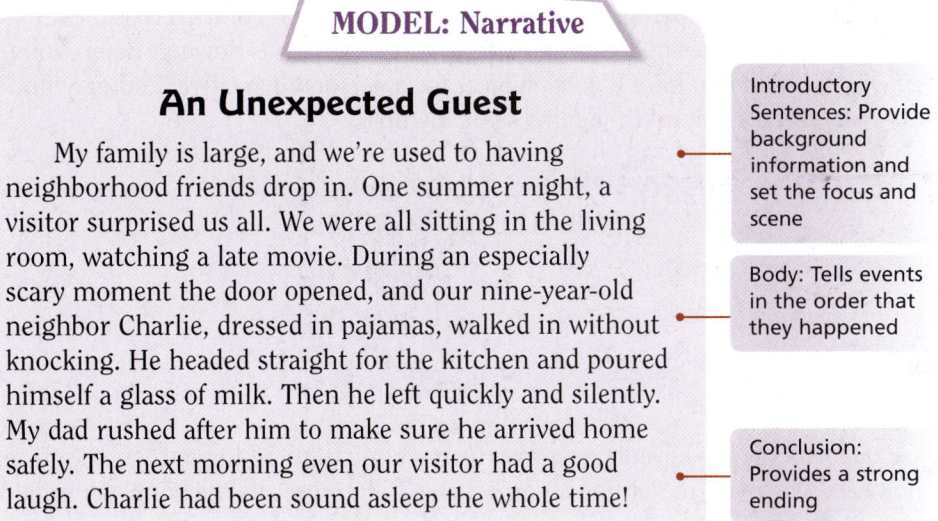

The following chart shows how each part of a narrative paragraph helps to tell a story.

STRUCTURE OF A NARRATIVE

- The **main idea statement** introduces the story by making a general statement, setting the scene, or capturing the reader's attention.
- The **body** tells the story event by event and answers the questions *Who? What? Where? Why? When?* and *How?*
- The **conclusion** ends the story by summarizing the events or making a point.

PROJECT PREP Analyzing Structure

With your writing group, develop a graphic organizer to represent a narrative. Make a large, neat copy of it and share it with the rest of the class. Post the various organizers around the room so they can be reminders of the structure of narratives.

Personal Narrative Writing

Reflecting on an Experience

During the prewriting stage, let your mind wander as you think about possible subjects for narrative paragraphs. Jot down any ideas that come to mind. Use brainstorming, clustering, and freewriting to help get ideas flowing. Before long you will find that you have a good subject for a personal narrative. You may find the following sources helpful in jogging your memory.

IDEA SOURCES FOR SUBJECTS OF PERSONAL NARRATIVES	
poems	family stories
short stories	favorite things
essays	journals

When you are experiencing events, you may be too close to them to see their significance. Later, however, when you reexamine an experience to interpret its meaning, you might complete a checklist like the one below.

 Checklist for Interpreting Experience

Experience: Hiking in the woods is something I love.

This experience is important to me because it

    helps me understand and appreciate living things.
    uses my mind and body.
✓ makes me feel good about my place in the world.
✓ gives me a sense of peace and contentment.
✓ offers me new ways of looking at things.

This experience is worth writing about because

    it will interest many readers.
    it is unique or extraordinary.
✓ writing will help me understand it better.

Interpretation: This is something that makes me feel happy. I am my best self when I am with nature. I enjoy learning about things in the wild.

Choosing and Focusing a Subject

After thinking about all the candidates for your narrative, you have to choose the best one. Pick one that you are excited about. Sometimes even an ordinary event can elicit strong emotion, such as the one Graham Salisbury relates in "Not Your Normal Beast." This type of experience can make an exceptional personal narrative.

Occasionally a subject is broad enough to fill an entire book. A slightly more specific subject may take up a whole chapter. A subject for a short narrative, however, must be very specific. Making your subject narrow enough to cover well is called **limiting** or **focusing** the subject. Look at the following examples.

BOOK LENGTH	CHAPTER LENGTH	SHORT NARRATIVE
my travels	one summer vacation	hiking in a bog
holidays	Thanksgiving	our dog eating the turkey
memories	moving to the country	the day I got lost in the woods

Considering Purpose and Audience

Once you have decided on a subject for your personal narrative, you need to think about your writing purpose. Personal narratives are usually written to express thoughts and feelings in a way that will interest readers. In a personal narrative, the purpose is to tell a story. Your writing can be funny or serious, depending on the personal story you choose to share with your readers.

Writing Tip

Think about your purpose and audience when writing a personal narrative to make sure that you capture and hold your readers' interest.

You must also think about your readers' interests and knowledge so you can make sure they will understand your purpose and meaning. For example, the details you include in writing intended for friends and classmates will be different from those included in writing meant for a younger audience.

PROJECT PREP   Interpreting   Focus

1. Using your work so far and your discussions and reading, develop an idea for a personal narrative. What is your primary focus? For example, what overall idea do you want to convey about the importance of an experience or the reasons behind it and the resultant consequences? What audience are you addressing?
2. Complete a checklist like the one on page 130 to help you interpret the experience.
3. Share your ideas with your writing group and give one another feedback.
4. Write a draft of your personal narrative based on feedback and your own judgment.

❷ First-Person and Third-Person Narratives

In personal narratives, the narrator's position in relation to the story is called the **point of view.** If the person telling the story is a character in the story, then the story is in the first person and pronouns such as *I, we, me, us, my,* and *our* are used. These narratives are called **first-person narratives.**

> **MODEL: First-Person Narrative**
>
> **I** was heading for the locker room when **my** friend Lydia shouted my name. She wanted to give **me** something before the big soccer game. She handed me a new ball. It was signed by Mia Hamm. I couldn't believe it was **mine**. I thanked Lydia about two thousand times!

Some narratives do not involve the writer at all. Writers telling a story about other people will refer to them with third-person pronouns. These stories are called **third-person narratives.**

> **MODEL: Third-Person Narrative**
>
> Laura and Tyron had planned a surprise party for **their** friend's birthday. **They** had thought of everything, and now everyone was waiting to yell surprise when Jake walked in. Then one of **them** remembered that **they'd** forgotten to invite Jake.

Writing Tip

Be sure to use the same **point of view** consistently throughout your personal narrative.

PROJECT PREP *Discussing* **Narrative Voice**

In your writing group, consider each writer's voice as the narrator. What emotions, perspective, knowledge, and other factors are evident from the narrative voice? Identify three or four specific words or phrases that indicate the writer's voice. For each author, suggest ways to make the narrative voice more effective. Then make revisions in your own work as you see fit.

❸ Organizational Strategy

The best way to organize a narrative is by relating a **sequence of events,** or telling the story in time order (also called **chronological order**).

You can use a chart like the one below to help you arrange your sequence of events or you can use a timeline. You might start by writing what happened first and what happened last and then fill in the remaining details in order.

Subject	Jake's surprise party
What happened first	set the date
What happened next	invited all the neighbors
What happened next	decorated the house and set out food
What happened next	everyone hid, ready to yell surprise
What happened last	forgot to tell Jake to come over

● Practice Your Skills

Arranging Events in Order

Write the subject. Then list the events in chronological order.

Subject	trying out for the soccer team
Events	• showing skills in both defense and offense
	• last test was a shoot-out on the goal
	• really nervous before tryouts began
	• very excited when I made the team

PROJECT PREP   Analyzing   Organization

In your writing group, focus on each author's arrangement of events. Do you get a clear sense of the sequence? Does the narrative follow the shape of the graphic organizer your group (or another group) developed? Point out any gaps and suggest ways to fill them clearly and improve the flow.

Think Critically

Recalling

To help you come up with the details you need for your narrative paragraph, you use the skill of **recalling.** Stored somewhere in the mysterious gray mass of your brain are fragments of virtually all the experiences you have ever had. Through active recall, you can bring some of these fragments to your memory—and use them to make your writing rich and lifelike.

Different writers use different techniques to retrieve memories, but the following strategies may help you tap into some nearly forgotten parts of your past.

Strategies for Recalling

- Relax. Shut down the part of your mind that usually disciplines your thoughts. Let one thought lead to another as you float on top of your general memory. Before you know it, you will probably have a flood of specific memories.
- Try to recall exactly one aspect of the experience you wish to remember. Focus your thoughts on that one single memory. Chances are good that other details will soon come to mind as well.
- Imagine you are looking at a photograph or video of the event. Little by little, let your mind fill in all the details in the picture or video until you can see it as clearly as if it really existed.

Thinking Practice

Think back to one of the most pleasant memories of your childhood. Use any or all of the strategies above to bring even the smallest details of that experience to mind. Jot down each detail as it occurs to you. Save your work in case you want to develop your memories into a composition later.

Personal Narrative Writing  Drafting

To write your first draft, take the details you listed in your prewriting activities and develop them into an organized narrative. Like other kinds of writing, personal narratives have an introduction, a body, and a conclusion.

 Introduction

In a narrative, the main idea is the event you are writing about. The tips below will help you write a good introduction.

 Tips for Drafting an Introduction

- Make clear the subject, purpose, and main idea of your narrative.
- Provide enough information for your reader to appreciate the situation.
- Capture readers' attention and try to sustain it throughout the narrative.

If you were writing a narrative about the time you tried to take pictures of Rags and her newborn pups, you might write the following main idea.

> **Main Idea**   Rags was a protective mother.

This sentence states the main idea, but readers would not know who Rags is. The following sentence does a better job.

> **Main Idea**   My dog Rags protected her pups from everyone—even me.

This statement is strong because it focuses attention on the subject and prepares the reader for what is to follow. Avoid openings such as "This narrative will be about . . ." or "In this narrative I will . . ."

The opening sentence in the narrative below sets the scene and defines the focus.

> **MODEL: Dramatic Opening Line**
>
> If you are looking for a pet that will be loyal and obedient, don't get a cat.

Personal Narrative Writing • Drafting

The following introductory passage, which includes a sentence fragment for effect, also does a good job of setting the scene and establishing the voice of the narrator.

STUDENT MODEL: *Strong Beginning*

Whipping, peeling, and cutting corners no bus had cut before. This was my morning, every morning, riding the yellow demon.

—Katie Smith, Canton South High School, Canton, Ohio

● **Practice Your Skills**

Drafting Main Idea Statements

Read the three lists of details for narrative compositions. Then write a main idea statement for each list. Save your work.

1. rained all day
   - lights went out
   - went to basement for candles
   - basement flooded
   - spent all evening drying things out

2. left at 4:00 A.M. on a fishing trip
   - drove for two hours
   - rented a boat
   - rowed out into lake
   - discovered I had left fishing gear at home
3. decided to paint a picture of my dog
   - bought paints and brushes
   - spilled paint on the rug
   - thought the dog looked like a seal
   - dog ran off with picture

PROJECT PREP *Evaluating* **Introduction**

In your writing group, focus on how each author begins the narrative. Can you picture the setting and characters clearly? Help each writer think about details that might help readers get a good sense of the location for the narrative.

Transitions

Presenting your ideas in order will help your readers follow the events in your narrative. Use transitional words and phrases to make sure that the order is clear. **Transitions** are words and phrases that show the passing of time.

In the following draft of a paragraph-long narrative, the transitions are highlighted.

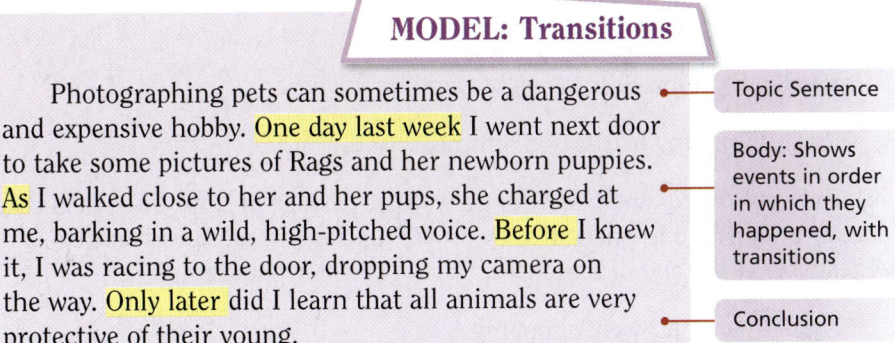

MODEL: Transitions

Photographing pets can sometimes be a dangerous and expensive hobby. **One day last week** I went next door to take some pictures of Rags and her newborn puppies. **As** I walked close to her and her pups, she charged at me, barking in a wild, high-pitched voice. **Before** I knew it, I was racing to the door, dropping my camera on the way. **Only later** did I learn that all animals are very protective of their young.

- Topic Sentence
- Body: Shows events in order in which they happened, with transitions
- Conclusion

Transitions can appear anywhere in a sentence. The following transitions are often used to show time order in narrative writing.

TRANSITION WORDS FOR TIME ORDER

before	finally	meanwhile
after	later	after a while
first	soon	one day
next	at last	last weekend
when	then	the next day

PROJECT PREP Drafting Transitions

In your writing group, help each author provide transitions to keep one event in the narrative flowing smoothly into the next.

editing

During the drafting stage you are concentrating on getting your ideas down, so you may find yourself overwriting. Look back at your draft when you feel it is complete and rewrite wordy sentences and delete unnecessary repetition.

Personal Narrative Writing • Drafting

The Power of Language

Adverbs: Fine Points

An adverb is a word that modifies a verb, an adjective, or another adverb. Adverbs can show *how* or *when* an action was done; they focus on the action and bring it into sharp focus. In these examples from Graham Salisbury's "Not Your Normal Beast," the adverbs, highlighted, come at the beginning of sentences.

Yesterday I was in a huge hurry to get home…

Finally, he stopped in the right-hand turn lane…

Instantly, all my frustration left me.

The adverbs *finally* and *instantly* convey the passage of time. They help readers better understand the narrative by providing transitions. Adverbs can also be used effectively at the end of sentences. Study the following examples.

My mother and I went shopping today.

We might watch a movie later.

The officer told the boys to leave immediately.

Try It Yourself

Write two sentences with adverbs at the beginning and two sentences with adverbs at the end. When you draft your narrative paragraph, use adverbs as transitions that convey the passage of time.

Punctuation Tip

If you want your reader to pause, put a comma after an introductory adverb. (See pages 841–843 on introductory elements.)

Personal Writing

③ Adding Specific Details: Zoom In

When you have a good, focused subject and an organization in place, you can give some thought to adding important details of the narrative, like those shown in highlighted text. You can find these details by *zooming in* for a closer look at your scene and subject.

Subject **Zoom in on Setting**	Rags and puppies	neighbor's kitchen/ sunny, bright
What happened first **Zoom in on Sensory Details**	I went into the kitchen.	gentle "wet dog" smell/bundles of fur snuggled up to their mom
What happened next **Zoom in on Actions and Sensory Details**	I walked up to Rags and the pups.	quiet footsteps/could feel my heart race because I was so eager to hold the puppies
What happened next **Zoom in on Actions**	Rags charged at me	Rags bared her teeth and snarled/bounded toward me fiercely/my litte scream
What happened next **Zoom in on Sensory Details/Thoughts**	I turned and ran.	I was afraid of getting bit/surprised at Rags' behavior/ran so fast I created a breeze
What happened last **Zoom in on Attitudes**	Rags would have done anything to protect her pups.	Rags was just following her instincts/I was actually touched by her devotion

By choosing your details (and the words that describe them) carefully, you breathe life into your writing. Your work becomes distinctive and meaningful.

● **Practice Your Skills**

Adding Details

Add a few details to each of the sentences below.

1. My dog is old.
2. Dad came into the room.
3. Stewart and I like music.

Writing Tip

As you develop details, be sure to keep the focus of your composition clear. Avoid distracting details that do not relate closely to your focused subject.

Personal Narrative Writing • Drafting

 Conclusion

A strong conclusion brings your writing to a close and leaves the reader satisfied. A concluding sentence may serve a variety of purposes.

Ways to Write a Conclusion

- Restate the main idea in fresh words.
- Sum up the events.
- Pull the supporting paragraphs together.
- Explain the importance of the experience.

Any of the following ideas would form the basis for a strong conclusion to the short narrative about Rags and her pups.

Concluding Ideas

Be careful when you approach a dog and her newborn puppies. (restates an idea from the focus statement)

Seeing how well Rags protected her puppies was an experience I will never forget. (sums up the narrative)

Rags may have thought her pups were in danger, but I knew I was! (pulls the supporting ideas together)

The experience with Rags gave me a first-hand look at just how strong animal instincts can be. (explains the importance of the experience)

● Practice Your Skills

Writing a Conclusion

Look over your work on the **Practice Your Skills** activity on page 139. Choose one of those topics and write a conclusion for the narrative.

PROJECT PREP Drafting Conclusion

In your writing group, help each author develop a satisfying ending. Consider ending with a moral, a quote, or an observation regarding the subject. Some members may decide that letting readers draw their own conclusions is the best way to go. Help each author come up with a conclusion that enhances the point of the piece.

Personal Narrative Writing

Revising a personal narrative involves attention to three important points.

- Have you developed your personal narrative in enough detail?
- Have you made your ideas and feelings clear?
- Have you maintained a consistent voice?

① Checking for Development of Ideas

Make sure you have included enough specific supporting details to make your reader clearly see and hear what you want to share. The following strategies will help.

HERE'S HOW

Strategies for Revising to Improve the Development of Ideas	
Events	Close your eyes and visualize the experience you are writing about. Write down the details that you "see" in your mind's eye.
People	Visualize each person you are writing about. Visualize the head and face of each person and slowly move down to the feet. Write down details as you "see" them.
Places	Visualize the place you are describing from left to right and from top to bottom, as well as from the foreground to the background.
Feelings	Imagine reliving the experience that you are writing about. As you relive the experience, focus on your thoughts and feelings.

● Practice Your Skills

Revising for Development of Ideas

Revise the following paragraph by adding details that would help readers visualize or understand the experience.

> I wanted to paint a picture. My dog would be a good subject. I bought paint and brushes. I began to paint. The dog knocked over the table. Paint spilled on the rug. My dog looked like a seal. He ran off with the painting.

PROJECT PREP Revising **Development of Ideas**

Based on the feedback from your writing group, write a new draft of your narrative, with attention to the development of your ideas with sensory details as well as thoughts and feelings.

Checking for Focus, Clarity, and Style

After revising your writing to be sure you have developed your ideas adequately, check for focus, clarity, and style. Writing in which all the sentences support the main idea has **focus,** or unity. Writing with **clarity** is easy to understand and is enjoyable to read. **Style** indicates a way of using language that makes your writing unique.

The following checklist will help you identify areas for improvement when you revise your personal narrative.

✓ Evaluation Checklist for Revising

Checking Your Narrative

- ✓ Does your narrative fulfill its purpose? (page 131)
- ✓ Is your narrative appropriate for your audience and occasion? (page 131)
- ✓ Does your story have all the features of the narrative genre? (pages 129–133)
- ✓ Does your introduction make a general statement, set the scene, or capture attention? (pages 135–136)
- ✓ Does the body of your narrative tell the story event by event and answer the questions *Who? What? Where? Why? When?* and *How?* (page 129)
- ✓ Does each paragraph support the main idea in some way, giving it focus? (page 142)
- ✓ Do the words you've used reflect your distinctive writing style and connect with the reader? (page 38)
- ✓ Does your narrative have an organizational strategy with appropriate transitions to give it clarity and coherence? (pages 133 and 137)
- ✓ Did you use first person if you are a character in the story? Did you use third person if your story is about something that happened to someone else? Did you stick with your point of view throughout the narrative? (page 132)
- ✓ Does your conclusion end the story by summarizing the events or making a strong point about the story? (page 140)

Checking Your Sentences

- ✓ Did you combine related sentences to avoid too many short, choppy sentences? (pages 64–72)
- ✓ Did you vary the length and beginnings of your sentences? (page 73)
- ✓ Did you avoid unnecessary repetition, empty expressions, and rambling sentences? (pages 75–78)

Checking Your Words

- ✓ Did you use specific words? (pages 44–46)
- ✓ Did you use words that appeal to the senses? (pages 47–53)

● **Practice Your Skills**

Revising for Focus, Clarity, and Style

Revise the following paragraph by adding details that help focus and clarify the writing and deleting anything that does not belong. Also add words and phrases that reflect a writing style suitable for this narrative.

> ## Skiing Ups and Downs
>
> All skis should read: "Skiing may be hazardous to your health." I should know, because I tried skiing for the first time yesterday. Many of my friends know how to ski. It looked like fun. I fell getting onto the chair lift. I fell getting off the chair lift. Then as soon as I started skiing, my skis crossed. I fell forward, lost my skis, and rolled halfway down the hill. We were skiing in the Green Mountains. Then I had to climb back up again to pick up my skis. After falling several more times and running into another skier, I finally reached the bottom of the hill.

PROJECT PREP   Revising   Checklist and Feedback

Exchange papers with a writing partner and read one another's narratives against the checklist on the previous page. Make suggestions to help the author prepare an effective revision of the story. Then, based on the feedback you have gotten from your writing group, write a new draft of your narrative. In this draft, take into account your partner's recommendations and also focus greater attention on grammar, punctuation, and spelling so that readers will easily be able to follow your writing.

Meet with your writing group. Discuss what you learned from the experience of writing a personal narrative. What did you learn about your writing style and about yourself?

In the Media

Television Talk Shows

One of the most popular media forms is the daytime talk show. The producers of these shows come up with a different situation for each show, a "hook" that tends to be moving, disturbing, or even shocking. Then the producers locate ordinary citizens who are willing to appear on national television to discuss their experiences. The result can be fascinating, touching, distasteful, maddening, or simply boring.

What usually makes the difference is the host. This role is one that requires a strong ability to talk through any situation, as well as a lively personality. The show's following is made up of people who find the host's personality compelling.

Media Activity

Work with several classmates. Ask your parents to help you choose a daytime talk show to watch. Videotape it, if possible, for several days. As you watch, notice the content and overall message, as well as how the message is presented.

Questions for Analyzing a Daytime Talk Show

- Who is the host? What is the best way to describe the host's personality?
- List the topic for each show you watched. How does the theme relate to the host's personality?
- How is the studio audience involved in the program? Does the host interview audience members throughout the show?
- Are there clips of background material or interviews? Are they effective?

Share your findings with your classmates.

Personal Narrative Writing — Editing

As you wrote and revised your personal narrative, you looked for ways to help your reader clearly see and hear what you wanted to share. You also checked for adequate development, clarity, and consistency of tone. Now you are ready to edit, or polish, your writing.

The Language of  Pronouns

Power Rule: Use subject forms of pronouns in subject position. Use object forms of pronouns in object position. (See pages 716–719.)

See It in Action The following sentence from "Not Your Normal Beast" shows subject and object pronouns used correctly.

> **I** was in a huge hurry, and a slow driver was in front of **me.** (*I* is the subject of the sentence, so the subject form is used. *Me* is the object of the preposition *in front of*, so the object form is used.)

Most people would not make the mistake of saying "the driver in front of I." However, many people would make the mistake of using *I* in the following.

> **I** was in a huge hurry, and a slow driver was in front of my passenger and **me.** (*I* is the subject of the sentence. Although it is now part of a compound object, *me* is still an object of the preposition *in front of*, so the object form is still used.)

If you notice a compound object like this one *(my passenger and me)* make sure you use the object form for the pronoun.

Remember It Record this rule and example in the Power Rule section of your Personalized Editing Checklist.

Use It Read through your narrative and circle all the pronouns. Check each one to make sure you have used the correct form.

PROJECT PREP Editing **Polish Your Work**

Exchange papers with a classmate. Read one another's work, looking for errors in grammar, usage, mechanics, and spelling. Point out ones you find.

Using a Six-Trait Rubric — Personal Narratives

Use an evaluation form like the one below to measure a personal narrative.

Ideas	**4** The topic and details powerfully convey the meaning of the experience to the intended audience and fulfill the intended purpose.	**3** The topic and details convey the meaning of the experience to the intended audience and fulfill the intended purpose.	**2** The topic and details do not convey the meaning of the experience to the intended audience or fulfill the intended purpose.	**1** The topic and details do not convey meaning and fail to address the audience and fulfill the purpose. Little effort was made to complete the assignment.
Organization	**4** The introduction sets the tone and captures attention; details in the body are in time order; the conclusion provides a powerful ending.	**3** The organization is mostly clear, but a few ideas seemed out of place or transitions were missing.	**2** Many ideas are out of place and transitions are missing. The introduction, body, and conclusion are weak.	**1** The organization is unclear and hard to follow. The introduction, body, and conclusion are ill formed.
Voice	**4** The voice sounds natural, engaging, and personal.	**3** The voice sounds natural, and personal.	**2** The voice sounds mostly unnatural with a few exceptions.	**1** The voice sounds mostly unnatural.
Word Choice	**4** Words are precise and create vivid images.	**3** Words are precise and some words appeal to the senses.	**2** Some words are overly general.	**1** Most words are overly general.
Sentence Fluency	**4** Varied sentences flow smoothly. Transitions are used effectively.	**3** Most sentences are varied and flowing. Transitions help coherence.	**2** Some sentences are not varied, and some are choppy. There are few transitions.	**1** Sentences are not varied and are choppy. There are very few transitions.
Conventions	**4** Punctuation, usage, and spelling are correct. The Power Rules are all followed.	**3** There are only a few errors in punctuation, usage, and spelling. The Power Rules are all followed.	**2** There are a number of errors in punctuation, usage, and spelling, but all Power Rules are followed.	**1** There are many errors and at least one failure to follow a Power Rule.

Personal Narrative Writing — Publishing

You may decide to complete the writing process by sharing your writing with someone who was part of your experience or who may have an interest in it.

PROJECT PREP   Publishing   Sharing Your Work

If you chose one of the forms listed on page 128 for your published work, meet with others in your class to discuss the publishing conventions of that form. For example, if you chose to write a letter, does your finished work have all the elements of a letter? In what ways did you need to adjust your narrative to fit the form you chose? How might you have done that better?

When you are satisfied that you have polished your personal narrative as well as you can, publish it through your chosen medium. If you wrote a letter, for example, share it with another person who was involved in your narrative account.

Personal Narrative Writing • Publishing 147

Writing Lab

Project Corner

Get Dramatic
Act It Out

In your writing group, use one of the narratives and **produce a brief drama** based on its content. Either perform the play live for an audience or record it and play it on a screen.

Think Creatively Write a Prequel

Write a prequel to one of the narratives written by a member of your class. A prequel is a story that takes place before an existing story and helps lead into it. Think about what might have taken place in order to set the stage for the events the author has recounted.

Get Artistic Try a Different Medium

Take an image from one of the personal narratives written by a classmate and **transform it into another artistic medium**, such as a drawing, painting, or sculpture. What is gained and lost through an interpretation in a different form?

In the Workplace
Electronic Bulletin Board Message

Apply And Assess

1. You are the owner of a goat farm. Recently, a group of seventh graders visited your farm on a field trip. You showed them the shelters and hay barns, the milking equipment, and the pastures. At the end of the morning, you provided a lunch that included goat cheese and goat milk. **Write a personal narrative** to be posted on an electronic bulletin board for farmers describing the field trip and reflecting on why it was important to you. Check for clarity, unity, and style.

For Oral Communication Personal Speech

2. You are a member of the seventh-grade Travel Club. Your group has recently been invited to speak to fourth graders about your travel experiences. Each of you will speak about a different aspect of travel, and you have chosen the topic of transportation. **Write a one-paragraph speech** describing the first trip you ever took. Narrate the events of that day and what you felt about the experience. Put your narrative in chronological order and include a topic sentence and concluding sentence. Check that you use transitions to help guide your listeners through the story. (You can find information on writing speeches on pages 435–440.)

Timed Writing Friendly Letter

3. Some people in your town consider the Peabodys "peculiar"—after all, their house is painted bright orange, and both husband and wife make frequent trips to the junkyard to decorate their lawn. On a recent sunny day, you stopped to speak to the Peabodys while they were working on their lawn, and you found them to be interesting and extremely nice. They showed you their many unusual and interesting possessions—old comic books, antique dolls, coins from around the world. They even shared the cookies they love to bake. **Write a letter** to a friend describing your time with the Peabodys. Put your narrative in chronological order. Tell your friend what happened, and include reflections on what the experience meant to you. Remember to use specific and colorful details in describing the Peabodys and their home. (You can find information on writing a letter on pages 419–429.) You have 25 minutes to complete your work.

Before You Write Consider the following questions: What is the subject? What is the occasion? Who is the audience? What is the purpose?

After You Write Evaluate your work using the six-trait evaluation form on page 146.

CHAPTER 7

Descriptive Writing

Descriptive writing creates a picture of a person, an object, or a scene through words.

A vivid description appeals to readers' senses. The descriptive writer goes out into the world with senses wide open, noticing the sharp edges of midday shadows, the scent of fresh-cut grass in the summertime, the irritating scratch of a new wool sweater, or the relentless hammering of rain on the roof. When you want your reader to see the world through your eyes, you use descriptive writing. Think about these examples of description in everyday life.

- **You write an e-mail pal in a foreign country,** describing your home, your neighborhood, and your school.
- **You describe your idea for a band T-shirt to an artist friend.** Your friend will draw the design you have imagined.
- **You write a letter to the student newspaper protesting the food served in the cafeteria.** You include a graphic description of the soggy vegetables and mystery meats.
- **You listen as a reporter describes the jubilation of people celebrating a political victory** to a television news anchor.
- **Knowing you miss home while you're at camp,** your mom sends you a detailed description of the activities that have taken place in your home.

Writing Project

The Comfort of the Ordinary Follow the directions below to write a description of a place you know well.

Think Through Writing Write about a familiar place in which you feel comfortable. It could be your room at home, a spot beside a creek, a street you take on your way home from school, a gym where you play sports, or any other place you know well. Write a description of this place, focusing on details that stand out to you.

Talk About It Share your writing with your writing group. What kinds of features did people include in their descriptions? Can you easily picture the area being described? Talk about other specific details that come to mind.

Read About It The following selection from *Julie of the Wolves* by Jean Craighead George describes the experience of Miyax, a 13-year old girl who gets lost in the Alaskan wilderness and attempts to communicate with a wolf to stave off starvation. Take note of the kinds of details included in this descriptive piece. Do you get a strong picture of the area?

MODEL: Descriptive Writing

From

Julie of the Wolves

Jean Craighead George

Miyax pushed back the hood of her sealskin parka and looked at the Arctic sun. It was a yellow disc in a lime-green sky, the colors of six o'clock in the evening and the time when the wolves awoke. Quietly she put down her cooking pot and crept to the top of a dome-shaped frost heave, one of the many earth buckles that rise and fall in the crackling cold of the Arctic winter. Lying on her stomach, she looked across a vast lawn of grass and moss and focused her attention on the wolves she had come upon two sleeps ago. They were wagging their tails as they awoke and saw each other.

> Striking colors grab the reader's attention.

> Readers see the scene from Miyax's point of view.

Her hands trembled and her heart-beat quickened, for she was frightened, not so much of the wolves, who were shy and many harpoon-shots away, but because of her desperate predicament. Miyax was lost. She had been lost without food for many sleeps on the North Slope of Alaska. The barren slope stretches for three hundred miles from the Brooks Range to the Arctic Ocean, and for more than eight hundred miles from the Chukchi to the Beaufort Sea. No roads cross it; ponds and lakes freckle its immensity. Winds scream across it, and the view in every direction is exactly the same. Somewhere in this cosmos was Miyax; and the very life in her body, its spark and warmth, depended upon these wolves for survival. And she was not so sure they would help.

> These details of touch help the reader share Miyax's fear.

Miyax stared hard at the regal black wolf, hoping to catch his eye. She must somehow tell him that she was starving and ask him for food. This could be done she knew, for her father, an Eskimo hunter, had done so. One year he had camped near a wolf den while on a hunt. When a month had passed and her father had seen no game, he told the leader of the wolves that he was hungry and needed food. The next night the wolf called him from far away and her father went to him and found a freshly killed caribou. Unfortunately, Miyax's father never explained to her how he had told the wolf of his needs. And not long afterwards he paddled his kayak into the Bering Sea to hunt for seal, and he never returned.

She had been watching the wolves for two days, trying to discern which of their sounds and movements expressed goodwill and friendship. Most animals had such signals. The little Arctic ground squirrels flicked their tails sideways to notify others of their kind that they were friendly. By imitating this signal with her forefinger, Miyax had lured many a squirrel to her hand. If she could discover such a gesture for the wolves she would be able to make friends with them and share their food, like a bird or a fox.

Propped on her elbows with her chin in her fists, she stared at the black wolf, trying to catch his eye. She had chosen him because he was much larger than the others, and because he walked like her father, Kapugen, with his head high and his chest out. The black wolf also possessed wisdom, she had observed. The pack looked to him when the wind carried strange scents or the birds cried nervously. If he was alarmed, they were alarmed. If he was calm, they were calm.

Long minutes passed, and the black wolf did not look at her. He had ignored her since she first came upon them, two sleeps ago. True, she moved slowly and quietly, so as not to alarm him; yet she did wish he would see the kindness in her eyes. Many animals could tell the difference between hostile hunters and friendly people by merely looking at them. But the big black wolf would not even glance her way.

A bird stretched in the grass. The wolf looked at it. A flower twisted in the wind. He glanced at that. Then

> This specific detail about how Miyax had communicated with animals in the past helps explain the kinds of sounds and movements she is looking for in the wolves.

> Descriptive writing is rarely done for its own sake. Instead, good descriptions help bring any written text to life. Here it is used to set the scene and enliven the story of Miyax alone in the wilderness.

> The stretching bird, twisting flower, and rippling ruff are such subtle motions that the reader might seem to be looking at the scene through a magnifying glass.

the breeze rippled the wolverine ruff on Miyax's parka and it glistened in the light. He did not look at that. She waited. Patience with the ways of nature had been instilled in her by her father. And so she knew better than to move or shout. Yet she must get food or die. Her hands shook slightly and she swallowed hard to keep calm.

Miyax was a classic Eskimo beauty, small of bone and delicately wired with strong muscles. Her face was pearl-round and her nose was flat. Her black eyes, which slanted gracefully, were moist and sparkling. Like the beautifully formed polar bears and foxes of the north, she was slightly short-limbed. The frigid environment of the Arctic has sculptured life into compact shapes. Unlike the long-limbed, long-bodied animals of the south that are cooled by dispensing heat on extended surfaces, all live things in the Arctic tend toward compactness, to conserve heat.

> Can you picture Miyax from this description?

The length of her limbs and the beauty of her face were of no use to Miyax as she lay on the lichen-speckled frost heave in the midst of the bleak tundra. Her stomach ached and the royal black wolf was carefully ignoring her.

"*Amaroq, ilaya*, wolf, my friend," she finally called. "Look at me. Look at me."

She spoke half in Eskimo and half in English, as if the instincts of her father and the science of the *gussaks*, the white-faced, might evoke some magical combination that would help her get her message through to the wolf.

> Miyax doesn't lie on just frost in the tundra. Adjectives say just what kind of frost and what kind of tundra: "lichen-speckled frost" and "bleak tundra."

Amaroq glanced at his paw and slowly turned his head her way without lifting his eyes. He licked his shoulder. A few matted hairs sprang apart and twinkled individually. Then his eyes sped to each of the three adult wolves that made up his pack and finally to the five pups who were sleeping in a fuzzy mass near the den entrance. The great wolf's eyes softened at the sight of the little wolves, then quickly hardened into brittle yellow jewels as he scanned the flat tundra.

> Vivid sights and feelings help the reader come to know the wolf as well as Miyax and the wilderness landscape.

Not a tree grew anywhere to break the monotony of the gold-green plain, for the soils of the tundra are permanently frozen. Only moss, grass, lichens, and a few hardy flowers take root in the thin upper layer that thaws briefly in summer. Nor do many species of animals live in this rigorous land, but those creatures that do dwell here exist in bountiful numbers. Amaroq watched a large cloud of Lapland longspurs wheel up into the sky, then alight in the grasses. Swarms of crane flies, one of the few insects that can survive the cold, darkened the tips of the mosses. Birds wheeled, turned, and called. Thousands sprang up from the ground like leaves in a wind.

> If you took this paragraph out, the story would still make sense. What does it add, however, that makes it worth keeping?

The wolf's ears cupped forward and tuned in on some distant message from the tundra. Miyax tensed and listened too. Did he hear some brewing storm, some approaching enemy? Apparently not. His ears relaxed and he rolled to his side. She sighed, glanced at the vaulting sky, and was painfully aware of her predicament.

Here she was, watching wolves—she, Miyax, daughter of Kapugen, adopted child of Martha, citizen of the United States, pupil at the Bureau of Indian Affairs School in Barrow, Alaska, and thirteen-year-old wife of the boy Daniel. She shivered at the thought of Daniel, for it was he who had driven her to this fate. She had run away from him exactly seven sleeps ago, and because of this she had one more title by gussak standards—the child divorcée.

The wolf rolled to his belly.

"Amaroq," she whispered. "I am lost and the sun will not set for a month. There is no North Star to guide me."

Amaroq did not stir.

"And there are no berry bushes here to bend under the polar wind and point to the south. Nor are there any birds I can follow." She looked up. "Here the birds are buntings and longspurs. They do not fly to the sea twice a day like the puffins and sandpipers that my father followed."

The wolf groomed his chest with his tongue.

"I never dreamed I could get lost, Amaroq," she went on, talking out loud to ease her fear. "At home on Nunivak Island where I was born, the plants and birds pointed the way for wanderers. I thought they

> The author sets up a pattern here: the wolf performs some simple action (rolled to his belly, did not stir, groomed his chest with his tongue), and in between these simple motions are Miyax's appeals to Amaroq for help and her explanations why she can't rely on her usual methods for finding her way. The structure makes it seem as if the two are having a conversation.

Descriptive Writing

did so everywhere . . . and so, great black Amaroq, I'm without a compass."

It had been a frightening moment when two days ago she realized that the tundra was an ocean of grass on which she was circling around and around. Now as that fear overcame her again she closed her eyes. When she opened them her heart skipped excitedly. Amaroq was looking at her!

Respond in Writing Respond to this description of the Alaskan wilderness. Imagine yourself in that place and write about what your senses would experience.

Develop Your Own Descriptive Strategies Work with your classmates to develop ideas that you might use in writing clear descriptive pieces about a place with which you are familiar and in which you feel comfortable.

Small Groups: In your small group, discuss the writing you have done. Answer the following questions about each writer's work.

1. Did the writer identify the place by name, location, and other identifiers?
2. What aspects of the place's physical appearance are included in the description?
3. In addition to what you can see, what other sensory details (smells, sounds, tastes, and feelings) are provided to characterize the place?
4. What kind of overall impression do the details form?

Project and Reading

Whole Class: Make a master chart of all of the answers generated by the small groups to see how different members of the class described their places.

Write About It You will next write a descriptive piece about a place that you know well and that makes you feel very comfortable. Your writing might concern any of the following possible topics, audiences, or forms.

Possible Topics	Possible Audiences	Possible Forms
• a place you go for peace and quiet • a place where you engage In important activities • a place you walk through or pass by frequently • a place that was the site of an important event	• residents of the area • newcomers to the area • the Chamber of Commerce • potential visitors to the area	• a Web-based guide • a pamphlet • a welcome brochure • an encyclopedia entry • a newspaper article

Elements of Descriptive Writing

Descriptive writing takes the reader into a world created entirely by words. Writers open the door to this world by using vivid sensory details. They also structure their writing so that readers get a clear picture of what is being described.

❶ Structure in Descriptive Writing

In the following description, the writer's purpose is to describe a barn. As you read the description, notice how each part works to create the picture.

MODEL: Descriptive Writing

The Old Barn

Their barn was a marvelous, solid structure with a sense of long ago about it. There were a couple of old horse stalls in there. There were even a few oats left in the feed bins and some wisps of old, shiny hay, dark with age. With a little imagination you could hear a gentle ghostly whinny and the restless stirring of iron shod hooves on the wide-board floors. People sometimes tried to buy the barn for lumber or to haul it away to someplace else and make a house out of it. The owners refused to sell. Barns like this, they said—once they are gone they do not come back.

—Mary Stolz, *The Edge of Next Year*

- Main Idea
- Supporting Details
- Strong Ending

The following chart summarizes the function of each part of a descriptive text.

Structuring Descriptive Writing

- In the **introduction,** present the subject of the description and suggest a general tone or impression of it. In paragraphs, the topic sentence does that job.
- In the **body,** provide details that bring the subject to life.
- In the **conclusion,** summarize the overall impression of the subject.

● **Practice Your Skills**

Writing Descriptive Main Idea Statements

For each subject, write a main idea statement that conveys an overall feeling.

Example	a cave
Possible Answer	The cave was dark and mysterious, full of sights from another world.

1. a porpoise
2. a city bus
3. a block party
4. a spring day
5. a seashore
6. a path in the woods
7. a pair of new shoes
8. a hockey game
9. an ice, snow, or rainstorm
10. a view from a rooftop

PROJECT PREP *Evaluating* Structure

With your writing group, evaluate the structure of what you have written. Chances are it is not very tightly organized because you were just doing exploratory writing. For each writer, make suggestions about how to provide a clear structure. Based on your group's feedback, make revisions. Share your new draft with your teacher.

❷ Specific Details and Sensory Words

If a description contains only vague ideas and general words, readers will soon lose interest. Specific details and words that appeal to the senses are the sparks that activate a reader's imagination.

Notice the sensory words used to describe the canyon in the following description.

MODEL: Specific Details and Sensory Words

The Santa Elena Canyon

<mark>Just before dawn one day, I stood at the mouth of the majestic Santa Elena Canyon, watching the sun come up.</mark> The Rio Grande, about 50 feet wide at this point, spilled out of the canyon. As the sun rose, the coloring of the canyon walls, reflected in the slow-moving waters, gradually changed. Faint blacks, browns, and warm, rusty reds faded into grayish white. Before long the sun moved on and left the canyon in shade. I felt dwarfed by the high, massive, sheer walls. More than anything I remember the sounds. Like a symphony, songs of birds and insects flowed from the lower canyon, then vibrated and echoed up and out of the sky. Looking up, following the sounds, I could see black vultures soaring up and down the canyon walls. It looked almost as if they were dancing to the songs.

—Tor Eigeland, *America's Majestic Canyons*

- Suggests general impression
- Sights
- Sounds

Writing Tip

Use **specific details** and **sensory words** to bring your description to life.

Elements of Descriptive Writing   159

● **Practice Your Skills**

Developing Sensory Details by Clustering

Using the following cluster diagram as a model, choose two of the subjects that follow it and make a new cluster diagram for each. Attach as many details as you can to each of the sensory circles.

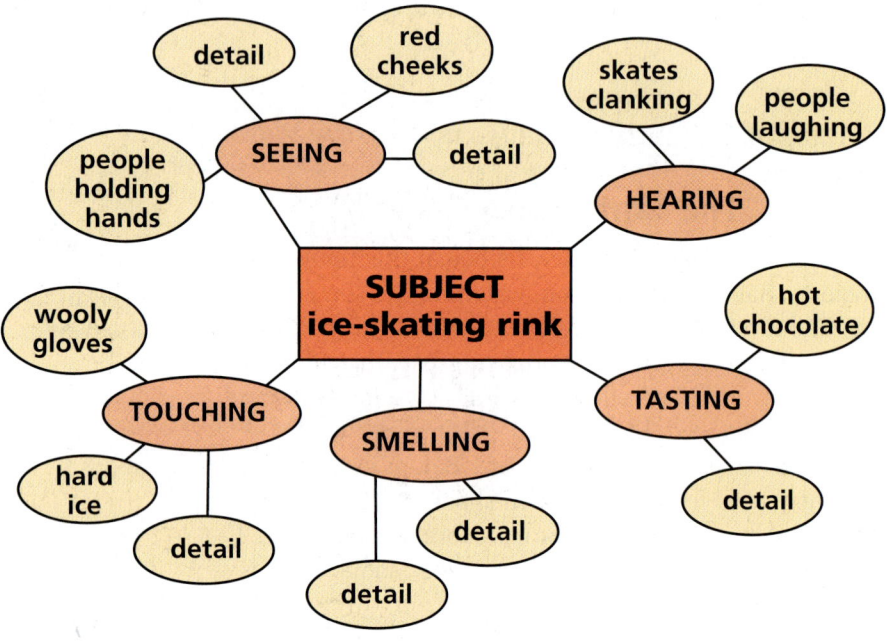

1. a windy day
2. a hayride
3. a parade
4. a locker room
5. a hospital

PROJECT PREP *Evaluating* **Details**

Bring your new draft to your writing group. Focus first on sensory details. Has each author described key aspects of the place in vivid detail? Help each author to identify places where new or expanded descriptions would help readers experience the place. Next, focus on the general impression. Do the details add up to the intended feeling? Is a general impression suggested early in the description? Based on your partners' feedback and feedback from your teacher, revise your description to improve the quality of the details and their support of a general impression.

Think Critically

Visualizing

When you completed the previous activities, how did you know what details to list? Chances are you did not actually go to each place and observe the scenes. By concentrating, you were able to remember or imagine some of the specific details that stand out in each place.

The process of seeing something in your "mind's eye" is called **visualizing.** Although visualizing usually refers to seeing, it can also refer to hearing, tasting, touching, and smelling. Visualizing is an important skill for any writer of description. The better you can visualize the person, place, or object you are describing, the better you can communicate your vision to readers.

You can strengthen your visualizing skills the same way an athlete strengthens muscles. Use them often and stretch them a little further each time. When writing, do not settle for a so-so, bland description. Let your "mind's eye" create a whole vivid scene as if you were watching a movie. Then record the details you have visualized.

Thinking Practice

Choose a fresh place to write about. Then concentrate as you let your mind's eye recreate it. As you are visualizing, jot down all the details you see. Even after you think you have enough details, close your eyes again and take a closer look: what have you left out? Then use your details to write a description of your place with plenty of specific details and words that appeal to the senses. Share your jottings with a partner and together come up with even more descriptive details for both of your places.

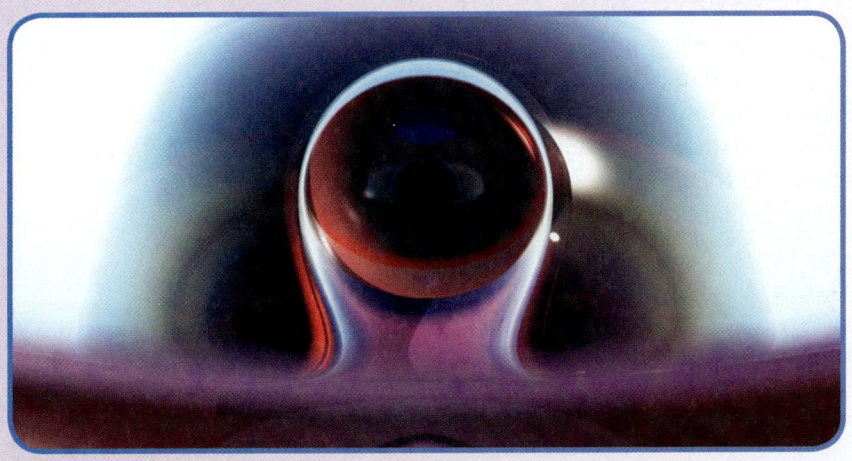

3 Spatial Order and Transitions

For readers to "see" what you are describing, your details must be arranged in a logical order. The most logical order for descriptions is usually spatial order.

Spatial order arranges details according to their location.

Transitions show the relationships between the details.

The following chart shows several types of spatial order and transitions.

SPATIAL ORDER	TRANSITIONS
near to far (or reverse)	close by, beyond, around, farther, across, behind, in the distance, near
top to bottom (or reverse)	at the top, in the middle, lower, below, at the bottom, above, higher
side to side	at the (far, near) left (right), in the middle, next to, beside, between, at one end, at the other end
inside to outside (or reverse)	within, in the center, (on the) inside, the next layer, further in/out, in between, (on the) outside

In the following description, the details are arranged from bottom to top. Notice how transitional words are used to show the spatial order.

MODEL: Spatial Order

The Singing Tower

Thousands of people have listened to the music of the bells at the Singing Tower in Lake Wales, Florida. **At the base** of the tower is a clear pool that reflects the entire 205-foot structure. **Reaching from the bottom of the tower to the top** are wide stripes of pink and gray marble. Florida plants and animals are carved in these marble stripes. **At the crown-shaped top** of the tower, a set of bells plays melodies. People from all over the country come to hear the bell chimes ring out over the surrounding park.

● **Practice Your Skills**

Using Spatial Order

Look at the picture below. Based on what you see, complete the paragraph that follows with the best transitions. Choose the transitions from the following list.

- in the left corner
- to the right of the bed
- across from the table
- on either side of the bed
- under the smaller window
- against the wall

This photo of a log cabin from 1690 shows the many uses of a single room. ■ is a sturdy wooden bed with a headboard, footboard, and colorful quilt. Windows ■ let in light but also drafts. ■ stands a small table with a pitcher and bowl. These were used for washing up. Homesteaders wouldn't have to go far for their dinners, for ■ was the dining area. The chair ■ and ■ would have been brought over to the dining room table for dinner.

PROJECT PREP *Evaluating* **Organization**

In your writing group, discuss the organization of each writer's description. Is it appropriate for the subject? Are there transitions to guide the reader from point to point? Make suggestions for improving organization and transitions. Based on the feedback from your peers, make revisions to tighten the organization and smooth out the transitions.

Elements of Descriptive Writing

The Power of Language

Parallelism: The Power of 3s

One way to help readers connect ideas and emphasize organization is to use parallelism. **Parallelism** is the use of the same kind of word or group of words, grammatically speaking, in a series. When Jean Craighead George is describing the black wolf, for example, and his relation to the other wolves in the pack, she set up parallel sentences:

> If he was alarmed, they were alarmed. If he was calm, they were calm.

Parallelism is especially effective if three or more parallel elements are presented together. Can you see the three parallel constructions in the following example from *Julie of the Wolves*?

> No roads cross it; ponds and lakes freckle its immensity. Winds scream across it, and the view in every direction is exactly the same.

Parallelism can show how thoughts are similar, as in the above examples. It can also heighten differences. The pattern leads the reader to expect another similar item, so when a contrast comes along, it's especially powerful.

> A bird stretched in the grass. The wolf looked at it. A flower twisted in the wind. He glanced at that. Then the breeze rippled the wolverine ruff on Miyax's parka and it glistened in the light. He did not look at that.

Try It Yourself

Write short passages imitating the structure of each of these parallel constructions. Then later, in your description, see if there are other places where you might use parallelism effectively.

Punctuation Tip

To be most effective, use the same punctuation pattern in the parallel elements.

Descriptive Writing

❹ Logical Order

Sometimes details for descriptive writing do not fall neatly into spatial order. How do you order the details in such cases? Ask yourself what makes the most logical sense. Suppose you are writing about a person. You could order your details based on your first impressions of that person, then your second impressions, and finally your later impressions as you looked more closely or got to know the person better.

Logical order should help the reader clearly and simply picture what you are trying to describe. Transitional words that work well with logical order include *first of all, most important, in addition, also, further, then, later, finally*.

● Practice Your Skills

Using Logical Order

Decide on a logical order for arranging the following details and write a sentence for each one. Then arrange the sentences into a descriptive paragraph, using transitional words to show the relationships among the details.

Purpose to describe water moccasins so people can recognize and avoid them

Audience people who fish or use boats

Details

- no strong pattern of colors
- between three and six feet long
- head shaped like a stone arrowhead
- brownish gray color
- often looks like a stick hanging from a tree limb
- nicknamed cottonmouth because its open mouth is white
- wide, flat body

PROJECT PREP *Evaluating* Organization

In your writing group, discuss other possible ways each writer could have ordered his or her description. Would any have been an improvement on the one you chose? If so, revise your description accordingly.

Elements of Descriptive Writing

In the Media

Classified Advertisement

Words can paint beautiful pictures, but sometimes these pictures can be deceiving. When it comes to classified advertising, the rule is, Consumer beware! Examine the photograph below of a house that is for sale. Then read the description of the house that appears in a real-estate advertisement.

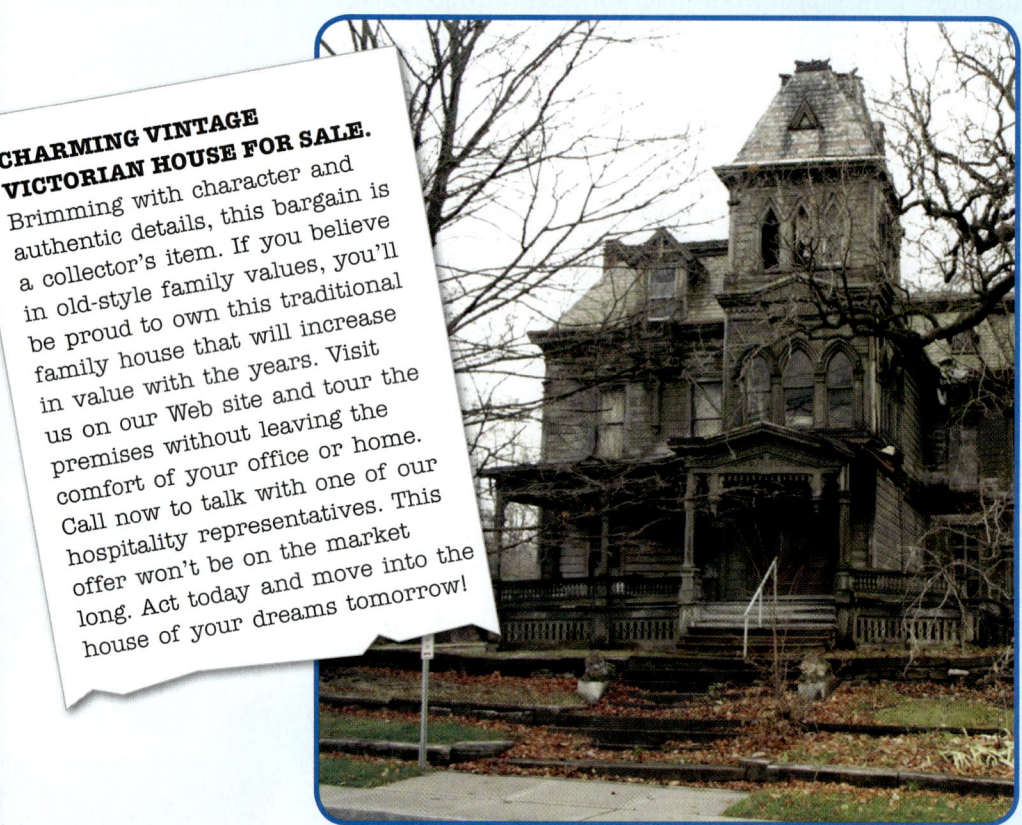

CHARMING VINTAGE VICTORIAN HOUSE FOR SALE. Brimming with character and authentic details, this bargain is a collector's item. If you believe in old-style family values, you'll be proud to own this traditional family house that will increase in value with the years. Visit us on our Web site and tour the premises without leaving the comfort of your office or home. Call now to talk with one of our hospitality representatives. This offer won't be on the market long. Act today and move into the house of your dreams tomorrow!

Media Activity

Analyze the language of this advertisement. List the words or phrases that convey a positive image. Next to each word or phrase, write the positive words or feelings that the phrase evokes. Explain how, with a few words, the truth is slightly twisted to make an old and run-down house sound like a real steal!

5 The Six Traits

Strong descriptive writing has the traits identified in the #4 column. Use this rubric to evaluate and revise your or others' descriptive writing.

	4	3	2	1
Ideas	The text conveys an overall impression with abundant vivid details and is well chosen for the purpose and audience.	The text conveys an overall impression with ample details and suits the purpose and audience.	The text conveys an overall impression with some vivid details and suits the purpose and audience.	The text does not convey an overall impression and fails to suit the purpose and audience.
Organization	The organization is clear with abundant transitions.	A few ideas seem out of place or transitions are missing.	Many ideas seem out of place and transitions are missing.	The organization is unclear and hard to follow.
Voice	The voice sounds natural, engaging, and personal.	The voice sounds natural and personal.	The voice sounds mostly unnatural with a few exceptions.	The voice sounds mostly unnatural.
Word Choice	Words are specific and powerful, rich in sensory images.	Words are specific and some appeal to the senses.	Some words are overly general.	Most words are overly general.
Sentence Fluency	Varied sentences flow smoothly and coherently.	Most sentences are varied and flow smoothly.	Some sentences are varied but some are choppy.	Sentences are not varied and are choppy.
Conventions	Punctuation, usage, and spelling are correct. The Power Rules are all followed.	Punctuation, usage, and spelling are mainly correct and Power Rules are all followed.	Some punctuation, usage, and spelling are incorrect but all Power Rules are followed.	There are many errors and at least one failure to follow a Power Rule.

CHECKING YOUR PURPOSE, AUDIENCE, OCCASION, AND GENRE

Always evaluate your writing to be sure it is appropriate for your writing purpose, audience, and occasion and that it meets the expectations readers will have for the genre you chose.

Elements of Descriptive Writing

The following checklist will remind you of the elements of good descriptive writing that will help you achieve your goals.

 Evaluation Checklist for Revising

Checking Your Overall Composition

- ✓ Does your introduction present the subject and suggest a general impression of it? (page 158)
- ✓ Does your body provide details that bring your description to life? (pages 158–160)
- ✓ Are your details in either spatial order or another logical order? (pages 162–165)
- ✓ Did you use transitions to give your writing both internal and external coherence? (page 162)
- ✓ Does your conclusion summarize the overall impression of the subject and provide a strong ending? (page 158)

Checking Sentences

- ✓ Did you combine related sentences to avoid too many short, choppy sentences in a row? (pages 64–72)
- ✓ Did you avoid rambling sentences? (pages 75–76)
- ✓ Did you avoid repetition and empty expressions? (pages 77–78)

Checking Words

- ✓ Did you use specific, lively words? (pages 42–46 and 56–57)
- ✓ Did you use words that appeal to the senses? (pages 47–53 and 159–160)

editing

As always, look over your writing to be sure you have expressed yourself in as few words as possible. For practice in eliminating unnecessary words, edit the following sentence.

> In my comfortable bed, I smell the familiar smell of the fragrance of the detergent my mom uses to wash the sheets, the point being that I feel so comfortable and relaxed in my bed.

The Language of Power *Verb Tense*

Power Rule: Use a consistent verb tense except when a change is clearly necessary. (See page 698.)

See It in Action In the following example from *Julie of the Wolves*, the author consistently uses past tense verbs.

> A bird **stretched** in the grass. The wolf **looked** at it. A flower **twisted** in the wind. He **glanced** at that. Then the breeze **rippled** the wolverine ruff on Miyax's parka and it **glistened** in the light. He **did** not look at that. She **waited.**

Notice how confusing the same paragraph is when the verb tenses are inconsistent.

> A bird **stretched** in the grass. The wolf **looks** at it. A flower **is twisting** in the wind. He **glanced** at that. Then the breeze **rippled** the wolverine ruff on Miyax's parka and it **glistens** in the light. He **did** not look at that. She **waits.**

Remember It Record this rule and example in the Power Rule section of your Personalized Editing Checklist.

Use It Read through your descriptive writing and circle or highlight all the verbs. Check to make sure you have used the same tense throughout your text except when a change is needed.

PROJECT PREP Polishing Final Draft

Exchange papers with a partner from your writing group and give each other final feedback using the rubric on page 167 and the checklist on page 168 as evaluation tools. Use your partner's suggestions to prepare a final, polished version of your description, checking for conventions as you prepare your work. Publish your description through an appropriate medium. You might, for instance, share your writing by reading it aloud to your classmates or posting it on the class bulletin board or writing wall.

In your Learning Log, write briefly about what you have learned about writing descriptions. How have you improved as a writer because of these activities? How can you apply what you've learned to other writing projects?

Elements of Descriptive Writing

Writing Lab

Project Corner

Experiment
Change Genres

Convert the images from your description to a poem that cuts out unnecessary words and depicts your chosen place strictly through a string of images.

Get Artistic
Represent Visually

Using conventional art supplies or computer software, **produce an artistic representation** of the place you have described. Share your work with the class. Explain what you could capture visually that you could not capture in words, and explain what you believe words were more effective at conveying than visuals.

Experiment
Tell a Story

Use the place you have described as the setting for a story. What might happen there? How would this setting provide a stimulating place for an interesting story to take place in? **Write a draft of the story** and share it with your class. (See pages 182–195 for help with writing stories.)

Apply and Assess

In Everyday Life
A Descriptive Conversation

1. You are on a two-week vacation with your family in a small seaside town. One morning you wake up before dawn and go to the beach to watch the sun rise. The scene is so breathtaking that you immediately call your best friend to describe every detail. *Improvise a telephone conversation* with your best friend in which you describe the sunrise. Include specific details and vivid sensory words to create an overall impression with your description. Be sure to use colorful words that will make your friend see, hear, smell, and feel what you are describing.

In the Workplace An Advertisement

2. You are the marketing director for a new music-themed restaurant. You are preparing an advertising brochure to mail to potential customers, inviting them to the grand opening. You know that your boss, the restaurant owner, has worked hard to make her café a place where people will enjoy both excellent food and a fun, lively atmosphere. *Write the ad copy* for the brochure. As you describe the restaurant, remember that you want readers to picture themselves having a great time there, so use vivid words that appeal to their senses. Organize your description in a logical order.

Timed Writing Letter

3. You have just been reelected for a second term as President of the United States. Newspapers and magazines all over the country are calling you the most popular President ever, and the Appreciation League has announced that they have raised enough money to re-create your childhood home. Unfortunately no one but you knows what your childhood home looked like. There is a fast-food restaurant where it once stood. Write a letter to the Appreciation League describing your childhood home. Fully describe both the outside and inside of the home so that the Appreciation League's re-creation is accurate. Use specific details and sensory words. Be sure that your letter includes an introduction to the subject, supporting details that bring your childhood home to life, and a conclusion that summarizes your overall impression. Organize the details in your letter in spatial order. You have 20 minutes to complete your work.

Before You Write Consider the following questions: What is the situation? What is the occasion? Who is the audience? What is the purpose?

After You Write Evaluate your work using the six-trait evaluation rubric on page 167.

Descriptive Writing Workshops

The power of observation is the mark of a good writer. Practice sharpening your senses. Think of yourself as a "sensitive recording device." Notice all the details of the environment around you. Look for precise words to record your observations. Your readers will savor the clarity and individuality of your perceptions.

Describing an Object

PREWRITING

Look at the picture below. What does it make you think of? How would you describe it? Talk with a classmate for five minutes, answering these questions. Then jot down notes from your discussion and make a plan for writing a description of this sculpture in Chicago.

DRAFTING

Use your plan to write a description of the sculpture. Be sure to include specific details that will create a clear picture in the mind of your reader. Keep an eye out for places to use parallelism. (See page 164.)

REVISING BY CONFERENCING

Exchange papers with a classmate. Read your partner's description carefully. Point out the parts that you like as well as the parts that could be improved. Make any revisions that are needed to improve your description.

EDITING AND PUBLISHING

When you have finished revising your draft, edit your work for mistakes in grammar, punctuation, usage, capitalization, and spelling. Read your description carefully and look for errors you may have missed at the revising stage. Use your Personalized Editing Checklist to avoid errors you tend to make. Then make a neat, final copy.

❷ Describing a Person

PREWRITING

Imagine that you are writing a science fiction story about someone living on a distant planet. Give your character a name. Then jot down answers to the following brainstorming questions. Visualize carefully to bring your character to life.

1. What does your character's face look like?
2. What do your character's hands look like?
3. What do your character's feet look like?
4. How does your character move around?
5. How does your character sound?

Use your brainstorming notes to create a plan for a descriptive sketch.

DRAFTING

Use your plan to write the first draft of a description of your character.

REVISING BY CONFERENCING

Exchange papers with a classmate. Draw a picture of the character described in your partner's draft. Give the picture and the draft back to your partner. Then look at the picture your partner drew. Does it accurately reflect your character? Revise your description to include anything that brings your written picture into sharper focus.

EDITING AND PUBLISHING

When you are satisfied with the substance of your description, edit your work for mistakes in grammar, punctuation, usage capitalization, and spelling. Look for errors you may have missed at the revising stage. Use your Personalized Editing Checklist to avoid errors you tend to make. Then make a neat, final copy.

CHAPTER 8

Creative Writing

Creative writing takes many forms. In addition to novels and short stories, the genre includes plays, poems, songs, movie scripts, and graphic novels. Creative writing may be humorous, serious, sad, suspenseful, or fantastic—if you can imagine it, you can write it.

Here are just a few ways people use creative writing.

- **A lyricist writes words** to accompany a tune for a new musical.
- **A screenwriter develops a story line** for a movie about a fantastic planet inhabited by strange creatures.
- **You engage in a humorous imaginary dialogue** with a friend on the telephone.
- **Your drama club writes a play** about an event in your town's 200-year history.
- **Your classmates write a funny sketch** about school life for a talent show.
- **A poet writes a humorous poem** about rap music and delivers it at a poetry slam.

Writing Project

Wishes Denied Write a story or a poem about someone who wanted something very much but did not get it.

Think Through Writing Did you ever want something very much, but were told by an adult that you couldn't have it? Write about an occasion when you were denied something you wanted for an "adult" reason: it was too expensive, for example, or it was inappropriate for your age. What were the circumstances? How did you feel?

Talk About It In your writing group, discuss the writing you have done. What sorts of things did you want? For what reasons were they denied to you? How did you feel about being denied your wish?

Read About It Read the following short story by Cynthia Rylant. As you read, think about how the author has developed her characters through the use of description, tone, and setting.

MODEL: Short Story

From

Stray

Cynthia Rylant

In January, a puppy wandered onto the property of Mr. Amos Lacey and his wife, Mamie, and their daughter, Doris. Icicles hung three feet or more from the eaves of houses, snowdrifts swallowed up automobiles and the birds were so fluffed up they looked comic.

> Chilly details help create the setting

The puppy had been abandoned, and it made its way down the road toward the Laceys' small house, its ears tucked, its tail between its legs, shivering.

Doris, whose school had been called off because of the snow, was out shoveling the cinderblock front steps when she spotted the pup on the road. She set down the shovel.

"Hey! Come on!" she called.

The puppy stopped in the road, wagging its tail timidly, trembling with shyness and cold.

> The puppy's arrival sets all the other events in motion.

Doris trudged through the yard, went up the shoveled drive and met the dog.

"Come on, Pooch."

"Where did *that* come from?" Mrs. Lacey asked as soon as Doris put the dog down in the kitchen.

Mr. Lacey was at the table, cleaning his fingernails with his pocketknife. The snow was keeping him home from his job at the warehouse.

"I don't know where it came from," he said mildly, "but I know for sure where it's going."

> Mr. Lacey's attitude sets up the story's main conflict.

Doris hugged the puppy hard against her. She said nothing.

Because the roads would be too bad for travel for many days, Mr. Lacey couldn't get out to take the puppy to the pound in the city right away. He agreed to let it sleep in the basement while Mrs. Lacey grudgingly let Doris feed it table scraps. The woman was sensitive about throwing out food.

By the looks of it, Doris figured the puppy was about six months old, and on its way to being a big dog. She thought it might have some shepherd in it.

Four days passed and the puppy did not complain. It never cried in the night or howled at the wind. It didn't tear up everything in the basement. It wouldn't even follow Doris up the basement steps unless it was invited.

It was a good dog.

Several times Doris had opened the door in the kitchen that led to the basement and the puppy had been there, all stretched out, on the top step. Doris knew it had wanted some company and that it had lain against the door, listening to the talk in the kitchen, smelling the food, being a part of things. It always wagged its tail, eyes all sleepy, when she found it there.

Even after a week had gone by, Doris didn't name the dog. She knew her parents wouldn't let her keep it, that her father made so little money any pets were out of the question, and that the pup would definitely go to the pound when the weather cleared.

> Time transitions help the reader follow the events.

Creative Writing

Still, she tried talking to them about the dog at dinner one night.

"She's a good dog, isn't she?" Doris said, hoping one of them would agree with her.

Her parents glanced at each other and went on eating.

"She's not much trouble," Doris added. "I like her." She smiled at them, but they continued to ignore her.

"I figure she's real smart," Doris said to her mother. "I could teach her things."

Mrs. Lacey just shook her head and stuffed a forkful of sweet potato in her mouth. Doris fell silent, praying the weather would never clear.

But on Saturday, nine days after the dog had arrived, the sun was shining and the roads were plowed. Mr. Lacey opened up the trunk of his car and came into the house.

Doris was sitting alone in the living room, hugging a pillow and rocking back and forth on the edge of a chair. She was trying not to cry but she was not strong enough. Her face was wet and red, her eyes full of distress.

Mrs. Lacey looked into the room from the doorway.

"Mama," Doris said in a small voice. "Please."

Mrs. Lacey shook her head.

"You know we can't afford a dog, Doris. You try to act more grown-up about this."

Doris pressed her face into the pillow.

Outside, she heard the trunk of the car slam shut, one of the doors open and close, the old engine cough and choke and finally start up.

> This is the high point of the conflict.

"Daddy," she whispered. "Please."

She heard the car travel down the road, and, though it was early afternoon, she could do nothing but go to her bed. She cried herself to sleep, and her dreams were full of searching and searching for things lost.

It was nearly night when she finally woke up. Lying there, like stone, still exhausted, she wondered if she would ever in her life have anything. She stared at the wall for a while.

But she started feeling hungry, and she knew she'd have to make herself get out of bed and eat some dinner. She wanted not to go into the kitchen, past the basement door. She wanted not to face her parents.

But she rose up heavily.

Her parents were sitting at the table, dinner over, drinking coffee. They looked at her when she came in, but she kept her head down. No one spoke.

Doris made herself a glass of powdered milk and drank it all down. Then she picked up a cold biscuit and started out of the room.

"You'd better feed that mutt before it dies of starvation," Mr. Lacey said.

Doris turned around.

"What?"

"I said, you'd better feed your dog. I figure it's looking for you."

> This is the outcome of the conflict.

Doris put her hand to her mouth.

"You didn't take her?" she asked.

"Oh, I took her all right," her father answered. "Worst looking place I've ever seen. Ten dogs to a cage. Smell was enough to knock you down. And they give an animal six days to live. Then they kill it with some kind of a shot."

Doris stared at her father.

"I wouldn't leave an *ant* in that place," he said. "So I brought the dog back."

Mrs. Lacey was smiling at him and shaking her head as if she would never, ever, understand him.

Mr. Lacey sipped his coffee.

"Well," he said, "are you going to feed it or not?"

Respond in Writing Write freely about the author's descriptions of the characters and setting in the story "Stray." How did these and the author's tone pull you into the story?

Develop Your Own Ideas Work with your classmates to develop ideas that you might use to write a story or poem about an interesting character in an imagined situation.

Small Groups: In your small group, discuss the writing you have done. Answer the questions below to help formulate your stories or poems.

- Who is your main character? What makes this person stand out? How does the character look, speak, walk, think, behave? Who are the supporting characters?
- What is the setting? What details of the setting will help readers see it clearly and feel as though they are there?
- How is the main character similar to you? How is he or she different from you?
- What are the plot elements of your story: conflict, rising action, climax, falling action, resolution?
- What sensory details will you use to round out the character and the setting?
- How does the story's ending wrap up the action?

Whole Class: Make a master chart of the ideas generated by the small groups to see who is writing a story and who is writing a poem. Then list the plot lines, main character, supporting characters, and setting of each story or poem.

Write About It: You will next write a short story about a young person who covets something—an item or a relationship—and is denied it by an adult. You may base it on your own experiences, on the experiences of someone you know or have read about, or on a situation that you make up.

Possible Topics	Possible Audiences	Possible Forms
• A present that you hoped to get but were told you would not get • Something that you found but were told you could not keep • Something that you wanted but were told you would not get • Something that you bought but were told you could not keep • A friendship you wanted but were told you could not develop	• Students in your class • Readers of the Internet • Adults • Your family	• A written short story • A graphic novel • A long poem • An animation

Analyzing a Story

A **short story** is a fictional account of characters resolving a conflict or situation.

In the process of personal writing, you have already gained practice in telling stories. Short stories usually have more details than personal narratives. They are also not true-life events. The events in a story may have actually happened to the writer or to someone the writer knows, but they are presented in an imaginative way.

You can learn more about narrative and descriptive writing on pages 126–149 and 150–173.

ELEMENTS OF A SHORT STORY

All short stories have three main sections: a beginning, a middle, and an end. Usually in the beginning of a story, the writer provides all the necessary background information that readers will need to understand and to enjoy the story. For example, readers will find out where the story takes place, who the main characters are, and what problem, or **conflict,** the main character has to solve or overcome.

The middle of the story develops the **plot;** that is, the writer tells what happens (usually in the order it happens) as a result of the conflict and how the characters react to those events.

As the conflict develops, the action rises until it hits its highest level, the **climax.** The climax involves a dramatic event that is the high point of the story. The ending of the story tells the outcome, or **resolution,** of the central conflict.

Plot and Central Conflict The plot is the story's core. It tells what happens as the characters meet and struggle to resolve the conflict. This conflict can come from within a character, such as a conflict of conscience; between characters, such as a conflict between friends; or between characters and the outside world, such as a struggle against the forces of nature. After resolving the conflict (or explaining why it remains unresolved), the story ends.

Characters Most short stories focus on one main character who has or faces the conflict, or on two main characters whose relationship is often the source of the conflict. The other characters in the story—the minor, or supporting, characters—either help or hinder the main character in resolving the crisis. In the best short stories, characters are colorful, authentic, and memorable to readers in some way. Authors develop characters through narration, description, and dialogue.

Setting The setting of a story is the environment in which the action takes place. It is like the scenery and props on a stage set. The setting also includes the time during which the story occurs. One of the functions of a setting is to create a mood and to establish the characters' environment. An author will often create settings that match the main character's mood or reflect his or her place in society. For example, intimate details between the lord and lady of the manor will probably take place in their drawing room or sitting room, while the lady's maids will share secrets in the kitchen or servants' area.

Narrator The person who tells a story is the narrator. Readers see the events of a story through the eyes of the narrator, or from the narrator's point of view. When the point of view is first person, the narrator is involved in the events of the story and refers to himself or herself using the pronoun *I*. A third-person narrator is an observer, relating events that happen to the characters and sometimes the characters' thoughts and feelings as well.

ELEMENTS IN A SHORT STORY

Narrator	the person telling the story; may be first person or third person
Setting	the time and place in which the story takes place
Tone	the mood; or the writer's attitude toward characters
Characters	the people involved in the story
Conflict	the problem at the heart of the story
Triggering Event	the event that starts the story rolling
Climax	the point in the story where the conflict or problem is most serious
Outcome	how the problem or conflict is solved
Dialogue	words spoken by the characters
Description	writing that helps the reader see, hear, feel, taste, or smell events

Theme Most short stories have a **theme,** or main idea. Often the theme is an idea or message about life, society, or human nature. The outcome of the story may then imply some lesson or moral about the theme, or it may affirm some meaningful observation or conclusion about life. However, some short stories aim chiefly to inform, surprise, or entertain readers rather than to convey a message.

WRITING OUTSTANDING STORIES

If all stories share the elements in the chart above, why are some better than others? The chart on the following page shows some of the characteristics of outstanding stories. Remember these as you write your own stories.

Writing an Outstanding Story

- Create interesting, "3-D" characters, showing their unique personalities through dialogue, actions, thoughts, and feelings.
- Create a believable, easy-to-imagine setting, rich in details that appeal to the senses.
- Base your story on an engaging plot, one that keeps the reader wanting to read on and know what happens next.
- Pace your story skillfully. Don't let the action of the story get bogged down in unnecessary information.
- Put your words to work for you. Pack your story with style and energy by using such literary devices as similes, metaphors, and other figures of speech.
- Show your attitude toward your characters and storyline through the tone you establish.

● **Practice Your Skills**

Analyzing Story Elements

Write answers to the following questions about "Stray" on pages 175–179.

1. What is the plot of the story? Briefly outline the main events.
2. What is the central conflict? Briefly describe it.
3. Who are all the characters in the story? Which one is the main character and how do you know that?
4. What is the setting? Describe it in a few sentences.
5. List a few of the descriptive passages that create sensory impressions.
6. What do you think the theme of the story is? Express the theme in a few sentences in your own words.
7. Using the chart above, would you say "Stray" was an outstanding story? Explain your reasons.

PROJECT PREP *Prewriting* **Story Sketch**

Based on the discussions you have had with your classmates, your reading of "Stray," and the charts in this section, sketch out the story you will write. Turn a piece of 8½" by 11" paper sideways and make three columns. In the first column, write the elements in a short story, using the chart on the previous page as a guide. In the second column, write ideas for your own story. In the third column, write the details that will help make your plot, setting, characters, and literary style outstanding. Share your chart with your writing group for feedback.

Analyzing a Story

Writing a Short Story *Prewriting*

"First sentences are doors to worlds," wrote the author Ursula K. LeGuin. When you invite your readers to share a good story, they are eager to step into your world. You can begin with dialogue, description, or action to draw them in, but what you really need is a compelling plot to sustain reader interest.

Building an Engaging Plot

Ideas for a plot can come from anywhere: something you've read, a dream you had last night, an experience a friend had, or one of your own. Plots thrive on imagination. The following strategies may stimulate your thinking about plot ideas.

Strategies for Developing an Engaging Plot

- Brainstorm for a list of story ideas based on conflicts you have read about, thought about, or experienced firsthand. Then use clustering or inquiring to develop plot details. For each conflict you think of, identify the triggering event and describe the resolution or outcome.
- Scan newspaper headlines and news items for an event you could build into a fictional story. Some items might suggest a dramatic or humorous story. Others might lead to a tale of mystery or romance.
- Think of conflicts or events in history—including your family history and local history—that might be interesting to develop in fiction writing.
- Observe people and events in your life. Sometimes even small events or snatches of conversation will suggest a conflict on which to build a plot. An argument that you overheard at school could become the basis of a story.

Once you have a story idea and a conflict, you can build the plot around it. A plot usually unfolds from the event that triggers the conflict to the event that resolves it. You will probably arrange the details of your plot so that they naturally unfold as the story progresses.

PROJECT PREP *Prewriting* **Conflict and Plot**

In your small group, talk through your stories, using your chart as a guide. Help one another add details to further advance the plot, especially the central conflict. Are there any surprising events in the plot? Should there be?

② Sketching Interesting Characters

Once you have your plot in place, you can begin to flesh out your characters. One good way to make your characters lifelike is to draw a word sketch of them. List all the characters in your story, briefly describing each one. Include physical features and personality traits. Below are traits for characters in the story "Stray."

Doris	Timid, lonely, emotional, only child, eleven to thirteen years old
Father	Not talkative, hardworking, strict, kind, head of the household
Mother	Not talkative, hardworking, thrifty
Puppy	Six-month-old puppy, part shepherd mix, a good dog

Physical descriptions can also go a long way to help paint the personality of your characters, as the example below shows.

STUDENT MODEL: *Characterization*

Whitney Freeman had bleach-blonde hair that hung below her shoulders and turned a macaroni-and-cheese orange when the light hit it just right. Her tanned skin was acquired in a tanning booth. She had a stick-thin figure that was dressed in a black denim mini skirt, white leather high-heeled boots, a hot pink V-neck shirt with a white cami underneath. She held a shiny black leather clutch in one hand, while a white styrofoam Starbucks cup occupied the other. Her friends Caylee and Kari stood by, comparing their French manicures quietly.

—Natalie Volpe, Canton South High School, Canton, Ohio

● Practice Your Skills

Writing Character Sketches

Write a brief character sketch of the following people.

1. yourself
2. a childhood friend
3. an older relative
4. your teacher
5. a neighbor
6. a salesperson

PROJECT PREP *Prewriting* Character Sketch

Write sketches of your characters and read them to your writing group members. Ask your partners: Do you find these characters interesting? Do you get a good sense of who they are and what they want? Keep notes of the feedback.

Writing a Short Story • Prewriting

Think Critically

Imagining

To create lifelike characters, you can observe people firsthand and try to capture all their characteristics in your story. You can also add your own imaginative details to your characters. The skill of imagining will help you create interesting, memorable characters. **Imagining** means creating mental pictures of something or someone you have never actually seen or experienced.

Both pretending and imagining require you to invent new places, people, things, and situations. In the process, however, you also draw on whatever related experiences you have had. Suppose, for example, you want to try to imagine what a newly discovered animal called the "frogaroocerous" looks like. Some of the sounds in the animal's name might make you think of frogs, kangaroos, and rhinoceroses. Drawing on what you know about these animals and their special characteristics, you would let your imagination put these characteristics together in a way that was all your own. You would use both your previous knowledge and your skill at imagining to create a whole new creature.

WHAT I KNOW	WHAT I IMAGINE
frog: green; croaks; hops	frogaroocerous: hops as high as a tree; keeps flies and berries in its pouch for munching on; has a horn smack on top of its head
kangaroo: large feet; hops; has pouch	
rhinoceros: large; horn on head	

Thinking Practice

Pretend that one of the characters in your story is a spoiled little kid. Draw on what you might already know about real-life spoiled children and let your imagination create a whole new character. Use a two-column chart to organize what you already know and what you can imagine. Write a brief sketch of your character, including physical appearance, personality traits, and even gestures that the character often uses.

Creative Writing

③ Creating a Believable Setting

The process of creating a setting is similar to the process of sketching characters. Most writers begin with the world they know and understand and build from there. The sensory details—colors, sounds, and textures—of this world are layered like paints on a canvas. You may want to create a setting using many details, or you may want to leave the details up to your reader's imagination. However you create your setting, it should reflect the characters' personalities and set the tone for the story.

As you create your setting, be clear in your own mind about when and where the story takes place. Readers respond when they recognize a setting as believable. Also impart the **tone** you intend. You can express the tone through a range of strategies, such as sensory details, dialogue, and narration. Below are some details of the setting of Cynthia Rylant's story "Stray." What tone do they help create?

Where
- a semirural area
- small house of hardworking people
- a girl's room, very plain, with few toys, books, or possessions
- a simple kitchen with a kitchen table

When
- January
- after a blizzard
- over the course of nine days
- anytime over the last fifty years

> **Writing Tip**
>
> Plot, characters, setting, and other story elements should all fit together so that the reader believes in the story and finds meaning in it.

PROJECT PREP *Prewriting* **Setting**

Write a description that helps readers see, feel, hear, smell, and/or taste the setting of your story. Then, in your group, discuss each author's settings. What sensory details could improve the believability of each setting?

Writing a Short Story • Prewriting

Ordering and Pacing Events

Most stories present the events that take place in **chronological order,** the order in which they occur. This order helps readers follow the events as they rise to their climax and are resolved at the end. Use the following questions to help you list all the separate events in your story in the proper order.

> **Listing Events in Chronological Order**
> - What happened to start the story rolling?
> - What conflict developed?
> - What happened after that?
> - What happened after that?
> - What happened after that?
> - What is the climax of the story?
> - What finally happened to resolve the conflict?
> - How does the story end?

Writing Tip

You might want to create a story map, which gives an overview of the plot of your story from start to finish. Write a sentence explaining each major event from beginning to end of the story.

Pace the events to keep the story moving. Try to avoid slow spots in the story. For example, you need to use dialogue to reveal character. However, if you have a long stretch of dialogue, the plot might come to a standstill. To avoid this problem, try to use the dialogue to move the plot along.

PROJECT PREP *Prewriting* **Order of Events**

In your writing group, talk through the events in your plot. Help each author sequence the events in chronological order. Then create a chronological list or story map that outlines the way in which the story will unfold. Think about places where you can advance the plot through dialogue so that you can keep the story moving crisply.

188 Creative Writing

The Power of Language

Participial Phrases: Getting into the Action

Using modifiers can help keep your creative writing lively and inventive. You know that sometimes modifiers of a noun come after the noun (page 540), but experiment to see what else you can do with participial phrases, or "*–ing* modifiers" for short. Participial phrases describe a person, thing, or action. (See pages 621–625.) Sometimes, a participial phrase comes at the beginning of a sentence.

> **Participial Phrase at the Beginning of a Sentence**
>
> Looking out the window, he saw the visitors before they rang the doorbell.
>
> Balancing three plates of steaming food, the waiter deftly sidestepped the toddler who darted in front of him.

In these examples, the participial phrase explains what the subject is doing before the main action of the sentence, so it makes sense to have the *–ing* phrase at the beginning. Often, however, writers will put participial phrases at the end of a sentence, as Cynthia Rylant does in these examples:

> **Participial Phrase at the End of a Sentence**
>
> The puppy stopped in the road, wagging its tail timidly, trembling with shyness and cold.
>
> Doris knew it had wanted some company and that it had lain against the door, listening to the talk in the kitchen, smelling the food, being a part of things.
>
> Doris was sitting alone in the living room, hugging a pillow and rocking back and forth on the edge of a chair.

Try It Yourself

Write one sentence with a participial phrase at the beginning and another with the participial phrase at the end. You may imitate these sentences if you wish. Write sentences on the topic you have chosen for your project and incorporate them into your draft if you can. During revision, try to add additional participial phrases.

Punctuation Tip

> When you add details to make your writing more interesting, be sure to separate the participial phrase from the main part of the sentence with a comma. If the participial phrase comes in the middle of the sentence, enclose it in two commas.

Writing a Short Story  Drafting

As you draft your short story, try to recall other stories you have enjoyed. Ask yourself what made those stories exciting or interesting. Were the characters special or fantastic in some way? Did they face problems that you have also faced? Did you care about what happened to them? As you write, use the following strategies, which are specific to short story writing.

 **Strategies for Drafting Your Short Story**

- Use vivid language and interesting details to introduce the characters and the central conflict.
- Use sensory details to create a mood.
- Use background details to set the time and place of the story and to capture your readers' interest.
- Aim for originality in your writing by avoiding stereotypes.
- Start the plot early in the story by introducing the triggering event.
- Reveal the characters and unfold the plot through a combination of description, narration, action, and dialogue.
- Maintain a clear and consistent point of view.
- Include only those events that have a direct bearing on the plot and the central conflict. Connect the events in your story by showing how each event in the plot relates naturally and logically to the central conflict.
- Use chronological order and transitions to show the passing of time and to build up tension.
- End your story in a way that makes the outcome clear and that leaves a strong emotional impression on your readers.

USING DIALOGUE

When you write the actual words that the characters speak, the characters spring to life. A conversation between characters in a story is called **dialogue.** Reread the dialogue in "Stray." Notice how natural it sounds and how much it tells you about each speaker. Consider, for example, the impression Mr. Lacey makes because of the way he lets Doris know she can keep the dog. If he had come home from the shelter, gone to Doris's room, and handed her the puppy, how would you have felt about him? Instead of doing that, he waits until Doris comes downstairs and then says, "You'd better feed that mutt before it dies of starvation." Choosing to tell Doris that way gives Mr. Lacey a unique personality and helps readers see him as a man who may feel uncomfortable expressing emotion or making a big "to-do" over such a thing, but who is happy when he does what he feels to be right and who cares very much for his daughter.

PUNCTUATING DIALOGUE

While drafting your story, you are busy concentrating on *what* your characters say. Also learn *how* to present your characters' words so your reader will know who is speaking and what is said. You will need to use proper dialogue form. A **direct quotation** is how a writer indicates the exact words of a person. You use quotation marks to enclose a person's exact words. The chart below sums up the rules.

Using Direct Quotations

- Capitalize the first word of a direct quotation.
- Use a comma to separate a direct quotation from a speaker tag. (A speaker tag is the "he said" or "she whispered" that often precedes or follows a quotation.) Place the comma after the speaker tag when it precedes a direct quotation. Place the comma inside the closing quotation marks when the speaker tag follows a direct quotation.
- Place a period inside the closing quotation marks when the end of the quotation comes at the end of the sentence.
- When writing dialogue, begin a new paragraph each time the speaker changes.

Writing Tip

Use natural-sounding **dialogue** to bring characters to life and to develop the plot. However, if you are creating a character who is affected or artificial in some way, then this character's dialogue should reflect that.

Practice Your Skills

Writing Dialogue

Imagine each of the following situations. Then select one of the situations or another of your choice and write a dialogue about eight lines long between or among the characters. You may want to review the correct form for writing dialogue in the chart above.

1. A messenger carrying a glowing box asks for directions to the aquarium.
2. A soda machine calls you over and demands all your quarters.
3. Two friends confront you about your "attitude."
4. Three teenagers discuss a friend's unusual outfit.
5. A mom and dad warn their offspring about the dangers of chewing gum.

ENHANCING THE PLOT

A writer's skill in developing the plot keeps you turning the pages. Use the devices below to make your plot engaging and well paced and to sustain reader interest.

DEVICES FOR ADDING INTEREST TO YOUR PLOT	
Flashback	an event from the past that is presented out of and interrupts the chronological order
Foreshadowing	clues that help the reader anticipate what is to come
Story within a Story	a story that is told during the telling of another story
Subplot	a secondary plot line that reinforces the main plot line
Juxtaposition	placing two normally unrelated events, characters, or words next to one another to create a surprise effect

PROJECT PREP Drafting Dialogue and Plot Techniques

After you review all your prewriting about character, setting, and plot, write the first draft of the short story you have been developing. Include dialogue and try using some devices from the chart above to enhance your plot and make it engaging and well paced. Where appropriate, use participial phrases to pack plenty of action into your story. Use a consistent point of view throughout.

192   Creative Writing

Writing a Short Story 

Most writers agree that their first drafts are good starting points but rarely good enough ending points. Usually the effort of just getting your ideas down in a smooth, flowing form takes all your concentration when drafting. Once your draft is on paper, however, you can stand back from it and concentrate on improving your story. Use the following checklist when revising your short story.

 Evaluation Checklist for Revising

✓ Does the beginning of your story describe the setting, capture attention, introduce characters, and include the triggering event? (pages 181 and 184)

✓ Does the middle develop the plot by making the central conflict clear and by using transition words to keep the action moving? (pages 181 and 184)

✓ Are events in the plot arranged in chronological order or in an order that makes the chronology of events clear? (page 188)

✓ Does the story build until the action reaches a climax? (page 181)

✓ Did you use dialogue and description to bring your characters to life? (pages 185 and 190–191)

✓ Did you use various strategies to enhance the style and tone? (page 187)

✓ Does the ending show how the conflict was resolved and bring the story to a close? (pages 181–182)

✓ Did you choose an appropriate point of view and stick to it throughout the story? (page 190)

✓ Does the story have a theme or express your reasons for writing it? Does it accomplish your specific purpose for creative writing? (pages 182 and 184)

PROJECT PREP  **Using a Checklist**

Pair off in your writing group and exchange papers. Use the checklist above to evaluate your partner's story. Revise your work based on your partner's feedback. Write a new draft of your story. In this version, in addition to your development of the setting, characters, and events of the story, make sure that your grammar, punctuation, and spelling are correct so that your readers may easily follow your plot.

Writing a Short Story — Editing and Publishing

Once you have drafted and revised your story to your satisfaction, you are ready to edit it. In the editing stage, you polish your story so that it reads just the way you want it and correct any additional errors in spelling, grammar, punctuation, and capitalization.

You may become so familiar with your work that you miss errors. Putting your writing aside long enough to give you some distance will help you see mistakes.

The Language of Power — Past Tense

Power Rule: Use mainstream past tense forms of regular and irregular verbs. *(See pages 680–688.)*

See It in Action Mistakes in irregular verb usage will distract your reader from focusing on your story. Knowing when to use the past or the past participle of some irregular verbs, such as *go, lie, bring*, and *take*, can be confusing, so it's a good idea to memorize these verb forms. In this sentence from "Stray," for example, the author correctly uses the past participle form of *go*.

> Even after a week had **gone** by, Doris didn't name the dog.

Although the following usage is considered unconventional, writers sometimes use such constructions in dialogue to show that a character uses non-mainstream English.

> "After a week had **went** by, Doris still didn't name the dog," her mom said.

Remember It Record this rule and example in the Power Rule section of your Personalized Editing Checklist.

Use It Read through your short story and circle all the irregular verbs. Check each one to make sure you have used the correct past tense form.

Creative Writing

Using a Six-Trait Rubric

Ideas	**4** The plot, setting, characters, and dialogue are original and creative.	**3** The plot, setting, characters, and dialogue are effective.	**2** Most aspects of the plot, setting, characters, and dialogue are effective.	**1** Most aspects of the plot, setting, characters, and dialogue are ineffective.
Organization	**4** The organization is clear with abundant transitions.	**3** A few events or ideas seem out of place or transitions are missing.	**2** Many events seem out of place and transitions are missing.	**1** The order of events is unclear and hard to follow.
Voice	**4** The narrator's voice sounds natural and the point of view is consistent.	**3** The narrator's voice sounds mostly natural and the point of view is consistent.	**2** The narrator's voice sounds unnatural at times and the point of view changes.	**1** The narrator's voice sounds mostly unnatural and the point of view changes.
Word Choice	**4** Specific words and sensory images help readers picture characters and setting.	**3** Words are specific and some words appeal to the senses to help readers picture characters and setting.	**2** Some words are overly general and do not bring characters or setting into focus.	**1** Most words are overly general and do not bring characters or setting into focus.
Sentence Fluency	**4** Varied sentences flow smoothly and dialogue reflects characters.	**3** Most sentences are varied and flow smoothly, and dialogue reflects characters.	**2** Some sentences are choppy and dialogue seems forced.	**1** Sentences are choppy and not varied, and dialogue seems forced or is missing.
Conventions	**4** Conventions are correct and Power Rules are followed except for effect.	**3** Conventions are mainly correct and Power Rules are followed except for effect.	**2** Some conventions are incorrect but Power Rules are followed except for effect.	**1** There are many errors and at least one accidental failure to follow a Power Rule.

PROJECT PREP *Evaluating* **Editing and Publishing**

Use the six-traits rubric to evaluate your story. Submit it to your teacher and make changes in response to his or her feedback. Create a class anthology of your finished stories.

Writing a Play

A play is a special type of creative writing because it is written to be performed by one or more actors on a stage. Plays and stories have some characteristics in common, such as characters, setting, and plot. However, unlike a story, the plot of a play develops through the actors' words and actions alone.

A **play** is a piece of writing intended to be performed on a stage by actors.

The playwright provides the words in a script along with information on how the characters should act. The actors and director then decide how they will deliver the words and carry out the actions. The playwright also provides information about the setting. This information becomes the basis for the set design used in the stage performance.

The following is from a scene from *The Dancers* by Horton Foote. As you read, notice how the dialogue and the stage directions bring the scene to life.

MODEL: Play Scene

The Dancers

The lights are brought up D.L. *on the living room of* INEZ STANLEY. HERMAN STANLEY *and his brother-in-law,* HORACE, *come in.* HERMAN *is carrying Horace's suitcase.* HERMAN *is in his middle thirties.* HORACE *is eighteen, thin, sensitive, but a likable boy.*

Herman: Inez. Inez. We're here. (*He puts the bag down in the living room.* INEZ *comes running in from R.*)

Inez: You're early.

Herman: The bus was five minutes ahead of time.

Inez: Is that so? Why, I never heard of that. (*She kisses her brother.*) Hello, honey.

Horace: Hello, Sis.

Inez: You look fine.

Horace: Thank you.

Inez: You haven't put on a bit of weight though.

Horace: Haven't I?

Inez: Not a bit. I'm just going to stuff food down you and put some weight on you while you're here. How's your appetite?

Horace: Oh, it's real good. I eat all the time.

Inez: Then why don't you put on some weight?

Horace: I don't know. I guess I'm just the skinny type.

Inez: How are the folks?

Horace: Fine.

Inez: Mother over her cold?

Horace: Yes, she is.

Inez: Dad's fine?

Horace: Just fine.

Inez: Oh, Herman, did you ask him?

Herman: Ask him what?

Inez: Ask him what? About his tux.

Herman: No, I didn't . . . .

Inez: Honestly, Herman. Here we have him a date with the prettiest and most popular girl in Harrison and Herman says ask him what. You did bring it, didn't you, Bubber?

Horace: Bring what?

Inez: Your tux.

Horace: Oh, sure.

Inez: Well, guess who I've got you a date with. Aren't you curious?

Horace: Uh. Huh.

Inez: Well, guess . . . . (*A pause. He thinks*)

Horace: I don't know.

Inez: Well, just try guessing . . . .

Horace: Well . . . uh . . . uh . . . (*He is a little embarrassed. He stands trying to think. No names come to him.*) I don't know.

Inez: Emily Crews. Now isn't she a pretty girl?

Horace: Yes. She is.

Inez: And the most popular girl in this town. You know her mother is a very close friend of mine and she called me day before yesterday and she said I hear Horace is coming to town and I said yes you were and she said that the boy Emily is going with is in summer school and couldn't get away this week-end and Emily said she wouldn't go to the dance at all but her mother said that she had insisted and wondered if you'd take her . . . .

Horace: Her mother said. Does Emily want me to take her?

Inez: That isn't the point, Bubber. The point is that her mother doesn't approve of the boy Emily is in love with and she likes you . . .

Horace: Who likes me?

Inez: Emily's mother. And she thinks you would make a very nice couple.

Horace: Oh. (*a pause*) But what does Emily think?

Inez: Emily doesn't know what to think, honey. I'm trying to explain that to you. She's in love.

Horace: Where am I supposed to take her to?

Inez: The dance.

Horace: But, Inez, I don't dance well enough . . . . I don't like to go to dances . . . yet . . .

Inez: Oh, Horace. Mother wrote me you were learning.

Horace: Well . . . I am learning. But I don't dance well enough yet.

Inez: Horace, you just make me sick. The trouble with you is that you have no confidence in yourself. I bet you can dance.

Horace: No, I can't . . . .

Inez: Now let's see. (INEZ *goes to the radio and turns it on. She comes back to him.*) Now, come on. Show me what you've learned . . . .

Horace: Aw, Sis . . .

Herman: Inez. Why don't you let the boy alone?

Inez: Now you keep out of this, Herman Stanley. He's my brother and he's a stick. He's missing all the fun in life and I'm not going to have him a stick. I've sat up nights thinking of social engagements to keep him busy every minute of these next two weeks—I've got three dances scheduled for him. So he cannot dance. Now come on, dance with me . . . . (*He takes her by the arm awkwardly. He begins to lead her around the room.*) Now, that's fine. That's just fine. Isn't that fine, Herman?

Herman: Uh. Huh.

Inez: You see, all you need is confidence. And I want you to promise me you'll talk plenty when you're with the girl, not just sit there in silence and only answer when you're asked a question . . . . Now promise me.

Horace: I promise.

Inez: Fine. Why, I think he dances real well. Don't you, Herman?

Herman: Yes, I do. Just fine, Inez.

Inez: Just a lovely dancer, all he needs is confidence. He is very light on his feet. And he has a fine sense of rhythm—why brother, you're a born dancer—

(HORACE *is smiling over the compliments, half wanting to believe what they say, but then not so sure. He is dancing with her around the room as the lights fade. They are brought up on the area* U. R. EMILY CREWS *is in her living room. She has on her dressing gown. She is crying.* ELIZABETH, *her mother, comes in from* U. R.)

Elizabeth: Emily.

Emily: Yes, ma'm.

Elizabeth: Do you know what time it is?

Emily: Yes, ma'm.

Elizabeth: Then why in the world aren't you dressed?

Emily: Because I don't feel good.

Elizabeth: Emily . . .

Emily: I don't feel good . . . (*She begins to cry.*) Oh, Mother. I don't want to go to the dance tonight. Please, ma'm, don't make me. I'll do anything in this world for you if you promise me . . .

Elizabeth: Emily. This is all settled. You are going to that dance. Do you understand me. You are going to that dance. That sweet, nice brother of Inez Stanley's will be here any minute . . . .

Emily: Sweet, nice brother. He's a goon. That's what he is. A regular goon. A bore and a goon . . . .

Elizabeth: Emily . . .

Emily: That's all he is. Just sits and doesn't talk. Can't dance. I'm not going to any dance or any place else with him and that's final. (*She runs out R.*)

Elizabeth: Emily . . . Emily . . . You get ready this minute . . . (*The doorbell rings. Yelling.*) Emily . . . Emily . . . Horace is here. I want you down those stairs in five minutes . . . dressed. (*She goes out L. and comes back in followed by* HORACE, *all dressed up. He has a corsage box in his hand.*) Hello, Horace.

Horace: Good evening.

Elizabeth: Sit down, won't you, Horace? Emily is a little late getting dressed. You know how girls are.

Horace: Yes, ma'm. (*He sits down. He seems a little awkward and shy.*)

Elizabeth: Can I get you something to drink, Horace?

Horace: No, ma'm. (*A pause.* ELIZABETH *is obviously very nervous about whether Emily will behave or not.*)

Elizabeth: How's your family?

Horace: Just fine, thank you.

Elizabeth: I bet your sister was glad to see you.

Horace: Yes, she was.

Elizabeth: How's your family? Oh, I guess I asked you that, didn't I?

Horace: Yes you did. *(ELIZABETH keeps glancing off R., praying that Emily will put in an appearance.)*

Elizabeth: I understand you've become quite an accomplished dancer . . . .

Horace: Oh . . . well . . . I . . .

Elizabeth: Inez tells me you do all the new steps.

Horace: Well—I . . .

Elizabeth: Excuse me. Let me see what is keeping that girl.

● **Practice Your Skills**

Analyzing Dramatic Elements

Write answers to the following questions about the scene from *The Dancers*.

1. Who are all the main characters in the story? Who are the supporting characters? How do you know?
2. What is the central conflict? Briefly describe it.
3. What is the setting? Describe it in a few sentences.

CHOOSING A CONFLICT OR PROBLEM

Like stories, plays are based on conflict. A conflict may be between two or more people, as between Emily and her mother in *The Dancers*. A conflict may also exist within a single person, as within Horace. For a conflict to be interesting in a play, it must be seen and heard on the stage.

SKETCHING CHARACTERS

Characters are usually the most important element of a play. In drama, the characters are brought to life by actors—artists who use their individual movements and tones of voice to perform the playwright's words in a unique way.

CREATING A SETTING

A story in a book or movie may have many scenes with different settings. One scene may take place inside a house during a rainy afternoon. Another scene may take place outside the house on a clear, starlit night. Still another scene may take place on a snowy ski slope.

Because of the difficulty in creating sets that can be changed quickly, most plays have only a few scenes with different settings. In fact, an entire play may take place in one room with the actors moving the props—chairs and tables, for example—to different positions. The playwright must create an interesting, dramatic story using scenery that can be changed easily and quickly.

WRITING DIALOGUE

Plays consist of live action; the audience is not reading descriptions of what is going on. Most plays, therefore, contain a great deal of dialogue. Dialogue is the way a playwright shows the development of the plot of a play through the characters' words.

As in a story, the dialogue in a play should seem real. Each character should have his or her own personal way of speaking. In addition, the dialogue needs to deliver information to the audience. Everything that the reader learns about the characters must be shown through action and dialogue. For example, if a character had been missing for two years and then returned home at the beginning of the play, some character in the play would probably say something like, "Where have you been for the last two years? We were so worried about you!" The need to express information and characterization at the same time makes the dialogue in plays particularly rich in content.

WRITING STAGE DIRECTIONS

Playwrights frequently supply directions in the script so the reader (and the actors and director) will know how the characters should speak and move around the stage. These stage directions usually appear in *italic* print.

Because the dialogue itself usually conveys almost everything the audience learns about the characters, most modern playwrights like to keep their stage directions short. For example, if a character's words convey anger, then the playwright is unlikely to include the stage direction *Angrily*.

Some stage directions are necessary, however. They indicate which character should enter or exit, or they express meaningful actions, such as one character taking another character's hand.

In addition to describing how the actors should speak or move, a playscript provides information on how the characters should look and dress. It also includes information on what the set, or physical design of the stage, should look like. Then the stage directions indicate which props, or physical objects, should appear within the set.

● **Practice Your Skills**

Writing Dialogue

Write a conversation between two friends in which they disagree about the actions of a third friend. Set the conversation in a home in a community like your own. Write at least two separate speeches for each character. Write only the dialogue; do not include descriptions.

In the Media

Movies and Plays

What makes a performance of a live play different from a movie? When you watch a movie, you are viewing a carefully edited sequence of events, actions, and dialogue that will be the same every time it is viewed. When you watch a play, however, each performance will be unique. Although the characters, setting, and script remain the same, the actors will interpret the dialogue and actions and respond differently from performance to performance.

In a movie the camera controls what the audience sees. Close-ups of actors create a sense of intimacy, while long, sweeping shots of scenery suggest the larger world. In a play people in the audience see the entire stage and can choose what they want to watch. It's up to the actors and the playwright to let the audience know what is important. A monologue (in which one person speaks for a long time) is one way of helping the audience realize that what someone is saying is important. The plot, or action in the play, is another way.

Media Activity

Work with several classmates to adapt the scene from *The Dancers* into a screenplay. Use the following questions as guides.

- Is there an image you could show that would tell the story more effectively than characters can tell or show it? What character or image do you want to see in each shot?
- Would you change the setting of the stage play for the screenplay? If so, to where?

Discuss how your ideas for a screenplay are different from the ideas of others in your group. What have you learned about the differences between a stage play and a screenplay?

editing

The parts of a film that end up on "the cutting room floor" are the pieces of unused footage—scenes that are edited out of the final version. Often these scenes are included as bonus extras on the DVD version of a movie. Rent and watch or recall a DVD with such features.

Choose one of the scenes that was edited out and write a paragraph explaining why the director made the cut and if it earned him or her the editing star for economy of expression.

USING A RUBRIC FOR A DRAMATIC SCENE OR PLAY

Use the rubric below as a guide to revising your dramatic scene.

Dramatic Elements	4 The plot, setting, characters, and dialogue are original and creative and express the writer's feelings.	3 The plot, setting, characters, and dialogue are effective and express the writer's feelings.	2 Most aspects of the plot, setting, characters, and dialogue are effective.	1 Most aspects of the plot, setting, characters, and dialogue are ineffective.
Stage Directions	4 The stage directions clearly indicate actions and states of mind and add depth.	3 The stage directions indicate actions and states of mind.	2 The stage directions indicate actions but do not go deeper.	1 There are few if any stage directions.

PROJECT PREP Changing Genre From Story to Play

Using your story as the basis, write a play or a scene from a play. Follow these steps:

1. Evaluate your plot, characters, setting, and dialogue to see where you would need to make changes to rewrite the story in a new genre.
2. Write a first draft and include stage directions as appropriate.
3. In your writing group, take turns reading one another's scenes aloud. Does the dialogue sound real? Are the stage directions and actions easy to carry out?
4. Based on feedback from your group, revise your script, cutting or adding lines in the dialogue. Make your stage directions more specific and descriptive.
5. Share your scene with your teacher. Use his or her feedback to make a final copy. Use the script for *The Dancers* on pages 196–200 as the model for your play format. Make extra copies of your script and give them to students who want to portray the characters. Have them perform the scene for the class.

Writing a Poem

Dig deeply into your feelings and experiences and you may find that you are inspired to write a poem rather than a short story. Poetry allows you to say something in an imaginative way.

Poetry is a writing form that expresses feelings through sound and the imaginative use of language.

Poems are an expression of the feelings and impressions of the poet. Some poems are dramatic or sad. Some are silly or use clever plays on words, like the following poem.

> **MODEL: Humorous Poem**
>
> If Mary goes far out to sea,
>   By wayward breezes fanned,
> I'd like to know—can you tell me?
>   Just where would Maryland?
> Two girls were quarreling one day
>   With garden tools, and so
> I said, "My dears, let Mary rake:
>   And just let Idaho."
>
> —Anonymous, "Stately Verse"

Notice what happens to the state names when you say them slowly—*Maryland* (Mary land) and *Idaho* (Ida hoe). The poet has used a play on words called a pun. A **pun** is a humorous use of a word that suggests two or more different meanings.

FINDING IDEAS FOR POEMS

To help you find ideas for poems, use a chart like the one below. In the first column list general subjects. Next to the subjects, write specific examples that come to mind. Then choose an example that interests you and brainstorm even more ideas.

IDEA CHART	
Events	sitting in a tree; listening to a song; drawing a picture
Scenes	a gnarled old tree; a back yard; the woods in winter
Sensations	the sound of a bird chirping; the wind in your hair; the feel of a kitten's fur

Creative Writing

Using Poetic Techniques

All creative writing makes use of the way words sound, but in poetry sound is basic. The full effect of a poem often comes through when it is read aloud. In the following poem, the poet has repeated the sounds of *fl* to create humor. The repetition of consonant sounds at the beginning of a series of words is called **alliteration.**

MODEL: Alliteration

A flea and a fly got caught in a flue.
Said the fly, "Let us flee."
Said the flea, "Let us fly."
So together they flew through a flaw in the flue.

—Anonymous, "The Flea and the Fly"

Below is a chart of other sound devices you can use when you write a poem.

SOUND DEVICES	
Onomatopoeia	Use of words whose sounds suggest their meaning *hum, splash, whistle, hoot, murmur, fizz*
Consonance	Repetition of a consonant sound or sounds, used with different vowel sounds, usually in the middle or at the end of words "the pi**tt**er pa**tt**er of li**tt**le feet"
Assonance	Repetition of a vowel "**o**ver the **o**range gr**o**ves and on to the **o**utback"
Repetition	Repetition of an entire word or phrase "The **rain** is **fall**ing all around/It **fall**s on field and tree It **rain**s on the umbrellas here,/And on the ships at sea." —Robert Louis Stevenson, "Rain"
Rhyme	Repetition of accented syllables with the same vowel and consonant sounds, especially at the end (*tree, sea*)
Rhythm	Arrangement of accented and unaccented syllables "The **rain** is **fall**ing **all** a**round**"

● **Practice Your Skills**

Using Poetic Techniques

Create an idea chart, like the one on the previous page to help you think of an idea for a poem. Then write a draft of the poem using at least three of the poetic techniques explained on this page. Exchange papers with a partner to identify the techniques your partner used and provide feedback.

RHYME SCHEMES

A rhymed poem has a pattern, or **rhyme scheme,** that can be shown by letters. The rhyme pattern for the poem below is ABAB. The first line rhymes with the third, and the second line rhymes with the last. Another common pattern is AABB, in which the first two lines rhyme and then the next two.

"Mother, may I go out to swim?"	*a*
"Yes, my darling daughter,	*b*
But hang your clothes on a hickory limb,	*a*
And don't go near the water."	*b*

Poetry that does not rhyme or have a regular meter is called **free verse.** The excerpt below from "Don't Let That Horse . . . " by Lawrence Ferlinghetti is an example.

> Don't let that horse
>   eat that violin
> cried Chagall's mother
>   But he
>   kept right on
>   painting

GRAPHIC ELEMENTS

Poets also use graphic elements such as line length, capitalization, and punctuation to help them express their meaning. The excerpt from "Don't Let That Horse . . . ," for example, shows a pattern of line length and breaks that creates space in the poem. Read the poem aloud to see how that presentation affects the poem, especially where pauses appear.

- **Practice Your Skills**

    Using Rhyme Scheme and Graphic Elements
    Review the poem you wrote in the previous activity. Decide if you want it to have a rhyme scheme or be in free verse and make revisions accordingly. Then think about the graphic presentation of the poem. What graphic elements—line length, capitalization, or punctuation—can you use to emphasize the meaning and feeling of the poem? For example, if you are writing about a crowded city street, might you *runsomewordstogether* to represent the feeling of being crowded? Make revisions and share your work with your partner for feedback.

Creative Writing

FIGURATIVE LANGUAGE

Poets sometimes try to express the nearly inexpressible. For this reason, they often look to figures of speech to help them give the reader an idea of what they mean. **Figures of speech** are expressions that stray from their literal meaning in order to make an impact. Figures of speech are also called **figurative language.** The chart below shows some common figures of speech.

FIGURATIVE LANGUAGE	
Simile	comparison using the words *like* or *as* An emerald is as green as grass,/A ruby red as blood" —Christina Rossetti, "Flint"
Metaphor	implied comparison that does not use *like* or *as* Life is a broken-winged bird That cannot fly. —Langston Hughes, "Dreams"
Imagery	use of visual details or details that appeal to other senses One thinks of all the hands/That are raising dingy shades/ In a thousand furnished rooms —T. S. Eliot, "Preludes"
Personification	use of human qualities to describe something non-human Because I could not stop for Death—He kindly stopped for me —Emily Dickinson, "Because I Could Not Stop for Death"

● **Practice Your Skills**

Developing Figurative Language for Poems

Add at least two figures of speech to your poem-in-process. Share the poem with your partner for feedback.

PROJECT PREP *Changing Genre* **From Story to Poem**

Carefully examine your original story looking for "poetry moments" and draft a poem. Decide what rhyme scheme, if any, you want it to have and make adjustments accordingly. Ask yourself where such poetic techniques as alliteration and onomatopoeia would be effective and make additional revisions. Decide how to use graphic elements to best present your poem and make a polished copy of your poem. Use the rubric on the next page to evaluate it.

TIME OUT TO REFLECT Did you enjoy the creative writing activities in this chapter? Why or why not? How might creative writing help you with other kinds of writing? Write your thoughts in your Learning Log.

Writing a Poem

Writing Lab

Project Corner

Speak and Listen Poetry Reading

Have a poetry reading in which each person reads his or her poem for the class. Read clearly and loudly and feel free to use gestures, pauses, and vocal variety to enhance the intent of your poem. Evaluate each poem using the rubric below.

	4	3	2	1
Poetic Techniques	The rhyme scheme (if used) and sound devices create a strong effect and help express a meaningful idea.	The rhyme scheme (if used) and sound devices create a strong effect and help express an idea.	The rhyme scheme (if used) is inconsistent but sound devices help express meaning.	The rhyme scheme (if used) is inconsistent and few if any sound devices are used.
Figurative Language	The poem is enriched by a wide variety of memorable figurative language.	The poem is enriched by a variety of figurative language.	The poem uses figurative language once or twice.	The poem uses no figurative language.
Graphic Elements	The poem uses line length, capitalization, and punctuation creatively to help express the ideas precisely.	The poem uses line length, capitalization, and punctuation to help express ideas.	The poem uses line length, capitalization, and punctuation in predictable and uninspired ways.	The poem's use of line length, capitalization, and punctuation seems unintentional.

Get Technical Multimedia Presentation

With your writing group, **create a multimedia poetry anthology.** Use your own poems as well as poems of your favorite poets. Decide on the type of technology you will use (PowerPoint™ or Keynote™, Movie Maker™ or iMovie™, or some other technology with multimedia capability) and collaborate to create your presentation. Determine the tasks involved and divide them up among your group members. Present your completed anthology to the class.

In Everyday Life
A Humorous Poem

Apply and Assess

1. Zack, a classmate of yours, is ill and recovering at home. Your teacher has suggested that Zack would appreciate receiving artwork, stories, or poems from his peers. You have decided to create a humorous poem for Zack to cheer him up. **Write the poem for Zack.** Begin by creating a cluster diagram to find your idea. When you have decided on a topic, write the poem, using at least one simile, one pun, and one example of alliteration in your lines. You might also want to consider an effective rhyme scheme. (You can find information on writing poetry on pages 204–207.)

For Oral Communication
Oral Presentation of a Play

2. You are the manager of Ziegfield's, a popular restaurant in town. Critics everywhere are raving about your expertly prepared dishes and friendly wait staff. Later this month, you will take on many new workers. You wish to teach them about the job and familiarize them with safety tips about working in a restaurant, and you have decided to write a short play for this purpose. **Write a short play** to be performed for the restaurant's new workers. Consider effective dramatic situations that could illustrate your points about safety on the job. Be sure to include vivid characters and an appropriate setting for the play. (You can find information on writing plays on pages 196–203.)

Timed Writing 🕐 Short Story

3. You volunteer once a week to help in a kindergarten class. The teacher has heard that you are a good storyteller and asks you to create an original story and present it to the class. Write a humorous short story for the kindergartners. The teacher has told you that the students like stories about animals the best, but she has left you to be as creative as you like. Your story should include as many colorful and vivid details as possible, and a beginning, middle, and ending. Include a main conflict and a humorous resolution. You have 30 minutes to write your story. (See pages 398–399 for help with budgeting time.)

Before You Write Consider the following questions: What is the situation? What is the occasion? Who is the audience? What is the purpose?

After You Write Evaluate your work using the six-trait evaluation rubric on page 195.

CHAPTER 9

Expository Writing

Expository writing presents information using facts and examples or offers an explanation by giving directions or listing steps in a process.

A well-written expository article offers stimulating ideas on an interesting subject. You can find examples of expository writing everywhere—on television, in books, on the Internet, and even in your own experiences. Consider these examples:

- **You write a report on the life cycle of a butterfly** for your science class.
- **A travel writer prepares copy for a brochure** describing the animals and vegetation of the Florida Everglades.
- **A theater critic provides background information** on a play to be included in the program.
- **A game developer writes instructions** on how to play a new video game.
- **A nutrition expert contributes a magazine article** reporting the latest research in healthful eating.
- **Your math teacher writes the explanations** for solving complex problems on the chalkboard.

Writing Project — Expository

Welcome to My World Write a multi-paragraph expository essay about your physical surroundings.

Think Through Writing Places can be described by their geography (the physical, biological, and cultural features of the earth's surface), landscape (the natural scenery), cityscape (the urban environment), and other distinctive features. What traits make your home area distinctive? Write freely about these traits, noting specific details for each one. Identify and expand on at least three traits.

Talk About It In your writing group, discuss the traits you identified. Be as specific as you can. What kinds of features did you and your group members include in the descriptions?

Read About It In the following newspaper article, the area around Austin, Texas, is described. Take note of the kinds of details included in this expository piece. Do you get a strong picture of the area? Are there details that would help you see it better?

MODEL: Expository Writing

From the *Austin American-Statesman*

Austin's archive of natural history

CARVED IN STONE

What caused the hills and terrain that make Austin, well, Austin? It all started millions of years ago, when the forces that cause the Earth's plates to move shoved ocean sediments north from what is now the Gulf of Mexico. Those mountains are now buried hundreds of feet below Austin, which has also been home to a lagoon crammed with sea life, a volcano and an earthquake-prone zone. Thankfully, things have settled down. But you can still see the results of these eons of geologic forces in the landscape around you. Here, a brief guide to our geologic past:

> Beginning with a question is one way to engage readers.

Loriola Texana
Rock formation: Glen Rose
Fossil size: 6/8" diameter, 2/8" thick
Estimated age: 107 million years
Location found: Travis County, near Turkey Foot

Project and Reading

What our region looked like millions of years ago

Approximate time periods

1,150–1,120 million years

The continents collide, seas cover and then recede from the region in repeated cycles. Rocks from this period (Precambrian) can be seen in West Texas and Llano because of erosion and uplifting.

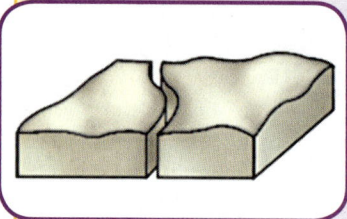

> The oldest event in the process is explained first.

322–290 million years

About 700 feet below present-day Austin is a mountain range that was formed when ocean sediments from the precursor of the Gulf of Mexico were shoved north and folded. Part of these ancient mountains can be seen north of Big Bend National Park.

> In explaining a process, the writer wisely chose to present the steps in the process in chronological, or time, order.

290–115 million years

Geologists don't have much detailed evidence of what was happening in Austin. Based on information from other parts of the United States and Mexico, geologists can deduce that Austin was hilly or mountainous. The Gulf of Mexico was a newly formed ocean. Austin was about 100 miles closer to the Gulf than it is now.

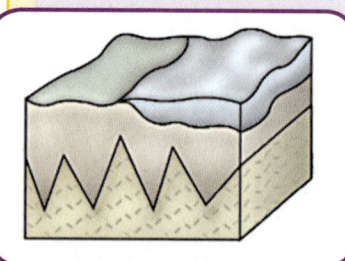

115–97 million years

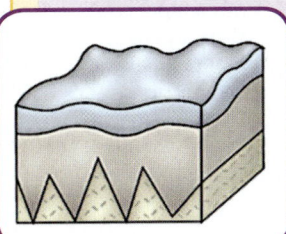

The ocean slowly flooded across Texas, forming a shallow sea. Imagine Austin as a large lagoon filled with abundant marine life and small islands with shell beaches. Rudists (see page 216) were main reef builders. During this period Glen Rose, Edwards, and Georgetown formations took shape.

The graphics help the reader picture otherwise hard-to-imagine events.

97–66 million years

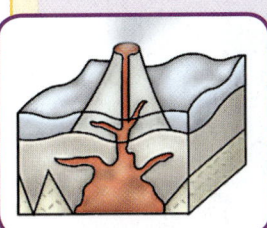

The ocean spread inland. Sharks swam above Austin. The Del Rio, Eagle Ford, Taylor, and Navarro formations took shape. Buda Limestone and Austin Chalk formed from bodies of plankton accumulated on the ocean floor. A volcano formed in what is now south Austin, now known as Pilot Knob.

24–21 million years

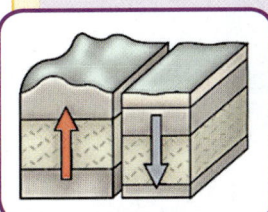

Earth's crust broke along the faults of the Balcones Fault Zone. (See map, page 215.) Austin may have experienced earthquakes at this time. One thousand feet of displacement took millions of years.

Heads in purple type help readers follow the progress through time.

11,000 years–present

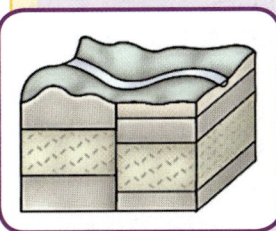

The modern Colorado River cuts its valley and deposits sand and gravel in bars and terraces. You can see this and older sand near Longhorn Dam. The Balcones Fault seems to be still now. Scientists have not detected any movement in the Balcones Fault today.

Project and Reading

Why is West Austin hilly . . .

The West

The Balcones Fault Zone separates the inland edge of the Coastal Plain from the Hill Country. The faulting created two distinct geological environments with distinct soils, distributions of plants and animals, and land appearance.

> The placement of elements on the page helps readers make comparisons. On this page, West Austin is discussed.

The view looking southwest from Mount Bonnell. Surrounding hills provide prime real estate.

214 Expository Writing

. . . and East Austin so flat?

The view looking south from U.S. 290 shows a different kind of landscape. Flat fields with rich soil provide for excellent farming and ranching.

The East

While West Austin was being pushed up, East Austin was held back by the drag of the Gulf of Mexico. The floor of the Gulf of Mexico sank because of loading by huge volumes of sediment poured into the Gulf from rivers and by the cooling of the ocean floor as it ages.

On this page, East Austin is discussed. Both regions also have photographs highlighting their unique features.

Rock composition

Chalk: Made from skeletons of floating algae
Limestone: Made from fragments of fossil shells
Dolomite: Similar to limestone, but includes magnesium from seawater
Altered tuff: Volcanic ash altered by sea water and air
Basalt: Hard black rock that forms when lava cools

Information is presented in a number of different ways in this article. Here is just a simple list of what different kinds of rocks are made of. Below is a cross-section map of the area.

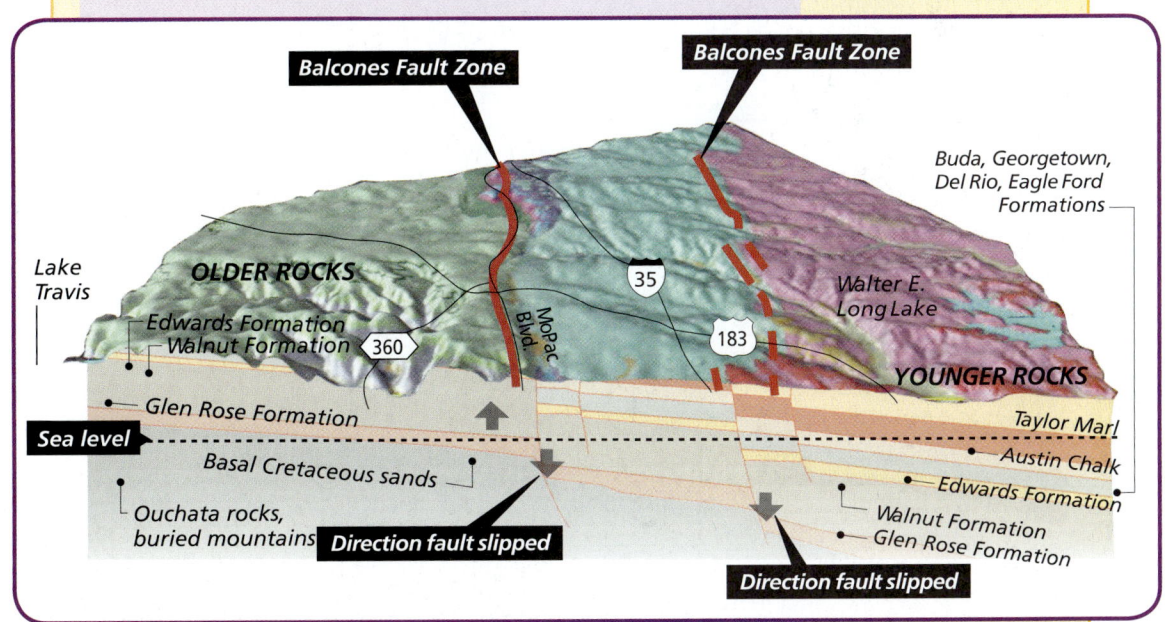

Project and Reading 215

Made in Central Texas

Common Austin area fossils

Eoradiolites (Rudists)

Rock formation: Edwards

Fossil size: 6 2/8" length, 1 2/8" wide, 1" thick

Estimated age: 105 million years

Location found: Bell County. Example shown was chosen for its size and detail. Rudists have been found in the RM 2222 and Loop 360 area.

These illustrations are accompanied by a "fact sheet" on each fossil.

Paracymatoceras

Rock formation: Georgetown

Fossil size: 3 4/8" longest length, 2 6/8" wide, 1 6/8" thick

Estimated age: 100 million years

Location found: East of Brodie Lane, on Oakdale Drive

Shark tooth

Rock formation: Taylor

Fossil size: 1/2" height, 1/2" across the base

Estimated age: 75 million years

Location found: Near Taylor

How fossils are formed

Imagine
Millions of years ago, Austin's current site was a sea filled with aquatic life.

Here another process is explained. It relies as much on graphics as it does on text.

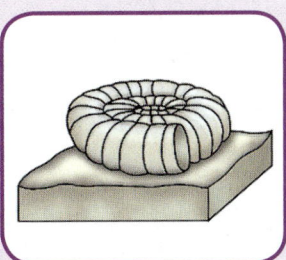

A Shellfish Dies
It drops to the seabed and the animal inside the shell decays.

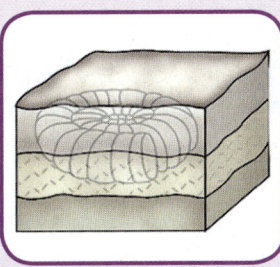

The Shell is Buried
Layers of ooze and sand fill with shell fragments. The composition of the shell slowly changes. Minerals replace organic material.

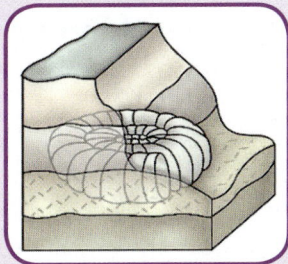

Years Pass
The sea recedes. Weather and water wear away the layers of sediment above the fossil, exposing the ancient fossil.

Respond in Writing Summarize the information about the geography of Austin that you learned from this piece. How would you evaluate the quality of this piece in conveying information?

Develop Your Own Ideas Work with your classmates to develop ideas that you might use in writing clear expository pieces about your area.

Small Groups: In your small group, discuss the brief descriptions you have written. Then make a list of categories of information you need to include in a description to make it well developed. Your list might include:

- identification of place by name, location, and other identifiers
- historical background
- physical features

Whole Class: Make a master chart of all of the categories generated by the small groups. You can refer to these categories as you write your description to help you narrow your subject and cover it adequately.

Write About It You will next write an expository text about the area in which you live. You might choose from any of the following possible topics, audiences, or forms.

Possible Topics	Possible Audiences	Possible Forms
• a neighborhood	• residents of the area	• a Web guide
• a whole geographic region	• newcomers to the area	• a pamphlet
• a city	• the Chamber of Commerce	• a welcome brochure
• a property lot	• potential visitors to the area	• an encyclopedia entry
• a section of a town or city		• a newspaper article

Developing Your Expository Writing Skills

Expository writing can serve two purposes. One is to provide information. Writing that explains what happens during a solar eclipse gives factual information. The second is to give directions. Writing that tells how to watch a solar eclipse safely gives directions.

 Paragraph and Essay Structure

The chart below shows the role of each sentence in an expository paragraph.

Structuring an Expository Paragraph
- In the **topic sentence,** state a main idea based on fact.
- In the **body of supporting sentences** provide facts, examples, or steps in a process.
- In the **concluding sentence,** summarize the main idea and add a strong ending.

The purpose of the following paragraph is to inform. Notice the clear structure.

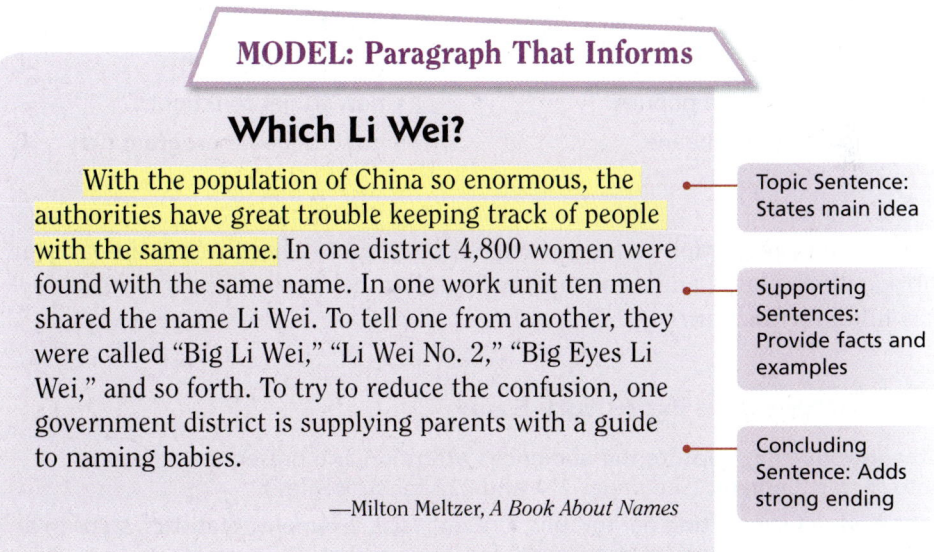

MODEL: Paragraph That Informs

Which Li Wei?

With the population of China so enormous, the authorities have great trouble keeping track of people with the same name. In one district 4,800 women were found with the same name. In one work unit ten men shared the name Li Wei. To tell one from another, they were called "Big Li Wei," "Li Wei No. 2," "Big Eyes Li Wei," and so forth. To try to reduce the confusion, one government district is supplying parents with a guide to naming babies.

—Milton Meltzer, *A Book About Names*

Topic Sentence: States main idea

Supporting Sentences: Provide facts and examples

Concluding Sentence: Adds strong ending

In the following paragraph, the writer's purpose is to explain by giving directions.

MODEL: Paragraph That Explains

How to Lace Your Ice Skates

Properly laced ice skates should be loose enough to let your toes stay warm and tight enough to support your ankles. First, remove all laces. Then, starting near the toe, thread the laces loosely through the first two eyelets. Next, slip your foot into the skate. Finally, thread the remaining eyelets securely over your instep and ankle. Skates laced this way will give your ankles support without pinching your toes.

— Topic Sentence: States main idea

— Supporting Sentences: Give steps in order

— Concluding Sentence: Summarizes

● **Practice Your Skills**

Writing Expository Topic Sentences

Choose two subjects from each list below. Under each subject write a topic sentence that suits the purpose.

PROVIDING INFORMATION
- what classes you have
- what a double play is
- why pets are popular
- what ROM means

GIVING DIRECTIONS
- how to make friends
- how to train a pet
- how to get to school
- how to load a program disk

Like all multi-paragraph essays, an **expository essay** has three main parts: an introduction, a body, and a conclusion. The chart below shows how to make each part fulfill its function.

Structuring an Expository Essay

- In the **introduction,** capture the audience's attention and present the **thesis or controlling statement**. (See pages 221 and 222 for strategies.)
- In the **body of supporting paragraphs,** present facts, examples, statistics, steps in a process, or other supporting details to back up your thesis statement.
- In the **conclusion,** drive home your thesis and try to leave a strong impression in the reader's mind. (See pages 94–95 for strategies.)

Like an expository paragraph, a strong expository essay presents information in a logical order with clear transitions. Each paragraph in the body of an expository essay develops one of the supporting ideas (or steps in a process) required to back up the thesis statement. A strong expository essay also has the following features.

QUALITIES OF A STRONG EXPOSITORY ESSAY

- It fulfills its purpose to present information or explain a process.
- It is appropriate for the audience and occasion.
- It states a thesis clearly and backs it up with ample supporting information and details.
- It has an engaging introduction, transitions connecting the body paragraphs to one another and to the introduction and conclusion, and a conclusion that brings the essay to a satisfying end.
- It may use reader-friendly formatting techniques such as bulleted or numbered lists and boldface heads.
- It may use graphics, such as charts and diagrams.
- It is free from errors in grammar, usage, and mechanics and follows all the Power Rules.

PROJECT PREP   Prewriting   *Thoughts onto Paper*

1. Based on your early writing and your discussions, identify and clearly state a purpose and controlling idea for your essay. (The master chart can help you decide which categories to include as your focus.) Then make a rough outline (see pages 344–345), assigning at least one paragraph to each of the topics you have decided to include.

2. Look over your outline and determine which topics will require outside sources. Plan to use at least two sources for this composition.

3. Find your sources and take notes on the information you need. (See pages 312–313 and 318–319.)

Developing Your Expository Writing Skills

In the Media

News Lead-ins

Learning the techniques of one medium can help you learn about another. Understanding the power of images on television, for example, can remind you to include strong description in your writing. Recognizing how different media present information can help you improve your expository writing.

Techniques for grabbing a reader's attention, or **lead-ins,** are especially useful to study and include in your work.

A newspaper story usually begins with the whole story summarized in the first sentence: *Bilco is being acquired by Zinc Enterprises for about $162 billion in stock in what would be the biggest corporate merger ever*. The rest of the story supplies the details, but the reader is drawn in by knowing the outcome.

A newsmagazine, in contrast, might begin with a descriptive paragraph setting the scene: *Surrounded by lawyers and looking weary but elated, Bilco CEO Jessica Zacks surveyed the mayhem around her. Barely two years after starting her outrageously successful Internet company, the 23-year-old executive was preparing for her biggest coup yet*.

Media Activity

Use the following guidelines to analyze different writing techniques in newspapers, newsmagazines, and the Internet. Skim through a newspaper, newsmagazine, and the Internet until you find a headline that interests you. Read only the first paragraph of the story. Then ask yourself these questions.

- Does the lead-in grab my attention?
- How did the writer get my attention?
- What is the implied or stated message? If it is stated, where is it placed in the introduction?

When you are finished, discuss your findings with your classmates. Apply any techniques you have learned through this activity to your compositions to make your introductions effective.

Methods of Development

The purpose of your composition will help you decide what kind of supporting details you need. When providing information, you use facts and examples. When giving directions, your supporting details will be the steps in the process.

FACTS AND EXAMPLES

Read the following thesis statement. Then ask yourself what kinds of supporting details you expect the rest of the composition to contain.

Thesis Statement	For many years disabled athletes have set milestones.

The questions probably raised in your mind are these: *Who were these athletes? What did they do to set new milestones?* Facts and examples will answer these questions.

Facts and Examples	Jack Robertson, an athlete with paralyzed legs, swam most of the English Channel.
	Bruce Jennings, an athlete with only one leg, bicycled three thousand miles across the United States.
	Two wheelchair athletes in the 1977 Boston Marathon finished in the top third.

● **Practice Your Skills**

Listing Facts and Examples

With a partner, talk through each thesis statement below and come up with specific facts or examples to back it up. Then, on your own, write each thesis statement. Under each one, list at least three facts or examples you identified.

Example	The Fourth of July is a holiday with many traditions.
Possible Answer	People usually watch firework displays.
	Many people have barbecues.
	Some towns have parades.

1. The parents of my friends have interesting jobs.
2. Most television comedy series have one male and one female lead character.
3. The only way to lose weight is to use up more calories than you take in.
4. Dogs express emotion in many ways.
5. The one invention I could never live without is the ▇. (Fill in your choice.)

Developing Your Expository Writing Skills

The Power of Language

Strong Verbs: In Living Color

Clear facts and examples will help your reader understand your subject. Descriptive verbs will provide additional clarity and also add interest to your expository writing. Verbs convey the action of a sentence. A dull verb may get the job done, but a strong, colorful verb will give your sentences life and movement.

The right verb will not only tell your readers what happened but also give them a sense of *how* it happened. Consider the following sentences:

Dull Verb	Weather and water affect the layers of sediment above the fossils.
Colorful Verb	Weather and water wear away the layers of sediment above the fossils.

In the first sentence, the reader gets the idea that the wind and water have done something to the earth but has no idea what has occurred. The second sentence, however, gives the reader a more specific sense of what takes place—erosion—and conveys the sense that this is a long-term process. The verb phrase *wear away* adds to the descriptive power of the writing.

The same can be said of the verb *cuts* in the following example.

Dull Verb	The Colorado River runs through the land.
Colorful Verb	The Colorado River cuts through the land.

Try It Yourself

Write four or five sentences that contain common verbs, such as *went, give, tried,* or *walk*. Then list other verbs you could use to add more meaning to those sentences. When you draft your own expository piece, try to add descriptive verbs and verb phrases. Then, as you revise your writing, look specifically for dull verbs that could be replaced with more descriptive ones.

STEPS IN A PROCESS

The following thesis statement introduces a composition that gives directions. What are the questions it raises?

Thesis Statement You can return tennis balls hit to you if you follow a few important steps.

Readers will wonder what these steps are. The following details give the steps in the process.

Steps in a Process
- First decide whether to use your forehand or backhand as the ball approaches.
- Then, turn your body to get into position.
- As you turn, bring your racket as far back as possible.
- Bend your knees and swing through with your whole body.
- Follow through on your stroke.

● Practice Your Skills

Listing Steps in a Process

With a partner, talk through the specific steps needed to accomplish the goals of each of the following controlling ideas. Then, on your own, write each thesis statement and list the steps in the process the reader will have to follow to accomplish each goal.

1. Learning how to ride a bicycle requires help at first.
2. Checking a book out of the library/media center is easy.
3. A good way to get downtown from my house is by bus.
4. I have found a way to get up on time every morning.
5. Following these steps can help you prepare for a test.

PROJECT PREP *Revising* **Facts, Examples, or Steps**

Use your prewriting work to write a first draft of your expository essay. Include the information you gathered from your two sources. Then read over your draft. Are there enough facts, examples, and/or steps in a process to clearly communicate your ideas? Does all the information relate directly to the thesis statement? Add, delete, substitute, or rearrange to make your essay well developed, unified, and coherent.

Think Critically

Analyzing

If the purpose of your expository essay is to give directions for performing a process, you will need to break down the process into separate, logical steps. To do so, you will use the skill of **analyzing.**

Think about the process of brushing your teeth. Analyze all your actions, and you become aware that you complete several smaller steps as part of the larger process. You start by holding the toothbrush a certain way to add toothpaste. Then you bring the toothbrush up to your mouth. After that you follow a pattern of movement to brush the teeth in different parts of your mouth. Then you probably rinse both your mouth and your toothbrush. Finally you put the toothbrush back in its holder. All these actions are the small steps that make up a larger process; here the end result is clean, sparkling teeth.

Thinking Practice

Using the map below, analyze the steps in the process of getting from the bus station to the stadium. Write the steps in order.

③ Logical Order and Transitions

Explanations that are presented in a logical order help readers understand your message. Two kinds of order often used in informative paragraphs are order of importance or size and sequential order.

ORDER OF IMPORTANCE OR SIZE

In compositions that offer information, details are often arranged in the order of least to most or most to least. Transitions point out the relationships among the details.

TRANSITIONS USED WITH ORDER OF IMPORTANCE OR SIZE		
first	larger	equally important
next	even larger	more important
finally	the largest	most important

Writing Tip

To provide information, use **order of importance or size** with appropriate **transitions**. Arrange the details in order of least to most or most to least.

MODEL: Order of Importance or Size

The five Great Lakes in North America vary significantly in size. The smallest is Lake Ontario, covering 7,340 square miles. Lake Erie is slightly larger, with an area of 9,910 square miles. Lake Michigan is the third largest lake. It is as big as Lake Erie and Lake Ontario combined. Next in size is Lake Huron. Its total area is 23,000 square miles. Lake Superior deserves its name as the largest of the Great Lakes. Its total area, in the United States and Canada, is 31,700 square miles. So important have the Great Lakes been to North Americans that even the smallest is great.

— Smallest first
— Size of lakes increases
— Largest lake presented last

Developing Your Expository Writing Skills

● **Practice Your Skills**

Arranging Details in Order of Size

Write each topic sentence. Then arrange the supporting details in the order of least to most or most to least.

1. Dogs come in many sizes.
- Midsized dogs, such as retrievers, hounds, setters, and huskies, usually weigh between 40 and 75 pounds.
- Small dogs, such as the Chihuahua and the Pekingese, often weigh between 10 and 40 pounds.
- Large dogs, such as the Great Dane, the Saint Bernard, and the Newfoundland, weigh up to 150 pounds.

2. Some branches of the armed services have many more people on active duty than do others.
- In May of 2009, the Air Force had 323,000 people on duty.
- The 2009 figure for the U.S. Army was 548,000.
- The Marines had 203,095 people in May 2009.
- The U.S. Navy had 332,000 in May 2009.

3. Humans have the longest life span of all mammals, living an average of about seventy years.
- A rabbit lives an average of five years.
- A leopard lives an average of twelve years.
- An opossum lives only one year.
- A lion lives an average of fifteen years.
- A gorilla lives twenty years, on average.
- A hippopotamus lives about twenty-five years.

SEQUENTIAL ORDER

In compositions that explain by giving directions, the supporting details must be presented in the proper sequence. This kind of order is called **sequential order.** In the following paragraph, the directions are clear because the steps are presented in the order in which the reader would do them. The transitions are printed in **bold** type.

> **MODEL: Sequential Order**
>
> ### How to Make a Magnifying Lens
>
> A simple magnifying lens can be made from a piece of wire and a drop of water. **First**, partly fill a container with water. **Then**, cut a piece of thin wire about six inches long. Bend one end of the wire, forming a small loop. **Next**, twist the wire at the bottom of the loop to hold it in place. **Now** you are ready to dip the loop into the water. **When** you do, a drop of the water will stay in the loop. **When** you look through the drop of water, you will see things magnified four or five times their real size. With only wire, water, and a little know-how, you have created a magnifying lens.

Steps in sequential order with transitions

> **Writing Tip**
>
> To explain by giving directions, use **sequential order** and appropriate **transitions.**

The following chart shows some useful transitions for sequential order.

TRANSITIONS FOR SEQUENTIAL ORDER			
first	before	while	finally
next	after	as soon as	as a last step
then	when	second	now

Developing Your Expository Writing Skills

● **Practice Your Skills**

Listing Steps in Sequential Order

The illustrations below show how to say in sign language, "Please write your name and address." Using the illustrations, rewrite the directions below in the proper sequence.

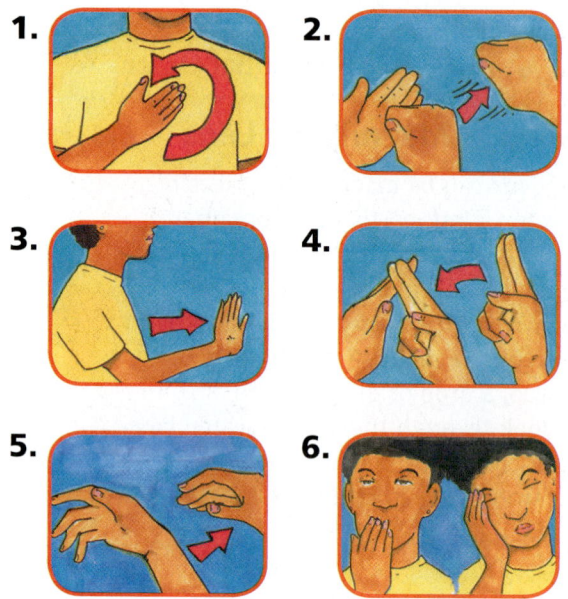

a. To make the sign for *name*, extend the second and third fingers of both hands while your hands are apart. Then bring the right hand over the left to form an X.

b. You can make the sign for *please* by rubbing in a circular motion on your chest with your right hand.

c. The sign for *address* is a combination of two signs that indicate eating and sleeping.

d. For the first part of the sign, bring your right hand up to your mouth, with all five fingers cupped together.

e. Make the sign for *and* by closing the fingers of your right hand as you move your hand to the right.

f. The second part of the sign is the right hand over the ear, signifying sleep.

g. *Your* is signed by pushing your open hand outward from the chest.

h. In the sign for *write*, your left hand acts as the paper, while your right hand slides outward from your palm to your fingers as if it were holding a pencil.

- **Practice Your Skills**

  Adding Transitions

  Use the following sentences and your work from the previous activity to write a brief, well-organized essay about sign language. Add transitions where necessary.

  Thesis Statement — Learning to sign the sentence "Please write your name and address" is one way to appreciate the sign language used by people who have a hearing impairment.

  Concluding Sentence — By learning to sign this sentence, you can appreciate the clarity of sign language.

PROJECT PREP *Revising* Order and Transitions

1. In your writing group, discuss the order in which each author presents information. Does the sequence of information make sense to you? Are the sentences organized clearly? Are the paragraphs organized clearly? Add effective transitions as needed so that the order is clear to the reader. Remove any extraneous, or unneeded, information.

2. When you think you have all of your information in the right order, create a new draft of your essay. Read it over to be sure that you have used ideas from several sources and represented them accurately. Check your sentence structures so that you have a combination of short and long sentences. Check that you have used rhetorical devices such as metaphors and similes to enliven your writing.

 **TIME OUT TO REFLECT** — What have you learned about expository writing so far? In your Learning Log make a list of five ideas to remember. Add to the list or change it as you learn more about expository writing. Use your list the next time you write to inform or explain.

Developing Your Expository Writing Skills

Using a Six-Trait Rubric — Expository Writing

Use the following rubric to evaluate your own or another's expository text.

Ideas	4 The main idea is clear and focused and the text conveys information powerfully.	3 The main idea is clear and the text conveys information.	2 Some aspects of the topic are not clear and/or well developed.	1 Most aspects are not clear and/or well developed.
Organization	4 The organization is clear and easy to follow. Transitions provide coherence.	3 The organization is clear, but a few ideas seem out of place or disconnected.	2 Many ideas seem out of place and transitions are missing.	1 The organization is unclear and hard to follow.
Voice	4 The voice sounds natural and knowledgeable and is appropriate for the audience. The tone is consistent.	3 The voice sounds mostly natural and knowledgeable and is right for the audience. The tone is consistent.	2 The voice sounds a bit unnatural and does not seem right for the audience. The tone seems to change in places.	1 The voice sounds mostly unnatural or is inappropriate for the audience. The tone is not appropriate or consistent.
Word Choice	4 Words are specific and figures of speech are used.	3 Words are vivid and specific.	2 Some words are overly general.	1 Most words are overly general.
Sentence Fluency	4 Sentences vary in structure and length and flow smoothly.	3 Most of the sentences are varied and flow smoothly.	2 Some sentence patterns are not varied and some sentences are choppy.	1 Sentences are not varied and are choppy.
Conventions	4 Punctuation, usage, and spelling are correct and all Power Rules are followed.	3 There are only a few errors in punctuation, usage, and spelling and no Power Rule errors.	2 There are several errors in punctuation, usage, and spelling and no Power Rule errors.	1 There are many errors and at least one Power Rule error.

PROJECT PREP — Editing — Final Revision

After using the rubric, make any needed revisions and corrections. Write a final version, and ask your teacher for feedback. Make further changes as needed.

Expository Presentations

Earlier, you read an article about the geology of the Austin, Texas, area. It included not only text but also graphics that played a big role in conveying the information. Sound and video also convey information powerfully. You can include visuals, sound, and text using presentation software to create an expository text that will make a strong impression.

BUILDING A USER-FRIENDLY PRESENTATION

Presentation software is easy to use and can produce some dazzling effects. However, make sure the technology you use genuinely serves your purpose. Fancy techniques can detract from the message, so use good judgment when creating slides.

Here are some other points to keep in mind as you prepare a reader-friendly expository presentation.

Tips for Creating Effective Multimedia Presentations

Content
1. Keep it simple. Keep text to a minimum.
2. Include only the most important information.
3. Limit the number of bullet points per slide. Three or four should be the maximum.

Images and Video
4. Make sure the images and video support your key points.
5. Do not use graphics just as decoration.

Language
6. Limit the number of words you use.
7. Use parallel language. For example, if the first bullet point is a complete sentence, the second should be too.

Fonts
8. Heavy fonts are easier to read from a distance than light ones.
9. Keep the font size large enough to be seen easily at the back of the room.
10. Use only two font styles per presentation.

PROJECT PREP   Publishing   Presentation

Prepare a multimedia presentation of your expository essay or of some key part of it. Begin by making a plan. Which points do you want to convey? What graphics, including videos, would help you convey your information? What style would present information most clearly? After you have a plan, use the software to create your presentation. Practice presenting it before you actually present it to the class.

Writing Lab

Project Corner

Picture It Photo Essay

A photo essay is a set of photographs designed to tell a story or evoke emotions in the viewer. **Produce a photo essay** to accompany the area you have written about so that you have a multimedia presentation about the area in which you live. You might include photos of buildings, landscapes, and overhead shots from an airplane or satellite.

Research It Dig Deeper

Conduct further research on the history of the area. You might go back in geological time, as illustrated in this chapter's opening account of Austin, Texas, to explain how the area was formed. You could also provide the human history of the area, including the effects of people on the landscape.

Map It Share Information

Collect together all of the descriptions written by all class members, and use them to **develop a descriptive map** of the school's region. In addition to the informational writing, you could supplement the project with a physical map of the area with each place identified and other types of texts (including photo essays) that would provide a clear picture of the school's region.

For Oral Communication
Television Presentation

Apply and Assess

1. You have been asked by a local cable station to appear on a show called Science Hour. You are to perform and explain the steps in the process of a science experiment. The show is always hosted by a school student. The current host is a high school senior, who will be graduating next spring. You hope to impress the station manager enough to become the next host. *Write the steps in the process* of performing a science experiment you know how to do. Be sure the steps are in sequential order and use transitions to connect ideas. Perform your experiment for the class, who will watch as the studio audience. Explain the steps (from your written explanation) as you perform them. (You can find information on giving oral presentations on pages 435–440.)

In Academic Areas
Personal History

2. In school it always seems that you are learning about people you do not know. In an attempt to personalize history, your social studies teacher has decided to publish a book about the history of the members of your class. *Write a short encyclopedia-like entry* about yourself and your past to be published in the class book. Inform readers about yourself and explain how you came to be in this particular class. Try to avoid opinions and use only facts to construct your history. Your work should have an interesting introduction and conclusion, as well as a body of supporting details. Arrange details in a logical order.

Timed Writing
Prepare for Debate

3. Your older brother, Brian, often ends arguments with you by shouting, "You don't know anything!" and slamming the door. You are determined to prove him wrong. You plan to show him exactly what you know. Choose a subject you know well. Write an expository essay about the subject to slip under Brian's door the next time he slams it. Your expository essay should include a thesis statement. Use facts and examples in the body of the work to support your thesis statement. Arrange your details in a logical order that will ensure progression and coherence. Use transitions between your supporting details. Your conclusion should summarize the information you have presented. You have 30 minutes to finish.

Before You Write Consider the following questions: What is the situation? What is the occasion? Who is the audience? What is the purpose?

After You Write Evaluate your work using the six-trait evaluation rubric on page 232.

Expository Writing Workshops

The activities on these pages will give you more practice writing expository texts. During prewriting, consider the needs of your audience as you plan your explanations. During drafting, put your thoughts in flowing sentences. As you revise and edit your work, look for any weaknesses or errors in your writing and correct them. The result should be an explanation that is easy for your intended audience to understand.

① Explaining Symbols

PREWRITING

You know what all the symbols on the American flag stand for. The white stars stand for the fifty states. The red and white stripes stand for the original thirteen colonies. Red, white, and blue are also the colors of the British flag. Each shape and color on that flag stands for something as well.

Now think about yourself. Think about the things that are important to you and that help identify you. Pair off with a partner and talk about these things. Help your partner come up with possible symbols for these interests.

After your conversation, write down your list of interests and decide what symbols you will use for each one. When you have created a number of symbols, design your own personal flag. Draw a picture of your flag, using colors that have special meaning for you. List the symbols you have drawn and choose an organizational strategy to present them in your essay.

DRAFTING

Draft an expository essay explaining each symbol and color on your flag. Since your readers will already have a picture of your flag, you do not need to describe it in your essay.

REVISING BY CONFERENCING

Exchange essays and pictures with a classmate. Read your partner's work carefully as you study the picture. Are any symbols or colors left out? Tell your partner about them. Also, let your partner know the answers to the following questions:

- Does the essay fulfill its purpose?
- Is it appropriate for the audience?
- Does it have the features of expository writing associated with that genre?

Make any revisions that would improve your writing. Use your partner's comments and the checklist below to help you.

 Evaluation Checklist for Revising

Checking Your Essay as a Whole
- ✓ Does the introduction set the tone and capture attention? (pages 114 and 220)
- ✓ Does the thesis statement make your main idea clear? (pages 220–221 and 281)
- ✓ Is your main idea well developed, with well-chosen details, facts, and examples? (pages 219–220 and 223–225)
- ✓ Does your essay have unity? Does the topic sentence of each paragraph relate directly to the thesis statement? (pages 22, 113–115, and 142)
- ✓ If you give directions, do your supporting sentences provide the steps in the process? (pages 225–226)
- ✓ Are the paragraphs arranged in a logical order? (pages 227–231)
- ✓ Do transitions smoothly connect the paragraphs? (pages 137 and 227–231)
- ✓ Did you use techniques for achieving external coherence between paragraphs? (pages 227–231)
- ✓ Do you have a strong concluding paragraph? (pages 219–221)
- ✓ Did you include a title? (page 116)
- ✓ Did you maintain a consistent tone throughout? (page 187)

Checking Your Paragraphs
- ✓ Does each paragraph have a topic sentence that is based on a fact? (pages 219–220)
- ✓ Does each paragraph use transitions to make it unified and achieve internal coherence? (pages 227–231)
- ✓ Are your details within each paragraph arranged in logical order? (pages 227–231)

Checking Your Sentences and Words
- ✓ Are your sentences varied? (pages 64–74)
- ✓ Are your sentences clear and concise? (pages 75–79)
- ✓ Did you combine related sentences to avoid too many short, choppy sentences in a row? (pages 64–72)
- ✓ Did you vary the beginnings of your sentences? (page 73)
- ✓ Did you avoid rambling sentences? (pages 75–76)
- ✓ Did you avoid repetition and empty expressions? (pages 77–78)
- ✓ Did you use precise words and sensory words? (pages 42–57)
- ✓ Did you include vivid images, figurative language, parallelism, and other rhetorical devices? (pages 42–56, 164, and 207)

Expository Writing Workshops

The Language of Power Past Tense

Power Rule: Use mainstream past-tense forms of regular and irregular verbs. (See pages 680–681 and 693–694.)

See It in Action When you write about events that have already happened, use past-tense verb forms. Add *–ed* or *–d* to regular verbs to form the past tense. Irregular verbs vary in how their past tenses are formed.

In the following example from "Carved in Stone," the highlighted verb shows the conventional use of an irregular past tense verb.

> Earth's crust **broke** along the faults of the Falcones Fault Zone.

Break is an irregular verb, so its past tense does not take the usual ending. You might want to memorize the forms of the most common irregular verbs.

Remember It Record this rule and example in the Power Rule section of your Personalized Editing Checklist.

Use It As you edit your work, highlight all the verbs and verb phrases. Then check each one to make sure you have used correct past-tense forms when needed.

EDITING AND PUBLISHING

Check over your essay for errors in spelling, grammar, mechanics, and usage. Pay special attention to the Power Rules. Then make a neat final copy. On a separate sheet of paper, make a fresh picture of your flag. Mount your essay and flag on a large sheet of construction paper. Display your finished work in your classroom or at home for others to enjoy.

❷ Giving Directions

PREWRITING
Think about exercises you know. Toe touches, knee bends, and jumping jacks might be a few. Write them down. Under each one, list all the steps you follow to complete that exercise. Then choose the exercise you most like to do. Write a sentence telling why that exercise is your favorite.

DRAFTING
Use your notes to draft a short essay giving directions on how to do the exercise you chose.

REVISING BY CONFERENCING
Pair off with a partner. Leave room to move around. Have your partner read his or her essay to you. Follow the directions as your partner reads them. Let your partner know if any parts of the directions are confusing. Use your partner's comments and the **Evaluation Checklist for Revising** on page 237 to help you revise your directions.

EDITING
Check over your essay for spelling, grammar, mechanics, and usage errors.

---

editing ⭐

Make the following directions easier to follow and more efficent by cutting back on the "calories" needed to get the point across.

> It's really very easy to do an upright row using resistance bands. The first step regards positioning. Position the center of the band under your foot, placing it right in the middle between your foot and the floor. Hold one end of the band in one hand and the other end of the band in the other. When you have the bands in both hands, you can begin.

PUBLISHING
Make a neat final copy using the publishing suggestions on page 218.

CHAPTER 10

Writing to Persuade

Persuasive writing states an opinion on a subject and uses facts, reasons, and examples to convince readers.

The ability to convince others of what you believe is one of the most valuable skills you can acquire. Being persuasive will aid you in work, school, and the world at large. Writing persuasive compositions is one way to develop and refine this skill. Here are some examples of ways people use persuasive writing in everyday life.

- **Students write a proposal to the principal** outlining plans for a proposed new after-school club.
- **Movie reviewers write articles** for magazines telling people why they should or should not see the newest releases.
- **Organizations protecting endangered species write pamphlets** presenting facts and statistics to persuade people to join the effort.
- **Residents write to the city council** in an effort to persuade the members to change their plans to pave over a playing field.
- **Political groups send e-mails urging support** of a reform bill in Congress.

Writing Project — Persuasive

Words into Deeds Write a persuasive composition that will spur others to action.

Think Through Writing When John F. Kennedy hoped to persuade the American public to support his plan to send the first astronaut to the moon, he quoted another great statesman, William Bradford, governor in the 1660s of Plymouth Colony: "Great and honorable actions are accompanied with great difficulties, and both must be enterprised and overcome with answerable courage." Think of a difficult task that you believe needs doing but would require courage to accomplish. How would you go about influencing the attitudes and actions of others on this issue? Write about this situation as though you are trying to convince someone that, in spite of the risks, people need to take action.

Talk About It In your writing group, discuss the writing you have done. What difficult tasks did members of your group feel need to be done? What challenges are involved? As you express your opinion, give at least three reasons for it. As you listen to your partners, are you persuaded that people should take the necessary risks to address the challenges they have identified? Why or why not? Give at least three reasons.

Read About It In the following passage, President Kennedy presents his case about why astronauts should fly to the moon. Think about the persuasive techniques he uses to influence attitudes and stimulate support for his goal.

MODEL: Persuasive Speech

From

Address at Rice University on the Nation's Space Effort

John F. Kennedy
Houston, Texas, September 12, 1962

We meet at a college noted for knowledge, in a city noted for progress, in a state noted for strength, and we stand in need of all three, for we meet in an hour of change and challenge, in a decade of hope and fear, in an age of both knowledge and ignorance. The greater our knowledge increases, the greater our ignorance unfolds.

> The opening paragraph sets a dramatic tone and stirs the interest of the audience.

Despite the striking fact that most of the scientists that the world has ever known are alive and working today, despite the fact that this nation's own scientific [workforce] is doubling every 12 years in a rate of growth more than three times that of our population as a whole, despite that, the vast stretches of the unknown and the unanswered and the unfinished still far outstrip our collective comprehension.

> Kennedy uses striking statistics to draw in the audience.

No [one] can fully grasp how far and how fast we have come, but condense, if you will, the 50,000 years of [humankind's] recorded history in a time span of but a half-century. Stated in these terms, we know very little about the first 40 years, except at the end of them advanced [humans] had learned to use the skins of animals to cover them. Then about 10 years ago, under this standard, [humans] emerged from . . . caves to construct other kinds of shelter. Only five years ago [humans] learned to write and use a cart with wheels. Christianity began less than two years ago. The printing press came this year, and then less than two months ago, during this whole 50-year span of human history, the steam engine provided a new source of power.

Newton explored the meaning of gravity. Last month electric lights and telephones and automobiles and airplanes became available. Only last week did we develop penicillin and television and nuclear power, and now if America's new spacecraft succeeds in reaching Venus, we will have literally reached the stars before midnight tonight.

> Kennedy puts space exploration in historical perspective to enlighten his audience and urge a continuing move forward.

This is a breathtaking pace, and such a pace cannot help but create new ills as it dispels old, new ignorance, new problems, new dangers. ==Surely the opening vistas of space promise high costs and hardships, as well as high reward.==

> This is Kennedy's thesis: that the challenge is worth the risk.

So it is not surprising that some would have us stay where we are a little longer to rest, to wait. But this city of Houston, this State of Texas, this country of the United States was not built by those who waited and rested and wished to look behind them. This country was conquered by those who moved forward—and so will space.

> Here, Kennedy refutes logical arguments against his proposal.

William Bradford, speaking in 1630 of the founding of the Plymouth Bay Colony, said that all great and honorable actions are accompanied with great difficulties, and both must be enterprised and overcome with answerable courage.

> See reference to William Bradford on page 240.

If this capsule history of our progress teaches us anything, it is that [humans], in [their] quest for knowledge and progress, [are] determined and cannot be deterred. The exploration of space will go ahead, whether we join in it or not, and it is one of the great adventures of all time, and no nation which expects to be the leader of other nations can expect to stay behind in the race for space.

Those who came before us made certain that this country rode the first waves of the industrial revolutions, the first waves of modern invention, and the first wave of nuclear power, and this generation does not intend to founder in the backwash of the coming age of space. We mean to be a part of it—we mean to lead it. For the eyes of the world now look into space, to the moon and to the planets beyond, and we have vowed that we shall not see it governed by a hostile flag of conquest, but by a banner of freedom and peace. We have vowed that we shall not see space filled with weapons of mass destruction, but with instruments of knowledge and understanding.

> Here Kennedy makes his strongest point.

Yet the vows of this Nation can only be fulfilled if we in this Nation are first, and, therefore, we intend to be first. In short, our leadership in science and in industry, our hopes for peace and security, our obligations to ourselves as well as others, all require us to make this effort, to solve these mysteries, to solve them for the good of all [people], and to become the world's leading space-faring nation.

We set sail on this new sea because there is new knowledge to be gained, and new rights to be won, and they must be won and used for the progress of all people. For space science, like nuclear science and all technology, has no conscience of its own. Whether it will become a force for good or ill depends on [humans], and only if the United States occupies a position of pre-eminence can we help decide whether this new ocean will be a sea of peace or a new terrifying theater of war. I do not say that we should or will go unprotected against the hostile misuse of space any more than we go unprotected against the hostile use of land or sea, but I do say that space can be explored and mastered without feeding the fires of war, without repeating the mistakes that [humankind] has made in extending [its] writ around this globe of ours.

> The metaphor of an ocean voyage leads nicely into the proposed launch into space.

There is no strife, no prejudice, no national conflict in outer space as yet. Its hazards are hostile to us all. Its conquest deserves the best of all [humankind], and its opportunity for peaceful cooperation may never come again. But why, some say, the moon? Why choose this as our goal? And they may well ask why climb the highest mountain? Why, 35 years ago, fly the Atlantic? Why does Rice play Texas?

> Kennedy draws his audience in on a very personal and entertaining level here.

We choose to go to the moon. We choose to go to the moon in this decade and do the other things, not because they are easy, but because they are hard, because that goal

Project and Reading

will serve to organize and measure the best of our energies and skills, because that challenge is one that we are willing to accept, one we are unwilling to postpone, and one which we intend to win, and the others, too.

It is for these reasons that I regard the decision last year to shift our efforts in space from low to high gear as among the most important decisions that will be made during my incumbency in the office of the Presidency. . . .

Within these last 19 months at least 45 satellites have circled the earth. Some 40 of them were "made in the United States of America" and they were far more sophisticated and supplied far more knowledge to the people of the world than those of the Soviet Union. . . .

> Mentioning the Soviet Union, a Cold War adversary, gives urgency to Kennedy's speech.

Transit satellites are helping our ships at sea to steer a safer course. Tiros satellites have given us unprecedented warnings of hurricanes and storms, and will do the same for forest fires and icebergs.

We have had our failures, but so have others, even if they do not admit them. And they may be less public.

To be sure, we are behind, and will be behind for some time in manned flight. But we do not intend to stay behind, and in this decade, we shall make up and move ahead.

The growth of our science and education will be enriched by new knowledge of our universe and environment, by new techniques of learning and mapping and observation, by new tools and computers for industry, medicine, the home as well as the school. Technical institutions, such as Rice, will reap the harvest of these gains.

> In this paragraph and the one that follows, Kennedy focuses on how the space race will benefit the nation (and Rice University).

And finally, the space effort itself, while still in its infancy, has already created a great number of new companies, and tens of thousands of new jobs. . . .

To be sure, all this costs us all a good deal of money. This year's space budget is three times what it was in January 1961, and it is greater than the space budget of the previous eight years combined. . . . But if I were to say, my fellow citizens, that we shall send to the moon, 240,000 miles away from the control station in Houston, a giant rocket more than 300 feet tall, the length of this

> Again Kennedy acknowledges oposition to his views.

football field, made of new metal alloys, some of which have not yet been invented, capable of standing heat and stresses several times more than have ever been experienced, fitted together with a precision better than the finest watch, carrying all the equipment needed for propulsion, guidance, control, communications, food and survival, on an untried mission, to an unknown celestial body, and then return it safely to earth, re-entering the atmosphere at speeds of over 25,000 miles per hour, causing heat about half that of the temperature of the sun—almost as hot as it is here today—and do all this, and do it right, and do it first before this decade is out—then we must be bold.

I'm the one who is doing all the work, so we just want you to stay cool for a minute. [laughter]

> A light note in a long speech or essay can give the audience some relief and keep them aligned with you.

However, I think we're going to do it, and I think that we must pay what needs to be paid. I don't think we ought to waste any money, but I think we ought to do the job. And this will be done in the decade of the sixties. It may be done while some of you are still here at school at this college and university. It will be done during the term of office of some of the people who sit here on this platform. But it will be done. And it will be done before the end of this decade. . . .

Many years ago the great British explorer George Mallory, who was to die on Mount Everest, was asked why did he want to climb it. He said, "Because it is there."

Well, space is there, and we're going to climb it, and the moon and the planets are there, and new hopes for knowledge and peace are there. And, therefore, as we set sail we ask God's blessing on the most hazardous and dangerous and greatest adventure on which [humankind] has ever embarked.

Thank you.

> The conclusion is positive and forthright and harkens back to the ocean voyage metaphor and the courageous explorers of the past.

Respond in Writing Respond to Kennedy's argument. Do you agree with him? Why or why not? What, if anything, has he persuaded you to think or do?

Develop Your Own Ideas Work with your classmates to develop ideas that you might incorporate into a persuasive essay in which you try to persuade people to do something that involves costs, risks, and challenges.

Small Groups: In your small group, discuss the challenging task each writer has recommended. Ask and discuss answers to the following questions about each.

- What need exists that justifies taking risks to meet the challenge?
- What views and concerns of others must be considered in taking on these risks?
- What gains do you foresee in accepting this challenge?
- What possible problems and losses might follow from accepting this challenge?
- In what way do the benefits outweigh the risks in trying to meet this challenge?
- What is the justification for taking on this challenge despite the risks?

Whole Class: Each group should prepare a summary of its conversation and select a member to share that summary with the rest of the class.

Write About It You will next write a persuasive essay in which you take a position on and present valid reasoning for taking a risk to reach an important goal. Your essay might use any of the following possible topics, audiences, and forms.

Possible Topics	Possible Audiences	Possible Forms
• a social issue, such as how to reduce pollution even though it may cost jobs and hurt the economy	• people who agree with your position	• an essay
• a scientific issue, such as funding a scientific procedure that could help many people while perhaps harming others	• people who disagree with your position	• a blog
	• people who are unfamiliar with the issues and only understand the situation as you explain it	• a newspaper opinion page
• a personal issue, such as enrolling in a very challenging class even though your grades might suffer	• people in authority who might have to make a decision depending on how well you argue your points	• a letter

Developing Your Skills of Persuasion

The ability to shape your opinion on a controversial subject into a reasonable and forceful argument is a very valuable skill. Writing persuasive essays will help you develop and refine this skill.

Structure

Like all essays, a persuasive essay has three main parts: an introduction, a body, and a conclusion. The chart below shows how to make each part fulfill its function.

Structuring a Persuasive Essay

- In the **introduction,** you capture the audience's attention, present the issue, and express your opinion in a **thesis statement.**
- In the **body of supporting paragraphs,** you present reasons, facts, examples, and expert opinions to support your opinion, or thesis. You also respectfully address the concerns of those who disagree with you and offer **counter-arguments** to their position.
- In the **conclusion,** you present a summary or strong conclusive evidence—logically drawn from the arguments—that drives home your thesis.

As you read the selections below from a draft of a persuasive essay by student Reanna Eckroad of Canton, Ohio, notice how each part carries out a persuasive purpose.

STUDENT MODEL: *Introduction*

It's Not Easy Being Green

Scientists have warned that what would come out of global warming would not be good. Glaciers are melting, giving polar bears and penguins little space to call home. Rivers have become home to trash and waste while carbon dioxide emissions from factories have polluted the air and caused global warming. Scientists and political leaders have established many options for people, but there is only one problem: humans do not want to take the time and money to save the Earth. This problem has led me to the conclusion that something radical must be done. **I propose that every person must "go green" no matter what his or her circumstance may be.**

Introduction captures attention with dramatic images.

Thesis statement identifies the position to be argued.

In the essay body, after explaining how the law would have an impact on water conservation, Reanna moves on to the impact of the law on air pollution.

STUDENT MODEL: *Body Paragraphs*

Another part of this law focuses on air pollution, which affects humans' respiratory systems and causes serious health problems. To reduce air pollution, under the new law every family must buy a hybrid car or carpool. A hybrid car can cost up to $23,384, so those families who cannot afford it can carpool. The reduction of air pollution will help the ozone layer to stay intact which will protect humans from harmful UV rays and cause humans to not breathe in as much polluted air. This step, along with the conservation of water, will help the environment and save lives.

This proposal may seem harsh, but it is what the people of the Earth have put upon themselves. Environmental scientists have agreed that this plan will help families become healthier, and a risk to the environment will be lifted.

- The word *another* is a transition.
- Possible objection is anticipated and answered.
- Referring back to water conservation helps give the essay coherence.
- Referring to scientists helps strengthen the case. In a later draft she will add specific names.

Reanna's conclusion provides a strong ending.

STUDENT MODEL: *Concluding Paragraph*

If the law is obeyed by every person, the natural consequence of health will follow. People will be able to breathe again, and non-renewable resources will be conserved.

PROJECT PREP *Analyzing* **Essay Structures**

1. In your writing group, share your first rough draft by reading it aloud. After each person reads, identify and evaluate the clarity of the author's thesis or position and the supporting ideas used to back up that position. Discuss any flaws in the argument you might see. Use the feedback to rework your thesis statement.
2. SInce the first draft was written freely, chances are it is not yet tightly organized. Help each author sketch out a clear organizational plan for the chosen topics.

❷ Facts and Opinions

Persuasive essays are primarily made up of two types of statements: facts and opinions. Facts can be proved. Opinions can be supported but not proved.

A **fact** is a statement that can be proved. An **opinion** is a belief or judgment that cannot be proved.

You can test whether a statement is factual in two ways. One way is to ask yourself whether you would be able to prove the statement through your own observation and experience.

> **Fact**   This year the profit on our corn crop was higher.
> (You can count the money you made to prove this.)

The second way is to ask yourself whether you could prove it by consulting accepted authorities.

> **Fact**   The yields and profits from corn crops in Iowa this year were 10% higher than last year.
> (You cannot use your experience to test this statement, but you can verify it by consulting a recognized expert or an almanac.)

Unlike facts, opinions cannot be proved. They are personal judgments, interpretations, preferences, and predictions that differ from person to person. Here are some examples.

> **Opinions**   This is the **best** tasting corn we've ever grown.
>
> Modifying our vegetables genetically is a **terrible** thing to do.
>
> Genetically modified crops are the **best** produce ever.

Sometimes you can recognize opinions by watching for some of the words below.

OPINION WORDS	
should	better
must	best
ought	worst
may	maybe

In persuasive essays the soundest opinions are those supported by factual evidence, logical arguments, or both.

Developing Your Skills of Persuasion   **249**

Unsupported Opinion Corn is easier to grow than soybeans.
(No supporting facts back up this statement.)

Supported Statement Iowa grows more corn than Texas.
(U.S. agricultural statistics support this statement.)

● **Practice Your Skills**

Identifying Facts and Opinions

For each statement write *F* if it is a fact or *O* if it is an opinion.

1. The Petronas Tower in Kuala Lumpur is the world's tallest building.
2. Hawaii became a state in 1959.
3. Cats make better pets than dogs.
4. Nothing tastes better than a glass of cold milk.
5. Milk contains both protein and calcium.
6. All the best movies are comedies.
7. Robert Frost was truly a great poet.
8. Yosemite is America's most beautiful national park.
9. Nathaniel Hawthorne wrote *The Marble Faun*.
10. Weeping willow trees do not really weep.

> **Writing Tip**
>
> An argument based on opinions is like a house built on sand. Use **facts** and **examples** to convince your readers.

● **Practice Your Skills**

Expressing Opinions

Pair off. With your partner, choose one of the topics to the right. Talk for about five minutes, expressing your opinions on it. After your discussion, identify five facts that could be used to support the opinions you expressed.

1. animal rights
2. bullying
3. gangs
4. music
5. technology

PROJECT PREP   *Revising*   Facts and Opinions

Read your essay draft, looking for facts and opinions. Identify each supporting point in your composition as either opinion or fact. Underline the opinions in red ink. Underline facts, examples, or reasons in blue ink. If you have more red than blue, gather more facts, examples, and reasons to back up your position and work them into your draft.

Writing to Persuade

In the Media

Opinions and Advertising

Advertisers know that opinions can be very persuasive. Commercials on television and advertisements in newspapers and magazines often use opinions to sell products. Advertisements are meant to convince you that one soda tastes better than another; or that the style of one car is more attractive than the style of another; or that one brand of jeans is cooler than another. If the advertisement is persuasive, you are more likely to buy the "better tasting" soda or "cooler" jeans. Try to spot all the opinions in the following advertisement.

As fast as the wind. As sleek as a racing cheetah. Tomorrow's car for today, built for speed and performance. The car that dreams are made of...

WINDSPRITE

This advertisement appeals to the emotions. It implies that owning a Windsprite will make dreams come true and will give the owner power. Although not a single fact is presented, the advertisement stirs strong feelings and could succeed in selling the Windsprite.

A different approach to selling the Windsprite would be to provide some facts about the car. The facts might include its gas mileage, leg room, trunk space, warranty policy, available colors, and price. Facts like these would help a person compare the features of the Windsprite with those of other cars.

Media Activity

Look through several magazines or newspapers to find examples of advertising that appeals to emotions and relies on opinions. Then create an advertisement promoting yourself as a friend. Use the same emotional tactics as the ads you've found. After that, create a "spec sheet" about yourself that would appeal to the reasonable rather than the emotional in people. Give factual personal information that might persuade someone to be your friend. Share your ads and spec sheets with the rest of the class. Compare the effectiveness of appeals to emotions and appeals to reason.

3 Other Points of View

If you don't know where your audience stands on the position you've taken, then you won't be able to shape an effective argument. For example, suppose you wanted to get a dog but your parents do not agree. You could make the case that all your other friends have a dog, but that would not likely be very persuasive to your parents. Instead, try to get inside their heads and understand their views and concerns, and be ready for their **counter-arguments.**

Parents' Opposition	How I Will Respond
Their views: They are in charge and they have the right to decide.	Response: They are right about that. I just want to give some good reasons for them to think about.
Their concerns: • A dog is a big responsibility, both in time and in money. • A dog requires training. • A dog creates extra household work.	Answers: • I will take on as much responsibility as I can so you won't have to. I can't earn enough money to provide medical care for the dog, but I could take a reduction in allowance if that would help. • There are cheap training classes at the park district and I would be more than willing to be the one that trains the dog. • I will vacuum once a week to help with dog hair removal.
Their counter-arguments: • The money we save by not getting a dog could go toward a family vacation. • A smaller pet like a fish or turtle would be more practical and would be easier on the household.	Answers: • We could do simpler things than a vacation away. We could spend time together in our own neighborhood. • Fish and turtles could never return the kind of love you get from dogs. Kids especially appreciate the idea that they are loved all the time, no matter what. Dogs are masters at that.

PROJECT PREP *Revising* **Counter-Arguments**

Make a chart like the one above on your topic for a persuasive essay. Identify your readers' concerns and views and anticipate their counter-arguments. Be ready to respond to each of those. Discuss your chart with your writing group members and give feedback to each author on improving the responses or identifying new opposing views.

Think Critically

Evaluating Counter-Arguments

Not all evidence is created equal. **Evaluate**, or judge, the facts and examples your opponents might use in their arguments. To evaluate the information and decide whether it supports the argument, use the criteria below.

Is the evidence:

- clearly related to the thesis?
- a fact or an expert opinion?
- from a reliable source?
- up to date?
- unbiased and objective?

Suppose you were putting together an argument for year-round school. Here is how you could evaluate evidence on this issue.

EVIDENCE	EVALUATION
Using the building all year would be cost effective.	Supports thesis if backed by research—indicates how year-round school would save money.
Many students would be opposed to going to school twelve months a year.	Does not support thesis—no evidence is given to support the thesis; may not be objective
Continuing school without a long break would help students better remember what they learn.	Supports thesis if true—reliable source needs to be verified

Thinking Practice

Find an interesting editorial in a recent magazine or newspaper online or in print. List the main points the author makes; then evaluate each one. Tell whether you agree or disagree with the opinions expressed in the editorial. Write a brief counter-argument to the editorial opinion.

Order of Importance and Transitions

The most common organization for persuasive essays is **order of importance**—beginning with the least important point and working up to the most important. This emphasis will help your audience remember your most convincing points.

As you develop your argument, also use transitional words and phrases to guide the reader from one point to the next. The following transitional words are strong when addressing a counter-argument or emphasizing contrasting ideas.

TRANSITIONS FOR ORDER OF IMPORTANCE

also	for example	moreover
another	in the first place	furthermore
besides	in the second place	in addition
finally	in the same way	more important
first	likewise	most important
second	to begin with	similarly

Notice the logical order in the following paragraph. The transitions are highlighted in yellow.

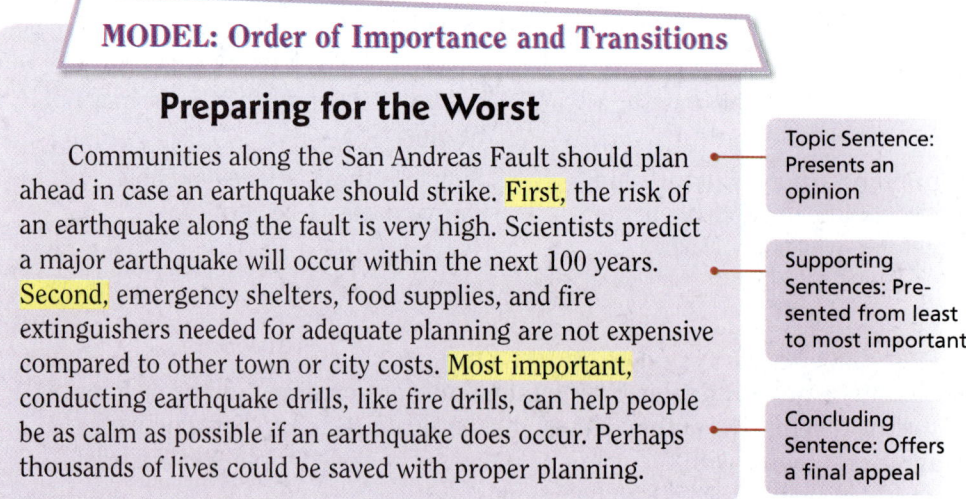

MODEL: Order of Importance and Transitions

Preparing for the Worst

Communities along the San Andreas Fault should plan ahead in case an earthquake should strike. First, the risk of an earthquake along the fault is very high. Scientists predict a major earthquake will occur within the next 100 years. Second, emergency shelters, food supplies, and fire extinguishers needed for adequate planning are not expensive compared to other town or city costs. Most important, conducting earthquake drills, like fire drills, can help people be as calm as possible if an earthquake does occur. Perhaps thousands of lives could be saved with proper planning.

- Topic Sentence: Presents an opinion
- Supporting Sentences: Presented from least to most important
- Concluding Sentence: Offers a final appeal

Counter-arguments can appear anywhere in a persuasive essay. They are often especially effective near the end, after you have established your own position clearly.

● **Practice Your Skills**

Using Transitions

In the paragraph below, the ideas are arranged in order of least to most important. The transitions, however, are missing. Using the list on the previous page, rewrite this paragraph to include transitions.

> ### Bicycle Lanes Are a Good Idea
>
> The city should paint bicycle lanes along Reston Street, Tower Avenue, and Madison Street. Having a safe place to bicycle might encourage more people to take their bikes rather than their cars to work. Fewer cars would mean less pollution. Fewer people would ride their bikes on the sidewalks, where they endanger pedestrians. Bicycle lanes promote safety by keeping cyclists away from cars and by reminding drivers that cyclists are on the road. The cost of having the lanes painted is low compared to the benefits.

Writing Tip

A good way to organize your ideas from least to most important is to use index cards. Write each of your ideas on a separate index card. You may even want to list supporting details under each point. Then you can move the cards around to decide the best order.

If you are composing on a computer, you can easily rearrange blocks of text with the Cut and Paste commands.

PROJECT PREP   Revising   *Order and Transitions*

In your writing group, help each author to consider the order in which the paragraphs are presented. Does this order make sense to you as a reader? Are there gaps that need to be filled with additional paragraphs so that the argument is more persuasive? Help each author write transition sentences that lead smoothly from one thought to the next.

Developing Your Skills of Persuasion

The Power of Language

Repetition: Say It Again

The organization of your essay and the transitions you use help your reader understand which of your ideas are most important. Another way to call attention to important ideas is to set up a pattern of repetition. In his address to the students and faculty of Rice Unversity, President Kennedy showed he knew the power of repeating key phrases. Near the conclusion of his address, Kennedy used repetition to emphasize the necessity of a staffed expedition to the moon.

> And **this will be done** in the decade of the sixties. **It may be done** while some of you are still here at school at this college and university. **It will be done** during the term of office of some of the people who sit here on this platform. But **it will be done**. And **it will be done** before the end of this decade. . . .

Repeating the phrases gives Kennedy's speech an emphatic and determined tone. The listener would have no doubt that what this man proposes will, indeed, come to pass.

In a speech, the volume and cadence a speaker uses to address the audience also help draw attention to important points. In Kennedy's case, physical gestures also added impact.

When you write, however, you have only your words to represent you and your ideas. In a persuasive piece, try adding emphasis to your most important point by repeating a key word or phrase.

Try It Yourself

Write a few sentences on your project topic or on a subject about which you have strong feelings. Use a pattern of repetition to enhance the persuasive appeal of your statements. Remember this technique as you draft a persuasive essay. When you revise, you will have another chance to add repetition of your most important points.

Persibuary Writing

As you prepare to evaluate and revise your persuasive essay, always begin with three questions.

- Does your essay fulfill its purpose? Is it persuasive?
- Does your essay have all the features readers expect in persuasive writing, such as a clear thesis statement or position, strong evidence, easy-to-follow structure, and a persuasive tone?
- Does your essay address and respond to the views of the audience, anticipate and answer its concerns, and provide thoughtful answers to counter-arguments?

When you are sure these fundamental questions are answered with a "yes," you can use the checklist below to evaluate and revise some of the other aspects of your essay.

 Evaluation Checklist for Revising

Checking Your Introduction
- ✓ Does the thesis statement present your opinion effectively? (page 247)
- ✓ Will your introduction convince the readers that your topic is important? (pages 114 and 247)

Checking Your Body Paragraphs
- ✓ Does each paragraph have a topic sentence? (page 254)
- ✓ Have you supported your main points with facts and examples, not more opinions? (pages 249–251)
- ✓ Have you organized your supporting material in the most logical way? (pages 254–255)
- ✓ Have you dealt with opposing views effectively? (pages 252–253)
- ✓ Have you used sound reasoning? (pages 249–251)
- ✓ Have you used transitions to help your reader follow your argument from point to point? (pages 254–255)

Checking Your Conclusion
- ✓ Does your conclusion summarize your main points and add a strong ending? (pages 247–248)

Checking Your Words and Sentences
- ✓ Have you used respectful language? (page 247)
- ✓ Have you combined short, choppy sentences into longer, more interesting ones? (pages 64–72)
- ✓ Have you used precise and lively words? (pages 42–46 and 56–57)

Carefully reread your revised draft for spelling, grammar, and usage. Put your writing aside for a time. Later, you will see mistakes that you missed.

The Language of Power *Negatives*

Power Rule: Use only one negative form for a single negative idea. (See page 784.)

See It in Action Probably the most common mistake with negatives is using *not* (or a contraction formed with *n't*) with another negative word.

Incorrect	Kaila did**n't** have **nothing** to do with the broken window.
Correct	Kaila had **nothing** to do with the broken window.
	Kaila did**n't** have anything to do with the broken window.

Reread this paragraph from Kennedy's speech. Notice the use of negatives.

> So it is **not** surprising that some would have us stay where we are a little longer to rest, to wait. But this city of Houston, this State of Texas, this country of the United States was **not** built by those who waited and rested and wished to look behind them. . . .

When *not* appears in a sentence, it should be the only negative word in that sentence. In the following sentence, double negatives confuse the issue.

Incorrect	. . . the United States was **not** built by **no one** who waited and rested. . . .

Remember It Record this rule and examples in the Power Rule section of your Personalized Editing Checklist.

Use It Read through your persuasive essay circling all the negative words, including *not* and contractions formed with *n't, nothing, no one,* and *never.* Rewrite any sentences that contain double negatives.

PROJECT PREP *Revising and Editing* Polish

Exchange papers with a member of your writing group. Use the evaluation checklist on the previous page to assess your partner's essay. Based on the feedback you receive, make additional revisions as you see fit. Add, delete, substitute, and rearrange until everything is in just the right order and is as well developed as possible. Then check your grammar, usage, mechanics, and spelling to be sure you have not made any mistakes. Pay special attention to the Power Rules, as always.

Using a Six-Trait Rubric

Use the following rubric to make a final evaluation of your persuasive essay.

Ideas	**4** The introduction clearly states an opinion. The text backs it up with abundant supporting facts or examples and addresses readers' concerns. The conclusion is strong.	**3** The introduction states an opinion. The text uses facts and examples and takes some readers' views into account. The conclusion is clear.	**2** The thesis statement is unclear. The text does not provide enough support for the stated opinion nor consider other views. The conclusion is unclear.	**1** The thesis statement is missing or unclear, or the text fails to support the stated opinion. The conclusion is missing or weak.
Organization	**4** The organization is clear with frequent transitions to guide the reader.	**3** A few ideas seem out of place or transitions are missing.	**2** Many ideas seem out of place and transitions are missing.	**1** The organization is unclear and hard to follow.
Voice	**4** The voice sounds natural, engaging, and forceful.	**3** The voice sounds natural and engaging.	**2** The voice sounds mostly natural but is weak.	**1** The voice sounds mostly unnatural and is weak.
Word Choice	**4** Words are precise and powerful. Language is respectful.	**3** Words are specific and language is respectful.	**2** Some words are too general and/or emotional.	**1** Most words are overly general.
Sentence Fluency	**4** Varied sentences flow smoothly.	**3** Most sentences are varied and flow smoothly.	**2** Some sentences are varied but some are choppy.	**1** Sentence structure is not varied or sentences are choppy.
Conventions	**4** Punctuation, usage, and spelling are correct. The Power Rules are all followed.	**3** Punctuation, usage, and spelling are mainly correct and the Power Rules are all followed.	**2** Some punctuation, usage, and spelling are incorrect but all Power Rules are followed.	**1** There are many errors and at least one failure to follow a Power Rule.

If you have written a persuasive essay earlier in the year, take it out and read it again. How does it differ from the work you just completed? What did you do better in your most recent work? Is there anything you did better before? Record your reflections in the Learning Log section of your journal.

Writing Lab

Project Corner

Listening Circle
Respond in Silence

With five other students, **form a listening circle** to express your opinions and feelings about the issues facing young people, such as equality, the environment, war, and the economy. When it's your turn to talk, express yourself freely for three to five minutes. Everyone else will listen in silence. Go around the circle until everyone has had a chance to talk. After the experience, write about it in your journal and identify possible topics for future persuasive writing.

Collaborate and Create Act It Out

In your writing group, select one student's argument and **create a drama** that illustrates the author's points about risks and rewards. Perform it live or film it and show it on a screen.

Cross-Cultural Connection Translation, Please

Translate the persuasive essay you have written into other languages, such as the one you may speak at home or one you are studying in school. Have someone who speaks that language well read it and comment on your ability to write in that language. Share your essay with other speakers of this language and ask for their response to your ideas.

For Oral Presentation
Persuasive Speech

Apply and Assess

1. The school water balloon team has not won a game all season. This afternoon you play the best water balloon team in the district. **Prepare a speech** to give to your teammates to convince them of the importance of winning this game. Take opposing views (such as the view that with such an embarrassing record, it will not matter anyway) into consideration. Deliver your speech to your classmates who will act as the team. (You can find information on preparing speeches on pages 435–438.)

In the Workplace Persuasive Note

2. One of the houses on your paper route is the house of Ms. Robin, who wants her paper placed in her mailbox. You are happy to do this. The problem: Ms. Robin lives in a tree house, and you have to climb the tree to get to her mailbox. **Write a note** to Ms. Robin persuading her to move her mailbox down to the ground. Support your opinion with reasons and examples. Anticipate any objections she might have and address them. Be sure to organize your ideas in order from least to most important. Remember to avoid highly charged or emotional language.

Timed Writing Persuasive Public Speech

3. The Recreation Commission of your town has recently established a Teen Center. You think it is a good idea, but the members of the commission have used the budget money to set up activities like Pick-up Sticks and Go Fish. They have also installed a television that only picks up one station—the all-macramé channel. Think of some ways the Teen Center could be improved. Write a speech to deliver to the Recreation Commission persuading them to make the center more interesting to teens. When preparing your remarks, be sure you create a clear, logical structure and support your points adequately. Use polite, reasonable language. Anticipate any objections the Commission may have and address them without taking weight away from your own points. You have 25 minutes to complete your work. (For help with budgeting time, see pages 398–399.)

Before You Write Consider the following questions: What is the situation? What is the occasion? Who is the audience? What is the purpose?

After You Write Evaluate your work using the six-trait evaluation rubric on page 259.

Persuasive Writing Workshops

When you plan a persuasive composition, think about the people who disagree with you. Why do they see things differently? If you were debating with these people, what points would they probably make to support their viewpoint? Having solid arguments to counter opposing viewpoints will help you win your case.

❶ Persuading with Examples

PREWRITING

Write a persuasive essay about the characters on your favorite TV show and why their true-to-life qualities help make the show the best on TV. Begin by pairing off with a partner and discussing your favorite TV shows. Listen carefully to your partner's comments, because they will help you shape your essay.

After the conversation, plan your essay by listing all the important characters in your favorite TV show. Then arrange your list in the order of least to most important or another order that seems more logical to you. For each character, elaborate with several examples that show how he or she is true to life.

Your audience for this assignment is your partner. You know now what he or she likes in TV shows and what possible counter-arguments you might expect. Consider your partner's views and anticipate his or her counter-arguments while you are developing your argument.

DRAFTING

Use your notes and the following thesis statement to write a draft of a persuasive essay.

> **Thesis Statement** [Your favorite show] is the best show on television because its characters are true to life.

Keep your partner's views and counter-arguments in mind as you draft so you can respond to them effectively. For example, if you know your partner likes the show "Fly by Night," you might write something like:

> While some may think that Rolly in "Fly by Night" is very true to life, he's less colorful and less distinctive than a character in "Bird's Nest" no viewer will ever forget—Ned.

REVISING BY CONFERENCING

Exchange papers with a different classmate. Read your revising partner's paper carefully. Does it convince you that his or her choice could be considered the best show on television? Check it against the checklist on page 257 and the rubric on page 259. Tell your partner what is good about the essay and what could be improved. After your paper has been returned, revise your essay to make it as convincing as possible.

EDITING AND PUBLISHING

When you are satisfied with the substance of your essay, check to make sure you have followed all the conventions of grammar, usage, mechanics, and spelling. Check your Personalized Editing Checklist for mistakes you tend to make, and refer to the Editing Checklist on page 28 to make sure you have covered everything. Be especially careful to follow all the Power Rules. (See pages 8–10.)

❷ Persuading with Facts

PREWRITING

A young boy you know often stays up late at night reading adventure stories. When he does, he seems tired and cranky the next day. Think of how to advise this boy to get to sleep at an earlier hour. The following facts will help you back up your advice. Arrange the facts in a logical order.

- Heartbeat slows down to about 56 beats per minute during sleep.
- People who do not get enough sleep are more likely to catch contagious diseases.
- Lungs and other organs rest during sleep.
- People who do not dream enough during the night do not perform well during the day.

Now think about concerns the boy might have about your advice. Make a list of objections he might have. Prepare yourself to answer his concerns and objections with convincing solutions.

DRAFTING

Using your prewriting notes, draft a persuasive e-mail advising the boy on the benefits of sufficient sleep. Be sure to include answers to any objections he may have.

REVISING BY CONFERENCING

Exchange papers with a classmate. As you read your partner's paper, pretend you are the boy receiving advice. Would you be convinced? Tell your partner why or why not. When your own paper is returned, revise it as needed to make it more persuasive.

EDITING AND PUBLISHING

Check over your e-mail to make sure you have not made any mistakes. Review your Personalized Editing Checklist for mistakes you have tended to make in the past. Check that you followed all the Power Rules as well. (See pages 8–10.)

Finally, go over your e-mail to be sure that it is presented in an appropriate way. See pages 469–470 for more information on writing e-mails.

3. Persuading with Reasons

PREWRITING

There's a growing problem at your school. Some students are teasing and bullying students they regard as different. Those being bullied are afraid to identify the offenders for fear of rough treatment if they do. The school is seeking recommendations from students, families, and faculty members on how to handle this problem. Working with a partner, brainstorm a list of several possible solutions. Talk through the pros and cons of each approach. Be sure to ask your partner to clarify anything you do not understand.

On your own, choose the solution you think is best and develop a list of reasons to convince school officials to select your solution. Next to each, indicate what concerns and counter-arguments your audience of school officials might have and be prepared to respond to them. Arrange your ideas in a logical order in an outline or graphic organizer.

DRAFTING

Using your prewriting notes, draft a proposal to your school officials. Use compelling reasons and wording. Be sure to use logical order and transitions and to anticipate and address their concerns.

REVISING

Using a Rubric Use the rubric on page 259 to evaluate your proposal. What score would it earn? Write a brief paragraph explaining how you arrived at your score. If it is lower than a 4, what can you do to improve your proposal? Make revisions as you see fit.

Conferencing Exchange papers with a partner. Read your partner's paper carefully. Tell your partner whether or not you agree with the order of importance given to each reason. When your own paper is returned, make further revisions as needed for clarity.

---

editing ★

Check over your persuasive writing to eliminate unnecessary words and phrases. Avoid the temptation to say "I think" or "I believe" or "In my opinion." Readers will understand that you think, believe, and hold the opinions in your composition because you are, after all, expressing them. Too many qualifiers like "I think" actually weaken an argument.

CHAPTER 11

Writing About Literature

A **literary analysis** presents an interpretation of a work of literature and supports that interpretation with evidence from the text, including quotations when necessary.

Writing about literature can take many forms. Here are some real-life examples.

- **Students select a play** to present to their class as a final project and write up their reasons for their choice.
- **A political candidate uses a famous quote** from literature in a speech to stir the audience.
- **An Internet company encourages users to post online reviews of books and movies** to guide other shoppers.
- **You want to tell your friends about a book** that had a strong impact on you.

Writing Project — Interpretive Response

Character Analysis Write a response to a literary work that uses evidence from the work to support a thoughtful interpretation of a character.

Think Through Writing Write about a character that you really like from a book you have enjoyed. What do you like about this character? How would you let other people know what makes this character special?

Talk About It In your writing group, discuss your writing. What kinds of characters did each of you choose? What did you like best about them? What feelings do the characters stir? Do you clearly understand what is special about the character in each student's writing?

Read About It The following story by Ray Bradbury takes place in 1862 in Tennessee during the Civil War. It is the night before the Battle of Shiloh—the deadliest battle in U.S. history at that point, with nearly 24,000 soldiers killed. Focus on the two main characters in the story and how Bradbury has depicted them.

MODEL: Historical Fiction

The Drummer Boy of Shiloh

Ray Bradbury

In the April night, more than once, blossoms fell from the orchard trees and lit with rustling taps on the drumskin. At midnight a peach stone left miraculously on a branch through winter, flicked by a bird, fell swift and unseen, struck once, like panic, which jerked the boy upright. In silence he listened to his own heart ruffle away, away, at last gone from his ears and back in his chest again.

After that, he turned the drum on its side, where its great lunar face peered at him whenever he opened his eyes.

His face, alert or at rest, was solemn. It was indeed a solemn time and a solemn night for a boy just turned fourteen in the peach field near the Owl Creek not far from the church at Shiloh.

". . . thirty-one, thirty-two, thirty-three . . ."

Unable to see, he stopped counting.

Beyond the thirty-three familiar shadows, forty thousand men, exhausted by nervous expectation, unable to sleep for romantic dreams of battles yet unfought, lay crazily askew in their uniforms. A mile yet farther on, another army was strewn helter-skelter,[1] turning slow, basting themselves with the thought of what they would do when the time came: a leap, a yell, a blind plunge their strategy, raw youth their protection and benediction.[2]

Now and again the boy heard a vast wind come up, that gently stirred the air. But he knew what it was, the army here, the army there, whispering to itself in the dark. Some men talking to others, others murmuring to themselves, and all so quiet it was like a natural element arisen from south or north with the motion of the earth toward dawn.

What the men whispered the boy could only guess, and he guessed that it was: Me, I'm the one, I'm the one of all the rest won't die. I'll live through it. I'll go home. The band will play. And I'll be there to hear it.

Yes, thought the boy, that's all very well for them, they can give as good as they get!

For with the careless bones of the young men harvested by night and bindled[3] around campfires were the similarly strewn steel bones of their rifles, with bayonets fixed like eternal lightning lost in the orchard grass.

Me, thought the boy, I got only a drum, two sticks to beat it, and no shield.

---

1 **helter-skelter:** Hurried, confused, and disorderly.
2 **benediction:** Blessing, especially one given at the close of a religious service.
3 **bindled:** Bedded.

There wasn't a man-boy on this ground tonight did not have a shield he cast, riveted, or carved himself on his way to his first attack, compounded of remote[4] but nonetheless firm and fiery family devotion, flag-blown patriotism, and cocksure immortality strengthened by the touchstone of very real gunpowder, ramrod, minié ball,[5] and flint. But without these last the boy felt his family move yet farther off away in the dark, as if one of those great prairie-burning trains had chanted them away never to return, leaving him with this drum which was worse than a toy in the game to be played tomorrow or some day much too soon.

The boy turned on his side. A moth brushed his face, but it was peach blossom. A peach blossom flicked him, but it was a moth. Nothing stayed put. Nothing had a name. Nothing was as it once was.

If he lay very still, when the dawn came up and the soldiers put on their bravery with their caps, perhaps they might go away, the war with them, and not notice him lying small here, no more than a toy himself.

"Well, by God, now," said a voice.

The boy shut up his eyes, to hide inside himself, but it was too late. Someone, walking by in the night, stood over him.

"Well," said the voice quietly, "here's a soldier crying *before* the fight. Good. Get it over. Won't be time once it all starts."

And the voice was about to move on when the boy, startled, touched the drum at his elbow. The man above, hearing this, stopped. The boy could feel his eyes, sense him slowly bending near. A hand must have come down out of the night, for there was a little rat-tat as the fingernails brushed and the man's breath fanned his face.

"Why, it's the drummer boy, isn't it?"

The boy nodded, not knowing if his nod was seen. "Sir, is that *you?*" he asked.

"I assume it is." The man's knees cracked as he bent still closer.

He smelled as all fathers should smell, of salt sweat, ginger tobacco, horse and boot leather, and the earth he walked upon. He had many eyes. No, not eyes, brass buttons that watched the boy.

He could only be, and was, the General.

"What's your name, boy?" he asked.

"Joby," whispered the boy, starting to sit up.

---

4 **remote:** Located far away.
5 **minié ball:** Cone-shaped rifle bullet that expands when fired.

"All right, Joby, don't stir." A hand pressed his chest gently, and the boy relaxed. "How long you been with us, Joby?"

"Three weeks, sir."

"Run off from home or joined legitimately,[6] boy?"

Silence.

"Damn-fool question," said the General. "Do you shave yet, boy? Even more of a damn-fool. There's your cheek, fell right off the tree overhead. And the others here not much older. Raw, raw, damn raw, the lot of you. You ready for tomorrow or the next day, Joby?"

"I think so, sir."

"You want to cry some more, go on ahead. I did the same last night."

"*You*, sir?"

"God's truth. Thinking of everything ahead. Both sides figuring the other side will just give up, and soon, and the war done in weeks and us all home. Well, that's not how it's going to be. And maybe that's why I cried."

"Yes, sir," said Joby.

The General must have taken out a cigar now, for the dark was suddenly filled with the smell of tobacco unlit as yet, but chewed as the man thought what next to say.

"It's going to be a crazy time," said the General. "Counting both sides, there's a hundred thousand men, give or take a few thousand out there tonight, not one as can spit a sparrow off a tree, or knows a horse clod from a minié ball. Stand up, bare the breast, ask to be a target, thank them and sit down, that's us, that's them. We should turn tail and train four months, they should do the same. But here we are, taken with spring fever, and thinking it blood lust, taking our sulfur with cannons instead of with molasses as it should be, going to be a hero, going to live forever. And I can see all of them over there nodding agreement, save the other way around. It's wrong, boy, it's wrong as a head put on hind side front and a man marching backward through life. It will be a double massacre if one of their itchy generals decides to picnic his lads on our grass. More innocents will get shot out of pure enthusiasm than ever got shot before. Owl Creek was full of boys splashing around in the noonday sun just a few hours ago. I fear it will be full of boys again, just floating, at sundown tomorrow, not caring where the tide takes them."

The General stopped and made a little pile of winter leaves and twigs in the darkness, as if he might at any moment strike fire to them to see his way

---

6 **legitimately:** In a lawful manner; in accordance with the law.

through the coming days when the sun might not show its face because of what was happening here and just beyond.

The boy watched the hand stirring the leaves and opened his lips to say something, but did not say it. The General heard the boy's breath and spoke himself.

"Why am I telling you this? That's what you wanted to ask, eh? Well, when you got a bunch of wild horses on a loose rein somewhere, somehow you got to bring order, rein them in. These lads, fresh out of the milkshed, don't know what I know, and I can't tell them: men actually die, in war. So each is his own army. I got to make *one* army of them. And for that, boy, I need you."

"Me!" The boy's lips barely twitched.

"Now, boy," said the General quietly, "you are the heart of the army. Think of that. You're the heart of the army. Listen, now."

And, lying there, Joby listened.

And the General spoke on.

If he, Joby, beat slow tomorrow, the heart would beat slow in the men. They would lag by the wayside. They would drowse in the fields on their muskets. They would sleep forever, after that, in those same fields, their hearts slowed by a drummer boy and stopped by enemy lead.

But if he beat a sure, steady, ever faster rhythm, then, then their knees would come up in a long line down over that hill, one knee after the other, like a wave on the ocean shore! Had he seen the ocean ever? Seen the waves rolling in like a well-ordered cavalry charge to the sand? Well, that was it, that's what he wanted, that's what was needed! Joby was his right hand and his left. He gave the orders, but Joby set the pace!

So bring the right knee up and the right foot out and the left knee up and the left foot out. One following the other in good time, in brisk time. Move the blood up the body and make the head proud and the spine stiff and the jaw resolute.[7] Focus the eye and set the teeth, flare the nostrils and tighten the hands, put steel armor all over the men, for blood moving fast in them does indeed make men feel as if they'd put on steel. He must keep at it, at it! Long and steady, steady and long! Then, even though shot or torn, those wounds got in hot blood—in blood he'd helped stir—would feel less pain. If their blood was cold, it would be more than slaughter, it would be murderous nightmare and pain best not told and no one to guess.

The General spoke and stopped, letting his breath slack off. Then, after a moment, he said, "So there you are, that's it. Will you do that, boy? Do you know now you're general of the army when the General's left behind?"

---

[7] **resolute:** Having or showing strong determination.

The boy nodded mutely.

"You'll run them through for me then, boy?"

"Yes, sir."

"Good. And, God willing, many nights from tonight, many years from now, when you're as old or far much older than me, when they ask you what you did in this awful time, you will tell them—one part humble and one part proud—'I was the drummer boy at the battle of Owl Creek,' or the Tennessee River, or maybe they'll just name it after the church there. 'I was the drummer boy at Shiloh.' Good grief, that has a beat and sound to it fitting for Mr. Longfellow. 'I was the drummer boy at Shiloh.' Who will ever hear those words and not know you, boy, or what you thought this night, or what you'll think tomorrow or the next day when we must get up on our legs and *move*!"

The general stood up. "Well, then. God bless you, boy. Good night."

"Good night, sir."

And, tobacco, brass, boot polish, salt sweat and leather, the man moved away through the grass.

Joby lay for a moment, staring but unable to see where the man had gone.

He swallowed. He wiped his eyes. He cleared his throat. He settled himself. Then, at last, very slowly and firmly, he turned the drum so that it faced up toward the sky.

He lay next to it, his arm around it, feeling the tremor, the touch, the muted thunder as, all the rest of the April night in the year 1862, near the Tennessee River, not far from the Owl Creek, very close to the church named Shiloh, the peach blossoms fell on the drum.

Respond in Writing Respond to the two main characters in this story. How do you feel about them? What do you learn about them? What clues does the author provide for you to understand the characters and their actions? How would you describe each character?

Develop Your Own Ideas for Analysis Work with your classmates to develop ideas you might use in writing a character analysis of the two main characters in this story.

Small Groups: In your small group, discuss the two main characters. Use the following graphic organizer to help you understand how the author has constructed each.

CHARACTER ANALYSIS	JOBY	THE GENERAL
What does the narrator reveal directly about the character?		
What indirect clues does the narrator provide about the character's personality?		
What do you infer about the character based on the clues?		
What does the story's ending tell you about the character?		
How do you feel about this character, based on your reading?		
What is your overall evaluation of this character?		

Whole Class: Make a master chart of all of the ideas generated by the small groups to compare the ideas about the two characters.

Write About It You will next write a character sketch of either Joby or the General. The chart below gives possibilities for topics, audiences, and forms.

Possible Topics	Possible Audiences	Possible Forms
• Joby • the General	• others who have read this story • people who haven't read it but are curious about it • English teachers • the author	• a blog entry • a review on a bookseller's Web site • a formal essay • a review for your school newspaper

Writing About Literature

Structure of a Literary Analysis

A common format for a literary analysis is an essay that has the following features.

STRUCTURE OF A LITERARY ANALYSIS	
Title	Identifies which aspect of the work the writer will focus on
Introduction	Names the author and the work; contains a **thesis statement** that expresses an interpretation of some aspect of the work
Body	Supports the statement with **evidence** and **direct quotations** from the work. In some instances the body contains quotations from other respected sources, such as literary critics and biographers. It may also include the author's personal comments and letters.
Conclusion	Summarizes, clarifies, or adds an insight to the thesis statement

There are many ways to organize the body of a literary analysis. The graphic organizer below shows one way to organize a character analysis.

Character Analysis Organizer

Introduction, including thesis statement

- Trait #1 → Evidence → Evidence → Evidence
- Trait #2 → Evidence → Evidence → Evidence
- Trait #3 → Evidence → Evidence → Evidence

Conclusion, drawing insights based on evidence

PROJECT PREP Evaluating Structure

In your writing group, discuss how you might structure an essay analyzing either of the characters in "The Drummer Boy of Shiloh" or another work of your teacher's choosing.

Responding to Literature

You have just read a work of literature—a short story. You have also already begun to think critically about it, by thinking about the characters' voices and generating questions about their roles. This kind of thinking helps you to understand and appreciate a literary work, and it is what you use when you write a literary analysis.

One type of literary analysis is a **character analysis,** a breakdown of the traits of a character in a story. To begin a character analysis, note your personal reactions to the character in the story. Then learn to recognize the clues that the author provides to the character's traits. To back up a statement you make about the character, you use details from the story itself.

Before you begin to write about the character, think about how you form your own responses to what you have read. The chart below lists several factors that influence a reader's response to a work of fiction.

FACTORS IN A READER'S RESPONSE TO LITERATURE

- the reader's age, gender, and personality
- the reader's cultural or ethnic origins, attitudes, and customs
- personal opinions, beliefs, and values of the reader
- life experiences and general knowledge acquired by the reader
- the reader's knowledge of literature and literary genres
- a knowledge of the historical and social climate in which the work was written
- the reader's reading and language skills

1 Responding from Personal Experience

When you read a book or story for the first time, you are probably forming judgments about each character as you read. You are most likely rooting for the "good guys" and hoping the "bad guys" will get caught in the end. Often there are characters in the work about whom you care strongly.

Much of your response to a story is based on your own personal experiences. One character, for example, might remind you of yourself when you faced a similar problem or conflict. Another might remind you of a kind uncle who always made you feel comfortable. Still another might call to mind a friend who hurt your feelings or treated you unfairly. How you feel about characters in a work is often related to how you feel about the people in your own life the characters bring to mind.

Writing About Literature

The following strategies will help you understand your personal responses to a literary work.

Personal Response Strategies

1. Freewrite answers to the following questions:
   - Where in the story, novel, play, or poem do you see yourself? In other words, with what character or characters do you most closely identify? Why? Do your feelings about the character or characters stay the same? Do they change? If so, when and why do they change?
   - What characters remind you of other people you know? In what ways are they like those real people? In what ways are they different? How has your experience with those real people influenced your reactions to the characters in the work?
   - If you were a character in the work, do you think you might have behaved any differently? Why or why not? What actions or behaviors puzzle you?
   - What experiences from your own life come to mind as you read this work? How are they similar to the events portrayed? How are they different? What feelings do you associate with the experiences?
   - What moved you in the work? How and why did it affect you?
2. Write a "personal response statement." In this statement, explain your feelings about the main character.
3. In small discussion groups, share your various reactions to the above questions. Feel free to adjust your reactions if your classmates suggest ideas that make good sense to you. After the discussion, write freely about how, if at all, your ideas about the work changed after talking them over with your classmates.

● **Practice Your Skills**

Responding from Personal Experience

Answers the question below.

1. What do you think of Joby in "The Drummer Boy of Shiloh"? Does he remind you of anyone you know? How would you describe his personality? What do you think of the General? Does *he* remind you of anybody you know?
2. When you were reading the story, did you predict the outcome? If not, why did you think it would end differently?
3. Write about times in your life that came to mind when you read the story.

PROJECT PREP *Prewriting* **Personal Responding**

Choose a character from "The Drummer Boy of Shiloh" or another work to serve as the topic of your character analysis. Write a personal response statement in which you explain your feelings about this character and why you feel this way, based on what the narrator tells you. Save your work for later use.

Responding to Literature 275

2 Responding from Literary Knowledge

To understand a specific literary work, you can use your knowledge of literary works in general. You know, for example, that most short stories have elements that work together. By studying these elements and their impact on the whole story, you can add to your understanding of a story.

The chart below shows the main elements of fiction, poetry, and drama. The elements listed under drama show only the features that differ from those of other kinds of literature.

ELEMENTS OF LITERATURE	
FICTION	
Plot	the events that lead up to a **climax** (high point) and to an outcome that resolves a central **conflict**
Setting	when and where the story takes place
Characters	the people in the story who advance the plot through their thoughts and actions
Dialogue	the conversations among characters that reveal their personalities, actions, and **motivations,** or reasons for behaving as they do
Tone	the writer's attitude toward her or his characters
Point of View	the "voice" telling the story—**first person** (*I*) or **third person** (*he* or *she*)
Theme	the main idea or message of the story
POETRY	
Persona	the person whose "voice" is saying the poem, revealing the character the poet is assuming
Meter	the pattern of stressed and unstressed syllables in each line
Rhyme Scheme	the pattern of rhymed sounds, usually at the ends of lines
Sound Devices	techniques for playing with sounds to create certain effects, such as **alliteration** and **onomatopoeia**
Poetic Techniques	**figurative language, similes,** and **metaphors** (which create images by making comparisons)
Shape	the way a poem looks on the printed page, which may contribute to the underlying meaning of the poet's thoughts and feelings
Theme	the underlying meaning of the poem

	DRAMA
Setting	the time and place of the action; lighting and stage sets, as described in the stage directions
Characters	the people who participate in the action of the play
Plot	the story of the play divided into acts and scenes and developed through the characters' words and actions
Theme	the meaning of a play, as revealed through the setting and the characters' words and actions

Ask yourself the questions below as you investigate the meaning of the story you will be examining. Pay particular attention to questions about analyzing characters.

Questions for Finding Meaning in Fiction

Plot
- What are the key elements of the plot, and how do these influence the characters? What is the central conflict of the story? What do the climax and the ending reveal about the theme?

Characters
- What is the main character's motivation, or reason for behaving? How does the narrator of the story describe the main characters? What do the characters' words and actions reveal about the characters' personalities? What does the dialogue reveal about the characters' personalities and motivations? How does the point of view of the story affect the characterizations?

Setting
- How does the setting contribute to the story and help define the characters? Which details of the setting are most important in the development of the plot? How do the characters relate to their setting?

Theme
- What passages and details in the story best express the main theme? How does the author communicate the theme through the development of setting, characters, and plot? Does this theme have meaning for me? What else have I read that has a similar theme?

PROJECT PREP *Prewriting* Responding from Literary Knowledge

Using the chart above, freewrite a literary response to "The Drummer Boy of Shiloh" or another work. Identify the literary elements the author uses to evoke your response. Also consider how the author's use of language, especially figures of speech and imagery, influences your response. Save your work for later use.

The Power of Language

Adjectives: Modifiers Come Lately

Adjectives give life and precision to nouns and pronouns. Writers use them to add descriptive details to the characters and to enrich the setting and plot. You can use them to enliven a character sketch.

Writers often place adjectives before the words they modify, but to add interest and impact to their sentences, they may use adjectives "come lately" after the words they modify. In the following sentence from Ray Bradbury's "The Drummer Boy of Shiloh," the subject of the sentence is *men*. Bradbury incorporates the adjectives *exhausted* and *unable* after the subject to offer details about the men.

> Beyond the thirty-three familiar shadows, forty thousand men, exhausted by nervous expectation, unable to sleep for romantic dreams of battles yet unfought, lay crazily askew in their uniforms.

Here is another example of adjectives come lately that modify the noun *tobacco*:

> The General must have taken out a cigar now, for the dark was suddenly filled with the smell of tobacco unlit as yet, but chewed as the man thought what next to say.

Try It Yourself

Write two or three sentences about the character you are analyzing that contain adjectives that come after the noun they modify. If you can, use these in your character analysis, or look for other ways to use adjectives come lately. When you revise your character analysis, you will have another opportunity to add variety to your sentences by placing adjectives after the nouns they modify.

Punctuation Tip

Use commas to set off adjectives in a series whether they come before or after the word they modify.

Example: Joby was still a boy, innocent, fearful, and ashamed.

Writing a Character Analysis

After exploring your personal responses to a work of literature, you are ready to begin an analysis of one of the characters in the story.

You will no doubt find the greatest amount to say about the main character in a story or book. However, you may feel a closer bond with one of the minor characters and choose to write about that character. One good way to help you choose a subject is to do some prewriting about the character for whom you have the strongest feelings.

❶ Choosing a Subject Related to Character

If a character has succeeded in stirring your feelings, chances are good that you will have much of genuine interest to say about that character. Another good way to choose the character for your paper is to decide which one puzzles you the most. Having to solve a puzzle for a paper about why a character behaves as he or she does will make you think (and feel) so keenly that your writing is bound to be good. The following questions will help you think of subjects related to characters that are interesting to you and appropriate for a literary analysis.

Questions for Choosing a Subject Related to Character

- What character moves me, surprises me, disappoints me, or angers me? Why does the character have that effect on me?
- What images or details about the character made a strong impression on me? What do they contribute to the overall work?
- With which character do I identify most? Why?
- What makes the characters distinct from one another? What motivates them?
- What parts of any characterization puzzle me? What would I like to understand better?
- What message does the work convey through the characters? What insight or understanding have I gained?

Before you decide on your focus, consider your audience. Will you assume that the audience is familiar with the character you are analyzing or will you have to fully explain your examples in the analysis?

● Practice Your Skills

Look at the chart above again. Which of the questions relate well to the character you are considering for your analysis? Pick two questions and write a statement addressing both questions.

LIMITING A SUBJECT

Once you have focused on a subject for your character sketch, take the time to be sure you can cover your subject in a short essay. One good way to limit your subject is to try to express it in a phrase. Ask yourself, "What do I plan to say about my subject?" When you can express the answer to that question in a phrase, you probably have a suitably limited subject.

In writing about *Julie of the Wolves,* one writer went through the following thought process.

MODEL: Limiting a Subject

Too General	Miyax
Ask Yourself	What do I plan to say about Miyax?
Possible Answer	How she handles herself
Limited Subject	How Miyax handles survival

PROJECT PREP Prewriting Limited Subject

In most stories you read, you will probably have many characters from which to choose. In "The Drummer Boy of Shiloh," you have only two, but they are both exceptional. Based on your group discussions, write freely about the character you have chosen. You might consider:
- the character's prominent traits (courage, responsibility, generosity)
- the character's actions (admirable, pathetic, incredible)
- the character's fate (sad, fulfilling)

When you are finished freewriting, look over your notes and go through a process like the one modeled above to limit your subject. Share your limited subject with your writing group and give feedback to one another on whether or not the subject seems appropriately limited. Revise your limited subject accordingly.

2 Developing a Thesis

Every good literary analysis has a thesis at its core. This **thesis,** or main idea, is the reason the writer is writing. Since how people interpret a work of literature can differ widely, your task in a literary analysis is to persuade the audience that your thesis is valid. You must be able to point to evidence in the work that supports your thesis.

Your limited subject is just a step away from your **thesis statement,** which is a statement that explains what you will be trying to show in your essay. To develop your limited subject into a clear thesis statement, express your main idea in a complete sentence. In the following example, the thesis statement makes a definite proposition that was only hinted at in the limited subject.

MODEL: Developing a Thesis

Focused, Limited Subject	How Miyax handles survival
Working Thesis Statement	"Miyax is frightened and desperate and does not have much chance for survival."

To convert your limited subject into a clear thesis statement, you can repeat the technique of asking yourself, "What exactly do I want to say about my subject?" The thesis statement at this stage should be precise enough to guide you through the rest of your planning. However, you should regard it as a working thesis statement only. You can change or adjust it as you continue to develop your essay.

Writing Tip

After you have focused and limited your subject, express it in a complete sentence as a **thesis statement.**

PROJECT PREP Prewriting Thesis Statement

To develop your working thesis statement, write your limited subject in the form of a sentence, which you can change or adjust as needed as you continue work on your character analysis. Share your thesis statement with your writing group and give feedback to one another on its suitability. Also discuss what kinds of evidence will be required to support each writer's thesis statement.

❸ Gathering Evidence

You already have a fairly clear idea of how you feel about the character you have chosen as your subject. On the basis of your personal and literary responses, you have decided such things as whether your character is likable or unlikable, proud or humble, genuine or manipulative, courageous or cowardly. Now, however, you need to put your reactions to a test. You need to gather evidence from the work itself to support your overall impression of the character.

To gather evidence for a character sketch, read the story, looking for clues about the character's personality. For each clue you come across, create an index card to record the information. Include the page number on which the clue can be found, so you can easily return to that part of the story if you need to. Make a brief note to yourself explaining what you think each clue means. You can also use sticky notes or a computer to make your notes.

The clues to a character's personality come in various forms. The following chart summarizes where you might find clues to a character.

Clues to Character Traits

External Traits
- What the character says about himself or herself
- What other characters say about the character
- What the narrator of the story says about the character
- How the character looks (physical description)
- What the character actually does

- **Internal Traits**
- What the character thinks about himself or herself
- What other characters think about the character
- What the narrator thinks or implies about the character

The note cards on the next page show how one writer looked for clues to the internal and external traits of the character Miyax in the excerpt from *Julie of the Wolves* on pages 151–155.

MODEL: Gathering Evidence

Text Portions

"Her hands trembled and her heart-beat quickened, for she was frightened, not so much of the wolves, who were shy and many harpoon-shots away, but because of her desperate predicament. Miyax was lost. She had been lost without food for many sleeps on the North Slope of Alaska. The barren slope stretches for three hundred miles from the Brooks Range to the Arctic Ocean, and for more than eight hundred miles from the Chukchi to the Beaufort Sea. No roads cross it; ponds and lakes freckle its immensity. Winds scream across it, and the view in every direction is exactly the same. Somewhere in this cosmos was Miyax; and the very life in her body, its spark and warmth, depended upon these wolves for survival. And she was not so sure they would help.–page 151.

"She had been watching the wolves for two days, trying to discern which of their sounds and movements expressed goodwill and friendship." –page 152.

"Propped on her elbows with her chin in her fists, she stared at the black wolf, trying to catch his eye. She had chosen him because he was much larger than the others, and because he walked like her father, Kapugen, with his head high

Note Cards

1. Miyax is afraid. In a desperate and life-threatening predicament, she is alone. The description of her exact geographic location explains just how alone she is: "The barren slope stretches for three hundred miles from the Brooks Range to the Arctic Ocean, and for more than eight hundred miles from the Chukchi to the Beaufort Sea. No roads cross it; ponds and lakes freckle its immensity. Winds scream across it, and the view in every direction is exactly the same."—page 151. Miyax is afraid that she may not be able to get the help she needs from the wolves: "...the very life in her body, its spark and warmth, depended upon these wolves for survival. And she was not so sure they would help."—page 151.

2. This passage shows that, despite her situation, Miyax has not lost her wits or panicked. She is very determined and patient. "She had been watching the wolves for two days, trying to discern which of their sounds and movements expressed goodwill and friendship."—page 152. She knows that to survive, she has to identify which wolf is the leader and get his help, as her father once did. She draws on past experience. She is also extremely observant. She chooses the black wolf to concentrate on because he is the largest and because "he walked like her father, Kapugen, with his head high and his chest out."—page 152.

Writing a Character Analysis • Prewriting

and his chest out. The black wolf also possessed wisdom, she had observed. The pack looked to him when the wind carried strange scents or the birds cried nervously. If he was alarmed, they were alarmed. If he was calm, they were calm."
—page 152.

She also chooses him because she observes that "he possessed wisdom"—page 152—and the rest of the wolf pack looks to him for their safety and leadership. The actions she takes, external traits, reflect her inner traits, patient and observant.

PROJECT PREP   Prewriting   Gathering Evidence

Gather evidence that would support your thesis. Use a graphic organizer like the one below to track the details of the evidence you gather. Write your thesis statement at the top of the organizer so you keep it clearly in mind as you gather evidence.

Character Detail	Describe Detail	How Detail Reveals Character
appearance		
thoughts		
belongings		
spoken words		
actions/responses		

284   Writing About Literature

Organizing Your Details

The final step before drafting a character sketch is to organize your supporting details in a logical order. One common approach is to present your supporting evidence in the order in which it appears in the story; this is called **chronological order.** Another good approach is to organize details according to the different character traits you identify in your character. For example, your main idea may be that your character is outwardly conceited but inwardly shy. So you may wish to arrange your details in an order that first presents evidence for conceit and then presents evidence for shyness.

On the other hand, if you give reasons why a character behaves in a certain way, using **cause-and-effect order** or **order of importance** would be a more effective way to organize your details. Order of importance is often thought to be the best way to set up the points that support your thesis. If you are interpreting two works or analyzing two characters in a work, you might want to use an organization associated with **comparison and contrast.** In all cases you need to order your supporting details so that they are arranged in the most effective way possible to support your thesis.

PROJECT PREP *Prewriting* Organizing

1. In your writing group, discuss the organizational strategies explained above to be sure you understand them. Ask questions if you are unclear about anything. Then help each author decide which pattern would be most effective for his or her character analysis.

2. After your discussion, arrange your evidence into categories and your categories into an appropriate order. For example, your categories might be 1) evidence from the beginning of the story; 2) evidence from the middle of the story; and 3) evidence from the end of the story. In that case, you would arrange them in chronological order, from beginning to end. Or maybe your categories are 1) one trait and all the evidence; 2) another trait and all the evidence; 3) a third trait and all the evidence. In that case, you would need to decide the order in which you will present the traits. Another possibility is that your categories might be 1) external traits; and 2) internal traits. Again, you would need to decide which of those to present first.

3. When you have decided on an organizational strategy, make a graphic organizer showing the structure of the body of your composition or create an outline (see pages 344–345).

Writing a Character Analysis

Before you began to gather evidence, you had already formed an overall impression of your character. Now that you have looked the story over carefully in search of clues, has your overall impression changed any? Did you find any details that made you rethink your first impression of your character? If so, rewrite the statement explaining your overall reaction to the character until it takes into account all the evidence you uncovered. The resulting statement will serve as the final main idea of your character analysis. The following examples show how the writer refined her reaction to Miyax in the excerpt from *Julie of the Wolves* after gathering evidence.

Working Thesis Statement	Miyax is frightened and desperate and does not have much chance for survival.
Refined Thesis Statement	Miyax is frightened and desperate, but she does not lose her head. She uses her strong power of observation to take steps for her survival. She has some chance for survival.

The following sample has already been revised and edited, so it is more polished than your first draft will be. Use it, though, as a guide as you write your character analysis.

MODEL: Character Analysis

A Chance for Survival

At the beginning of the excerpt from *Julie of the Wolves* by Jean Craighead George, Miyax appears to be helpless, in a hopeless situation. By the end of the selection, however, Miyax has proven to be extremely resourceful, patient, and determined. She has a chance of survival, and it rests on her own courage and initiative.

Miyax's extreme predicament is presented in the opening paragraphs of the selection. She is lost, "lost without food for many sleeps on the North Slope of Alaska." The author's description of the landscape emphasizes just how alone Miyax is. She writes, "The barren slope stretches for three hundred miles from the Brooks Range to the Arctic Ocean, and for more than eight hundred miles from the Chukchi to the Beaufort Sea. No roads cross it; ponds and lakes freckle

- Title: Identifies focus
- Introduction: Identifies title and author
- Refined main idea
- First Body Paragraph: Analyzes Miyax's traits at beginning of selection

its immensity. Winds scream across it, and the view in every direction is exactly the same." It is not surprising, then, that Miyax is afraid. Her internal state of mind mirrors her external situation. She knows, however, that the wolves can help her. Her father once got help from wolves. Yet she is afraid that she may fail where her father succeeded.

Miyax's efforts to get the wolves to help her show her internal traits, namely, her patience and power of observation. She has been watching the wolves for two days, "trying to discern which of their sounds and movements expressed goodwill and friendship." She singles out the big black wolf to focus on based on careful observation. He is not only the biggest wolf, but he also walks "like her father, Kapugen, with his head high and his chest out. The black wolf also possessed wisdom, she had observed. The pack looked to him when the wind carried strange scents or the birds cried nervously. If he was alarmed, they were alarmed. If he was calm, they were calm." Miyax draws on past experience to help her in this crisis. She recalls how her father got wolves to help him. She remembers her own experiences with animals. She demonstrates courage and patience.

> Second Body Paragraph: Analyzes Miyax's traits in the body of the selection

By the end of the selection, Miyax has been watching and observing the wolf for a long time. She has observed his every move and tried to get him to look at her. Finally, she begins to speak to him. She tells him how she got lost on the tundra, and how there are none of the familiar signs to guide her. She says, "I am lost and the sun will not set for a month. There is no North Star to guide me." She continues, "At home on Nunivak Island where I was born, the plants and birds pointed the way for wanderers. I thought they did so everywhere . . . and so, great black Amaroq, I'm without a compass." She remembers the moment when she realized she was lost. Fear closes in on her again and she closes her eyes.

> Third Body Paragraph: Analyzes Miyax's traits at end of selection

Just when she thinks her efforts will never be rewarded, she opens her eyes to find the wolf finally looking at her. Her efforts have paid off and she has gained the wolf's trust. In a situation where she has no one to turn to but herself, Miyax draws on her own strengths and knowledge. It now appears that she has a chance for survival.

> Conclusion: Reinforces main idea

Writing a Character Analysis • Drafting

You may find the following guidelines helpful as you draft a character analysis.

Guidelines for Drafting a Character Analysis

- Find out whether your readers are familiar with the work you are writing about.
- In your introduction, identify the title and author of the work you are discussing, as well as the character on whom you are focusing.
- Include your thesis statement somewhere in the introduction, revised if needed and worked in as smoothly as possible.
- Develop paragraphs for the body of your character analysis based on the internal and external traits you have identified. Include evidence as supporting details. Use transitions to show how one detail relates to another within paragraphs. Use transitions to move smoothly from one paragraph to another. Use direct quotes from the story if they strengthen your points. Always enclose direct quotes in quotation marks.
- Add a conclusion that provides a strong ending to your character analysis.
- Add a title that makes the focus of your character analysis clear.

Project Prep Drafting Character Analysis

If you have found details that have caused you to rethink your thesis, rewrite your thesis statement until it takes into account all the evidence you uncovered. The resulting statement will serve as the thesis of your character analysis. Save your work. Then, using the guidelines above and the evidence you have assembled and organized, draft your character analysis of a character from "The Drummer Boy of Shiloh" or another work. Based on what you write, add a concluding paragraph that drives home your main point about your character. Save your work for later use.

Writing About Literature

In the Media

Evaluating Performances

When stories are performed, they offer a new way for audiences to interpret them. In fact, both the audience *and* the performer can often understand a work more fully through the art of performance. An audience can respond to both visual and spoken clues that they wouldn't derive from reading. The actor, in turn, can learn from the way a live audience responds to a performance. In the case of a film performance, an actor may learn from movie reviews how popular the movie is. In these ways, a play or movie version can create a new, exciting life for a book.

Many books are adapted for film. For example, three novels in the series *The Chronicles of Narnia* by C.S. Lewis have been made into movies. For many years, Lewis refused to give permission to turn the books into movies. He feared no movie could capture the fantasy elements effectively. In recent years, with the advent of CGI animation, permission was finally granted.

How *do* you evaluate a performance version of a beloved novel or series of novels, such as *The Chronicles of Narnia* or *The Lord of the Rings,* whose words have created indelible images in readers' minds for decades? The following activity will help answer that question.

Media Activity

Rent or check out from your local library one of the novels in *The Chronicles of Narnia* or *The Lord of the Rings* as well as the movie based on it. Use the following questions to help you as you evaluate the film after you watch it.

- Did the film move you?
- Did the film make confusing parts of the book seem clearer?
- Was the film true to the book? Was there anything left out that you think should have been there?
- Were camera angles, lighting, sequencing, and music used effectively? How do they contribute to the overall effect?

Writing a Character Analysis 

The following checklist will help you improve your character analysis. You may also wish to share your work with a peer reader to find out where you could strengthen your character's description. Make as many drafts as you feel necessary to refine your main idea and find the supporting details.

 Evaluation Checklist for Revising

Checking Your Essay
- ✓ Do you have a strong introduction that identifies the author and work you will discuss? (page 273)
- ✓ Does your introduction contain a clear thesis? (pages 281 and 288)
- ✓ In the body of your essay, have you provided ample details from the work to support your thesis? (pages 273 and 282)
- ✓ Did you quote the work to strengthen your points? (pages 273 and 288)
- ✓ Does your conclusion summarize the details in the body of your essay and reinforce your thesis statement? (page 288)
- ✓ Does your whole essay have unity and coherence? (page 288)
- ✓ Did you add a title showing the focus of your essay? (pages 273 and 288)
- ✓ Does your essay meet the requirements for your purpose and audience?

Checking Your Paragraphs
- ✓ Does each paragraph have a topic sentence? (pages 219–220)
- ✓ Is each paragraph unified and coherent? (page 288)

Checking Your Sentences and Words
- ✓ Are your sentences varied and concise? (pages 64–79)
- ✓ Did you use lively, specific language? (pages 42–46 and 56–57)

PROJECT PREP *Revising* **Using a Checklist**

Exchange the draft of your character sketch with a partner. Comment on the strengths and weaknesses of your partner's paper. Consider your partner's comments as you use the **Evaluation Checklist for Revising** to improve your draft. Also take into account any comments you have received from your teacher.

Writing a Character Analysis *Editing*

When you are satisfied with your character analysis, you can begin to polish it for presentation to readers. Since you are writing about a character from another published work, the following information about using titles may be helpful as you edit your work.

SPECIAL TREATMENT OF TITLES

Italicize (or underline in handwritten work) the titles of long works, including books, magazines, newspapers, full-length plays, movies, long poems, operas, symphonies, recordings, paintings, and sculptures.

Example   I took my brother to see <u>Prince Caspian</u> (or *Prince Caspian*).

Use quotation marks to enclose the titles of chapters, articles, stories, one-act plays, short poems, and songs.

Examples   I am writing a poem called "The Phantom School Bus."

I finished reading "The Drummer Boy of Shiloh" by Ray Bradbury.

I can play "Stars and Stripes Forever" on the kazoo.

The Language of Power    *Of* v. *Have*

Power Rule: Use the contraction *'ve* (not *of*) when the correct word is *have*, or use the full word *have*. (See page 790.)

See It in Action   Confusing *of* for *have* is a common mistake because the two words sound alike in speech. Problems arise most often after the words *would, could, might,* and *should*.

Incorrect	We **should of** turned left at the last intersection.
Correct	We **should've** turned left at the last intersection.
Incorrect	James **might of** missed his train.
Correct	James **might have** missed his train.

Remember It   Record this rule and example in the Power Rule section of your Personalized Editing Checklist.

Use It   Check the words *would, could, might,* and *should* to be sure you did not follow any of them with the word *of* instead of *have*.

Using a Six-Trait Rubric — Interpretive Response

Ideas	**4** The thesis statement is clear. Evidence and inferences are solid. The analysis goes beyond mere summary.	**3** The thesis statement is clear. Most evidence and inferences are solid. The analysis goes beyond mere summary.	**2** The thesis statement could be clearer. Some evidence is solid, but there is too much simple summary.	**1** The thesis statement is missing or unclear. There is little supporting evidence, and the ideas rarely go beyond summary.
Organization	**4** The organization is clear with abundant transitions.	**3** A few ideas seem out of place or transitions are missing.	**2** Many ideas seem out of place and transitions are missing.	**1** The organization is unclear and hard to follow.
Voice	**4** The voice sounds natural, engaging, and persuasive.	**3** The voice sounds natural and engaging.	**2** The voice sounds mostly natural but is weak.	**1** The voice sounds mostly unnatural and is weak.
Word Choice	**4** Words are specific and powerful. Language is appropriate.	**3** Words are specific and language is appropriate.	**2** Some words are too general and/or inappropriate.	**1** Most words are overly general and inappropriate for the purpose and audience.
Sentence Fluency	**4** Varied sentences flow smoothly.	**3** Most sentences are varied and flow smoothly.	**2** Some sentences are varied but some are choppy.	**1** Sentences are choppy. Sentence structure is not varied.
Conventions	**4** Punctuation, usage, and spelling are correct. Titles are handled correctly. The Power Rules are all followed.	**3** Punctuation, usage, and spelling are mainly correct and Power Rules are all followed.	**2** Some punctuation, usage, and spelling are incorrect but all Power Rules are followed.	**1** There are many errors and at least one failure to follow a Power Rule.

PROJECT PREP — Editing — Conventions

Reread your paper carefully, looking for errors. Refer to your Personalized Editing Checklist to make sure you are not repeating errors you have made in the past. The rubric above will help you edit your work. You may also want to ask a classmate to exchange papers with you. In the process of editing your own and your peer's papers, use the proofreading marks on page 11 as a quick shorthand. After checking your work in any of the ways suggested here, prepare a final draft in the manuscript form shown on page 31.

Writing a Character Analysis Publishing

You have arrived at the final stage of the writing process. You now want to consider how to share your work with readers. Remember when you begin a writing assignment, one of the first things you do is consider who your audience might be. Now you want to connect with your audience and make sure they get a chance to read what you have written. When you have caught any errors you may have made, prepare a neat final copy of your character analysis to present to readers. Some possible ways of publishing your paper are listed below.

- Publish a class anthology of critical compositions. Decide how to organize, illustrate, bind, and circulate your anthology.
- Hold a reader's roundtable. At this meeting, each participant reads his or her character analysis aloud. The rest of the group responds with questions and varying interpretations of the same character.
- Draw a picture of your character in one of the scenes from the selection. Post both your picture and your character analysis on a bulletin board or Web site.

Before submitting your work for publication, read your work one last time. You may find that there is yet a sentence or two you can refine. How would you edit the following sentence to make it just a bit better?

> Bradbury creates two characters who exchange just a few moments on a starlit night that neither of them will ever forget—nor will we, the readers.

PROJECT PREP Publishing Options

At the beginning of this chapter, you were given the choice of several different publishing formats to use:
- a blog entry
- a review on a bookseller's Web site
- a formal essay
- a review for your school newspaper

Discuss with your writing group what the requirements are for each format and prepare your final copy accordingly.

Writing a Book Report

A **book report** offers a brief summary of the book and an opinion about the quality of the book.

Writing a book report is another way for you to write about literature. If you are writing about a nonfiction book, you will briefly summarize the author's main point in your own words. If you are writing about a fiction book, you will briefly summarize the story in your own words.

As you prepare to draft a book report, think about how you felt while reading the book. Skim the book, jotting down specific details that led to your overall feeling about it. Then use the following guidelines to organize your ideas.

Structure of a Book Report

Introduction
- gives the title and the author's name
- tells the subject of the book
- may give background information about the author
- identifies the time and location of the story
- expresses its writer's opinion of the book

Body
- offers specific reasons and examples from the book to support the writer's opinion
- includes highlights from the book

Conclusion
- restates the writer's opinion in new words
- adds a strong ending

When you write a book report, assume that your readers are not familiar with the book. Include a brief summary of what the book is about, but do not reveal any plot points that your readers will probably rather learn on their own by reading the book. Do not try to retell the whole story, either. You will soon run out of room for your opinion of the book if you give too many details.

Also, watch your writing for unnecessary shifts in tense. If you are telling what happened to a character, use the present tense and stick to it. ("The main character, Mark, *tries* to find his father and *searches* throughout the West.")

Think Critically

Summarizing

Although you should not try to retell the whole story in your book report, you will need to provide a clear summary of what happens in the book. **Summarizing** means selecting the most important information for a short version of the original.

When you summarize, you actually call on other thinking skills as well. Suppose, for example, you were summarizing the fairy tale "Snow White." You would call on your skill of recalling to bring the whole story to mind. Then you would call on the skill of analyzing to remember all the parts of the story. Next you might use your skill of evaluating to decide which points in each part of the story are most important and which could be left out. Finally, you might use the skill of generalizing to tell the main ideas without having to give all the details.

Summary of "Snow White"

"Snow White" is the story of a princess whose evil stepmother, the Queen, is jealous of her beauty. The Queen wants Snow White killed, but the man she hires cannot bring himself to slay the young girl. He leaves her in the forest, where she finds shelter in the home of seven friendly dwarfs. But the Queen finds out in her magic mirror that Snow White is not dead. She puts on a disguise, finds Snow White, and gives her a poisoned apple that causes her to sleep as if dead. Only the kiss of her true love can save her. A handsome prince eventually comes, fights off the forces of evil, and restores Snow White to life with a kiss.

Thinking Practice

Write a brief summary of a fairy tale that you remember from your childhood. Tell only the most important parts of the story, leaving out most of the details.

MODEL: Book Report

Journeys Through Space and Time

A Wrinkle in Time by Madeleine L'Engle is a novel about a young girl's voyages through space and time to find her father. Along the way she also finds appreciation of her true self. The girl, Meg, and her brother, Charles Wallace, are accompanied by their friend, Calvin O'Keefe. They are aided by three magical spirits, Mrs. Whatsit, Mrs. Who, and Mrs. Which. These three loving spirits transport the young people through wrinkles in time, called tesseracts. The suspenseful story, the variety of interesting characters, and the theme of individuality make A Wrinkle in Time a very enjoyable book.

Introduction: Identifies title and author

At the beginning of the book, Meg is a troubled girl. She becomes angry and belligerent in school, and she dislikes her plain appearance and her inability to control her feelings. As the story progresses, she is put to test after test. On the evil planet of Camazotz, where everyone is a carbon copy dominated by a single brain called IT, Meg learns the value of individuality, of just being herself. Later, on a gray planet called Ixchel, she learns the enormous power of love from a sightless, tentacled creature named Aunt Beast. Meg uses her power to love in a daring rescue of Charles Wallace, who is trapped by the evil power of IT on Camazotz.

Body: States an opinion

Body: Provides examples and reasons to support opinion

The interesting characters in the book reinforce the theme of individual differences. Charles Wallace, believed to be dim-witted by some of the neighbors, is actually gifted with special mind-reading powers. Calvin, a popular boy in school, learns that he has been denying an important, different part of himself. The three spirits, Aunt Beast, and a soulful character called the Happy Medium are each unique.

When you finish reading A Wrinkle in Time, you feel glad that people are as different as they are from one another. You also feel that the powers of love and goodness are strong enough to keep IT and other evils in check.

Conclusion: Reinforces opinion in new words

Writing About Literature

Writing Tip

When writing a book report, briefly summarize the plot of the book you are writing about, but avoid retelling the whole story.

Time Out to REFLECT

Use your knowledge of literary analysis and your experience analyzing characters to gauge how your understanding of literature has changed. Date the writing you did for this chapter. Continue to take notes as you read all kinds of literature. Examine how your understanding of literature has deepened. How has this affected the way you read and write about literature? Record your thoughts in your Learning Log.

Writing Lab

Project Corner

CHAPTER 11

Communicate Across Differences
Compare Literary Responses

Pair off with someone in your class who you think might be different from you in some way. Together, review the factors that influence literary response on page 274. Decide which factors you have in common and which are different. Then **discuss your interpretations** of "The Drummer Boy of Shiloh." In what ways are they different? Do you think the differences you identified in your discussion affected your responses? Prepare a summary of your conversation to report to the rest of the class.

Research and Write Historical Fiction

The short story "The Drummer Boy of Shiloh" is Ray Bradbury's fictionalization of a real battle of the American Civil War. **Write your own story based on an actual historical event.** Include two to four characters in a realistic setting. Be sure to keep the characters and dialogue true to the situation or the event. Use your local or school library or the Internet to help you do research.

Get Creative Write a Very Short Story

With a partner, **write a very short story** that, like Bradbury's, has only two characters and a vivid setting. Before you write, discuss the characters fully so that you understand their traits. Also discuss how you can show, not tell, readers about those traits. What can your characters do, say, and think to reveal their traits? Try to keep your story under 400 words. (You can use your computer to count the words easily. Select your text and go to Tools->Word Count.)

In the Workplace
Movie Review

Apply and Assess

1. Your older brother has come up with a great idea to make money: he is starting a newspaper, *The Cucumber Bulletin,* which will be distributed for free. All costs are to be paid by advertisers who are hoping to gain access to the local youth market. Your brother invites you to write the movie reviews, knowing how much time you spend in the theater on weekends. **Write a review** of a movie you have seen recently for *The Cucumber Bulletin.* Tell whether you liked the movie or not, and why. Then summarize the plot. Support your points with descriptions of the characters, setting, and main conflict.

In Academic Areas Character Analysis Essay

2. A national software company has announced an upcoming competition for seventh-grade students. The guidelines state that entrants should write an essay about a character from a book who provides a good role model for students. The essay writers are to describe what makes this character a good role model. One hundred winners get a new home computer, and you really want to win! **Write a draft of your essay** for the contest. Choose a character from literature, and draft a thesis statement that describes this character. Jot down a list of admirable character traits and specific details that reveal those traits.

Timed Writing 🕐 Essay on Literature

3. You volunteer one hour a week as an assistant to a third-grade teacher. It is often your job to read to the third graders, as well as to recommend books for them. Lately, the young students have been asking you questions such as, "If fiction isn't true, why do we have to read it?" When you posed this same question to your seventh-grade teacher, he decided to assign it as the topic of your end-of-year composition. Write the composition for your class assignment. Directly address the question posed by the third-grade students, and explain your feelings about the insights you have gained from fiction. Organize your supporting details, gathering specific examples from literature to back up your points. Consider the elements of plot, character, and setting in the books you choose to answer the question. You have 30 minutes to complete your work.

   Before You Write Consider the following questions: What is the situation? What is the occasion? Who is the audience? What is the purpose?

   After You Write Evaluate your work using the six-trait evaluation rubric on page 292.

Unit 3

Research and Report Writing

Chapter 12 Research: Planning and Gathering Information 302

Research Companion *322*

Chapter 13 Research: Synthesizing, Organizing, and Presenting 340

The driving force behind research of all kinds is a question, or a set of questions. What computer should I get? How do I care for my new pet rabbit? Why did farming develop at about the same time in far distant parts of the world? What lies beneath the surface of everyday objects? Are there any particles smaller than an atom? Researching and writing reports are two ways to satisfy the desire to find answers to your questions.

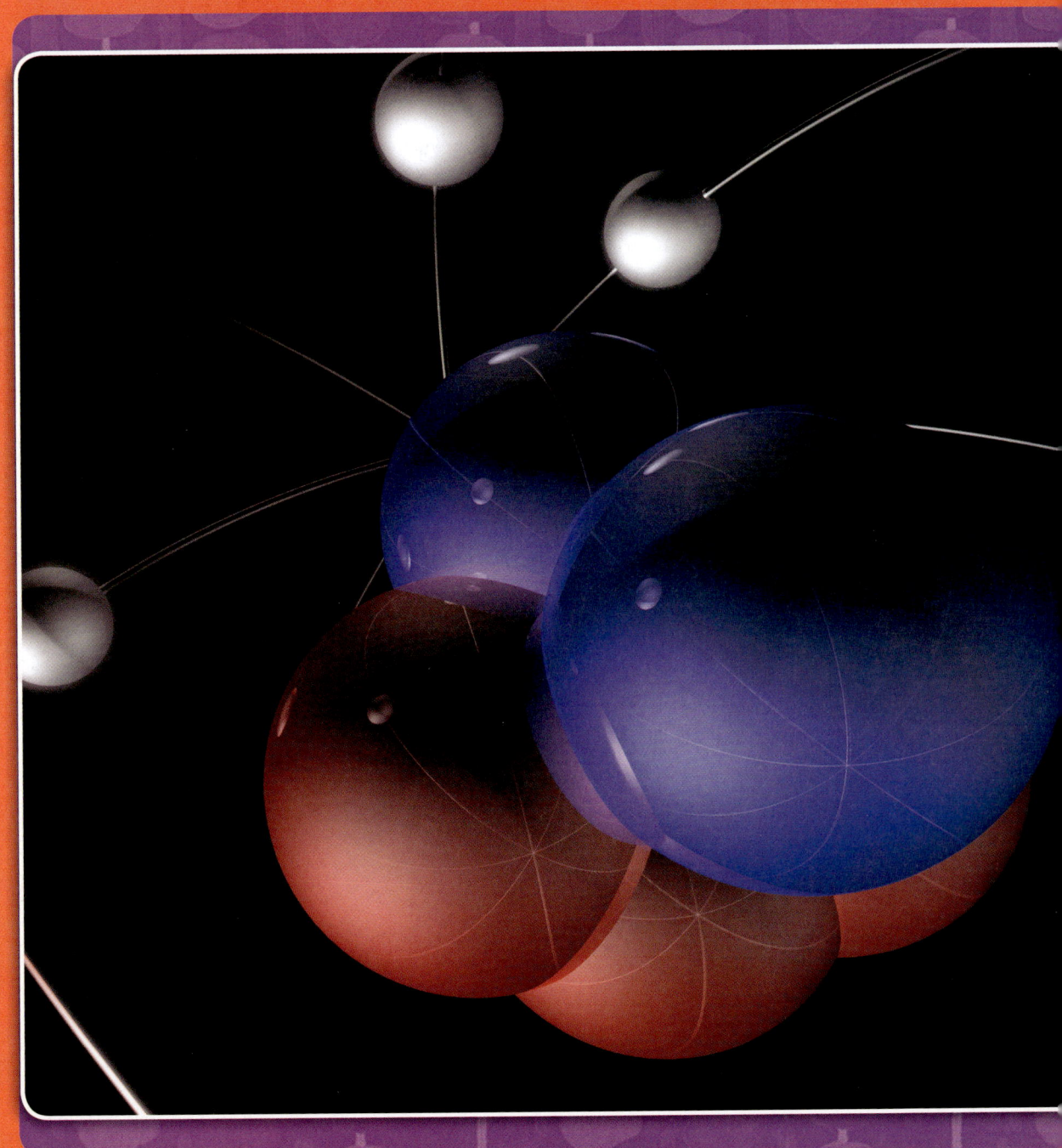

If we knew what it was we were doing, it would not be called research, would it? — Albert Einstein

CHAPTER 12

Research: Planning and Gathering Information

A research report is a composition based on information from books, magazines, the Internet, and other sources.

Research reports include collections of facts—information gathered under one roof. However, the roof is only as strong as the structure beneath it, and a research report must be built on the writer's own clear ideas. In other words, a report is not just a collection of facts for the sake of collecting facts. Instead, the facts in a research report are presented to back up a writer's thesis. You can find research reports everywhere you turn.

- **A middle-school student creates a page** for the school Web site on the history of soccer at her school.
- **A newspaper reporter writes a story** about the work of a local food bank.
- **A famous chef updates his Web site** with historical information about chocolate.
- **A local historian gives a presentation** about Abraham Lincoln's visit to your city.
- **A travel writer posts information on her blog** about the best amusement parks in the United States.
- **A journalist writes a magazine article** that suggests ways families can help fight global warming.

Writing Project — Research Report

Don't Let Me Be Misunderstood Write a research report presenting the facts about a misunderstood person, place, animal, thing, or event.

Think Through Writing Think of something that you think is misunderstood and needs to be explained truthfully. It could be a person, such as a famous person who is often criticized unfairly. It could be a whole group of people, such as a sports team considered by some to be cheaters yet you believe plays fairly, or an ethnic group that behaves differently from the ways it is stereotyped.

It could be an animal, such as the blue jay, which is believed by many people to be a "bad" bird. It could be an activity, such as synchronized swimming, which is believed by many not to be a real sport. Write about possible topics you could research so you could then overturn myths by explaining the facts.

Talk About It In your writing group, discuss the topics you have noted. What sorts of interests did you identify? In your opinion, which topics would be interesting to pursue through research, and why? Which topics would have enough written about them to serve as a good research subject? Which topics might be trimmed from the list for any reason?

Read About It In the following selection from the Web site of an environmental organization, myths about the Endangered Species Act are categorically rejected and facts are put forward. Think about your topics and which you might want to write about as you read through this report.

MODEL: Research Report

Myths and Facts About the Endangered Species Act

Myth: The Endangered Species Act doesn't work.

Fact: The Endangered Species Act is filled with success stories of species that have been recovered or are on their way to recovery. The creation of the Act has stopped many species from becoming extinct such as the bald eagle, brown pelican, Aleutian Canada goose, peregrine falcon, and Peninsular bighorn sheep and led to the restoration of animals such as the masked bobwhite quail and gray wolf to the wild.

Myth: The Endangered Species Act does not recover species; very few species have been taken off the list.

Fact: Many species such as the brown pelican, Aleutian Canada goose, and peregrine falcon have recovered. Others, such as the bald eagle, have improved to the point that they have been moved from the endangered to the threatened list. Still more plants and animals, such as the Peninsular bighorn sheep, have seen dramatic increases in their number since they were listed and are on the road to recovery.

Myth: Extinction is part of the natural order.

Fact: The current extinction rate is vastly accelerated mostly because of human development; the rate is

The format of this report is not the traditional written composition. Instead, the report is presented in a pattern of myth v. fact and uses "chunked" sections of text suitable for a Web site. Nonetheless, it has a clear thesis statement, which is highlighted.

Abundant examples and facts are offered in support of the thesis statement.

Project and Reading

estimated to be around 1,000 times higher than what would occur without human interference.

Myth: There is too much land designated for Critical Habitat[1] that is not needed for species survival.

Fact: Critical habitat is an important tool in efforts to recover listed species. Analysis of U.S. Fish and Wildlife Service data shows that species with critical habitat designated are twice as likely to be increasing in number than species without designated critical habitat. Less than 2% of the nation's total land area is designated as critical habitat and much of that is on existing protected public lands such as national parks, forests, and wildlife refuges.

> The report refers to data collected by a reliable and unbiased agency, the U.S. Fish and Wildlife Service.

Myth: The Endangered Species Act places animal needs before human needs.

Fact: One of the goals of the Act is to maintain healthy lands and waters that are essential to human health and commerce. Healthy ecosystems are very beneficial. They help keep the air clean and take pollutants out of the water by way of water filtration. They also help reduce land erosion and provide beautiful places for tourists to visit and preserve wilderness for future generations. Many listed species, such as wild salmon, also have economic and cultural benefits for people.

Myth: The Endangered Species Act is harmful to development.[2]

Fact: The Act has protected endangered species without impeding development. Less than 1% of all development projects in the United States are reviewed for harms they might do to endangered species. According to the National Association of Homebuilders, more than two million new homes have been built in the United States in the second quarter of 2005 alone.

> This reference is to another respected source of information, one that the reader might even conclude would have an economic advantage without the Act.

Myth: The Endangered Species Act only hurts the economy and does not bring any economic benefits.

---

1 **critical habitat:** specific areas of land set aside for conservation
2 **development:** turning noncommercial land into commercial land through building

Fact: One of the main goals of the Act is to create healthy ecosystems that provide many economic benefits from tourism and recreation activities. During 2001 alone 39% of the population participated in fish and wildlife recreational activities and spent $110 billion dollars, which is equal to 1.1% of the nation's Gross Domestic Product, on these activities.[3]

Myth: Agency scientists use "junk" science when making decisions.

Fact: The Endangered Species Act requires that agency biologists use the best scientific information and methods available. Additional agency policies set standards for the quality of information that can be used in decision making and subject agency work to peer review.

> As an article on a Web site, this report does not provide a conclusion. Instead, it saves one of the most important points—the reliability of the science behind the Act—for the end.

[3] "2001 National Survey of Fishing, Hunting, and Wildlife-Associated Recreation (National Overview)." May 2001. U.S. Fish and Wildlife Service.

Respond in Writing Respond to this debunking of myths surrounding the Endangered Species Act. How might you apply what you have learned here to your own research into the truth about a misunderstood person, place, thing, animal, or event?

Develop a Topic Evaluation Worksheet Work with your classmates to develop ideas that will help you research a misunderstood person, place, thing, animal, or event and explain why it is different from what many people think.

Small Groups: In your writing group, use the following graphic organizer to help you identify a good topic for your research.

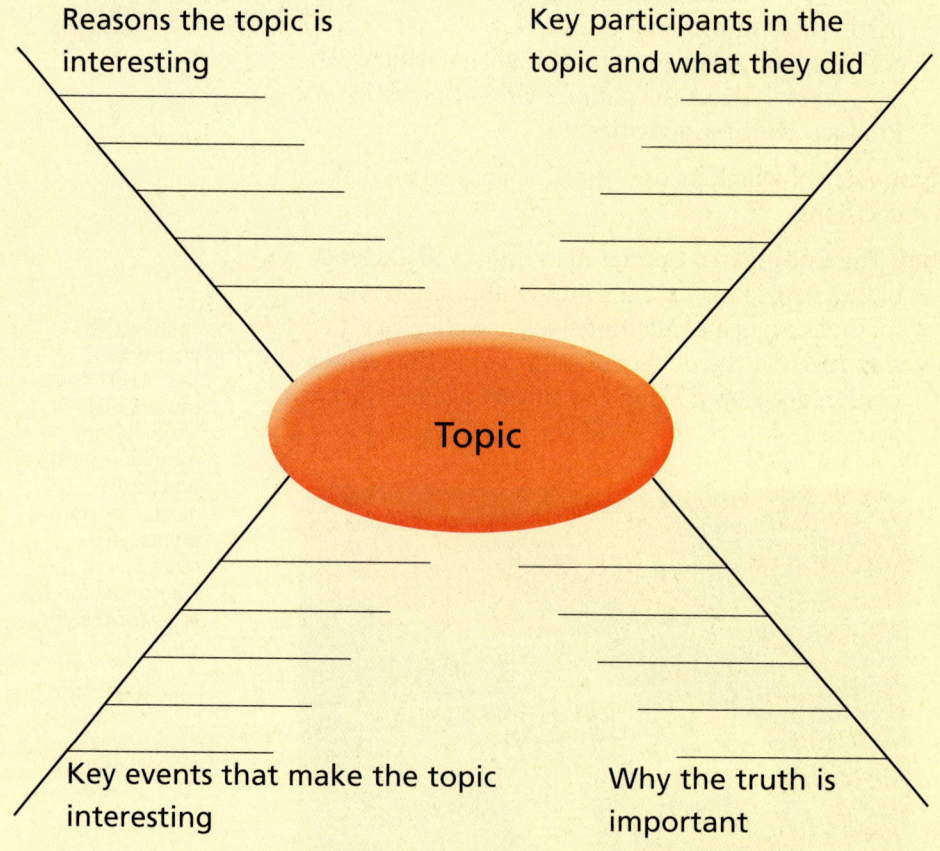

Whole Class: Make a master chart of all of the topics generated by the small groups, and discuss which topics would make good research subjects and what sorts of information would be good to include in a research report.

Write About It You will next write a research report that exposes the facts about a misunderstood person, place, animal, thing, or event. Your writing may take any of the following possible topics, audiences, and forms.

Possible Topics and Examples	Possible Audiences	Possible Forms
• an animal such as a pit bull, which is believed by many to be dangerous and aggressive yet which can make a good pet in some cases • a group of people such as rappers, who are believed by many to be toughs yet who include many nonviolent and respectable citizens • a single person such as a coach, who is assumed to be abusive toward players yet whose players respect him or her • an activity such as dancing, which some believe is frivolous yet which involves athleticism, practice, and dedication	• politicians who make laws • people who criticize the topic of your report • people who are unfamiliar with the topic of your report • your classmates	• a written report • a multimedia presentation • an oral report • an investigative newspaper report

CHAPTER 12

Project and Reading 307

Writing a Research Report

In some ways writing a research report is like working on a puzzle. The first step in solving it is finding pieces of information from various print and electronic sources. The second step is fitting those pieces together into an organized whole. To help you keep track of all the pieces of information, gather the supplies you will need. If you will be working by hand, you will need a folder with pockets, index cards, paper clips, and rubber bands. If you are working on a computer, you will need a good system for naming files and perhaps a flash drive on which to store your work.

❶ Structure of a Report

The three main parts of a report are the introduction, the body, and the conclusion. In addition, a report has a title and a page that lists your sources of information. Each part of the report has a special purpose.

STRUCTURE OF A REPORT

Title	Suggests the subject of the report
Introduction	Captures the reader's attention
	Provides any background information that the reader may need to know
	Contains a sentence expressing the main idea of the report
Body	Supports the main idea stated in the introduction
	Follows the order of your outline
	Includes specific information from your sources
Conclusion	Brings the report to a close
	Summarizes the main idea
	Includes a comment that shows the importance of your subject
Sources Page	Lists your sources of information
	Appears at the end of the report

PROJECT PREP Analyzing Report Structure

With your writing group, re-read the opening report on the Endangered Species Act. How would you describe its structure? Does it have all the elements shown in the chart above? If it differs in any way, how might you explain the difference? What formatting techniques does the report use to help readers follow? Discuss these questions and share your answers with the rest of the class.

 Choosing and Limiting a Subject

Compare the following subjects. Only those that require research are suitable for a report.

PERSONAL EXPERIENCE	RESEARCH
how to practice the piano	the history of the piano
my best Thanksgiving	the first Thanksgiving
why I like sports	televising a sports event
my experience during an earthquake	the San Francisco earthquake of 1989

There are many ways to find ideas for subjects for research reports. **Brainstorming** about things that interest you or things you've always wondered about is one good way. **Talking with your classmates, a teacher, or a librarian** might also give you possible subjects. (See Chapter 1, pages 13–17 for more strategies for finding a subject.)

Once you have several ideas, use the following strategies to help you choose a subject.

Strategies for Choosing a Subject

- Choose a subject you would like to know more about.
- Choose a subject your reader might like to know more about.
- Choose a subject that can be covered adequately in a short report.
- Choose a subject that you can research in the library or on the Internet.

After you have decided on a major research topic or general subject that requires research, the next step is to limit it. Your subject should be limited enough to allow you to cover it completely in a short report. The chart below shows ways to limit a subject.

	WAYS TO LIMIT A SUBJECT	
Divide the general subject into its smaller parts.	Subject	televising a sports event
	Parts	setting up the camera crew
		selling commercials
		choosing announcers
Limit the subject to a certain time or place.	Subject	the history of the piano
	Time	pianos in Mozart's time
	Place	pianos made in Japan

Writing a Research Report • Planning

● **Practice Your Skills**

Limiting a Subject

For each general subject, write two limited subjects that would be suitable for a short report.

General Subject   whales

Limited Subjects   how whales breathe
                        training whales to perform

1. city life
2. Native Americans
3. games
4. television shows
5. football
6. zoos
7. computers
8. driving

PROJECT PREP *Prewriting* *Choosing a Subject*

In your writing group, consider the topics you have identified as possible subjects for research reports. Discuss which would have appropriate information available through print and media sources. Based on this discussion, decide which one interests you most, which one your readers will find most interesting, and which one is likely to have the most information available. Limit your topic so that you can adequately cover it in a report.

③ Developing Research Questions

After you have limited your subject, decide what you already know about it. Then pose questions you still need to answer in order to complete your report. These questions will serve as a research plan for gathering more information. By summarizing your questions into one major research question, you can focus your efforts and thoughts. The chart below shows how this questioning process works.

Suppose you decide to write a report on protecting the bald eagle. You might ask the following questions. They will lead you to your major research question, the question that will guide your research and writing. The **major research question** is the broad question you seek to answer. The other questions address only part of the topic.

FORMULATING A MAJOR RESEARCH QUESTION	
Limited Subject	protecting bald eagles
Focus Questions	**Possible Answers**
What do I already know about protecting bald eagles?	I saw a documentary about how they became endangered through pesticides.
What more do I want to find out?	What has been done to protect bald eagles? How many bald eagles are left? Are there laws that protect bald eagles? How did people try to help the bald eagles?
Major Research Question	What has been done to protect bald eagles?

PROJECT PREP — Prewriting — Formulating a Major Research Question

1. With your topic selected, generate with your writing group a list of facts you already know about your subject and a list of questions you would like to answer through your research. Help one another ask questions that are appropriate to the topic, that may be answered through research, and that are limited enough so they can be answered without writing a book.

2. When you have exhausted the questions, discuss each writer's list and help each writer come up with a major research question that encompasses all the other questions. Write your major research question clearly, since that is what will guide your research. Brainstorm ways you will be able to locate information that will help you answer your question and, in a short paragraph, sketch out a rough research plan.

Writing a Research Report • Planning

Writing a Research Report — Gathering Information

❶ Finding Sources

With your questions in mind you can write a plan for answering them. The following strategies will help you find the answers by gathering information from a wide variety of sources.

Strategies for Gathering Information

- Begin by checking an encyclopedia in print or online. This will give you an overview of your subject. It may also contain a list of books and other references with more information.
- Use the library catalog to find more books on your subject.
- Check your library's online databases or a news index such as *Facts on File* for magazine and newspaper articles.
- Look on the Internet using a search engine to find Web sites related to your subject.
- Make a source card for each of your sources. Use a 3-by-5-inch note card to record the necessary information. For each source, record the proper information in the proper format.

Search Tip

When you are searching the Web, start with sites that have been reviewed by librarians. At the American Library Association's Web page *Great Web Sites for Kids* <http://www.ala.org/greatsites> you can search by subject or keywords. Results show which sites are best for middle school students.

The examples that follow show how to prepare source cards so they contain all the needed information. If you cannot find all the information for a source, include the information you have.

Encyclopedia

> James W. Grier, "Eagle," World Book Encyclopedia, 2009 ed.

Book

> The Bald Eagle by Cheryl L. DeFries, Berkeley Heights, NJ: Enslow, 2003, J598.943 DEF

312 Research: Planning and Gathering Information

Magazine

"Endangered!" by Sean Price, <u>National Geographic Kids</u>, Dec. 2005, p. 16. MAS Ultra - School Edition, EBSCO, library database, 2 Mar. 2009.

Web

"Eagle Facts/Bald Eagle: The U.S.A.'s National Symbol." American Eagle Foundation, 06 December 2007. 2 Mar 2009 <http://www.eagles.org/moreabout.html>

(The last update to this Web page was December 6, 2007. The material was accessed on March 2, 2009.)

● **Practice Your Skills**

Using Source Cards

Use the library or media center to find three sources for each subject. At least one source should be a magazine. Use source cards, like the ones below, to record your findings.

1. formations on Mars

"Mars Express Probes Red Planet's Unusual Deposits" <u>NASA</u>, 1 Nov. 2007. 3 April 2009 <http://www.nasa.gov/mission_pages/mars/news/marsis-20071101.html>

"Mars' dynamic, icy past," by Daniel Pendick, <u>Astronomy</u>, Sep. 2008, Vol 36 Issue 9, p. 18. <u>MAS Ultra - School Edition</u>. EBSCO, library database. 2 April 2009

2. police dogs
3. creating Web pages

PROJECT PREP *Prewriting* **Gathering Information**

Use the **Strategies for Gathering Information** on page 312 to find the information you need for your subject. Your sources should include at least one article from a magazine and one from an encyclopedia. Check your source cards to be sure you have accurately recorded the necessary information. The call number or Internet address is especially important since it will help you find your source again quickly.

In the Media

Documentary

Documentaries use images, interviews, and narration to create a powerful report. Their subjects may range from coal miners to cartoonists. Documentaries can make the public more aware of a social condition. One example would be a film on terrible working conditions in another country. Such a documentary might cause people to write to government leaders, who in turn might appeal to the leaders of that country to make changes.

Media Activity

Check your school library or media center for a documentary to watch. As you are watching, think about how a visual report is different from a written one. As you watch, take notes on the way the director uses the camera, lighting, and music. How do these affect the overall impact of the show? How well does the script convey information? Are there scenes that interrupt the flow of the show? Discuss your findings with your classmates.

Next, work with several classmates to think of a topic that you think is important. There may be an issue at school or in your neighborhood that concerns or interests you. Prepare an outline for a documentary about the topic. Use the following guidelines as you work.

Guidelines for Outlining a Short Documentary

- Brainstorm with your partners about what should be included in your documentary. Identify people you would interview and live-action or background footage you would shoot.
- Use note cards to organize your ideas. Use the guidelines for preparing an outline on pages 344–345.
- Be critical. What do you need to put your concept on video? Music? Narration? Titles? Add these elements to your outline.

Now share your outline with your class and ask for feedback. When you are satisfied with your plan, work with your team to create the documentary. For more information on making a video, see *Electronic Publishing,* pages 456–461.

Research: Planning and Gathering Information

❷ Evaluating Sources

As you begin the research process, keep in mind that not all sources of information you discover will be equally useful to you. Before using a source, you need to evaluate it critically with some basic guidelines in mind. Regardless of your specific topic, all of your sources should be relevant, reliable, up-to-date, and unbiased.

EVALUATING PRINT SOURCES

Just because a certain print source is in your library catalog or database doesn't mean that it's appropriate for your project. You still need to decide if it's relevant to your subject and whether the information is up-to-date and appropriate to the kind of report you are writing. The following guidelines can help you evaluate print sources.

Guidelines for Evaluating Print Sources

- **Who's the authority?**
  Find out the author's background. A library catalog entry or online book reviews may give information about the education or experience that makes the author an expert. Magazine or newspaper articles often provide a brief summary of their author's credentials. Get recommendations from a teacher, librarian, or someone else who is knowledgeable about the topic.

- **Who's behind it?**
  See if the author is associated with a particular organization and whether that organization might be biased. Find out who published the book. If the publisher is unfamiliar, do an online search to find out more about it. A librarian can lead you to the best sources for particular types of information.

- **What's right for you?**
  Make sure the book or article is relevant to your limited subject. Some sources may be too general or too specific for what you are trying to accomplish. They may be written at a level that is either too simple or too complex for a student researcher.

- **Look inside.**
  Check the publication date to make sure the information is current. Read the book jacket or an inside page to find out about the author's background. Look at the table of contents and index to see whether your particular topic is covered in appropriate detail. Skim relevant sections to see if sources are given to back up the facts presented. Does the author support his or her opinions with solid evidence?

EVALUATING ONLINE SOURCES

When you check out a book from the library, a librarian or a committee of educators has already evaluated the book to make sure it's a reliable source of information. But remember, no one owns or regulates the Internet. Just because you read something online doesn't mean it's true. How can you tell the difference? Here are a few guidelines on how to evaluate an online source.

Writing a Research Report • Gathering Information   **315**

Guidelines for Evaluating Online Sources

- **Play the name game.**
  First, find out who publishes the site. Does the URL end in ".com" (which means it's a commercial company)? If so, is it a large, reputable company, or one you've never heard of that might just be trying to sell you something? An educational site in which the URL ends in ".edu," such as a college or university, might be a more reliable choice. A site sponsored by a well-known organization with a URL that ends in ".org," such as the American Red Cross <http://www.redcross.org>, would also probably be a credible source.

- **Scope it out.**
  Click around the site and get a feel for what it's like. Is the design clean and appealing? Is it easy to get around the site and find information? Are the sections clearly labeled? Does the site accept advertising? If you think the site seems disjointed or disorganized, or you just have a negative opinion of it, listen to your instincts and move on to another one.

- **Says who?**
  Suppose you find an article on the Web that seems chock-full of great information. The next question you need to ask yourself is, "Who is the author? Is the person an acknowledged expert on the subject?" If you don't recognize the author's name, you can do a search on the Web, using the author's name as the keyword to get more information about him or her. In some cases, an article won't list any author at all. If you don't find an author's name, be skeptical. A credible site clearly identifies its authors and usually lists the person's professional background and credentials.

- **Check point of view.**
  Might the Web site have a bias, or particular slant, on a topic? For example, the article on the Endangered Species Act is from the Sierra Club Web site. The Sierra Club is known for its environmental activism.

- **Is this old news?**
  If you are doing research on the pyramids, it's probably all right if the information wasn't posted yesterday. But if you're looking for information in quickly changing fields, such as science and politics, be sure to check the publication date before you accept the data as true.

- **Original language?**
  Is the Web site you are viewing in its original language or might it be a translation from another language? Translations can often misrepresent the original. Use English-language Web sites or sites in another language you know well enough to read in the original.

- **Ask around.**
  Reliable Web sites frequently provide e-mail addresses or links to authors and organizations connected to the content on the site. Send off a quick e-mail to a few of these sources, tell them what you are writing, and ask them: "Is this material accurate?"

Perhaps the best way to find out if the information on any Web site or the information in any article (signed or unsigned) is accurate is to check it against another source—and the best source is your local library or media center.

You can learn more about using the Internet for research on pages 337–339.

Creating a chart like the one below can help you compare the reliability of your sources.

Evaluation Chart for Research Sources						
Source Title	Reputable Name?	Well designed?	Authors named?	Bias?	Date published?	Original language?
1						
2						
3						

PROJECT PREP *Prewriting* *Evaluating Sources*

In your writing group or with a research partner, discuss the sources you have found to locate verifiable facts for your research. For each writer, make a source evaluation chart like the one above. When you have completed such a chart for each writer, help one another decide which sources are trustworthy and which are not, and focus your research using the reliable sources.

Writing a Research Report • Gathering Information

Writing a Research Report — Taking Notes

Before you begin taking notes, skim your sources, looking for information that will answer your research questions. In light of the information you are previewing, be prepared to narrow or broaden your major research question as you learn more about your subject. For example, if you are finding only a small amount of information on your subject, broaden your question so that you can include information from a wider field.

When you find the part of the source that answers your questions, read it carefully, looking for the main ideas. Then write those ideas on your card in your own words. Read the following excerpt from *World Book Encyclopedia* on the subject of bald eagles. The sample note card that follows shows how the information can be summarized on an index card.

> United States federal law has protected the species since 1940 in the lower 48 states and since 1959 in Alaska. But the continued shooting and trapping of birds, as well as accidental collisions with vehicles, caused further population declines. The number of bald eagles also dropped because of the pollution of lakes and rivers with pesticides, especially DDT, and industrial wastes. Some of these pollutants built up in the bodies of fish that the eagles ate. In most cases the pollutants did not kill the birds, but they interfered with the birds' ability to reproduce. By the mid-1970s, there were only about 2,000 to 3,000 bald eagles making nests in the lower 48 states.

Sample Note Card

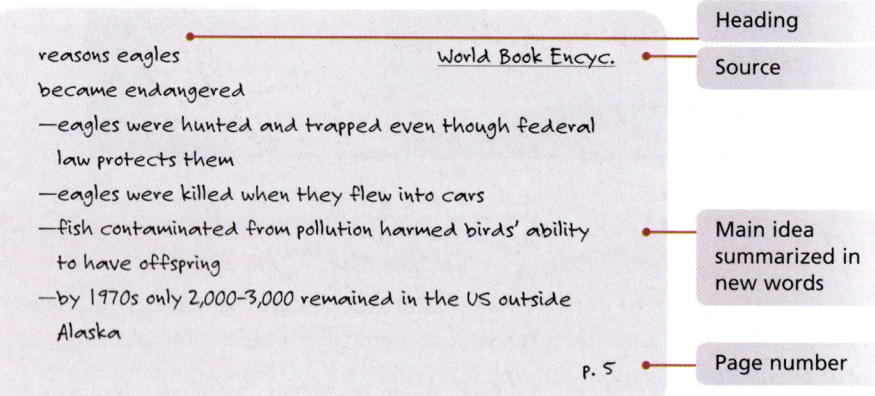

You can learn about taking notes from visuals on pages 333 and 334.

To help you later when you sort your notes, be sure to prepare your card according to the following guidelines.

Taking Notes

- Write the title of your source in the upper right-hand corner of your note card.
- Write a heading in the upper left-hand corner of your card to identify the part of the subject being discussed.
- Begin a new card whenever you start taking notes on a different part of your subject.
- Summarize main points in your own words.
- Record the page number from which your information is taken.
- Clip together all cards from the same source. Later you will sort them into categories.

PARAPHRASE, DON'T PLAGIARIZE

If your sources are good, their authors will have taken time to think and write carefully about the subject. In fact, you are likely to come across a word, phrase, or short passage that is so well worded you would like to use it yourself. In those cases, write what you would like to use on your note card, and place quotation marks around it to remind you the words belong to someone else. Presenting someone else's words as your own is **plagiarism,** a serious and unlawful action. When you are drafting your report, you can include the quoted material as long as you place it in quotation marks and credit the source. (See pages 349–350 and 353–355.) Otherwise, rewrite or paraphrase the material that interests you. When you **paraphrase,** you put something in your own words.

Original	The female was full-grown, and the span of her broad wings was greater than any man's height.—N. Scott Momaday
Quoted	The wing-span of a grown female eagle can be "greater than any man's height."
Paraphrased	The wing-span of a grown female eagle can be longer than 6 feet.

PROJECT PREP *Prewriting* Taking Notes

Use your reliable sources to continue to locate information that will help you answer your research questions, taking notes when you find information that you can use in your report. Use the above procedures for using note cards, computer technology, and other tools for conducting your research.

Writing Lab

Project Corner

Think Critically Take Stock

With your writing group, **evaluate your progress** so far in working on your research project. You may want to consider such questions as:

- Is my topic genuinely interesting to me?
- Is my major research question open enough to allow room for me to adapt my main idea according to the information I find in my research?
- Have I identified a variety of reliable sources?
- Do my notes contain enough information so that I do not need to find the source and page number again when I am drafting?

If you answer "no" to any of these questions, rethink your topic and adjust your research accordingly.

Chart It From Visual to Print

Interpret the chart on this page by writing a paragraph explaining the percentages of threatened and endangered animals by type.

Speak and Listen Conduct an Interview

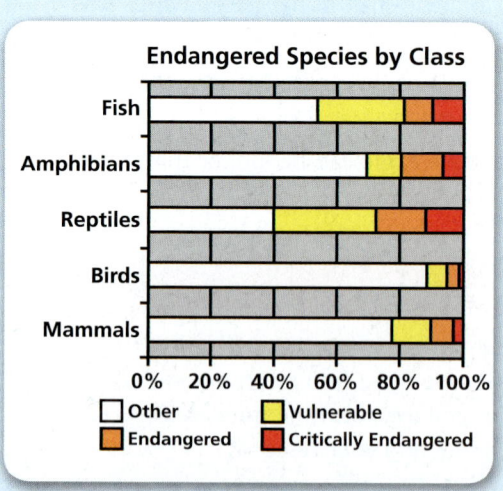

Not all sources for reports are found in the library or online. People themselves are often good sources, and you can find out what they know related to your subject by conducting an interview. Think of a person you know who might be able to offer you helpful information about your topic, or direct you to someone else who can. **Set up and conduct an interview to gain information.** Take notes (or, with your interviewee's permission, record the interview) so you will remember what was said.

Apply and Assess

In Everyday Life
A Persuasive Note

1. For your birthday your parents will let you attend a concert, but only if you bring your little brother and you let him choose the musical group that you are going to see. Unfortunately your brother has his heart set on seeing his favorite band, the Lip Synch Boys. **Write a note** to your brother explaining why your favorite band is the better choice. Research your favorite band on the Web and collect information that will persuade your little brother.

For Oral Communication
Notes for a Speech

2. Your class has been assigned the creation of an exhibit about foods of South America for a culture fair at your school. Your teacher asks you to head the team that will research information for the exhibit. **Prepare notes for a short speech** to the rest of your team about how you plan to conduct the research. Formulate a major research question to address your topic. Outline the types of sources you plan to consult. Explain why it's best to use sources from both the library or media center and the Internet.

Timed Writing
Memo to the Mayor

3. You are an intern working for Mayor Stanton. She wants the city to spend $8 million on a new stadium to encourage a new professional football team, the Turf Monsters, to move to the city. She needs information on the cost of the stadium versus the revenues it will create.

   Write a memo to the mayor outlining how you plan to research the experiences of other cities that have built new sports stadiums. Develop a major research question to focus your search for information. Plan to include interviews with some of the city's "citizens" (your classmates) and information from a variety of other sources that address the topic of the costs and benefits of new stadiums. You have 25 minutes to complete your memo. (For help budgeting time, see pages 398–399.)

   Before You Write Consider the following questions: What is the subject? What is the occasion? Who is the audience? What is the purpose?

   After You Write Evaluate your work by reviewing your plan and checking that your sources are reliable as outlined on pages 315–317.

Research Companion

When you walk into a library or media center, you are entering a place where centuries of knowledge are gathered under one roof. These places are storehouses of information and ideas—invaluable resources for any writer. Libraries answer your questions and help you figure out what questions to ask next. In the past, when people thought about the library, they mostly thought of it as a place to find books. Today, however, most libraries operate as media centers where, in addition to books, you can find magazines, newspapers, and a wide range of reference materials in print, online, or in electronic formats.

Library Arrangement

A library arranges books on the shelves so you can find them easily. Books of fiction are organized in alphabetical order. Nonfiction books are arranged by numbers and filed in a separate section.

FICTION

Books of **fiction** include novels and stories that are partly or totally imaginary. These books are put on the shelves in alphabetical order by the author's last name. The following rules will help you find books of fiction.

Guidelines for Finding Fiction

- Two-part names are alphabetized by the first part of the name.
  DaRosa   **Mac**Mahon   **O'**Leary   **Van** Dam
- Names beginning with *Mc* or *St.* are alphabetized as if they began with *Mac* or *Saint*.
- Books by the same author are alphabetized by title, skipping *a, an* and *the* at the beginning.

Research: Planning and Gathering Information

- **Develop Research Skills**

  Arranging Fiction

  Write this list of novels in the order that they should be placed on the shelves.

  M. C. Higgins, the Great, Virginia Hamilton

  Across Five Aprils, Irene Hunt

  Little Women, Louisa May Alcott

  Dr. Doom: Superstar, T. Ernesto Bethancourt

  Tina Gogo, Judie Angell

  Arilla Sun Down, Virginia Hamilton

  The Wolves of Willoughby Chase, Joan Aiken

  The Empire Strikes Back, Donald F. Glut

  The Wonderful Wizard of Oz, L. Frank Baum

  The Blind Colt, Glen Rounds

- **Develop Research Skills**

  Solving Shelving Problems

  Write the following list of fiction authors in the order that their books would appear on the shelves.

Mary O'Hara	Madeleine L'Engle
J. K. Rowling	Robert O'Brien
Scott O'Dell	Helen MacInnis
Patricia A. McKillip	Scott O'Neill
Jean Van Leeuwen	Betty MacDonald
Walter Dean Meyers	Virginia Hamilton
Lawrence Yep	Gary Soto

NONFICTION

Nonfiction books contain factual information and document events. Most libraries use the Dewey decimal system to arrange nonfiction books on the shelves. In this system each book is assigned a call number according to its subject.

A **call number** is a number and letter code used to identify a book by subject and category.

There are ten general categories in the Dewey decimal system. This system makes it easy to find a book about a certain subject. For example, a subject that falls under science—such as astronomy—is assigned a number between 500 and 599. A book about robots

Research Companion

would be listed under technology. It would be assigned a number between 600 and 699. This number is written on the **spine**—the part of the book that faces you when it is on the shelf. The books are then arranged on the shelves in numerical order.

DEWEY DECIMAL SYSTEM	
000–099	General Works (reference books)
100–199	Philosophy
200–299	Religion
300–399	Social Science (law, education, economics)
400–499	Language
500–599	Science (mathematics, biology, chemistry)
600–699	Technology (medicine, inventions)
700–799	Fine Arts (painting, music, theater)
800–899	Literature
900–999	History (biography, geography, travel)

BIOGRAPHIES AND AUTOBIOGRAPHIES

Biographies and autobiographies are usually kept in a separate section. Most libraries label each book with a *B* for biography or with the Dewey decimal number 920. Biographies and autobiographies are arranged in alphabetical order by the last name of the subject, not the author.

Develop Research Skills

Understanding the Dewey Decimal System

For each of the following nonfiction books, write the range of numbers and the category each falls under in the Dewey decimal system. Use the chart on page 324.

Example The History of Rock 'n' Roll
Answer 700–799 Fine Arts

1. *Laws, Courts, and Lawyers*
2. *The Life of John F. Kennedy*
3. *The Philosophy of Plato*
4. *The Invention of Ordinary Things*
5. *Religions of the World*
6. *Math and Logic Games*
7. *Heart Transplants*
8. *Hit Broadway Plays*
9. *You Can Speak French*
10. *Famous American Poets*

Develop Research Skills

Solving Shelving Problems

Write the following Dewey decimal numbers and book titles in the order that the books would appear on the shelves. Remember that nonfiction books are arranged in numerical order, not in alphabetical order.

590.7 *A Zoo for All Seasons*
581.4 *The Life of a Forest*
598.2 *Birds of the Ocean*
594.5 *Kingdom of the Octopus*
582.3 *What's in the Names of Flowers?*
591.9 *Animals of the Antarctic*
595.7 *Familiar Insects of America*
586   *Plants Without Leaves*
597.3 *The Natural History of Sharks*
593.9 *The Living Wilderness*

THE LIBRARY CATALOG

In order to find a book on the shelves of the library, you need to know the book's call number. You can find the call number of a book in the catalog of the library or media center. The online catalog is a computerized catalog that provides information on all the materials available in a library or media center. You use it by entering the title, author, or subject you are seeking. The computer will then display the results of your search. Some online catalogs can also tell if the material you are seeking is held by the library or media center you are using, whether it is currently available to check out, and whether other libraries have it.

ONLINE CATALOG RECORD	
The backyard astronomer's guide	Dickinson, Terence.
Personal Author:	Dickinson, Terence.
Title:	The backyard astronomer's guide/Terence Dickinson & Alan Dyer.
Edition:	3rd ed., rev. & expanded
Publication info:	Richmond Hill, Ont. : Firefly Books, 2008.
Physical descrip:	368 p. : ill. ; 29 cm.
General Note:	"Revised and expanded."
Subject term:	Astronomy—Amateurs' manuals.
Added author:	Dyer, Alan, 1953-

You may also find a simpler record of the book that may appear as follows. This type of catalog entry tells you where you can find the book in the library.

ITEM INFORMATION ENTRY			
The backyard astronomer's guide	Dickinson, Terence.		
Publisher:	Firefly Books,		
Pub date:	2008.		
Pages:	368 p. :		
ISBN:	9781554073443		
Item info:	1 copy available at Columbia Public Library.		
Holdings			
Columbia Public Library	Copies	Material	Location
522 DIC 3RD ED.	1	Book	Nonfiction

Research: Planning and Gathering Information

Search Tip

When the library's online catalog displays the results of a search, instead of taking notes by hand, you can print out the information you need using the Print command. This will save you time and ensure that the information you are using to find a book is accurate.

HERE'S HOW — Strategies for Finding Books

- Find out if the library has the book you want by looking it up in the online catalog.
- Read the screen to see if the book is likely to contain the information you need. Check the copyright date to see how current the information is.
- On a slip of paper, copy the call number, the title, and the name of the author for each book you want to find or print out the information.
- Use the call number to find each book. The first line of the call number tells which section of the library or media center to look in.

F or FIC	fiction section
B or 920	biography section
call number	nonfiction section

- Then find each book on the shelves by looking for its call number, located on the spine.

● Develop Research Skills

Searching Online Catalogs

Use the online catalog in your local or school library to find call numbers for the following books.

1. a nonfiction book about flowers
2. a book by Margaret Miller
3. *The Diary of Anne Frank*

Research Companion

PARTS OF A BOOK

Books are organized in a way that will allow you to find the information you need quickly and easily. In order to find information in a book, you need to know how to use the parts of a book. The following chart lists the different parts found in most books and the information available in each.

INFORMATION FOUND IN PARTS OF A BOOK	
PART	**INFORMATION**
Title Page	gives the full title, the name of the author or authors, the publisher, and the place of publication
Copyright Page	gives the date of the first copyright and of any revisions
Table of Contents	lists titles of chapters and sections and their starting page numbers
Appendix	provides additional information about the book's subjects; sometimes contains maps and charts
Glossary	defines difficult words or terms used in the book (in alphabetical order)
Bibliography	lists sources used in writing the book; sometimes provides titles of materials on related topics
Index	lists topics mentioned in the book and the page numbers where they can be found; sometimes lists in alphabetical order the page where a certain illustration can be found

● **Develop Research Skills**

Using the Parts of a Book

Use this book, along with the chart on this page, to answer the following questions.

1. Who is the publisher of this book?
2. In what year was this book copyrighted?
3. How many chapters does this book include?
4. What does the word *brainstorming* mean?
5. Where can you find information about writing business letters?

Print and Nonprint Reference Materials

Reference books, such as encyclopedias, dictionaries, atlases, and almanacs, are kept in a separate section of the library. Usually, these books cannot be checked out, and you must use them while you are in the library.

Now libraries and media centers are also often the best way to find the most reliable online reference sources. Most libraries subscribe to **online databases** that can be accessed through computers in the library. Often, anyone with a library card may use a computer at home to search the databases through the library's Web site. These databases provide a wealth of information that is not usually available for free just by searching on the Internet. Some databases are especially designed for students.

PERIODICALS—MAGAZINES AND NEWSPAPERS

Periodicals, including magazines and newspapers, are excellent sources for current information. You can usually search for periodical titles in the library's online catalog, but you cannot search for individual articles. The library may keep copies of a daily newspaper for a few months and copies of weekly or monthly magazines for a few years.

By subscribing to online databases, libraries now make it easy to find articles in a wide variety of magazines and newspapers. A librarian or media specialist can help you determine which databases are best for your research project. You can search in a database using keywords as you would with an Internet search engine. Database entries provide an abstract or short summary of the article so you can decide if it would be useful to read the full text. Full text is available for many articles from the 1990s onward. These full-text articles can be downloaded or printed. Most databases allow you to save your search results in folders for future reference.

You can learn more about searching with keywords on pages 337–338.

Following are some results from a search of an online database especially designed for students. The search used the keywords *electronic mail messages* and limited the results to full-text articles from the past year. The search also limited the results to materials with the right reading level for students in grades 6–8.

1. Find Your Perfect Pen Pal! *Girls' Life*, Feb/Mar2009, Vol. 15 Issue 4, p6–6, 2/3p; Reading Level (Lexile): 1040; (*AN 36379418*)
   HTML Full Text
2. MURPHY, MEET OUR NEW DEPARTMENT. By: Copeland, Sue H. *Horse & Rider*, Jan2009, Vol. 48 Issue 1, p6–6, 1p; Reading Level (Lexile): 910; (*AN 35942647*)
   HTML Full Text PDF Full Text (577KB)
3. Ask the Experts. *PC Magazine*, Jan2009, Vol. 28 Issue 1, p78–79, 2p, 3 color; Reading Level (Lexile): 950; (*AN 35764052*)
   HTML Full Text PDF Full Text (910KB)

Research Companion

4. WE NEED TO CHAT! By: Blyth, Catherine. *Daily Mail*, 11/10/2008, p13, 1p; (*AN 35177891*)

    HTML Full Text

5. A SELECTION OF LETTERS FROM THE FRONT. By: Carroll, Andrew. *Military History*, Nov/Dec2008, Vol. 25 Issue 5, p36–42, 7p; Reading Level (Lexile): 1020; (*AN 35572164*)

    HTML Full Text   PDF Full Text   (3.1MB)

6. Adam Grosser's Arresting e-mail. *Business Week Online*, 10/13/2008, p9–9, 1p; Reading Level (Lexile): 1010; (*AN 34848150*)

    HTML Full Text

7. Facebook Blows It. By: Karlgaard, Rich. *Forbes*, 9/15/2008, Vol. 182 Issue 4, p31–31, 1/4p; Reading Level (Lexile): 1000; (*AN 34173046*)

    HTML Full Text

8. Now that summer's over, it's time for a homework assignment. By: Iezzi, Teressa. *Advertising Age*, 9/8/2008, Vol. 79 Issue 33, p18–18, 2/5p; Reading Level (Lexile): 1070; (*AN 34247573*)

    HTML Full Text

9. Why Chrome Won't Crash Windows. By: Beal, Andy. *Business Week Online*, 9/4/2008, p6–6, 1p; Reading Level (Lexile): 1100; (*AN 34252514*)

    HTML Full Text

10. YOU ARE WHAT YOU e-mail. By: Bachel, Beverly. *Career World*, Sep2008, Vol. 37 Issue 1, Special section p16–19, 4p; Reading Level (Lexile): 1090; (*AN 34474213*)

    HTML Full Text   PDF Full Text   (1.4MB)

● Develop Research Skills

Using Online Databases

Use the search results on pages 329–330 to answer the following questions.

1. Which article has the most recent publication date?
2. What are the titles of two articles in *Business Week Online*?
3. Which article is about a social networking site?
4. What article would you read to find out how soldiers use e-mail?
5. What is the date of the publication in which an article by Catherine Blyth appears?
6. What volume of *PC Magazine* contains an article by computer experts?
7. What is the title of the article of interest to people with horses?
8. Who is the author of the article "Why Chrome Won't Crash Windows"?

9. What are the titles of three magazine articles that are more than one page long?
10. Which of the articles has the lowest reading level?

ENCYCLOPEDIAS

When you are gathering information for a report, encyclopedias are a good place to start. These works contain general information on a wide variety of subjects.

The information in most encyclopedias is arranged alphabetically by subject. Guide letters on the spine show which letter or letters are covered in each volume. Guide words at the top of each page help you find your subject.

When looking for information in an encyclopedia, be sure to check the index. It will tell you if your subject is discussed in more than one volume or if it is listed under another name.

Online encyclopedias are arranged in the same manner as printed encyclopedias—alphabetically, but there are no guide words or indexes. Instead, in order to find information on a particular subject, you enter the subject in a search box. The best online encyclopedias are the ones available through your library's databases. Beware of open source encyclopedias that have unsigned articles that can be changed without being reviewed by an expert.

Print and Online Through Libraries and Media Centers	*Compton's by Encyclopedia Britannica* *World Book Encyclopedia* *Encyclopedia Americana* *Grolier Multimedia Encyclopedia*
Online	*Columbia Encyclopedia* *Microsoft Encarta Concise Encyclopedia*
Reliable Free Encyclopedia	http://www.bartleby.com/65/

SPECIALIZED ENCYCLOPEDIAS

Specialized encyclopedias have the same organization as general encyclopedias. The specialized encyclopedias, however, concentrate on one specific subject. They provide more extensive information than general encyclopedias do. Just like general encyclopedias, specialized encyclopedias come in print and online versions.

Following are some specialized encyclopedias.

Print	*World Sports Encyclopedia*
	Encyclopedia of Animals
	International Wildlife Encyclopedia
	Encyclopedia of American Facts and Dates
	The DC Comics Encyclopedia
	The World Encyclopedia of Coins & Coin Collecting
	The McGraw-Hill Encyclopedia of Science and Technology
Online	*Encyclopedia Smithsonian*
	http://www.si.edu/Encyclopedia_SI/default.htm
	A collection of almost 50 different encyclopedias
	http://www.encyclopedia.com

GENERAL BIOGRAPHICAL REFERENCES

Biographical reference works give you information about the lives of famous people. Check your library or media center to see which of the following biographical references it has. Your library may also have an online biographical database.

Print	*Current Biography*
	Who's Who in America
	Merriam-Webster's Biographical Dictionary
	Dictionary of American Biography
	American Men and Women of Science
Online	Biography http://www.biography.com

● Develop Research Skills

Using General Biographical References

Each of the following Americans was the first at what he or she did. Using a biographical reference, briefly explain what this famous first was.

1. Jackie Robinson
2. Sally Ride
3. Guion Bluford
4. Geraldine Ferraro
5. Robert E. Peary
6. George Washington
7. Sandra Day O'Connor
8. Neil Armstrong
9. Amelia Earhart
10. Charles Lindbergh

ATLASES

An atlas is a collection of maps. Atlases also contain facts about oceans, deserts, mountains, climate, population, and natural resources. They do not all contain the same maps and information. The pages at the front of each printed atlas and the home page of each online atlas will tell you what the atlas contains and how the information is presented. Following is a list of commonly used atlases.

- **Print**
  - *The Times Atlas of the World*
  - *Hammond Odyssey World Atlas*
  - *Rand McNally International World Atlas*
  - *Goode's World Atlas*
  - *The National Geographic Atlas of the World*
- **Online**
  - *National Atlas of the United States* http://www-atlas.usgs.gov/

Taking Notes from Visuals Sometimes, as in atlases, the information you want will be in the form of visuals—charts, graphs, tables, diagrams, and maps. They often contain a wealth of information and present it more clearly than text alone might do. Suppose you were working on a report on the water resources of Fort Worth, Texas. You come across the following map.

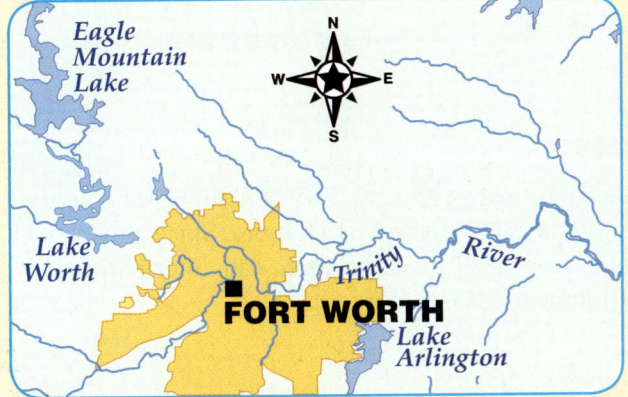

Research Tip

For each source you use, record the bibliographic information (such as title, date, and author) on every note card you create. You will then have all the information you need to cite your sources accurately.

Using the information on the map, including the compass rose, you might make the following note card.

Sample Note Card

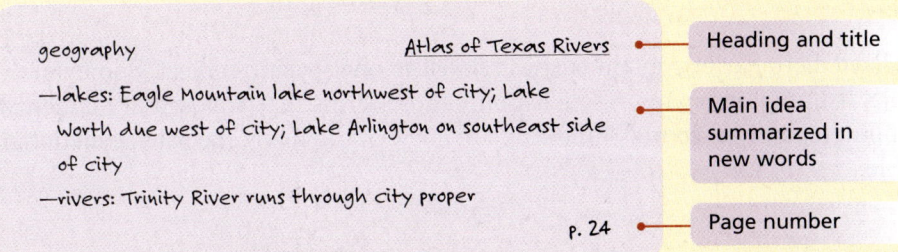

- Heading and title
- Main idea summarized in new words
- Page number

Research Companion

Converting Print to Visuals You can also take notes in the form of a visual. For example, if the source you are reading contains a brief geological history of rivers, you might record that information on a notecard in the form of a timeline.

● **Practice Your Skills**

Converting Print to Visual

Using the excerpt below, draw a map of Bismuth Island. Label all of its significant features (like Mt. Mooselip), and give the island's dimensions (its length and width). Also, add compass points to show where the island is in relation to other geographic features.

> The legendary island of Bismuth is 25 miles off the coast. It is shaped roughly like an outline of a fish—its western end looks like the fish's tail and the eastern end resembles the fish's body. The western end of the island is dominated by the island's tallest point, Mt. Mooselip. Bismuth is 8 miles long and 4 miles at its widest point. Off the shore of the easternmost end of the island, there is another tiny island, called Orson's Crag, where islanders harvest wild lavender.

ALMANACS AND YEARBOOKS

Almanacs and yearbooks include facts about many subjects. They contain world records, noteworthy achievements, facts about famous people, and much more. Since almanacs and yearbooks are published every year, they usually contain up-to-date information. Following are the names of some well-known almanacs and yearbooks.

Print	*Information Please Almanac*
	World Almanac and Book of Facts
	Guinness Book of World Records
Online	*The Old Farmer's Almanac,* http://www.almanac.com
	Infoplease http://www.infoplease.com/

SPECIALIZED DICTIONARIES

Specialized dictionaries contain entries related to one specific subject. Some, for example, list only synonyms. Some list only those terms that are used in mathematics, or computers, or even sports. Following are a few of the many specialized dictionaries available.

- **Print**

  Roget's 21st Century Thesaurus in Dictionary Form
  Merriam-Webster Dictionary of Synonyms and Antonyms
  American Heritage Student Science Dictionary
  Dictionary of American History

- **Online**

  English and foreign language dictionaries
  http://dictionary.reference.com/
  Roget's Thesaurus http://thesaurus.reference.com/

● Develop Research Skills

Using Specialized Reference Materials

Following is a list of library resources. Write the name of the best source for answering each question.

specialized encyclopedia   atlas
specialized dictionary   almanac or yearbook
biographical reference

1. For which president's inauguration did Maya Angelou write a poem?
2. Who is the subject of Andrew Wyeth's famous painting *Christina's World*?
3. How many people can the Rose Bowl in Pasadena, California, seat when it is filled to capacity?
4. Lorraine Vivian Hansberry was the first black woman to have a play produced on Broadway. What was the name of the play?
5. In tennis, what is a foot fault?
6. During what years was the American buffalo nickel made?
7. Name the countries partly covered by the Alps.
8. What cities were sites of the Olympic Games in 1992 and 2008?
9. In what state is Kalamazoo, and what large city is directly north of it?
10. In music, what does the term *rockabilly* mean?

● Develop Research Skills

Finding Facts in Reference Materials

Use appropriate reference materials to find answers to the ten questions listed above.

VERTICAL FILES

Libraries keep pamphlets, catalogs, newspaper clippings, and other kinds of leaflets. These are usually kept in a filing cabinet called the **vertical file.** The items are placed in folders and arranged alphabetically by subject.

Microforms

To save space, many libraries store older issues of some magazines and newspapers in **microform:** either **microfilm** (a reel of film) or **microfiche** (a sheet of film). You can view these types of film by using a special projection machine. Check with a librarian to see if there are indexes such as the *Readers' Guide to Periodical Literature* or newspaper indexes to help you locate articles on specific topics.

Recorded Materials

Most libraries have a section where the recorded materials are kept. These usually include CDs and DVDs, and perhaps audiotapes, records, videos, and CD-ROMs. You will find these materials indexed in the online catalog. Some of the recorded materials may be borrowed and others can only be used in the library. Many libraries and media centers have listening, viewing, and computer rooms where these types of materials can be used.

You have seen that some information in a library or media center is in print form, while other information is in electronic form. Each format has its own advantages. What advantages did you find in using the Internet to gather information instead of going to print or bound materials? Were there any advantages to looking in books instead of going online? In what situations would each form of information be most useful? Record your reflections in your Learning Log.

Using the Internet for Research

The Information Superhighway could be the best research partner you've ever had. It's fast, vast, and always available. But like any other highway, if you don't know your way around, it can also be confusing. It takes time to learn how to navigate the Net and zero in on the information you need. The best thing to do is practice early and often. Don't wait until the night before your paper is due to learn how to do research on the Internet.

GETTING STARTED

Just as there are several different ways to get to your home or school, there are many different ways to arrive at the information you're looking for on the Internet.

Internet Public Library Perhaps the best place to start your search for reliable information on the Web is to go to the Internet Public Library (ipl2) site <http://www.ipl.org/>. The IPL is a virtual reference library that provides links to Web sites that have been reviewed and recommended by librarians. The home page is organized with links to sections much like those at your local library or media center. There are even special sections for kids and teens. Clicking on the links that relate to your topic will take you to a list of suggested resources.

Search Bar Another good first step is your browser's search bar. Type a word or short phrase that describes the topic you are researching. Then select the search tool you wish to use. You can usually customize your browser by adding the search tools you use most often to the drop-down menu. Some of these tools, sometimes referred to as **search engines,** include:

AltaVista—http://www.altavista.com/

Ask—http://www.ask.com/

Bing—http://www.bing.com/

Dogpile—http://www.dogpile.com/

Google—http://www.google.com/

Lycos—http://www.lycos.com/

Yahoo!—http://www.yahoo.com/

Search services usually list broad categories of subjects, plus they may offer other features such as "Random Links" or "Top 25 Sites," and customization options. Each one also has a search field. Type in a **keyword,** a word or short phrase that describes your area of interest. Then click Search or press the Enter key on your keyboard. Seconds later a list of

Web sites known as "hits" will be displayed containing the word you specified in the search field. Scroll through the list and click the page you wish to view.

The tricky part about doing a search on the Internet is that a single keyword may yield a hundred or more sites. Plus, you may find many topics you don't need.

For example, suppose you are writing a paper about the planet Saturn. If you type the word *Saturn* into the search field, you'll turn up some articles about the planet, but you'll also get articles about NASA's Saturn rockets and Saturn, the automobile.

SEARCH SMART

Listed below are a few pointers on how to narrow your search, save time, and search smart on the Net. Not all of the following strategies will work with all of the search engines.

Guidelines for Smart Searching

- The keyword or words that you enter have a lot to do with the accuracy of your search. Focus your search by adding the word "and" or the + sign followed by another descriptive word. For example, try "Saturn" again, but this time, add "Saturn + space." Adding a third word, "Saturn + space + rings" will narrow the field even more.
- On the other hand, you can limit unwanted results by specifying information that you do *not* want the search engine to find. If you type "dolphins not football," you will get Web sites about the animal that lives in the ocean rather than the football team that uses Miami as its home base.
- Specify geographical areas using the word "near" between keywords as in "islands near Florida." This lets you focus on specific regions.
- To broaden your search, add the word "or" between keywords. For example, "sailboats or catamarans."
- Help the search engine recognize familiar phrases by putting words that go together in quotes such as "Tom and Jerry" or "bacon and eggs."
- Sometimes the site you come up with is in the ballpark of what you are searching for, but it is not exactly what you need. Skim the text quickly anyway. It may give you ideas for more accurate keywords. There might also be links listed to other sites that are just the right resource you need.
- Try out different search engines. Each service uses slightly different methods of searching, so you may get different results using the same keywords.
- Check the spelling of the keywords you are using. A misspelled word can send a search engine in the wrong direction. Also, be careful how you use capital letters. By typing the word *Gold*, some search services will only bring up articles that include the word with a capital *G*.

Research: Planning and Gathering Information

SAVING A SITE FOR LATER

You may want to keep a list handy of favorite Web sites or sites you are currently using in a project. This will save you time because you can just click on the name of the site in your list and return to that page without having to retype the URL.

Different browsers have different names for this feature. For example, AOL's Netscape™ calls it **My Links,** Mozilla's Firefox™ calls it a **bookmark,** while Microsoft's Internet Explorer™ calls it **favorites.**

INTERNET + MEDIA CENTER = INFORMATION POWERHOUSE

Although the Internet is a limitless treasure chest of information, remember that it's not catalogued. It can be tricky to locate the information you need, and sometimes that information is not reliable. The library is a well-organized storehouse of knowledge, but it has more limited resources. If you use the Internet and your local media center, you've got everything you need to create well-researched articles, reports, and papers.

Using the Internet and Media Center

Use the Internet to
- get great ideas for topics to write about;
- gather information about your topic from companies, colleges and universities, and professional organizations;
- connect with recognized experts in your field of interest;
- connect with other people who are interested in the same subject and who can put you in touch with other sources.

Use the Media Center to
- find reliable sources of information either in print or online;
- get background information on your topic;
- cross-check the accuracy and credibility of online information and authors.

Research Companion

CHAPTER 13

Research: Synthesizing, Organizing, and Presenting

When you are a gardener, you need to plan what you want to grow, prepare the soil, and gather your seeds before planting. In the previous chapter you have begun the "gardening" process for your research report. You have:

- chosen and limited a subject;
- posed a major research question;
- written a research plan;
- used your library and media center to find sources;
- evaluated those sources; and
- taken notes.

The activities in this chapter will take you through the rest of the process of preparing a research report.

Writing Project — Research Report

Don't Let Me Be Misunderstood *Complete your research report that exposes the facts on a misunderstood person, place, animal, thing, or event.*

Review So far you have identified and narrowed your topic, created a research plan to guide both your research and your writing, and located the information that will go into your report. You have also collaborated with classmates to find and evaluate sources and to consider your organizational plan for your research. You have used your research questions to establish what you need to find, remaining flexible in case your research leads to a different question or modified version of your question. Next you will use all your prewriting work to create a written report.

Writing a Research Report  Synthesizing

To prevent your report from being a mere collection of facts, you need to synthesize what you have learned to develop your own insights. To **synthesize** means to merge together information from different kinds of sources and your own experience and understanding. The following diagram shows the steps you can take to synthesize information.

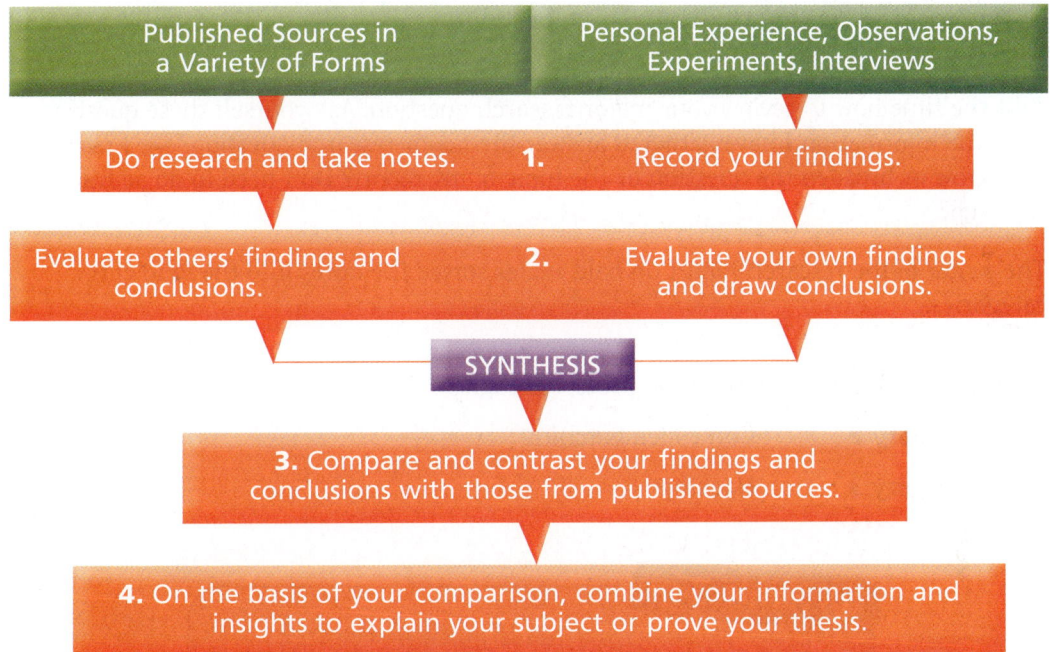

PROJECT PREP *Prewriting* Synthesis

Review your research question and all the notes you took as you conducted research. Follow the steps in the diagram above to synthesize the information, beginning with step #2. Write a brief paragraph evaluating the findings and conclusions of others, and explain why some of your sources may be more useful than others. Write a second brief paragraph evaluating your own views on the subject. Then complete steps #3 and #4. Write a few sentences explaining how you combined the various sources of information for the understanding you now have.

Writing a Research Report

① Organizing Your Notes

As you take notes, you will start to see how ideas belong together. You can group ideas that relate to a similar theme into a single category. Building a system of categories helps you see the bigger picture of the information you gathered. Categorizing is the first step in organizing your notes into an outline.

The headings on your note cards can help you organize your information into categories. Then you can easily sort through your notes and clip together all the cards that belong in each category.

Take the time now to review your major research question. Ask yourself these questions: Does the information I have gathered answer the major research question? Do I need to narrow or broaden the question or the topic of my report? Do I need to do additional research?

The writer of the research report on bald eagles sorted the notes into the following categories.

Category 1	Laws that protected eagles
Category 2	Controlled hatching
Category 3	Hacking

> **Writing Tip**
>
> Group your notes into three to five main categories that are broad enough to include all your information.

PROJECT PREP *Prewriting* **Organization of Information**

Sort the notes for your report so that they fit into categories. (You have already begun this process by marking the aspect of the topic each note covers.) Look for big ideas that cover the important themes in your notes to identify the broad categories. Look at your major research question and see if you need to make it broader or narrower. Sketch out a "map" of the information you have, showing the categories you have developed.

Think Critically

Classifying

Grouping ideas into categories is called **classifying.** When you classify, you look for ways in which items are similar enough to belong to the same category. For example, scientists classify cows, dogs, and humans as mammals. Although cows, dogs, and humans are different, they are all warm-blooded, they have backbones, and the females produce milk for their young.

By taking notes, you have already started classifying. The heading at the top of each note card shows how it fits into your subject. When you are ready to classify your note cards, you can use these headings to create categories.

Thinking Practice

Imagine that you are writing a report on animal behavior. In your research you have come up with a list of notes. Give each of the following facts about amazing animals a heading suitable for a note card. Then create two categories into which you can classify these details.

A cat in Lawrence, Kansas, moved all her kittens days before a cyclone came and knocked down their old home.

In April 1961, bees from Sam Rogers's hives in England came to his funeral and sat in funeral wreaths for a half hour.

Redsy, an Irish Setter, refused to get on a boat, saving owner William H. Montgomery from a hurricane in 1938.

John Gambill once nursed a wounded goose back to health; when Gambill died, a flock of geese circled and honked over the hospital.

❷ Outlining

Now that your notes are categorized, you are ready to organize them into an outline or some other organizational tool for the body of your report.

Preparing an Outline

- Use the headings on your note cards to group the cards into a few categories. Save the cards that do not fit into any category for possible use in the introduction or conclusion.
- Make a list of your categories. Then, using Roman numerals (I, II, III, etc.), arrange your categories in a logical order. (pages 227–231)
- Use the categories as the main topics in your outline.
- Using your note cards, list subtopics under each main topic. (Capitalize the first letter of each subtopic.)

The outline for the body of the report on eagles might appear as follows.

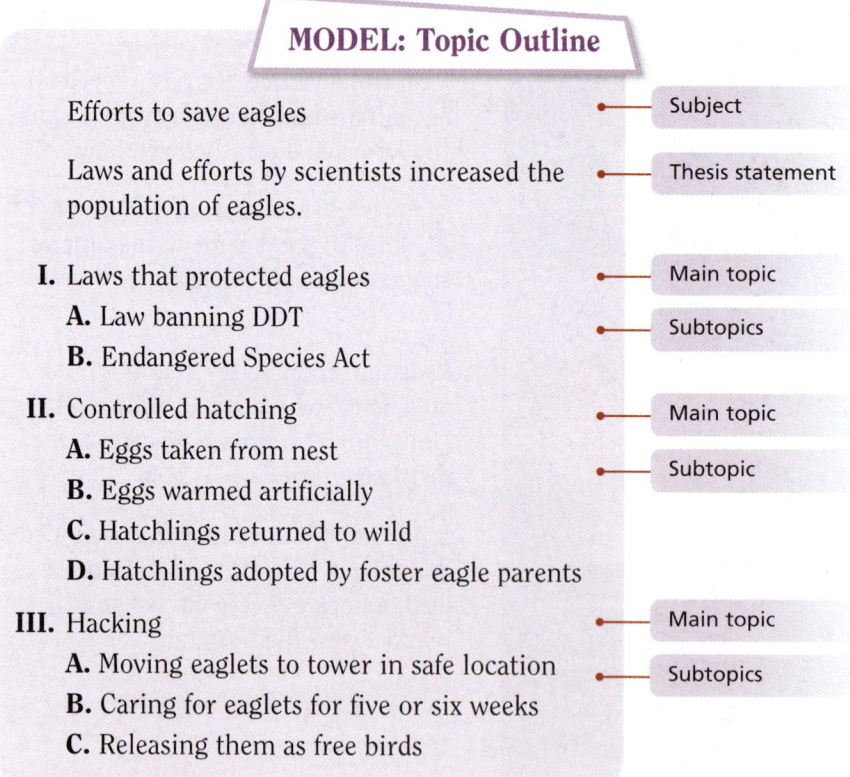

After you have finished your outline, use the following guidelines to check its form.

Outline Form

- Include a title and a statement of the main idea.
- Use a Roman numeral and a period for each main topic.
- Use a capital letter and a period for each subtopic.
- Always include at least two subtopics under each main topic.
- Indent as shown in the above model.
- Capitalize the first word of each entry.

You can also make an informal outline or use some other graphic organizer to get your thoughts straight. Maybe you will find something like the following easier for you to use in planning and organizing your report.

Writing Tip

Use your note-card categories as the main topics of an outline. Then use your notes to add subtopics to the outline.

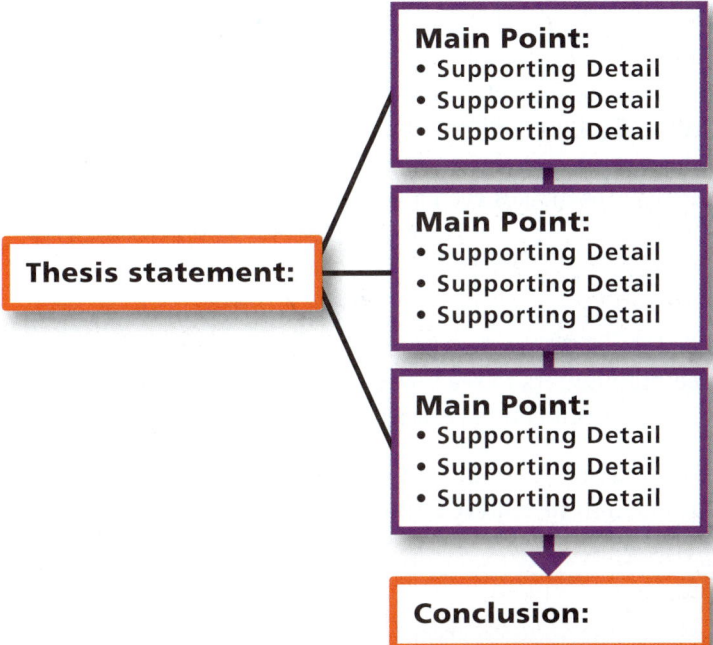

PROJECT PREP *Prewriting* **Outline**

Use your note cards—and your skill at classifying—to shape up the outline for your report. Now that you have assembled the information you will use, does the outline still serve your purposes? Discuss with your writing group whether or not you need to revise your outline before finalizing it. When you have settled on a final form of the outline, you can begin drafting your report.

The Power of Language

Fluency: Let It Flow

You have learned various ways of adding information and details to your sentences and using grammatical structures to enhance your writing style. Fluent writing—writing that flows—requires still more. To keep your sentences flowing smoothly, you need to vary their length and structure.

Read the following passage from a fact sheet put out by the U.S. Fish and Wildlife Service about an animal that went on the threatened list in 2008.

> Female polar bears prepare small dens on the mainland or on sea ice where they will give birth and spend winter. Usually two cubs are born in December or January. While the cubs are born blind, hairless, and no bigger than squirrels, they grow very rapidly.

You can probably easily tell that the middle sentence is considerably shorter than the first and third. The beginnings of the sentences are also different. The first sentence begins with the subject. The second begins with an adverb, and the third begins with a subordinating conjunction. The first and third sentences are complex sentences; the second is a simple sentence. This variety in sentence length, beginning, and structure makes even a government document fluent and easy to read.

Try It Yourself

Write a passage of about five sentences on the topic of your research report. Use different colored highlighters to see how you started your sentences. If you have only one color, revise until you have at least three.

Also count the number of words in each. If they are all about the same, look for ways to vary their length to achieve a smoother flow.

Research: Synthesizing, Organizing, and Presenting

Writing a Research Report  Drafting

Your goal in writing the first draft of your report is to structure your information into an introduction, a body, and a conclusion. The model you will see in the pages that follow will help you structure your report. Note, however, that this model has already been revised and edited. Do not worry if your first draft is less polished than the model.

You can learn more about the structure of a report on page 308.

Drafting the Introduction

A good introduction is like a promise to your readers. It focuses your readers' attention on the main idea and leads them to expect certain details in the rest of the report. Use the following guidelines to write a strong introduction.

Writing the Introduction

A strong introduction
- captures the reader's attention.
- provides any background information needed.
- contains a sentence expressing the main idea of the report.

Read the following introduction to a report on eagles. Then read the introduction on the next page. Both capture attention and provide background information. The first introduction, however, fails to focus the reader's attention on the main idea.

MODEL: Introduction of a Report (Unfocused)

The bald eagle has been the symbol of the United States since 1782. Some early Americans, including Benjamin Franklin, did not like that choice. However, since the eagle is found only in North America, it was voted to receive the high honor of representing the United States. Two hundred years later, President Ronald Reagan declared 1982 "the Year of the Eagle." The eagle is indeed a magnificent bird of prey.

— No clear main idea

MODEL: Introduction of a Report (Focused)

For more than 200 years, the bald eagle has been the symbol of the United States. In the early 1700s, there may have been as many as 500,000 bald eagles in North America ("Bald Eagle"). By the early 1970s, however, only about 2,000–3,000 remained in the United States outside of Alaska (Grier 5). Fear for the dwindling population led to laws protecting eagles in all states, including Alaska. In addition, scientists found creative ways to increase the eagle population.

— Main idea clearly stated

Notice that all of the sentences in the second introduction build up to the main idea. No unrelated ideas are included. This introduction provides a clear promise to the readers.

PROJECT PREP Drafting Introduction

1. Write an introductory paragraph that explains what the report will be about. You can use your major research question to help you write a thesis statement for the introduction. If, for instance, your major research question is "Is it true, as many people think, that most immigrants entered the United States illegally?" you could rephrase it as your thesis statement as follows: "Many people believe that most recent immigrants have entered the U.S. illegally, yet the facts reveal that many immigrants have crossed our borders through legal means." Your introduction should then explain this assertion briefly.

2. When you have drafted your introductory paragraph, bring it to your writing group. Critique one another's introductory paragraphs and help one another state a clear thesis that sets the stage for the remainder of the paper.

348   Research: Synthesizing, Organizing, and Presenting

❷ Drafting the Body

When you draft, use your outline or graphic organizer as a guide. The body of the report is where you present the evidence to explain your topic. You will summarize or paraphrase what you have learned in a systematic way. Make sure that the information you include from different sources is consistent. Give relevant reasons for any conclusions that you draw. Use transitions to help guide your readers from idea to idea. Notice how the following report body follows the outline on page 344.

Also notice how the writer used source material. Quotes and paraphrases are worked into the sentences and paragraphs smoothly and systematically. Sources are cited in parentheses. This method of citing sources is called **parenthetical citation.** A parenthetical citation briefly identifies the source and page number whenever the source of information must be credited. You will learn more about citing sources in Lesson 5.

MODEL: Body of a Report

Two laws passed in the early 1970s were "the two main reasons for the recovery of the bald eagle" (DeFries 43). The first was the law that banned the use of the pesticide DDT. This pesticide got into the food that eagles ate and caused damage to their eggs. The second important law was the Endangered Species Act. This law protected eagles and other species that were in danger of disappearing (DeFries 29–31). *—From Roman numeral I in outline*

One of the most effective ways of increasing the eagle population was by controlling the hatching of eggs. At a research center in Maryland, eggs laid by captive eagles were taken away from the nest. They were then kept warm artificially. Meanwhile, the mother soon laid more eggs. If she had her original brood to watch, she would not lay more eggs. In this way more eaglets could be born from each mother (Wyss 19–20). In some cases the eggs laid by captive eagles were taken into the wild and placed in the nests of other eagles. Most wild eagles seemed willing to adopt and care for the new eggs. By 1988 this program was no longer needed because eagles were able to hatch enough eggs successfully in the wild again (DeFries 40). *—From Roman numeral II*

Another technique for increasing the eagle population is called hacking. Hacking involves moving young birds to a new, safe habitat. In most cases eaglets were taken from their birthplace and moved to a caged tower in the new location. There, workers fed the eaglets. To prevent these wild birds from becoming dependent on humans, the workers never got close enough for the birds to see them. When they were old enough to survive on their own, the eagles were released (DeFries 40–41). *—From Roman numeral III*

A good report has no unnecessary parts and no unnecessary words in its sentences. When you draft, you may not be thinking too much about the most economical way to express something. You can trim away unnecessary elements during revising and editing. For practice, revise the following passage from a report about television talent shows.

> Television talent shows have been broadcast on TV for more than 50 years going back to Ted Mack who had a talent show called The Original Ted Mack Amateur Hour, which aired in the 1950s.

PROJECT PREP   Drafting   Body

1. Use your outline and notes to draft the body of your report. Summarize your findings and present the evidence that explains your topic in an organized way. Your outline should help you decide what order you should present your information in, what the topic of each paragraph should be, and what information and facts should be included to support that topic. Make sure the information is consistent throughout the report. Give reasons for your conclusions. Add a parenthetical citation each time you include a quotation or an idea that is not your own. Simply identify the source and page number in parentheses, as in the model. As long as you know which source you mean, you can rewrite each citation in the proper form if necessary when you revise your draft.

2. When you have drafted the body paragraphs in which you specifically address misconceptions about your topic, bring your draft to your writing group. Help one another evaluate the extent to which each paragraph is dedicated to a clear and specific topic that helps you answer your research questions.

3. Drafting the Conclusion

A strong conclusion provides a wrap-up of the details in the body of a report. Use the following guidelines whenever you write a conclusion to a report.

Writing a Conclusion

- Restate your main idea in new words.
- Include a comment that shows the importance of your subject.
- Round out the report by referring to an idea in the introduction without repeating it exactly.
- Draw your own conclusions based on the research you have done.
- Avoid adding a completely new idea.

Avoid such phrases as "Now you have seen . . ." or "I have just told you . . ." Notice how the following conclusion follows these guidelines.

MODEL: Conclusion of a Report

By 1995 all these efforts had been so successful that eagles were no longer listed as an endangered species (Price). In 2007 they were taken off the list of threatened species ("Bald Eagle"). The population had recovered to about 30,000 in the lower 48 states and about 100,000 in Alaska and Canada (Grier 5). The combination of strong laws to protect eagles and the work of scientists to increase the survival of more eaglets led to this environmental success story. Destruction of areas where eagles live and water pollution still pose a danger to the birds and require continued monitoring (DeFries 38). There is now every reason to expect, however, that this majestic national symbol will celebrate its 300th birthday in 2082.

PROJECT PREP Drafting Conclusion

1. Using the guidelines and model, write a strong conclusion for your report. Your conclusion should leave no doubt that your topic has indeed been misunderstood. It should also showcase the conclusions you have drawn from your research.

2. When you have drafted your concluding paragraph, bring it to your writing group. Help one another evaluate the conclusion. Does it clearly give an answer to the major research question? Are you persuaded that each writer's topic has indeed been misunderstood?

Writing a Research Report • Drafting   351

④ Including Visuals

Many reports can be enhanced with the use of visuals. Visuals can include illustrations, photos, graphs, and charts. In the case of a report that is to be published on a Web page, movie clips may also be included. If you are using a word processing program to prepare your report, and you have a scanner, you can scan the images directly into your document. With some programs, you can also enter data and the program will prepare a graph or table of your choosing.

The most important thing to remember when deciding whether to include a visual in your report is that it must clarify or extend the meaning of your text. In other words, all visuals must be relevant to your topic and be included for a reason. Visuals can help deepen your reader's understanding if used and placed properly.

WRITING A TITLE

Once you have finished your first draft, give your report an interesting title. Your title should catch your reader's interest and indicate what your report is about.

PROJECT PREP *Drafting* **Visuals and Title**

Reread your report and add any visuals that might make your text clearer or add to its meaning. Then give your report an interesting title that alerts readers to the subject of your report. Save your draft for later use.

5 Citing Sources

When you write a report, you usually research your topic by investigating other people's ideas. You may even quote an author directly. When you use the words or ideas of other people in your report you must give them proper credit. A note that gives this credit is called a **citation.**

Laws protect authors, illustrators, photographers, and publishers whose materials have been copyrighted. Using another person's words, pictures, or ideas without giving proper credit is called **plagiarism,** a serious offense. For this reason, you must give credit to the authors whenever you use source materials—even if you only paraphrase. You have already taken steps to avoid plagiarism by taking notes in your own words and by recording the author, the page number, and the exact words of any quotation you plan to use. The easiest method of citing sources is parenthetical citations.

Parenthetical Citations

A **parenthetical citation** is a brief note in parentheses that is placed immediately after the words or ideas you have borrowed. Readers can then refer to the works-cited page at the end of your report for complete information about each source. Use the following examples for the correct form of parenthetical citations.

MODERN LANGUAGE ASSOCIATION (MLA) STYLE GUIDELINES	
Book or Article by One Author	Give author's last name and page number(s): (DeFries 29–31).
Book or Article by Two or More Authors	Give all of the authors' names and page number(s): (Bair and Wright 24).
Article; Author Unnamed	Give a shortened form of the title of the article (unless title is already short) and page number(s), unless the article is a single page: ("Eagles Fly High").
Article in a Reference Work; Author Unnamed	Give title (full or shortened). No page number is necessary if the article is a single page from an encyclopedia arranged alphabetically: ("Eagle").
Online Article; Author Named	Give author's last name; include a page or paragraph number only if the online source includes them; do not use page references from a print version of the article: (Price).
Online Article or Web Page; Author Unnamed	Give title of article (full or shortened) or Web page, as used on the works-cited page: ("Bald Eagle").

Writing a Research Report • Drafting

You should keep parenthetical citations as close as possible to the words or ideas being credited. To avoid interrupting the flow of the sentence, place them at the end of a phrase, clause, or sentence. If you have used information from the exact same source in several sentences in a row, it is okay to place the citation at the end of the last sentence. See examples in the model report on page 349.

WORKS-CITED PAGE

A **works-cited page** is a list of sources at the end of your report that you include regardless of the style of citation you use in the body of the report. The works-cited page lists complete information about each source you have used to write your paper. The sources are listed alphabetically by the author's last name or by the title if there is no author listed.

Sometimes your teacher may ask you to include a works-consulted page—often called a **bibliography**—on which you include all the works you consulted but did not necessarily cite in your research report. A works-consulted page or bibliography uses the same form as the works-cited page.

The model shows the works-cited page for the report on bald eagles. The works-cited list gives the details for the sources in the parenthetical citations.

MODEL: Works-Cited Page

Works Cited

"Bald Eagle: The U.S.A.'s National Symbol." *American Eagle Foundation*, 06 Dec. 2007. Web. 2 Mar. 2009.

DeFries, Cheryl L. *The Bald Eagle*. Berkeley Heights: Enslow, 2003. Print.

Grier, James W. "Eagle." *World Book Encyclopedia*. 2009 ed. Print.

Price, Sean. "Endangered!" *National Geographic Kids* Dec. 2005: 16. *MAS Ultra - School Edition*. Web. 2 Mar. 2009.

Wyss, Hal H. *Eagles: A Portrait of the Animal World*. New York: Smithmark, 1997. Print.

On a works-cited page, page numbers are usually given for articles but not for books. In each example note the order of information, the indentation, and the punctuation. When citing online sources, always give the date you accessed the site. Use the following examples to help you create a works-cited page.

MLA GUIDE TO WORKS-CITED PAGE

General Reference Works	Grier, James W. "Eagle." *World Book Encyclopedia*. 2009 ed. Print.
Books by One Author	DeFries, Cheryl L. *The Bald Eagle*. Berkeley Heights: Enslow, 2003. Print.
Books by Two or More Authors	Bair, Diane, and Pamela Wright. *Eagle Watching*. Mankato: Capstone, 2000. Print.
Articles in Magazines	Conn, Heather. "Explore: A Wild Place." *Sierra* Jan. 2009: 16–17. Print.
Articles, Author Unnamed	"Eagles Fly High." *Scholastic Action* 10 Nov. 2008: 3. Print.
Articles in Newspapers	DePalma, Anthony. "Bald Eagles in Catskills Show Increasing Mercury." *New York Times* 25 Nov. 2008: A2. Print.
Articles from Online Databases	Price, Sean. "Endangered!" *National Geographic Kids* Dec. 2005: 16. *MAS Ultra - School Edition*. Web. 2 Mar. 2009.
Articles from Web Sites	"Bald Eagle: The U.S.A.'s National Symbol." *American Eagle Foundation*, 06 Dec. 2007. Web. 2 Mar. 2009.

These entries follow the style recommended in the *MLA Handbook for Writers of Research Papers* (7th ed.). Notice that the citation includes the medium for each source—print or Web. The MLA no longer recommends including URLs, or Web site addresses, for most online sources because they change so frequently. If your teacher asks you to include a URL, enclose it in angle brackets as the last entry in the citation.

Example

"Bald Eagle: The U.S.A.'s National Symbol." *American Eagle Foundation*, 06 Dec. 2007. Web. 2 Mar. 2009. <http://www.eagles.org/programs/eagle-facts/more-about-bald-eagles.php>.

PROJECT PREP Drafting Parenthetical Citations, Works-Cited Page

Review what you have learned about citing sources correctly. Then reread the first draft of your report and write the parenthetical citations in the proper form. Place the citations so they do not disrupt the flow of the sentences. Finally, prepare a works-cited page to add at the end of your report. If you have a source that does not fit one of the categories described above, refer to the *MLA Handbook for Writers of Research Papers* for information on how to cite the source correctly. Save your completed draft for revising.

Writing a Research Report  Revising

In the process of writing your report, you may not have been able to concentrate on all the elements of clear writing. During the revising stage, you can stand back from your report and try to read it with a fresh eye. Have the seeds you planted come up in the form you intended? Does your work need weeding or thinning? Ask yourself if you have achieved the purpose of your report. Did you keep your audience in mind as you wrote? The following checklist can help you improve your first draft.

 Evaluation Checklist for Revising

Checking Your Report
- ✓ Does your introduction contain a sentence expressing the main idea of the report? (pages 347–348)
- ✓ Does the body of your report support the thesis statement with specific evidence and examples and answer your major research question? (pages 349–350)
- ✓ Did you draw conclusions and give relevant reasons for your conclusions? (page 351)
- ✓ Did you use your own words, paraphrasing systematically? (pages 319 and 349)
- ✓ Did you use a variety of transitions? (pages 137 and 227–231)
- ✓ Does your report have unity and internal and external coherence? (pages 6, 119, and 248)
- ✓ Does your report fulfill its purpose and suit your chosen audience? (pages 15–16 and 104–105)
- ✓ Does your conclusion add a strong ending? (page 351)
- ✓ Does your report have a title? (page 352)
- ✓ Does your report have citations and a works-cited page? (pages 353–355)

Checking Your Paragraphs
- ✓ Does each paragraph in the body have a topic sentence? (pages 349–350)
- ✓ Is each paragraph unified and coherent? (pages 6, 119, and 248)

Checking Your Sentences
- ✓ Did you use a variety of sentence structures? (pages 64–73)
- ✓ Are your sentences concise? (pages 75–78)
- ✓ Did you use such devices as figurative language and parallelism? (pages 164 and 207)

PROJECT PREP Revising **Using Feedback**

Based on the feedback from your writing group and on the checklist above, write a new draft of your research report. Then exchange work with a member of your writing group and give each other suggestions for further revision. Listen to all suggestions and revise your work as you feel necessary. Save your work for further revising and for editing.

Research: Synthesizing, Organizing, and Presenting

Writing a Research Report — Editing

One of the final stages in writing a research report is to edit your work for proper grammar, mechanics, spelling, and usage.

The Language of  Fragments

Power Rule: Use sentence fragments only the way professional writers do, after the sentence they refer to and usually to emphasize a point. Fix all sentence fragments that occur before the sentence they refer to and ones that occur in the middle of a sentence. (See pages 662–667.)

See It in Action In the first draft, the writer of the report on bald eagles wrote:

> By 1988 this program was no longer needed. Because eagles were able to hatch enough eggs successfully in the wild again (DeFries 40).

The writer had seen "eagles were able to hatch enough eggs" as a complete sentence since it has a subject (*eagles*) and verb (*were able*). However, it also has a subordinating conjunction, the word *because,* which makes the clause unable to stand alone. So during editing, the writer removed the period and capital letter and joined the two clauses.

> By 1988 this program was no longer needed because eagles were able to hatch enough eggs successfully in the wild again (DeFries 40).

Remember It Record this rule in the Power Rule section of your Personalized Editing Checklist.

Use It Read through your research report to make sure you have no unintended sentence fragments.

PROJECT PREP — Editing — Checking for Conventions

Check your work for grammar, usage, mechanics, and spelling. As you edit your research report, refer to your Personalized Editing Checklist. When you are finished, use the rubric on the following page to measure the strength of each of the six traits in your writing.

Using a Six-Trait Rubric — Research Reports

Ideas	4 The text conveys a thesis statement with abundant supporting details and is well-chosen for the purpose and audience.	3 The text conveys a thesis statement with ample details and suits the purpose and audience.	2 The text conveys a thesis statement with some supporting details and suits the purpose and audience.	1 The text does not convey a thesis statement and fails to suit the purpose and audience.
Organization	4 In each paragraph and the report as a whole, the organization is clear with abundant transitions.	3 In most paragraphs as well as the report as a whole, a few ideas seem out of place or transitions are missing.	2 Many ideas seem out of place and transitions are missing.	1 The organization is unclear and hard to follow.
Voice	4 The voice sounds engaging and is appropriate for purpose and audience.	3 The voice sounds natural and is appropriate for purpose and audience.	2 The voice sounds mostly unnatural with some exceptions.	1 The voice sounds mostly unnatural.
Word Choice	4 Words are precise. All terms are explained or defined.	3 Words are precise and some terms are explained or defined.	2 Some words are overly general and some technical terms are not explained.	1 Most words are overly general.
Sentence Fluency	4 Varied sentences flow smoothly.	3 Most sentences are varied and flow smoothly.	2 Some sentences are varied but some are choppy.	1 Sentences are not varied and are choppy.
Conventions	4 Punctuation, usage, and spelling are correct. The Power Rules are all followed.	3 Punctuation, usage, and spelling are mainly correct and Power Rules are all followed.	2 Some punctuation, usage, and spelling are incorrect but all Power Rules are followed.	1 There are many errors and at least one failure to follow a Power Rule.

PROJECT PREP  **Peer Evaluation**

Conduct a final reading of your report and make all necessary changes.

Writing a Research Report — Publishing

Publishing is an important part of report writing—the whole purpose of writing in this form is to present information. During the process of writing a research report, the writer learns about his or her subject in order to pass the information on to an interested reader. When deciding how to publish a research report, keep in mind the subject and who might benefit from reading about it.

The chart below suggests several publishing options for a research report. Each of the suggested formats has its own unique requirements for presentation.

PUBLISHING OPTIONS FOR RESEARCH REPORTS

A written report	Requirements: Clear, well-organized writing with smooth transitions presented in a neat, error-free copy with citations handled appropriately; illustrations may help explain some of the ideas; reader-friendly formatting techniques such as bullet points and headings can help convey information
A multimedia presentation	Requirements: Unified blend of print, sound, video, and/or other media that uses the best features of each medium to make the points clear; the print portion as well as the presentation as a whole should not include unnecessary details or information
An oral report	Requirements: Clear writing that will be easy for a listener to understand without re-readings; visual aids as needed; delivery that uses voice, gesture, and a range of speaker strategies to convey information clearly
An investigative newspaper report	Requirements: A "lead" that gets readers involved in the report right away; short paragraphs to look good in newspaper columns

PROJECT PREP — Publishing — Adjusting for Format

Present a final copy of your research report, making adjustments as needed to meet the requirements of your chosen format. With your teacher's direction, display your reports on a table in your school library or media center for interested parties to read.

TIME OUT TO REFLECT

In what ways have your skills in researching and writing reports improved after going through this process? Record your thoughts in your Learning Log.

Writing Lab

Project Corner

Speak and Listen
Class Discussion

With your classmates, **discuss** how people, places, animals, things, and events can become misunderstood. What should people do to stay informed about the realities of the situation? How can they tell bad information from good, rumor from truth, propaganda from reality? (See pages 434–435 for information on group discussions.)

Present It Slide Show

Use the information you have gathered to **prepare a slide show,** using presentation software. How could you use graphics to emphasize your points? What features of the software will enable you to convey your information clearly to viewers? (See pages 456–461 for information on multimedia presentations.)

Communicate Across Cultures Translate

If you are learning another language or if you speak another language at home, **translate your report** into that language. Have a speaker of that language evaluate your translation for accuracy and fluency.

Experiment
Try a Different Form

Review the suggested project forms on page 359. Think about how your project would be different if it were in one of those forms you didn't use or another that you can think of. Choose a part of your project and **recast it in that new form.** What changes would you need to make? Write a brief paragraph explaining those changes.

In Everyday Life
A Concert Review

Apply and Assess

1. Return to the information you gathered about your favorite band (see page 321). You and your brother attended the concert and now you want to write about it. **Write a review** of the concert for your school newspaper. Summarize the event and include background information on the band from your research. Mention the reasons you think this band's concerts are great. Consider adding quotes from people you interviewed at the concert.

In Spoken Communication   A Speech at a Culture Fair

2. Review the research plan you outlined earlier to find out about foods of South America. Choose a particular type of food or the food of a particular country to research. **Prepare a short speech** on the subject you chose. Use your note cards to organize your ideas thematically. Describe the food, the country or region it comes from, and the occasions when it is most often eaten. Then present your speech to your classmates. Consider using visuals to make your presentation clearer or more informative.

Timed Writing   Report to the Mayor

3. Build on the research plan you developed earlier about the costs and benefits of a new sports stadium for your city (see page 321). Follow your research plan by collecting information about other cities and interviewing your classmates. **Write a report** for the mayor that she can use to present her ideas to the people of the city. The mayor believes that a new stadium will bring a renewed sense of civic pride to the city and encourage economic growth. Provide information about the costs of the stadium and the revenue it will generate. Draw conclusions about whether your evidence supports the mayor's beliefs. Work quotations from the citizens you interviewed into your report smoothly. Include citations so the mayor knows the sources of your information. You have 35 minutes to complete your work after you have gathered all the necessary information from sources and have completed the interviews with your classmates. (For help with budgeting time, see pages 398–399.)

   Before You Write Consider the following questions: What is the subject? What is the occasion? Who is the audience? What is the purpose?

   After You Write Evaluate your work using the Six-Trait Rubric on page 358.

Guide to 21st Century

School and Workplace Skills

Part I
Critical Thinking and Problem Solving for Academic Success — 364

- **A.** Learning Study Skills — 366
- **B.** Taking Standardized Tests — 372
- **C.** Taking Essay Tests — 391

Part II
Communication and Collaboration — 400

- **A.** Vocabulary — 402
- **B.** Letters and Forms — 418
- **C.** Directions and Speeches — 432

Part III
Media and Technology — 447

- **A.** Electronic Publishing — 449
- **B.** Using the Internet — 464

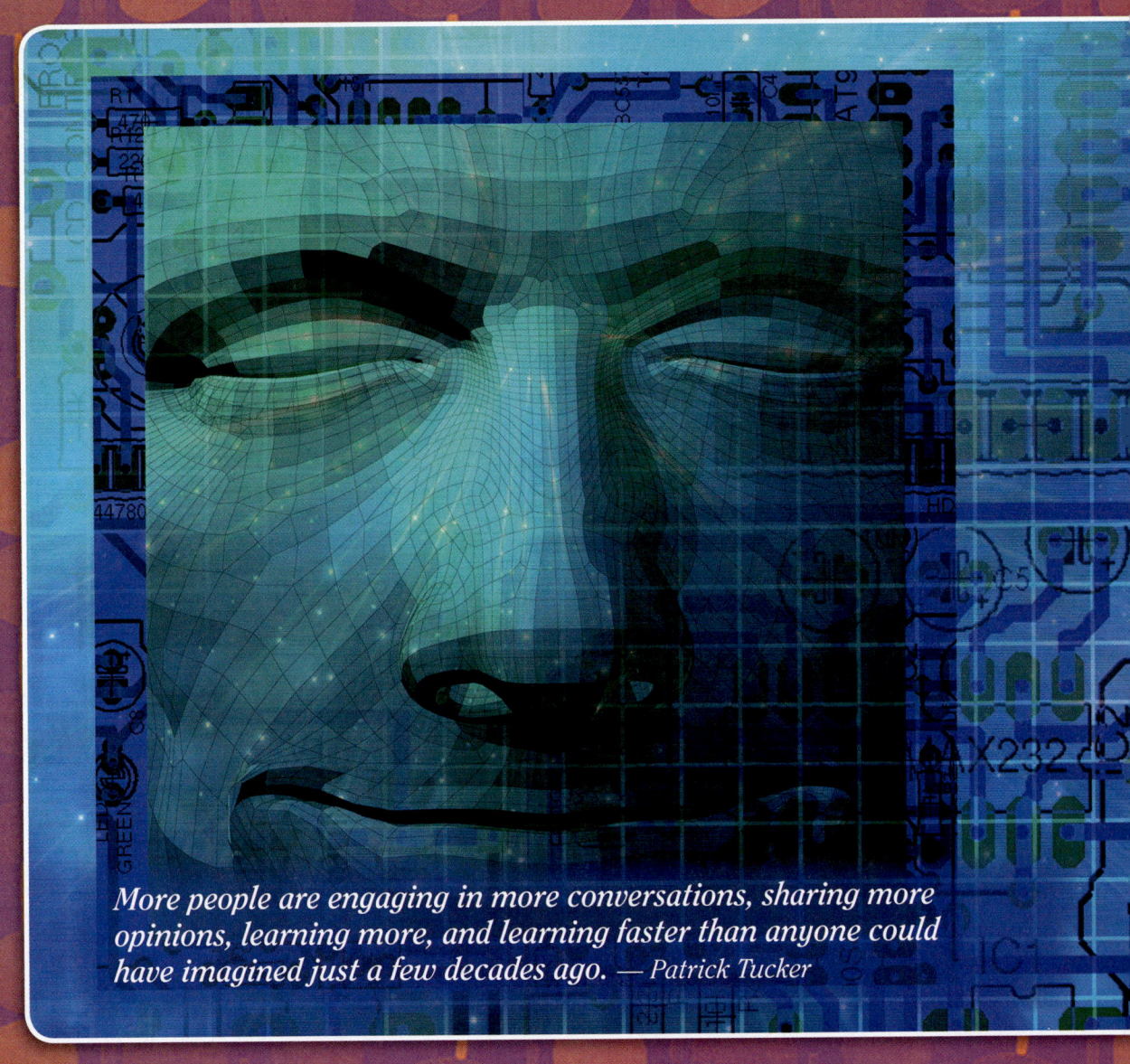

More people are engaging in more conversations, sharing more opinions, learning more, and learning faster than anyone could have imagined just a few decades ago. — Patrick Tucker

Students, citizens, and workers face new challenges in the global and technological world of the 21st century. While developing technology skills is essential, developing human relations skills—the ability to collaborate and communicate with people across cultures, to solve problems, to think creatively—may be even more important.

PART I

Critical Thinking and Problem Solving for Academic Success

> **Part I** Critical Thinking and Problem Solving for Academic Success
> **Part II** Communication and Collaboration
> **Part III** Media and Technology

Essential Skills

Every day in school, you are asked to use your **critical thinking** and **problem-solving skills.** In Part I of this guide, you will learn how to apply these skills in order to succeed academically.

Critical Thinking

USING REASONING

The word *reasoning* refers to the process of making inferences, making judgments, or drawing conclusions. In your social studies class, for example, you use reasoning to determine the causes of a rebellion. Using sound reasoning is essential for every task you perform in school. Always check for errors in your reasoning. Make sure that your reasoning is logical and is based on facts, examples, or other types of support. (See pages 223, 226, and 249.)

ANALYZING OUTCOMES

In your academic subjects, you often examine cause-and-effect relationships. In your social studies class, you may explore how events and other factors led to the passing of a law. In your science class, you may study the interaction between chemicals or the parts of a system, such as an ecosystem. Understanding these relationships and interactions is essential for analyzing outcomes, or results. It will help you gain insight into how systems and processes work.

EVALUATING AND DRAWING CONCLUSIONS

Thinking critically means much more than simply understanding information. You need to analyze and evaluate evidence, claims, and different points of view. You need to make inferences and interpret information. You should also make connections and synthesize information. Then you should draw conclusions. Critical thinking also involves reflecting on your learning in order to evaluate your skills and methods. Learning how to evaluate information effectively and draw logical conclusions will help you make sound judgments and decisions in school and in your daily life.

You can learn more about specific critical thinking skills on the following pages:

Elaborating, page 54	Imagining, page 186
Seeing Relationships, page 72	Analyzing, page 226
Generalizing, page 89	Evaluating Counter-Arguments, page 253
Ordering, page 110	Summarizing, page 295
Recalling, page 134	Classifying, page 343
Visualizing, page 161	

❷ Developing Solutions

SOLVING PROBLEMS

To solve problems, you should use sound reasoning, analyze outcomes, and evaluate and draw conclusions. In other words, you should use your critical thinking skills. For example, when you encounter a problem on a test, first look for connections between it and other problems you have solved in the past. Next decide if the solution should follow certain conventions or patterns. Remember to use logical reasoning, and then draw conclusions to determine the correct solution. When you have to solve complex problems, ask questions. Then synthesize and evaluate information and different viewpoints to produce strong, creative solutions. Developing and applying your problem-solving skills in school will prepare you for resolving problems in other areas of your life.

A. Learning Study Skills

Part I Critical Thinking and Problem Solving for Academic Success	**A.** Learning Study Skills 366
Part II Communication and Collaboration	**B.** Taking Standardized Tests 372
Part III Media and Technology	**C.** Taking Essay Tests 391

Apply Critical Thinking Skills

When you use your critical thinking skills, you think actively about what you read and hear. Critical thinking involves asking questions, making connections, analyzing, and interpreting. Critical thinkers also evaluate and draw conclusions. When you interpret the theme of a short story or distinguish between fact and opinion, you are using your critical thinking skills.

Thinking critically also involves reflecting on your learning. Evaluating the methods you use to study and prepare for assignments and tests will help you identify your strengths. It will also help you determine how you can learn more effectively.

In this section, you will develop your study skills. Improving these skills will help you become a better critical thinker and help you succeed in school.

Developing Effective Study Skills

Adopting good study habits will help you complete your daily classroom assignments. Improve your study habits by using the following strategies.

Strategies for Effective Studying

- Choose an area that is well lighted and quiet.
- Equip your study area with everything you need for reading and writing. You can easily access a dictionary and thesaurus online, but you may want to have print versions of these resources on hand.
- Keep an assignment book for recording due dates.
- Allow plenty of time to complete your work. Begin your assignments early.
- Adjust your reading rate to suit your purpose.

1 Adjusting Reading Rate to Purpose

Your reading rate is the speed at which you read. Depending on your purpose in reading, you may choose to read certain materials more quickly than others.

If your purpose is to get a quick impression of the contents of a newspaper, you should scan the headlines. If you want to identify the main ideas of an article, you should skim it. If your purpose is to learn new facts or understand details, you should read the article closely.

Whether you are reading a newspaper, an article in a periodical, or a textbook, you can read with greater effectiveness and efficiency if you adjust your reading rate to suit your purpose for reading.

SCANNING

Scanning is reading to get a general impression and to prepare for learning about a subject. To scan, you should read the title, headings, subheadings, picture captions, words and phrases in boldface or italics, and any focus questions. Using this method, you can quickly determine what the material is about and what questions to keep in mind. Scanning is also a way to familiarize yourself with everything a book has to offer. Scan the table of contents, appendix, glossary, and index of a book before reading.

SKIMMING

After scanning a chapter, a section, or an article, you should quickly read—or skim—the introduction, the topic sentence of each paragraph, and the conclusion. **Skimming** is reading quickly to identify the purpose, thesis, main ideas, and supporting details of a selection.

Close Reading

Most of your assignments for school will require close reading, which is an essential step for critical thinking. You use **close reading** for locating specific information, following the logic of an argument, or comprehending the meaning or significance of information. After scanning a selection or chapter, read it more slowly, word for word, to understand the text's meaning fully. You can then apply your critical thinking skills to analyze and interpret information and ideas. Be sure to evaluate points and draw conclusions so that you can make judgments and decisions. Pose questions based on your close reading to help you solve problems.

Reading a Textbook—SQ3R

When you read a textbook, you should combine the techniques of scanning, skimming, and close reading by using the SQ3R study strategy. This method helps you understand and remember what you read. The *S* in *SQ3R* stands for *Survey,* the *Q* for *Question,* and the *3R* for *Read, Recite,* and *Review.*

	THE SQ3R STUDY STRATEGY
Survey	First get a general idea of what the selection is about by scanning the title, headings, subheadings, and words that are set off in a different type or color. Also look at maps, tables, charts, and other illustrations. Then read the introduction and conclusion or summary.
Question	Decide what questions you should be able to answer after reading the selection. You can do this by turning the headings and subheadings into questions or by looking at any study questions in the book.
Read	Now read the selection. As you read, try to answer your questions. In addition, find the main idea in each section, and look for important information that is not included in your questions. After reading, review the important points in the selection and take notes. (See pages 369–371.)
Recite	Answer each question in your own words by reciting or writing the answers.
Review	Answer the questions again without looking at your notes or at the selection. Continue reviewing until you answer each question correctly.

● **Practice Your Skills**

Choosing a Reading Strategy

Think of all the reading you have to do in the next week in order to complete assignments and prepare for tests. For example, you may need to do research for a social studies project, study for a science test, or read several poems. Choose one of these tasks, and decide whether you will use scanning, skimming, close reading, or the SQ3R study strategy to complete it. Then use the strategy to complete the task. When you are done, write a brief paragraph reflecting on what you learned from this activity. Did you choose the correct strategy? Why or why not?

❷ Taking Notes

Taking notes when reading a textbook or listening to a lecture will help you identify and remember important points. It will also prepare you to engage in critical thinking. Once you identify and record key information, you can make connections, evaluate points, and draw conclusions. Three methods for taking notes are the informal outline, the graphic organizer, and the summary.

In an **informal outline,** you use words and phrases to record main ideas and important details. Notes in this form are helpful in studying for an objective test because they emphasize specific facts.

In a **graphic organizer,** words and phrases are arranged in a visual pattern to indicate the relationships between main ideas and supporting details. The graphic organizer is an excellent tool for studying information for an objective test, for preparing an open-ended assessment, or for writing an essay. The visual organizer allows you instantly to see important information and its relationship to other ideas.

In a **summary,** you use sentences to express important ideas in your own words. A summary should not simply restate the ideas presented in the textbook or lecture. Instead, a good summary should express relationships between ideas and state conclusions. For this reason, summarizing is useful for preparing for an essay test.

In the following passage from a textbook, the essential information about snow leopards is underlined. Following the passage are examples of notes in the form of an informal outline, a graphic organizer, and a summary.

MODEL: Essential Information

The harsh Himalaya Mountains are home to the snow leopard. Beautiful and rare, this creature lives and hunts alone. Its beautiful, thick winter coat has rows of charcoal gray spots on a light gray to white background. Large paws thickly padded with hair and powerful back legs give the snow leopard protection and great hunting ability. Unfortunately, it has been hunted almost to extinction.

Despite laws against either owning or selling its fur, the snow leopard is still a target for poachers.

Informal Outline

The Snow Leopard

1. Lives in the Himalaya Mountains
2. Lives and hunts alone
3. Has a white or light gray coat with charcoal spots
4. Has large paws and powerful back legs—great hunting ability
5. Has been hunted almost to extinction by poachers

Graphic Organizer

The Snow Leopard

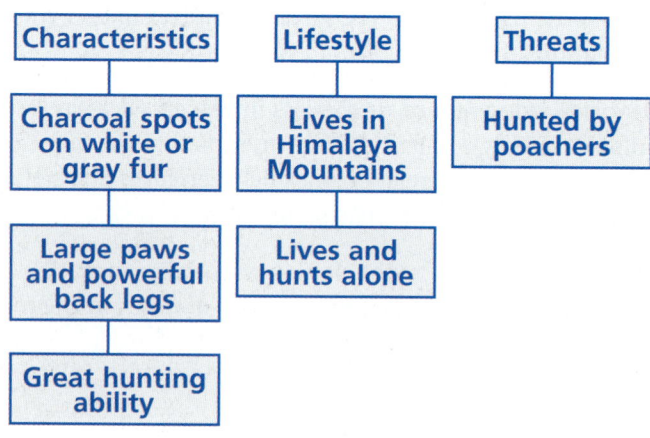

A. Learning Study Skills

Summary

The Snow Leopard

The snow leopard is a beautiful animal that lives and hunts alone in the Himalaya Mountains. Its coat is white or light gray with charcoal gray spots. The snow leopard, with its large paws and powerful back legs, is an excellent hunter. Unfortunately, poachers have hunted the snow leopard almost to extinction.

Whichever note-taking method you use, the following strategies will help you make your notes clear and well organized.

Strategies for Taking Notes

- Label your notes with the title and page numbers of the chapter or the topic and date of the lecture.
- Record only the main ideas and important details.
- Use the title, headings, subheadings, and words in special type to help you select the most important information.
- Use your own words; do not copy word for word.
- Use as few words as possible.

● **Practice Your Skills**

Taking Notes

Choose one of your reading assignments for the next week. Select two of the three methods of note-taking—an informal outline, a graphic organizer, or a summary—and take notes on the reading using each of these two methods. Then write a paragraph comparing and contrasting the two methods you used. Was one method more effective than the other? Why or why not?

Developing Effective Study Skills

B. Taking Standardized Tests

Part I Critical Thinking and Problem Solving for Academic Success	**A.** Learning Study Skills 366
Part II Communication and Collaboration	**B.** Taking Standardized Tests 372
Part III Media and Technology	**C.** Taking Essay Tests 391

Applying Your Critical Thinking and Problem-Solving Skills

To succeed on standardized tests, you should become familiar with the kinds of questions you will be asked. Learning test-taking strategies will help you become a better test taker as well.

Applying your critical thinking skills is also essential for success. Standardized test questions, such as analogies, require you to use reasoning to determine the correct answer. Other types of test items, such as reading comprehension questions, ask you to analyze, infer, interpret, make connections, and draw conclusions.

For all types of test questions, you need to use your problem-solving skills. You must determine what a question is asking and how you should arrive at the correct answer. You should decide if a particular question is a familiar type. If it is, decide if the answer should match certain conventions or patterns.

Learning to apply your critical thinking and problem-solving skills effectively will help you not only when taking tests but also when completing your daily classroom assignments. Using these skills effectively will help you in all aspects of your daily life as well.

In this section, you will develop your skills in taking standardized tests. Improving these skills will help you do your best on classroom, school-wide, or state-wide standardized tests.

Strategies for Taking Standardized Tests

A standardized test measures your academic progress, skills, and achievement in such a way that the results can be compared with those of other students who have taken the same test. Standardized tests that assess your verbal skills, or your ability to use language, include vocabulary tests, analogy tests, sentence-completion tests, reading comprehension tests, and tests of Standard written English.

The best way to do well on standardized tests is to work consistently on your school subjects throughout the year, to read widely, and to learn test-taking strategies.

Strategies for Taking Standardized Tests

- Relax. Although you can expect to be a little nervous, concentrate on doing your best.
- Read the test directions carefully. Answer the sample questions to be sure you understand what the test requires.
- Preview the whole test; skim it to get an overview of the kinds of questions on it.
- Plan your time carefully. Note how much time is allotted for each part of the test.
- Answer first the questions you find easiest. Skip hard questions, coming back to them later if you have time.
- Read all choices before you choose an answer. If you are not sure of the answer, try to eliminate choices that are obviously wrong. Educated guessing often helps.
- If you have time, check your answers. Be sure you have correctly marked your answers.

❶ Vocabulary Tests

One kind of vocabulary test asks you to find **antonyms**—words that mean the opposite of other words. For instance, in the following test item, you must find the antonym for *weary* among the five choices.

WEARY: (A) tired (B) energetic (C) sleepy
        (D) worn   (E) exhausted

(The answer is (B) because *energetic* is an antonym for *weary*. The other choices are wrong because each has a similar meaning to *weary*.)

Test items about **synonyms** have the same format. However, instead of choosing the opposite of a given word, you choose the word that has the same meaning.

AMAZE: (A) astonish (B) heavy (C) fast
        (D) bore   (E) weary

(The answer is (A) *astonish*, which means the same as *amaze*.)

In the following item, the answer is *(A) gleam*, which means the same as *shimmer*.

SHIMMER: (A) gleam (B) shake (C) dance
          (D) bore   (E) dull

Practice Your Skills

Recognizing Antonyms

Write the letter of the word that is most nearly opposite in meaning to the word in capital letters.

1. PERISHABLE:
- (A) everlasting
- (B) dislike
- (C) thin
- (D) tasty
- (E) decayed

2. ORDINARY:
- (A) uncommon
- (B) usual
- (C) funny
- (D) noble
- (E) regular

3. CHOPPY:
- (A) calm
- (B) rough
- (C) sharp
- (D) brief
- (E) loose

4. PROLONG:
- (A) shorten
- (B) lengthen
- (C) close
- (D) disturb
- (E) run

Practice Your Skills

Recognizing Synonyms

Write the letter of the word that is most similar in meaning to the word in capital letters.

1. VESSEL:
- (A) blood
- (B) slave
- (C) container
- (D) stop
- (E) tomb

2. EMOTIONAL:
- (A) fierce
- (B) comical
- (C) violent
- (D) excitable
- (E) happy

3. ORIGIN:
- (A) name
- (B) society
- (C) owner
- (D) beginning
- (E) end

4. EMBRACE:
- (A) learn
- (B) hug
- (C) fear
- (D) batter
- (E) fight

❷ Analogies

Analogy questions test your skill at figuring out relationships between words. To complete an analogy, you need to use reasoning. Your first step is to decide how the given words—the first pair of words, usually in capital letters—are related to each other. The next step is to decide which other pair has the same kind of relationship as the given pair.

The single colon in an analogy question stands for the words *is to,* and the double colon stands for the word *as.*

> COMPOSER : SONG :: painter : portrait

The above example reads, "Composer is to song as painter is to portrait." That is, a composer has the same relationship to a song as a painter has to a portrait. A composer and a painter are both artists, and a song and a portrait are items they create. Explaining an analogy to yourself in one sentence can help you to figure out the answer. In the following example, you might say, "A snake is a kind of reptile."

> SNAKE : REPTILE ::
> (A) lion : tiger   (B) wood : hard
> (C) diamond : gem   (D) ceiling : roof
> (E) language : Spanish
>
> (The answer, *(C) diamond : gem,* expresses the same item-to-category relationship.)

The word order in an analogy is very important. If the given pair of words in the analogy expresses a part-to-whole order, for example, the words in the correct answer should also appear in the order of part to whole.

Some analogies are written in sentence form.

> *Calm* is to *peaceful* as *sorrow* is to ▪.
> (A) anger   (B) joy
> (C) sadness   (D) confusion
> (E) illness
>
> (The first two italicized words are synonyms. Therefore, the correct answer is *(C) sadness,* a synonym for *sorrow.*)

Strategies for Taking Standardized Tests   375

Knowing some of the common types of analogies, like those in the following chart, will help you figure out word relationships. In the first step for completing an analogy, determining whether the relationship between the words is one of the familiar, conventional types will make it easier to select the correct answer.

COMMON TYPES OF ANALOGIES

Analogy	Example
word : synonym	competition : contest
word : antonym	fail : succeed
part : whole	screen : television
cause : effect	sun : heatstroke
worker : tool	speaker : microphone
worker : product	chef : meal
item : purpose	crane : lift
item : category	baseball : sport

● Practice Your Skills

Recognizing Analogies

Write the letter of the word pair that has the same relationship as the word pair in capital letters.

1. WHISPER : SHOUT ::
   (A) foretell : predict   (B) lessen : increase
   (C) wish : desire   (D) decay : organism
   (E) friend : ally

2. SHIMMER : SHINE ::
   (A) smile : grin   (B) cry : laugh
   (C) walk : ride   (D) needle : thread
   (E) boring : interesting

3. CUNNING : SLYNESS ::
   (A) beauty : ugliness   (B) bravery : courage
   (C) emptiness : fullness   (D) game : tennis
   (E) smart : student

4. FLEXIBLE : RIGID ::
   (A) modern : old-fashioned   (B) similar : alike
   (C) reliable : trustworthy   (D) doctor : profession
   (E) pencil : paper

5. CONFIDENTIAL : SECRET ::
   (A) nervous : calm
   (B) rainy : dry
   (C) lifeless : dead
   (D) telephone : message
   (E) scared : bold

● Practice Your Skills

Completing Analogies

Use the chart on page 376 to determine the relationship of the first pair of words. Then complete the analogy by writing the letter of the word that best completes the sentence.

1. *Oven* is to *heat* as *lid* is to ▭.
   (A) decorate
   (B) food
   (C) cover
   (D) save
   (E) liquid

2. *Drawer* is to *dresser* as *branch* is to ▭.
   (A) tree
   (B) leaves
   (C) roots
   (D) strong
   (E) arm

3. *Firefighter* is to *hose* as *fishers* is to ▭.
   (A) fish
   (B) river
   (C) catch
   (D) net
   (E) water

4. *Poetry* is to *literature* as *documentary* is to ▭.
   (A) director
   (B) theater
   (C) film
   (D) novel
   (E) truth

5. *Carpenter* is to *cabinet* as *tailor* is to ▭.
   (A) sewing machine
   (B) pants
   (C) model
   (D) designer
   (E) fabric

Strategies for Taking Standardized Tests

3 Sentence-Completion Tests

Sentence-completion tests measure your ability to comprehend what you read and to use context correctly. Each item consists of a sentence with one or more words missing. First read the entire sentence. Then read the answer choices. Use logical reasoning to select the answer that completes the sentence in a way that makes sense. Read the following item, and then find the word that most appropriately completes the sentence.

The new cars are very ▪; they burn no more fuel than they absolutely need.

(A) small (B) expensive
(C) efficient (D) reliable
(E) colorful

(The answer is *(C) efficient*. Efficient cars use only the fuel they need.)

Some sentence-completion questions have two blanks in the same sentence, with each answer choice including two words. Find the correct answer in this example.

Her long illness left Maria ▪ and ▪.

(A) happy . . . rested (B) scarred . . . smiling
(C) cheery . . . homesick (D) thin . . . tired
(E) sleepy . . . careful

(The answer is *(D) thin . . . tired*. The other choices do not make sense.)

● Practice Your Skills

Completing Sentences

Write the letter of the word that best completes each of the following sentences.

1. The cloud ▪ itself around the mountain like a shawl around giant shoulders.
   (A) wrapped (B) opened
   (C) left (D) pounded
   (E) tickled

2. The twins were ▪ in every way, from the dimples in their cheeks to the color of their hair.
   (A) annoyed (B) identical
   (C) young (D) sisters
   (E) happy

378   B. Taking Standardized Tests

3. The doctor was pleased to announce that the patient had made a complete ▇ and showed no sign of illness.
   (A) recovery   (B) sickness
   (C) diagnosis   (D) operation
   (E) coma

4. Something is missing in the egg salad; I must have ▇ an ingredient.
   (A) doubled   (B) omitted
   (C) chopped   (D) mixed
   (E) bought

5. The ▇ of the house was run-down, but the interior of the house was beautifully maintained.
   (A) outside   (B) roof
   (C) basement   (D) paint
   (E) kitchen

● **Practice Your Skills**

Completing Sentences with Two Blanks

Write the letter of the words that best complete each of the following sentences.

1. Deep-sea ▇ keep warm by wearing suits that water cannot ▇.
   (A) skiers . . . immerse   (B) boats . . . freeze
   (C) divers . . . penetrate   (D) boaters . . . wrinkle
   (E) fishers . . . drink

2. To avoid being ▇, always use your hand to ▇ the water before entering the shower to make sure it is not too hot.
   (A) scalded . . . test   (B) wet . . . drink
   (C) cleaned . . . touch   (D) cold . . . freeze
   (E) sleepy . . . splash

3. Sheryl was ▇ and shy, while her sister was loud and ▇.
   (A) boisterous . . . meek   (B) quiet . . . outgoing
   (C) social . . . boisterous   (D) timid . . . shy
   (E) lonely . . . scared

Strategies for Taking Standardized Tests

4. After paying all our expenses, our club has a ▢ of $45, which we are going to donate to ▢.
   (A) wallet . . . ourselves
   (B) surplus . . . charity
   (C) bowl . . . spend
   (D) wish . . . families
   (E) purse . . . groceries

5. Jason became ▢ and gave up quickly, but Ben was ▢ and, after hours of work, finally solved the brainteaser.
   (A) happy . . . angry
   (B) wonderful . . . talented
   (C) frustrated . . . persistent
   (D) eager . . . confused
   (E) cheerful . . . lost

4 Reading Comprehension Tests

Reading comprehension tests assess your ability to understand and to analyze written passages. The information you need to answer the test questions may be either directly stated or implied in the passage. You must use your critical thinking skills to make inferences as you read, to analyze and interpret the passage, and to draw conclusions in order to answer the questions. The following strategies will help you answer questions on reading comprehension tests.

HERE'S HOW Strategies for Reading Comprehension Questions

- Begin by skimming the questions that follow the passage so you know what to focus on as you read.
- Read the passage carefully. Notice the main ideas, organization, style, and key words.
- Study all possible answers. Avoid choosing one answer the moment you think it is a reasonable choice.
- Use only the information in the passage when you answer the questions. Do not rely on your own knowledge or ideas on this kind of test.

Most reading comprehension questions focus on one or more of the following characteristics of a written passage.

- **Main Idea** At least one question will usually focus on the central idea of the passage. Remember that the main idea of a passage covers all sections of the passage—not just one section or paragraph.

- **Supporting Details** Questions about supporting details test your ability to identify the statements in the passage that back up the main idea.

- **Implied Meanings** In some passages not all information is directly stated. Some questions ask you to infer or interpret in order to answer questions about points that the author has merely implied.

- **Purpose and Tone** Questions on purpose and tone require that you interpret or analyze the author's purpose for writing and his or her attitude toward the subject.

Practice Your Skills

Reading for Comprehension

Read the following passage, and write the letter of the correct answer to each question that follows it.

> The amount of the sun's energy that a place receives varies because of the way the earth moves in space. In many places, including most of the United States, winters are colder than summers. Other places may have hot or cold weather all year round. The differences are caused by changes in the earth's position in relation to the sun.
>
> As it travels through space, the earth spins like a top. This spinning motion is called rotation. The earth rotates on its axis. The axis is an imaginary line through the center of the earth from one pole to the other. The axis is tilted at an angle. Because of this angle, one half of the earth is tilted toward the sun and therefore receives more direct sunlight. There it is summer, and temperatures are warmer. The other half is tilted away from the sun and receives less direct solar energy. There it is winter, and temperatures are cooler.
>
> In addition to spinning on its axis, the earth travels around the sun. In this motion, called revolution, the earth follows a nearly circular path, or orbit, around the sun. The earth takes about 365 days to make one complete revolution around the sun. As it revolves, it remains tilted at the same angle. Therefore, the half of the earth that was tilted toward the sun and experiencing summer will, half a year later, be tilted away from the sun and having winter. The opposite is true of the other half of the earth. It will now be tilted toward the sun and enjoying summer.

1. The best title for this passage is
   (A) Earth's Movement and the Sun.
   (B) Earth and Its Moon.
   (C) Our Incredible Solar System.
   (D) The History of the Sun.
   (E) My Trip to the Moon.

2. Changes in temperature on the earth's surface are due to
   (A) the temperature of the sun.
   (B) the tilt and movement of the earth.
   (C) the distance of the moon from the earth.
   (D) earth's position in the galaxy.
   (E) the position of people on the earth.

3. The passage indicates that the United States
   (A) is not the only country to have differences in temperature.
   (B) is warm all year.
   (C) has hot winters and cold summers.
   (D) has the same temperatures as the countries at the equator.
   (E) always receives the same amount of energy from the sun.

4. This passage would most likely appear in
   (A) a science textbook.
   (B) a news magazine.
   (C) an article on a travel Web site.
   (D) a book about the history of space travel.
   (E) a novel.

THE DOUBLE PASSAGE

You may be asked to read a pair of passages, called the double passage. Then you will be asked questions about each passage individually and about the relationship between the two passages. The two passages may present similar or opposing views, or they may complement each other in various ways. A brief introduction preceding the passages may help you anticipate the relationship between them. Questions about double passages require you to use your critical thinking skills in order to make connections and synthesize information.

All of the questions follow the second passage. The first few questions relate to Passage 1, the next few questions relate to Passage 2, and the final questions relate to both passages. You may find it helpful to read Passage 1 first and then immediately answer the questions related only to it. Then read Passage 2 and answer the remaining questions.

- **Practice Your Skills**

  Reading for Double-Passage Comprehension

  The following passages are about uniforms for schoolchildren in the United States. Read each passage, and answer the questions that follow.

  ## Passage 1

  The recent increase in school violence has led teachers, parents, and students to consider uniforms for public-school children in America. In doing so, these proponents of similar fashion are squashing our schoolchildren's self-esteem. As children mature, they seek their individuality—they want to know *who* they are. Wearing a uniform to a school in which every other student is wearing the same outfit limits a student's self-expression. If students can't express themselves, they cannot possibly understand who they are. Although they might believe they are protecting children from school violence, those who force students to wear uniforms are stifling the individual personalities, creativity, and freedom of America's children.

  ## Passage 2

  Peer pressure for America's schoolchildren is overwhelming. Most children today are caught between pleasing their friends and following the rules. As unusual as it may seem, much peer pressure involves clothing. Children are harassed, berated, and attacked because of their choice of clothing. One solution to the problem is to require all schoolchildren to wear uniforms. If all the students in a school wear the same clothes, no one will be singled out for his or her choices. Wearing uniforms will give students relief from the pressures of deciding what to wear and the fear of wearing the "wrong" outfit. It's a simple solution with a valuable result.

  1. According to the author of Passage 1, which of the following best explains the reason that schoolchildren should not wear uniforms?
     (A) Wearing uniforms stifles a student's individuality.
     (B) Students like to wear expensive clothes.
     (C) Clothing should not play a significant role in students' lives.
     (D) Students need to look the same.
     (E) Uniforms are cost effective.

Strategies for Taking Standardized Tests

2. The purpose of Passage 1 is to
   (A) inform readers about self-esteem.
   (B) persuade people to require uniforms.
   (C) entertain readers with humorous stories about uniforms.
   (D) persuade people not to require uniforms.
   (E) inform the reader of the cost of uniforms.

3. According to the author of Passage 2, which of the following is a result of wearing uniforms?
   (A) relief from peer pressure
   (B) an increase in violence against students
   (C) a decrease in students' self-esteem
   (D) an increase in choices of clothing
   (E) an increased laundry bill

4. The tone of Passage 2 is
   (A) lighthearted.
   (B) insistent.
   (C) mean-spirited.
   (D) humorous.
   (E) optimistic.

5. Which of the following is not mentioned by either author?
   (A) School uniforms can decrease the amount of peer pressure faced by children.
   (B) Wearing uniforms will not eliminate all problems faced by children.
   (C) School uniforms might be a solution to problems faced by children in school.
   (D) Expressing individual tastes in clothing can increase self-esteem.
   (E) Students who wear uniforms will not be singled out for their choices.

5 Tests of Standard Written English

Objective tests of Standard written English assess your knowledge of the language skills used for writing. They may contain sentences with underlined words, phrases, and punctuation. The underlined parts may contain errors in grammar, usage, mechanics, vocabulary, or spelling. These tests ask you to use your problem-solving skills to find the error in each sentence or to identify the best way to revise a sentence or passage.

FINDING ERRORS

The most familiar way to test students' knowledge of grammar, usage, capitalization, punctuation, word choice, and spelling is by asking them to find errors in sentences. A typical test item of this kind is a sentence with five underlined choices. Four of the choices suggest possible errors in the sentence. The fifth choice states that there is no error. Read the following sentence and identify the error, if there is one.

> There <u>are</u> about 20,000 <u>islands</u> in the Pacific <u>ocean</u>, the <u>largest</u> ocean in
>   A   B   C   D
> the world. <u>No error</u>
>   E
>
> *(The answer is (C). The word* ocean *should be capitalized as part of the proper name* Pacific Ocean.*)*

The list below shows errors to watch for on a test of Standard written English.

- lack of agreement between subject and verb
- lack of agreement between pronoun and antecedent
- incorrect spelling or use of a word
- missing, misplaced, or unnecessary punctuation
- missing or unnecessary capitalization
- misused or misplaced italics or quotation marks

Sometimes you will find a sentence that contains no error. Be careful, however, before you choose *E (No error)* as the answer. It is easy to overlook a mistake, since common errors are the kind generally included on this type of test. Parts of a sentence that are not underlined are presumed to be correct. You can use clues in the correct parts of the sentence to help you search for errors in the underlined parts.

● Practice Your Skills

Recognizing Errors in Writing

Write the letter of the underlined word or punctuation mark that is incorrect. If the sentence contains no error, write *E*.

(1) Volcanoes <u>occur</u> when <u>pressure</u> builds up <u>under neath</u> the <u>earth's</u>
                A   B   C   D
surface. (2) <u>Usually</u> a volcano warns that <u>its</u> going to <u>erupt</u> by <u>rumbling</u>.
             A   B   C   D
(3) The <u>eruption</u> can take <u>two</u> <u>forms</u> <u>both impressive.</u> (4) Either the volcano
          A   B   C   D
<u>shoots</u> out chunks of burning debris <u>or</u> it sends out a flow of <u>liquid rock</u><u>,</u>
 A   B   C   D
called lava. (5) Lava may seem <u>scaryer</u><u>,</u> but the <u>flying</u> debris can be more
                                        A B   C
<u>dangerous</u>. (6) <u>Because</u> lava <u>move</u> slowly, it is not <u>impossible</u> to <u>avoid</u>.
      D   A   B   C   D
(7) Flying chunks of <u>rock</u> on the other hand<u>,</u> can travel far and <u>ignite</u>
                    A   B   C
<u>roofs</u> instantly.
 D

SENTENCE-CORRECTION QUESTIONS

Sentence-correction questions assess your ability to recognize appropriate phrasing. Instead of locating an error in a sentence, you must use your problem-solving skills to select the most appropriate and effective way to write the sentence.

In this kind of question, a part of the sentence is underlined. The sentence is then followed by five different ways of writing the underlined part. The first way shown, *(A)*, simply repeats the original underlined portion. The other four choices present alternative ways of writing the underlined part. The choices may differ in grammar, usage, capitalization, punctuation, or word choice. Consider all answer choices carefully. If there is an error in the original underlined portion, make sure the answer you choose solves the problem. Be sure that the answer you select does not introduce a new error and does not change the meaning of the original sentence. Look at the following example.

Maria seen that movie at the theater last night.

(A) seen that movie at the theater
(B) seen that movie, at the theater
(C) saw that movie, at the theater
(D) saw that movie at the theater
(E) saw that movie. At the theater

(The correct answer is *(D)*. Choices *(A)* and *(B)* are incorrect because they use the past participle of *see* instead of the past form of the verb. In *(B)*, as well as in *(C)* and *(E)*, punctuation is used incorrectly.)

● **Practice Your Skills**

Correcting Sentences

Write the letter of the most appropriate way of phrasing the underlined part of each sentence.

1. Harry hasn't said nothing since breakfast.
(A) hasn't said nothing
(B) hasnt said nothing
(C) hasn't said, nothing
(D) hasn't said anything
(E) has not said nothing

2. The first person off the plane was aunt bea.
   (A) the plane was aunt bea.
   (B) the plane was Aunt bea.
   (C) the Plane was Aunt Bea.
   (D) the plane was Ant Bea.
   (E) the plane was Aunt Bea.

3. The weather forecast called for sleet snow and rain.
   (A) called for sleet snow and rain.
   (B) called for sleet, snow, and rain.
   (C) call for sleet, snow, and rain.
   (D) called for sleet, snow, and, rain.
   (E) called for sleet and snow. And rain.

4. Last night I finished reading the story Today.
   (A) reading the story Today.
   (B) reading, the story Today.
   (C) reading the story Today.
   (D) reading the story "Today."
   (E) read the story Today.

5. All the boys carried theirs own suitcases.
   (A) carried theirs own suitcases.
   (B) carried his own suitcases.
   (C) carried their own suitcases.
   (D) carried him own suitcases.
   (E) carried them own suitcases.

REVISION-IN-CONTEXT

Another type of multiple-choice question that appears on some standardized tests is called revision-in-context. Such questions are based on a short passage and assess your reading comprehension skills, your writing skills, and your understanding of Standard written English. The questions following the passage ask you to choose the best revision of a sentence, a group of sentences, or the essay as a whole. To select the correct answer, use your critical thinking skills to evaluate the relative merits of each choice. You may also be asked to identify the writer's intention. To do so, you will need to analyze the passage carefully to determine the writer's purpose.

Strategies for Taking Standardized Tests

MODEL: Correcting Sentences

(1) The explorers found themselves in a barren land. (2) No signs of life were nowhere. (3) The sun parched the earth. (4) Water was nowhere to be found. (5) Suddenly they heard the rattle of a snake. (6) The explorers fled for safety. (7) Snakes were not the only kind of hazard these newcomers would have to face.

1. Which of the following is the best revision of sentence 2?
   (A) There were no signs of life anywhere.
   (B) Signs of life were anywhere.
   (C) Nowhere is signs of life.
   (D) Signs of life wasn't anywhere to be found.
   (E) There were no signs of life no where.

(The correct answer is *(A)*, which does not contain the double negative found in sentence 2. Choice *(B)* does not express the same meaning as sentence 2. *(C)* and *(D)* contain errors in subject-verb agreement. *(E)* contains a double negative and a spelling error.)

2. Which of the following is the best way to combine sentences 3 and 4?
   (A) The sun parched the earth, and water was nowhere to be found.
   (B) The sun parched the earth and found water nowhere.
   (C) The sun parching the earth and finding water nowhere.
   (D) The sun was parching the earth and water was nowhere to be found.
   (E) The sun parched the earth, water was nowhere to be found.

(The correct answer is *(A)*. In *(B)* and *(C)*, *sun* is incorrectly made the subject of both verbs. In addition, incorrect verb forms are used in *(C)* as well as in *(D)*, which also lacks a comma. *(E)* is a run-on sentence.)

B. Taking Standardized Tests

3. In relation to the rest of the passage, which of the following best describes the writer's intention in sentence 7?
   (A) to restate the opening sentence
   (B) to interest the reader in the story
   (C) to persuade the reader to avoid snakes
   (D) to summarize the paragraph
   (E) to provide supporting details about snakes

(The correct answer is *(B)*, which can be determined by the process of elimination. Sentence 7 does not serve the purposes described in the other answer choices.)

● **Practice Your Skills**

Correcting Sentences

Carefully read the following passage about rain forests. Write the letter of the correct answer to the questions that follow.

> **(1)** The rain forests hold secrets of many possible cures for illnesses that need to be cured. **(2)** Scientists believing that the cure for many illnesses including cancer, may come from plants. **(3)** There are so many species of plants. **(4)** Many thousands of plants are still not studied. **(5)** Some cures might even come from plants that have not yet been discovered. **(6)** That's why scientists argue to protect rain forests and their natives, the people.

1. The best revision of sentence 1 is
   (A) The rain forests hold the secrets to many possible cures for illnesses.
   (B) The rain forests, holding secrets of many possible cures, can cure illnesses.
   (C) The rain forests possibly held the secrets to many cures.
   (D) The rain forests—hold secrets of many possible cures—can cure illnesses.
   (E) The rain forests hold secrets and cure illnesses.

2. The best revision of sentence 2 is
   (A) Scientists believe that the cures for many illnesses including cancer, may come from a plant.
   (B) Scientists believe, that the cures for many illnesses including cancer, may come from a plant.
   (C) Scientists believe that the cures for many illnesses, including cancer, may come from plants.
   (D) Scientists believe that illnesses, including cancer, may come from a plant with a cure.
   (E) Coming from a plant, scientists believe is the cure for illnesses like cancer.

3. What is the best way to combine sentences 3 and 4?
   (A) There are so many species of plants, many thousands are still not studied.
   (B) There are so many species of plants, and many thousands of plants are still not studied.
   (C) Many thousands of plants have still not been studied although there are so many species.
   (D) There are so many species of plants that many thousands have still not been studied.
   (E) Many thousands of many species of plants are still not studied.

4. What is the purpose of sentence 5?
   (A) to inform readers about the typical characteristics of plants
   (B) to persuade readers to learn more about illnesses like cancer
   (C) to motivate readers to travel to rain forests
   (D) to provide support for sentence 1
   (E) to create interest by presenting an unusual fact

5. What is the best revision of sentence 6?
   (A) This is reason enough, scientists argue, to protect rain forests and their people.
   (B) This reason is to protect rain forests and their native people.
   (C) Scientists argue about protecting the rain forest's native people.
   (D) This reason, scientists argue, protects rain forests, their natives, and their people.
   (E) This is reason to protect rain forests, their native people.

C. Taking Essay Tests

Part I	Critical Thinking and Problem Solving for Academic Success	A. Learning Study Skills	366
		B. Taking Standardized Tests	372
Part II	Communication and Collaboration	C. Taking Essay Tests	391
Part III	Media and Technology		

Applying Critical Thinking Skills

Essay tests are designed to assess both your understanding of important ideas and your critical thinking skills. You will be expected to analyze, connect, and evaluate information and draw conclusions. You may be asked to examine cause-and-effect relationships and to analyze outcomes. Some questions may address problems and solutions. Regardless of the type of question you are asked, your essay should show sound reasoning. You must be able to organize your thoughts quickly and to express them logically and clearly.

In this section, you will develop your skills in taking essay tests. Your critical thinking skills are essential in performing well on these tests.

❶ Kinds of Essay Questions

Always begin an essay test by reading the instructions for all the questions. Then, as you reread the instructions for your first question, look for key words.

NARRATIVE, DESCRIPTIVE, AND PERSUASIVE PROMPTS

Following are some sample essay prompts and strategies for responding to them.

Narrative Writing Prompt

Trying new things is the only way to learn, but it sometimes takes courage. Think of a time you tried something new, such as learning to ride a bike or performing on stage, and needed courage to accomplish it. Tell what happened in this experience and what you learned from it.

Analyze the Question The key words in this question are "tell what happened." That is your cue that you will be relating a story.

Sketch Out the Key Parts You may want to make a chart like the following to be sure that you include all the necessary parts. Refer to the question for the headings in the chart.

STORY PLANNING SKETCH	
New thing I tried and the circumstances for trying it	
Why it took courage	
What happened as I tried	
The outcome and what I learned	

Use What You Know About Narrative Writing Think of other narratives you have written and remember their key features: an attention-getting beginning that introduces a conflict; a plot that unfolds chronologically and often includes dialogue; a resolution to the conflict. Draft accordingly.

Save Time to Revise and Edit Read over your essay and look for any spots where adding, deleting, rearranging, or substituting would improve your essay. Edit it for correct conventions. Pay special attention to punctuation with dialogue.

Descriptive Writing Prompt

Think of field trips you have taken. Choose one place you have visited that left a strong impression in your mind. Write a well-organized, detailed description of that place using words that appeal to the senses.

Analyze the Question The key words in this question are "detailed description." The directions to use "words that appeal to the senses" is another important item. It sets forth the expectation that you will include vivid sights, sounds, smells, tastes, and feelings.

Sketch Out the Key Parts You may want to make a chart like the following to be sure that you include all the necessary parts. Refer to the question for the headings in the chart.

DESCRIPTION PLANNING SKETCH	
Identification of place	
Vivid sights	
Vivid sounds	
Vivid smells, tastes, and feelings	

Use What You Know About Descriptive Writing Call to mind the key features of descriptive writing: a main idea that represents an overall attitude toward the subject;

sensory details that support that overall feeling, often organized spatially; a conclusion that reinforces the main impression of the place. Draft accordingly.

Save Time to Revise and Edit Read over your essay and look for any spots where adding, deleting, rearranging, or substituting would improve your essay. Edit it for correct conventions.

Persuasive Writing Prompt

Your school is considering making 20 hours of community service (helping out in organizations in your community) a requirement for graduation. Do you think that should be a graduation requirement or not? Write an essay expressing your opinion on that question and backing up your opinion with persuasive facts, examples, and reasons.

Analyze the Question The key words in this question are "expressing your opinion." Those words tell you that you will be writing a persuasive text to convince people to do or believe something.

Sketch Out the Key Parts You may want to make a chart like the following to be sure that you include all the necessary parts. Refer to the question for the headings in the chart.

PERSUASIVE PLANNING SKETCH	
What you are trying to persuade about	
Reason #1	
Reason #2	
Reason #3	
Why your opinion will lead to the best possible benefits for the students and community	
Counter-arguments	

Use What You Know About Persuasive Writing Call to mind the key features of persuasive writing: a main idea that expresses an opinion; facts, examples, reasons, and other supporting details arranged in logical order, often order of importance; a look at why other opinions are not as sound; a conclusion that reinforces your opinion.

Save Time to Revise and Edit Read over your essay and look for any spots where adding, deleting, rearranging, or substituting would improve your essay. Edit it for correct conventions.

EXPOSITORY WRITING PROMPTS

Probably most of the essay tests you will take will ask you to address an expository writing prompt. Look for the key words in each of the following kinds of expository essay questions.

KINDS OF ESSAY QUESTIONS	
Analyze	Separate into parts and examine each part.
Compare	Point out similarities.
Contrast	Point out differences.
Define	Clarify meaning.
Discuss	Examine in detail.
Evaluate	Give your opinion.
Explain	Tell how, what, or why.
Illustrate	Give examples.
Summarize	Briefly review main points.
Trace	Show development or progress.

As you read the instructions, jot down everything that is required in your answer, or circle key words and underline key phrases in the instructions, as in the following example.

> (Explain) the <u>destruction of the rain forest</u>, the <u>history behind the destruction</u>, and the <u>effects</u> experienced by people around the world. Write (three paragraphs,) giving (specific examples) or (illustrations.)

● Practice Your Skills

Interpreting Essay Test Items

Write the key direction word in each item. Then write one sentence explaining what the question asks you to do.

Example   Trace the life cycle of a tree.

Possible Answer   *Trace*—Show the development of a tree by describing, in order, the stages in its growth.

1. In your own words, define *precipitation*.
2. How does the appearance of a wolf compare with that of a coyote?
3. Briefly summarize the novel *Where the Red Fern Grows*.
4. John F. Kennedy said, "Humankind must put an end to war or war will put an end to humankind." Discuss his meaning.
5. Evaluate one of Ray Bradbury's short stories.

C. Taking Essay Tests

Writing an Effective Essay Answer

The steps in writing a well-constructed essay are the same for an essay test as they are for a written assignment. The only difference is that in a test situation you have a strict time limit for writing. As a result, you need to plan how much time you will spend writing and how much time you will devote to each step in the writing process. As a rule of thumb, for every five minutes of writing, allow two minutes for planning and organizing and one minute for revising and editing.

PREWRITING

Begin planning your essay by brainstorming for main ideas and supporting details. Then decide how you will organize your ideas. For example, you may decide to describe events in the order in which they happened. To help you organize your answer, create a simple informal outline or a graphic organizer. Your outline or graphic organizer will help you to present your ideas in a logical order, to cover all your main points, and to avoid omitting important details.

Informal Outline

Destruction of the Rain Forest

1. explanation of the history
2. reasons for destruction
3. effects of destruction

Graphic Organizer

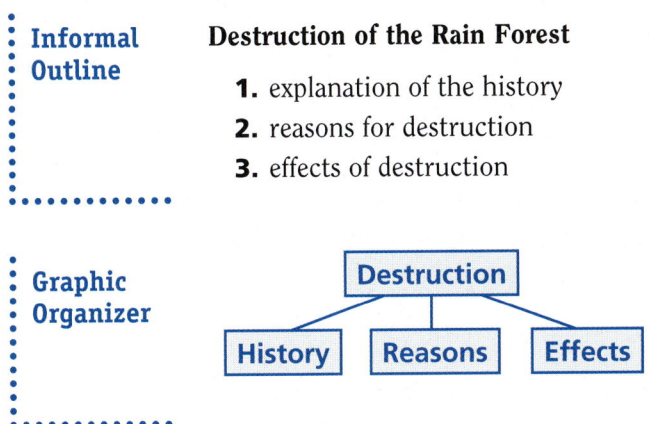

Your next step is to write a thesis statement that expresses your main idea and covers all of your supporting ideas. Often you can write a suitable thesis statement by rewording the test question.

Essay Question

Explain the destruction of the rain forest, the history behind the destruction, and the effects experienced by people around the world. Write three paragraphs, giving specific examples or illustrations.

Thesis Statement

The destruction of the rain forest in recent history will have lasting effects on humanity.

DRAFTING

As you write your essay answer, keep the following strategies in mind.

Strategies for Writing an Essay Answer

- Write an introduction that includes the thesis statement.
- Follow the order of your outline or graphic organizer. Write one paragraph for each main point, beginning with a topic sentence.
- Be specific. Back up each main point by using supporting details, such as facts and examples.
- Use transitions to connect your ideas and examples.
- End with a strong concluding statement that summarizes your main ideas or brings your essay to a close.
- Write clearly and legibly because you will not have time to copy your work.

MODEL: Essay Test Answer

The destruction of the rain forest in recent history will have lasting effects on humanity. The riches of the rain forest are invested in its plants, trees, and living creatures. Beneath them, the soil is thin and poor for growing crops. Nonetheless, for centuries, the few people living in the forests have cleared patches of land and farmed. After a few years, the land would harden and grow nothing, so the people would move on and start again. Then the forest could start to heal the old, wounded clearing, sending up new plants to restore the growth. — Thesis Statement

Then things began to change. Cities strained at the seams with poor people. Industries grew. Suddenly, like a plague, the rain forests were filling up with humans. They came not to live from the wealth of its fruits and plants and animals, but to wipe them from the land. They cleared spaces for homes, farms, ranches, and mines. They cut trees for lumber. Millions of acres were destroyed each year. The smoke from hundreds of thousands of fires lifted into the sky.

More time passed. No one seemed to understand what was being lost. Thousands of species of plants and animals were disappearing. Life-giving oxygen was being replaced by carbon dioxide from fires. Even the ashes of the burned trees, rich with nutrients, were washed away. Today, perhaps the world is beginning to understand and act to preserve remaining rain forests. Areas have been set aside where no one may harm the forest. World summits have been convened to consider the problem. **Has the world acted in time?** — Concluding Statement

396 C. Taking Essay Tests

REVISING

Leave time to revise and edit your essay answer. To keep your paper as neat as possible, mark any corrections or revisions clearly, and write additional material in the margins. As you revise, consider the following questions.

Checklist for Revising an Essay Answer

- ✓ Did you follow the instructions completely?
- ✓ Did you interpret the question accurately?
- ✓ Did you begin with a thesis statement?
- ✓ Did you include facts, examples, or other supporting details?
- ✓ Did you organize your ideas and examples logically in paragraphs, according to your informal outline or graphic organizer?
- ✓ Did you use transitions to connect ideas and examples?
- ✓ Did you end with a strong concluding statement that summarizes your main ideas or brings your essay to a close?

EDITING

After you have made any necessary revisions, quickly read your essay to check for mistakes in spelling, usage, or punctuation. As you edit, check your work for accuracy in the following areas.

Check your work for:

- ✓ the Power Rules (Chapter 1, pages 8–11)
- ✓ agreement between subjects and verbs (Chapter 26, pages 738–760)
- ✓ forms of comparative and superlative adjectives and adverbs (Chapter 27, pages 768–773)
- ✓ capitalization of proper nouns and proper adjectives (Chapter 28, pages 807–817)
- ✓ use of commas (Chapter 29, pages 835–852)
- ✓ use of apostrophes (Chapter 31, pages 880–889)
- ✓ division of words at the end of a line (Chapter 31, pages 897–898)

Writing an Effective Essay Answer

3. Timed Writing

Throughout your school years, you will be tested on your ability to organize your thoughts quickly and to express them in a limited time. Your teacher may ask you to write a twenty-minute, two-hundred-word essay that will then be judged on how thoroughly you covered the topic and organized your essay. To complete such an assignment, you should consider organizing your time in the following way.

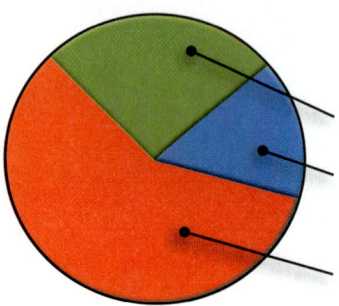

- 5 minutes: Brainstorm and organize ideas.
- 3 minutes: Revise your work and edit it for mistakes.
- 12 minutes: Write a draft.

The more you practice writing under time constraints, the better prepared you will be for writing effectively on tests.

Strategies for Timed Tests

- Listen carefully to instructions. Find out if you may write notes or an outline on your paper or in the examination book.
- Find out if you should erase mistakes or cross them out by neatly drawing a line through them.
- Plan your time, keeping in mind your time limit.

You will find timed writing prompts on all of the following pages.

TIMED WRITING PROMPTS	
Chapter 2	Paragraph Revision, page 59
Chapter 3	Magazine Contest Entry, page 81
Chapter 4	Make Suggestions, page 99
Chapter 5	Party Planner, page 123
Chapter 6	Friendly Letter, page 149
Chapter 7	Letter, page 171
Chapter 8	Short Story, page 209
Chapter 9	Prepare for Debate, page 235
Chapter 10	Persuasive Public Speech, page 261
Chapter 11	Essay on Literature, page 299
Chapter 12	Memo to the Mayor, page 321
Chapter 13	Report to the Mayor, page 361

● **Practice Your Skills**

Completing a Timed-Writing Assignment

Give yourself twenty minutes to write an essay on the following topic.

In one school district, students and parents complained that girls did not have the same opportunity to play sports as boys had. How do you think the district should solve this problem? For example, should teams be made coed, or should more girls' teams be added? Be sure to support your answer with specific reasons.

Begin by creating an informal outline or a graphic organizer and writing a thesis statement. As you draft your essay, follow the Strategies for Writing an Essay Answer on page 396. Be sure to revise and edit your essay.

Timed Writing 399

PART II

Communication and Collaboration

Part I	Critical Thinking and Problem Solving for Academic Success
Part II	**Communication and Collaboration**
Part III	Media and Technology

Essential Skills

In Part II of this guide, you will learn effective communication and collaboration skills. These skills are essential for success in the diverse world of the 21st century.

1 Communication

THE PURPOSE OF COMMUNICATION

In all areas of your life, you communicate for a variety of purposes—to inform, instruct, motivate, and persuade, for example. In school, you might give a speech to motivate your teammates before a championship game. You might persuade your principal to let you start a new club. In the future, you might work as a camp counselor and give instructions and directions to campers. You might send an invitation to inform people about a fundraising event for a charity. Having a clear purpose is essential for communicating your ideas successfully in both speech and writing.

EXPRESSING IDEAS EFFECTIVELY

In school and in your future career, you will use a variety of forms of communication, such as e-mail, a speech, or a letter. You will communicate in a variety of contexts, such as a school assembly or a group discussion. No matter what the form or context is, your goal is to express your thoughts and ideas as effectively as possible. Use words precisely and correctly, and state your ideas in a specific, concise manner. Suit your tone to your purpose and audience. Provide valid support for your ideas, and present information in a logical order. In a speech or presentation, use facial expressions, gestures, and other forms of nonverbal communication to help convey your message.

USING MEDIA AND TECHNOLOGY EFFECTIVELY

On a daily basis, you can use many forms of media and technology to help you communicate. You can e-mail, text message, or Twitter a friend, and complete business forms online. To prepare a speech, you can look up words in an online dictionary and research your subject on the Internet. You can use PowerPoint™ to make a presentation. To use media and technology effectively, you should make sure they suit the purpose and context of your communication.

LISTENING EFFECTIVELY

To listen effectively, you need to do much more than simply understand what words mean. Your goal is to gain knowledge and to identify the speaker's purpose, values, and attitudes. Skillful listeners also evaluate the speaker's message, views, and intentions. Listening effectively means listening actively so that you can understand, appreciate, evaluate, and remember what you have heard.

COMMUNICATING IN A DIVERSE WORLD

You probably attend school with people from diverse social and cultural backgrounds whose lifestyle, religion, and first language may be different from your own. To communicate effectively in school and in your future job, listen actively in order to understand different traditions, values, and perspectives. Be sure to respect these differences when you express your thoughts and ideas.

❷ Collaboration

ACHIEVING A COMMON GOAL

In school and in the workplace, you often collaborate with others on diverse teams. To be an effective team member, you need to be open-minded and flexible. Make sure that all team members have an equal opportunity to be heard, and respect and value differences. Remember to maintain a positive attitude and to put the group's needs before your own. Help the group resolve conflicting opinions and work toward a compromise in order to achieve its goal. By sharing responsibility, team members will collaborate successfully.

A. Vocabulary

Part I	Critical Thinking and Problem Solving for Academic Success	**A. Vocabulary**	**402**
Part II	Communication and Collaboration	B. Letters and Forms	418
Part III	Media and Technology	C. Directions and Speeches	432

Apply Communication Skills

Words are powerful. The more words you know, the more "word power" you have. Having a large vocabulary will help you to write and speak well. You will be able to choose words that best express your ideas and suit your purpose, your audience, and the context. Developing your vocabulary will also help you to read and listen effectively. You will be able to understand the precise meanings of words so that you can comprehend an author's or a speaker's ideas and intentions.

This section will discuss the origins of the English language. You will also learn ways to figure out the meanings of unfamiliar words and to expand your vocabulary. The more words you know and use correctly, the more successful you will be. You will become a more effective communicator and a more skillful reader and listener—in and out of school.

The Growth of the English Language

Just like people, languages are born and then develop. Many factors can influence the development of a language. Immigration, technology, and popular culture are some of the factors that have greatly influenced the English language. To better understand the vocabulary you use, you need to understand where English comes from and how the language has changed.

Origins

The English language and all other languages come from a single language that was spoken thousands of years ago. At some point in history, a form of English branched off as a separate language. If you were to hear someone speak this early form of English, it would probably sound like a foreign language and not at all like the English you speak today. This is because English has developed over the centuries. Words have been added, and spellings, meanings, and pronunciations have changed.

BORROWED WORDS

Many of the words you use come from Latin and Greek. The English language, however, also contains words from many other languages and cultures. The words *chocolate, helicopter,* and *trampoline* illustrate the diverse origins of English words.

chocolate—a Spanish word from the Nahuatl word *xocolatl* (Nahuatl is the language of the Indian peoples of central Mexico). *Xocolatl* comes from two words: *xococ* (meaning "bitter") + *atl* (meaning "water").

helicopter—from the French word *hélicoptère,* which comes from two Greek words meaning "spiral" and "wing"

trampoline—from the Spanish word *trampolín* and the Italian word *trampolino,* from *tràmpoli,* meaning "stilts," which has a German origin

WORDS WITH UNUSUAL ORIGINS

Borrowing words from other languages is only one way English has grown. New words come into the language in a variety of other ways. Some words, called **compound words,** are formed by combining two words.

birthday	moonlight	sunglasses	weekend

Some words are a blend of two words.

breakfast + lunch = brunch

guess + estimate = guesstimate

smoke + fog = smog

Some words are shortened forms of longer words.

Shortened Form	Longer Form
fan	fanatic
plane	airplane
sub	submarine

Some words imitate sounds.

hiss	Ping-Pong	pitter-patter	sizzle	crash

Some names of people have also become words.

Levi Strauss—maker of Levi's blue jeans

Louis Pasteur—first to pasteurize milk

21ST CENTURY

The Growth of the English Language

Some words are acronyms. **Acronyms** are words that are formed from the first letters or syllables of other words.

- **NASA** — **N**ational **A**eronautics and **S**pace **A**dministration
- **Radar** — **ra**dio **d**etecting **a**nd **r**anging
- **Vista** — **V**olunteers **i**n **S**ervice **t**o **A**merica

● **Practice Your Skills**

Finding Unusual Origins

Tell how each of the following words came into the English language by writing *compound, blend, shortened form, sound, person's name,* or *acronym*. Use a dictionary (see pages 405–410) and the examples on pages 403–404 to help you.

1. whoosh
2. moped
3. raincoat
4. scuba
5. tangelo
6. newspaper
7. lab
8. motel
9. saxophone
10. deli

❷ Spelling

Although some words have stayed the same, the spelling of many English words has changed over the years. Even today, there are alternate spellings of the same word. *(To learn more about alternate spellings, see pages 407–408.)*

CHANGES IN SPELLING				
MODERN	center	music	plow	three
ORIGINAL	centre	musik	plough	threo

❸ Pronunciation

Just as the spelling of English words has changed over centuries, so too has the pronunciation of many words. These changes in pronunciation can sometimes account for what might seem like the odd spelling of words. For example, the silent *k* in many modern English words is left over from the time when those words used to be pronounced with hard *c* or strong *k* sounds at the beginnings of the words. At one time the *k* in *knife, knight,* and *knee* was pronounced and was not a silent letter. Eventually, the pronunciation of the words changed, but the spelling stayed the same, reflecting the words' history.

A. Vocabulary

④ Meaning

The meanings of words have also changed over the years. For example, the word *fear* today usually means "to be afraid of," but at one time it also meant "to respect." The word *surf* had referred to a water sport until the Internet came along. Now *surf* can also refer to exploring different Web sites.

Developing Your Dictionary Skills

Whenever you need to know the meaning, spelling, pronunciation, or part of speech of a word, you can look up the word in a dictionary. You can also use a dictionary to research the origin of a word. Some dictionaries provide lists of synonyms (words with similar meanings) as well. Dictionaries come in book form, but you can also access many dictionaries online. Learning how to use a print or an online dictionary will help you to communicate effectively.

① Word Location

Most dictionaries are organized similarly. The structure of a dictionary lets you quickly find the information you need.

ALPHABETICAL ORDER

A dictionary lists words in alphabetical order. Words that start with the same letter are then alphabetized by the second, third, and following letters in each word. Two-word and hyphenated compound words are alphabetized as if they were one word with no space or hyphen between the two words. Note the alphabetized list below.

Single Word	space
One-Word Compound	spacecraft
Two-Word Compound	space station
Hyphenated Compound	space-time

The dictionary also lists proper nouns, prefixes, suffixes, phrases, and abbreviations. Abbreviations are alphabetized letter by letter and not by the word they stand for. For example, the abbreviation *Rd.* for *road* is one of many entries that fall between *razor* and *read*. It is not placed next to *road*.

GUIDE WORDS

The two words printed in heavy type at the top of each page in a print dictionary are called **guide words.** Each pair of guide words shows the first and last words defined on the page. The guide words *pinch/pioneer,* for example, show you that *pine* and *pinto bean* would be listed on that page. The words *pistachio* and *pit,* however, would appear on a later page.

- **Practice Your Skills**

    Using Guide Words and Alphabetical Order

    Follow these steps to place the words below in the correct order.

    1. Make two columns on your paper. Write the words *babble/badminton* at the top of the first column and *baffle/balloon* at the top of the second column. These word pairs will serve as guide words.
    2. Write each word below in the correct column.
    3. Number the words in each column to show how you would arrange them if you were placing them in alphabetical order.

    | baboon | Bahamas | babysit |
    | bachelor | baggage | backyard |
    | backgammon | balance | bagpipe |
    | bacteria | balcony | ballerina |
    | badly | backpack | ballet |
    | Badlands | bald eagle | ballad |
    | bakery | badger | bacon |

406 A. Vocabulary

❷ Information in an Entry

In a dictionary, all of the information given for a word is called an **entry.** The four most important parts of the entry are (1) the entry word, (2) the pronunciation, (3) the definitions, and (4) the word origin. The following entry for the word *disk* shows these four main parts. In this section, you will learn about these four parts as well as other information that may be included in an entry.

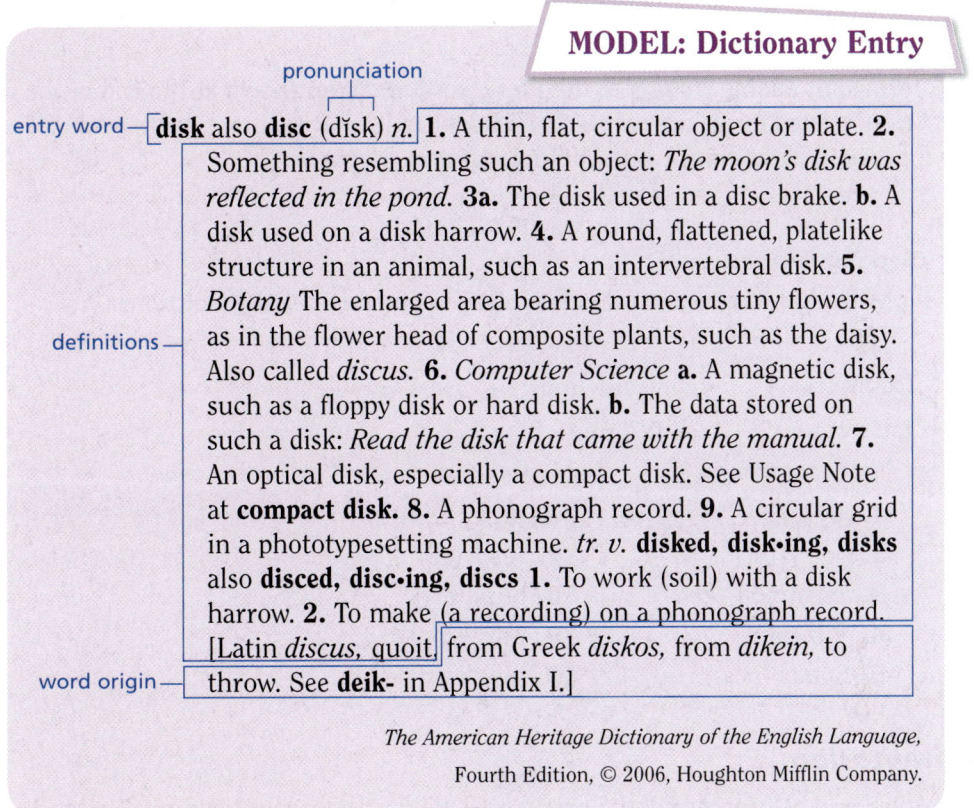

MODEL: Dictionary Entry

entry word — **disk** also **disc** (dĭsk) *n.* **1.** A thin, flat, circular object or plate. **2.** Something resembling such an object: *The moon's disk was reflected in the pond.* **3a.** The disk used in a disc brake. **b.** A disk used on a disk harrow. **4.** A round, flattened, platelike structure in an animal, such as an intervertebral disk. **5.** *Botany* The enlarged area bearing numerous tiny flowers, as in the flower head of composite plants, such as the daisy. Also called *discus.* **6.** *Computer Science* **a.** A magnetic disk, such as a floppy disk or hard disk. **b.** The data stored on such a disk: *Read the disk that came with the manual.* **7.** An optical disk, especially a compact disk. See Usage Note at **compact disk. 8.** A phonograph record. **9.** A circular grid in a phototypesetting machine. *tr. v.* **disked, disk•ing, disks** also **disced, disc•ing, discs 1.** To work (soil) with a disk harrow. **2.** To make (a recording) on a phonograph record. [Latin *discus,* quoit, from Greek *diskos,* from *dikein,* to throw. See **deik-** in Appendix I.]

The American Heritage Dictionary of the English Language,
Fourth Edition, © 2006, Houghton Mifflin Company.

THE ENTRY WORD

The entry word provides three kinds of information. It shows (1) how to spell the word, (2) whether the word should be capitalized, and (3) how to divide the word into syllables.

Spelling

The entry word shows you the correct spelling of the word. Some words have more than one correct spelling. The most common spelling, called the **preferred spelling,** is given first. The second spelling is called the **variant spelling.** Always use the preferred spelling of a word in your writing. In the model dictionary entry for *disk* above, *disk* is the preferred spelling and *disc* is the variant spelling.

A dictionary entry also shows how to spell the plurals of nouns, the principal parts of verbs, and the comparative and superlative degrees of adjectives and adverbs. Usually these words or parts are given only if the spelling or forms are irregular.

Principal Parts   o•mit (ō-mĭt') *tr. v.* o•mit•ted, o•mit•ting, o•mits
Noun Plural   goose (goos) *n., pl.* geese (gēs)
Adjective Forms   crisp•y (krĭs'pē) *adj.* –i•er, –i•est

Words formed by adding a suffix to the entry word are often shown at the end of the entry. These related forms are called **derived words.** For example, at the end of the entry for *lazy* in a dictionary, you will find *lazily* and *laziness*.

● **Practice Your Skills**

Checking Spelling

Write each word with the ending given in parentheses. Use a dictionary to check your spelling.

Example   continue (ing)
Answer   continuing

1. spy (s)
2. wolf (s)
3. tomato (s)
4. quiz (s)
5. cloudy (ness)
6. satisfy (ed)
7. refer (ed)
8. busy (er)
9. bury (ing)
10. monkey (s)

Capitalization

If a word should be capitalized, the entry word will be printed with a capital letter. If a word is capitalized only when it is used in certain ways, the word will be shown with a capital letter near the appropriate definition.

Syllables

When you write, you sometimes need to divide a word at the end of a line. You cannot divide the word in the middle of a syllable. Instead, you must break it after a syllable. The entry word shows you how a word breaks into syllables.

ar • ti • cle   jus • ti • fy   re • source • ful

A. Vocabulary

PRONUNCIATION

If you are not sure how to pronounce a word, you can look it up in the dictionary. A **phonetic spelling** appears in parentheses after each entry word, as in the model dictionary entry for *disk* on page 407. The phonetic spelling shows how to pronounce the word correctly.

At the front of a print dictionary, a pronunciation key is provided to help you understand the letters and symbols used in phonetic spellings. Many dictionaries also provide a shortened form of the key on every other page for easy reference.

In the phonetic spellings of words, there may be marks over some vowels. These marks are called **diacritical marks.** They show the different sounds a vowel can make. For example, in the phonetic spelling of *disk* in the model entry, the diacritical mark tells you that the *i* should be pronounced as a short *i*. Use the key to find out how to pronounce a vowel with a diacritical mark.

Accent Marks An accent mark (') shows which syllable should be stressed in the pronunciation of a word. Accent marks appear in the phonetic spelling of a word.

> pa • per (pa'–pər)   like • a • ble (līˈ kə-bəl)

Some words have two accent marks. The darker one, called the **primary accent,** tells you which syllable receives more stress. The lighter one, called the **secondary accent,** tells you which syllable receives slightly less stress.

> sci • en • tif • ic (sīˈ ən-tĭfˈ ĭk)   primary accent / secondary accent

● **Practice Your Skills**

Practicing Pronunciation

Some of the following words might be new to you. Look them up in a dictionary to learn their meaning and pronunciation. Then in pairs, take turns pronouncing them. Keep practicing until you have the pronunciation just right.

1. invigorate
2. sabatoge
3. feint
4. sleuth
5. dungeon
6. thwart
7. barbecue
8. wistful
9. qualm
10. quotient

Developing Your Dictionary Skills

DEFINITIONS

Most words have more than one meaning. The model entry for *disk* on page 407 gives thirteen definitions. To find the definition that fits a particular context, read all of the definitions carefully. Then decide which meaning makes sense in the sentence. Sometimes dictionaries include example sentences or phrases, as in the model for *disk*. Read these examples carefully as well because they show how the words are used.

Parts of Speech Dictionaries use the following abbreviations to tell what part of speech a word is.

n.	noun	*pron.*	pronoun
v.	verb	*prep.*	preposition
adj.	adjective	*conj.*	conjunction
adv.	adverb	*interj.*	interjection

Since many words can be more than one part of speech, two or more abbreviations may appear in a single entry, as in the entry for *disk* on page 407. Be sure that you first find the right part of speech in an entry when you search for the definition of a word. Then read all the definitions for that part of speech in order to find the appropriate definition.

Synonyms Words with almost the same meaning are called **synonyms.** Dictionaries often list synonyms at the end of an entry and explain how the meanings of the synonyms differ from that of the entry word. These lists can come in handy when you are writing or preparing a speech. You can use the lists to find the most appropriate words to express your meaning and intention.

WORD ORIGINS

As you learned in the beginning of this chapter on pages 402–405, words have entered the English language in many different ways. The dictionary provides information about the history, or origin, of words. This information is usually in brackets and may appear at the beginning or the end of an entry. For example, the model entry for *disk* on page 407 tells you that the word comes from the Greek word *dikein,* meaning "to throw." In the front or back of a print dictionary, you can find an explanation of the symbols and abbreviations used to tell about word origins.

Expanding Your Vocabulary

What do you do when you come across words that are new to you? Suppose you came across this sentence.

> The short story takes place in a bucolic setting, and the main character is a farmer.

Perhaps you know that *bucolic* means "rural" or "country-like." However, it is more likely that the word is unfamiliar to you. One way to learn its meaning is to look it up in a dictionary. In this section you will learn several other ways to unlock the meaning of a new word and to expand your vocabulary.

❶ Context Clues

Often you can pick up clues about a word's meaning from its **context.** The **context** of a word is the sentence, the surrounding words, or the situation in which the word is used.

In the sentence above about the bucolic setting of the story, the words "the main character is a farmer" act as a context clue. They help you figure out that *bucolic* means "country-like."

There are several kinds of context clues. You probably have seen the following types in your reading.

Definition	Animals that feed on plants are **herbivores.**
Example	**Conifers,** such as cone-bearing pine and spruce trees, are found in cooler climates.
Synonym	The **Isle** of Wight lies off the coast of England. The island is famous for its scenery and mild climate.

In the first item, the word *herbivores* is defined in the sentence. In the second item, examples of conifers appear in the sentence. In the third item, a synonym for the word *isle*—the word *island*—is used in the following sentence. All of these items show how the surrounding words can be used to determine the meanings of unfamiliar words.

● **Practice Your Skills**

Using Paragraph Context Clues

Write each underlined word and its meaning. Use the context of the paragraph to help you define the words. Then check your answers in a dictionary.

> The aging <u>monarch</u> sat on his throne with his head bowed. Outside, the thunder of distant armies carried an <u>ominous</u> warning. The king knew that soon he would have to <u>yield</u> his throne to his enemies, who were now strong enough to overpower him. His only hope was the band of loyal, brave soldiers who had been <u>summoned</u> from fighting in a distant land. Would his soldiers arrive in time to <u>thwart</u> the attack? Suddenly the quiet of the throne room was shattered by a great <u>commotion</u> outside the palace. Were the cheers and hoofbeats those of his <u>valiant</u> troops—or the victory sounds of his <u>treacherous</u> enemies? <u>Rousing</u> himself, the king raced toward the gate to <u>ascertain</u> his fate.

● **Practice Your Skills**

Practicing Pronunciation

Use a print or online dictionary to look up the pronunciation of the words in the previous activity. Then in pairs, take turns pronouncing them. Keep practicing until you have the pronunciation just right.

② Base Words, Prefixes, and Suffixes

BASE WORDS

Another way to determine the meanings of unfamiliar words is to break the words down into their parts. Suppose, for example, that you come across the word *disobey*. Chances are you recognize one part of this word, *obey*. This part is called the base word. A **base word** is a complete word that can stand alone. Other word parts can be added to a base word to make new words. The base words in the following examples are in boldface type.

Base Words   pre**judge**   un**drink**able   **fight**er   **joy**ful

PREFIXES

The part of the word that comes before the base word is called a **prefix.** A prefix can have one or more syllables. In the word *disobey,* the prefix is *dis-*. If you know that *dis-* means "not," then you can figure out that *disobey* means "not obey." The following chart contains some common prefixes and their meanings.

A. Vocabulary

PREFIX	MEANING	EXAMPLE
anti–	against	anti + freeze = antifreeze
dis–	not	dis + agree = disagree
in–	not	in + human = inhuman
mis–	bad, badly, wrong, wrongly	mis + spell = misspell
pre–	before	pre + school = preschool
re–	again	re + appear = reappear
sub–	under	sub + way = subway
un–	not	un + healthy = unhealthy

● **Practice Your Skills**

Practicing Pronunciation

Use a print or online dictionary to look up the pronunciation of the complete words in the right-hand column of the chart above. Then in pairs, take turns pronouncing them until you have the pronunciation just right.

● **Practice Your Skills**

Combining Prefixes and Base Words

For each item, write the prefix that has the same meaning as the underlined word. Then write the complete word that is defined after the equal sign.

Example again + copy = copy again

Answer re–, recopy

1. before + view = to see something ahead of time
2. against + war = opposed to war
3. wrongly + pronounce = to use the wrong pronunciation
4. again + freeze = to freeze a second or third time
5. not + approve = to judge unfavorably
6. wrong + print = an error in a published work
7. not + popular = not liked or approved of by most people
8. under + basement = a floor below the basement of a building
9. not + direct = not straight
10. again + capture = to seize again

SUFFIXES

The part of a word that comes after the base word is called a **suffix.** Like prefixes, suffixes can be added to base words to make new words and can have more than one syllable. Unlike prefixes, many suffixes form a word that is a different part of speech from the base word.

Noun Suffixes	Meaning	Examples
–ance, –ence	state of	depend + ence
–er, –or	one who or that	sing + er
–ment	state of	resent + ment
–ness	state of	kind + ness
Verb Suffixes	**Meaning**	**Examples**
–en	make, become	strength + en
–ize	make, cause to be	final + ize
Adjective Suffixes	**Meaning**	**Examples**
–able	capable of	break + able
–ful	full of	cheer + ful
Adverb Suffixes	**Meaning**	**Examples**
–ly	in a certain way	slow + ly

● **Practice Your Skills**

Using Suffixes to Form Words

Write each base word twice, each time adding a different suffix. Then write the part of speech of each new word. Use the list of suffixes above to help you.

Example bright

Possible Answers brighten—verb, brightly—adverb

1. fair
2. employ
3. light
4. visual
5. deep
6. rude
7. treat
8. moral
9. legal
10. govern

A. Vocabulary

❸ Synonyms

Because the English language has so many words, you can choose words that express your meaning exactly. Sometimes two or more words have similar meanings. A word that has nearly the same meaning as another word is called a **synonym.**

In the following sentences, the words *tall* and *towering* are synonyms. Although they have similar meanings, *towering* paints a more precise picture than *tall* does.

> The shade from the **tall** tree kept us cool.
> The shade from the **towering** tree kept us cool.

In the following sentences *sat* and *perched* are synonyms. Which word gives you a clearer picture of the bird's position?

> The bird **sat** on the ledge of my windowsill.
> The bird **perched** on the ledge of my windowsill.

When you write and speak, choose words that will help you express your ideas precisely and vividly. You can use a dictionary to find synonyms. *(See page 410.)* You can also use a thesaurus. *(See page 46.)*

● Practice Your Skills

Choosing the Better Word

Write the synonym in parentheses that better fits the meaning of each sentence. Use a dictionary for help.

1. Our friends were so deep in (conversation, discourse) that they barely noticed us.
2. Lara has a (shiny, brilliant) mind.
3. Samuel (spotted, detected) a hint of disapproval in his father's voice.
4. The glass figurines were (flimsy, fragile).
5. In his report Ian included an interesting (representation, picture) of Mexico City.
6. Marissa hoped a (lullaby, song) would calm her baby sister.
7. The speaker bored everyone with his (repetitious, monotonous) reading of the poem.
8. The decorator chose (neutral, indifferent) colors for the living room.
9. Kim's library books are (delayed, overdue).
10. The baby (scribbled, wrote) all over the mural.

Expanding Your Vocabulary

● **Practice Your Skills**

Using Synonyms

Write as many synonyms as you can for the underlined word in each phrase.

1. a nice person
2. a big boat
3. a great day
4. a sad movie
5. a little fish
6. a funny speech
7. a bad time
8. a hot sun
9. a happy story
10. a good game

④ Antonyms

An **antonym** is a word that means the opposite of another word. Dictionaries may list antonyms for some words. The following pairs of words are antonyms.

amateur—professional   reduce—increase

continuous—interrupted   resemble—differ

discard—save   vanity—modesty

Antonyms show a contrast between extremes. Often, however, there are words in between the two extremes that show a smaller degree of contrast. For example, the words *damp, moist,* and *humid* fall between the extremes of *wet* and *dry*. Knowing the whole range of words you can use to express an idea will help you choose exactly the right word when you write.

● **Practice Your Skills**

Recognizing Antonyms

Write the letter of the answer choice that is most nearly opposite in meaning to the capitalized word. Then check your answers in a dictionary.

1. Suspicion: (A) crime (B) trust (C) worry (D) suspense (E) kindness
2. Triumphant: (A) victorious (B) disappointed (C) musical (D) defeated (E) loud
3. Villain: (A) character (B) joker (C) hero (D) criminal (E) narrator
4. Thorough: (A) total (B) narrow (C) straight (D) lasting (E) incomplete
5. Strict: (A) tight (B) old (C) permissive (D) striped (E) rigid
6. Mature: (A) wise (B) eager (C) childish (D) ripe (E) respected
7. Gallant: (A) courteous (B) friendly (C) daring (D) cowardly (E) similar

A. Vocabulary

8. Changeable: (A) steady (B) unreliable (C) nervous (D) cranky (E) upset

9. Blunt: (A) dull (B) rude (C) wide (D) heavy (E) sharp

10. Exhale: (A) relax (B) snore (C) inhale (D) greet (E) decline

B. Letters and Forms

Part I	Critical Thinking and Problem Solving for Academic Success	**A.** Vocabulary	402
Part II	**Communication and Collaboration**	**B.** Letters and Forms	418
Part III	Media and Technology	**C.** Directions and Speeches	432

Apply 21st Century Communication Skills

In the 21st century, people are communicating and sharing information much more than they have in the past. To communicate effectively, always have a clear purpose in mind and use technology wisely.

Real-World Communication

In this section, you will develop skills for making your communication with others suit your purpose, audience, and occasion.

1 Communicating for a Purpose

In your personal life and in the business world, you communicate and share information for a variety of purposes: to inform, instruct, motivate, or persuade, for example. You might write a friendly letter, filled with words of encouragement, to motivate a good friend who lacks confidence. You might send a letter of regret, a type of social letter, to inform a friend that you can't attend her party. In a letter of complaint, a type of business letter, you might persuade a company to correct a billing error. When you complete a business form, your purpose is to inform a company or an organization by providing specific facts and details.

Whether you are writing a letter or filling out a form, you should always keep your purpose in mind. Your goal is to write in a clear, concise manner because you want your readers to know exactly what you mean.

2 Using Technology to Communicate

In the 21st century, you have many ways to communicate. You can text or tweet a friend, e-mail a request, or post a complaint online. With all these options, electronic communication—particularly e-mail—has replaced letter writing to a great extent. However, writing a letter can be more effective or appropriate than sending an e-mail depending on your purpose, the context, and the impact you want to make. Use these guidelines to determine whether to send a letter or an e-mail.

Send a letter in the following circumstances:

- You want to express sincere, serious emotions, such as get-well wishes or thanks for a favor or a gift.
- You want to show that you have put thought and care into communicating.
- You want to introduce yourself formally or make an impact on your audience by using impressive stationery, for example.
- You are including private, confidential information. Keep in mind that e-mail is not a private form of communication, and you should never include confidential information in an e-mail. A recipient can forward an e-mail to others without your knowledge, and companies can read their employees' e-mails. Also, hackers can break into e-mail systems and steal information.
- You need to have formal documentation of your communication, or you are sending authentic documents.

Send an e-mail in the following circumstances:

- You want to communicate quickly with someone.
- You want to send a message, perhaps with accompanying documents, to several people at once.
- You have been instructed by a business or an organization to communicate via e-mail.

The Purpose and Format of Letters

Letters fall into two general categories: personal letters and business letters. In each category, letters can serve many different purposes. Regardless of your purpose, your goal when you write a letter is to convey ideas, opinions, and information in an effective way.

1 Writing Personal Letters

You probably text a friend when you want to send a brief, quick message. You may use e-mail for fast, but more extended communication. However, if you want to express your feelings or provide a personal touch or if the occasion is formal, you should write a personal letter. Friendly letters and social letters are two types of personal letters. When you write a friendly or a social letter, make sure you convey your ideas, opinions, and feelings precisely. Include whatever information is necessary to make your message clear and complete, and provide closure at the end.

Friendly Letters

A **friendly letter** is an informal letter that you write to a friend or a relative. In your letter, you might convey your ideas and opinions, describe your feelings, or include important information. Although friendly letters are casual in style, they still follow certain conventions. All friendly letters have five main parts: the heading, salutation, body, closing, and signature. A friendly e-mail, like a letter, should contain a proper salutation and closing.

The parts of a friendly letter are explained in the following chart.

PARTS OF A FRIENDLY LETTER	
Heading	The heading includes your full mailing address with your ZIP code. Use the two-letter abbreviation for your state. Always include the date after your address. Follow the rules for capitalizing proper nouns and using commas in an address.
Salutation	The salutation is your greeting. It is followed by a comma. Capitalize the first word and any proper nouns. **D**ear **U**ncle **H**ugh, **D**ear **D**ad,
Body	The body is the main part of the letter. It includes your conversational message. Remember to indent the first line of each paragraph.
Closing	End your letter with a brief personal closing followed by a comma. Capitalize the first word only. **L**ove always,
Signature	Sign your name below the closing.

B. Letters and Forms

The following model shows the correct format for a friendly letter.

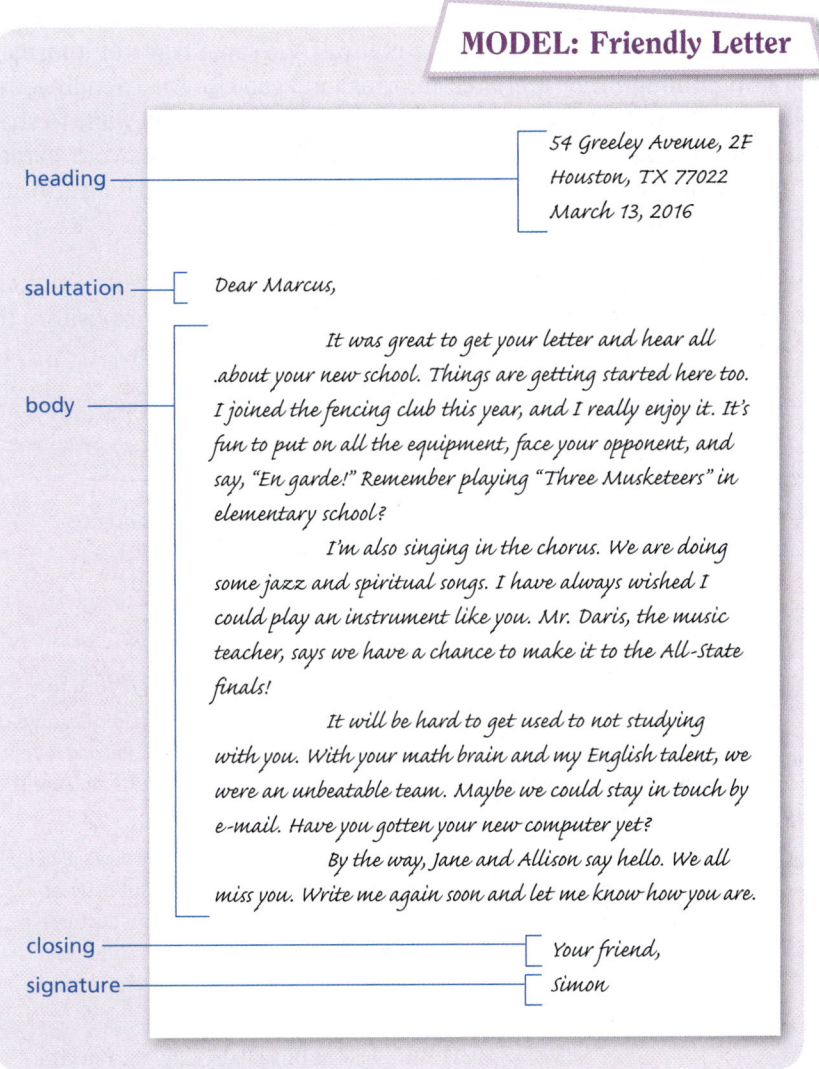

The envelope for a friendly letter may be handwritten. It should contain the same information as that on the envelope for a business letter. (See page 427.) Be sure both your address and the receiver's address are clear and complete.

● **Practice Your Skills**

Writing a Friendly Letter

Write an informal letter to a friend or a relative that reflects your opinion about an event in your life. Think of a way to encourage an answer from the person to whom you are writing. Be sure to follow the conventions of a friendly letter. Send your letter, and remember to reply in a timely fashion when you receive a response.

INFORMATIONAL LETTERS

Sometimes you might want to convey interesting ideas or important information in a letter. These **informational letters** have many of the same traits of informational or expository writing, though they are often informal and can use the friendly letter format. For example, you might have a great new idea for a video game and want to share it with your cousin, who programs video games for a living. As you describe your game to him, you would use the same techniques you would use an expository text: clear organization, lots of supporting ideas, and a natural sounding voice.

You might also have occasion to send important information in a letter. Once again, you would need to take the same care in your letter as you would in an expository text.

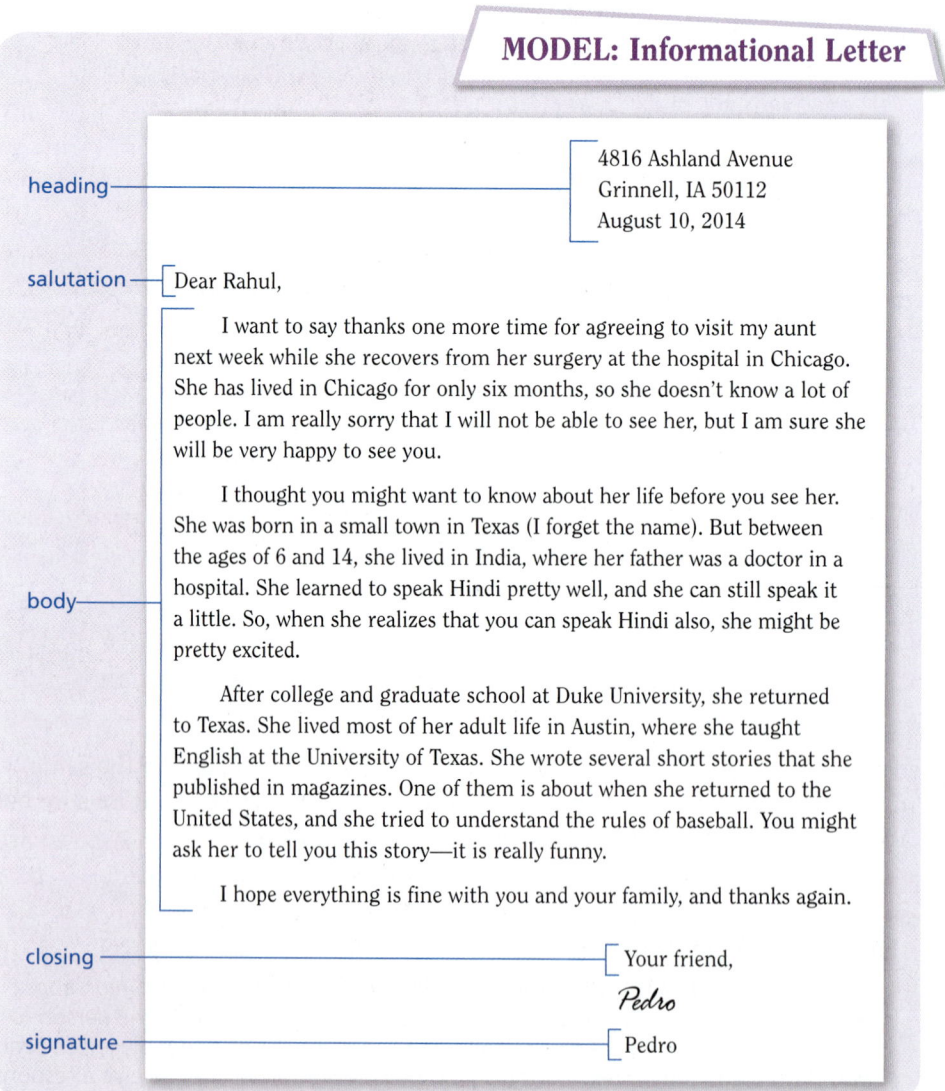

MODEL: Informational Letter

heading
4816 Ashland Avenue
Grinnell, IA 50112
August 10, 2014

salutation
Dear Rahul,

body
I want to say thanks one more time for agreeing to visit my aunt next week while she recovers from her surgery at the hospital in Chicago. She has lived in Chicago for only six months, so she doesn't know a lot of people. I am really sorry that I will not be able to see her, but I am sure she will be very happy to see you.

I thought you might want to know about her life before you see her. She was born in a small town in Texas (I forget the name). But between the ages of 6 and 14, she lived in India, where her father was a doctor in a hospital. She learned to speak Hindi pretty well, and she can still speak it a little. So, when she realizes that you can speak Hindi also, she might be pretty excited.

After college and graduate school at Duke University, she returned to Texas. She lived most of her adult life in Austin, where she taught English at the University of Texas. She wrote several short stories that she published in magazines. One of them is about when she returned to the United States, and she tried to understand the rules of baseball. You might ask her to tell you this story—it is really funny.

I hope everything is fine with you and your family, and thanks again.

closing
Your friend,
Pedro

signature
Pedro

● **Practice Your Skills**

Writing an Informational Letter

Imagine a friend is visiting from out of town, and you have gotten sick. Your friend is going to the library to get you a book to read. Write the directions for how to get from your house to the library. Then exchange directions with a partner. Ask your partner if he or she would be able to follow the directions you have written. After you and your partner have shared feedback, revise your letter as necessary.

● **Practice Your Skills**

Writing a Letter to Share Ideas

Think of a song or musical group that you have heard recently that you liked very much. Write a letter to a friend with whom you have enjoyed talking about music, explaining what you liked so much about the song or group. Use the conventions of a friendly letter and provide a meaningful closure.

SOCIAL LETTERS

Social letters have a specific purpose. They are sent, for example, to thank someone for a gift, to invite someone to an event, or to express regret for being unable to do something. Social letters have a more formal tone than friendly letters, but they follow the same conventions.

Get-Well Letters A get-well letter is short and to the point. Such letters let people know that you are wishing for their fast recovery. Keep the tone sensitive but upbeat.

Thank-You Letters A thank-you letter lets someone know how much you appreciate a gift or a favor. A letter carries more weight than a verbal thank-you because it shows that you took the time to sit down and write out your thoughts.

Invitations An invitation informs someone about an event you would like that person to attend. It includes the time and place and any other important information your guests need to know. This information might tell how to get to the event by car or public transportation or how to dress (formally or informally). Sometimes invitations tell the receivers whether they may bring a guest or whether they should bring food or a gift.

Letters of Regret When you are unable to attend an event to which you have been invited, you write a letter of regret. In it, you explain why you will be unable to attend, and you express your regret. Invitations that say "RSVP" (an abbreviation for "please reply") often require a written response. You should respond in a timely fashion to an invitation so that the person planning the event knows how many people to expect.

● **Practice Your Skills**

Writing Social Letters

1. Imagine that a friend has gotten a bad case of the flu and has been hospitalized. Write a get-well letter to send to your friend.
2. Imagine that someone took the time, expended energy, or spent money to do something for you. Write a thank-you letter in which you express your thoughts about the importance of this person's actions. Follow appropriate conventions in writing your letter.
3. Imagine that you are giving a party. Draft an invitation to your party that identifies the occasion for the party, the time and place for the party, and any additional information guests need to know. Exchange letters with a partner. Check that your partner followed the appropriate format and did not omit any important information. After you and your partner have shared feedback, revise your letter as necessary.
4. Imagine that you have received an invitation to a birthday party for a friend. Using the appropriate conventions, write a letter of regret explaining why you will be unable to attend.

❷ Writing Business Letters

A **business letter** is a formal letter that calls for some action on the part of the receiver. Letters of request, order letters, and letters of complaint are three types of business letters. The most effective business letters state their purpose and convey ideas simply and directly. They are concise; they include important information and leave out unnecessary details.

Most of the business letters you write will be sent to a company. When a business letter arrives at a company, it is often taken out of the envelope before it reaches the person addressed in the letter. For this reason, a business letter has one more part than a friendly letter. This part is called the inside address. The inside address contains the name and address of the person to whom you are writing.

There are many formats or styles for business letters. In the modified block style, the heading, closing, and signature are on the right. The inside address, salutation, and body all start at the left margin. A blank line is left between each paragraph in the body of the letter, and the first line of each paragraph is indented. The models of business letters in this chapter are in the modified block style.

Tips for Writing Business Letters

- Use white stationery, preferably 8½ by 11 inches.
- Leave margins at least 1-inch wide on all sides.
- Keep an electronic copy or a hard copy of each business letter you write.

The parts of a business letter are explained in the following chart.

PARTS OF A BUSINESS LETTER

Heading	The heading of a business letter is the same as that of a friendly letter. Include your full address followed by the date. Follow the rules for capitalizing proper nouns and using commas in an address.
Inside Address	Start the inside address two to four lines below the heading. Write the name of the person who will receive the letter if you know it. Use *Mr., Ms., Mrs.,* or *Dr.* before the name. If the person has a title, such as Vice President, write it on the next line. Then write the receiver's address. Follow the rules for capitalizing and punctuating addresses.
Salutation	Start the salutation two lines below the inside address. Use a colon after the salutation. If you do not know the person's name, use *Sir or Madam*. Dear Mr. Timberlake: Dear Sir or Madam:
Body	The body begins two lines below the salutation. Skip a line between paragraphs, and indent the first line of each new paragraph.
Closing	Use a formal closing. Start the closing two lines below the body. The closing lines up with the heading. Capitalize the first letter of the first word, and use a comma at the end of the closing. Sincerely, Very truly yours,
Signature	In a business letter, your name appears twice. Type or print your name four lines below the closing. Then sign your name in the space between the closing and your typed or printed name. Do not refer to yourself as *Mr.* or *Ms.*

The following model shows the correct format for a business letter.

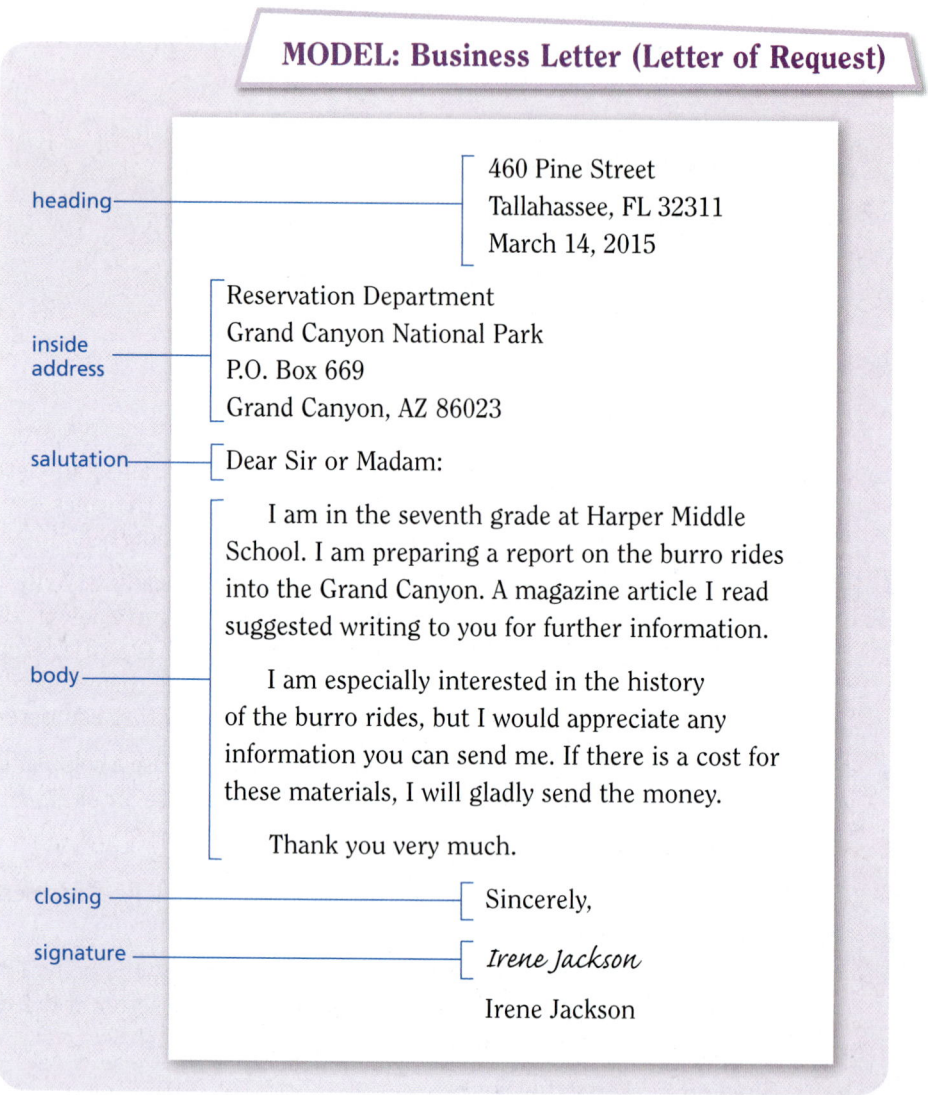

Business Envelopes The following model shows the correct format for a business envelope. If you use a word-processing program to type the letter, you should also type the envelope. If you handwrite the letter, you can handwrite the envelope neatly. Place your name and address in the upper left-hand corner. The receiver's address, which is the same as the inside address in a business letter, is centered on the envelope.

Use a business-sized envelope that matches the stationery on which you wrote your letter. Fold the letter in thirds, and place it in the envelope so that the receiver will take it out right-side up.

MODEL: Business Envelope

Irene Jackson
460 Pine Street
Tallahassee, FL 32311

— sender's address

Reservation Department
Grand Canyon National Park
P.O. Box 669
Grand Canyon, AZ 86023

— receiver's address

BUSINESS E-MAILS

A business letter sent via e-mail should be just as formal as a letter sent by mail. Follow these guidelines when sending a business e-mail.

Guidelines for Writing a Business E-mail

- Include a formal salutation and closing. Format the body of the letter correctly.
- Use proper grammar and punctuation.
- Check your spelling. (Some e-mail programs have their own spell-check function. Use it!)
- Double-check the person's e-mail address to be sure you have typed it correctly.
- In the subject line of the e-mail, remember to specify the topic you are writing about.

LETTERS OF REQUEST

Requesting information is one common purpose of a business letter. When requesting information, be specific about the information you need. Include appropriate facts and details, but be sure to exclude extraneous information. Remember to state your request politely and express your thanks in order to give closure to your letter. (For a model of a letter of request, see page 426.)

● **Practice Your Skills**

Writing a Letter of Request

Imagine that you are researching life on the ocean floor. Write a letter to a museum or an aquarium to request information. You may want to find the name and address of a museum or an aquarium in your area. Be specific about the kind of information you wish to receive. Remember to express your thanks to give closure to your letter. Be sure to follow the conventions of a business letter.

ORDER LETTERS

You can also use a business letter to order merchandise from catalogs and advertisements. Because your reader needs specific information to fill your order accurately, you should include important information about the merchandise such as the description, size, order number, price, and the quantity of the items you want. If you enclose payment for your purchase, your letter should state the amount you have enclosed. Check your arithmetic to be sure you have included the proper amount.

MODEL: Order Letter

333 Westmont Drive
Ramer, TN 38367
July 15, 2015

Stowaway Supplies
42 Ridge Avenue
Agoura Hills, CA 91301

Dear Sir or Madam:

Please send me the following items from your 2015 summer catalog:

2 student book bags—	
1 green, 1 red	
Order # 356—AZ5	
$9.99 each	$19.98
1 navy blue sweatshirt—	
size medium	
Order # 455—AM2	
$17.50	$17.50
TOTAL:	$37.48

I have enclosed a check for $42.98 to cover the cost of the merchandise plus $5.00 for shipping and handling.

Sincerely,

Martin J. Conway
Martin J. Conway

- **Practice Your Skills**

    Writing an Order Letter

    Imagine that you are the set director for a play called *The Haunted Castle*. You have only one hundred dollars to spend for props. Choose from the following items advertised in the Theater Supplies fall catalog, and order the props you need. The address of Theater Supplies is 45 Highland Avenue, Lexington, MA 02173. Add $7.50 for shipping and handling. In your letter, state your purpose clearly. Include all the important information your reader needs in order to fill your order. Be sure this information is well organized. Remember to follow the conventions of a business letter.

Item	Number	Price
creaking stairway	#368-B	$65.00
bushel of cobwebs	46-9z	9.00
drawbridge	55-C	82.00
dungeon cell	116-V	47.50
black curtains	99-D	24.00
ghoulish-laughter tape	20-A	3.75
torches (light bulbs included)	67-A	7.50 each
portrait with moving eyes	21-B	35.00
motorized rats	56-X	12.00 each

LETTERS OF COMPLAINT

When you write a letter of complaint, you should state the problem politely and provide complete information about it. Then tell how you think the problem might be corrected. For example, if you receive an item that is missing some parts, you should state what the item is, what parts are missing, and what you expect the company to do about the problem. Remember to use a professional, courteous tone, no matter how angry you might be.

- **Practice Your Skills**

    Registering a Complaint

    Write an e-mail in which you register a complaint to an imaginary company because you received a defective item in the mail. Include a description of the problem, and suggest a solution. Review your e-mail to make sure you haven't left out any important information. Remember to use a professional, polite tone and to follow the conventions of a business e-mail.

The Purpose and Format of Letters

Completing Business Forms

You will need to fill out business forms for a variety of reasons. For example, you might send a money order or register for a class at a community center. Today, you can often complete forms online. However, there are still many occasions when you will be asked to fill out a paper form. Follow these guidelines when you complete a paper form.

Completing Business Forms

- Read all of the directions carefully before you begin to fill out the form.
- If the form is long or complex, you may want to write the answers on a separate sheet of paper first. Then copy the answers onto the form in ink.
- Check both sides of the form to make sure you do not miss any questions written on the back.
- Do not leave blanks. If a question does not apply to you, write *N/A* (not applicable) in the space provided.
- Always use blue or black pen.
- Be sure to print neatly and clearly.
- Remember to sign the form if needed.
- Check your work when you are finished.

The model on the next page is an example of a form that you might complete if you wanted to submit an original work to a magazine that publishes student writing.

SUBMISSION FORM

Student Information

Student's Name: _____

Home Address: _____

Telephone Number: _____

E-mail Address: _____

Age: _____

Grade in School: _____

School Information

School Name: _____

School Address: _____

School Telephone Number: _____

Name of English Teacher: _____

Name of Principal: _____

Submission Information

Title of Work:

Genre (check one box): ☐ fiction ☐ nonfiction ☐ poetry ☐ drama

I certify that this submission is my original work. It has not been copied from another work. Any material used from another source has been properly cited.

Student's Signature: Date:

● **Practice Your Skills**

Completing a Business Form

Copy the Submission Form above onto a sheet of paper. Make up the title of a work to submit to the magazine, and choose a genre (fiction, nonfiction, poetry, or drama). Then complete the form. Be sure to print neatly using a blue or black pen. Check your work carefully.

C. Directions and Speeches

Part I	Critical Thinking and Problem Solving for Academic Success	**A.** Vocabulary	402
Part II	**Communication and Collaboration**	**B.** Letters and Forms	418
Part III	Media and Technology	**C. Directions and Speeches**	**432**

Apply 21st Century Communication and Collaboration Skills

To communicate effectively, two things have to happen: A speaker must send a clear message, and a listener must hear and understand it.

In the diverse world of the 21st century, you will communicate with people from various social and cultural backgrounds. When you give a speech, the members of your audience may have diverse views and beliefs. You may listen to a speaker who has a perspective very different from your own. You may collaborate in a group discussion with classmates from a variety of backgrounds. In all these cases, you should respect the varied opinions and values of others. Doing so will enrich your understanding and help you communicate and collaborate effectively.

You can practice and improve your speaking, listening, and collaborating skills just like any other skills. This section will help you sharpen these skills, which are important for school and all other areas of your life.

Developing Your Informal Speaking Skills

In your day-to-day life, there is not much time for making formal speeches. For example, if a friend calls you for advice or if someone asks you for directions, you will not have a chance to prepare a formal speech. That is why much of our speaking is informal. **Informal speaking** is a form of speech that is suitable for everyday use or for casual occasions. Although informal speeches are short and require little or no advance preparation, you still must use language effectively to communicate your message. Remember to keep your purpose in mind as you speak. Take the time to organize your thoughts and use precise language so that your message is clear and to the point.

❶ Giving Directions

If you have ever been lost, you know how important a clear set of directions can be. Compare the two sets of directions to the concert hall that follow.

Unclear   The concert hall is not too far from here. Just go down the main street for a while. Turn at the traffic light, go down that street a short way, and it is on your right.

Clear   To get to the concert hall, continue on Central Street for two blocks. At the second traffic light, take a right onto Grove Avenue. Follow Grove Avenue for about half a mile. You will cross a small bridge, and the concert hall will be on your right.

Notice that the second set of directions gives specific details, such as distances, street names, and landmarks. The first set of directions does not provide enough information.

The following strategies will help you give clear, concise directions.

Guidelines for Giving Directions

- Use words like *right, left,* and *straight* rather than *north, south, east,* or *west*.
- Use the names of streets or highway numbers if you know them.
- Mention landmarks whenever possible.
- Include the approximate number of blocks or miles if you know this information.
- If possible, draw a map.
- Do not give directions for a difficult shortcut.
- If you are unsure of the correct directions, do not guess. Help the other person find someone else to ask for information.
- Speak clearly and slowly.
- Look directly at the other person as you give him or her directions.
- Pay attention to the other person's facial expressions and body language. They may indicate that he or she does not understand your directions.
- Repeat the directions, or have the other person repeat the directions to you.

When you give directions, keep in mind that most people cannot easily remember more than three to five steps. If the directions are long and complicated, sometimes the best thing to do is to give directions to a halfway point. Then tell the person to ask for additional directions from there.

Developing Your Informal Speaking Skills

● **Practice Your Skills**

Improving Directions

List five errors in the following directions. Then rewrite the directions using specific details of your own choice.

> To get to the Crown Building, go south on the main street through the town for a while. Turn at the streetlight and go for another mile or so. After you cross a bridge, go north. The Crown Building should be on your left.

Giving and Following Directions

Write directions from your classroom to the following places in your school. Include as many specific details as possible. Then take turns with a partner as one of you reads aloud your directions and the other follows them. If parts of the directions are unclear, ask questions to clarify them. Discuss ways in which the directions could be improved.

1. main entrance
2. water fountain
3. library
4. nurse's office

❷ Participating in Group Discussions

In a group discussion, you collaborate with others. You share ideas and information and exchange opinions in order to accomplish a goal. Your goal might be to solve a problem or to reach a decision. By developing your group discussion skills, you will learn to state your ideas effectively and to listen carefully to others' ideas. You will also learn to collaborate respectfully with others. Keep the following guidelines in mind the next time you are in a group discussion—at home or at school.

Guidelines for Participating in Group Discussions

- Keep to the subject of the discussion.
- Support your ideas and opinions with facts or examples if you can.
- Listen carefully to what others have to say, and do not interrupt.
- Keep an open mind, and appreciate diverse perspectives.
- Respond respectfully to others' views. If you disagree with someone's point, do it politely and explain why you disagree.
- Ask questions if you do not understand information or another person's views.
- Keep in mind that everyone in the group should have an equal opportunity to speak.
- Be flexible and try to help your group accomplish its goal, whether that involves drawing a conclusion or reaching a decision or consensus.

C. Directions and Speeches

- **Practice Your Skills**

    Participating in a Group Discussion

    Form a group with three or four classmates, and hold a group discussion. Discuss your favorite movies. Your goal is to choose one movie that you have all seen to recommend to a friend. Be sure to follow the Guidelines for Participating in Group Discussions. Present the results of your discussion to the rest of the class. Tell which movie your group recommends and why.

Developing Your Formal Speaking Skills

Have you ever given an oral report in your social studies class or made a speech during a school election? If you have, then you have given a formal speech. A **formal speech** is usually longer than an informal speech, and it requires careful preparation. You will have many opportunities in school and in your future career to deliver speeches. Learning to express your ideas well and to use media and technology effectively will help you deliver a successful speech.

① Preparing Your Speech

The steps that you follow when you prepare a formal speech are very similar to those that you follow when you prepare a written report. (See pages 308–311.) The main difference is that you will practice your speech and deliver it orally rather than present your ideas in writing.

CHOOSING AND LIMITING A SUBJECT

To choose a subject for your speech, first make a list of subjects that you know well. Then choose one that will interest both you and your audience. For example, if you were speaking to younger students about your school, you might tell them about the courses your school offers. If you were speaking to your classmates, however, this subject would not interest them. A better subject for your classmates might be new courses the school should offer in the coming year.

Once you have chosen a subject, think about how much time you have to deliver your speech. If you have only ten minutes, you will need to limit your subject and talk about just one aspect or part of it. For example, you could limit the subject of new courses your school should offer by talking about just the importance of offering computer classes.

● **Practice Your Skills**

Choosing and Limiting a Subject

Write the subject of a speech for each item below. Then limit each subject so that it is suitable for a ten-minute speech.

Example   food
Possible   Subject: food rich in vitamins
Answer   Limited Subject: citrus foods rich in vitamin C

1. great musicians
2. heroines
3. Olympic events
4. world leaders
5. oceans
6. great books

UNDERSTANDING YOUR PURPOSE

The purpose of your speech determines the points you make and the way you present your information. Most speeches have one of the following three purposes: to inform, to persuade, or to entertain. The purpose of a speech may also be to motivate or to instruct.

PURPOSES OF SPEECHES	
Purpose	**Examples**
To Inform	• to explain how the Special Olympics began • to explain how the Egyptian pyramids were built • to explain how electricity works
To Persuade	• to encourage people to vote for a candidate for president • to encourage others to try out for the school musical • to convince others to visit Canada
To Entertain	• to tell about the time you forgot your lines during a play • to tell about the time you went sailing without a sail • to tell about the first time you went ice-skating

● **Practice Your Skills**

Choosing a Subject and Purpose for Your Speech

You will be presenting a ten-minute speech to your class. The topic is "Someone I Admire." Brainstorm or freewrite to choose a subject that suits your audience and the length of your speech. Then select a purpose for your speech. Write down your subject and purpose, and save your work for later use.

● **Practice Your Skills**

Determining a Purpose for a Speech

Label the purpose of each speech *to inform*, *to persuade*, or *to entertain*.

1. to explain how exercise and diet affect people's health
2. to explain key events in the life of an athlete
3. to encourage students to attend school events
4. to tell about the time you went fishing and ended up swimming instead
5. to convince your listeners to buy Wam-o running shoes

GATHERING AND ORGANIZING YOUR INFORMATION

The next steps in preparing your speech are to gather and organize information. These steps are similar to those you follow when writing a report. (See pages 312–319 and 341–345.) You should also collect audiovisual aids. Follow these guidelines to complete these steps.

Gathering Information

- List what you already know about your subject.
- Gather more information from books and magazines in the library or from Internet sources. You may also want to interview someone who is knowledgeable about the subject.
- Find interesting examples and quotations to include.
- Take notes on the information you find. Writing information on index cards will make it easy to organize your notes as you prepare your outline. Use a new card for each new idea. Be sure to note the source for your information in case you need to find it again.

Collecting Audiovisual Aids

- Decide whether any audiovisual aids, such as maps, pictures, PowerPoint™ slides, CDs, or DVDs, will add to the impact of your speech. Keep in mind that audiovisual aids should be used to add to points or to help make points clear. They should never be distracting to your audience.
- Make sure that any audiovisual aids you choose suit the purpose and context of your speech.
- Plan how and when you will use the aids in your speech.
- Gather or create the audiovisual aids you will use.

Organizing Information

- Make an outline of your speech. Unlike an outline for a report, an outline for a speech should include your introduction and your conclusion.
- The introduction of your speech should capture the attention of your audience. It should also include the main idea of your speech.
- The body of your speech should include your supporting points. Arrange your points in a logical order. Think of the transitions you will use to connect your ideas when you speak.
- The conclusion of your speech should summarize your main idea.

● **Practice Your Skills**

Gathering Information with Note Cards

The following paragraph about George Lucas is from *Encyclopedia Britannica Online*. Use index cards to take notes on the paragraph as if you were preparing a speech about Lucas's life. Sample notes have been started for you.

> Lucas became interested in filmmaking while in high school. He received encouragement from the cinematographer Haskell Wexler and gained admission to the film department of the University of Southern California (B.A., 1966). Lucas's first full-length film was *THX 1138* (1971), a grim fantasy about a robotized, dehumanized society in the distant future. His second film, *American Graffiti* (1973), a sympathetic recollection of adolescent American life in the early 1960s, was a surprise success at the box office.

Source: Encyclopedia Britannica Online
— *first full-length film:* THX 1138
— *1971*
— *about future robot society*

● **Practice Your Skills**

Gathering and Organizing Information for Your Speech

Look back at the subject and purpose you chose for your speech. Write what you know about your subject on note cards. Next, find information for at least four more note cards by using Internet or library resources. Then organize your cards, and write an outline of your speech. Prepare any audiovisual aids you will use.

❷ Practicing Your Speech

Practicing your speech aloud is a very important step for delivering it successfully. Use the following guidelines as you practice your speech.

Guidelines for Practicing Your Speech

- Read your outline several times until you are familiar with all the information and feel comfortable presenting your points.
- Practice in front of a long mirror so that you will be aware of your facial expressions and gestures.
- Practice looking around the room as you talk.
- Practice using your audiovisual aids.
- Time the length of your speech. If it is too long, decide what information you can omit. If it is too short, you should find more information.
- Practice over a period of several days.

● Practice Your Skills

Practicing Your Speech

Practice your speech alone several times. Then, with a partner, take turns practicing your speeches in front of each other. Share your feedback with each other. Use your partner's comments to revise and improve your speech.

❸ Delivering Your Speech

If you have followed the guidelines for preparing and practicing your speech, you will be prepared to deliver it. Follow these guidelines to deliver an effective speech.

Guidelines for Delivering Your Speech

- Be well prepared and have all the materials you need, such as your outline and audiovisual aids or equipment.
- Wait until your audience is quiet and settled.
- Take a deep breath and begin.
- Stand with your weight divided between both feet. Avoid swaying back and forth.
- Look directly at the people in your audience, not over their heads. Try to make eye contact.
- Speak slowly, clearly, and loudly enough to be heard.
- Use gestures and facial expressions to emphasize your main points.
- Make sure that everyone in your audience can see your audiovisual aids.

● Practice Your Skills

Delivering Your Speech

Present the speech you have practiced before a group of classmates. Then, in your journal, list what you think you did well and what you would like to improve in your next speech. You may want to use the Oral Presentation Assessment Form on page 446 to assess your speech or to provide feedback to your classmates about their speeches.

Developing Your Listening Skills

Most people spend over 50 percent of each day just listening. Surprisingly, however, most people remember only about one fourth of what they hear. This section will help you improve your listening skills.

Guidelines for Listening to an Oral Presentation

During the Presentation:
- Pay attention.
- Do not interrupt or make unnecessary noise.
- Listen to understand, appreciate, and evaluate.
- Notice how the speaker may use pauses to make points.
- Observe how the use of gestures, voice, and facial expressions adds to the message.
- Listen for changes in volume, intonation, and pitch used to emphasize important ideas.

After the Presentation:
- If possible, ask the speaker to explain anything you did not understand.
- If the speaker is available, thank him or her for the presentation.

● Practice Your Skills

Listening Carefully

Watch ten minutes of a news program or an interview on TV, or watch a video of a news story or an interview on a news organization's Web site. Next, write a few sentences summarizing what you heard. Then describe how the speaker(s) used pauses, gestures, facial expressions, or voice to emphasize points or add to the message.

❶ Listening to Enjoy and Appreciate

One of the most important aspects of listening is enjoying and appreciating a presentation. You will remember more about a presentation you enjoyed than about one that does not interest you. Paying attention and listening carefully will help you to enjoy a presentation. You will also better appreciate what the speaker is trying to say and accomplish.

● **Practice Your Skills**

Listening to Enjoy and Appreciate

With a partner, take turns reading the following poem aloud. While you are listening to your partner read, try to enjoy and appreciate the poem. Close your eyes if that helps you focus as you listen. When you have each heard the poem, answer the questions that follow it.

> **"I am the creativity"**
>
> I am the dance step
> of the paintbrush singing
> I am the sculpture
> of the song
> the flame breath
> of words
> giving new life to paper
> yes, I am the creativity
> that never dies
> I am the creativity
> keeping my people
> alive
>
> —Alexis De Veaux

- Did you enjoy the poem? Why or why not? Even if you did not enjoy the poem, did you appreciate what the poet was trying to convey? Why or why not?

❷ Listening for Information and Taking Notes

When you listen to gain information, focus your attention on the main idea and supporting ideas of the speech. You should also determine the speaker's purpose, whether it is to inform, instruct, motivate, or persuade.

LISTENING FOR THE MAIN IDEA AND PURPOSE

In a well-planned speech, the main idea, along with the speaker's purpose, will be in the introduction. Often the speaker will state both directly in a single sentence. For example, if you heard the sentence *Using a computer makes writing easier than composing by hand,* you would know that the speech is about the advantages of using a computer for writing. You would also know that the speaker's purpose is to persuade you to use a computer rather than writing your work by hand.

Be alert during the introduction because the speaker does not always state the main idea and purpose directly. Instead, the speaker may convey the main idea and purpose through a question, a quotation, or a personal example.

LISTENING FOR SUPPORTING IDEAS

Once you have identified a speaker's main idea and purpose, listen for the major supporting ideas in the speech. Pay attention to clues such as *There are three reasons that . . .* or *I will explain the four main causes of. . . .* Such phrases often introduce major supporting ideas. A speaker may also signal major supporting ideas by using transitional expressions like *first, second, third, moreover, most important,* or *finally*.

As each major supporting idea is introduced, listen for supporting details that the speaker offers to clarify or drive home the major idea. These supporting details often take the form of facts and examples, such as statistics, quotations from experts, and anecdotes. In some cases a speaker will alert you to an important supporting detail by introducing it with a phrase such as *for example, studies show that,* or *according to one expert*.

Keep in mind that not all details are important. As you listen to the speech, focus on major supporting ideas and details that help you understand and evaluate the speaker's main idea. If any points are unclear and the speaker is available after the presentation, ask questions to clarify the points.

TAKING NOTES WHILE LISTENING

Taking notes on speeches helps you to listen carefully. To take notes, you need to listen for important points and then organize the information clearly. Use the following guidelines to help you take notes.

Guidelines for Taking Notes on Speeches

- Write the main idea presented in the introduction.
- Write the main topics, using Roman numerals (I, II, III) in an outline form.
- Under each main topic, write the main supporting ideas, using capital letters (A, B, C). These are the subtopics.
- At the end of the outline, write a restatement of the main idea. This is the summary.

The following notes in outline form are based on a speech about designing video games.

MODEL: Notes in Outline Form

Designing video games is a complex, carefully planned procedure. — **Main Idea**

I. Games developed around one theme — **Main Topic**
   A. Ideas from books, magazines, movies, dreams, life experience — **Subtopic**
   B. Ideas suggested by other popular games

II. Idea or theme developed on paper
   A. Sequence of sketches or drawings called storyboards
   B. Flow charts or block diagrams showing a game in words and boxes

III. Game programmed into computer
   A. Game coded in assembly or machine computer language
   B. Assembly languages give game its speed and exactness

IV. Game tested and marketed
   A. Children play new games, and their reactions are studied
   B. Games put in arcades and records kept on use
   C. If popular, game produced in large quantities and sold for home use

Designing video games includes several steps. They are **(1)** developing a theme, **(2)** putting it down on paper, **(3)** programming the game into the computer, and **(4)** testing and marketing the game. — **Summary Statement**

When you take notes, do not try to write everything down. If you do, you might miss important points. Write only the information that is necessary for remembering the most important points accurately. Your notes will then help you remember the other details.

● **Practice Your Skills**

Listening for Information and Taking Notes

Pair up with a classmate who attends another class with you. During the next class discussion, take notes. Then compare notes and discuss any differences.

❸ Listening Critically

When you listen, your goal is not only to understand but also to evaluate what the speaker is saying. To listen critically, you need to listen very carefully and pay close attention to the speaker's choice of words.

Guidelines for Listening Critically

- Identify the speaker's purpose and intentions. Is the speaker trying to persuade you to do or buy something, for example?
- Think about the values and attitudes expressed by the speaker. What principles or qualities are important, according to the speaker? How does the speaker feel about the topic?
- Consider how the speaker's purpose, values, and attitudes affect the way he or she talks about the topic.

Be on the lookout for the following types of techniques and statements that may be used to mislead or influence you.

To learn more about the techniques of persuasion, see Writing to Persuade, *pages 240–265.*

FACT AND OPINION

A **fact** is a statement that can be proved. An **opinion** is a personal feeling or judgment. Because opinions are often stated as facts, you must listen carefully to tell them apart.

Fact	Austin is the capital of Texas.
Opinion	Austin is a wonderful city.

● Practice Your Skills

Understanding Fact and Opinion

Label each statement *fact* or *opinion*.

1. Our school has a girls' basketball team.
2. Our school is the oldest school in the city.
3. Everyone should go to college.
4. Our cafeteria serves terrible food.
5. Water expands when it is frozen.

BANDWAGON

Commercials and advertisements sometimes include a bandwagon statement. A **bandwagon statement** leads you to believe that everyone is using a certain product. In other words, everyone is "jumping on the bandwagon." A bandwagon statement can be misleading because it suggests that if you do not jump on the bandwagon, you will be different from everyone else.

Bandwagon Statement	Read *Success the Easy Way*, and join millions of people who have turned their dreams into reality.

C. Directions and Speeches

TESTIMONIAL

In a **testimonial** a famous person encourages you to buy a product. A testimonial can be misleading because it suggests that if a famous person uses the product, it must be worth buying.

Testimonial Statement   I'm Sienna Javits. A busy star like me needs a reliable cell phone. That's why I use a Cello.

LOADED WORDS

Another type of statement that may mislead or influence you is one that contains loaded words. **Loaded words** are ones that are carefully chosen to appeal to your hopes or fears rather than to reason or logic. In the following advertisement, the word *confidence* was chosen to stir up the listener's emotions.

Loaded Word   Shop at Maxine's, and walk into your next job interview with confidence.

● **Practice Your Skills**

Evaluating for Misleading Information

Label each statement *bandwagon*, *testimonial*, or *loaded words*.

1. I'm Mitchell Judson. A star like me knows that Sparkle works better than any other toothpaste.
2. For a safe, stress-free vacation, book a trip with International Travel Pros.
3. Find out why audiences across the country are raving about the new thriller *Double Cross*.
4. Smart shoppers everywhere head straight to Bargain Warehouse to find the lowest prices.

④ Listening to Evaluate

After you have listened to a speech in class, you can assess the speech for its effectiveness. Through self-assessment, your classmates' feedback, and assessing the speeches of others, you can improve your speaking and listening skills and help your classmates to improve theirs. You may want to use the following Oral Presentation Assessment Form to assess a speech.

ORAL PRESENTATION ASSESSMENT FORM

Subject: _____

Speaker: _____ **Date:** _____

Content

Was the subject appropriate for the audience?
Was the subject appropriate for the length of the speech?
Was the purpose clear? Was it appropriate for the audience?
Was the main idea clear?
Did all the ideas clearly relate to the subject?

Organization

Was the introduction clear and interesting?
Did the introduction include the main idea?
Did the ideas in the body of the speech follow a logical order?
Were transitions used between ideas?
Did the conclusion summarize the main idea?

Presentation

Was the speaker well prepared?
Did the speaker use an outline well?
Did the speaker talk loudly and clearly enough?
Did the speaker talk at a good speed?
Did the speaker make eye contact with the audience?
Did the speaker use an appropriate pitch and tone of voice?
Did the speaker use gestures and pauses effectively?
If the speaker used audiovisual aids, were they effective?

Comments: _____

_____

_____

_____

_____

_____

PART III

Media and Technology

> **Part I**   Critical Thinking and Problem Solving for Academic Success
> **Part II** Communication and Collaboration
> **Part III** Media and Technology

Essential Skills

You already understand the importance of literacy, or the ability to read and write. In the 21st century, literacy—meaning "knowledge of a particular subject or field"—in the areas of information, media, and technology is also essential. Part III of this guide will help you develop literacy in these three areas. This knowledge will help you succeed in school and in your future jobs.

❶ Information Literacy

Today, a tremendous amount of information is available at your fingertips. To acquire information literacy, you must know how to access, manage, evaluate, and use this wealth of information. Learning advanced search strategies will help you locate information efficiently and effectively from a range of relevant print and electronic sources. Evaluating the reliability and validity of sources will help you assess their usefulness. Then you can synthesize information in order to draw conclusions or to solve a problem creatively. Understanding the difference between paraphrasing and plagiarism and knowing how to record bibliographic information will ensure that you use information in an ethical, legal manner. Part III of this guide will help you build your information literacy skills by showing you how to use the Internet to access information.

You can learn more about information literacy on pages 322–339.

❷ Media Literacy

Media messages serve a variety of purposes. They can have a powerful influence on your opinions, values, beliefs, and actions. Part III of this guide will help you develop your media literacy skills by showing you how to use both print and nonprint media to communicate your message. You will learn how to use these media to create effective messages that suit your audience and purpose. You will also learn about the types of tools available for creating media products.

You can learn more about media literacy on pages 43, 74, 97, 117, 144, 166, 202, 222, 251, 289, and 314.

❸ Technology Literacy

In the 21st century, knowing how to use technology to research, evaluate, and communicate information is essential. You must also know how to use different forms of technology, such as computers and audio and video recorders, to integrate information and create products. Part III of this guide will show you how to use technology effectively to access information and to publish and present your ideas in different media.

You can learn more about technology literacy on pages 448–463.

A. Electronic Publishing

Part I	Critical Thinking and Problem Solving for Academic Success	**A.** Electronic Publishing	449
Part II	Communication and Collaboration	**B.** Using the Internet	464
Part III	Media and Technology		

Apply Media and Technology Literacy

Everything you may ever have to say or write requires some medium through which you express it and share it with others. The ability to use available media and technology to their fullest potential will enable you to communicate your ideas effectively and to a widespread audience. For now, most academic and workplace communication still depends on print technology. By using that to its full capability, you will prepare yourself for the inevitable improvements and upgrades that will be a feature of communication in the future.

In this section, you will develop your skills in using available technology in your communication.

Digital Publishing

The computer is a powerful tool that gives you the ability to create everything from newsletters to multimedia reports. Many software programs deliver word-processing and graphic arts capabilities that once belonged only to professional printers and designers. Armed with the knowledge of how to operate your software, you simply need to add some sound research and a healthy helping of creativity to create an exciting paper.

WORD PROCESSING

Using a standard word-processing program makes all aspects of the writing process easier. Use a word-processing program to:

- create an outline;
- save multiple versions of your work;
- revise your manuscript;
- proof your spelling, grammar, and punctuation;
- produce a polished final draft document.

Using a Spell Checker

You can use your computer to help you catch spelling errors. One way is to set your Preferences for a wavy red line to appear under words that are misspelled as you type. You can also set your Preferences to correct spelling errors automatically.

A second way to check your spelling is to choose Spelling and Grammar from the Tools menu. Select the text you want to check and let the spell checker run through it looking for errors. While a spell checker can find many errors, it cannot tell you if a correctly spelled word is used correctly. For example, you might have written *The books were over their*. The spell checker will not identify an error here, even though the correct word is *there*, not *their*.

Fascinating Fonts

Once your written material is revised and proofed, you can experiment with type as a way to enhance the content of your written message and present it in a reader-friendly format. Different styles of type are called **fonts** or **typefaces**. Most word-processing programs feature more than 30 different choices. You'll find them listed in the Format menu under Font.

Or they may be located on the toolbar at the top left of your screen.

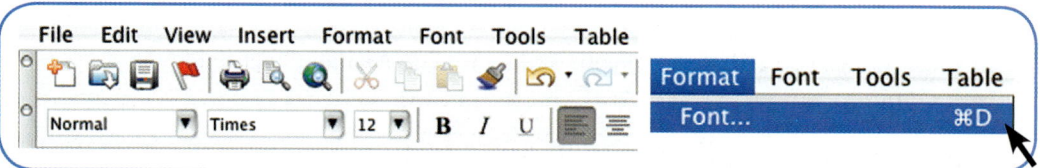

Most fonts fall into one of two categories: **serif** typefaces or **sans serif** typefaces. A serif is a small curve or line added to the end of some of the letter strokes. A typeface that includes these small added curves is called a serif typeface. A font without them is referred to as sans serif, or in other words, without serifs.

> Times New Roman is a serif typeface.
> Arial is a sans serif typeface.

In general, sans serif fonts have a sharp look and are better for shorter pieces of writing, such as headings and titles. Serif typefaces work well for body copy.

Each typeface, whether serif or sans serif, has a personality of its own and makes a different impression on the reader. Specialized fonts, like the examples in the second paragraph on page 451, are great for unique projects (posters, invitations, and personal correspondence) but less appropriate for writing assignments for school or business.

A. Electronic Publishing

Since most school writing is considered formal, good font choices include Times New Roman, Arial, Helvetica, or Bookman Antiqua. These type styles are fairly plain. They allow the reader to focus on the meaning of your words instead of being distracted by the way they appear on the page.

With so many fonts to choose from, you may be tempted to include a dozen or so in your document. Be careful! Text printed *in* multiple fonts can be EXTREMELY *confusing* to *read*. Remember that the whole idea of using different typefaces is to enhance and clarify your message, not muddle it!

A Sizable Choice

Another way to add emphasis to your writing and make it reader-friendly is to adjust the size of the type. Type size is measured in points. One inch is equal to 72 points. Therefore, 72-point type would have letters that measure one inch high. To change the point size of your type, open the Format menu and click Font.

Or use the small number box on the toolbar at the top left side of your screen.

For most school and business writing projects, 10 or 12 points is the best size of type for the main body copy of your text. However, it's very effective to increase the type size for titles, headings, and subheadings to highlight how your information is organized. Another way to add emphasis is to apply a style to the type, such as **bold,** *italics,* or underline. Styles are also found in the Format menu under Font.

Or look for them—abbreviated as **B** for bold, *I* for italics, and U for underline—in the top

Digital Publishing

center section of the toolbar on your screen.

If you have access to a color printer, you may want to consider using **colored type** to set

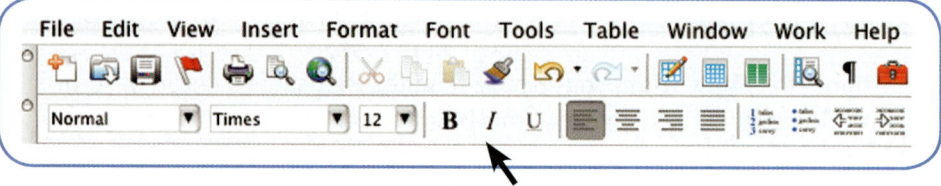

your heading apart from the rest of the body copy. Red, blue, or other dark colors work best. Avoid yellow or other light shades that might fade out and be difficult to read.

Use different type sizes, styles, and colors sparingly and consistently throughout your work. In other words, all the body copy should be in one style of type. All the headings should be in another, and so on. Doing so will give your work a unified, polished appearance.

TEXT FEATURES

Text features such as **bulleted lists** and **numbered lists** are useful ways to organize information and give it a reader-friendly format. If you create pages of text in which information isn't broken up in any way, your readers may lose focus or have trouble identifying your main points. Instead, use bulleted or numbered lists to highlight important information and present it clearly and simply. To create these lists, open the Format menu and click on Bullets and Numbering. You can also click on the numbered or bulleted list on the toolbar at the top right of your screen.

A sidebar is another useful text feature for presenting information. A **sidebar** is a section of text that is placed alongside the main copy. Often the text in a sidebar appears in a box. Use sidebars to present additional, interesting information that relates to your main topic but doesn't belong in the body of your report or paper.

LAYOUT HELP FROM YOUR COMPUTER

One way to organize the information in your document is to use one of the preset page layouts provided by your word-processing program. All you have to do is write your document using capital letters for main headings and uppercase and lowercase letters for subheadings. Set the headings apart from the body copy by hitting the "return" key. Then open the Format menu and click the Autoformat heading. Your copy will probably look like the illustration on the next page.

You can probably use this automatic, preset format for most of the writing you do in school. You'll also find other options available in the File menu under Page Setup.

A. Electronic Publishing

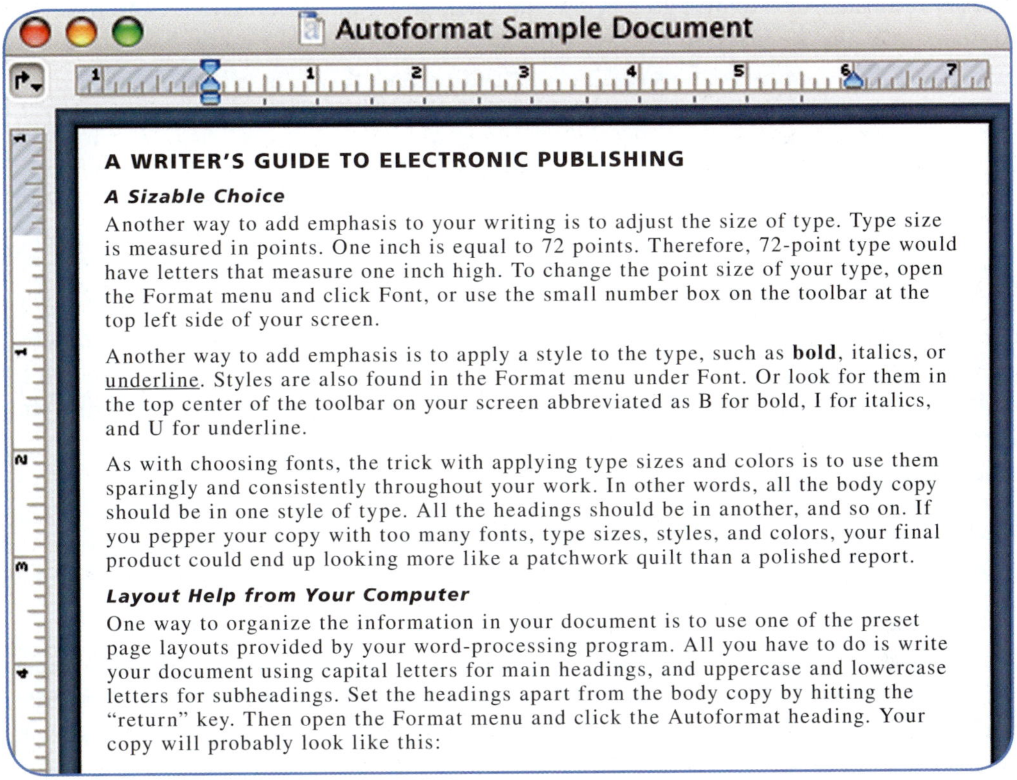

AUTOFORMAT SAMPLE DOCUMENT

A WRITER'S GUIDE TO ELECTRONIC PUBLISHING

A Sizable Choice

Another way to add emphasis to your writing is to adjust the size of type. Type size is measured in points. One inch is equal to 72 points. Therefore, 72-point type would have letters that measure one inch high. To change the point size of your type, open the Format menu and click Font, or use the small number box on the toolbar at the top left side of your screen.

Another way to add emphasis is to apply a style to the type, such as **bold**, italics, or underline. Styles are also found in the Format menu under Font. Or look for them in the top center of the toolbar on your screen abbreviated as B for bold, I for italics, and U for underline.

As with choosing fonts, the trick with applying type sizes and colors is to use them sparingly and consistently throughout your work. In other words, all the body copy should be in one style of type. All the headings should be in another, and so on. If you pepper your copy with too many fonts, type sizes, styles, and colors, your final product could end up looking more like a patchwork quilt than a polished report.

Layout Help from Your Computer

One way to organize the information in your document is to use one of the preset page layouts provided by your word-processing program. All you have to do is write your document using capital letters for main headings, and uppercase and lowercase letters for subheadings. Set the headings apart from the body copy by hitting the "return" key. Then open the Format menu and click the Autoformat heading. Your copy will probably look like this:

21ST CENTURY

Here you can change the margins and add headers, footers, and page numbers. Headers and footers are descriptive titles that automatically appear at the top or bottom of each page without your having to retype them each time. For example, you may wish to add the title of your project and the date as a header or footer to each page.

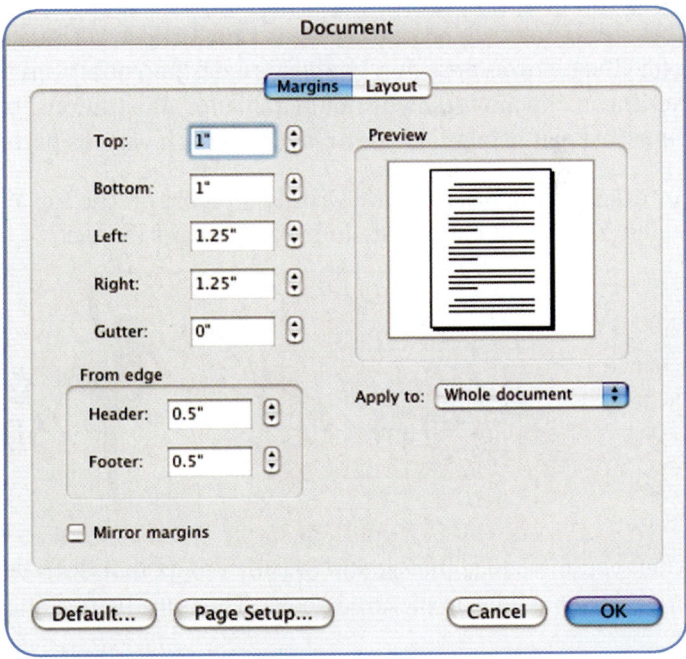

Digital Publishing   453

To insert a header or a footer, go to View and click on Header and Footer. Note that page numbers may also be inserted by way of the Insert option on your menu bar.

```
Header
Project Title Here
Date Here
```

LET'S GET GRAPHIC

The old saying "A picture is worth a thousand words" is particularly true when it comes to spicing up papers and reports. Publishing and presentation software programs give you the ability to include photographs, illustrations, and charts in your work that can express your ideas more clearly and succinctly than words alone.

The key to using graphics effectively is to make sure each one conveys a message of importance. Don't use them just for decoration. Be sure they add something meaningful, or you'll actually detract from your written message.

Drawings Many paint and draw programs allow you to create an illustration or **import** (bring in from another program) one into your document. Drawings can help illustrate concepts that are difficult to describe, such as mechanical parts or procedures. Cartoons can also add a nice touch. If you use them sparingly, they can lighten up an otherwise dry, technical report.

Clip Art Another kind of drawing is called clip art. These simple, black-and-white or color line pictures are often included in desktop publishing or word-processing programs. Pre-drawn clip art usually is not suitable for illustrations, but it does work well as graphic icons that can help guide your reader through various parts of a long report.

For example, suppose you are writing a report on the top arts programs in the United States. You might choose the following clip art for each of the sections:

When you introduce the section of your report that deals with music, you might use the large sized music icon pictured above. Then, in the headings of all the following sections that deal with music, you might use a smaller version of the icon that looks like this:

Music Trends

Using clip art as icons in this manner lets your readers know at a glance which part of the report they are reading.

Charts and Graphs One of the best ways to communicate information about numbers and statistics is by using charts and graphs. Programs such as Microsoft PowerPoint™ allow you to create bar graphs, pie charts, and line graphs that can communicate fractions, figures, and comparative measurements much more powerfully than written descriptions.

Photographs With the widespread availability of digital cameras and scanners, adding photos to your project is an easy and effective way to enhance your content. Using a digital camera or a scanner, you can load photos directly into your computer. Another option is to shoot photographs with a regular camera, but when you have them developed, specify that they be returned to you as "pictures on disc," which you can open on your computer screen.

Photographic images are stored as bits of data in an electronic file. Once you have the photos in your computer, you can use a graphics program to manipulate the images in a variety of ways and create amazing visual effects. You can crop elements out of the photo, add special filters and colors, combine elements of two different pictures into one—the possibilities are endless.

After you have inserted the edited photo into your document, be careful when you print out your final draft. Standard printers often don't reproduce photographs well. You may want to take your document on disc to a professional printing company and have it printed out on a high-resolution printer to make sure you get the best quality.

Captions and Titles While it's true that a single photo can say a great deal, some pictures still need a little explanation in order to have the strongest impact on your reader. Whenever you include an illustration or photograph in a document, also include a simple caption or title for each image.

Add captions in a slightly smaller type size than the body copy and preferably in a sans serif typeface. Use the caption to add information that isn't immediately apparent in the photo. If there are people in the picture, tell readers who they are. If the photo features an odd-looking structure, explain what it is. Be smart with your captions. Don't tell readers the obvious. Give them a reason to read your caption.

Stand-Alone Graphics Occasionally you may include well-known graphics or logos in a report. These graphics convey powerful messages on their own and don't require captions. Examples of these logos or symbols include:

Nonprint Media—Audio and Video

The world we live in is becoming increasingly more multimedia-savvy. Many businesses rely extensively on multimedia presentations to market their products or convey messages to consumers and employees. Exciting opportunities exist for people who can produce clear, concise messages in audio and visual formats.

PRE-PRODUCTION—PUT IT ON PAPER FIRST

Although the final presentation of your subject material may be an audio recording or a video, your project needs to begin on paper first. When you write down your ideas, you do four things:

- Organize your thoughts.
- Narrow your focus.
- Isolate the main messages.
- Identify possible production problems.

Resist the urge to grab an audio recorder or camcorder and run off to record your project. That's a sure-fire way to create an unorganized mess. Take the time to plan your production.

Concept Outline The first task in the writing process is a short, one-page document that describes the basic idea of the project. Ideally this should be three paragraphs—one paragraph each describing the beginning, the middle, and the end. Do not go forward until you have clearly identified these three important parts of your project.

Brief Next write one to two pages that describe in detail the point of your project: how it will be used, who the intended audience is, what the purpose is, and what you hope to achieve with the presentation. Do you want your audience to be informed about something? Motivated to do something? Emotionally moved in some way?

Treatment The next phase of the writing process fleshes out the ideas you expressed in your outline and brief. The treatment is several pages long. It contains descriptions of the characters, dialogue, and settings and describes the presentation scene by scene. Include in your treatment descriptions of the mood and the tone of your piece. If your project is a video, set the stage by describing the overall look and feel of the production.

Script Once you've completed the first three steps, you are ready to go to script. Everything that is mentioned in the script will wind up in the audio recording or on the screen. Conversely, anything that is left out of the script will likely be overlooked and omitted from the final production. So write this document carefully.

For an audio recording, the script contains all narration, dialogue, music, and sound effects. For a video, it contains all of these elements plus descriptions of the characters, any sets, props, or costumes, plus all camera shots and movements, special visual effects, and onscreen titles or graphic elements. In short, the audio script encompasses everything that is heard, and the video script covers everything that is seen and heard.

Storyboard Last, for video productions, it's also helpful to create storyboards—simple frame-by-frame sketches with explanatory notes jotted underneath—that paint a visual picture of what the video will look like from start to finish.

Pre-Production Tasks The final stages of pre-production include assembling all the elements you will need before you begin producing your audio recording or video. Here's a general checklist.

Pre-Production Checklist

Audio Tasks

- ✓ Arrange for audio recording equipment
- ✓ Cast narrator/actors
- ✓ Find music (secure permission)
- ✓ Arrange for sound effects
- ✓ Set up recording schedule
- ✓ Coordinate all cast and crew
- ✓ Arrange for transportation if needed
- ✓ Rehearse all voice talent

Video Tasks

- ✓ Arrange for video equipment (including lighting and sound recording equipment)
- ✓ Cast narrator/host/actors
- ✓ Find music (secure permission)
- ✓ Arrange for sound/visual effects
- ✓ Set up shooting schedule
- ✓ Coordinate all cast and crew
- ✓ Arrange for transportation if needed
- ✓ Set up shooting locations (secure permission)
- ✓ Arrange for costumes, props, sets
- ✓ Arrange for make-up if needed
- ✓ Rehearse all on-camera talent

Video Production Schedule Tucked into the list of pre-production tasks is "Set up recording/shooting schedule." For a video, this means much more than just deciding what day and time you will begin shooting.

During the video production phase of your project, the idea is to shoot everything that your script calls for in the final production. Often the most efficient way to do this is what is called "out-of-sequence" filming. This means that, rather than shooting scenes sequentially (that is, in the order that they appear in the script), you shoot them in the order that is most convenient. Later you will edit them together in the correct order in post-production.

For example, your video might begin and end in the main character's office. Rather than shoot the first office scene, then move the cast and crew to the next location, then later at the end of the day return to the office, it might be easier to shoot both office scenes back-to-back. This will save a great deal of time and effort involved in moving people, lights, and props back and forth.

Lighting may be a factor in the order in which you shoot your scenes. For example, scenes 3, 4, and 7 may take place in the daytime, and scenes 1, 2, 5, and 6 may take place at night.

To accommodate all of these factors, you will need to plan your shooting schedule carefully. The difference between a smooth shoot day and chaos is a well thought-out shooting schedule.

Last, for video or audio recording, it's also a good idea to assemble your team for a pre-production meeting before you begin. This is your chance to read through the script together, go over time schedules, review responsibilities of each person involved, and answer any questions or discuss potential problems before you begin the production process.

PRODUCTION

At last, it's production time! There are a number of different formats you can use for audio and video recording. Talk to the AV expert in your school or check with the media center for help in selecting the best format to use. Get tips, as well, for how to use the audio or video equipment to achieve the best results and produce a polished, professional project.

Next, if you are producing a video, think carefully about how you will shoot it. Consider the kinds of camera shots, camera moves, and special effects you will use.

Camera Shots To hold the interest of your audience, use a variety of camera shots and angles. Check your local library or media center for good books on camera techniques that describe when and how to use various shots—from long shots to close-ups, from low angles to overhead shots. As a rule, every time you change camera shots, change your angle slightly as well. This way, when the shots are edited together, you can avoid accidentally putting two nearly identical shots side-by-side, which creates an unnerving jarring motion called a "jump cut."

Do some research on framing techniques as well to make sure you frame your subjects properly and avoid cutting people's heads off on the screen.

Camera Moves Learn about ways to move the camera in order to keep your audience interested. Three common, but effective camera moves are panning, tracking, and zooming. **Panning** means moving the camera smoothly from one side of the scene to another. Panning works well in an establishing shot to help orient your audience to the setting where the action takes place.

Tracking means moving the camera from one place to another in a smooth action as well, but in tracking, the camera parallels the action, such as moving alongside a character as he or she walks down the street. It's called tracking because in professional filmmaking, the camera and the operator are rolled forward or backward on a small set of train tracks alongside the actor or actress.

Zooming means moving the camera forward or back, but zooming actually involves moving the lens, rather than the camera. By touching the zoom button, you can focus in on a small detail that you would like to emphasize, or you can pull back to reveal something in the background.

The important factor in any kind of camera move is to keep the action fluid and, in most cases, slow and steady. Also, use camera movement sparingly. You want to keep your audience eager and interested, not dizzy and sick!

Cuts Another good way to keep your presentation moving is to use frequent cuts. While the actual cuts will be done during post-production, you need to plan for them in production. Professional filmmakers use the word *coverage* for making sure they have ample choices for shots. You can create coverage for your production by planning shots such as those on the following pages.

Here are three kinds of video shots:

- **establishing shot** — This shot sets up where the action of the story will take place. For example, if your story takes place inside an operating room, you might begin with an establishing shot of the outside of the hospital.

- **reaction shot** — It's a good idea to get shots of all on-camera talent even if one person does not have any dialogue but is listening to, or reacting to, another character. This gives you the chance to break away from the character who is speaking to show how his or her words are affecting other people in the scene.

- **cutaway shot** — The cutaway shot is a shot of something that is not included in the original scene, but is somehow related to it. Cutaways are used to connect two subjects. For example, the first shot may be of a person falling off a boat. The second shot could be a cutaway of a shark swimming deep below the water.

Special Effects If you are adventurous, you may want to try some simple special effects. For instance, dry ice can create smoke effects. You can also have your actors freeze; then stop the camera, remove an object from the set, and restart the camera. This technique will make objects seem to disappear as if by magic. Other effects can be achieved by using false backdrops, colored lights, and filters.

> **Technology Tip**
>
> You may already have video editing tools on your computer or your school's computer. Many computers come equipped with free video editing software. These programs are simple to use and can produce very effective videos or slide shows that are coordinated with music and narration and that feature interesting transitional elements like fades and dissolves. (See next page.) These programs also allow you to edit your video in a way that makes for easy uploading to video file-sharing sites. There are also free video editing tools online. Check out the computer you use most often to see what video tools it may have on it, and follow a tutorial to learn how to use the tool.

A. Electronic Publishing

POST-PRODUCTION—EDITING

Once all of your video recording is complete, it's time to create the final cut—that is, your choice of the shots you wish to keep and the shots you wish to discard. Be choosy and select the footage with only the best composition, lighting, focus, and performances to tell your story.

There are three basic editing techniques:

in-camera editing — In this process you edit as you shoot. In other words, you need to shoot all your scenes in the correct sequence and in the proper length that you want them to appear. This is the most difficult editing process because it leaves no margin for error.

insert editing — In insert editing you transfer all your footage to a new video. Then you record over any scenes that you don't want with scenes that you do want in the final version.

assemble editing — This process involves electronically copying your shots from the original source in your camera onto a new blank source, called the edited master, in the order that you want the shots to appear. This method provides the most creative control.

Consider including effects such as a dissolve from one shot to another instead of an abrupt cut. A *dissolve* is the soft fading of one shot into another. Dissolves are useful when you wish to give the impression that time has passed between two scenes. A long, slow dissolve that comes up from black into a shot, or from a shot down to black, is called a *fade* and is used to open or close a show.

In addition to assembling the program, post-production is the time to add titles to the opening of your program and credits to the end of the show. Computer programs, such as Adobe Premiere™, can help you do this. Some cameras are also equipped to generate titles. If you don't have any electronic means to produce titles, you can always mount your camera on a high tripod and focus it downward on well-lit pages of text and graphics placed on the floor. Then edit the text frames into the program.

Post-production is also the time to add voiceover narration and music. Voiceovers and background music should be recorded separately and then edited into the program on a separate sound track once the entire show is edited together. Video editing programs for your computer, such as Adobe Premiere™, allow you to mix music and voices with your edited video.

After post-production editing, your video production is ready to present to your audience or upload to a video file-sharing site.

Publishing on the Web

You may become a part of the Web community by building and publishing a Web site of your own. In fact, you may already have a Web presence with your account on a social network such as Facebook, which provides a medium for publishing your thoughts and linking to the sites of those you have designated as your "friends." Maybe you have even created your own social network through Ning or communicated with other members of your school on Twitter. Many businesses now have a presence in one or more social networks, appreciating the opportunity to interact with customers and collaborators.

Traditional Web sites, however, are still the main medium through which most organizations and businesses communicate. Web sites have universal access; the ability to use photos, illustrations, audio, and video; unlimited branching capabilities; and the ability to link with related content.

If you are going to create a Web site, take advantage of all of these features. Your goal should be to make your site interesting enough that visitors will want to stay, explore, and come back to your site again—and that takes thought and planning.

Planning Your Site

First you need to capture your thoughts and ideas on paper before you publish anything. Start with a one-page summary that states the purpose of your Web site and the audience you hope to attract. Describe in a paragraph the look and feel you think your site will need in order to accomplish this purpose and hold your audience's attention.

Make a list of the content you plan to include in your Web site. Don't forget to consider any graphics, animation, video, or sound you may want to include.

Next go on a Web field trip. Ask your friends and teachers for the URLs of their favorite Web sites. (URL stands for Universal Resource Locator.) Visit these sites, and ask yourself, "Do I like this site? Why or why not?" Determine which sites are visually appealing to you and why. Which sites are easy to navigate and why? Chances are the sites you like best will have clean, easy-to-read layouts, be well written, contain visually stimulating graphic elements, and have intuitive **interfaces** that make it simple to find your way around.

One sure drawback in any Web site is long, uninterrupted blocks of text. Decide how to break up long passages of information into manageable sections. Will there be separate sections for editorial content? News? Humor? Feedback? Which sections will be updated periodically and how often?

Make a few rough sketches for your site. How do you envision the home page of your site? What will the icons and buttons look like? Then give careful thought to how the pages will connect to each other, starting with the home page. Your plan for connecting the pages is called a **site map**.

Because the Web is an interactive medium, navigation is critical. Decide how users will get from one page to another. Will you put in a navigation bar across the top of the page or down the side? Will there be a top or home page at the beginning of each section?

Once you have planned the content, organized your material into sections, and designed your navigation system, you are ready to begin creating Web pages.

PUTTING IT ALL TOGETHER

Writing for the Web is different from writing for print. The Web is a fast medium. Keep your messages succinct and to the point. Use short, punchy sentences. Break up your copy with clever subheads. Try not to exceed 500 to 600 words in any single article on any one page.

In order to turn text into Web pages, you need to translate the text into a special language that Web browsers can read. This language code is called HTML—HyperText Markup Language. There are three methods available:

- You can use the Save As HTML feature in the File menu of most word-processing programs.
- You can import your text into a Web-building software program and add the code yourself if you know how.
- You can easily find free software programs online that will do the work for you. Web-building software programs are referred to as WYSIWYG (pronounced "Wiz-E-Wig"), which stands for "What You See Is What You Get."

Web-building software also allows you to create links to other Web pages using a simple process called **drag and drop**. Be sure to read the directions that come with your software package for complete instructions.

BLOGS

Blogs (short for Web logs) are a type of Web page. In many ways, they are like online diaries or journals, where "bloggers" post the latest events of their lives and their thoughts and feelings on a wide range of subjects. Some blogs have other purposes, such as to promote community among speakers of certain languages or to influence politics. Among the most popular blogs are those devoted to celebrity news and to animal photos with funny captions. The most popular blog software is free and easy enough to use so that anyone with Web space can build one.

B. Using the Internet

Part I	Critical Thinking and Problem Solving for Academic Success	**A.** Electronic Publishing	449
Part II	Communication and Collaboration	**B.** Using the Internet	464
Part III	**Media and Technology**		

Apply Information and Technology Literacy

The "age of information" dawned in the last half of the 20th century. Success in the 21st century requires the ability to access, evaluate, and wisely use the abundance of information made available by advances in technology. Developing an understanding of the changing technologies and skill in putting them to work for your purposes are key competencies for the rest of your schooling and for your adult life ahead.

In this section, you will develop your skills for understanding and making the most of what the Internet has to offer.

How Does the Internet Work?

The Internet is made up of thousands of networks all linked together around the globe. Each network consists of a group of computers that are connected to one another to exchange information. If one of these computers or networks fails, the information simply bypasses the disabled system and takes another route through a different network. This rerouting is why the Internet is so valuable to agencies such as the U.S. Department of Defense.

No one "owns" the Internet, nor is it managed in a central place. No agency regulates or censors the information on the Internet. Anyone can publish information on the Internet as he or she wishes.

In fact, the Internet offers such a vast wealth of information and experiences that sometimes it is described as the Information Superhighway. So how do you "get on" this highway? It's easy. Once you have a computer, a modem, and a telephone or cable line, all you need is a connection to the Internet.

THE CYBERSPACE CONNECTION

A company called an Internet Service Provider (ISP) connects your computer to the Internet. Examples of ISPs that provide direct access are Microsoft

Network, Earthlink, Comcast, and AT&T. You can also get on the Internet indirectly through companies such as America Online (AOL).

ISPs charge a flat monthly fee for their service. Unlike the telephone company, once you pay the monthly ISP fee, there are no long-distance charges for sending or receiving information on the Internet—no matter where your information is coming from, or going to, around the world.

ALPHABET SOUP—MAKING SENSE OF ALL THOSE LETTERS

Like physical highways, the Information Superhighway has road signs that help you find your way around. Each specific group of information on the World Wide Web is called a **Web site** and has its own unique address. Think of it as a separate street address of a house in your neighborhood. This address is called the URL, which stands for Uniform Resource Locator. It's a kind of shorthand for where the information is located on the Web.

Here's a typical URL: **http://www.perfectionlearning.com.**

All addresses, or URLs, for the World Wide Web begin with **http://.** This stands for HyperText Transfer Protocol and is a programming description of how the information is exchanged.

The next three letters—**www**—let you know you are on the World Wide Web. The next part of the URL—**perfectionlearning**—is the name of the site you want to visit. The last three letters, in this case **com**, indicate that this Web site is sponsored by a **com**mercial company. Here are other common endings of URLs you will find:

- "org" is short for **org**anization, as in http://www.ipl.org, which is the URL of the Web site for the Internet Public Library, ipl²: Information You Can Trust.
- "edu" stands for **edu**cation, as in the Web address for the Virtual Reference Desk, http://thorplus.lib.purdue.edu/reference/index.html, featuring online telephone books, dictionaries, and other reference guides.
- "gov" represents **go**vernment-sponsored Web sites, such as http://www.whitehouse.gov, the Web site for the White House in Washington, D.C.

To get to a Web site, you use an interface called a **browser**. Two popular browsers are Microsoft Internet Explorer and Mozilla Firefox. A browser is like a blank form where you fill in the information you are looking for. If you know the URL of the Web site you want to explore, all you have to do is type it in the field marked Location, click Enter on your keyboard, and wait for the information to be delivered to your computer screen.

Basic Internet Terminology

Here are some of the most frequently used words you will hear associated with the Internet.

address
The unique code given to information on the Internet. This may also refer to an e-mail address.

bookmark
A tool that lets you store your favorite URL addresses, allowing you one-click access to your favorite Web pages without retyping the URL each time.

browser
Application software that supplies a graphical interactive interface for searching, finding, viewing, and managing information on the Internet.

chat
Real-time conferencing over the Internet.

cookies
A general mechanism that some Web sites use both to store and to retrieve information on the visitor's hard drive. Users have the option to refuse or accept cookies.

cyberspace
The collective realm of computer-aided communication.

download
The transfer of programs or data stored on a remote computer, usually from a server, to a storage device on your personal computer.

e-mail
Electronic mail that can be sent all over the world from one computer to another.

FAQs
The abbreviation for Frequently Asked Questions. This is usually a great resource to get information when visiting a new Web site.

flaming
Using mean or abusive language in cyberspace. Flaming is considered to be in extremely poor taste and may be reported to your ISP.

FTP
The abbreviation for File Transfer Protocol. A method of transferring files to and from a computer connected to the Internet.

home page
The start-up page of a Web site.

HTML The abbreviation for HyperText Markup Language—a "tag" language used to create most Web pages, which your browser interprets to display those pages. Often the last set of letters found at the end of a Web address.

http The abbreviation for HyperText Transport Protocol. This is how documents are transferred from the Web site or server to the browsers of individual personal computers.

ISP The abbreviation for Internet Service Provider—a company that, for a fee, connects a user's computer to the Internet.

keyword A simplified term that serves as subject reference when doing a search.

link Short for Hyperlink. A link is a connection between one piece of information and another.

network A system of interconnected computers.

online To "be online" means to be connected to the Internet via a live modem connection.

plug-in Free application that can be downloaded off the Internet to enhance your browser's capabilities.

podcast An audio or video file on the Internet that is available for download to a personal media device.

real time Information received and processed (or displayed) as it happens.

RSS A format for distributing content to people or Web sites. It stands for "Really Simple Syndication." With an RSS "feed," users can get updates from sites of interest without having to go to the sites for the information.

search engine A computer program that locates documents based on keywords that the user enters.

server A provider of resources, such as a file server.

site A specific place on the Internet, usually a set of pages on the World Wide Web.

social network An online community of people who share interests and activities, usually based on the Web.

spam	Electronic junk mail.
surf	A casual reference to browsing on the Internet. To "surf the Web" means to spend time discovering and exploring new Web sites.
upload	The transfer of programs or data from a storage device on your personal computer to another remote computer.
URL	The abbreviation for Uniform Resource Locator. This is the address for an Internet resource, such as a World Wide Web page. Each Web page has its own unique URL.
Web 2.0	The so-called second generation of the World Wide Web, which promotes programming that encourages interaction and collaboration.
Web site	A page of information or a collection of pages that is being electronically published from one of the computers in the World Wide Web.
Wiki	Technology that holds together a number of user-generated Web pages focused on a theme, project, or collaboration. Wikipedia is the most famous example. The word *wiki* means "quick" in Hawaiian.
WWW	The abbreviation for the World Wide Web. A network of computers within the Internet capable of delivering multimedia content (images, audio, video, and animation) as well as text over communication lines into personal computers all over the globe.

Communicating on the Internet

E-mail, mailing lists, and newsgroups are all great ways of exchanging information with other people on the Internet. Here's how to use these useful forms of communication, step-by-step.

❶ Using E-mail

Any writer who has ever used e-mail in his or her work will agree that sending and receiving electronic messages is one of the most useful ways of gathering information and contacts for writing projects.

Once you open your e-mail program, click on the command that says Compose Mail or New Message. This will open a new blank e-mail similar to the one pictured below. Next, fill in the blanks.

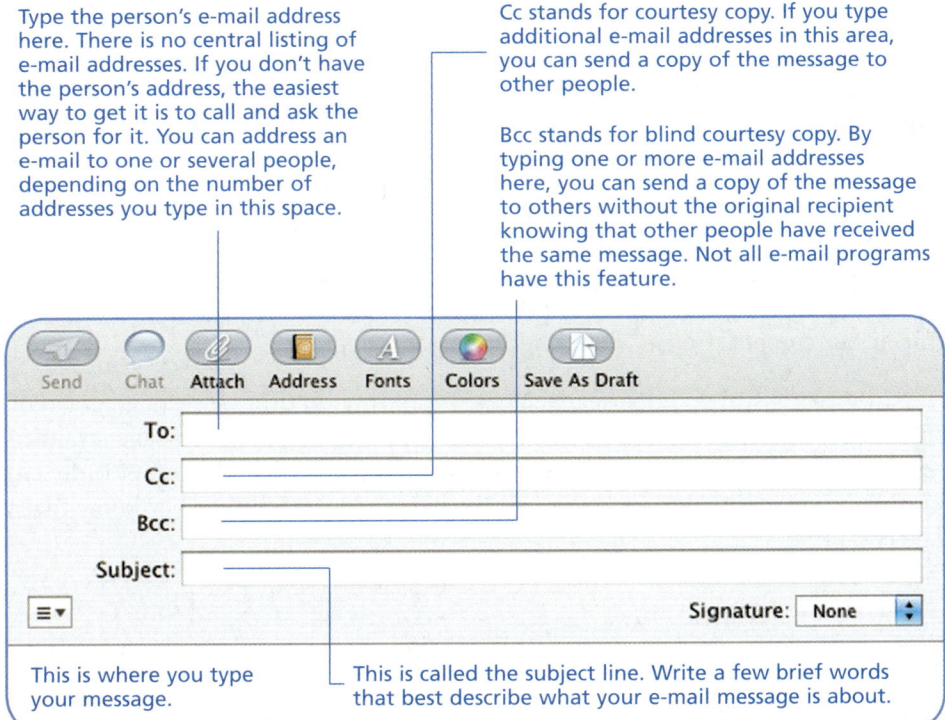

Type the person's e-mail address here. There is no central listing of e-mail addresses. If you don't have the person's address, the easiest way to get it is to call and ask the person for it. You can address an e-mail to one or several people, depending on the number of addresses you type in this space.

Cc stands for courtesy copy. If you type additional e-mail addresses in this area, you can send a copy of the message to other people.

Bcc stands for blind courtesy copy. By typing one or more e-mail addresses here, you can send a copy of the message to others without the original recipient knowing that other people have received the same message. Not all e-mail programs have this feature.

This is where you type your message.

This is called the subject line. Write a few brief words that best describe what your e-mail message is about.

SAY IT WITH STYLE

Like regular letters, e-mail can assume different tones and styles, depending on to whom you are writing. Usually informal e-mails and instant messages (IMs) to close friends are light, brief, and to the point. In the case of more formal e-mails, such as a request for information from an expert or a museum, keep the following guidelines in mind.

Guidelines for Writing E-mails

- Make sure your message is clear and concise.
- Use proper grammar and punctuation.
- Check your spelling. (Some e-mail programs have their own spell-check function—use it!)
- Double-check the person's e-mail address to be sure you've typed it correctly.

ATTACH A LITTLE SOMETHING EXTRA

When you send e-mail, you can also send other information along with your message. These are called **attachments**. Depending on your e-mail program's capabilities, you can attach documents, photos, illustrations—even sound and video files. Click Attach, and then find and double-click on the document or file on your computer that you wish to send.

After you have composed your message and added any attachments you want to include, click the Send button. Your message arrives in the other person's mailbox seconds later, regardless of whether that person lives right next door or on the other side of the world.

FOLLOW UP

Just because you have sent a message, you shouldn't automatically assume that the other person has received it. Internet Service Providers (ISPs) keep all messages that are sent until the recipient requests them. The person you sent your e-mail to might be away from his or her computer or may not check messages regularly.

Also, the Internet is still an imperfect science. From time to time, servers go down or other "hiccups" in electronic transmissions can occur, leaving your message stranded somewhere in cyberspace. If you don't get a reply in a reasonable amount of time, either resend your original e-mail message or call the person and let him or her know that your message is waiting.

YOU'VE GOT MAIL

When someone sends you an e-mail message, you have several options:

Reply Click Reply, and you can automatically send back a new message without having to retype the person's e-mail address. (Be sure you keep a copy of the sender's e-mail address in your Address Book for future use.)

Forward Suppose you receive a message that you would like to share with someone else. Click Forward, and you can send a copy of the message, plus include a few of your own comments, to another person.

Print In some instances, you may need to have a paper copy of the e-mail message. For example, if someone e-mails you directions to a party, click Print to take a hard copy of the instructions with you.

Store Do you want to keep a message to refer to later? Some e-mail programs allow you to create folders to organize stored messages.

Delete You can discard a message you no longer need just by clicking Delete. It's a good idea to throw messages away regularly to keep them from accumulating in your mailbox.

2 Other Online Communication

Another way to communicate online is Internet Relay Chat (IRC), or "chat rooms" for short. Chat rooms focus on a large variety of topics, so it's possible you'll be able to find a chat room where people are discussing the subject you are writing about.

"Chat" is similar to talking on the telephone except, instead of speaking, the people in the chat room type their responses back and forth to each other. As soon as you type your comment, it immediately appears on the computer screen of every person involved in the "conversation." There are also more advanced forms of chat available on the Net, such as video chat and voice chat.

One-to-one chatting, or instant messaging, is probably something you use frequently. With instant messaging, you need to "accept" as a buddy or contact each person you will communicate with.

In contrast, anyone in a chat room can talk to you, and the anonymous nature of a chat room can make people less inhibited than they might otherwise be in person. If you sense that one of the participants in your chat room is responding inappropriately, ask your parents or teacher to step in, or simply sign off.

JOIN THE GROUP

Mailing lists and newsgroups are larger discussion forums that can help you get even more information about a specific subject.

Mailing Lists To find a directory of available mailing lists, enter "mailing list directory" in a search engine. If you find a mailing list that interests you and wish to subscribe to it, just send a message to the administrative address. You will start to receive messages from the mailing list within a few days.

Remember, mailing lists use e-mail to communicate, so be sure to check your e-mail often because once you subscribe to a list, it's possible to receive dozens of messages in a matter of days.

Another good idea is to read the messages in your new mailing list for a week or so before submitting a message of your own. This will give you a good idea of what has already been discussed so you can be considerate about resubmitting old information.

You can reply to a message any time you wish. However, it doesn't do anyone any good to respond by saying "Yes, I agree." Get in the habit of replying to messages only when you have something important to add. Also, be sure to repeat the original question in your reply so that people understand which message you are responding to.

Be sure that you really want to belong to a mailing list before you subscribe. Unwanted e-mail can be a nuisance. Fortunately, if you change your mind, you can always unsubscribe to mailing lists at any time.

Newsgroups To join a newsgroup, check with your ISP. Service providers frequently list available topics under the heading "Newsgroups." Newsgroups are named with two or more words separated by a period. For example, there is a newsgroup named rec.sport.baseball.college. The first three letters—"rec"—defines the main subject, in this case recreation. Each word that follows—sport, baseball, and college—narrows the scope of the subject to an increasingly more specific area of interest.

As with mailing lists, you can always unsubscribe to newsgroups at any time.

As in any social setting, there are a few guidelines to follow when you are talking to people online—via e-mail, in a chat room, or in a newsgroup. This conduct is called **netiquette**. Netiquette requires that you refrain from harsh or insulting language and from writing in all uppercase letters, which can feel like shouting. It requires you to respect other people's privacy, ideas, and work. Don't forward a message or attach documents written by someone else without first asking the author's permission. Don't send spam, unwanted messages for the purpose of selling something.

Online Collaboration and Web 2.0

The Web is always changing. One big change from its earliest days is the ease with which people can collaborate online. For example, your writing group could use Google Docs (http://docs.google.com) to work together on writing projects: to share drafts, to edit your peers' work and to set schedules and guidelines. Through Google Docs, everyone who is invited to do so can have access to documents and edit them online.

Another useful tool for collaboration is the **wiki**, a platform for creating linked pages on a common theme or for a common project. Wikipedia is the best known example. You can start your own free wiki at wiki.com and explore how you can use it in your learning.

Cyberbullying

More than half of teenagers recently surveyed reported that they have been the victim of online bullying, also called cyberbullying, or known someone who has been. **Cyberbullying** is the use of such technology as the Internet and cell phones to deliberately hurt or embarrass someone. Cyberbullies often assume fake identities to trick people. They also knowingly spread lies and often post pictures of someone without his or her permission. Cyberbullies can trick their victims into revealing personal information which is then abused.

Victims react in different ways. Some take such reasonable measures as blocking an offending user or refusing to read comments that might be hurtful and deleting them as soon as they arrive. Some seek help from adults, who sometimes help the victim report the problem to the appropriate authorities. Other teens have a more negative and painful reaction. They might withdraw from their usual pastimes and suffer from problems with self-esteem. Or they might get caught up in the negative swirl and try to bully back.

The National Crime Prevention Council (NCPC) makes these suggestions to teens to stop cyberbullying.

- Refuse to pass along cyberbullying messages.
- Tell friends to stop cyberbullying.
- Block communication with cyberbullies.
- Report cyberbullying to a trusted adult.

The NCPC developed a slogan to summarize what to do: "Delete cyberbullying. Don't write it. Don't forward it."

Unit 4

Grammar

Chapter 14	The Sentence	476
Chapter 15	Nouns and Pronouns	502
Chapter 16	Verbs	520
Chapter 17	Adjectives and Adverbs	536
Chapter 18	Other Parts of Speech and Review	558
Chapter 19	Complements	578
Chapter 20	Phrases	598
Chapter 21	Verbals and Verbal Phrases	616
Chapter 22	Clauses	636
Chapter 23	Sentence Fragments and Run-ons	660

Grammar, as Joan Didion says, has power. The ability to use grammatical elements—the sentences (simple and compound) that contain nouns, verbs, phrases, and clauses—gives you a way to create meaningful language. Additionally, the terms used in grammar provide a way to discuss and analyze that language. Knowing the rules and how to apply them will help you use grammar powerfully, whether you play by ear or by the book.

Grammar is a piano I play by ear. All I know about grammar is its power. — Joan Didion

CHAPTER 14

The Sentence

How can you create fluency in your writing by using a variety of sentence types?

The Sentence: Pretest 1

The first draft below is hard to read because it contains many sentence errors. Revise the draft so that it reads more smoothly. The photograph above might help you figure out some of what is missing. The first error has been corrected as an example.

> The rainforest is an amazing place. It is incredibly green. *Plants* Grow close together. Moss on tree trunks. The ground is blanketed with leaves. Are chirping and perching in trees. Small animals scurry among the trees and plants. Grow tall and straight. Thousands of kinds of insects everywhere. It rains almost every day in the rainforest. Streams and waterfalls down the mountain. Most rainforests are found in areas with hot climates. Also temperate rainforests in some places. Wherever they are found, rainforests are wet, beautiful, and full of life.

The Sentence: Pretest 2

Directions
Write the letter of the term that correctly identifies the underlined word or words in each sentence.

(1) <u>My family and I</u> drove across the country last summer. (2) We <u>headed south to the Grand Canyon</u>. (3) <u>Have you seen</u> this incredible sight? (4) <u>Incredible walls of red rock</u>. (5) <u>A group of Girl Scouts, two teachers, and my family</u> rode down the canyon on mules. (6) <u>I</u> could not <u>believe</u> the bumpiness of the ride. (7) <u>Down the canyon went we and our mules!</u> (8) The quiet in the canyon <u>was</u> eerie. (9) We <u>could see a hawk circling lazily far above us</u>. (10) The only sound <u>was the roar of the river below</u>.

1. **A** simple subject
   B compound subject
   C simple predicate
   D complete predicate

2. **A** simple subject
   B simple predicate
   C compound subject
   D complete predicate

3. **A** inverted order
   B compound subject
   C simple subject
   D complete predicate

4. **A** simple predicate
   B complete predicate
   C sentence fragment
   D simple subject

5. **A** simple subject
   B compound subject
   C sentence fragment
   D complete predicate

6. **A** simple subject
   B complete predicate
   C verb phrase
   D sentence fragment

7. **A** inverted order
   B sentence fragment
   C complete subject
   D complete predicate

8. **A** complete predicate
   B simple predicate
   C simple subject
   D inverted order

9. **A** compound subject
   B verb phrase
   C complete predicate
   D complete subject

10. **A** simple predicate
    B compound subject
    C verb phrase
    D complete predicate

A Sentence — Lesson 1

One of the keys to good speaking and writing is understanding the parts of a complete sentence.

14 A A **sentence** is a group of words that expresses a complete thought.

Following are examples of sentences—groups of words that express a complete thought.

> Every morning my dad cooks breakfast.
> I need to get to school on time.
> My best friend and his sister are going to camp this summer.

From time to time, people use a group of words that does not express a complete thought.

14 A.1 A group of words that expresses an incomplete thought is called a **sentence fragment.**

Following are examples of sentence fragments—groups of words that do *not* express a complete thought.

> The dog next door.
> A bowl of cereal.
> Wants to come with us.

You can learn more about sentence fragments on pages 662–667.

Good sentences are the building blocks of good writing.

When You Speak and Write

When you talk to a friend or a family member, you probably use slang and other informal language. You may also speak quickly and in incomplete sentences. People often use sentence fragments when they speak informally. When you are speaking or writing formally, however, your audience will appreciate your use of complete sentences.

Look back at a recent piece of formal writing and be sure you did not use informal language.

Complete and Simple Subjects

To express a complete thought, a sentence must have a subject.

14 B   The **subject** of a sentence names the person, place, thing, or idea that the sentence is about.

Complete Subjects

Aunt Hilda's washing machine groaned. The complete subject of this sentence is *Aunt Hilda's washing machine,* a total of four words.

14 B.1   A **complete subject** includes all the words used to identify the person, place, thing, or idea that the sentence is about.

To find a complete subject, ask yourself either *Who or what is doing something?* or *About whom or what is a statement being made?*

       ┌──────── complete subject ────────┐
The heavy blue catfish on the end of my line does not want to be caught.
(Who or what does not want to be caught? *The heavy blue catfish on the end of my line* is the complete subject.)

       ┌────── complete subject ──────┐
The hungry snapping turtle in the pond is huge.
(What is huge? *The hungry snapping turtle in the pond* is the complete subject.)

● **Practice Your Skills**

Finding Complete Subjects

Write each complete subject.

1. Schools of fish stay together for protection.
2. An average goldfish lives four years.
3. The horseshoe crab existed in its current form 500 million years ago.
4. A small trout swims faster than a person.
5. The upside-down catfish floats on its back.
6. The huge whale shark eats only small plants and small water animals.
7. The world's smallest frog fits inside a thimble.
8. The common sponge is a sea animal with a soft skeleton.
9. The basket starfish has more than 80,000 arms up to fifteen inches long.
10. Scientists around the world have identified about 21,000 species of fish.

Simple Subjects

Within each complete subject, there is one main subject, called the simple subject. It answers the question *Who or what is doing something?* or *About whom or what is a statement being made?*

14 B.2 A **simple subject** is the main person, place, or thing in a complete subject.

The complete subject is in bold type, and the simple subject is underlined.

That big black <u>cloud</u> on the horizon signals rain.
(Who or what is doing something in the sentence? The simple subject is *cloud*.)

The simple subject can have more than one word, as in some names of people or places.

<u>Sports Plus</u> in the mall has a sale on umbrellas.

Sometimes a complete subject and a simple subject are the same word.

<u>Marianna</u> danced in the rain.

Throughout the rest of this book, the simple subject will be called the subject.

Practice Your Skills

Finding Complete and Simple Subjects

Write each complete subject. Then underline each simple subject.

1. China is the third-largest country in the world.
2. *Viking I* took pictures of the surface of Mars.
3. A healthy person can take twelve to eighteen breaths per minute.
4. Hair on your head grows about 1/100 of an inch daily.
5. Robert Fulton built the first successful steamboat.

Connect to Writing and Speaking: Drafting

Using Complete and Simple Subjects

Write a sentence using a complete subject and a simple subject for the topics below. Read your sentences aloud to a partner.

1. swimming in a pool
2. sledding down a hill

Complete and Simple Predicates

To express a complete thought, a sentence must have a **predicate.**

14 C The **predicate** tells what the subject is or does.

Complete Predicates

As with the complete subject, a complete predicate can include several words.

14 C.1 A **complete predicate** includes all the words that tell what the subject is doing or that tell something about the subject.

To find a complete predicate, first find the subject. Then ask yourself either *What is the subject doing?* or *What is being said about the subject?*

The cat **purred loudly in the quiet room.**

(The subject is *cat*. What did the cat do? *Purred loudly in the quiet room* is the complete predicate.)

Our dog **has a brand-new collar.**

(The subject is *dog*. What is being said about the dog? *Has a brand-new collar* is the complete predicate.)

● **Practice Your Skills**

Finding Complete Predicates

Write each complete predicate.

1. That zany zebra plays the zither.
2. A big bear with a balloon bolted through the barn.
3. Furry foxes fought fiercely for food.
4. The giant giraffes greeted me graciously.
5. Lazy llamas from Liberia licked the lemons.
6. Chilly chipmunks chattered cheerfully.
7. The brown baboons banged on the bongo drums.
8. The round raccoons raced the reindeer.
9. The timid tiger tripped on a torn tuxedo.
10. Pudgy pandas played the piano with precision.

Simple Predicates, or Verbs

Each complete predicate has one main word or phrase that tells what the subject is doing or that tells something about the subject. This main word or phrase is called a **simple predicate,** or **verb.**

14 C.2   A **simple predicate,** or **verb,** is the main word or phrase in the complete predicate.

In the following sentences, the complete predicate is in bold type and the simple predicate, or verb, is underlined twice.

> My father **cooked Italian food last night.**
> (What is the main word in the complete predicate? What did the subject do? The verb is *cooked.*)
> Jody **wants a trip to Mexico for her birthday.**

Some verbs tell what the subject is doing. These are **action verbs.** Some action verbs—such as *run, talk,* and *drive*—show physical action. Other action verbs—such as *dream, think,* and *worry*—show mental action.

Sometimes verbs do not show action. These verbs tell something about a subject. The following is a list of some common verb forms that are used to make a statement about a subject.

COMMON VERBS THAT MAKE STATEMENTS				
am	is	are	was	were

> My map **is in the trunk of your car.**
> The geography test **was unusually long yesterday.**

A complete predicate and a simple predicate can be the same.

> The happy child **giggled.**

You can learn about subject-verb agreement on pages 738–765.

482   The Sentence

● **Practice Your Skills**

Finding Complete Predicates and Verbs

Write each complete predicate. Then underline each verb.

1. The largest state in the United States is Alaska.
2. The Alaskan pipeline transports crude oil over land.
3. The Underground is the name of London's busy subway system.
4. Columbus's discoveries in 1492 led to the European settlement of the Americas.
5. The Pyrenees Mountains separate France from Spain.
6. Lafayette sailed from France to America on March 26, 1777.
7. The Black Sea lies along the northern coast of Turkey and below the Ukraine.
8. The Mississippi River divides the country's eastern states from the western states.
9. The Rio Grande borders Mexico and Texas.
10. The Pacific Ocean defines California's coastline.

● *Connect to Writing and Speaking:* **Revising**

Expanding Sentences

Revise the following sentences, which do not contain enough information, by adding information to the simple predicate. Read two of your completed sentences to a partner.

1. The catcher missed.
2. John hit.
3. Myra batted.
4. The shortstop tagged.
5. I play.
6. Samantha pitched.

● *Connect to Writing:* **News Article**

The editor of your school newspaper has asked you to write a news story about tonight's baseball game. Be sure to include interesting verbs and predicates. Don't forget to tell which team won the game! When you have finished, underline the complete predicates and circle the verbs in your story.

 **Verb Phrases**

The verb of a sentence sometimes needs help to make a statement or to tell what action is taking place. Words that help a verb are called **helping verbs,** or **auxiliary verbs.**

14 C.3 The main verb and any helping verbs make up a **verb phrase.**

The following is a list of common helping verbs.

COMMON HELPING VERBS	
be	am, is, are, was, were, be, being, been
have	has, have, had
do	do, does, did
Other verbs	may, might, must, can, could, shall, should, will, would

The verb phrases in the following examples are underlined twice; the helping verbs are in bold type.

The cast **is** practicing hard for next week's play.

John **has been** acting for years.

The Baldwins **must have** seen a different play.

You can learn about subject-verb agreement with verb phrases on pages 745–746.

● **Practice Your Skills**

Finding Verb Phrases

Write each verb phrase.

1. Drew might audition for a part in the school play.
2. Sarah may be singing in the talent show tomorrow.
3. Karen can memorize almost anything.
4. Next month I will volunteer as a set painter.
5. The drama club does practice an hour every afternoon after school.
6. The director should have warned us about the trap door on the set.
7. By the first rehearsal, cast members had memorized most of their lines.
8. Susan did get the lead in the play.
9. My family has invited the cast to a party after the performance.

Interrupted Verb Phrases

A verb phrase is often interrupted by one or more words. The verb phrases below are in bold type.

> A compass **can** easily **locate** true north.
> I **have** never **hiked** this canyon before.

Not and its contraction *n't* are never part of a verb phrase.

> Pearl **is** not **going** with us.
> Paulo **did**n't **hear** the weather report.

In some questions the subject comes in the middle of a verb phrase. To find the verb phrase in a question like this, turn the question around to make a statement.

> **Does** Terry **know** the date of his trip?
> (Terry *does know* the date of his trip.)

Throughout the rest of this book, a verb phrase will be called a verb.

● Practice Your Skills

Finding Verb Phrases

Write each verb phrase.

1. We couldn't find the tent.
2. Will your brother drive us to the campground in Sumter County?
3. Does the campfire begin at sunset?
4. My sister can easily cook over an open fire.
5. Campers will often toast marshmallows.
6. Does Gina like camp life?
7. I have never been to this campground before.
8. Sabrina wouldn't help with the extra gear.
9. Would you swim in this lake?
10. Tom could certainly bring his canoe along with us.
11. The boys can't forget their warm jackets.
12. Did you pack the lantern?
13. Molly has only brought enough food for dinner tonight and breakfast tomorrow.

● *Connect to Writing and Speaking:* **Drafting**

Writing Sentences Using Helping Verbs

Write a sentence for each verb. Include the helping verb *has* or *have* in at least two of your sentences. Then underline each subject once and each verb twice. Read two of your sentences to a partner.

1. paddled
2. tumbled
3. raced
4. waded
5. sunk
6. sailed

✓ *Check Point:* **Mixed Practice**

Write the subject and verb in each sentence.

1. James Naismith was teaching physical education at the YMCA in Springfield, Massachusetts.
2. This dedicated teacher wanted an indoor sport for city children in the winter.
3. Winter shouldn't end all possibility of having fun!
4. In 1891, Naismith created a new game with two peach baskets.
5. He had based many of the rules on football, field hockey, and other outdoor sports.
6. Naismith mounted the baskets overhead.
7. Soon, eager players were throwing balls into those baskets.
8. Naismith had invented the game of basketball.
9. The popularity of Naismith's new game was soon sweeping across the country.

● *Connect to Writing:* **Letter of Applications**

Using Interrupted Verb Phrases

Your scout leader has recommended you to serve as an assistant day camp counselor for first- and second-grade children. Write a letter to the head counselor, explaining why you are interested in the job. Use verb phrases and interrupted verb phrases in your letter. Be prepared to identify all the verbs you used.

The Sentence

Different Positions of Subjects

14 D   The subject of a sentence can appear in different positions or be understood.

14 D.1   When the subject appears before the verb, a sentence is said to be in **natural order.**

- The <u>audience</u> <u>cheered</u> the performers.
- In April the <u>teachers</u> <u>stage</u> a show.

14 D.2   When the verb comes before the subject, the sentence is in **inverted order.**

To find the subject in such a sentence, turn the sentence around to its natural order.

Inverted Order	Over the noise <u>sang</u> <u>Mr. Davis</u>.
Natural Order	<u>Mr. Davis</u> <u>sang</u> over the noise.

Questions are usually written in inverted order. To find the subject easily in a question, change the question into a statement.

Question	<u>Has</u> <u>Roberta</u> <u>operated</u> these lights before?
Statement	<u>Roberta</u> <u>has</u> <u>operated</u> these lights before.
Question	<u>Did</u> <u>you</u> <u>finish</u> your costume?
Statement	<u>You</u> <u>did</u> <u>finish</u> your costume.

Sentences beginning with *there* or *here* are also in inverted order. To find the subject in such a sentence, turn it around to its natural order.

Inverted Order	There <u>are</u> some <u>mittens</u> in the chest.
Natural Order	Some <u>mittens</u> <u>are</u> in the chest. (Sometimes *there* must be dropped for the sentence to make sense.)
Inverted Order	Here <u>is</u> the <u>script</u>.
Natural Order	The <u>script</u> <u>is</u> here.

You can learn about subject-verb agreement with inverted order on pages 749–751.

Understood Subjects

Subjects sometimes do not even appear in a sentence. In a command or a request, the subject *you* is rarely stated.

> **14 D.3** The unstated *you* in a command or request is called the **understood subject.**

Command or Request
(you) Wait for me!
(you) Smile for the camera.
(you) Enjoy the show.

● Practice Your Skills

Finding Subjects and Verbs

Write the subject and verb in each sentence. If the subject is an understood *you*, write *you* in parentheses.

1. Did Nathan see a snowflake under his microscope during lab period today?
2. Write an entry in your journal every day this week about your science experiments.
3. During third period today, Mr. Brown will invite a guest speaker to our science class.
4. Along the edge of the glass beaker were dozens of tiny crystals.
5. Deliver the results of my science experiment to Mr. Brown.
6. Read to the class your journal entry about our experiment with the hamster.
7. At the front of the class sat Mr. Brown.
8. Is Denise taking life science again this year?
9. Answer the question quickly.
10. There are traces of saline in our solution.

● *Connect to Writing and Speaking:* Revising

Using Different Positions of Subjects

Rewrite any five of the preceding sentences so that they are in natural order. Read two of your revised sentences aloud to a partner. Then listen to two of your partner's sentences. Check each other's work.

Check Point: Mixed Practice

Write the subject and verb in each sentence. If the subject is an understood *you*, write *you* in parentheses.

1. Do you know the poems of Edgar Allan Poe?
2. Have you ever read any of his short stories?
3. You can discover more about his personality.
4. There are many fans of his detective stories.
5. Didn't the Allans adopt him at the age of three?
6. Into his schoolwork plunged the young Poe.
7. At the beginning of his writing career, there were hundreds of publishing opportunities for his poetry.
8. Write an essay about "The Raven."
9. After the poems came fiction.
10. Did you ever read "The Masque of the Red Death"?
11. Here are some of his first detective stories.
12. To many literary publications, Poe contributed articles.
13. On your paper, write a description of C. Auguste Dupin, the main character in Poe's detective stories.
14. Poe worked as an editor throughout his life.

Power Your Writing: Let It Flow

Good writing has fluency. That is, it flows smoothly from sentence to sentence. Sentences that are well structured in various ways keep the reader interested and involved. Using inverted order and presenting images in an organized way are two ways to create fluid sentences. Read the passage below. Notice that the second sentence is in inverted order.

> This old man wore a blue denim coat buttoned to the throat with brass buttons, as all men do who wear no shirts. Out of the sleeves came strong bony wrists and hands gnarled and knotted and hard as peach branches. The nails were flat and blunt and shiny.
> —John Steinbeck, *The Red Pony*

Check one of your own compositions for fluency. You may want to revise by converting several sentences to inverted order, but be sure your sentences sound natural.

Different Positions of Subjects • Lesson 4

Compound Subjects and Verbs

14 E Sentences can contain **compound subjects** and **compound verbs**.

➤ Compound Subjects

Some sentences have two or more subjects joined by the conjunction *and* or *or*. These subjects together are called a *compound subject*.

14 E.1 A **compound subject** is two or more subjects in one sentence that have the same verb and are joined by a conjunction.

Notice that each subject in the following examples shares the same verb—*attended*.

One Subject   The children attended the performance.

Compound Subject The children and their parents attended the performance.

You can learn about subject-verb agreement of compound subjects on pages 752–753.

● Practice Your Skills

Finding Compound Subjects

Write each compound subject. Remember that *and* and *or* are not considered part of the subject.

1. At the circus, clowns and acrobats will be featured.
2. Lions and elephants do not often appear in the same act.
3. Dancers and jugglers were photographed during the parade to the center ring.
4. Popcorn and cotton candy taste good at the circus.
5. Did horses, dogs, or lions perform in the show?
6. Only dedicated performers and gifted artists work for the circus.
7. A trapeze performance and a clown act are scheduled.
8. The ringmaster and the bandleader have arrived.
9. A tiger and a lion will perform tricks.
10. At today's circus were clowns, lions, and horses.
11. The dogs and the silly seals barked to the audience.
12. A magician and a bunny entertained the crowd.

➤ Compound Verbs

Some sentences have two or more verbs joined by the conjunction *and, or,* or *but.* These verbs together are called a *compound verb.*

14 E.2 A **compound verb** is two or more verbs that have the same subject and are joined by a conjunction.

Notice that each verb in the following examples shares the same subject—*Patty*.

One Verb   Patty is sunning herself.

Compound Verb   Patty is sunning herself and will swim in the ocean later.

A sentence can include both a compound subject and a compound verb.

The parents and their children talked with the lifeguards and toured the beach.

● Practice Your Skills

Finding Compound Verbs

Write each compound verb.

1. Ashanti has packed a lunch and will spend the day at the beach.
2. She will take pictures and develop them quickly.
3. Guy played in the sand and built a sand castle.
4. Mark walked the beach and looked for shells.
5. Brian fished for bait and caught a turtle.
6. Jean will run and will swim at the beach.
7. Shirley caught the beach ball and threw it back.
8. Blake will take the boat to the repair shop or will fix it himself.
9. Angel took a soda from the ice chest and drank it.
10. Mia removed her sunglasses and applied sunscreen.

● *Connect to Writing and Speaking:* Revising

Using Compound Subjects and Verbs

Choose five sentences from the two previous exercises, and write them so that they include both a compound subject and a compound verb. Read two of your sentences aloud to a partner. Then listen to your partner's sentences. Check each other's work.

Connect to Writing and Speaking: Persuasive Paragraph

Using Compound Subjects and Verbs

Your parents are in charge of choosing a location for the family reunion this year. You would like for it to be at the same place it was last year because you and your cousins really enjoyed yourselves. Prepare a persuasive paragraph for your parents in which you state that you would like to return to the same place for the reunion.

- Brainstorm a few good reasons why the reunion should be held at the same place.
- Consider details about the location, shelter, facilities, and your family's needs.
- Give examples of activities you and your cousins enjoyed to support your choice.

Use compound subjects, compound verbs, and a combination of the two in your sentences. Then exchange your paper with a partner. Find and read aloud the sentences with compound subjects and compound verbs in each other's paragraphs.

✓ *Check Point:* Mixed Practice

Write the subject and verb in each sentence

1. In 1951, a powerful hurricane and heavy winds were heading for Bermuda.
2. By noon the storm was nearing the coast and was causing much damage.
3. Water flooded buildings and eroded the beach.
4. Then a weather forecaster stopped and noticed something very strange.
5. A second hurricane was building and was traveling toward the island.
6. Eventually the second storm reached the first storm and smashed into it.
7. The collision weakened both hurricanes and threw them off course!
8. The storms changed course and headed toward the ocean.
9. Scientists and weather observers seldom have witnessed anything like those two hurricanes.
10. The buildings and the people of the island survived both hurricanes.

Kinds of Sentences — Lesson 6

14 F There are four different kinds of sentences, each with a different purpose.

A sentence can make a statement, ask a question, give a command, or express strong feeling. The purpose of a particular sentence determines which end mark will go at the end of that sentence.

14 F.1 A **declarative sentence** makes a statement or expresses an opinion and ends with a period.

> The California Gold Rush occurred in 1849. (statement)
> Gold makes people greedy. (opinion)

14 F.2 An **interrogative sentence** asks a question and ends with a question mark.

> Have you ever panned for gold?
> How many people traveled to California to search for gold?

14 F.3 An **imperative sentence** makes a request or gives a command and ends with either a period or an exclamation point.

> Please follow me along Route 6 to the gold museum.
> (This imperative sentence ends with a period because it is a mild request.)
> Catch that gold nugget!
> (This imperative sentence ends with an exclamation point because it is a strong command.)

14 F.4 An **exclamatory sentence** expresses strong feeling and ends with an exclamation point.

> That's the biggest piece of gold I have ever seen!
> What a thrilling discovery that was!

- **Practice Your Skills**

    Classifying Sentences

    Using the abbreviations below, label each sentence and write the correct end marks.

    declarative = *d.*　　　　imperative = *imp.*
    interrogative = *int.*　　　exclamatory = *ex.*

    1. What an amazing place gold has had in legend and history
    2. It was partly responsible for the rapid settlement of the West
    3. Do you know when the Gold Rush started
    4. Is gold still mined in the United States
    5. Gold is a metal that never rusts or tarnishes
    6. Read the story about Croesus
    7. Wasn't he a wealthy ruler in ancient times
    8. Yes, gold filled every room in the house
    9. How proud he was of his golden throne
    10. At the library look for pictures of his house

- *Connect to Writing and Speaking:* **Peer Interaction**

    Reviewing Content

    With a partner, list the grammar terms introduced in this chapter. (Hint: new terms are printed in purple.) Quiz each other until you know the definitions of all the new words and concepts.

- ✓ **Check Point:** **Mixed Practice**

    Using the following abbreviations, label each sentence and write the correct punctuation.

    declarative = *d.*　　　　imperative = *imp.*
    interrogative = *int.*　　　exclamatory = *ex.*

    1. Diamonds are the hardest natural stone on Earth
    2. Are they used to cut gemstones
    3. Where are most diamonds found
    4. Most diamonds are mined in Africa
    5. How beautiful they are
    6. Diamonds are cut into many different shapes
    7. Do you like that marquis-shaped stone
    8. Look at that amazing red diamond
    9. Diamonds can be found in an array of colors

Sentence Diagraming

 ## Diagraming Subjects and Verbs

A diagram to a buried treasure would show you where the roads and landmarks that lead to the treasure are. A **sentence diagram** is very similar. It uses lines and words to help you find, identify, and analyze all the parts of a sentence.

Subjects and Verbs All sentence diagrams begin with a baseline—a straight, horizontal line that is the base of the diagram. A straight vertical line separates the subject (or subjects) on the left from the verb (or verbs) on the right. Capital letters are included in a diagram, but punctuation is not. In the second example that follows, notice that the whole verb phrase is written on the baseline.

Flies buzzed.

| Flies | buzzed |

John had been winning.

| John | had been winning |

Questions A question is diagramed as if it were a statement.

Was Donna listening? (Donna was listening.)

| Donna | Was listening |

Understood Subjects When the subject of a sentence is an understood *you*, as in a command or a request, place *you* in parentheses in the subject position.

Listen.

| (you) | Listen |

Sentence Diagraming   495

Compound Subjects and Verbs Place the parts of a compound subject or a compound verb on parallel horizontal lines. Then put the conjunction connecting each part on a broken line between them.

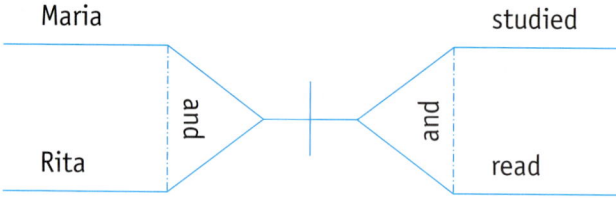

- **Practice Your Skills**

    Diagraming Subjects and Verbs

    Diagram the following sentences or copy them. If you copy them, draw one line under each subject and two lines under each verb. If the subject is an understood *you*, write *you* in parentheses.

    1. Weeds grow.
    2. Shutters are banging.
    3. Are you looking?
    4. Stop!
    5. Raul and Martin are coming.
    6. Everyone ran and ran!

Chapter Review

Assess Your Learning

Finding Subjects and Verbs

Write the subjects and verbs in the following sentences. Label each word *S* for subject or *V* for verb. If the subject is an understood *you*, write *you* in parentheses.

1. The science club has chosen bird study for its summer project this year.
2. The members have recently read some books about birds.
3. Has Jeff read your bird-watching book?
4. Kali has started a collection of stamps with bird pictures on them.
5. Other members are now constructing a simple ceramic birdbath.
6. We don't need a fancy concrete one.
7. A garbage can cover on a wooden post would work just as nicely.
8. We will always have water in it for the birds.
9. Many different birds will use the birdbath.
10. The members have also planned some food stations.
11. Our teacher gave several pairs of binoculars to the club.
12. Look at that beautiful bluebird!
13. Through his binoculars Andy spotted a warbler.
14. There is a raven at the birdbath now.
15. A bird sanctuary has always been a joy to both birds and people.

Understanding Kinds of Sentences

Write each sentence, using the correct end mark. Then label each sentence *declarative, interrogative, imperative,* or *exclamatory.*

1. Some people research their family history
2. What do they do with the information
3. They chart a family tree
4. Look at my family tree
5. At the top are my great-grandparents
6. That chart is very impressive
7. Where is your name
8. Be patient

9. I haven't gotten that far yet

10. I can hardly wait to start my family tree

Writing Sentences

Write ten sentences that follow the directions below. (The sentences may come in any order.) Write about one of the following topics or a topic of your choice: Little League baseball, girls in sports, a sport you enjoy.

1. Write a declarative sentence.

2. Write an interrogative sentence.

3. Write an imperative sentence.

4. Write an exclamatory sentence.

5. Write a sentence with a verb phrase.

6. Write a sentence with an interrupted verb phrase.

7. Write a sentence with a compound subject.

8. Write a sentence with a compound verb.

9. Write a sentence with a compound subject and a compound verb.

10. Write a sentence that starts with the word *there*.

Underline each subject once and each verb twice. Then check for capital letters and end punctuation.

The Sentence: Posttest

Directions
Write the letter of the term that correctly identifies the underlined word or words in each sentence.

(1) Our <u>entry</u> in our class's science fair was a model of a volcano. (2) <u>Carlotta</u> and I built the volcano. (3) <u>Was tall and colorful</u>. (4) Lucy <u>mixed the chemicals for a grand eruption</u>. (5) The exhibit <u>looked great</u>. (6) <u>All the other contestants</u> admired our lifelike miniature volcano. (7) <u>There were some other really amazing entries, too</u>. (8) <u>One of the other entries</u> was an interesting homemade barometer. (9) <u>Could</u> we <u>beat</u> such a great project? (10) <u>All three of us</u>.

1. **A** simple subject
   B simple predicate
   C compound subject
   D complete predicate

2. **A** inverted order
   B compound subject
   C complete subject
   D complete predicate

3. **A** simple predicate
   B complete predicate
   C sentence fragment
   D simple subject

4. **A** simple subject
   B compound subject
   C sentence fragment
   D complete predicate

5. **A** simple subject
   B complete predicate
   C verb phrase
   D sentence fragment

6. **A** inverted order
   B sentence fragment
   C complete subject
   D complete predicate

7. **A** complete predicate
   B simple predicate
   C sentence fragment
   D inverted order

8. **A** compound subject
   B verb phrase
   C complete predicate
   D complete subject

9. **A** simple subject
   B compound subject
   C verb phrase
   D complete predicate

10. **A** sentence fragment
    B inverted order
    C verb phrase
    D complete subject

Writer's Corner

Snapshot

14 A A **sentence** is a group of words that expresses a complete thought. (page 478)

14 B The **subject** names the person, place, thing, or idea that the sentence is about. (pages 479–480)

14 C The **predicate** tells what the subject is or does. (pages 481–486)

14 D When the subject comes before the verb, a sentence is in **natural order.** When the subject comes after the verb, a sentence is in **inverted order.** (page 487)

14 E A **compound subject** is two or more subjects in one sentence that have the same verb and are joined by a conjunction. A **compound verb** is two or more verbs that have the same subject and are joined by a conjunction. (pages 490–492)

14 F There are four different kinds of sentences: **declarative, interrogative, imperative,** and **exclamatory.** (pages 493–494)

Power Rules

 A sentence must have a subject and a predicate to express a complete thought. **Add the missing subject or verb** to fix sentence fragments. (pages 662–663)

Before Editing
My brother to the store.

Ran as fast as she could.

After Editing
My brother *went* to the store.

My sister ran as fast as she could.

 Use a conjunction and/or use punctuation when connecting two sentences. Revise run-on sentences. (pages 668–670)

Before Editing
Carlo is 12 his sister is 18.

Our new puppy is so cute we can hardly wait to teach him tricks.

After Editing
Carlo is 12; his sister is 18.

Our new puppy is so cute. We can hardly wait to teach him tricks.

Editing Checklist

Use this checklist when editing your writing.

✓ Does each sentence include a subject? (See pages 479–480.)
✓ Does each sentence include a predicate? (See pages 481–486.)
✓ Do all my subjects and verbs match in every sentence? (See pages 738–765.)
✓ Did I use the correct end mark for each sentence? (See pages 493–494 and 830–831.)

Use the Power

Discuss with a classmate what you have learned about sentence structure in this chapter. Summarize the most important points, including the four kinds of sentences and how to correct sentence fragments.

Study the diagram. It shows the correct way to diagram this sentence:

Snoopy and Bear ran and played.

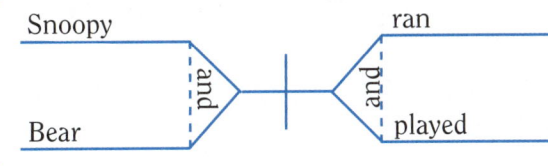

Now diagram this nonsense sentence.

Rufus and Rooster relmped and crenelled.

Create two nonsense or imaginative sentences for your partner to diagram. Go over each other's diagrams and share them with your teacher and classmates.

Nouns and Pronouns

CHAPTER 15

Why is it important to use nouns and pronouns correctly?

Nouns and Pronouns: Pretest 1

The following first draft is hard to read because it contains several noun and pronoun errors. Revise the draft so that it reads more smoothly. The first error has been corrected as an example.

> Theodore Roosevelt was the 26th president of the United States. ~~Theodore Roosevelt~~ He loved the out-of-doors. One time, conservationist John Muir and himself traveled through untouched parts of the country. They hiked together into the area that is now yosemite national park. Moved by the beauty of the wilderness, roosevelt passed laws to protect wild places. He protected the grand canyon. Hisself set aside 194 million acres of land to be protected. Because of all they did, theodore roosevelt national park in North Dakota was named in his honor.

Nouns and Pronouns: Pretest 2

Directions
Write the letter of the term that correctly identifies the underlined word or words in each sentence.

(1) My father and I went on <u>our</u> yearly camping trip last week. (2) We each carried a <u>backpack</u> and a water bottle. (3) We started hiking at the foot of <u>Hunter Mountain</u>. (4) For hours, we pushed <u>ourselves</u> to hike uphill. (5) <u>Several</u> of the climbs required crawling over rocks. (6) After a long period of continuous hiking, <u>we</u> sat down for a rest. (7) Later we climbed the <u>foothills</u> of the Berkshires. (8) <u>Everyone</u> we passed looked exhausted. (9) We <u>ourselves</u> were getting pretty tired, too. (10) <u>Those</u> were the highest mountains I'd ever climbed.

1. A proper noun
   B personal pronoun
   C compound noun
   D common noun

2. A proper noun
   B compound noun
   C personal pronoun
   D intensive pronoun

3. A common noun
   B personal pronoun
   C intensive pronoun
   D proper noun

4. A personal pronoun
   B intensive pronoun
   C reflexive pronoun
   D demonstrative pronoun

5. A indefinite pronoun
   B interrogative pronoun
   C intensive pronoun
   D reflexive pronoun

6. A intensive pronoun
   B personal pronoun
   C common noun
   D demonstrative pronoun

7. A proper noun
   B personal pronoun
   C common noun
   D reflexive pronoun

8. A intensive pronoun
   B reflexive pronoun
   C demonstrative pronoun
   D indefinite pronoun

9. A personal pronoun
   B intensive pronoun
   C reflexive pronoun
   D demonstrative pronoun

10. A reflexive pronoun
    B proper noun
    C demonstrative pronoun
    D interrogative pronoun

Nouns — Lesson 1

All of the words in the English language can be divided into eight groups called the parts of speech. Each **part of speech** does a different job in a sentence.

THE EIGHT PARTS OF SPEECH

noun (names)	preposition (relates)
pronoun (replaces noun)	conjunction (connects)
verb (states action or being)	interjection (expresses strong feeling)
adjective (describes, limits)	adverb (describes, limits)

The most common part of speech is the noun. Nouns are sometimes called naming words because they name people, places, things, and ideas.

15 A A **noun** is a word that names a person, a place, a thing, or an idea.

NOUNS

People	boy, pilot, family, Mr. Jenkins, Pamela
Places	classrooms, park, theater, Arizona, lake
Things	bells, water, Mars, oxygen, memory
Ideas and Qualities	honesty, kindness, peace, truth, wisdom, hope, independence, freedom, loyalty

15 A.1 **Concrete nouns** name things that can be seen or touched; **abstract nouns** name things that cannot be seen or touched.

CONCRETE AND ABSTRACT NOUNS

Concrete Nouns	boy, theater, bell, park, water
Abstract Nouns	memory, honesty, kindness, hope

When You Write

Many times a writer will try to use a very specific, concrete noun to help create a vivid picture or scene. Notice the underlined specific nouns in the following passage. Think about the items they name.

> He stood his <u>hoe</u> against the split-rail fence. He walked down the <u>cornfield</u> until he was out of sight of the <u>cabin</u>. He swung himself over the fence on his two hands. Old Julia the <u>hound</u> had followed his father in the wagon to Grahamsville, but <u>Rip</u> the <u>bull-dog</u> and <u>Perk</u> the new <u>feist</u> saw the form clear the fence and ran toward him. Rip barked deeply, but the voice of the small <u>mongrel</u> was high and shrill.
>
> —Marjorie Kinnan Rawlings, *The Yearling*

Go back to a composition you are working on. Underline ten nouns. Replace at least two vague general nouns with more specific concrete nouns.

● **Practice Your Skills**

Finding Nouns

Write each noun. (There are 45 nouns.)

1. At one time dinosaurs were rulers of the earth.
2. Some of these creatures were as big as houses.
3. Other dinosaurs were as small as turkeys.
4. Many of these animals walked on two legs and used their hands to hold things.
5. Their brains were tiny—no bigger than a walnut.
6. We know about these reptiles from footprints and from fossils such as eggs, bones, and teeth.
7. Some bones have been formed into whole skeletons.
8. Experts can tell from fossils whether dinosaurs ate plants or meat.
9. Many questions, however, still have no answers.
10. One mystery is that we have no knowledge of what color these ancient creatures were.
11. Scientists guess that their colors might have been similar to those of living reptiles.
12. Another unsolved mystery concerns what caused dinosaurs to become extinct.
13. One popular theory is that Earth was struck by a large asteroid.
14. The impact would have sent a thick cloud of dust into the atmosphere.

● **Connect to Writing: Revising**

Using Specific Nouns

Rewrite each sentence, replacing the underlined word or words with a more specific noun.

1. The <u>big lizards</u> are a very popular attraction at the museum.
2. <u>Small humans</u> seem to enjoy lizards and snakes the most.
3. <u>My science teacher</u> is an expert on dinosaurs.
4. Even <u>my best friend</u> likes learning about them.
5. Do you believe that a dinosaur could be the size of a <u>small dog</u>?

➤ Compound Nouns

15 A.2   A noun that includes more than one word is called a **compound noun.**

For example, *city* is one noun, but *city hall* is also one noun because it names one place. Compound nouns can take one of three different forms: separate, hyphenated, or combined. If you are unsure of the form of a compound noun, check a dictionary.

COMPOUND NOUNS	
Separate	compact disc, fire truck
Hyphenated	father-in-law, great-grandmother
Combined	carpool, notebook, sidewalk

● **Practice Your Skills**

Finding Compound Nouns

Write the compound noun or nouns in each sentence.

1. A man in a raincoat directed us to the picnic area.
2. My great-grandfather was able to attend.
3. My aunt brought her golden retriever.
4. Some of my cousins played on the sidewalk.
5. A cloudburst made all of us run for shelter.
6. Susie, my older sister, volunteered to be a babysitter while my aunts prepared the food.
7. My uncles played football.
8. After lunch we all watched the sailboats.

● *Connect to Writing:* **Editing**

Writing Compound Nouns

Write correctly the underlined compound noun in each sentence. If the noun is correct, write C. Use a dictionary to check your spelling.

1. My Aunt Sally used to be a <u>cheer-leader</u>.
2. Uncle Tom has been promoted to <u>firechief</u>.
3. By the next family reunion, I will have a new <u>brother in law</u>.
4. My dad got hurt sliding into <u>home plate</u>.
5. Mom attached the <u>fish-hook</u> to the end of the line.

Common and Proper Nouns

15 A.3 A **common noun** names any person, place, or thing. A **proper noun** names a particular person, place, or thing.

Proper nouns always begin with a capital letter.

COMMON AND PROPER				
Common Nouns	teacher	lake	country	dog
Proper Nouns	Mrs. Gray	Lake Erie	Canada	Buck

Some proper nouns such as *Lake Erie* are made up of more than one word. *Lake Erie* is still considered one noun because it is the name of one place.

✓ Check Point: Mixed Practice

Write each noun and label it common or proper. (A date is considered a noun.)

1. In 1785, Thomas Pool presented the first circus in the United States.
2. It is not popcorn or elephants that have made circuses last all these years.
3. The excitement has come from original acts and unusual performers.
4. Five brothers once gathered some entertainers and traveled by wagons to various cities.
5. Their name was Ringling.
6. Later P. T. Barnum offered three shows at the same time in different rings.
7. Americans always loved Emmett Kelly, a clown with a sad face.
8. Miguel Vazquez first performed four somersaults through the air to a catcher.
9. Tom Thumb was less than a yard tall.
10. President Lincoln invited him to the White House.

● Connect to Writing: Letter

Using Common and Proper Nouns

Your class is reading *The Call of the Wild*. Your teacher has asked you to find out more about Alaska. Write a business letter to the Chamber of Commerce in Fairbanks, Alaska. Request information about the history and climate of the area. Be sure to use common and proper nouns correctly in your letter.

Pronouns — Lesson 2

Notice the differences between these sentences.

> Rafael asked Jill if Jill would help Rafael with Rafael's soccer techniques.
>
> Rafael asked Jill if **she** would help **him** with **his** soccer techniques.

The second sentence is clearer because pronouns have been substituted for nouns.

15 B A **pronoun** is a word that takes the place of one or more nouns.

 ## Pronoun Antecedents

In the preceding example about Rafael and Jill, the pronoun *she* replaces *Jill,* and the pronouns *him* and *his* replace *Rafael.*

15 B.1 The noun that a pronoun replaces, or refers to, is called its **antecedent.**

An antecedent usually comes before the pronoun. It may be in the same sentence as the pronoun or in another sentence. In the following examples, arrows point from the pronouns to their antecedents.

> Rosalie dribbled the **ball** and kicked **it.**
>
> **Tim** made a nice score. **He** saved the game.
>
> **Kara** played **her** best game yet.

A pronoun can have more than one antecedent.

> **Mary** and **Dan** timed **their** defense perfectly.

You can learn more about pronouns and antecedents on pages 726–732.

● **Practice Your Skills**

Finding Antecedents

Write the antecedent of each underlined pronoun.

1. Michelle Akers, a star soccer player, is never sure how <u>she</u> will feel each day.
2. Michelle knows that <u>she</u> suffers from chronic fatigue syndrome.
3. The disease literally steals energy from <u>its</u> hosts.
4. Her coach, Tony DiCicco, says <u>he</u> is never sure how long Michelle will be able to play.
5. Michelle's family members say <u>they</u> worry about her health.

Personal Pronouns

15 B.2 There are several kinds of pronouns, including personal, reflexive, intensive, and indefinite. **Personal pronouns** are used as substitutions for proper or common nouns.

PERSONAL PRONOUNS		
	Singular	**Plural**
First Person (speaker)	I, me, my, mine	we, us, our, ours
Second Person (person spoken to)	you, your, yours	you, your, yours
Third Person (person or thing spoken about)	he, him, his, she, her, hers, it, its	they, them, their, theirs

First Person Pronouns	I have **my** butterfly net with **me**.
	We left **ours** at the cottage.
Second Person Pronouns	Did **you** take **your** hat with you?
	These boots must be **yours**.
Third Person Pronouns	**She** finished **her** hike first.
	They put **their** backpacks by the door.

Reflexive and Intensive Pronouns

15 B.3 **Reflexive** and **intensive pronouns** refer to or emphasize a noun or another pronoun.

These pronouns are formed by adding *-self* or *-selves* to certain personal pronouns.

REFLEXIVE AND INTENSIVE PRONOUNS

Singular myself, yourself, himself, herself, itself
Plural ourselves, yourselves, themselves

Megan taught **herself** to identify different kinds of butterflies and cocoons.
(The reflexive pronoun *herself* tells who Megan taught.)

Gardeners **themselves** supported the new butterfly exhibit at the park.
(The intensive pronoun *themselves* emphasizes who supported the idea.)

You should never use reflexive or intensive pronouns by themselves. They must always have an antecedent. Also, never use *hisself* or *theirselves*.

● Practice Your Skills

Finding Personal, Reflexive, and Intensive Pronouns

Write each personal, reflexive, and intensive pronoun. Label each one **P** for personal, **R** for reflexive, or **I** for intensive.

1. Our science class has enjoyed itself learning about butterflies and moths.
2. I am writing a report about monarch butterflies.
3. I looked up their migration information on the Internet myself.
4. David Millard studies the habitats of butterflies and their predators.
5. Millard himself gave me much information for my science report.

● *Connect to Writing:* Revising

Replacing Nouns with Pronouns

Rewrite the following sentences, replacing some of the nouns with pronouns. Add reflexive or intensive pronouns wherever possible.

1. Mary said that Mary would help Charlotte hatch some butterfly eggs.
2. The students are going to present Mary with a special award for Mary's careful, accurate work with the butterflies.
3. David said that David would like to be able to present the special award to Mary.
4. Charlotte will take a picture of David and Mary in the new butterfly garden.
5. Will the students be able to enjoy the garden that the students created?

Indefinite Pronouns

15 B.4 **Indefinite pronouns** refer to unnamed people, places, things, or ideas.

COMMON INDEFINITE PRONOUNS					
all	anyone	either	few	none	several
another	anything	everybody	many	no one	some
any	both	everyone	most	nothing	someone
anybody	each	everything	neither	one	something

No one knew how to fold the flag.

Everything I know about the flag I learned in Boy Scouts.

There must be **something** we can do to help.

Few wanted to take the first step.

You can learn about indefinite pronouns used as antecedents on pages 728–729.

● **Practice Your Skills**

Finding Indefinite Pronouns

Write each indefinite pronoun.

1. Few know that flags first appeared in ancient China.
2. Most of the flags before then were actually poles with carved symbols on top.
3. Each of the units in the Roman army had a flag.
4. Someone discovered an Aztec flag made from feathers.
5. Many of the flags have important symbols on them.

Demonstrative and Interrogative Pronouns

15 B.5 **Demonstrative pronouns** point out a specific person, place, thing, or idea.

DEMONSTRATIVE PRONOUNS			
this	that	these	those

The pronouns *this* and *these* are used to point out people or things that are close by. *That* and *those* are used to point out items in the distance.

512 Nouns and Pronouns

This is my best speech so far.

I want to buy **these** for the rally.

That is the place for the debate.

Those are the buses for the band members.

15 B.6 **Interrogative pronouns** are used to ask questions.

INTERROGATIVE PRONOUNS				
what	which	who	whom	whose

What did you do then?

Who was at the rally?

● **Practice Your Skills**

Finding Pronouns

Write each pronoun.

1. Either of the candidates will make a good class president for seventh grade.
2. What has Rebecca said about the campaign speech?
3. Who is running for treasurer?
4. All of the students are voting today.
5. These were found in the voting area.
6. Many voted for class historian.
7. What did Mrs. Thompson do with the extra ballots?
8. A campaign promise like this will be hard to keep.
9. Which is the ballot for the seventh-grade officers?
10. Whom did David tell about the new voting rules?

➤ Relative Pronouns

15 B.7 **Relative pronouns** are used to relate an adjective clause to the noun or the pronoun that the clause describes.

RELATIVE PRONOUNS				
who	whom	whose	which	that

In the example below, the relative pronoun is used to relate and combine two sentences.

Two Sentences   Mary is a writer. Mary is researching the Apollo program.

Combined with Relative Pronoun   Mary is a writer **who** is researching the Apollo program.

● Practice Your Skills

Finding Pronouns

Write each relative pronoun.

1. *Apollo* was the name of a space program that was started during the presidency of Dwight D. Eisenhower.
2. John F. Kennedy was the president who first promoted the program.
3. *Apollo 4* was an early test flight that succeeded in orbiting Earth and reentering.
4. *Apollo 17* was the last mission that included a manned landing on the moon.
5. Tom Hanks is one of the famous actors who appeared in the movie *Apollo 13,* which was released in 1995.

You can learn about relative pronouns on pages 513–514 and 643–645.

Check Point: Mixed Practice

Write each pronoun.

1. No germs from the moon were found on *Apollo 11* or its astronauts.
2. The doctors examined each of the astronauts.
3. This was the moment everyone had waited for.
4. They landed their spacecraft in the Pacific Ocean on July 24, 1969.
5. Which was the first astronaut to walk on the moon?
6. Neil Armstrong was the first person who walked on the moon.
7. He said, "That's one small step for man, one giant leap for mankind."
8. That was a great human achievement.
9. Who did not land on the moon?
10. Michael Collins was the astronaut who stayed in orbit around the moon.
11. All of the astronauts made important discoveries.
12. These came from their mission.

Chapter Review

Assess Your Learning

Finding Nouns

Make two columns on your paper. Then write the common nouns in one column and the proper nouns in the other column. (There are 40 nouns.)

1. The army once recruited some kids at Fort Belvoir in Virginia.
2. These kids were actually goats, and their job was to eat the grass and weeds.
3. Officers preferred them to lawn mowers because goats didn't give off sparks that start fires.
4. That was important because at that time Fort Belvoir stored ammunition.
5. These helpful animals worked hard at this military base for many years.
6. It all began with only a few goats, but they quickly multiplied into a large herd.
7. Neither sunshine nor snowfall seemed to bother them, and they never had a single complaint.
8. During the winter a person from a nearby town would feed them, and a veterinarian would give them regular check ups.
9. The goats were always treated with respect and appreciation.
10. The United States Army had many requests from other branches of the armed services—from Alaska to Germany—for these hard workers.

Finding Pronouns and Their Antecedents

Write each pronoun. Then beside each one, write its antecedent.

1. Are Andrew and Emily visiting their cousin?
2. Emma's parents can't see the play because they will be out of town.
3. No United States coin shows its denomination in numbers.
4. Are Cora and Lily still good friends? Lately they don't spend much time together.
5. The players themselves were the happiest about the championship.

6. Jonathan said that he won't be taking the bus tomorrow.
7. Fleas don't have wings; they have powerful legs.
8. On Saturday Tara will fly her kite in the park.
9. Kevin kept telling himself that he could make the team.
10. Dawn waited until she heard the school bell.

Using Nouns and Pronouns

Write five sentences that follow the directions below. (The sentences may come in any order.) Write about the following topic or a topic of your own choice: an interesting story about a brother, sister, or friend.

1. Write a sentence that includes nouns that name a person, a place, and a thing.
2. Write a sentence that includes a proper noun that names a place.
3. Write a sentence that includes an indefinite pronoun.
4. Write a sentence that includes several personal pronouns.
5. Write a sentence that includes a reflexive pronoun.

Put an *N* over each noun and *P* over each pronoun.

Nouns and Pronouns: Posttest

Directions
Write the letter of the term that correctly identifies the underlined word or words in each sentence.

(1) In the Northeast where <u>I</u> live, fall is always a wonderful season. (2) This year there was a wet <u>spring</u> and dry summer with a lot of sunshine. (3) Scientists <u>themselves</u> admit they can't predict the fall colors perfectly. (4) <u>Many</u> think that a wet spring and dry summer produce the best effects. (5) Whatever the reason, the <u>leaves</u> are spectacular now. (6) Tourists flock to the <u>Green Mountains</u> to see the colorful foliage. (7) Almost <u>everyone</u> in our area makes a living from tourism. (8) <u>My</u> parents run a bed-and-breakfast. (9) <u>Which</u> is their best season? (10) For <u>them</u>, as for many others, it is the autumn.

1. A proper noun
   B compound noun
   C personal pronoun
   D intensive pronoun

2. A common noun
   B personal pronoun
   C compound noun
   D proper noun

3. A personal pronoun
   B intensive pronoun
   C reflexive pronoun
   D demonstrative pronoun

4. A indefinite pronoun
   B interrogative pronoun
   C intensive pronoun
   D reflexive pronoun

5. A intensive pronoun
   B personal pronoun
   C common noun
   D demonstrative pronoun

6. A proper noun
   B personal pronoun
   C common noun
   D reflexive pronoun

7. A intensive pronoun
   B reflexive pronoun
   C demonstrative pronoun
   D indefinite pronoun

8. A personal pronoun
   B intensive pronoun
   C reflexive pronoun
   D demonstrative pronoun

9. A reflexive pronoun
   B proper noun
   C demonstrative pronoun
   D interrogative pronoun

10. A proper noun
    B personal pronoun
    C compound noun
    D common noun

Writer's Corner

Snapshot

15 A A **noun** is a word that names a person, a place, a thing, or an idea. (page 504)

15 B A **pronoun** is a word that takes the place of one or more nouns. (page 509)

Power Rules

 Use standard ways to make nouns possessive. When you use a **noun to show ownership,** add an *'s* to singular nouns and plural nouns that don't end in an *s*. Add only an apostrophe to plural nouns ending in an *s*. (pages 880–883)

Before Editing	After Editing
I wanted to get my *friends* address.	I wanted to get my *friend's* address.
The *neighbors's* dogs barked all night.	The *neighbors'* dogs barked all night.

 Use **subject forms of pronouns** in subject position. Use the **object form** when the pronoun is a direct object, indirect object, or object of a preposition. (pages 710–720)

Before Editing	After Editing
Randy and *me* are going to the store.	Randy and *I* are going to the store.

Editing Checklist

Use this checklist when editing your writing.

- ✓ Did I use specific nouns where appropriate? (See pages 504–506.)
- ✓ Did I use compound nouns appropriately? (See pages 506–507.)
- ✓ Did I make sure each pronoun had an antecedent? (See pages 509–510.)
- ✓ Did I use the reflexive or intensive pronouns correctly? (See pages 510–511.)

Use the Power

In many board games, players use a game piece as a substitute. The game piece represents the player on the game board. In a similar manner, a pronoun represents a noun.

Player (noun/antecedent)	Game piece (pronoun)
Juanita Sanchez	**she**, **her**
Empire State Building	**it**
brothers-in-law	**they**, **them**

Juanita Sanchez walked toward the Empire State Building. **It** was towering over **her** when **she** saw **her** brothers-in-law. **They** were waiting for **her** to take **them** on a tour of the famous building.

Review a piece of writing you have completed recently. Underline all pronouns once and underline all antecedents twice. Revise sentences or paragraphs in which pronoun antecedents are missing or unclear.

Writer's Corner

CHAPTER 16

Verbs

How can you add color to your writing by using just the right verbs?

Verbs: Pretest 1

The following first draft lacks life and interest because of the overuse of colorless verbs. Revise the draft to make it more interesting. The first sentence has been revised as an example.

    The Chicago Botanic Garden is *has become* one of the city's top tourist spots. In every season, the garden is remarkably beautiful. In the spring, flowers are in every flower bed. In the summer, the Rose Garden is beautiful. The roses are wonderful, their perfume scenting the air. On the main island of the Japanese Garden, the moss garden is cool even in summer. In the Fruit and Vegetable Garden, the samples of honey are good. In the autumn, the leaves are red and gold. In the Nature Center, you can touch some of the plants. Some are soft, while some are prickly. You may want to be there all day.

Verbs: Pretest 2

Directions
Write the letter of the term that correctly identifies the underlined word or words in each sentence.

Every year we visit a lake in the Adirondacks. **(1)** The lake <u>has</u> always <u>been</u> quiet and peaceful. **(2)** The loudest sound <u>is</u> the call of the loons. **(3)** This year, jet skis <u>came</u> to the lake. **(4)** Their loud roar <u>echoed</u> from the mountain peaks. **(5)** At first, I <u>liked</u> the jet skis. **(6)** They <u>seemed</u> fun and exciting. **(7)** Soon, though, they <u>had</u> chased away the loons. **(8)** The moose <u>were</u> no longer <u>coming</u> around in the early mornings either. **(9)** People along the lake also <u>became</u> angry about the noise. **(10)** They <u>wrote</u> letters to the local newspaper and argued in the stores and on the street.

1. **A** helping verb
   B action verb
   C verb phrase
   D transitive verb

2. **A** transitive verb
   B action verb
   C helping verb
   D linking verb

3. **A** transitive verb
   B intransitive verb
   C helping verb
   D linking verb

4. **A** verb phrase
   B helping verb
   C linking verb
   D action verb

5. **A** verb phrase
   B intransitive verb
   C transitive verb
   D helping verb

6. **A** helping verb
   B action verb
   C linking verb
   D verb phrase

7. **A** helping verb
   B action verb
   C linking verb
   D verb phrase

8. **A** transitive verb
   B linking verb
   C helping verb
   D verb phrase

9. **A** helping verb
   B action verb
   C linking verb
   D verb phrase

10. **A** helping verb
    B transitive verb
    C intransitive verb
    D linking verb

Action Verbs — Lesson 1

Without a verb, a group of words cannot be a sentence.

16 A   A **verb** is a word used to express an action or a state of being.

There are several kinds of verbs, including helping verbs, linking verbs, and action verbs. Action verbs are easy to recognize because they show action or movement.

16 A.1   An **action verb** tells what action a subject is performing.

To find an action verb, first find the subject of the sentence. Then ask yourself, *What is the subject doing?*

> Carl **drove** the dogsled fast.
> (The subject is *Carl*. What did Carl do? *Drove* is the action verb.)

Some action verbs show physical action. Others show mental action.

> **Physical Action**
> Sandy **pulled** the sled team to a stop.
> The large sled **toppled** over.
>
> **Mental Action**
> Belinda always **thinks** positively before a race.
> She **believes** in her dogsled team.

Other action verbs, such as *have* and *own,* show ownership or possession.

> **Ownership**
> Lilly **has** two tickets to the race.
> The Russos **own** a dogsled.
> The huskies **belong** to Peyton.

You can learn about regular and irregular verbs on pages 680–688.

Connect to Writing: E-mail Message

Action Verbs

Through your social studies class, you have been keeping up with an Iditarod racer over the Internet. You send her an e-mail message asking about a particular part of the race. Be sure to use vivid action verbs in your message.

When You Write

Writers often use vivid action verbs to help create a picture of a character. Notice the action verbs—in bold type—in this passage by Ray Bradbury.

> The car **churned** off into the dust. The boy **rose** and **cupped** his hands to his mouth and **shouted** one last time at Teece: "Mr. Teece, Mr. Teece, what *you* goin' to do nights from now on? What you goin' to *do* nights, Mr. Teece?"
> —Ray Bradbury, *The Martian Chronicles*

Review a composition you completed recently. Underline the action verbs in three of the paragraphs. Revise at least three sentences by changing the original verbs to more specific action verbs.

Practice Your Skills

Finding Action Verbs

Write each action verb.

1. Every year dogsled drivers race across the frozen landscape of Alaska.
2. The course stretches more than a thousand miles from Anchorage to Nome.
3. Weather conditions often create severe hazards for the racers.
4. Snow and storms sometimes hide the trails.
5. Each driver carries snowshoes, a sleeping bag, and food for the dogs.
6. Drivers even take boots for the dogs' feet.
7. Veterinarians examine the dogs at checkpoints along the route.
8. Host families welcome the racers into their homes.
9. They feed the drivers and their dogs.
10. Most competitors complete the race within twelve or thirteen days.

Connect to Writing: Revising

Revising with More Specific Verbs

For each sentence, replace the underlined verb with a more specific verb.

1. The sleds <u>moved</u> across the frozen ground.
2. The dogs <u>went</u> past the spectators.
3. The injured dog <u>walked</u> to the rest station.
4. With plenty of time to spare, the winning team <u>crossed</u> over the finish line.
5. The weary sled dogs <u>came</u> into camp.

Transitive and Intransitive Verbs

Lesson 2

All action verbs can be either transitive or intransitive.

16 B A **transitive verb** expresses action directly toward a person or a thing. An **intransitive verb** expresses action that is not directed at a person or a thing.

To decide whether an action verb is transitive or intransitive, say the subject and verb. Then ask the question *What?* or *Whom?* A word that answers either question is called an **object.** An action verb that has an object is **transitive.** An action verb that does not have an object is **intransitive.**

Transitive   Kevin **answered** the difficult history question.
(Kevin answered what? *Question* is the object. Therefore, *answered* is a transitive verb.)

Granddad **took** us to the Alamo.
(Granddad took whom? *Us* is the object. Therefore, *took* is a transitive verb.)

Intransitive   Jim Bowie **died** at the Alamo.
(Jim Bowie died what? Jim Bowie died whom? Because there is no object, *died* is an intransitive verb.)

Some verbs can be transitive in one sentence and intransitive in another sentence.

Transitive   Jim Bowie **explored** parts of Texas.
(Jim Bowie explored what? *Parts* is the object.)

Intransitive   Jim Bowie **explored** often.
(Jim Bowie explored what or whom? There is no object.)

You can learn more about objects on pages 580–583 and 716–717.

● **Practice Your Skills**

Understanding Transitive and Intransitive Verbs

Write the verb in each sentence. Label the verb *T* for transitive or *I* for intransitive.

1. Jim Bowie lived in Tennessee and Louisiana during his childhood.
2. He inherited his parents' adventurous spirit.
3. During his childhood, he rode alligators.
4. Bowie learned from his mother.
5. He learned French and Spanish.
6. At the age of eighteen, Bowie sought his fortune.
7. He worked hard.
8. He made a profit from the work on his farm.
9. Jim Bowie received recognition as a frontiersman.
10. He arrived in Texas in 1828.
11. He searched Texas for silver.
12. He searched throughout Bexar County in Texas.
13. He led American settlers against the Mexican government.
14. Bowie's courage prevailed throughout the revolution.
15. Bowie defended the Alamo.

Power Your Writing: Getting into the Action

A **participle** is a word formed from a verb. It acts like an adjective by modifying a noun. A participle can be turned into a participial phrase by joining it with other words. **Participial phrases** are useful for creating a vivid sense of events that are happening as you read. Consider the example below.

> **Treading carefully,** the researchers made their way through the fragile ecosystem.

By using a participial phrase, the author provides a telling detail about the way research scientists approach a sensitive environment. The example below shows how you can use a participial phrase to combine two simple sentences and highlight the relationship between ideas.

Two Sentences	The notes were written in Sanskrit. They were impossible for us to read.
Combined	The notes, **written in Sanskrit,** were impossible for us to read.

Transitive and Intransitive Verbs • Lesson 2

Helping Verbs — Lesson 3

16 C A **helping verb,** or auxiliary verb, is a verb that is combined with a main verb to form a verb phrase.

16 C.1 A **verb phrase** is made up of a main verb and one or more helping verbs.

The following is a list of common helping verbs.

COMMON HELPING VERBS	
be	am, is, are, was, were, be, being, been
have	has, have, had
do	do, does, did
Others	may, might, must, can, could, shall, should, will, would

A verb phrase may have one or more helping verbs. The helping verbs in the examples below are in bold type.

> Birds **have** flown north for the spring.
> The flower baskets **will be** hanging on the front porch.

Sometimes a verb phrase is interrupted by other words.

> Julio **must** not **be** coming to the spring dance.
> I **have**n't heard any birds yet.

You can learn about contractions on pages 722–723 and 746–747.

To find the verb phrase in a question, turn the question around to make a statement.

> **Question**   **Have** they joined the garden club?
> **Statement** They **have** joined the garden club.

When you look for a verb in a sentence, always include helping verbs.

● **Practice Your Skills**

Finding Verb Phrases

Write each verb phrase. A verb phrase may be interrupted by one or more words.

1. This rain shower should stop in a few minutes.
2. We will not go on a picnic in the rain.
3. Flowers have been appearing early this year.
4. The weather has not turned cooler today.
5. Rachel is planting her garden.
6. Have you seen any robins yet?
7. My parents will be cleaning the whole house soon.
8. We were planning a party this afternoon.
9. I haven't seen any dogwoods in bloom yet.
10. Will Kara be happy with the warmer weather?

 Check Point: Mixed Practice

Write each verb.

1. Tigers live in Asia.
2. The tiger's distinctive black stripes provide excellent camouflage.
3. The Bengal tiger is smaller than other tigers.
4. The male grows to an adult weight of about 400 pounds.
5. Tiger cubs might stay with their parents for two years.
6. The father tiger does not help with the care of the cubs.
7. The Bengal tiger combines great power with lethal slyness.
8. A tiger can kill a water buffalo nearly four times its own weight.
9. Project Tiger was launched in India's Corbett National Park in 1972.
10. More than forty tiger reserves were created.

Linking Verbs

Some verbs that show being *link* the subject with another word in the sentence. These are the linking verbs.

16 D A **linking verb** links the subject with another word that renames or describes the subject.

Jessica **was** captain of our sailboat.
(*Was* links *captain* with *Jessica*. *Captain* renames the subject.)

The wind **will be** strong tomorrow.
(*Will be* links *strong* to *wind*. *Strong* describes the wind.)

COMMON FORMS OF *BE* USED AS LINKING VERBS

be	was	could be	have been
is	were	should be	has been
am	shall be	may be	could have been
are	will be	might be	must have been

Practice Your Skills

Finding Linking Verbs

Write each linking verb. Then write the words that the verb links.

1. The giraffe is the world's tallest animal.
2. Earth's first space traveler was a dog.
3. In some parts of the world, cattle are still wild.
4. The whale is a mammal, not a fish.
5. Wild horses may be dangerous.

➤ Additional Linking Verbs

Forms of the verb *be* are not the only linking verbs. The following words can also be used as linking verbs.

ADDITIONAL LINKING VERBS

appear	feel	look	seem	sound	taste
become	grow	remain	smell	stay	turn

Lucy **became** the new conductor.
(*Became* links *conductor* and *Lucy*. *Conductor* renames the subject.)

The old sheet music **smelled** musty.
(*Smelled* links *musty* and *music*. *Musty* describes the subject.)

Like action verbs, these linking verbs can also have helping verbs.

My flute **did sound** a little flat.

It **may have sounded** flat because of our long practice session.

Did your flute **stay** warm for too long?

In the preceding sentences, flat *and* warm *are subject complements. You can learn more about subject complements on pages 584–587.*

● **Practice Your Skills**

Finding Linking Verbs

Write each linking verb. Then write the words that the verb links.

1. Mozart's music appears difficult.
2. He became famous throughout Europe at a very young age.
3. His music does sound wonderful.
4. After the death of his father, Mozart's music turned darker.
5. *Don Giovanni* must have seemed scary to his audiences.
6. Mozart's music grew more complex.
7. His musical scores look perfect.
8. Did he ever feel successful?

▶ Linking Verb or Action Verb?

Some of the linking verbs listed on the previous page can also be action verbs. If the verb links two words, it is a linking verb. If the verb shows action, it is an action verb.

Linking Verb   The research boat **looked** new.
(*Looked* links *new* and *boat*. *New* describes the boat.)

Action Verb   Angie **looked** for the whales.
(*Looked* shows action. It tells what Angie did.)

Linking Verbs • Lesson 4

● **Practice Your Skills**

Distinguishing Between Linking Verbs and Action Verbs

Write each verb. Then label each one *A* for action or *L* for linking.

1. The biggest dinosaur on Earth appeared smaller than a blue whale.
2. Blue whales stay calm in most situations.
3. Blue whales appeared after dinosaurs.
4. These huge mammals stay underwater for periods as long as twenty minutes.
5. During the summer, blue whales remain in arctic and antarctic waters.

● *Connect to Writing:* **Drafting**

Writing Sentences with Linking and Action Verbs

Write two sentences for each of the following verbs. First use the verb as a linking verb; then use it as an action verb. Label each verb *A* for action or *L* for linking.

1. look 2. feel 3. taste 4. smell 5. sound 6. stay

● **Check Point: Mixed Practice**

Write each verb. Then label each one *A* for action or *L* for linking.

1. Many people had not heard about El Niño before 1998.
2. El Niño means "the boy" in Spanish.
3. El Niño has been responsible for unusual weather conditions around the world.
4. Florida was one state with problems from El Niño.
5. In the winter months, the ground in Florida normally becomes dry.
6. The ground does not remain dry for long, though.
7. In May and June, the afternoon showers begin.
8. In 1998, the afternoon showers stayed away.
9. People looked for rain.
10. The ground grew drier.
11. By the end of June, the air smelled smoky.
12. Wildfires spread through grass and trees and across highways.
13. The situation was a dangerous one.
14. Some people lost their homes to the flames.
15. Finally, El Niño turned away.

Chapter Review

Assess Your Learning

Finding Verbs

Write each verb. Then label each one *A* for action or *L* for linking.

1. For millions of years, dinosaurs ruled the land.
2. The apatosaurus was a huge animal.
3. This dinosaur reached a weight of thirty or forty tons!
4. Because of its size, it ate a tremendous amount.
5. Massive legs took the pressure of the animal's weight.
6. Its tail was long and whiplike.
7. The large tail also protected it from its enemies.
8. The apatosaurus looked fierce and mean.
9. Actually, it was never a threat to other dinosaurs.
10. This huge animal ate only vegetation.

Finding Verb Phrases

Write the verb or verb phrase in each sentence.

1. My brother will be home by noon.
2. Because of the storm, we might not go to the concert.
3. During your lifetime your brain may store up to 100 million bits of information.
4. Cars with front-wheel drive are becoming very popular.
5. At sunset the fire was still burning out of control.
6. The first public railroad was not built until 1825.
7. Robins have been appearing early this spring.
8. Haven't they become friends quickly?
9. Don't these lilies smell wonderful?
10. People have been wearing glasses for over seven hundred years.

■ Finding Verbs

Write each verb or verb phrase. Then label each *A* for action or *L* for linking.

1. Have you ever heard this story about a dog with ESP?
2. Jim was a black-and-white setter.
3. He apparently could guess the thoughts in people's minds.
4. Experts at a college in Missouri tested the dog.
5. At first the experts didn't believe the incredible stories about Jim.
6. One professor told Jim in French the number on a license plate.
7. Instantly Jim was standing beside the license plate.
8. The tests then grew harder.
9. The results, nevertheless, were always exactly the same.
10. By the end of the session, the professors had become believers in Jim's unusual ability.

■ Writing Sentences

Write five sentences that follow the directions below. (The sentences may come in any order.) Write about one of the following topics or a topic of your own choice: the funniest situation or the scariest situation you have ever been in.

Write a sentence that…

1. includes an action verb.
2. includes a linking verb.
3. includes an action verb with one or more helping verbs.
4. includes a linking verb with one or more helping verbs.
5. includes an interrupted verb phrase.

After writing the sentences, underline each verb or verb phrase.

Verbs: Posttest

Directions
Write the letter of the term that correctly identifies the underlined word or words in each sentence.

(1) A local company <u>wanted</u> to mine a mountainside near Jenna's house. (2) However, there <u>could</u> be a nest of rattlesnakes nearby. (3) The rattlesnakes <u>are</u> an endangered species. (4) Mining there <u>might destroy</u> the rattlesnake community. (5) The mining company <u>asked</u> the government for a permit to mine. (6) Jenna <u>was</u> writing letters and staging demonstrations. (7) She and some friends <u>organized</u> the local homeowners into a protest group. (8) The group <u>was</u> quick to contact their government representatives. (9) They <u>did</u> not <u>leave</u> anything to chance. (10) They <u>hired</u> a rattlesnake specialist.

1. **A** helping verb
   B action verb
   C verb phrase
   D linking verb

2. **A** transitive verb
   B intransitive verb
   C helping verb
   D linking verb

3. **A** transitive verb
   B action verb
   C helping verb
   D linking verb

4. **A** verb phrase
   B helping verb
   C linking verb
   D intransitive verb

5. **A** verb phrase
   B intransitive verb
   C transitive verb
   D helping verb

6. **A** helping verb
   B action verb
   C linking verb
   D verb phrase

7. **A** helping verb
   B action verb
   C linking verb
   D verb phrase

8. **A** action verb
   B linking verb
   C helping verb
   D verb phrase

9. **A** helping verb
   B intransitive verb
   C linking verb
   D verb phrase

10. **A** helping verb
    B transitive verb
    C intransitive verb
    D linking verb

Writer's Corner

Snapshot

16 A A **verb** is a word used to express an action or a state of being. (page 522)

16 B A **transitive verb** expresses action directly toward a person or a thing. An **intransitive verb** expresses action that is not directed at a person or a thing. (pages 524–525)

16 C A **helping verb,** or auxiliary verb, is a verb that is combined with a main verb to form a **verb phrase.** (pages 526–527)

16 D A **linking verb** links the subject with another word that renames or describes the subject. (pages 528–530)

Power Rules

 Use verbs that agree with the subject. (pages 738–760)

Before Editing
The *batter run* to first base.

The *students tries* to do their work.

After Editing
The *batter runs* to first base.

The *students try* to do their work.

 Do not use the word *of* in the place of *have* or its contraction *'ve*. (pages 790–791)

Before Editing
I *should of* already started.

Mom *might of* been right about my saving money.

We *could of* been swimming all summer.

After Editing
I *should've* already started. (*should have*)

Mom *might have* been right about my saving money.

We *could've* been swimming all summer. (*could have*)

Editing Checklist

Use this checklist when editing your writing.

✓ Did I use action verbs effectively? (See pages 522–523.)
✓ Did I use transitive and intransitive verbs effectively? (See pages 524–525.)
✓ Did I use the correct helping verbs in verb phrases? (See pages 526–527.)
✓ Did I use the correct form of the verb *be*? (See page 528.)
✓ Did I use linking verbs effectively? (See pages 528–530.)

Use the Power

A linking verb connects a subject with another word like a link in a chain.

Noun (Subject)	Linking Verb	Other Word
wagon	is	red
tree	grows	taller
students	are	happy
I	feel	sick

An action verb is like concentrated ink, a small drop of which can color an entire glass of water. Both sentences are correct in the example below, but notice how a single action verb carries the descriptive power of two words that say the same thing.

Verb with Adverb   The boy **walked hurriedly** across the square.
Strong Action Verb   The boy **hurried** across the square.

Revise a recent composition by replacing weak verbs and wordy descriptions with more colorful and descriptive action verbs.

CHAPTER 17

Adjectives and Adverbs

How can you add interest and detail to your writing with adjectives and adverbs?

Adjectives and Adverbs: Pretest 1

The following first draft is dull because it has no effective adverbs and adjectives. Revise the draft by suggesting more interesting adjectives and adverbs. An adjective has been added to the first sentence as an example.

    I just got back from a *wonderful* vacation to the Sonora Desert in Arizona. It was a fascinating place. There were mountains. We saw saguaro cactus. There was wildlife. I saw a wolf. I saw lizards. Near a stream, we saw trees growing. There were flowers. While we were there, we visited the Arizona-Sonora Desert Museum to learn more about the plants and animals of this area. At the museum, I saw a mountain lion. There were also birds, such as hummingbirds and owls. There was a garden of local plants. It was a vacation.

Adjectives and Adverbs: Pretest 2

Directions
Write the letter of the term that correctly identifies the underlined word in each sentence.

(1) The seventh-grade class gave a <u>fashion</u> show last week. (2) All of <u>the</u> class had a hand in designing, sewing, or modeling the clothes. (3) <u>Some</u> of the clothes were truly amazing. (4) The colors were <u>bold</u> and unusual. (5) The models stepped <u>jauntily</u> onto the stage. (6) Dion Clemens designed a hat that looked like a <u>frozen</u> dinner. (7) <u>That</u> got the loudest applause from the audience. (8) He was <u>very</u> proud of his creation. (9) There was loud <u>African</u> music playing during the show. (10) A <u>local</u> newspaper took pictures and wrote up a story.

1. **A** adjective
   B article
   C adverb
   D pronoun

2. **A** noun
   B article
   C adverb
   D pronoun

3. **A** adjective
   B article
   C adverb
   D pronoun

4. **A** adjective
   B article
   C adverb
   D pronoun

5. **A** proper adjective
   B article
   C adverb
   D pronoun

6. **A** adjective
   B verb
   C adverb
   D noun

7. **A** adjective
   B article
   C adverb
   D pronoun

8. **A** adjective
   B article
   C adverb
   D pronoun

9. **A** proper adjective
   B article
   C adverb
   D proper noun

10. **A** adjective
    B article
    C adverb
    D pronoun

Adjectives — Lesson 1

Two of the eight parts of speech are called modifiers. A **modifier** makes the meaning of another word more precise. Modifiers are important because they add color and exactness to writing and speaking. One kind of modifier is an adjective.

17 A An **adjective** is a word that modifies a noun or pronoun.

An adjective answers the questions *What kind? Which one? How many?* or *How much?* about nouns and some pronouns. Adjectives in the following examples are in **bold** type. An arrow points to the noun or pronoun each adjective modifies.

ADJECTIVES

What Kind?	**famous** hurricane	**heavy** rainfall
Which One?	**these** boats	**those** few
How Many?	**three** tornadoes	**several** records
How Much?	**little** damage	**much** work

When You Write

Writers know that choosing the right adjective can make a difference. In the following passage, notice how Mildred Taylor uses specific adjectives to help describe the scene the children are witnessing. (The adjectives are underlined.)

>   Beyond the <u>Avery</u> house <u>bright</u> lights appeared far away on the road near the Granger mansion. For a <u>breathless</u> second they lingered there, then plunged suddenly downward toward the Averys'. The <u>first</u> set of lights was followed by a <u>second</u>, then a <u>third</u>, until there were <u>half a dozen</u> sets of headlights beaming over the trail.
>   "Wh-what's happening?" cried Christopher-John.
>   For what seemed an <u>interminable</u> wait, we stood watching <u>those</u> lights drawing nearer and nearer before Stacey clicked off the flashlight and ordered us into the forest. Silently, we slipped into the brush and fell flat to the ground. <u>Two</u> pickups and <u>four</u> cars rattled into the yard, their lights focused like spotlights on the <u>Avery</u> <u>front</u> porch. <u>Noisy</u>, <u>angry</u> men leaped from the cars and surrounded the house.
>
>   —Mildred Taylor, *Roll of Thunder, Hear My Cry*

Practice Your Skills

Finding Adjectives

Write each adjective. Beside each one, write the word it modifies. Do not write the articles *a, an,* and *the.*

(1) A fierce hurricane begins over the ocean in the hot parts of the world. (2) Strong winds come from opposite directions and smash together. (3) Then the wild winds move in a circular pattern. (4) The calm center of the hurricane is called the eye. (5) The eye has light breezes and puffy clouds. (6) If the mighty winds of a hurricane hit land, they can cause severe damage. (7) Sturdy buildings have collapsed because of the huge waves or terrible winds of a severe hurricane. (8) With a hurricane comes heavy rain that often causes additional damage to property. (9) The rains often cause many rivers to overflow. (10) The powerful storm may weaken after it hits land.

Connect to the Writing Process: Revising

Adding Specific Adjectives

Rewrite the following sentences, adding specific adjectives wherever possible.

1. The winds damaged the homes.
2. The boats rode out the storm on the ocean.
3. The storm ruined businesses.
4. People were without power for hours.
5. After the storm the winds calmed down.

Different Positions of Adjectives

An adjective usually comes right in front of the word it modifies. Occasionally, however, an adjective will follow the word it modifies. An adjective can also follow a linking verb.

Before a Noun   A **huge, beautiful** flower was the subject of the painting.

After a Noun   A flower, **huge** and **beautiful,** was the subject of the painting.

After a Linking Verb   The flower in the painting was **huge** and **beautiful.**

Notice that more than one adjective can modify the same noun.

You can find lists of common linking verbs on pages 528 and 584.

PUNCTUATION WITH TWO ADJECTIVES

Sometimes you will write two adjectives together before or after the noun they describe. If those two adjectives are not connected by *and* or *or*, you might need to put a comma between them. To decide if a comma belongs, read the adjectives with the word *and* between them.

- If the adjectives read naturally, put a comma in to replace the word *and*.
- If the adjectives do not read well with the word *and* between them, do not add a comma.

Comma Needed   It was a long, hard day.
(*It was a long and hard day* reads well.)

Comma Not Needed   It was a dry summer day.
(*It was a dry and summer day* does not read well.)

Usually no comma is needed after a number or after an adjective that refers to size, shape, or age.

number   **six** blue flowers
size   a **large** sunny painting

You can learn more about commas before nouns on pages 835–838.

540   Adjectives and Adverbs

 Articles

17 A.1 The words *a*, *an*, and *the* form a special group of adjectives called **articles.**

A comes before words that begin with a consonant sound. *An* comes before words that begin with a vowel sound.

> Marcy wrote **a** report about **an** artist.
>
> (*A* comes before a consonant sound such as the *r* in *report*, and *an* comes before a vowel sound such as the *a* in *artist*.)

You will not be asked to list articles in the exercises in this book.

● Practice Your Skills

Finding Adjectives

Write each adjective. Beside each one, write the word it modifies. (Do not include articles or the possessive pronoun *her*.)

(1) Georgia O'Keeffe is a famous artist of the twentieth century. **(2)** Her famous flower paintings, large and colorful, appeared in the art scene of the mid-1920s. **(3)** She also painted precise and geometric city scenes. **(4)** In 1929, she moved to New Mexico, where she painted beautiful and unusual still lifes and landscapes. **(5)** Her paintings reflected the colorful desert of the Southwest. **(6)** A teacher once told Georgia that her drawings were small and dark. **(7)** As a result, she always painted everything large and bright. **(8)** Her unique style increased her popularity as an artist. **(9)** She enjoyed a long career. **(10)** Her bold, inspirational paintings are still popular today.

Proper Adjectives

A proper noun is the name of a particular person, place, or thing. A proper adjective is formed from a proper noun.

17 A.2 A **proper adjective** is used to describe a noun or a pronoun and always begins with a capital letter.

> **Proper Nouns** China, Europe, Democrat, England, Switzerland
>
> **Proper Adjectives** **Chinese** history, **European** countries, **Democratic** candidate, **English** sheepdog, **Swiss** watch

You can learn more about capitalization of proper adjectives on pages 816–817.

● **Practice Your Skills**

Finding Adjectives

Write each proper adjective. Beside each one, write the word it modifies.

1. Mr. Taylor told us, in his best English accent, that we would be participating in the school's cultural fair.
2. Nancy Coleman brought a German clock for our booth.
3. I saw wonderful African masks at the booth next to ours.
4. We ate Greek food at the fair.
5. While at the festival, José bought a souvenir at the Italian booth.
6. The Chinese embroidery that Ming brought was very delicate.
7. The local Republican candidate helped us open the fair.
8. We could hear the Mexican musicians playing mariachi music.
9. A Congressional representative also came to the fair.
10. She was surprised to win a Hawaiian vacation at the raffle.

● *Connect to the Writing Process:* **Editing**

Capitalizing Proper Adjectives

Write the following sentences, capitalizing each proper adjective. If a sentence is correct, write **C**.

1. My mother can speak the french language very well.
2. Did you get to see the irish dancers?
3. My favorite part of the fair was the performance of the Scottish pipers.
4. John liked the spanish flamenco dancers.
5. Did Sara like the african storyteller?

● *Connect to Writing:* **Advertisement**

Using Proper Adjectives

Your class has been asked to make posters for the school's cultural fair, which will also be one of the school's largest fund-raisers for this year. Think about what kinds of booths the fair will have. What types of activities will interest people of all ages? Then make a poster that will be placed in business windows throughout the community to advertise the fair. Be sure to use proper adjectives correctly in your advertisement.

Adjectives and Adverbs

Adjective or Noun?

A word's part of speech depends on how it is used in a sentence. For this reason the same word can be a noun in one sentence and an adjective in another sentence.

Noun	Let's watch some **baseball** today.
Adjective	Did you lose your **baseball** bat?
Noun	The coach caught my **cold.**
Adjective	He took some **cold** medicine before the game.
Noun	The first game of the baseball season is always in the **spring.**
Adjective	Most professional baseball teams hold **spring** training in Arizona or Florida.

● **Practice Your Skills**

Distinguishing Between Adjectives and Nouns

Write **A** for adjective and **N** for noun to identify each underlined word.

1. How many gallons of <u>paint</u> will we need for the dugout?
2. I will need a new <u>spring</u> jacket before we start practice.
3. The <u>baseball</u> soared over center field and into the bleachers.
4. On which <u>train</u> car will the team eat?
5. Getting enough <u>practice</u> can be a problem for me.
6. Can the <u>paint</u> stains be removed from the dugout floor?
7. The <u>train</u> was empty except for our team.
8. This <u>spring</u> we have had better practices.
9. Our coach knows some great <u>practice</u> drills.
10. Why did you join the <u>baseball</u> team this year?

● *Connect to the Writing Process:* **Drafting**

Writing Sentences with Nouns and Adjectives

Write two sentences for each of the following words. Use the word as an adjective in the first sentence. Use the word as a noun in the second sentence. Label the use of each one.

1. radio
2. art
3. silver
4. city
5. apple

Adjective or Pronoun?

Some words can be used as either pronouns or adjectives. A word such as *these* is a pronoun if it stands alone and takes the place of a noun. The same word can be an adjective if it modifies a noun or a pronoun.

Adjective	**That** plane belongs to Orville.
	(*That* modifies *plane*.)
Pronoun	**That** belongs to Orville.
	(*That* takes the place of the noun *plane*.)
Adjective	**Which** plane do you want?
Pronoun	**Which** do you want?
Adjective	**Many** onlookers stayed to congratulate Orville.
Pronoun	**Many** stayed to congratulate Orville.

All of the following words can be used as pronouns or adjectives.

WORDS USED AS PRONOUNS OR ADJECTIVES

Demonstrative	Interrogative	Indefinite		
that	what	all	either	neither
these	which	another	few	other
this	whose	any	many	several
those		both	more	some
		each	most	

544 Adjectives and Adverbs

● **Practice Your Skills**

Distinguishing Between Adjectives and Pronouns

Label each underlined word as an adjective or a pronoun.

1. <u>Few</u> people realize that Wilbur and Orville Wright made bicycles before airplanes.
2. They experimented with <u>many</u> designs before their historic flight at Kitty Hawk.
3. <u>Which</u> brother made the first flight?
4. <u>Few</u> understand the dangers of the first flight.
5. <u>That</u> airplane of the Wright brothers began as a glider.
6. <u>What</u> challenges did they face in December 1903?
7. <u>Both</u> brothers continued to make airplanes.
8. <u>Many</u> wanted to fly after Wilbur and Orville's successful flight.
9. <u>What</u> did Wilbur do?
10. <u>Several</u> people helped the Wright brothers with their first flight on December 17, 1903.

● *Connect to the Writing Process:* **Drafting**

Drafting Sentences for Adjectives and Pronouns

Write two sentences for each of the following words. Use the word as an adjective in the first sentence. Use the word as a pronoun in the second sentence. Then label the use of each one.

1. some
2. this
3. which
4. these
5. all

Check Point: Mixed Practice

Write each adjective. Beside each one, write the word it modifies. Do not list articles. (There are twenty-four adjectives.)

(1) Gorillas live in small family groups. (2) They roam many miles each day in search of food for the family group. (3) Some eat fruits, while others prefer green leafy plants. (4) Toward evening they construct rough nests for sleeping. (5) Usually the male leader builds his leafy nest on the ground. (6) The leader is the strongest and protects the other members of the group. (7) Gorillas with short hair live in the hot, damp areas of the Congo River valley. (8) The faces of these gorillas are hairless and shiny. (9) Gorillas with coarse hair live in the cool air of the African mountains. (10) Most gorillas live in and around the central part of Africa.

Power Your Writing: Adjectives Come Lately

Usually adjectives come before the word they modify. But you can create variety in your writing by placing adjectives and other modifiers after the words they modify. In the following sentence from "The Drummer Boy of Shiloh," the subject of the sentence is *men*. Ray Bradbury uses the adjectives *exhausted* and *unable* after the subject to describe the men.

> Beyond the thirty-three familiar shadows, forty thousand <u>men</u>, **exhausted** by nervous expectation, **unable** to sleep for romantic dreams of battles yet unfought, lay crazily askew in their uniforms.

When you place adjectives and adjective phrases after the word they modify, surround them with commas.

Adverbs — Lesson 2

Another kind of modifier is an adverb. Adverbs make writing more precise. Notice in the following examples how the second sentence gives more information with the addition of two adverbs.

> Jonathan is running the marathon.
> Jonathan is **carefully** running the marathon **now**.

17 B An **adverb** is a word that modifies a verb, an adjective, or another adverb.

Many adverbs are easy to recognize because they end in –*ly*.

> Run **quickly** and grasp the baton **firmly**.
> Did Ruth **finally** complete her training session **successfully**?

The following chart shows, however, that some common adverbs do not end in –*ly*.

COMMON ADVERBS			
again	far	never	soon
almost	fast	next	still
already	hard	not (n't)	then
also	here	now	there
always	just	often	too
down	late	quite	very
even	more	rather	well
ever	near	so	yet

Remember that *not* and its contraction *n't* are always adverbs.

> The stopwatch is **not** working.
> I have**n't** run the mile.

Adverbs • Lesson 2

Adverbs That Modify Verbs

Most adverbs modify verbs. To find these adverbs, first find each verb. Then ask yourself *Where? When? How?* or *To what extent?* about each verb. The answers to these questions will be adverbs. Notice that an adverb can appear anywhere in the sentence.

Where?	The old fence fell **down.**
When?	**Then** the runners jumped.
How?	The track meet ended **abruptly.**
To What Extent?	Stacy **almost** won the race.

If the verb contains helping verbs, the adverb modifies the entire verb phrase.

He has packed the equipment **carefully.**

Soon the heavy rains will begin **again.**

She can run **quickly.**

Uncle Ray has **not** met my track coach.

Does Jenny **often** compete at track?

Don has **not yet** arrived for the meet.

Notice in the preceding examples that an adverb can interrupt a verb phrase.

● **Practice Your Skills**

Finding Adverbs

Write each adverb and the word or words it modifies.

1. Our track team rarely loses.
2. Stephanie rushed forward to the finish line.
3. Lately the team has been practicing in the morning.
4. Danny was quickly tying his shoes.
5. Did you really forget your discus?
6. Finally the meet has begun.
7. Mira is practicing the long jump again.
8. We have looked everywhere for a new stopwatch.

9. Ellis will never run there.
10. Don't stop now!

Connect to the Writing Process: Drafting

Writing Sentences with Adverbs

Using adverbs, write sentences that follow each direction. Underline each adverb.

1. Describe how a friend talks.
2. Describe how a detective enters a dark, scary house.
3. Describe how a toddler walks.
4. Describe how you do your homework.
5. Describe how you eat spaghetti.

Adverbs That Modify Adjectives and Other Adverbs

An adverb that modifies an adjective or another adverb is called an **intensifying adverb.** Such an adverb answers the question *To what extent?* of the word it modifies.

Modifying an Adjective	Barry's compliments were **truly** sincere. (*Sincere* is an adjective. *Truly* tells how sincere Barry's compliments were.)
Modifying an Adverb	Ada finished her lines **very** quickly. (*Quickly* is an adverb. *Very* tells how quickly Ada finished.)

You can learn about using adjectives and adverbs for comparisons on pages 768–773.

Practice Your Skills

Finding Adverbs

Write each adverb. Beside each one, write the word it modifies.

1. The actors were extremely nervous.
2. You should whisper very quietly backstage.
3. It rained quite often during the month of outdoor performances.
4. The actors were truly responsible.
5. Rita arrived too early for her cue.

● **Connect to Writing: Drafting**

Writing Sentences with Adverbs

Use each word as an adverb in a sentence. Then rewrite the sentence, putting the adverb in a different part of the sentence.

1. calmly
2. finally
3. never
4. soon
5. quickly

✓ **Check Point: Mixed Practice**

Write each adverb. Beside each one, write the word or words it modifies.

(1) Giraffes glide gracefully and noiselessly across the plains of Kenya in Africa. (2) There they search hungrily and eagerly for the acacia tree. (3) A family of giraffes will often feed from the same tree. (4) Drinking water is the most difficult job for a giraffe. (5) This unusually tall animal drinks slowly and awkwardly. (6) Carefully it bends its knees and its neck and laps cautiously at the cool water. (7) The giraffe's very long neck contains the same number of bones as the neck of a guinea pig. (8) These neck bones are much longer in the giraffe than in the guinea pig. (9) The neck bones are also bigger in the giraffe. (10) The giraffe seldom uses its quite unusual voice. (11) Ordinarily, a giraffe will not attack other creatures. (12) Daily a giraffe will eat acacia leaves on the grassy plains. (13) Other animals rarely threaten the giraffe's survival. (14) Lions occasionally bother giraffes. (15) Sometimes visitors to Kenya's national parks see the giraffes.

● **Connect to Writing: Review**

Using Adverbs

The adviser to the school newspaper has invited students to write reviews. Write a review for the school paper of a movie, television show, CD, concert, or play that interests you. Be sure to use adverbs to modify verbs, adjectives, and other adverbs.

Sentence Diagraming

Diagraming Adjectives and Adverbs

Adjectives and adverbs are both diagramed on a slanted line below the words they modify.

Eventually the poor tree fell.

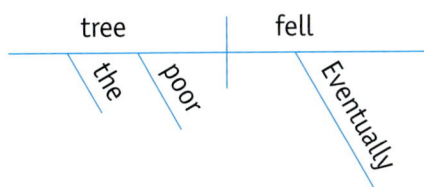

An adverb that modifies an adjective or another adverb is also connected to the word it modifies. It is written on a line parallel to the word it modifies.

Evening arrived very quickly.

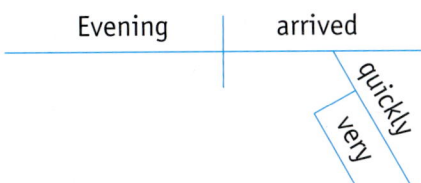

Frighteningly dark clouds floated by.

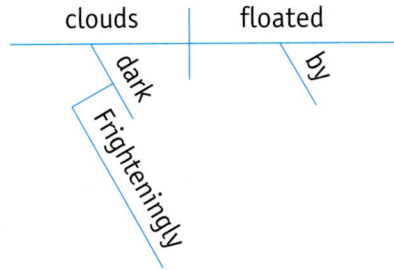

The unusually bright stars glittered quite intensely.

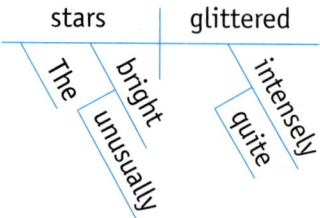

● **Practice Your Skills**

Diagraming Adjectives and Adverbs

Diagram the following sentences or copy them. If you copy them, draw one line under each subject and two lines under each verb. Then label each modifier *Adj.* for an adjective or *Adv.* for an adverb.

1. Three chickens have escaped.
2. Julia worked steadily.
3. Suddenly the brilliant sun disappeared.
4. Fierce winds blew daily.
5. An elephant can move noiselessly.
6. The strong batter grinned confidently.
7. The rather large ball bounced high.
8. She writes quite often.
9. Have the three workers finished so soon?
10. Very young kittens run quite awkwardly.
11. The proud horse flung its mane back and snorted loudly.
12. The Davis family moved recently.
13. We don't know the next winner yet.
14. Moviegoers were really frightened.
15. The antique cars moved very slowly.

Chapter Review

Assess Your Learning

Finding Adjectives and Adverbs

Make two columns on your paper. Label the first column <u>adjectives</u> and the second column <u>adverbs</u>. Then in the proper column, write each adjective and adverb.

1. Finally we finished the new doghouse for Tex.
2. The Irish soccer team has often won.
3. Lee spoke slowly and calmly.
4. A car skidded dangerously on the icy road.
5. The French diplomats were formally introduced.
6. The ride was too scary for me.
7. Did you bring that warm jacket?
8. They left the dance unusually early.
9. You should not drive the car through the deep water.
10. The English nurse is extremely thoughtful.

Identifying Adjectives and Adverbs

Write each adjective and adverb. Then beside each one, write the word or words each one describes.

1. Jody answered the first question correctly.
2. The spring concert will begin soon.
3. Slowly Jeff opened the old window.
4. Karen has never tasted a green apple.
5. Occasionally Mom does research for large companies.
6. I haven't seen that movie.
7. Muffy often eats small grasshoppers.
8. Now we should listen to the latest news.

Distinguishing Among Different Parts of Speech

Write each underlined word. Then label each one **N** for noun, **P** for pronoun, or **A** adjective.

1. The words of that song are funny.
2. Use these to wash the car windows.
3. I always enjoy watching the news on television.
4. Which is the best buy for each of us?
5. Several of the musicians knew the song title.
6. We will need a bicycle rack for the car.
7. These news bulletins just arrived for the President.
8. Which television station do you watch?
9. That is the bicycle for me.
10. Each runner ate several bananas.

Writing Sentences

Write five sentences that follow the directions below. (The sentences may come in any order.) Write about one of the following topics or a topic of your choice: the best or the worst birthday present you ever received or gave.

Write a sentence that…

1. includes two adjectives before a noun.
2. includes an adjective after a linking verb.
3. includes two adjectives after a noun.
4. includes a proper adjective.
5. includes *that* as an adjective.

Adjectives and Adverbs: Posttest

Directions
Write the letter of the term that correctly identifies the underlined word in each sentence.

(1) The Finellis traveled to Iceland over the summer. (2) It was an unusual place. (3) There are very few trees, and the land is strewn with huge volcanic rocks. (4) In many places they could see steam escaping from the earth between rocks. (5) Iceland is full of geothermic springs. (6) These bring heat to most of the country without polluting the air. (7) The Finellis swam in one hot spring while sleet fell on their chilly heads. (8) Geysers spray hot water high into the sky. (9) The Icelandic language is ancient, and many great stories have been written in it. (10) Iceland is on a spot where two great tectonic plates meet and rub against each other, causing earthquakes.

1. A noun
   B article
   C adverb
   D pronoun

2. A adjective
   B article
   C adverb
   D pronoun

3. A proper adjective
   B article
   C adverb
   D pronoun

4. A adjective
   B article
   C adverb
   D pronoun

5. A adjective
   B article
   C adverb
   D pronoun

6. A adjective
   B article
   C adverb
   D pronoun

7. A adjective
   B article
   C adverb
   D pronoun

8. A noun
   B article
   C adverb
   D pronoun

9. A proper adjective
   B article
   C adverb
   D proper noun

10. A adjective
    B article
    C adverb
    D pronoun

Writer's Corner

Snapshot

17 A   An **adjective** is a word that modifies a noun or pronoun. (page 538)

17 B   An **adverb** is a word that modifies a verb, an adjective, or another adverb. (page 547)

Power Rules

Avoid double negatives. Some adverbs have a negative meaning. Be careful not to use such adverbs with negative words. (pages 777–778 and 790)

Before Editing

Jane *doesn't hardly* care where they sit as long as she gets to see the concert.

They *couldn't scarcely* see the stage because their seats were so far away.

She was so excited after the show that she *wasn't barely* able to sleep.

After Editing

Jane *doesn't* care where they sit as long as she gets to see the concert.

They *could scarcely* see the stage because their seats were so far away.

She was so excited after the show that she *was barely* able to sleep.

Editing Checklist

Use this checklist when editing your writing.

✓ Did I use specific adjectives to modify nouns and pronouns effectively? (pages 538–540)
✓ Did I capitalize proper adjectives? (pages 541-542)
✓ Did I use commas to separate adjectives when necessary? (pages 540, 837–838)
✓ Did I use adverbs to make verbs, adjectives, and other adverbs more precise? (pages 547–550)

Use the Power

Using an adjective or an adverb is similar to adding color to a picture. Modifiers add additional information about the people, places, or things you are describing. Is she **tall, smart, shy**? Does she walk **quickly, slowly, ponderously**?

Review a piece of creative writing you have completed recently. Have you used adjectives and adverbs effectively? Revise your work to include modifiers that add color to your writing.

CHAPTER 18

Other Parts of Speech and Review

How can you create fluency in your writing by using prepositions, conjunctions, and interjections?

Other Parts of Speech and Review: Pretest 1

The following first draft is dull because the writer repeats one preposition over and over. Revise the draft by replacing the repeated preposition. The first one has been replaced as an example.

Kangaroo Island, ~~near~~ *off* the south coast of Australia, is a wonderful place to visit. You can visit Seal Bay, where hundreds of sea lions are sunning near the sea's edge. Everywhere, there are koalas near the trees. Small, local kangaroos gather near the picnic tables, hoping they will get a handout. Tall birds called emus are near the kangaroos. Near the coast, you can see the Remarkable Rocks, which are wind- and water-carved boulders. Near the south end of the island, you can tour Kelly Hill Caves. Near the entrance, you begin to see amazing crystal formations. Near the center of the island, farms alternate with forests. Kingscote, the largest city and capital of the island, is near the northernmost point of the island. Near the city's edge, there are trees that have been twisted by the wind. Near these trees, fishing boats wait to go out and catch spiny lobsters.

Other Parts of Speech and Review: Pretest 2

Directions
Write the letter of the term that correctly identifies the underlined word or words in each sentence.

(1) We hiked <u>to</u> the top of Mt. Greylock. (2) Mt. Greylock is a mountain <u>in</u> Massachusetts. (3) <u>Neither</u> Jayson <u>nor</u> I had ever climbed it before. (4) We climbed <u>upward</u> for hours. (5) <u>From a distance</u> Mt. Greylock looks like a whale. (6) <u>Wow!</u> I believe that the mountain inspired Herman Melville to write *Moby-Dick*. (7) We climbed on the hottest day <u>of</u> summer. (8) Our legs were trembling <u>and</u> weak. (9) <u>"Yikes!"</u> Jayson yelled. "I don't think we can make it!" (10) I told him it wasn't <u>much</u> farther.

1. **A** preposition
   B adverb
   C conjunction
   D interjection

2. **A** preposition
   B adverb
   C conjunction
   D interjection

3. **A** prepositions
   B adverbs
   C conjunctions
   D interjections

4. **A** preposition
   B adverb
   C conjunction
   D interjection

5. **A** prepositional phrase
   B adverb
   C verb phrase
   D interjection

6. **A** adjective
   B adverb
   C conjunction
   D interjection

7. **A** preposition
   B adverb
   C conjunction
   D interjection

8. **A** preposition
   B adverb
   C conjunction
   D interjection

9. **A** preposition
   B adverb
   C conjunction
   D interjection

10. **A** preposition
    B adverb
    C adjective
    D noun

Prepositions

Prepositions can change the entire meaning of a sentence.

> Please hand me the first-aid kit **on** the table.
> Please hand me the first-aid kit **near** the table.
> Please hand me the first-aid kit **under** the table.

18 A A **preposition** is a word that shows the relationship between a noun or a pronoun and another word in the sentence.

The following is a list of common prepositions. Notice that some prepositions are more than one word.

COMMON PREPOSITIONS		
about	beyond	over
above	by	past
according to	down	since
across	during	through
after	except	throughout
against	for	to
along	from	toward
among	in	under
around	in front of	underneath
at	inside	until
because of	into	up
before	like	upon
behind	near	up to
below	of	with
beneath	off	within
beside	on	without
between	out of	

● **Practice Your Skills**

Supplying Prepositions

Write two prepositions that could fill each blank in the following sentences.

1. The narrow road ran ___ the cliffs.
2. A huge boulder was lying ___ the path.
3. The scouts camped ___ the lake.
4. I found my compass ___ the stream.
5. Kathleen found the missing backpack ___ the tent.
6. Our guide looked for a bear ___ the bushes.
7. A huge falcon flew ___ the clouds.
8. The hikers climbed ___ the rocks.

Prepositional Phrases

A preposition is always the first word of a group of words called a **prepositional phrase.**

18 A.1 A **prepositional phrase** is a group of words made up of a preposition, its object, and any words that modify the object.

Prepositional Phrases	In *July* the islands are often crowded. (*July* is the object of the preposition *in*.) An iguana stood **in front of *us*.** (The pronoun *us* is the object of the preposition *in front of*.) Put the binoculars **inside *the small backpack*.** (*Backpack* is the object of the preposition *inside*. *The* and *small* modify *backpack*.)

Sometimes a preposition has more than one object. Then the prepositional phrase has a **compound object of the preposition.**

Compound Object of a Preposition	All the scientists **except *Kevin* and *Brianna*** have arrived.

Prepositions • Lesson 1

Some sentences may include more than one prepositional phrase.

> The penguin eggs **on the islands** usually hatch **around May.**
> **After dinner** we went **to the island.**

Prepositional phrases are used to convey location, time, and direction or to provide details.

Location	Bats are known to hibernate **in caves.**
Time	Many bats migrate **in the spring.**
Direction	They will migrate **toward their summer habitat.**
Provide Details	Most bats have a diet **of insects.**

You can learn more about prepositional phrases on pages 600–606.

● Practice Your Skills

Finding Prepositional Phrases

Write each prepositional phrase. Underline the preposition and circle its object. (There are fifteen phrases.)

1. The trunk of an elephant is like a hose.
2. Elephants inhale water through their trunks.
3. Then they curl their trunks and shoot the water into their mouths.
4. Elephants eat food in a similar way.
5. With their trunks elephants also spray water onto their backs.
6. They like water and can swim for six hours.
7. During the hottest hours, elephants often huddle under trees.
8. Elephants also throw mud over their bodies.
9. With their trunks elephants can break large branches from trees.
10. In a wildlife park, an elephant can live for sixty-five years.

● *Connect to Writing:* Drafting

Writing Sentences

Write five sentences about an animal that lives in the wild. Use at least one prepositional phrase in each sentence.

Preposition or Adverb?

Certain words, such as *inside,* can be a preposition in one sentence and an adverb in another. Such a word is a preposition when it is part of a prepositional phrase. It is an adverb when it stands alone.

Preposition Carolyn and Jackie went *inside the hotel.*
(*Inside the hotel* is a prepositional phrase.)

Adverb Carolyn and Jackie went *inside.*
(*Inside* is an adverb that tells where Carolyn and Jackie went. It is not part of a prepositional phrase, and it has no object.)

Preposition Climb *up the ladder* and check on the luggage.
Adverb Climb *up* and check on the luggage.

Preposition His very last quarter rolled *down the aisle.*
Adverb She rolled the window *down.*

Preposition She drove *past the house.*
Adverb She drove *past.*

● **Practice Your Skills**

Distinguishing Between Prepositions and Adverbs

Label each underlined word *P* for preposition or *A* for adverb.

1. We drove through Chicago in less than an hour.
2. The mountains of home were a long way off.
3. We ate our lunch near Lake Michigan.
4. Every morning Dad checked around the car.
5. Did you drive straight through?
6. Lisa left the tickets behind.
7. My suitcase rolled off the roof rack.
8. Don't come near, for I have to focus the camera.
9. Did you look around?
10. The spare tire may have rolled behind that bush.

● ***Connect to Writing:*** **Drafting**

Drafting Sentences with Prepositional Phrases and Adverbs

Write two sentences for each of the following words. Use the word as a preposition in the first sentence and as an adverb in the second sentence. Label the use of each one.

1. in
2. across
3. below
4. up
5. along

● **Check Point:** **Mixed Practice**

Write the prepositional phrases in the following paragraphs.

> **(1)** Does a monster really hide in Loch Ness? **(2)** For many centuries people have reportedly seen this strange creature. **(3)** The Loch Ness monster first had its picture taken in 1934. **(4)** Dr. R. K. Wilson was driving along the shore. **(5)** Suddenly he saw movement in the water and grabbed his camera. **(6)** The result is a very famous, very blurry photograph of a mysterious object. **(7)** The fuzzy picture just *might* show a strange animal with an extremely long neck. **(8)** Some people, however, are not convinced by this photograph.
>
> **(9)** With special underwater cameras, scientists have searched more recently for the Loch Ness monster. **(10)** Unfortunately, the new pictures also show little except fuzzy shapes. **(11)** Most scientists do not believe in the monster. **(12)** Possible explanations for the monster include a large fish, an unusual wave, and a giant seal. **(13)** Believers, though, think that a dinosaur may have survived from prehistoric times. **(14)** Without better evidence the Loch Ness mystery will remain unsolved.

Loch Ness

Power Your Writing: Fine Points

In "Learning English: My New Found Land," Julia Alavarez recounts how Sister Bernadette inspired her to find her place in the English language.

> "Here's a simple sentence: *The snow fell*." Sister Bernadette pointed with her chalk, her eyebrows lifted, her wimple poked up. "But watch what happens if we put an adverb at the beginning and a prepositional phrase at the end: *Gently the snow fell on the bare hills*."

Notice in the examples below how the prepositional phrase and adverb add emotion and detail to the sentences.

> I had never had the faintest desire to go to school.
>
> **Up until this moment,** I had never had the faintest desire to go to school.

> I shook my head.
>
> **Regretfully,** I shook my head.

Follow Sister Bernadette's advice: add prepositional phrases and adverbs to your sentences. Revise a composition you completed recently by adding prepositional phrases and adverbs.

Connect to Writing: Postcard

Using Prepositions and Adverbs

While driving with your family on vacation, you purchased a postcard. Write a short message to your grandmother, telling her about your trip and the things you have been doing. Consider these questions before you write your message.

- What did you do yesterday?
- What do you plan to do today?
- What has made this trip special or fun?

Be sure to use prepositional phrases and adverbs to make your writing interesting.

Conjunctions and Interjections

18 B A **conjunction** connects words or groups of words; an **interjection** shows strong feeling.

➤ Conjunctions

There are three kinds of conjunctions: coordinating, correlative, and subordinating.

18 B.1 Both **coordinating conjunctions** and **correlative conjunctions** connect words or groups of words.

COORDINATING CONJUNCTIONS			
and	but	or	yet

Connecting Words	I have *rods* **and** *reels*. (connects nouns)
	He **or** *I* will meet Tim. (connects pronouns)
	The wind *blew* **and** *howled*. (connects verbs)
	Get *blue* **or** *green* worms. (connects adjectives)
	He spoke *firmly* **yet** *kindly* about my poor skills. (connects adverbs)
Connecting Groups of Words	Tad looked *in the boat* **and** *outside the boat*. (connects prepositional phrases)
	Everyone was here early for the fish fry, **but** *the special guest was late.* (connects complete ideas)

Correlative conjunctions come in pairs. They also connect groups of words.

CORRELATIVE CONJUNCTIONS		
both/and	either/or	neither/nor

Connecting Words	**Both** *bass* **and** *catfish* are tender. (connects nouns)
	The two fish **neither** *look* alike **nor** *swim* alike. (connects verbs)
Connecting Groups of Words	**Either** *Raymond will come here,* **or** *I will go to the pond.* (connects complete ideas)

The third kind of conjunction is a subordinating conjunction. It will be covered on pages 640–641.

Conjunctive Adverbs

In the last chapter you learned about adverbs, which modify verbs, adjectives, and other adverbs. There are some words that act both as adverbs and conjunctions. These words are called **conjunctive adverbs.**

18 B.2 A **conjunctive adverb** is an adverb that acts as a conjunction connecting complete ideas.

Following is a list of some common conjunctive adverbs.

COMMON CONJUNCTIVE ADVERBS				
accordingly	consequently	however	namely	then
again	finally	indeed	nevertheless	therefore
also	furthermore	likewise	otherwise	
besides	hence	meanwhile	similarly	

A conjunctive adverb can come in the middle of a sentence, connecting two ideas, or it can come at the beginning of a sentence. When a conjunctive adverb appears within a sentence, a semicolon is used to link the two main ideas. A comma always follows a conjunctive adverb.

> Martha and Carlos did not do their homework; **consequently,** they were not prepared for the test.
>
> **Finally,** they decided to study together.

● **Practice Your Skills**

Connecting Ideas with Conjunctive Adverbs

Combine each set of related sentences by using one of the conjunctive adverbs listed in the blue box above. Use semicolons and commas correctly.

1. I forgot to write down the assignment. I didn't turn it in on time.
2. We were supposed to write about a family member. I couldn't think of anyone.
3. I thought about my mom and my dad. I thought about Uncle Ben.
4. I decided to write about Uncle Ben. I didn't know that much about him.
5. First I talked to my mom about Uncle Ben. I interviewed him via e-mail.

Parallelism with Conjunctions

18 B.3 **Parallelism** refers to the use of similar grammatical constructions for similar ideas.

When using a conjunction, be sure the groups of words you are connecting are parallel in structure. Otherwise your writing can become confusing and hard to read.

Not Parallel	Beth likes to fish and jogging.
Parallel	Beth likes **fishing** and **jogging.**
Not Parallel	Andrew likes to help out by cooking and preparing the bait. (Is Andrew cooking the bait?)
Parallel	Andrew likes to help out by **cooking** and **by preparing** the bait.

● Practice Your Skills

Identifying and Using Parallelism

Rewrite the following sentences, fixing faulty parallelism. If a sentence is parallel, write **C**.

1. Chi likes to write poetry and composing piano music.
2. The group decided on practicing on Saturday or to see a movie on Sunday.
3. The drummer is Randy and Echo is singing.
4. Chi neither arrives on time nor focuses on the music while in practice.
5. The group can't decide whether they are a classical music group or to play jazz.

➤ Transitions

Conjunctive adverbs can also be used as **transitions,** connecting the ideas in one sentence or paragraph to the ideas that came before.

18 B.4 A **transition** is a word or phrase that shows how two subjects or ideas are related.

Mary practiced her lines. **Meanwhile,** the rest of us began painting the sets.

[first sentence of a paragraph] **Finally,** we need to put these ideas into action.

Note that when a conjunctive adverb forms a transition at the beginning of a sentence or paragraph, a comma separates it from the rest of the sentence.

When You Write

Good writing uses transitions effectively. A transition says, "Here is an idea that is related to what you just read." The relationship can be time (*then, finally*), order of importance (*larger still, more importantly*), cause-and-effect (*consequently, as a result*), or disagreement (*nevertheless, on the other hand*).

Look for transitions in a recent piece of writing. Revise to improve the flow of ideas by using effective conjunctive adverbs and transitions.

● Practice Your Skills

Using Transitions

As you rewrite the paragraph, replace each blank with one of these transition words: *after, until, the next morning, before they left, last summer, for two hours.*

I was a gardener for two days ___ when my parents went away on vacation. ___, they told me to water the fruit trees every morning without fail. ___ I was about to water the trees when I had a great idea. I pushed the hose down into the ground so the water would reach the roots more quickly. My idea worked ___ I tried to pull the hose back out. It would not budge. ___ tugging at it ___, I had to cut it off. I ended up spending my whole allowance on a new hose.

▶ Interjections

18 B.5   An **interjection** is a word that expresses strong feeling.

The following is a list of some common interjections.

COMMON INTERJECTIONS					
aha	hooray	oops	ugh	wow	yikes
goodness	oh	ouch	well	yes	yippee

An interjection at the beginning of a sentence is followed by an exclamation point or a comma.

Wow! That was the best catch of the day.

Oh, I love my new puppy!

Do not overuse interjections. They can tire the reader.

Parts of Speech Review

Along with the definitions of words, the dictionary includes abbreviations such as *n., adj.,* and *v.* The word *work,* for example, would first be labeled *n.* for *noun.* This label does not mean that *work* is always a noun. It means that *work* may be used as a noun. A word does not become a part of speech until it is used in a sentence. *Work* can, as a matter of fact, be used as three different parts of speech.

Noun	Success often depends on hard **work.**
Verb	Justin **work**ed very hard.
Adjective	Celia's **work** schedule was tremendous.

To find a word's part of speech, ask yourself, *What is the word doing in this sentence?*

Noun — Is the word naming a person, a place, a thing, or an idea?
Most **farmers** who grow **lettuce** live in **California.**
Compassion is important to all **nurses.**

Pronoun — Is the word taking the place of a noun?
Lana believed **she** would find a job that was good for **her.**

Verb — Is the word showing action? Does it link the subject with another word in the sentence?
Everyone **read** about the American Revolution.
Ben Carson's life story **is** remarkable.

Adjective — Is the word modifying a noun or pronoun? Does it answer the question *What kind? Which one? How many?* or *How much?*
The **gentle** girl became a **famous** nurse.
That flag has a **red** cross.

Adverb — Is the word modifying a verb, an adjective, or another adverb? Does it answer the question *How? When? Where?* or *To what extent?*
Nurses work **quite calmly** in **unusually** difficult situations.

570   Other Parts of Speech and Review

Preposition Is the word showing a relationship between a noun or pronoun and another word in the sentence? Is it a part of a phrase?
During the afternoon we watched a film **about** Pearl Harbor.

Conjunction Is the word connecting words or groups of words?
Go find the iodine **and** some clean bandages.
My brother wanted a new car, **but** Dad decided to fix the old one.

Conjunctive Adverb (adverb used as a conjunction) Is the word creating a transition between two complete ideas?
We were out of milk; **therefore,** we had to go to the store.
The twins had never been on an airplane before. **Indeed,** they'd never seen one before last week.

Interjection Is the word expressing strong feeling?
Wow! I received my first-aid badge.
Hooray! I passed the math test.

● Practice Your Skills

Determining Parts of Speech

Write each underlined word. Then write how it is used in the sentence, using the following abbreviations:

noun = **n.**   adverb = **adv.**   verb = **v.**
preposition = **prep.**   adjective = **adj.**   pronoun = **pro.**
conjunction = **conj.**   interjection = **inter.**   conjunctive adverb = **con. adv.**

1. As a <u>young</u> child, Clara Barton proved to be good <u>at</u> studies.
2. <u>Everyone</u> loved her, <u>and</u> her family encouraged her many interests.
3. Her father <u>sometimes</u> told her exciting adventure stories.
4. <u>Oh</u>, she loved those stories!
5. <u>She</u> owned a turkey and a snapping turtle that <u>frequently</u> frightened children.
6. <u>Goodness</u>, she <u>one</u> day healed a sick dog!
7. Soon, children from other farms <u>brought</u> their <u>dogs</u> to Clara.
8. As a young <u>woman</u>, she cared for wounded soldiers <u>during</u> the Civil War.
9. Many soldiers were saved by the <u>gentle</u> nurse; <u>indeed</u>, she was often called "The Angel of the Battlefield."
10. In later years, <u>Clara</u> <u>founded</u> the American Red Cross.

Parts of Speech Review

● **Practice Your Skills**

Determining Parts of Speech

Write each underlined word. Then identify how it is used in the sentence, using the following abbreviations:

noun = *n.*   adverb = *adv.*   verb = *v.*
preposition = *prep.*   adjective = *adj.*   pronoun = *pro.*
conjunction = *conj.*   interjection = *inter.*   conjunctive adverb = *con. adv.*

During the Middle Ages, most people had only one name. That was fine, as long as everyone stayed put. When cities eventually began to grow, people moved from their farms and villages to the cities. Yikes! Soon there were twenty Marys in one city. That became confusing. Therefore, a solution was needed. Most people began adding information to their names. They generally used one of four methods.

First, a son might take the name of his father. As a result, Henry would become Henry, son of John. Over time, this became Henry Johnson.

Second, people could be named for their features or personalities. A strong person could be named Henry Strong. A person with red hair might take the last name of Reed or Reid. The names Wise, Grim, Moody, and Sharp came about in the same way.

Third, people became identified with the place of their birth. The Woods or the Atwoods, for example, lived near a forest. The Fairbanks family would have come from the edge of a beautiful river or stream.

Fourth, people were named for their occupations. A town's blacksmith might be called Henry the Smith. Later this would become Henry Smith. Similarly, the man who made thatched roofs would be Henry Thatcher, but the man who milled grain into flour would be Henry Miller.

Chapter Review

Assess Your Learning

Finding Prepositions, Conjunctions, Conjunctive Adverbs, Interjections, and Prepositional Phrases

Write each sentence. Label each preposition (**prep.**), conjunction (**conj.**), conjunctive adverb (**con. adv.**), or interjection (**inter.**). Then underline each prepositional phrase.

1. Both pineapple and watermelon were served after dinner.
2. Underneath our car a small kitten was sleeping.
3. Congratulations! You won first prize for your sculpture.
4. Roberto can sing and dance; however, he will not be in the variety show.
5. All members were present, yet no vote was taken.
6. Ouch! A hornet just stung me on my arm and my hand.
7. On a long journey, wild geese often fly in a V-shaped formation.
8. Those strawberries were big but tasteless.
9. Within five minutes the firefighters had the fire under control.
10. Because of so much rain, neither the bananas nor the peaches were ripe.
11. Golf balls were once stuffed with feathers.
12. No! Don't lean against the wet paint.
13. We will get a ride or take the bus.
14. Within ten minutes I will be ready.
15. That box is large but light.
16. Hurray! We won the championship for the second year.
17. Pepper, nutmeg, and mustard are all made from seeds.
18. That wonderful story was written by Raymond.

■ Identifying Parts of Speech

Write each underlined word. Then beside each one, write its part of speech: *noun, pronoun, verb, adjective, adverb, preposition, conjunction,* or *interjection.*

1. Louis, a young boy <u>of</u> five, <u>became</u> the king of <u>France</u> in 1643.
2. <u>He</u> <u>was</u> the king, <u>but</u> he didn't rule.
3. <u>His</u> mother and <u>other</u> adults <u>made</u> the decisions.
4. During <u>much</u> of the boy's <u>childhood</u>, his life was in <u>danger</u>.
5. A <u>group</u> of people <u>wanted</u> a change in the <u>government</u>.
6. <u>Once</u>, the <u>royal</u> family was trapped in the <u>palace</u>.
7. <u>Outside</u>, people <u>yelled</u> and threatened the young king <u>and</u> his family.
8. <u>At</u> sixteen Louis <u>finally</u> <u>became</u> king.
9. He was called the Sun King, and <u>his</u> court was <u>very</u> <u>fancy</u>.
10. <u>According to</u> history books, he acquired <u>much</u> land for France <u>during</u> his reign.

■ Writing Sentences

Write ten sentences that follow the directions below. Then label the use of each word in the sentence.

1. Use *television* as a noun and an adjective.
2. Use *glue* as a noun and a verb.
3. Use *all* as a pronoun and an adjective.
4. Use *over* as an adverb and a preposition.
5. Use *one* as a pronoun and an adjective.
6. Use *inside* as an adverb and a preposition.
7. Use *picture* as a noun and an adjective.
8. Use *these* as a pronoun and an adjective.
9. Use *well* as a noun, an adverb, and an interjection.
10. Use *paper* as a noun, a verb, and an adjective.

Other Parts of Speech and Review: Posttest

Directions
Write the letter of the term that correctly identifies the underlined word or words in each sentence.

(1) The Jarmans took a trip <u>to</u> Portugal. (2) They loved the twisted cobblestone streets <u>and</u> whitewashed houses of Lisbon. (3) One evening, they listened to *fado*, a sad, haunting music that speaks <u>of</u> love and loss. (4) They had never heard anything like it <u>before</u>. (5) The next day, they drove <u>out of</u> the city and into the countryside. (6) <u>Well</u>! They had some adventures there! (7) First, their car broke down <u>outside the palaces</u> of Sintra. (8) The townspeople, <u>friendly</u> and concerned, helped them find a new rental car. (9) The Jarmans spoke no Portuguese, and the townspeople spoke no English, <u>yet</u> they managed to communicate. (10) Finally, the Jarmans were <u>on their way</u> again.

1. **A** preposition
   B adverb
   C conjunction
   D interjection

2. **A** preposition
   B adverb
   C conjunction
   D interjection

3. **A** preposition
   B adverb
   C conjunction
   D interjection

4. **A** preposition
   B adverb
   C conjunction
   D interjection

5. **A** preposition
   B adverb
   C conjunction
   D interjection

6. **A** preposition
   B adverb
   C conjunction
   D interjection

7. **A** prepositional phrase
   B adverb
   C conjunction
   D verb phrase

8. **A** preposition
   B adverb
   C adjective
   D noun

9. **A** preposition
   B adverb
   C conjunction
   D interjection

10. **A** prepositional phrase
    B adverb
    C verb phrase
    D interjection

Writer's Corner

Snapshot

18 A A **preposition** is a word that shows the relationship between a noun or a pronoun and another word in the sentence. (pages 560–565)

18 B A **conjunction** connects words or groups of words; an **interjection** shows strong feeling. (pages 566–569)

Power Rules

 Use **subject forms of pronouns** in the subject position. Use **object forms of pronouns** when the pronoun is a direct object, an indirect object, or an object of a preposition. (pages 710–720)

Before Editing

Them and *me* are in the spring play.

Mom made lunch for Shelby and *he*.

After Editing

They and *I* are in the spring play.

Mom made lunch for Shelby and *him*.

 Check for **run-on sentences** and separate them by adding a conjunction and/or punctuation. (pages 668–670)

Before Editing

I need to get my homework done, I don't have the books I need.

We could go to a movie, maybe we could go to the park instead.

After Editing

I need to get my homework done, *but* I don't have the books I need.

We could go to a movie, *or* maybe we could go to the park instead.

Editing Checklist

Use this checklist when editing your writing.

✓ Did I use precise prepositions to show relationships? (See pages 560–562.)
✓ Did I write sentences using prepositions and adverbs? (See pages 560–565.)
✓ Did I use conjunctions to connect words and ideas? (See page 566.)
✓ Did I use conjunctive adverbs to create transitions and show the relationships between ideas? (See page 567.)
✓ Did I use interjections when necessary to show strong emotions or feelings? (See page 569.)
✓ Did I use the parts of speech correctly? (See pages 570–571.)

Use the Power

Prepositions are often used to add location information to a sentence. Compare these two sentences.

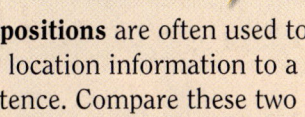

Alfonso thought he saw a bat.

Alfonso thought he saw a bat **outside his bedroom window.**

Play a preposition game. With a partner, select a small object such a pencil. Then give each other directions that include prepositional phrases: "Place the pencil under the table." "On your hand, balance the pencil."

Select a piece from your portfolio and highlight the transitions. If there are no transitions, add some! Experiment by using different conjunctive adverbs until you get the relationship between your ideas just right.

Complements

How can you use complements to focus your writing?

Complements: Pretest 1

The following first draft makes no sense because several sentences are incomplete. Revise the draft so that it makes more sense. The first incomplete sentence has been edited as an example.

> The final baseball game of the season had begun. The crowd was *excited*. The school team wore. They looked. The rival team was. In the second inning, the school team was up, and the bases were loaded. Justin hit. It sailed out over right field. Would the right fielder catch? No, he missed. The right fielder scooped up and threw. One player had already run home, and another was rounding third base. Justin reached third base as another player ran. However, the catcher now had, so Justin stayed on third. The cheers were. With three runs, the school team was.

Complements: Pretest 2

Directions
Write the letter of the term that correctly identifies the underlined word in each sentence.

(1) One of the greatest ancient Greek arts was architecture. **(2)** The Greeks built Athena a temple. **(3)** *Parthenon* is the name of this temple. **(4)** The Parthenon is very beautiful. **(5)** The Greeks constructed the Parthenon between 447 and 432 B.C. **(6)** Much Greek art glorified humans. **(7)** It also gave the gods thanks for life and fortune. **(8)** Their sculptures showed the perfection of humans. **(9)** The ancient Greeks also produced great thinkers. **(10)** Socrates was a famous philosopher.

1. **A** direct object
   B indirect object
   C predicate nominative
   D predicate adjective

2. **A** direct object
   B indirect object
   C predicate nominative
   D predicate adjective

3. **A** direct object
   B indirect object
   C predicate nominative
   D predicate adjective

4. **A** direct object
   B indirect object
   C predicate nominative
   D predicate adjective

5. **A** direct object
   B indirect object
   C predicate nominative
   D predicate adjective

6. **A** direct object
   B indirect object
   C predicate nominative
   D predicate adjective

7. **A** direct object
   B indirect object
   C predicate nominative
   D predicate adjective

8. **A** direct object
   B indirect object
   C predicate nominative
   D predicate adjective

9. **A** direct object
   B indirect object
   C predicate nominative
   D predicate adjective

10. **A** direct object
    B indirect object
    C predicate nominative
    D predicate adjective

Kinds of Complements

A sentence must have a subject and a verb. Some sentences, however, need another word to complete the meaning of the sentence. By themselves, the following subjects and verbs are not complete statements.

> Birds build.
>
> Lions seem.

19 A A **complement** is a word that is necessary to complete the meaning of a sentence.

> Birds build **nests.**
>
> Lions seem **hungry.**

There are four common kinds of complements. **Direct objects** and **indirect objects** follow action verbs. **Predicate nominatives** and **predicate adjectives**, called **subject complements**, follow linking verbs.

Direct Object	The robin built a **nest**.
Indirect Object	The robin fed its **young**.
Predicate Nominative	The robin is my favorite **bird**.
Predicate Adjective	The robin is **glorious**.

Direct and Indirect Objects

All direct objects are usually nouns or pronouns.

19 B A **direct object** is a noun or pronoun that answers the question *What?* or *Whom?* after an action verb. An **indirect object** is a noun or pronoun that answers the question *To or for whom?* or *To or for what?* after an action verb.

To find a direct object, first find the subject and the action verb in a sentence. Then ask yourself, *What or whom receives the action of the verb?* The answer to the question will be a direct object. In the example sentences below, subjects are underlined once and verbs are underlined twice. Notice that the direct object comes after the verb.

Direct Objects
Sharks have many **teeth.**
(Sharks have what? *Teeth* is the direct object.)

Predators know **them** very well.
(Predators know whom? *Them* is the direct object.)

To find the direct object in a question, change the question into a statement.

Question Did you see the eagles?
Statement You did see the **eagles.**

Two or more direct objects together are called a **compound direct object.**

Compound Direct Object
Adam bought a **camera** and **binoculars.**
(Adam bought what? The compound direct object is *camera* and *binoculars.*)

Verbs that are followed by a direct object are called transitive verbs. You can learn more about action verbs and transitive verbs on pages 522–525.

● Practice Your Skills

Finding Direct Objects

Write each direct object.

1. Ducks will lay eggs only in the morning.
2. You can make eleven omelets with an ostrich egg.
3. Chimpanzees use twigs and rocks as tools.
4. A robin has almost three thousand feathers.
5. Did you see eagles on your trip to the lake?

To find an indirect object, first find the direct object. Then ask yourself, *To whom? For whom? To what?* or *For what?* about the direct object. The answer to any of these questions will be an indirect object. Remember that in order to have an indirect object, a sentence must have a direct object.

Indirect Object	Ken bought **Nathan** three hamburgers. (*Hamburgers* is the direct object. Ken bought the hamburgers for whom? *Nathan* is the indirect object.)
Indirect Object	The yellow paint gave the **playscape** a bright appearance. (*Appearance* is the direct object. The paint gave a bright appearance to what? *Playscape* is the indirect object.)

Notice that an indirect object always comes before a direct object in a sentence. To find the indirect object in a question, change the question into a statement.

Question	Will you show everyone that watermelon?
Statement	You will show **everyone** that watermelon. (i.o., d.o.)

Two or more indirect objects together are called a **compound indirect object.**

Compound Indirect Object	Dad gave **Gene** and **Lani** his old football. (i.o., i.o., d.o.) (Dad gave the football to whom? The compound indirect object is *Gene* and *Lani*.)

When You Write

Sometimes using an indirect object is awkward. A prepositional phrase can often make the sentence read more clearly.

Indirect Object	Ted brought **the children** ice cream sandwiches.
Prepositional Phrase	Ted brought ice cream sandwiches **for the children.**

Review a recent composition. Revise awkward indirect objects by changing them to prepositional phrases.

Complements

● *Connect to Writing:* **E-mail Message**

Using Direct and Indirect Objects

Your mother is away on business and wants to know what you have been doing in school. Compose an e-mail message that tells her what you have learned this week. Use direct and indirect objects in your message.

● **Practice Your Skills**

Finding Indirect Objects

Write each indirect object.

1. We fed the ducks bread crumbs.
2. Dad cooked us hamburgers on the grill.
3. Sara showed us the delicious dessert.
4. Will you pass me the ketchup?
5. My mom found everyone at the picnic a shady spot for lunch.

✔ **Check Point:** **Mixed Practice**

Write each complement in the following sentences. Then label each one *direct object* or *indirect object*.

1. Have you ever eaten an artichoke or an avocado?
2. I tasted both at the food fair.
3. Anton cooked everyone a Mexican meal.
4. Grandmother made Martina and me sweet potato candy.
5. For decoration, people sometimes put flowers on cakes.
6. Please pass us the egg rolls and the chopsticks from the Asian display.
7. Did you show him the stuffed pitas?
8. Two new students were nibbling scones and biscuits at the fair.
9. Anna showed Peter and Maria her cooking project.
10. Mrs. Pallone kept the same booth as last year.

Direct and Indirect Objects • Lesson 2

Predicate Nominatives and Predicate Adjectives

Direct and indirect objects follow action verbs. Two other kinds of complements follow linking verbs. They are called **subject complements** because they identify, rename, or describe the subject. One kind of subject complement is called a predicate nominative, and the other is called a predicate adjective.

> **19 C** A **predicate nominative** is a noun or a pronoun that follows a linking verb and identifies, renames, or explains the subject. A **predicate adjective** is an adjective that follows a linking verb and modifies the subject.

To find subject complements, you must be able to recognize linking verbs.

You can learn more about linking verbs on pages 528–530.

COMMON LINKING VERBS	
Be Verbs	is, are, am, was, were, be, being, been, shall be, will be, can be, should be, would be, may be, might be, has been
Others	appear, become, feel, grow, look, remain, seem, smell, sound, stay, taste, turn

To find a predicate nominative, first find the subject and the verb. Check to see if the verb is a linking verb. Then find the noun or the pronoun that identifies, renames, or explains the subject. This word will always be a predicate nominative. In the following examples, the arrows point to the subjects and the predicate nominatives.

Predicate Nominatives That park is a **preserve**.
(The predicate nominative *preserve* renames the subject *park*.)

The U.S.A. has become a powerful **country**.
(The predicate nominative *country* renames the subject *U.S.A.*)

Two or more predicate nominatives together are called a **compound predicate nominative**.

Compound Predicate Nominative The states of most interest were **Texas** and **New York**.
(Both predicate nominatives, *Texas* and *New York,* rename the subject *states*.)

Notice that a predicate nominative can never be part of a prepositional phrase.

Iceland is **one** of the islands near the Arctic Circle.
(The predicate nominative *one* identifies the subject *Iceland*. *Islands* is not the predicate nominative because it is part of the prepositional phrase *of the islands*.)

● **Practice Your Skills**

Finding Predicate Nominatives

Write each predicate nominative.

1. Diamonds are extremely hard and rare stones.
2. The prairie sunsets were spectacular sights.
3. Those huge trees are maples.
4. The main resources of South Asia are soil, water, and climate.
5. The longest rivers in the world are the Amazon and the Nile.

● **Practice Your Skills**

Supplying Predicate Nominatives

Write a predicate nominative that completes each sentence. Beside the predicate nominative, write the word it renames. If you use a pronoun as a predicate nominative, use only *I, you, he, she, it, we,* or *they.*

1. My favorite musician is ___.
2. My favorite musical instrument is the ___.
3. My brother Roy will become a ___.
4. The instrument featured is a ___.
5. Their soloist is a ___.
6. Eric is a ___.
7. Mrs. Davis is my ___.

● *Connect to Writing:* **Revising**

Revising Sentences with Predicate Nominatives

Rewrite the following sentences so that they contain a different predicate nominative.

(1) When I grow up, I want to be a musician. **(2)** My favorite instrument is the piano. **(3)** My favorite types of music are classical and jazz. **(4)** One of the best schools for the study of music is Juilliard.

Predicate Nominatives and Predicate Adjectives • Lesson 3

Predicate Adjectives

The second kind of a subject complement is the **predicate adjective**.

To find a predicate adjective, first find the subject and the verb. Check to see if the verb is a linking verb. Then find an adjective that follows the verb and describes the subject. This word will be the predicate adjective.

| **Predicate Adjectives** | The bear's den was very **warm**. (The predicate adjective *warm* describes the subject *den—warm den*.)

 Recently the weather has become **warmer**. (The predicate adjective *warmer* describes the subject *weather—warmer weather*.) |

Two or more predicate adjectives together are called a **compound predicate adjective**.

| **Compound Predicate Adjectives** | These bears are **big** and **powerful**. (The predicate adjectives *big* and *powerful* both describe the subject *bears*.)

 The dens of the bears look **dark** and **warm**. (The predicate adjectives *dark* and *warm* both describe *dens*.) |

You can learn more about adjectives on pages 538–546 and 766–780.

● **Practice Your Skills**

Finding Predicate Adjectives

Write each predicate adjective. (Some sentences may have a compound predicate adjective.)

1. That polar bear is hungry again.
2. Its claws are long and sharp.
3. Polar bears seem cuddly.
4. The Arctic winter is dark and cold.
5. The mother polar bear appears thin after the long winter season.

● **Practice Your Skills**

Supplying Predicate Adjectives

Write a predicate adjective that completes each sentence. Avoid overused adjectives such as *good, nice,* and **wonderful.**

1. All of the original poems that Terry wrote are ___.
2. During her oral presentation, Dawn looked ___.
3. The poet was ___.
4. After waiting thirty minutes for the presentation to start, the class became ___.
5. After finishing her writing projects, Natalie always seemed so ___.
6. After her presentation, Alana appeared ___.
7. That new poem sounds ___.

✓ **Check Point: Mixed Practice**

Write each complement in the following sentences. Label each complement **predicate nominative** or **predicate adjective.**

(1) Television became very popular in the 1950s. (2) *Howdy Doody* was a favorite children's program of the time. (3) The characters Howdy Doody and Clarabelle the Clown were comical. (4) For more than twenty million teenagers, the most popular show in the late 1950s was *American Bandstand*. (5) Davy Crockett was one of the most admired TV characters of the decade. (6) Davy Crockett was a frontiersman. (7) Popular clothes for boys during those years were chino pants and motorcycle jackets. (8) Pedal pushers, bobby socks, and poodle skirts were fashionable for girls. (9) Hula hoops became a fad in 1958. (10) TV dinners in little aluminum foil dishes first became popular in 1954.

● *Connect to Writing:* **Field Notes**

Using Predicate Nominatives and Predicate Adjectives

Your science club has assigned you to research the bats that live in your area. Write a short paragraph that describes the habitat and behavior of the bats of your region. If feasible, observe bats in your neighborhood and include your notes in your report. Use at least one predicate nominative and one predicate adjective in your paragraph.

Sentence Patterns

Nearly every sentence you write follows one of five different patterns. Each pattern may be expanded by adding modifiers and prepositional phrases.

PATTERN 1: S-V (subject–verb)

    S   V
Clocks chime.
        S   V
Certain clocks in the store chime on the hour.

PATTERN 2: S-V-O (subject–verb–direct object)

    S   V   O
Roots prevent erosion.
      S   V   O
The roots of trees often prevent erosion of the soil.

PATTERN 3: S-V-I-O (subject–verb–indirect object–direct object)

     S   V   I   O
Aunt May sends me postcards.
      S   V   I   O
My Aunt May frequently sends me postcards from Idaho.

PATTERN 4: S-V-N (subject–verb–predicate nominative)

    S   V   N
Dogs are friends.
      S   V   N
Dogs of all sizes usually are excellent friends.

PATTERN 5: S-V-A (subject–verb–predicate adjective)

    S   V   A
Books are expensive.
     S   V   A
Books about art are often quite expensive.

To find the pattern of a certain sentence, drop all the modifiers and prepositional phrases.

             S   V   O
~~My~~ grandparents own ~~a small~~ farm ~~in Nebraska~~.

● **Practice Your Skills**

Determining Sentence Patterns

Write the sentence pattern that each sentence follows.

1. The branches of the old tree swayed in the wind.
2. Everyone in the audience grew very restless.
3. A hen often turns its eggs.
4. One of my neighbors is a farmer.
5. The small kitten raced around the room.
6. Some Chinese typewriters have 5,700 keys.
7. The blacksmith gave the black horse a new shoe.
8. The evening air suddenly felt very cold.
9. The secretary in the office gave me an application.
10. That song is this week's top single.

● **Practice Your Skills**

Expanding Sentence Patterns

Expand each sentence by adding modifiers or prepositional phrases or both.

1. (S-V) Eagles fly.
2. (S-V-O) Judges presented medals.
3. (S-V-I-O) Friends gave us presents.
4. (S-V-N) Neighbors are students.
5. (S-V-A) Photographs are old.
6. (S-V) Jake studies.
7. (S-V-O) Ms. Ubach reads stories.
8. (S-V-I-O) Mom sent Dad flowers.
9. (S-V-N) We have been friends.
10. (S-V-A) Hikers were weary.

● *Connect to Writing:* **Introductions**

Using Sentence Patterns

The guidance counselor has asked you to introduce a new student to your classmates and show the newcomer around the school tomorrow. You decide to write a few notes that will help you remember what to tell the new student. Write introductions about some of the people in your class. Use all five of the sentence patterns listed on the previous page. Label the parts of each sentence.

Sentence Diagraming

Diagraming Complements

A subject, a verb, and sometimes a complement make up the **sentence base**. Complements are diagramed on the baseline or are attached to it.

Direct Objects A direct object is placed on the baseline after the verb. The direct object and the verb are separated by a short vertical line. Notice in the second example that the parts of a compound direct object are placed on parallel horizontal lines. The conjunction is placed on a broken line.

That camera takes clear pictures.

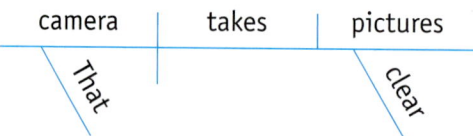

The team manager thoroughly cleaned the uniforms and the equipment.

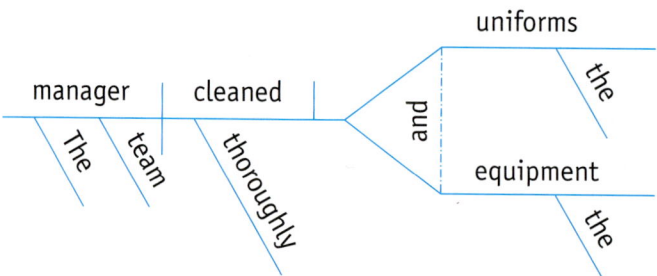

Indirect Objects An indirect object is diagramed on a horizontal line that is connected to the verb by a slanted line. Notice in the second example that the parts of a compound indirect object are diagramed on parallel horizontal lines. The conjunction is placed on a broken line.

The school counselor gave Beth some good advice.

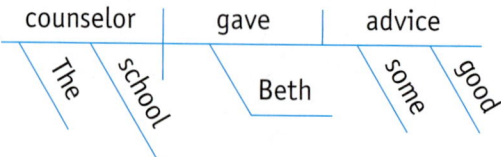

Complements

Give Carla and Rick our concert tickets.

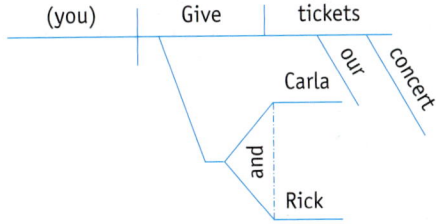

Subject Complements The predicate nominative and the predicate adjective are diagramed alike. They are placed on the baseline after the verb. These subject complements are separated from the verb by a slanted line that points back toward the subject. The first example below shows how to diagram a predicate nominative. The second example shows how to diagram a predicate adjective.

The trophies were small bronze statues.

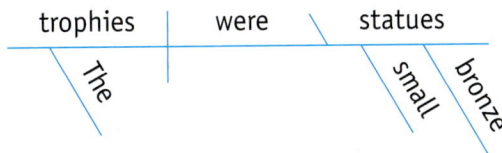

Our house is very old.

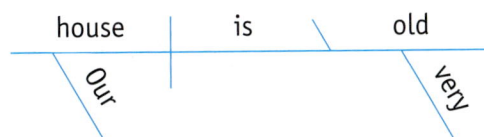

Notice in the next example that the parts of a compound subject complement are placed on parallel lines. The conjunction is placed on a broken line.

His favorite foods are corn dogs and hamburgers.

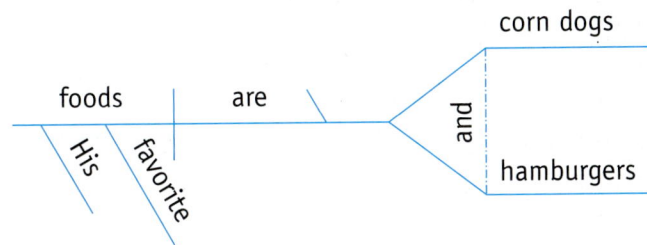

Sentence Diagraming 591

Each of the following examples has a compound predicate adjective. The two adjectives are placed on parallel lines. The conjunction is placed on a broken line.

The leather belt feels soft and smooth.

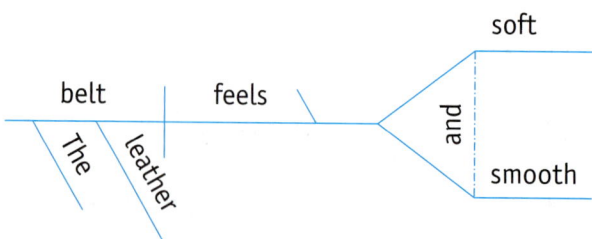

The soup was cold and watery.

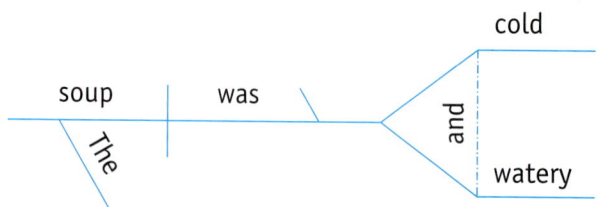

● **Practice Your Skills**

Diagraming Complements

Diagram the following sentences or copy them. If you copy them, draw one line under each subject and two lines under each verb. Then label each complement with the following abbreviations:

direct object = **d.o.**   predicate nominative = **p.n.**
indirect object = **i.o.**   predicate adjective = **p.a.**

1. Animals set boundaries.
2. These boundaries are exact.
3. Usually a territory is a safe place.
4. They give animals courage.
5. A small dog will chase a larger dog.
6. A territory usually includes space and food.
7. The spring day was clear and crisp.
8. The bird songs were signals and markers.
9. Have you heard these beautiful melodies?
10. Our teacher promised the other students and me more information about boundaries.

Chapter Review

Assess Your Learning

■ Finding Direct and Indirect Objects

Write each complement. Then label each one *direct object* or *indirect object.* (Some sentences have compound complements.)

1. Christopher Columbus brought cattle to America on his second voyage.
2. The director gave the actors their scripts for the play.
3. The United States once issued a five-cent bill.
4. I have the key to the apartment.
5. Mr. David gave Marita and me a project.

■ Finding Subject Complements

Write each complement. Then label each one *predicate nominative* or *predicate adjective.* (Some sentences have compound complements.)

1. Many animals are record holders.
2. The giraffe's neck, for example, is the longest.
3. The outstanding feature of the albatross is its wings.
4. Its twelve-foot wingspan is quite impressive.
5. The puma appears normal on the ground.
6. Then this cat becomes a bird or an Olympic jumper.
7. The remarkable puma is the champion of the twenty-three-foot-high jump from a standing position.
8. The tiger is also athletic and energetic.
9. The tiger, however, remains a distant second to the puma.
10. The tiger's highest jump is only thirteen feet.

■ Identifying Complements

Write each complement. Then label each one *direct object, indirect object, predicate nominative,* or *predicate adjective.*

1. Samuel Wilson was only a boy in 1775.
2. Nevertheless, he played an important role in the American Revolution.
3. Immediately after Paul Revere's ride through town, Sam told the people in each house the bad news.
4. His father and brother were Minutemen.

5. Years later the government gave Sam the job of meat inspector.
6. Uncle Sam became his nickname.
7. Someone drew a picture of Sam.
8. This picture eventually became a symbol of the United States.
9. "Uncle Sam" was famous overnight.
10. The workers in the meat plant were proud of their old friend with the white pointed beard.

Using Complements

Write five sentences that follow the directions below. (The sentences may come in any order.) Write about one of the following topics or a topic of your own choice: a recent movie you have seen or book you have read.

Write a sentence that . . .
1. includes a direct object.
2. includes an indirect object and a direct object.
3. includes a predicate nominative.
4. includes a predicate adjective.
5. includes a compound predicate adjective.

Then underline and label each complement.

Complements: Posttest

Directions
Write the letter of the term that correctly identifies the underlined word in each sentence.

(1) Marianne ran her first <u>marathon</u> in October. (2) Marianne was the youngest <u>racer</u> in her group. (3) The other runners in the competition seemed much <u>older</u>. (4) Marianne stretched her <u>muscles</u> first. (5) She gave <u>herself</u> fifteen minutes to warm up. (6) The official blew his <u>whistle</u>. (7) Marianne's pace was <u>slow</u> at first. (8) The course was very <u>hilly</u>. (9) Several hills on the path were a real <u>challenge</u> for Marianne. (10) People on the sidelines passed <u>Marianne</u> glasses of water.

1. **A** direct object
   B indirect object
   C predicate nominative
   D predicate adjective

2. **A** direct object
   B indirect object
   C predicate nominative
   D predicate adjective

3. **A** direct object
   B indirect object
   C predicate nominative
   D predicate adjective

4. **A** direct object
   B indirect object
   C predicate nominative
   D predicate adjective

5. **A** direct object
   B indirect object
   C predicate nominative
   D predicate adjective

6. **A** direct object
   B indirect object
   C predicate nominative
   D predicate adjective

7. **A** direct object
   B indirect object
   C predicate nominative
   D predicate adjective

8. **A** direct object
   B indirect object
   C predicate nominative
   D predicate adjective

9. **A** direct object
   B indirect object
   C predicate nominative
   D predicate adjective

10. **A** direct object
    B indirect object
    C predicate nominative
    D predicate adjective

Writer's Corner

Snapshot

19 A A **complement** is a word that is necessary to complete the meaning of a sentence. (page 580)

19 B A **direct object** is a noun or pronoun that answers the question *What?* or *Whom?* after an action verb. An **indirect object** is a noun or pronoun that answers the question *To or for whom?* or *To or for what?* after an action verb. (pages 581–583)

19 C A **predicate nominative** is a noun or a pronoun that follows a linking verb and identifies, renames, or explains the subject. A **predicate adjective** is an adjective that follows a linking verb and modifies the subject. (pages 584–587)

Power Rules

 When writing a sentence that renames the subject, be sure you use the **subject form** of the pronoun. (pages 583, 713–715)

Before Editing

The best student is *him*.

It will be *them* who will finish the project.

The winners are *her* and *me*.

After Editing

The best student is *he*.

It will be *they* who will finish the project.

The winners are *she* and *I*.

Editing Checklist

Use this checklist when editing your writing.

✓ Did I complete each idea, wherever complements were needed? (See page 580.)

✓ Did I use the object form of a pronoun for a direct or an indirect object? (See pages 581–583.)

✓ Did I use the subject form of a pronoun for a predicate nominative? (See page 585.)

Use the Power

Complements help you add variety and detail to your sentences. Without them the English language would be a rather poor vehicle for communicating ideas. Consider these sentences.

The opossum is. The female carries.

Complements allow you to complete the ideas.

The opossum is a **marsupial.** The female carries **her young.**

By modifying complements you can add a great deal of detail.

The opossum is the only North American **marsupial.** The female carries **her young** in a pouch.

Review a composition you completed recently. Underline and identify complements in five sentences. Can you provide more detail by modifying the complements?

CHAPTER 20

Phrases

How can you add precision and variety to your writing with phrases?

Phrases: Pretest 1

The following first draft is difficult to read because several phrases have been misplaced. The first phrase error has been corrected as an example. Revise the draft so that all phrases are used correctly.

This week the students *in our class* visited the city zoo ~~from our class~~. We arrived early and headed first to see the chimpanzee house. A sign said that a chimpanzee had just been born near the entrance. Among the tree branches we watched the chimps playing. A picture of a lion showed us where the big cats could be found on the map. In the enclosure we watched the tiger pace back and forth. At feeding time, the zookeeper gave big pieces of meat to the big cats with special vitamins added. In one building, a huge window let us see into a lake. Underwater we could see what life was like. I hope we can go to the zoo again.

Phrases: Pretest 2

Directions
Write the letter of the term that correctly identifies the underlined word or group of words in each sentence.

(1) Galen, <u>a Greek physician</u>, made many important observations in Egypt. (2) <u>Because of</u> Galen's studies, medicine became a part of European science. (3) Arabs <u>of the Middle East</u> also studied medicine. (4) Persian doctors practiced <u>in Baghdad</u> in the 700s. (5) They traveled <u>from town to town</u> with their medical offices. (6) These Persians, <u>skillful doctors</u>, rode camels. (7) The Muslims moved <u>into</u> Spain in 711 with their medical knowledge. (8) There, students <u>of medicine</u> learned the Persian techniques. (9) Italian professors, <u>teachers of the Roman methods</u>, added Muslim medical knowledge to their curriculum. (10) Arab scholars were also known <u>for mathematics</u>.

1. A preposition
   B adjectival phrase
   C adverbial phrase
   D appositive phrase

2. A preposition
   B adjectival phrase
   C adverbial phrase
   D appositive phrase

3. A preposition
   B adjectival phrase
   C adverbial phrase
   D appositive phrase

4. A preposition
   B adjectival phrase
   C adverbial phrase
   D appositive phrase

5. A preposition
   B adjectival phrase
   C adverbial phrase
   D appositive phrase

6. A preposition
   B adjectival phrase
   C adverbial phrase
   D appositive phrase

7. A preposition
   B adjectival phrase
   C adverbial phrase
   D appositive phrase

8. A preposition
   B adjectival phrase
   C adverbial phrase
   D appositive phrase

9. A preposition
   B adjectival phrase
   C adverbial phrase
   D appositive phrase

10. A preposition
    B adjectival phrase
    C adverbial phrase
    D appositive phrase

Prepositional Phrases

Unlike a sentence, a phrase does not have a subject or a verb. A **phrase** is a group of related words that acts as a single part of speech.

20 A A **prepositional phrase** is a group of words that begins with a preposition, ends with a noun or a pronoun, and is used as an adjective or adverb.

Since all prepositional phrases begin with a preposition, you should be familiar with the following list of common prepositions. Notice that some prepositions have more than one word. These prepositions, such as *because of,* are called **compound prepositions.**

COMMON PREPOSITIONS

about	below	inside	to
above	beneath	into	toward
according to	beside	like	under
across	between	near	underneath
after	beyond	of	until
against	by	off	up
along	down	on	upon
among	during	out of	up to
around	except	over	with
at	for	past	within
because of	from	since	without
before	in	through	
behind	in front of	throughout	

Prepositional Phrases

The story **of Cesar Chavez** is interesting.

He worked **throughout his lifetime.**

Practice Your Skills

Finding Prepositional Phrases

Write each prepositional phrase.

1. Cesar Chavez was born in 1927 in the Southwest near Yuma, Arizona.
2. He would later become an important leader of farm workers.
3. After the stock market crash in 1929, the Chavez family became migrant farm workers.
4. Chavez enlisted in the Navy during World War II.
5. In 1952, he was recruited by Fred Ross as a worker for the Community Service Organization, or CSO.
6. With the CSO, Cesar Chavez worked for the aid of the poor.
7. By 1958, Cesar Chavez had become the national director of the CSO.
8. He resigned from the CSO in 1962 and started a farm workers' union.
9. Cesar Chavez changed the system through nonviolent means.
10. With his dedication, he helped many migrant farm workers.

Adjectival Phrases

An adjectival phrase is a prepositional phrase used like a single adjective.

Single Adjective   A **quiet** street borders the Seine riverbank.

Adjectival Phrase   A street **with many cafes** borders the Seine riverbank.

Notice that both the adjective *quiet* and the prepositional phrase *with many cafes* tell something about the word *street*.

20 A.1 An **adjectival phrase** is a prepositional phrase that modifies a noun or pronoun.

An adjectival phrase also answers the same question that a single adjective answers: *Which one?* or *What kind?* In the following sentences, an arrow goes from each adjectival phrase to the word it describes.

Which One?   The postcard **of Paris** is mine.

I prefer the picture **of the** *Mona Lisa*.

What Kind?   James likes stories **about medieval Paris.**

We need a hotel room **with four beds.**

An adjectival phrase comes directly after the noun it modifies. Of course, a sentence can have more than one adjectival phrase. An adjectival phrase can also modify a pronoun, as in the first example below.

One **of my friends** wrote a report **about Paris.**

The Louvre **in Paris** is a museum **of exceptional quality.**

● **Practice Your Skills**

Finding Adjectival Phrases

Write each adjectival phrase.

1. The most famous city in France is Paris.
2. Paris is the capital of France.
3. It is one of the largest French cities.
4. Paris is also one of the major European cities.
5. Each of the twenty districts within Paris has its own mayor.
6. The most famous painting at the Louvre is the *Mona Lisa*.
7. The street in front of the Louvre is called the Triumphal Way.
8. A famous architect completed a renovation of the Louvre.
9. The view from the Eiffel Tower is breathtaking.
10. The sidewalk beneath the tower is a popular tourist area.

● **Practice Your Skills**

Finding the Words Adjectival Phrases Modify

Write each adjectival phrase. Then write the word that the phrase modifies.

1. The lake beyond those hills has an excellent sailing course.
2. One of my friends owns a sailboat.
3. The dock across the lake is vacant.
4. Six friends on the committee organized a pancake breakfast for the sailors.
5. The sailboat with the torn sail left the race.

● *Connect to Writing:* **News Article**

Using Adjectival Phrases

Your sports club has asked you to write an article about your team for the local newspaper. Describe different team members and their positions. Be sure to use adjectival phrases in your description. Underline the phrases you used.

Misplaced Adjectival Phrases

An adjectival phrase should never get too far from the word it describes.

20 A.2 When an adjectival phrase is placed too far from the word it describes, it is called a **misplaced modifier.** A misplaced modifier can confuse readers.

Misplaced Modifiers	The teacher gave the popcorn to the children **without butter or salt.** (Because the phrase is misplaced, the sentence seems to be saying that only children without butter or salt got the popcorn.)
	On the moon Tad gave a talk about the huge craters. (Because of this misplaced modifier, a reader would think that Tad was on the moon.)

To correct a misplaced modifier, place the adjectival phrase next to the word it describes.

Correct Modifiers	The teacher gave the popcorn **without butter or salt** to the children. (The popcorn is without butter or salt, not the children.)
	Tad gave a talk about the huge craters **on the moon.** (Now the craters, not Tad, are on the moon.)

● **Practice Your Skills**

Finding Misplaced Adjectival Phrases

Write each misplaced adjectival phrase.

1. Our teacher in the cafeteria talked about good manners.
2. The librarian gave books without library cards to the children.
3. Our school has many activities for students with no sports emphasis.
4. The school has an excellent academic record beyond that street.
5. That unusually large classroom is vacant across the hall.
6. The best teacher is Mrs. Emerson in the English department.
7. The shady area is called the Peace Garden in front of our school.
8. That student was lost from another school.

● *Connect to Writing:* **Editing**

Correcting Sentences with Misplaced Adjectival Phrases

Rewrite five of the sentences above fixing the misplaced adjectival phrases.

Adverbial Phrases

Like a single adverb, a prepositional phrase can describe a verb. This kind of phrase is called an **adverbial phrase.**

Single Adverb   The snail crawled **slowly.**

Adverbial Phrase   The snail crawled **at a slow pace.**

The adverb *slowly* and the adverbial phrase *at a slow pace* tell how the snail crawled.

20 A.3   An **adverbial phrase** is a prepositional phrase that is used mainly to modify a verb.

Because an adverbial phrase does the same job as a single adverb, it also answers the same questions: *Where? When?* or *How?* Occasionally an adverbial phrase will also answer the question *Why?*

Where?   Everyone went **to the garden.**

              The snail crept **toward the house.**

When?   They waited **for a few minutes.**

              Within the hour the snail arrived.

How?   **With a smile** Maria watched the snail.

              Without any directions the snail found the garden.

Why?   He waited **because of the terrible storm.**

              Snails eat plants **for survival.**

As the preceding examples show, an adverbial phrase can come anywhere in a sentence. In the following example, notice that the phrase modifies the whole verb phrase.

During science class I must finish this snail project.

Just like adjectival phrases, more than one adverbial phrase can be in a sentence, and two or more adverbial phrases can modify the same verb.

For three hours snails have been eating **in the garden.**

PUNCTUATION WITH ADVERBIAL PHRASES

If a short adverbial phrase comes at the beginning of a sentence, usually no comma is needed. However, a comma should be placed after an introductory adverbial phrase of four or more words or one that ends in a date.

No Comma	**From the deck** you can see the garden.
Comma	**From the front deck,** you can see the garden.
	In 1998, only a few snails lived in the garden.

● **Practice Your Skills**

Finding Adverbial Phrases

Write each adverbial phrase. Beside each one, write the word it modifies.

(1) The baseball whizzed by the batter. **(2)** A hush descended over the crowd. **(3)** Within a few innings, David Cone would have pitched a perfect baseball game. **(4)** Toward the eighth inning, the fans became quiet. **(5)** Cone looked around the baseball field carefully. **(6)** The catcher sent the signals across the field. **(7)** Anxious faces appeared in the dugout. **(8)** David Cone pitched the entire game without a base runner. **(9)** After the game he celebrated and thanked the fans. **(10)** This perfect baseball game will live forever in sports history.

● *Connect to Writing:* **Editing**

Punctuating Adverbial Phrases

Edit the following sentences for proper use of commas with adverbial phrases. If a sentence is correct, write **C**.

(1) In Cooperstown, you will find the Baseball Hall of Fame. **(2)** Until last week, I had no idea where it was, although **(3)** on several occasions, my sister has visited there. **(4)** In the spring my family toured it. **(5)** In the famous hall we learned about the players.

Connect to Writing: Friendly Letter

Using Adverbial Phrases

Your family watches a baseball game in this large stadium as part of your vacation. Write a letter to your cousin that tells about the stadium and the game you saw there. Use adverbial phrases correctly.

✓ Check Point: Mixed Practice

Write each prepositional phrase. Label each one as an adjective or an adverb.

(1) Basketball was invented in 1891. (2) At the time no major sport was played in winter. (3) A man at a Massachusetts YMCA school had an idea. (4) This man was James A. Naismith, the father of basketball. (5) Naismith had no money for fancy equipment. (6) In a hall he nailed peach baskets on opposite walls. (7) The game's name came from the peach baskets.

Appositives and Appositive Phrases

20 B An **appositive** is a noun or pronoun that identifies or explains another noun or pronoun in the sentence.

When you write, you often need to explain or identify a noun or a pronoun for your reader. To do this, add another noun or pronoun called an appositive.

Next is Gino's favorite class, **physical education.**
(*Physical education* is the appositive. It explains what Gino's favorite class is.)

Leroy and Guy, **the captains,** meet with the coach.
(*The captains* identifies who Leroy and Guy are. *The captains* is the appositive.)

When an appositive has one or more modifiers, it is called an **appositive phrase.**

That shoe, **the one with the black sole,** belongs to my brother.
(*The one with the black sole* is the appositive phrase. It explains which shoe.)

Ask Mr. Berry, **the director of the band,** for tickets to the game.
(*The director of the band* is the appositive phrase. It explains who Mr. Berry is.)

These examples show that a prepositional phrase can be part of an appositive phrase.

When You Write

When you finish a piece, go back over it to make sure everything will be clear to someone who doesn't know the subject. Often, inserting an appositive or appositive phrase can make the difference between writing that leaves readers wondering and writing that gives readers just what they need to know.

Needs information: Mr. Smith yelled at us to pick up the pace.

Enough information Mr. Smith, the coach for the running team, yelled at us to pick up the pace.

Select a composition from your portfolio. Look for places you can insert an appositive or appositive phrase to add needed information.

Appositives and appositive phrase are often, but not always, enclosed in commas. See the chart below for guidance in using commas with appositives and appositive phrases.

PUNCTUATION WITH APPOSITIVES AND APPOSITIVE PHRASES	
If the information in the appositive is **essential** to the complete meaning of the sentence, no commas are needed. If the information is **not essential** to the complete meaning, the appositive should be set off with one or two commas.	
Essential (no commas)	The movie *Brian's Song* is about football. (*Brian's Song* is the appositive. If it were dropped, the sentence would not have enough information.)
Nonessential (commas)	*Brian's Song,* **a movie about football,** is a very sad movie. (If the appositive phrase were dropped, the sentence would still contain the main information.)

● **Practice Your Skills**

Finding Appositives and Appositive Phrases

Write each appositive or appositive phrase.

1. Mr. Rich, our football coach, is looking forward to a great season this year.
2. Todd, the team captain, has been working hard all summer.
3. Tomorrow is the game against our rival school, Central.
4. The referee, the one with the black hat, gave our team a penalty.
5. The song "Fire Away" will be our fight song this year.

● *Connect to Writing:* **Editing**

Punctuating Sentences with Appositives or Appositive Phrases

Write each sentence, using commas correctly with appositives or appositive phrases. If a sentence is correct, write C.

1. My brother, Bob, likes to read.
2. The book, *The Adventures of Tom Sawyer,* is one of his favorites.
3. *The Adventures of Huckleberry Finn* a book by Mark Twain is also a favorite.
4. Tom my younger brother enjoys building models with his friends.
5. His favorite model, the *Titanic,* is on display in his room.

Sentence Diagraming

 Diagraming Phrases

Study the diagrams that follow to understand how phrases are diagramed.

Prepositional Phrases An **adjectival phrase** is connected to the noun or pronoun it modifies. An **adverbial phrase** is connected to the verb it modifies. Notice that prepositional phrases are diagramed beneath the word they modify.

The boy on the red bike waved.

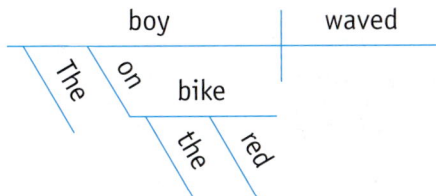

For an hour the wind blew steadily.

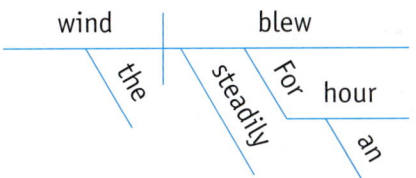

Appositives and Appositive Phrases An appositive is diagramed in parentheses next to the word it identifies or explains.

We like Ben Rosen, a baseball player for a local team.

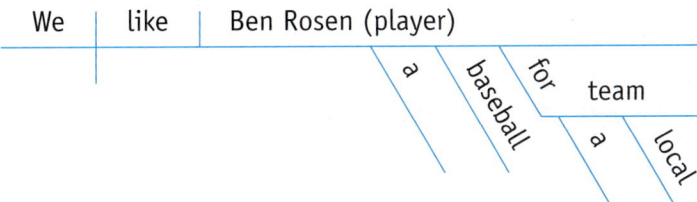

Sentence Diagraming 609

That watch, the gold one, is a present from my grandmother:

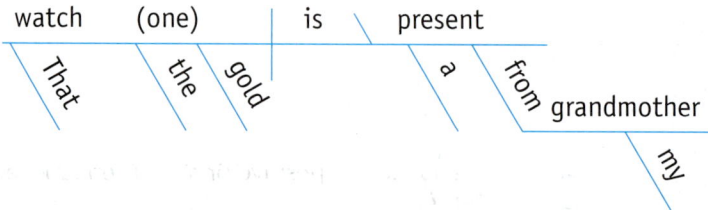

● **Practice Your Skills**

Diagraming Phrases

Diagram the following sentences or copy them. If you copy them, draw one line under each subject and two lines under each verb. Put parentheses around each phrase. Then label each one *adjectival, adverbial,* or *appositive*.

1. The Great Ice Age, a time of much change, occurred over two million years ago.
2. During this time huge ice sheets formed.
3. They covered large portions of the earth.
4. One glacier in New York was mammoth.
5. It covered the tops of the Catskill Mountains.
6. These mountains, an eastern range, are quite high.
7. The glaciers acted like rivers of ice.
8. They ground everything in their paths.
9. Minnesota and Wisconsin, two Midwestern states, have many lakes because of glacial melt.
10. States with great glacial erosion include New York and Ohio.

Chapter Review

Assess Your Learning

Finding Phrases

Write each prepositional phrase and each appositive phrase. Then label each one *adjectival, adverbial,* or *appositive.*

1. *Voyager 2* discovered huge ice cliffs on Miranda, Uranus's moon.
2. Pluto, a dwarf planet, was not discovered until 1930.
3. Because of the *Apollo* space missions, the moon has been mapped quite accurately.
4. Without a telescope you can see approximately fifteen hundred stars in a clear night sky.
5. The first record of an eclipse of the sun was in China on October 22, 2136 B.C.
6. In 1865 Jules Verne, a French writer, wrote a story about space travel to the moon.
7. According to his book, the launch site for this journey was Florida.
8. After one hundred years, his story actually happened.
9. The future of space travel is being planned now by scientists.
10. During the next fifty years, people might be traveling between Earth and another planet.
11. Would you travel to another planet?
12. Mars, the red planet, would be an interesting choice.
13. Saturn with its rings is farther away.
14. Venus can often be seen in the night sky.
15. The planet closest to the sun is Mercury.

Identifying Phrases

Write each phrase. Then write the word the phrase modifies, describes, or renames.

1. New York was named after an English royal family.
2. Monaco, a Mediterranean principality, has a total population of only 29,000 people.
3. The horse went to the creek and took a drink.
4. Jamie owns a cat without a tail.

5. Swifts, the world's fastest flyers, may spend weeks in the air.
6. Little League Baseball began in 1939.
7. A grove of cherry trees grew along the riverbank.
8. The classic book *Gulliver's Travels* was written by Jonathan Swift, an Irish clergyman.
9. The big oak door near us swung slowly open.
10. Comets travel around the sun in egg-shaped paths.

Using Phrases

Write five sentences that follow the directions below. (The sentences may come in any order.) Write about one of the following topics or a topic of your own choice: recommendations for making homeroom, study hall, or the cafeteria better.

Write a sentence that . . .
1. includes an adjectival phrase.
2. includes an adverbial phrase.
3. includes an introductory adverbial phrase.
4. includes an appositive.
5. includes an appositive phrase.

When you have finished, underline and label each phrase. Then check for correct punctuation in each sentence.

Phrases: Posttest

Directions
Write the letter of the term that correctly identifies the underlined word or group of words in each sentence.

(1) The movie, <u>a science-fiction thriller</u>, had some famous actors in it. (2) For days the crew set up scenes <u>around town</u>. (3) <u>Because of</u> their work, there were traffic jams everywhere. (4) A scene <u>about an alien</u> was shot at our school. (5) It was shot <u>on a weekend</u>, but the students came and acted as extras. (6) Early Saturday morning the crew pulled lights and props <u>out of boxes</u>. (7) The star, <u>a handsome man</u>, wouldn't look at any of us. (8) He sat alone <u>in a corner</u> and rehearsed his lines for the day's scene. (9) In our part of the movie, the alien was moving <u>toward</u> us. (10) We couldn't really see the alien, <u>a horrible, slimy beast</u>, because it would be added later with a computer.

1. A preposition
   B adjectival phrase
   C adverbial phrase
   D appositive phrase

2. A preposition
   B adjectival phrase
   C adverbial phrase
   D appositive phrase

3. A preposition
   B adjectival phrase
   C adverbial phrase
   D appositive phrase

4. A preposition
   B adjectival phrase
   C adverbial phrase
   D appositive phrase

5. A preposition
   B adjectival phrase
   C adverbial phrase
   D appositive phrase

6. A preposition
   B adjectival phrase
   C adverbial phrase
   D appositive phrase

7. A preposition
   B adjectival phrase
   C adverbial phrase
   D appositive phrase

8. A preposition
   B adjectival phrase
   C adverbial phrase
   D appositive phrase

9. A preposition
   B adjectival phrase
   C adverbial phrase
   D appositive phrase

10. A preposition
    B adjectival phrase
    C adverbial phrase
    D appositive phrase

Writer's Corner

Snapshot

20 A A **prepositional phrase** is a group of words that begins with a preposition, ends with a noun or a pronoun, and is used as an adjective or adverb. (pages 600–606)

20 B An **appositive** is a noun or pronoun that identifies or explains another noun or pronoun in the sentence. When an appositive has modifiers, it is called an **appositive phrase.** (pages 607–608)

Power Rules

Check your writing for these language patterns and make changes as needed.

 A phrase that is punctuated as a sentence is a phrase fragment. Fix a **phrase fragment** by adding a subject and a verb or by combining it with a related sentence. (See pages 664–665.)

Before Editing	After Editing
On the beach. My brother and I found a seashell.	On the beach my brother and I found a seashell.
In the evening. We played with our dog.	In the evening we played with our dog.

Use **subject forms of pronouns** in subject position. Use object forms of pronouns in object position. (See pages 712, 716–719.)

Before Editing	After Editing
We sent a package to Martha and *she*.	We sent a package to Martha and *her*.
Mom made cookies for *he* and his friends.	Mom made cookies for *him* and his friends.

Editing Checklist

Use this checklist when editing your writing.

✓ Are there any misplaced modifiers, or are all my adjectival phrases placed close to the words they describe? (See page 603.)
✓ Did I punctuate adverbial phrases correctly? (See page 605.)
✓ Did I punctuate appositives and appositive phrases correctly? (See page 608.)

Use the Power

Think of phrases as colors. Adding phrases to sentences makes your writing more vivid.

> On Saturday, Clara and Max ran at full speed to the concert hall. They were eager to buy tickets to see The Cranks, their favorite band. The hall was not a place with many seats, so they had to hurry.

Appositives are one of the best tools in the writer's toolbox. They provide a quick and easy way to add detail in a piece of writing.

Revise a composition you completed recently by adding appositives and appositive phrases.

Writer's Corner

CHAPTER 21

Verbals and Verbal Phrases

How can you use verbals and verbal phrases to add fluency to your writing?

Verbals and Verbal Phrases: Pretest 1

The following first draft contains many short, choppy sentences. Revise the draft so that it reads more smoothly by adding verbals or verbal phrases. The second and third sentences have been combined as an example.

Many people consider Captain James Cook to be the greatest explorer in history. He sailed into the Southern Hemisphere. He found and charted all of New Zealand. Next, he charted the 2,000-mile coast of Australia. He sailed up Australia's coast. The boat hit the Great Barrier Reef. His boat was damaged. He sailed into a bay along the coast to repair the damaged boat. Today, the place he stopped is known as Cooktown. He pushed farther south. Captain Cook reached Antarctica. The ropes and sails were frozen. Those ropes and sails made work difficult. They were surrounded by icebergs. The boat could hardly move. Of course, this is just one small part of what Captain Cook discovered. He sailed into the South Pacific. He discovered many islands, including Hawaii. Captain James Cook changed the map of the world more than anyone else in history.

Verbals and Verbal Phrases: Pretest 2

Directions
Write the letter of the term that correctly identifies the underlined word or group of words in each sentence.

(1) Our school worked hard to put on a carnival. (2) The carnival was to raise money for a new gym. (3) Each class was responsible for an activity. (4) The class had to plan a booth and set it up. (5) Acting wisely, our class decided on a dart game. (6) To win, you had to hit a balloon with a dart. (7) We had great stuffed animals to give to the winners. (8) Fortunately, the sun decided to shine on the day of the carnival. (9) The excited crowd milled around the booths. (10) A boy sitting on a board could be dunked into a vat of water at one popular booth.

1. **A** participle
    B participial phrase
    C infinitive
    D prepositional phrase

2. **A** participle
    B participial phrase
    C infinitive phrase
    D prepositional phrase

3. **A** participle
    B participial phrase
    C infinitive phrase
    D prepositional phrase

4. **A** participle
    B participial phrase
    C infinitive phrase
    D prepositional phrase

5. **A** participle
    B participial phrase
    C infinitive phrase
    D prepositional phrase

6. **A** participle
    B participial phrase
    C infinitive
    D infinitive phrase

7. **A** participle
    B participial phrase
    C infinitive phrase
    D prepositional phrase

8. **A** participle
    B infinitive
    C infinitive phrase
    D prepositional phrase

9. **A** participle
    B participial phrase
    C infinitive
    D prepositional phrase

10. **A** participle
    B participial phrase
    C infinitive phrase
    D prepositional phrase

Participles and Participial Phrases

A **verbal** is a verb form that serves as another part of speech—such as an adjective or a noun.

The examples below show the verbals *yelping* and *wounded*. *Yelping* is a form of the verb *yelp*; *wounded* is a form of the verb *wound*. In these sentences they serve as adjectives, not verbs.

> The **yelping** coyote attracted the scientists' attention.
>
> Lee found a **wounded** coyote.

In this chapter you will learn about two kinds of verbals: **participles** and **infinitives.** Often these verbals are linked with related words to form **verbal phrases.** Verbals pack a lot of detail into a small package and make your writing livelier and more interesting.

➤ Participles

Participles are probably the most often used verbals. In fact, the words *yelping* and *wounded* in the examples above are both participles.

21 A A **participle** is a verb form that is used as an adjective.

There are two forms of a participle: **present participles** and **past participles.** Present participles are easy to recognize because they always end in *-ing*. Past participles usually end in *-ed* or *-d*. Some, however, have irregular endings, such as *-n, -t,* or *-en*.

Verb	Present Participle	Past Participle
move	moving	moved
shout	shouting	shouted
blow	blowing	blown
lose	losing	lost
freeze	freezing	frozen

Since a participle is used as an adjective, it describes a noun or pronoun. It also answers the adjective question *Which one?* or *What kind?*

We were too near that **snarling** coyote.
(Which coyote?)

The **shouting** man disrupted the wildlife meeting.
(Which man?)

The **blowing** wind howled all night at the game preserve.
(What kind of wind?)

The **lost** pup was found very quickly.
(Which pup?)

The scientists ate **frozen** dinners.
(What kind of dinners?)

You can learn more about forming past participles on pages 680–691.

● Practice Your Skills

Finding Participles

Write each participle.

1. The scientists could hear the howling coyotes.
2. The coyote's expanding range presents a challenge for scientists.
3. A coyote can live anywhere from the frozen mountains to the hot deserts.
4. A starving coyote will scavenge in trash cans.
5. A coyote will change its breeding habits for adaptation.
6. Controlled hunts wiped out the coyote population in central Texas and much of North Dakota.
7. Lost pets often become prey for coyotes.
8. A hunting coyote will stalk its prey patiently.

● Practice Your Skills

Finding Participles

Write each participle.

1. A determined schoolteacher made an unusual bicycle trip.
2. Byron Vouga has no functioning kidneys.
3. Two failed transplants resulted in dialysis three times a week.
4. The courageous Vouga planned an exhausting cross-country bicycle trip.

Participles and Participial Phrases • Lesson 1

5. Vouga endured blistering heat and many other trials as a fund-raiser for the fight against kidney disease.
6. Scheduled stops at clinics for Vouga's dialysis were part of the trip.
7. Vouga met many unrecognized heroes who live with kidney disease every day.
8. One person has been on dialysis for twenty years and still works at a towing service.
9. Byron Vouga is truly an amazing man and an inspiration to others.
10. His challenging task brings hope to many people with kidney disease.

Participle or Verb?

It is very easy to confuse a participle with the verb of a sentence because a participle is a form of a verb and looks very much like a verb. To be a verb, a participle would have to have one or more helping verbs.

Participle	The **glowing** lights up ahead were bright.
Verb	The tiny candles **were glowing** in the dark room.
Participle	Clean up the **splattered** paint before the show.
Verb	The paint **was splattered** across the stage floor.

● Practice Your Skills

Distinguishing Between Participles and Verbs

Label each underlined word *P* for participle or *V* for verb.

1. The dancing children delighted the audience.
2. Marcie had spoken to the audience about the show.
3. Clap your hands with the syncopated rhythm.
4. The singers were standing under the bright lights.
5. By the end of the show, everyone was singing!
6. We gave the actors a standing ovation.
7. Everyone was dancing in the aisles.
8. Beth's spoken monologue went well.
9. Mrs. Owen syncopated the soprano part.
10. The singing dog was a great addition to the show.

Participial Phrases

More often than not, participles are joined with related words to form a participial phrase.

21 A.1 A **participial phrase** is a participle joined with related words. The related words in a participial phrase often include a complement, an adverb, or a prepositional phrase.

Participle with a Complement	The explorer, **strumming his guitar,** sang softly.
Participle with an Adverb	**Sitting up,** Sacajawea noticed several Shoshones.
Participle with a Prepositional Phrase	She found her people **living near the Rockies.**

PUNCTUATION WITH PARTICIPIAL PHRASES

A participial phrase that comes at the beginning of a sentence is always followed by a comma.

> **Listening carefully,** Sacajawea translated for the men.

Participial phrases that come in the middle or at the end of a sentence may not need commas. Use the following test: If the information in the phrase is **essential,** no commas are needed. If the information in the phrase is **not essential,** commas are needed to separate it from the rest of the sentence.

A phrase is nonessential if it can be removed from the sentence without changing the basic information of the sentence.

Essential	The boat **tied to the pier** was damaged. (Commas are not needed because the participial phrase is needed to identify which boat was damaged. *The boat was damaged* is not clear by itself.)
Nonessential	Sacajawea, **dancing joyfully,** recognized her people. (Commas are needed because the participial phrase could be removed from the sentence without changing the basic meaning: *Sacajawea recognized her people.*)

You can learn more about essential and nonessential phrases on page 608.

● **Practice Your Skills**

Recognizing Participial Phrases as Modifiers

Write each participial phrase. Then write the word each phrase modifies.

1. Viewed through a telescope, Saturn is one of the most unusual objects in the sky.
2. Saturn, named for an ancient Roman god, is yellow and gray.
3. Known as the ringed planet, Saturn is easily recognized.
4. Saturn is one of the giant outer planets characterized by large size and low density.
5. Composed mostly of hydrogen and helium, Saturn's atmosphere is not fit for human life.
6. Saturn's rings, first seen by Galileo in 1610, make it a unique planet.
7. Looking through a telescope, you can see six of Saturn's twenty satellites.
8. The largest satellite rotating around Saturn is called Titan.
9. Titan's diameter is about 3,200 miles, measuring larger than Mercury and Pluto.
10. Discovered in 1655, Titan has a substantial atmosphere.

When You Write

Writers often use participles and participial phrases to combine shorter sentences and make their writing smoother. The verb or verb phrase in one sentence is turned into a participle or participial phrase and inserted into the second, related sentence. This creates one longer sentence, rather than two short sentences.

Two sentences	That man was carrying several boxes. He tripped and fell.
Combined	The man carrying several boxes tripped and fell.
Two sentences	That building was burned. It will be rebuilt.
Combined	The burned building will be rebuilt.
Two sentences	They waded into the water. They discovered that the current was swift.
Combined	Wading into the water, they discovered that the current was swift.

It is good to have a variety of sentence lengths in your writing. Review a composition you have completed recently. Look for places you can use participial phrases to combine two short sentences.

Power Your Writing: Getting into the Action

You've learned how participial phrases are modifiers that can make your writing come alive and get your reader "into the action." The author Maya Angelou uses participial phrases both at the beginning of sentences as introductory phrases and at the end of sentences. In this example, she uses an introductory phrase to describe her actions as a young girl trying to be polite.

> **Remembering my manners,** I took nice little lady-like bites off the edges.

In the example below, Angelou put the participial phrase at the end for variety.

> She had the grace of control to appear warm in the coldest weather, and on the Arkansas summer days it seemed she had a private breeze which swirled around, **cooling her.**

Review a composition from your portfolio. Add participial phrases to the beginning of two sentences and to the end of two other sentences.

Connect to Writing: Descriptive Paragraph
Using Participles and Participial Phrases

After a trip to the local planetarium, your class has decided to help plan a planetarium for the local elementary school. Your group has been asked to write descriptions of planets and stars for the display. Write a descriptive paragraph about a planet, star, or constellation for elementary school children. Use some participles and participial phrases in your description.

● **_Connect to Writing:_ Editing**

Punctuating Participial Phrases

Rewrite each sentence, adding or deleting commas with participial phrases. If a sentence is correct, write **C**.

1. Wandering through the planetarium, we learned many amazing facts about the beautiful night sky.
2. Tom reading from one of the displays learned about stars and sailors.
3. Ancient sailors navigating without fancy instruments used the stars for guidance across the ocean.
4. Ancient navigators were also helped by the full moon shining above.
5. Shaking his head in amazement Mr. Guerrero said that ancient people must have been brave.

Misplaced Participial Phrases

In the last chapter, you learned that an adjectival phrase that is placed too far away from the word it describes is called a **misplaced modifier.** A participial phrase—like the one that follows—also becomes a misplaced modifier if it is placed too far away from the word it describes.

Misplaced Modifier	We saw a beautiful swan **riding along in our car.** (This sentence says that the swan was riding in our car.)
Misplaced Modifier	**Drinking a soda,** the gorilla watched Tim. (This sentence says that the gorilla was drinking a soda.)

To correct a misplaced modifier, find the word that the phrase describes. Place the phrase next to that word.

Correct Modifier	**Riding along in our car,** we saw a beautiful swan. (Because the participial phrase is close to the word it is describing, the sentence now makes sense. It is we who are riding, not the swan.)
Correct Modifier	The gorilla watched Tim **drinking a soda.** (Now it is Tim, not the gorilla, who is drinking the soda.)

Verbals and Verbal Phrases

● **Practice Your Skills**

Finding Participial Phrases

Write **C** for each participial phrase that is placed correctly and **I** for each participial phrase that is placed incorrectly. Then rewrite five of the incorrect sentences by moving the misplaced participial phrases.

1. Maria and Keisha watched a camel waiting for their popcorn.
2. Tanya, tired from the long walk on the trail, noticed a bobcat.
3. Singing clearly and loudly, Rico heard the rare bird.
4. Shawna took a picture of a lion panting in the hot sun.
5. Walking through the city zoo, Chen saw a ferocious tiger.
6. Tony enjoyed the seal swimming in its pool.
7. Morgan watched a raccoon talking quietly with her friends.
8. Swinging from the trees, the children laughed at the chimpanzee.
9. The elephants eyed the children spraying water from their trunks.
10. A giraffe, chewing on some leaves, cautiously watched Nita.

Participles and Participial Phrases • Lesson 1

Infinitives and Infinitive Phrases

An infinitive is another type of verbal. An infinitive usually begins with the word *to*.

21 B An **infinitive** is a verb form that usually begins with *to*. It is used as a noun, an adjective, or an adverb.

Noun   **To relax** isn't easy during a big shopping trip.
(*To relax* is the subject. It tells what the sentence is about.)

My brother likes **to shop.**
(My brother likes what? *To shop* is the direct object.)

Adjective   The best movie **to see** is at Cinema City.
(*To see* describes the movie. It tells which movie.)

Which is the best CD **to buy?**
(*To buy* describes the CD. It tells which CD.)

Adverb   They went to the mall **to plan.**
(*To plan* tells why they went to the mall.)

Gary will stay here **to eat.**
(*To eat* tells why he will stay.)

● **Practice Your Skills**

Recognizing Infinitives

Write each infinitive.

1. Kathy really likes to shop.
2. The best mall to visit is the Northgate Mall.
3. I visited the mall only to look.
4. To shop isn't the only reason for visiting the mall.
5. Danny likes to eat.

Infinitive or Prepositional Phrase?

Infinitives can be confused with prepositional phrases that begin with *to*. An infinitive is the word *to* plus a verb form. A prepositional phrase is the word *to* plus a noun or pronoun.

626   Verbals and Verbal Phrases

Infinitive	It is important **to succeed.**
	(The phrase ends with a verb form, *succeed.*)
Prepositional Phrase	They have already gone **to school.**
	(The phrase ends with a noun, *school.*)

● **Practice Your Skills**

Distinguishing Between Infinitives and Prepositional Phrases

Label each underlined phrase *I* for infinitive or *PP* for prepositional phrase.

1. There are many different factors that contribute <u>to research</u>.
2. It is important <u>to plan</u> your research paper very carefully.
3. Once you have completely developed your plan, get <u>to work</u>.
4. <u>To research</u> for any topic will require some supplies.
5. Organize all of your research information according <u>to type</u>.

Infinitive Phrases

Infinitives can be combined with modifiers or complements to form an infinitive phrase.

21 B.1 An **infinitive phrase** is an infinitive with its modifiers and complements—all working together as a noun, an adjective, or an adverb.

An infinitive phrase can be made up of several different combinations of words.

With an Adverb	At the rink we want **to skate quickly.**
With a Prepositional Phrase	Nelson hopes **to qualify for the Olympics.**
With a Complement	During practice we tried **to set a record.**

● **Practice Your Skills**

Finding Infinitive Phrases

Write each infinitive phrase.

1. Two-year-old Bonnie Blair learned to skate from her siblings.
2. They did not want Bonnie to use double runners on her skates.
3. Double runners make it easier for a child to stand up on skates.
4. Bonnie quickly learned to take a few steps on the skates.
5. She always wanted to skate in the Olympics.

Parallelism with Verbals — Lesson 3

21 C **Parallelism** refers to the use of similar grammatical constructions for similar ideas.

When forming a list of two or more verbals or verbal phrases, be sure the verbals are parallel in structure.

Not Parallel	Melissa likes **to play** tennis and **jogging** in the park.
Parallel	Melissa likes **to play** tennis and **to jog** in the park.
Not Parallel	Antonio likes **gaining** experience in networks and **to repair** computers.
Parallel	Antonio likes **gaining** experience in networks and **repairing** computers.

Practice Your Skills

Identifying and Using Parallelism

Rewrite the following sentences, fixing faulty parallelism. If a sentence is parallel, write **C**.

1. Jeb plans to study biology and taking computer programming.
2. Mindy is becoming an expert problem solver and taking computers apart.
3. Samuel finds it hard to think like a computer and programming.
4. Maria plans to study history and helping at her mother's store.
5. Mr. Hinman likes to say "Read the manual" and repeating over and over, "Garbage in; garbage out."

Check Point: Mixed Practice

Write each verbal or verbal phrase. Then label each one *participle, participial phrase, infinitive,* or *infinitive phrase.*

1. Searching the ocean floor carefully, treasure hunters look for remains of old ships.
2. Stolen treasure is rumored to be near the town of Wellfleet, Massachusetts.
3. Barry Clifford hopes to find the remains of the pirate ship *Whydah*.
4. The *Whydah*, laden with heavy treasure, sank in a storm on April 26, 1717.
5. The storm caused the ship to break apart.

Sentence Diagraming

Diagraming Verbals and Verbal Phases

Before diagraming a sentence with a verbal in it, you will have to determine how the verbal is used.

Participial Phrases Because a participial phrase is always used as an adjective, it is diagramed under the word it describes—the same way an adjective would be diagramed. The participle, however, is written in a curve. Notice in the sentence below that the second participial phrase, *making a nest*, has a direct object. It is diagramed like a regular direct object with a line between it and the verb form *making*.

Looking out the window, we watched a bird making a nest.

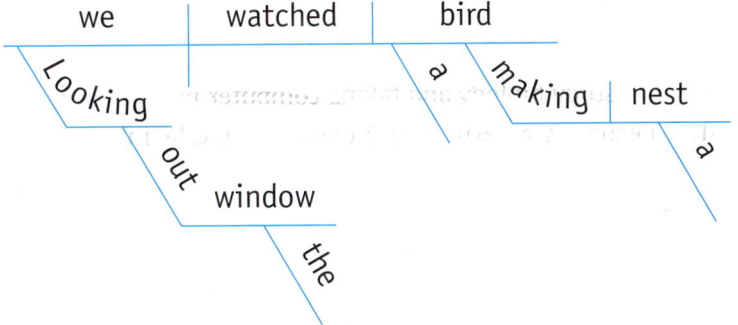

A single participle is diagramed exactly the same way the participle *looking* or *making* is diagramed above—except it would have no complement or modifiers.

Infinitive Phrases Because an infinitive phrase can be used as an adjective, an adverb, or a noun, it is diagramed in several ways. The first example shows how to diagram an infinitive phrase that is used as a noun, the subject of a sentence. Notice that *to make* has the direct object *impression* that is diagramed like a regular direct object with a line between it and the verb form *to make*. The second example shows how to diagram an infinitive phrase that is used as an adjective.

To make a good impression is very important.

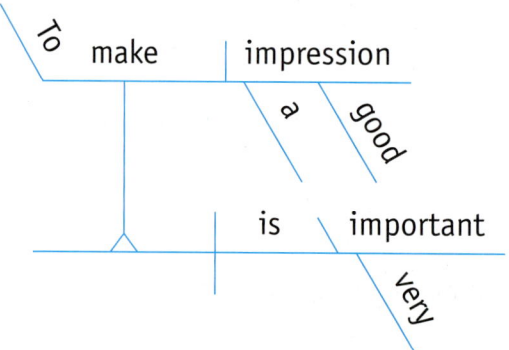

These are the best directions to get to my house.

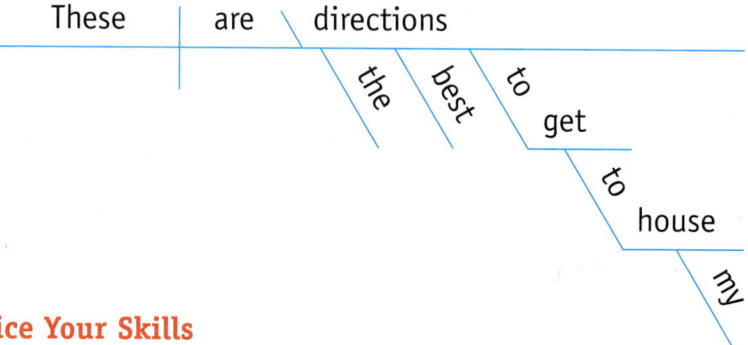

● **Practice Your Skills**

   Diagraming Verbal Phrases

   Diagram the following sentences or copy them. If you copy them, draw one line under each subject and two lines under each verb. Then put parentheses around each verbal phrase and label each one participial or infinitive.

   1. My father planted the lemon tree growing in our yard.
   2. He wanted to plant it.
   3. He likes to eat the lemons.
   4. Looking at the tree, my father remembered his old home.
   5. To keep the tree alive is very important.
   6. I plan to water it.
   7. The lemons, picked in the summer, are helpful.
   8. We used them to make lemonade.
   9. Sipping that delicious drink, I am cool.
   10. The tree, surviving for years, might last forever.

Verbals and Verbal Phrases

Chapter Review

Assess Your Learning

Finding Participial Phrases

Write each participial phrase.

1. The Sahara, covering approximately 3.5 million square miles, is the largest desert in the world.
2. Extinct volcanoes, crossing the Sahara from west to east, form a chain of mountains.
3. Scattered along the base of the Atlas Mountains, narrow strips of good soil break up the enormous stretch of desert.
4. These fertile areas, called oases, are rest areas for travelers.
5. Linked to the world by small air fields, some oases have grown into towns or villages.

Finding Infinitive Phrases

Write each infinitive phrase.

1. In a famous experiment at Yale University, chimpanzees learned to operate a "Chimp-O-Mate."
2. To earn chips to buy food from the machine, the chimpanzees performed certain kinds of work.
3. Some chimpanzees were willing to put off their purchases until the next day.
4. Others would grow impatient and try to shake the machine for oranges or bananas.
5. To the delight of the scientists, however, the chimpanzees quickly learned to use the right method.

■ Finding Verbal Phrases

Write each verbal phrase. Then label each one *participial* or *infinitive*. If a sentence does not have a verbal phrase, write *none*.

1. Have you ever traveled to Connecticut?
2. To see all the sights, my family visited the state last summer.
3. Harriet Beecher Stowe, known for her book *Uncle Tom's Cabin*, once lived in Hartford, the capital of Connecticut.
4. Living next door to her, Mark Twain also wrote many of his books in Hartford.
5. Also in Hartford, the first cookbook written by an American was published in 1796.
6. We went to see the home of Noah Webster.
7. His first book, published in 1783, was *Blue-Backed Speller*.
8. Later, of course, Webster published his famous dictionary, used now throughout the world.
9. His name is still remembered today.
10. Known for its charm, Connecticut is a great place.

■ Using Verbal Phrases

Write five sentences that follow the directions below.

1. Include the participial phrase *singing at the top of his lungs* at the beginning of a sentence.
2. Include the participial phrase *won by the girls' basketball team* in a sentence.
3. Include the participial phrase *falling asleep early* at the beginning of a sentence.
4. Include the infinitive phrase *to prevent the flu* at the beginning of a sentence.
5. Include the infinitive phrase *to see a rodeo* in a sentence.

When you have finished, underline and label each phrase.

Verbals and Verbal Phrases: Posttest

Directions
Write the letter of the term that correctly identifies the underlined word or group of words in each sentence.

(1) The growth of railroads brought new growth <u>to Europe and America</u>. (2) The steel industry also began <u>to grow</u>. (3) People such as farmers and tradesmen found their jobs <u>disappearing quickly</u>. (4) Factory work began <u>to replace other work</u>. (5) <u>Working</u> conditions were often harsh and difficult. (6) <u>Repeated</u> activity led to many injuries. (7) Children <u>in the factories</u> could not go to school. (8) These children often had no fresh food or milk <u>to eat and drink each day</u>. (9) Factory workers, <u>working fourteen-hour days</u>, often didn't make enough money to live. (10) They were forced <u>to live in the same dwelling with many other people</u>.

1. A participle
   B participial phrase
   C infinitive phrase
   D prepositional phrase

2. A participle
   B participial phrase
   C infinitive
   D infinitive phrase

3. A participle
   B participial phrase
   C infinitive phrase
   D prepositional phrase

4. A participle
   B participial phrase
   C infinitive phrase
   D prepositional phrase

5. A participle
   B participial phrase
   C infinitive phrase
   D prepositional phrase

6. A participle
   B participial phrase
   C infinitive phrase
   D prepositional phrase

7. A participle
   B participial phrase
   C infinitive phrase
   D prepositional phrase

8. A participle
   B participial phrase
   C infinitive phrase
   D prepositional phrase

9. A participle
   B participial phrase
   C infinitive phrase
   D prepositional phrase

10. A participle
    B participial phrase
    C infinitive phrase
    D prepositional phrase

Writer's Corner

Snapshot

A **verbal** is a form of a verb that is used as another part of speech, such as an adjective or a noun. (page 618)

21 A A **participle** is a verb form that is used as an adjective. A **participial phrase** is a participle joined with related words. (pages 618–625)

21 B An **infinitive** is a verb form that usually begins with *to*. It is used as a noun, an adjective, or an adverb. An **infinitive phrase** is an infinitive with its modifiers and complements, all working together as a noun, an adjective, or an adverb. (pages 626–627)

21 C **Parallelism** refers to the use of similar grammatical constructions for similar ideas. (page 628)

Power Rules

A **participial phrase** that is separated from the sentence to which it relates is an ineffective sentence fragment. **Fix such sentence fragments** by joining them to a related sentence. (pages 664–665)

Before Editing

Walking through the forest. The girls saw birds and squirrels.

We watched the boys. *Playing baseball in the park.*

After Editing

Walking through the forest, the girls saw birds and squirrels.

We watched the boys playing baseball in the park.

Editing Checklist

Use this checklist when editing your writing.

✓ Did I punctuate participial phrases correctly? (See page 621.)
✓ Did I use participles or participial phrases to combine choppy, short sentences and make my writing smoother? (See pages 622–623.)
✓ Did I place participial phrases near the words they modify? (See pages 624–625.)

Use the Power

Participial phrases are participles combined with modifiers and complements—all working together as an adjective. Participial phrases add descriptive details to writing.

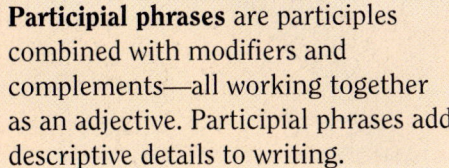

Running hard and waving her arms, Felicia tried to catch up with her mother, who was leaving without her in the car.

Infinitives usually begin with the word *to*. The famous phrase "To be, or not to be" contains no verbs, just infinitives.

Felicia's mother vowed **to check** the back seat before leaving rest stops.

Use verbals to add spice to your writing. Review a piece of writing you have completed recently. Add participial phrases to the beginning and to the end of several sentences. If possible, use participial phrases to combine short sentences and to add sentence variety to your piece.

CHAPTER 22

Clauses

Dr. Benjamin Carson

How can you use clauses to create a smooth flow and express ideas precisely?

Clauses: Pretest 1

The following first draft is hard to read. There are many fragments, and many of the sentences are short and choppy. Revise the draft so that it flows more smoothly. The first two sentences have been combined as an example.

    Benjamin Carson was born in Detroit. *where h* His early life was not easy. Because his parents were divorced. His mother Sonya had to work two and three jobs to support her sons. Sonya could barely read. She valued education. She made Benjamin and his brother read more books. Benjamin began to do better in school. He fell in love with learning. He studied hard. He graduated with honors. He went to Yale University. He went to medical school at the University of Michigan. He became one of the world's leading neurosurgeons. In 2008, he received the Presidential Medal of Freedom. That is the highest civilian honor in the United States.

Clauses: Pretest 2

Directions
Write the letter of the term that correctly identifies the underlined group of words in each sentence.

(1) <u>When we finished breakfast,</u> we visited the Raptor Center. (2) The Raptor Center is a place <u>that the county funds.</u> (3) <u>When people find hurt birds,</u> they bring them there. (4) <u>Vets help cure the birds,</u> and they are released. (5) <u>Some birds are too badly hurt to return to nature.</u> (6) These birds, <u>which can still fly short distances,</u> are trained to perform. (7) <u>The trainers show us some birds, and the birds perform for us.</u> (8) <u>When we last visited,</u> there was an injured owl. (9) The owl ignored us, but <u>it knew we were watching.</u> (10) An amazing thing <u>that the owl does</u> is to swivel its head nearly 360 degrees.

1. **A** adjectival clause
   B adverbial clause
   C independent clause
   D simple sentence

2. **A** adjectival clause
   B adverbial clause
   C independent clause
   D simple sentence

3. **A** adjectival clause
   B adverbial clause
   C independent clause
   D simple sentence

4. **A** adjectival clause
   B adverbial clause
   C independent clause
   D simple sentence

5. **A** compound sentence
   B complex sentence
   C independent clause
   D simple sentence

6. **A** adjectival clause
   B adverbial clause
   C independent clause
   D simple sentence

7. **A** compound sentence
   B complex sentence
   C independent clause
   D simple sentence

8. **A** adjectival clause
   B adverbial clause
   C independent clause
   D simple sentence

9. **A** adjectival clause
   B adverbial clause
   C independent clause
   D simple sentence

10. **A** adjectival clause
    B adverbial clause
    C independent clause
    D simple sentence

Independent and Subordinate Clauses

In this chapter you will learn about three kinds of sentences: simple, compound, and complex. Before you can fully understand these sentence types, you must know about a group of words called a **clause.**

22 A A **clause** is a group of words that has a subject and a verb.

Unlike the phrase, the clause has a subject and a verb. In the following examples, subjects of each clause are underlined once, and verbs are underlined twice.

> **Phrase**   We will eat **after lessons.**
> **Clause**   We will eat **after we finish our lessons.**

There are two kinds of clauses: independent and subordinate. First we will look at the independent clause.

22 A.1 An **independent, or main, clause** can stand alone as a sentence because it expresses a complete idea.

When an independent clause stands by itself, it is called a sentence. It only becomes an independent clause when it appears in a sentence with another clause.

> independent clause   independent clause
> Sara looked for shells, but the tide came in.

These two clauses are independent; they both can stand alone as single sentences.

> Sara looked for shells. The tide came in.

The second kind of clause is called a **subordinate clause,** or **dependent clause.** Because it is dependent, it needs another clause to give it meaning. In other words, a dependent clause cannot stand alone as a sentence.

22 A.2 A **subordinate, or dependent, clause** cannot stand alone as a sentence because it does not express a complete thought.

Notice that the subordinate clauses in the following examples do not express a complete thought—even though they have both a subject and a verb.

subordinate clause   independent clause
After we swam, we ate a huge lunch.

independent clause   subordinate clause
I just had the salad that my mother prepared.

Practice Your Skills

Distinguishing Between Main and Subordinate Clauses

Label each underlined clause *I* for independent or *S* for subordinate.

1. If the sky is dark and cloudy, you should bring an umbrella.
2. Unless you call first, I will leave for the beach at noon.
3. I like this beach because it is almost never crowded.
4. Since the tide is in, the water is high.
5. We will eat when Terry and Yolanda finally get here.
6. Although it was raining almost the entire afternoon, we stayed at the beach.
7. Before the rain started, we played a game of volleyball.
8. Sometimes we surf while we are at the beach with our friends.
9. I watched television after I got home from the beach.
10. Someone knocked on the door as soon as I got home.

Uses of Subordinate Clauses

22 B A **subordinate clause** can be used as an adverb or as an adjective.

➤ Adverbial Clauses

A subordinate clause can be used in the same way as a single adverb or adverbial phrase. Such a clause is called an **adverbial clause**.

Single Adverb	The eagles arrived **late.**
Adverbial Phrase	The eagles arrived **after the first storm.**
Adverbial Clause	The eagles arrived **after the snow had begun.**

22 B.1 An **adverbial clause** is a subordinate clause used mainly to modify a verb.

An adverbial clause answers the adverb question *How? When? Where? How much?* or *To what extent?* In addition, an adverbial clause answers the question *Under what circumstances?* or *Why?* Notice in the following examples that an adverbial clause modifies the whole verb phrase.

How?	The eagle flew **as if it were suspended in the sky.**
When?	**When the guide arrives**, the eagle watch will begin.
Where?	Eagles roost **where they can find good hunting.**
To What Extent?	Eagles search for prey **until they are successful.**
Why?	You should bring your binoculars **so that you can see the eagles.**

Subordinating Conjunctions

Adverbial clauses begin with a subordinating conjunction. A few of the subordinating conjunctions in the following box—such as *after, before, since,* and *until*—can also be used as prepositions. Remember that those words are subordinating conjunctions if they are followed by a group of words with a subject and a verb.

COMMON SUBORDINATING CONJUNCTIONS

after	as though	since	until
although	because	so	when
as	before	so that	whenever
as far as	even though	than	where
as if	however	though	wherever
as long as	if	thus	while
as soon as	in order that	unless	

When the eagles return to the nest, they will feed their babies.

The eagle has keen eyesight **so that** it can easily spot prey.

PUNCTUATION WITH ADVERBIAL CLAUSES

Always place a comma after an adverbial clause that comes at the beginning of a sentence.

Because we were early, we saw many eagles.

● **Practice Your Skills**

Supplying Subordinating Conjunctions

Write a subordinating conjunction to replace each blank to create a subordinate clause.

1. ___ the bald eagle is our national bird, it is protected from hunters.
2. ___ the bald eagle has been our national symbol since 1782, many people want to protect it.
3. ___ pesticides were used, many eagles died in the 1970s.
4. ___ the bald eagle became an endangered species, scientists studied it carefully.
5. It proved to be a relatively easy task ___ eagles reuse the same nest sites.
6. Eagles are convenient to study ___ several pairs of eagles nest in a small area.

Uses of Subordinate Clauses • Lesson 2

● **Practice Your Skills**

Finding Adverbial Clauses

Write the adverbial clause in each sentence. Then write the word or words that the adverbial clause modifies.

1. Although Detroit is called "the Motor City," its football team is named after an animal.
2. Because George Richards owned a radio station, he held a contest to name the new football team.
3. The team became the Detroit Lions after the contest had ended.
4. When the team won many games the first season, fans cheered.
5. After the Lions won the Western Division title in 1935, they advanced to the championship.
6. New York fans were disappointed when the Lions beat the Giants.
7. As soon as the game was over, Detroit celebrated.
8. Though they had won the championship in 1935, Detroit was 7–3 in 1936.
9. It would be several seasons before the Lions had another championship.
10. Until the team acquired some new players, winning seasons would be scarce.

● *Connect to Writing:* **Editing**

Punctuating Sentences with Adverbial Clauses

Rewrite the following sentences, adding or removing commas where needed. If a sentence is correct, write **C**.

1. Whenever I watch football I like to cheer for my team.
2. While the game is on, you shouldn't talk to my dad.
3. As soon as it's halftime we will get a pretzel at the snack bar.
4. Our team should spend some time on fundamentals unless they want to repeat last year's performance.
5. We should get our tickets before the game is sold out.

Adjectival Clauses

A subordinate clause can also be used like a single adjective or an adjectival phrase. Such a clause is called an **adjectival clause.**

Single Adjective It is a **great** story.
Adjectival Phrase It was a story **beyond our expectations.**
Adjectival Clause It was a story **that we will never forget.**

22 B.2 An **adjectival clause** is a subordinate clause that is used to modify a noun or a pronoun.

An adjectival clause answers the adjective question *Which one?* or *What kind?* Usually an adjectival clause will modify the noun or pronoun directly in front of it.

Which One? The story **that tells how Arthur found Excalibur** is my favorite.

What Kind? It is a legend **that is often repeated.**

Relative Pronouns

22 B.3 Most adjectival clauses begin with a relative pronoun. A **relative pronoun** relates an adjective clause to the noun or the pronoun that the clause describes.

RELATIVE PRONOUNS				
who	whom	whose	which	that

In some sentences the relative pronoun just begins the adjective clause; in other sentences, the relative pronoun also serves as the subject of the adjectival clause.

I haven't read another story **that I like.**

I haven't read another story **that is like Arthur's story.** (*That* is the subject of the clause *that is like Arthur's story.*)

PUNCTUATION WITH ADJECTIVAL CLAUSES

No punctuation is used with an adjectival clause that contains information that is essential to identify a person, place, or thing in the sentence.

Essential   A story **that was written about King Arthur** won the writing contest.

Arthur was a great leader **who united the British people.**

One or two commas should set off an adjectival clause that is nonessential. A clause is nonessential if it can be removed from the sentence without changing the basic meaning of the sentence. A clause is usually nonessential if it modifies a proper noun.

Nonessential   Thomas Malory, **who wrote many King Arthur stories,** lived hundreds of years after King Arthur.

Arthur, **whose adventures were many,** may have actually lived during the Dark Ages.

The relative pronoun *that* is used in an essential clause and *which* is usually used in a nonessential clause.

The play **that is about King Arthur** is *Camelot*.

Camelot, **which is about King Arthur,** is my favorite play.

● **Practice Your Skills**

Identifying Adjectival Clauses

Write each adjectival clause. Underline the relative pronoun once. Then write the word or words that each adjectival clause describes.

1. Joan, who is reading a book about Robin Hood, enjoys legends.
2. It was her love of old legends that interested me in the King Arthur stories.
3. Marco, whose report about the Dark Ages was excellent, wants to write his own book about King Arthur.
4. Missy's report, which was about castles, contained many details.
5. The report that Mrs. Johns liked the best was about ancient legends.
6. Mrs. Johns, who reads widely about historical people and events, learned something new about the Dark Ages from Sue's report.
7. Rahul, who wants to be an archaeologist, wrote about the search for Camelot.
8. The ancient castle, which has never been found, might be fictitious.

9. Jonathan, whose paper was written on the bus, did not hope for a good grade.
10. The paper, which had not been well researched, needed more work, additional information, and a great deal more thought.

Connect to Writing: Editing

Punctuating Sentences with Adjectival Clauses

Rewrite the following sentences, adding or removing commas where needed. If a sentence is correct, write C.

1. Our school library which is huge is a good place for research.
2. Mrs. Engel, who is our librarian, is a wonderful resource person.
3. The place in the library that I like best is the technology room.
4. Jim whose knowledge of computers is amazing is a good friend to take to the library.
5. Mrs. Engel whom I respect highly always finds the right book for me.

Check Point: Mixed Practice

Label each underlined clause *adverbial* or *adjectival*.

1. <u>Although he had been diagnosed with cancer in 1996,</u> Lance Armstrong overcame the disease.
2. Lance Armstrong, <u>who looks to his mother for inspiration</u>, trained hard for the 1999 Tour de France.
3. Armstrong was not discouraged <u>though doctors had given him only a 50–50 chance for recovery.</u>
4. <u>When Armstrong crossed the finish line at the end of the race</u>, he had accomplished the impossible.
5. The Tour de France, <u>which is a cycling event</u>, takes place every year in July.
6. <u>Even though Armstrong was in good physical condition</u>, doctors credit his recovery to his positive attitude.
7. Armstrong says, "<u>If you ever get a second chance in life</u>, you've got to go all the way."
8. Lance Armstrong, <u>who held a commanding lead after three stages of the event</u>, rode hard every day.
9. <u>As soon as he crossed the finish line</u>, a great cheer went up.
10. Many Americans, <u>who interrupted their vacations</u>, congratulated Armstrong.

Misplaced Adjectival Clauses

22 B.4 A **misplaced adjectival clause** is placed so far from the word it modifies that it creates unintended meaning.

To avoid confusion, put an adjectival clause next to the word it describes.

Misplaced	Miriam saw a duck **who had a pair of binoculars.**
	(This sentence says that the duck had the binoculars.)
Correct	Miriam, **who had a pair of binoculars,** saw a duck.
	(Now Miriam has the binoculars.)
Misplaced	The duck wanted the food **that was swimming in the water.**
	(This sentence says that the food was swimming.)
Correct	The duck **that was swimming in the water** wanted the food.
	(Now the duck is swimming.)

● Practice Your Skills

Recognizing Misplaced Adjectival Clauses

Write *C* if an adjectival clause is placed correctly and *I* if an adjectival clause is placed incorrectly. Rewrite the sentences, placing modifiers correctly and using commas where needed.

1. Bethany, who had a bag of bread crumbs, watched a pigeon.
2. A goose that had a bump on its head lunged for the bag.
3. David threw some crumbs to a duck who enjoys feeding the birds.
4. A grackle that was flying overhead wanted some food.
5. A dog that had no collar chased some of the ducks.
6. My sister that had been abandoned observed a nest.
7. Koreen threw some crumbs to the swans who had an extra bag.
8. A turtle that was eager to investigate climbed to the shore.
9. Marta explored the pool whose love of wildlife is well known.
10. Deb saw a duck who never really wanted to come along.
11. The duck, which was following its mother, lagged behind.
12. People waited in line who wanted to ride the paddleboats.
13. The line, which curved around several times, was very long.
14. Stephen, who was holding his brother's hand, became impatient.
15. He picked up some tiny pebbles and threw them into the water that were on the ground.

Kinds of Sentences

When you understand the different kinds of sentences, you will be able to add variety to your writing.

22 C There are three basic kinds of sentences: **simple, compound,** and **complex.**

➤ Simple and Compound Sentences

A simple sentence is the foundation on which the other kinds of sentences are built.

22 C.1 A **simple sentence** has one subject (or a compound subject) and one verb.

In the following examples, subjects are underlined once; verbs are underlined twice.

| One Subject, One Verb | Softball is my favorite sport. |

In a simple sentence, either the subject or the verb, or both, can be compound.

| Compound Subject | Amelia and her team flew to the softball championships in New York City. |
| Compound Verb | Mia-Lu threw the first pitch and struck the first batter out. |

Two or more related simple sentences can be joined into a **compound sentence.**

22 C.2 A **compound sentence** is made up of two or more simple sentences, usually joined by a comma and a coordinating conjunction: *and, but, or,* or *yet.*

As the examples below show, when the comma and the conjunction are dropped from a compound sentence, two simple sentences will remain.

| Compound Sentence | The game will begin at four o'clock, **but** the buses will leave at two o'clock. |
| Simple Sentences | The game will begin at four o'clock. The buses will leave at two o'clock. |

- **Practice Your Skills**

    Recognizing Simple and Compound Sentences
    Label each sentence *simple* or *compound*.

    1. Softball began in Chicago in 1887.
    2. Softball fields require less space than baseball fields.
    3. A game of softball is similar to a game of baseball, but the bases on a softball field are closer together.
    4. Softball bases are sixty feet apart, but baseball requires ninety feet between bases.
    5. A softball pitcher stands 40 to 46 feet from home plate, but the distance in baseball is 60.5 feet.
    6. The circumference of a softball usually measures twelve inches and is larger than a baseball's circumference.
    7. A baseball is about nine inches in circumference.
    8. Baseball players usually leave the base before a pitch, but softball players always wait for a pitch.
    9. Baseball allows a choice of pitches, but softball pitchers always throw underhand.
    10. A softball team has nine or ten players and plays only seven innings.

Compound Sentence or Compound Verb?

Sometimes you can mistake a sentence with a compound verb for a compound sentence. Just remember that a compound sentence must have two sets of subjects and verbs. In the following examples, subjects are underlined once and verbs are underlined twice.

Compound Sentence   The children cheered, and Mom gave them some pie.

Compound Verb   The children cheered and pointed at the chocolate pie.

PUNCTUATION WITH COMPOUND SENTENCES

There are several ways to connect the independent clauses in a compound sentence. One way is to join them with a comma and a conjunction.

Chocolate is the most popular flavor, **but** vanilla runs a close second.

You can also join independent clauses with a semicolon and no conjunction.

Chocolate is the most popular flavor; vanilla runs a close second.

You can learn more about punctuating compound sentences on pages 839–841 and 890–891.

● **Practice Your Skills**

Distinguishing Between Simple and Compound Sentences

Label each sentence *simple* or *compound.*

1. Yogurt is a good source of calcium, and cheese contains calcium, too.
2. On advice from the Indians, the Pilgrims planted corn and found many uses for it.
3. Potato leaves are definitely poisonous, but the potato itself is not.
4. Spinach is a good source of iron and other minerals and can be eaten raw.
5. Three types of roots are onions, turnips, and parsnips.
6. Tomatoes are categorized as fruits, but many people think of tomatoes as vegetables.
7. Trout is a very nutritious fish; it contains many nutrients.
8. Raw carrots are crunchy, tasty, and good for you too.
9. Ice cream contains vitamin D but has a great deal of fat.
10. Chocolate was once considered junk food, but now its health benefits are understood.

● *Connect to Writing:* **Drafting**

Writing Simple and Compound Sentences

Use the independent clauses below to form four simple or compound sentences. You may use a clause more than once.

1. the hamburgers smell delicious
2. they are cooked perfectly
3. the picnic starts at one o'clock
4. I don't have a ride

Kinds of Sentences • Lesson 3

Connect to Writing: Editing

Punctuating Compound Sentences

Rewrite the following compound sentences. Be sure that commas, conjunctions, and semicolons are used properly. If a sentence is punctuated correctly, write **C**.

1. Jennifer wanted to have watermelons at the picnic; but they weren't in season.
2. Ashley made a chocolate cake but she left it at home.
3. Brian cooked the hot dogs he burned only a few.
4. Bob wanted to bring cantaloupe yet he couldn't find any.
5. Michael made brownies; they were delicious.

Complex Sentences

You can recognize complex sentences if you understand independent and subordinate clauses.

22 C.3 A **complex sentence** consists of one main, or independent, clause and one or more subordinate clauses.

┌─subordinate clause─┐ ┌───main clause───┐
Before the rain started, I closed the car windows.

┌───main clause───┐ ┌────subordinate clause────┐
We stayed in the cabin that we had rented the year before.

┌──────main clause──────┐ ┌─────subordinate clause─────┐
Dan and I hiked to the general store, which was about a mile away.

When You Write

Writers often use many different kinds of sentences in their writing. This technique keeps the reader from getting bored because it creates variety. Notice how the writer uses simple, compound, and complex sentences in the following passage.

> At the end of the fourth period, the score was 47–32. Coach made the boys do three laps around the gym before he let them shower. On the last lap, Coach joined them and tried to be jolly, but the teams just looked at the floor, breathing hard. The cheerleaders were gone. The shafts of sunlight that had blazed on the gym floor were gone. The heater was off, and the janitor was pulling the windows shut.
>
> —Gary Soto, *Taking Sides*

Practice Your Skills

Identifying Main and Subordinate Clauses

Underline each main clause once and each subordinate clause twice.

1. Although many people associate Benjamin Franklin only with the discovery of electricity, he had many other accomplishments as well.
2. Even though he had only two years of formal schooling, Franklin was an avid reader.
3. After Franklin found a job as a printer, he began to publish *Poor Richard's Almanac*.
4. His business expanded further when he did government printing.
5. While he operated a bookshop, he became a clerk of the Pennsylvania Assembly.
6. Franklin, who served as postmaster of Philadelphia, retired at the age of forty-two.
7. Franklin began another career in 1740 when he invented the Franklin stove.
8. After reading papers about electricity, he began his own series of experiments.
9. Franklin became famous when the Royal Society in London published his discoveries.
10. Even though Benjamin Franklin was famous, few people recognize the breadth of his achievements.

Connect to Writing: Editing

Punctuating Complex Sentences

Rewrite the following sentences, adding commas where needed. If a sentence is correct, write **C**.

1. As Franklin traveled throughout the colonies he reorganized the American postal system.
2. In October 1776, Franklin sailed for France, where he gained French aid.
3. Though he was nearly eighty years old Benjamin Franklin became the first United States government minister to France.
4. Franklin outfitted John Paul Jones who owned the ship the *Bonhomme Richard*.
5. When Franklin returned home in 1785 he accepted his election as president of the Pennsylvania Executive Council.

Kinds of Sentences • Lesson 3

● *Connect to Writing:* **Summary**

Writing Complex Sentences

Your social studies class is creating a display for the local history museum. Because space is limited, only a few important people from history can be included. Persuade your teacher to include a display about a historical figure you admire by writing a short summary about that person. Include at least five complex sentences in your summary.

✓ *Check Point:* **Mixed Practice**

Label each sentence *simple*, *compound*, or *complex*. If a sentence is complex, write the subordinate clause.

1. Hans Christian Andersen was born in 1805 and died almost seventy years later.
2. He wrote 156 fairy tales, but his most famous tale was "The Ugly Duckling."
3. Andersen grew up in Denmark and lived in a one-room house.
4. Although his father was a shoemaker, he could not afford leather shoes for his own children.
5. Andersen was tall and lanky, and his hands and feet were large.
6. His eyes were small and very close together, and his nose was too big for his face.
7. People made jokes about him or ignored him.
8. As he played by himself, he carved a tiny theater.
9. He made up short plays and acted out all the parts.
10. After he saw a real play at the age of seven, he longed for the stage.
11. Later he went to Copenhagen, but no theater there would hire him.
12. When he wasn't successful, Andersen went back to school and earned good grades.
13. When he wrote his first fairy tale at the age of thirty, he never expected success.
14. People all over the world loved his stories, and they still read them today.

Sentence Diagraming

Diagraming Sentences

Each clause must have its own baseline in a diagram. As a result, only a simple sentence will have one baseline.

Compound Sentences A compound sentence is diagramed like two simple sentences, but the diagrams are connected by a broken line. The broken line joins the two verbs. The conjunction that joins the two sentences is written on this line.

You prepare the salad, and I will cook the stew.

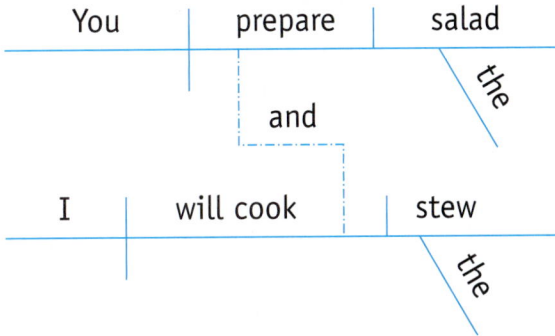

Complex Sentences An adverbial clause is diagramed beneath the independent clause, regardless of the order in a sentence. The subordinating conjunction belongs on a broken line that connects the verb in the adverbial clause to the word the clause modifies in the independent clause.

If you finish your homework, you can go to the movies.

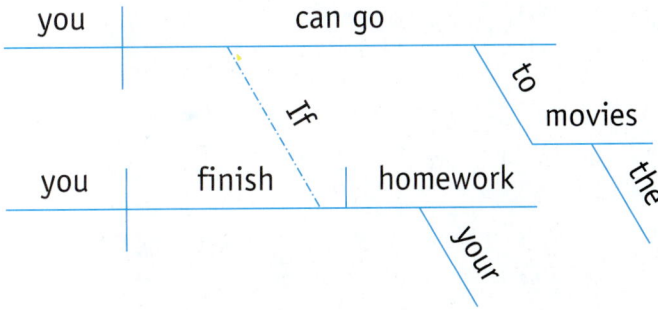

An adjectival clause is also diagramed beneath the independent clause. The relative pronoun is connected by a broken line to the noun or the pronoun the clause modifies. Keep in mind that a relative pronoun can also be the subject of an adjectival clause.

We liked the movie that is playing at the new theater.

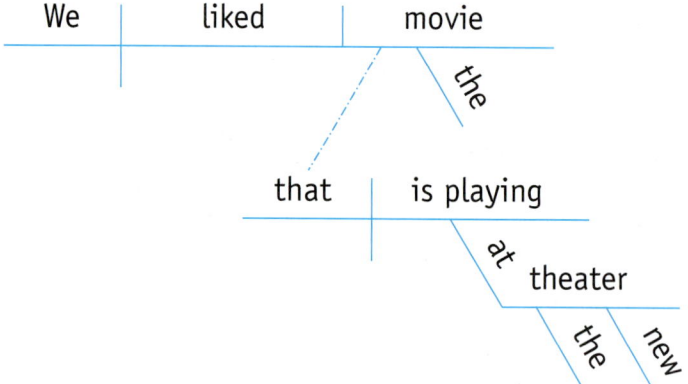

- **Practice Your Skills**

    Diagraming Sentences

    Diagram the following sentences or copy them. If you copy them, draw one line under each subject and two lines under each verb. Put any subordinate clauses in parentheses and draw arrows to the words they modify.

    1. Virginia became the tenth state when it joined the Union in 1788.
    2. Virginia is rich in history, and it is the birthplace of eight U.S. presidents.
    3. It has many historical sites that have been preserved.
    4. Williamsburg, which is a colonial village, is an unusual place.
    5. In the workshops blacksmiths make iron products, and weavers and glassblowers give demonstrations.

Chapter Review

Assess Your Learning

Finding Adverbial Clauses

Write each adverbial clause. Then write the word or words the clause describes.

1. Although there are no trees on the Aleutian Islands, other plants grow there.
2. As it sped through the air, the arrow hissed like a snake.
3. When the automobile was new and strange in 1896, it was shown in Barnum and Bailey's Circus.
4. Wrap the glasses carefully so that they don't break.
5. Mexican jumping beans jump because bugs live inside them.

Finding Adjectival Clauses

Write each adjectival clause. Then write the word or words the clause describes.

1. According to research there is no nation that does not enjoy music.
2. Clay pipes and wooden drums are often found in the graves of people who died thousands of years ago.
3. Musicians who lived in the Middle Ages often played a flute and beat a drum at the same time.
4. The bagpipe, which is generally considered a Scottish instrument, is also found in Africa and Asia.
5. Many folksongs that have been sung for centuries have only lately been written down.

Identifying Subordinate Clauses

Write each subordinate clause. Then label each one *adv.* for adverbial or *adj.* for adjectival.

1. Those who dwell among the beauties and mysteries of the earth are never alone or weary of life.—Rachel Carson
2. Big Red could do anything because a dog with his brains could be taught anything.—James Kjelgaard

3. Slang is language that rolls up its sleeves, spits on its hands, and goes to work.—Carl Sandburg
4. Home is all the words that call you in for dinner, over to help, into a hug, and out of a dream.—Michael J. Rosen
5. When I was a babe, I was warmed by the sun, rocked by the winds, and sheltered by the trees.—Geronimo

Using Sentence Structure

Write five sentences that follow the directions below. (The sentences may come in any order.) Write about the following topic or a topic of your choice: a job or occupation that sounds interesting to you and why you might choose that profession for yourself one day.

1. Write a simple sentence.
2. Write a complex sentence with an introductory adverbial clause.
3. Write a complex sentence with an adjectival clause.
4. Write a compound sentence joined by a comma and a conjunction.
5. Write a compound sentence joined by a semicolon.

When you have finished, label each sentence. Then check the punctuation of each one.

Clauses: Posttest

Directions
Write the letter of the term that correctly identifies the underlined group of words in each sentence.

(1) An ancient civilization, <u>which existed around 2500 B.C.</u>, was based in the Indus Valley. (2) <u>Archaeologists found the remains of two cities there.</u> (3) <u>Although the cities were built thousands of years ago,</u> they were laid out in a modern way. (4) <u>Streets intersected at right angles, and they were broad and long.</u> (5) <u>Each home had a sewer system,</u> so sewage disposal wasn't a problem. (6) The cities, <u>which were twin capitals of the area,</u> were called Harappa and Mohenjo-Daro. (7) <u>Because the cities were not rivals,</u> archaeologists think a strong central government must have existed. (8) <u>The cities were built of bricks that were dried in ovens.</u> (9) <u>The city of Harappa contained a huge granary,</u> which held grain to feed the population. (10) <u>The people of the area made cloth and pottery, and they also farmed.</u>

1. A adjectival clause
   B adverbial clause
   C independent clause
   D simple sentence

2. A compound sentence
   B complex sentence
   C independent clause
   D simple sentence

3. A adjectival clause
   B adverbial clause
   C independent clause
   D simple sentence

4. A compound sentence
   B complex sentence
   C independent clause
   D simple sentence

5. A adjectival clause
   B adverbial clause
   C independent clause
   D simple sentence

6. A adjectival clause
   B adverbial clause
   C independent clause
   D simple sentence

7. A adjectival clause
   B adverbial clause
   C independent clause
   D simple sentence

8. A compound sentence
   B complex sentence
   C independent clause
   D simple sentence

9. A adjectival clause
   B adverbial clause
   C independent clause
   D simple sentence

10. A compound sentence
    B complex sentence
    C independent clause
    D simple sentence

Writer's Corner

Snapshot

22 A A **clause** is a group of words that has a subject and a verb. An **independent, or main, clause** can stand alone as a sentence; a **subordinate, or dependent, clause** cannot stand alone as a sentence because it does not express a complete thought. (pages 638–639)

22 B A **subordinate clause** can be used as an adverb or as an adjective. An **adverbial clause** is a subordinate clause that is used mainly to modify a verb; an **adjectival clause** is used to modify a noun or a pronoun. (pages 640–646)

22 C There are three basic kinds of sentences: **simple, compound,** and **complex.** (pages 647–652)

Power Rules

 A **subordinate clause** must have something to relate to, or else it is a **sentence fragment.** Create a complete idea by connecting the fragment to a related sentence. You can also eliminate the subordinating conjunction and create two complete sentences. (pages 666–667)

Before Editing

Dad stopped the car. *Because* he wanted to check the map.

The children ran to the park. *Where* they played on the swings.

After Editing

Dad stopped the car *because* he wanted to check the map.

The children ran to the park. They played on the swings.

Editing Checklist

Use this checklist when editing your writing.

- ✓ Did I include a subject and verb in each clause? (See pages 638–639.)
- ✓ Did I use subordinating conjunctions where necessary to clearly show the relationships between ideas? (See pages 640–642.)
- ✓ Did I punctuate my adverbial clauses correctly? (See pages 641–642.)
- ✓ Did I use the correct relative pronoun to start my adjectival clauses? (See pages 643–645.)
- ✓ Did I punctuate my adjectival clauses correctly? (See pages 644–646.)
- ✓ Did I position the adjectival clauses so it is clear what they modify? (See page 646.)

Use the Power

Anticipate and answer readers' questions by using subordinate clauses in complex sentences. The subordinating words are highlighted.

Questions	Examples
How?	She left the test center as though she had run a marathon.
When?	She was exhausted after she finished the long exam.
Where?	Wherever she looked she saw answer bubbles.
To what extent?	As much as she tried to stay awake, she fell asleep on her couch later that day.
Why?	Because she missed the last test date, she had to take the test early in the morning.
Which ones?	Her experience only proves once again that early morning tests are the worst.

Select a composition from your portfolio. Underline the complex sentences. Then revise your paper by adding at least two complex sentences.

Writer's Corner 659

CHAPTER 23

Sentence Fragments and Run-ons

How can you clarify your meaning and add sentence variety by fixing unintended sentence fragments and run-ons?

Sentence Fragments and Run-ons: Pretest 1

The following first draft is hard to read because it contains fragments and run-on sentences. How would you revise the draft so that it reads more smoothly? The first run-on sentence has been corrected as an example.

In February, we visited Iceland. Iceland is very far north, *but* the Gulf Stream keeps the weather from getting too cold. Winter temperatures range around 32 degrees. We needed warm coats. Volcanoes under Iceland. People use the volcanoes to provide heat, this is called geothermal heat. We visited the Blue Lagoon, where the water is heated geothermally. After a long swim. We dried off and went to dinner. At a Viking restaurant. While in Iceland, we saw many interesting things. We visited an area with many geysers, *geyser* is actually an Icelandic word. Icelandic horses on the farms. Saw waterfalls. We stayed in Reykjavik, the capital of Iceland we visited other towns, as well. Fishing is very important in Iceland. A salmon river right through Reykjavik. It was a great trip, and we hope to go back someday.

Sentence Fragments and Run-ons: Pretest 2

Directions
Read the passage. Write the letter of the best way to write each group of underlined words. If the underlined words contain no error, write **D**.

Peppers are used **(1)** <u>in cooking. Throughout the world.</u> **(2)** <u>Some peppers are sweet some have sharp, spicy flavors.</u> Although they are high **(3)** <u>in vitamins A and C, peppers are low</u> in calories. Different kinds of **(4)** <u>peppers varying from</u> mild to extremely hot. Peppers are named after their place of origin. For example, El Paso chilies **(5)** <u>come from the city of El Paso in Texas.</u>

1. **A** in cooking, throughout the world.
   B in cooking throughout the world.
   C In cooking throughout the world.
   D No error

2. **A** Some peppers are sweet, some have sharp, spicy flavors.
   B Some peppers are sweet or some have sharp, spicy flavors.
   C Some peppers are sweet. Some have sharp, spicy flavors.
   D No error

3. **A** in vitamins A and C, and peppers are low
   B in vitamins A and C. Peppers are low
   C in vitamins A and C but peppers are low
   D No error

4. **A** peppers. Varying from
   B peppers vary from
   C peppers that vary from
   D No error

5. **A** come from the city of El Paso. In Texas.
   B coming from the city of El Paso in Texas.
   C come from the city of El Paso, it is in Texas.
   D No error

Sentence Fragments

You have learned that a sentence must have a subject and a verb to express a complete thought. A group of words punctuated as a sentence that is missing either a subject or a verb is called a **sentence fragment**.

23 A A **sentence fragment** is a group of words punctuated as a sentence that does not express a complete thought.

To be complete, a sentence must have both a subject and a verb and must express a complete thought. In each of the following examples, the subject is underlined once and the verb is underlined twice.

No Subject	**Spoke** to the band after the show. (*Who* spoke to the band?)
Complete Sentence	Brenda spoke to the band after the show. (Now the sentence has a subject.)
No Verb	Joe's **cousin** from Detroit. (What does Joe's cousin do?)
Complete Sentence	Joe's cousin from Detroit **plays** in a band. (Now the sentence has a verb.)

When you edit, check for any missing subjects or missing verbs.

When You Write

Writers often use fragments in fiction and drama for dialogue or for incomplete thoughts. Fragments, however, are almost never appropriate in formal writing, such as school assignments and business letters.

● **Practice Your Skills**

Identifying Sentence Fragments

Label each group of words **S** for sentence and **SF** for sentence fragment.

1. No one thought the Beatles had much talent in the early 1960s.
2. Said they were a musical disaster.
3. The band began its career in England.
4. Their unusual style.
5. The Beatles' arrival in America.

6. Their appearance on *The Ed Sullivan Show* was one of the highest-rated programs of its day.
7. Their music was a hit.
8. Thousands of fans.
9. Sold 2.5 million albums and singles in four weeks' time.
10. The fans went crazy.
11. Dozens of girls fainted at the Beatles' appearances across America.
12. The Beatles were the first rock-and-roll band to play at Carnegie Hall.
13. Had an amazing tour across most of the United States.
14. Apparently the critics were wrong.
15. Changed rock-and-roll music forever.

Connect to Writing: Revising

Correcting Sentence Fragments

Rewrite the sentence fragments from the preceding exercise to make complete sentences.

Check Point: Mixed Practice

Write **S** if the fragment is missing a subject or **V** if the fragment is missing a verb.

1. The reed for the clarinet.
2. Dropped the case on the ground.
3. Had sprung open.
4. My new clarinet.
5. Picked it up and tried the mouthpiece.
6. A crack on the mouthpiece.
7. Told my band teacher.
8. My mom and dad.
9. The price for the repairs.
10. My allowance for the next ten weeks.
11. Once dropped.
12. Plays the trumpet.
13. Practices every day.
14. My brother.

Phrase Fragments — Lesson 2

A sentence must have a subject and a verb to be complete. Since a phrase does not have either a subject or a verb, it can never stand alone as a sentence. When phrases are written alone, they result in **phrase fragments.** The phrase in **bold** type in the example below is a phrase fragment. Notice that it is punctuated as if it were a sentence.

> **Phrase Fragment**   **To keep your plants healthy.** You must care for your garden daily.

23 B A **phrase fragment** is a group of words standing alone without a subject or a verb.

You can correct a phrase fragment in one of two ways: add a subject and a verb to make it a separate sentence, or attach it to a related group of words that has a subject and a verb.

Prepositional Phrase Fragment	We waited for them for an hour. **At the edge of the garden.**
Corrected	We waited for them for an hour **at the edge of the garden.** (attached to a sentence)
Appositive Phrase Fragment	Have you ever met Mrs. Cho? **The famous gardener.**
Corrected	Have you ever met Mrs. Cho? **She is the famous gardener.** (subject and verb added)
Participial Phrase Fragment	The children watched the rabbits. **Nibbling on some lettuce.**
Corrected	The children watched the rabbits **nibbling on some lettuce.** (attached to a sentence)
Infinitive Phrase Fragment	**To keep your plants healthy.** You must care for your garden daily.
Corrected	**To keep your plants healthy,** you must care for your garden daily. (attached to a sentence)

Sentence Fragments and Run-ons

● **Practice Your Skills**

Identifying Phrase Fragments

Label each group of words *S* for sentence or *PF* for phrase fragment.

1. In the garden on a hot day.
2. The cucumber plants are very green this year.
3. Watering the garden with a hose.
4. I saw the birds eating the tomatoes again.
5. To stop them from eating all my plants.
6. I work hard to guard against bugs.
7. For the best gardener in my family.
8. My dad knows how to make plants grow.
9. At the end of a hot day.
10. We enjoy fresh vegetables from our garden.

● **Practice Your Skills**

Identifying Phrase Fragments

Label each group of words *S* for sentence or *PF* for phrase fragment.

1. George Washington Carver was a professor of agriculture.
2. At the Tuskegee Institute.
3. George Washington Carver was an ecologist.
4. To teach people about using the soil productively.
5. Carver spent much of his childhood tending the family vegetable garden.
6. Collecting new flowers.
7. As a quiet child.
8. Soon young Carver was known as the "plant doctor."
9. To help people take care of the land.
10. Carver's work resulted in many new uses for the peanut plant.

● *Connect to Writing:* **Revising**

Correcting Phrase Fragments

Rewrite the phrase fragments from the preceding exercise to make complete sentences.

Clause Fragments — Lesson 3

When a subordinate clause stands alone, it becomes a **clause fragment** because it does not express a complete thought. The clause in **bold** type below is a fragment. Notice that it is punctuated as if it were a complete sentence.

Clause Fragment   **Before the hunt began.** The dogs played with the pups.

23 C   A **clause fragment** is a subordinate clause punctuated as a sentence.

Ways to Correct Clause Fragments

You can correct clause fragments in one of two ways: change the subordinate clause to an independent clause, or attach a clause fragment to a related sentence next to it.

Adverbial Clause Fragment	We stayed behind. **So that we could observe the pups more carefully.**
Corrected	We stayed behind. **That way we could observe the pups more carefully.** (made into an independent clause)
Adjectival Clause Fragment	Is this the dog? **That we should tag for the scientist?**
Corrected	Is this the dog **that we should tag for the scientist?** (attached to a sentence)

When You Write

Listen to yourself when you talk with your friends. You will probably notice that you use fragments all the time. Writers imitate such normal conversation so that their writing sounds natural. Notice the fragments in the following excerpt.

> "And how old is this kid?"
> "About twelve, maybe a little older."
> "And for this you swore me to secrecy?"
>
> —Walter Dean Myers, *The Mouse Rap*

Review a piece of fiction or a play you have worked on recently. Add sentence fragments to the dialogue to create a natural feel to the piece.

Practice Your Skills

Recognizing Clause Fragments

Label each group of words **S** for sentence or **CF** for clause fragment.

1. Since it is called a wild dog.
2. Wild dogs are not house pets gone bad.
3. Tim McNutt spent many years researching African wild dogs.
4. Who is a wildlife biologist.
5. Wild dogs are most like wolves.
6. Which are nearly as endangered as the black rhino.
7. People mistakenly believe that wild dogs are bad animals.
8. Although they live in a pack.
9. Wild dogs sometimes make kills by themselves.
10. Because they have a tightly structured social system.

Practice Your Skills

Recognizing Clause Fragments

Label each group of words **S** for sentence or **CF** for clause fragment. Then rewrite five clause fragments to make complete sentences.

1. Jean Craighead George wrote *Julie of the Wolves*.
2. Since the author studied wolf behavior.
3. Many people have learned much about wolves.
4. After they have read *Julie of the Wolves*.
5. Julie, who is the main character.
6. She runs away from home.
7. The setting of the story is not a friendly one.
8. Which is located in the frozen North.
9. The wolves find her and save her life.
10. Before she freezes to death.

Connect to Writing: E-mail Message

Clause Fragments

Your family has just visited a nature preserve, and you think it would be a good place for your science class to visit. Write an e-mail message to your science teacher describing your trip. Explain that you would like to have your class visit the nature preserve. Give enough details to convince your teacher, and be sure to avoid using clause fragments.

Run-on Sentences

When people write too fast, they sometimes combine several thoughts together as one sentence. The result is a run-on sentence.

23 D A **run-on sentence** is two or more sentences that are written together as one sentence by incorrectly connecting them with a comma or with no mark of punctuation at all.

In each of the following examples, the subject of the sentence is underlined once, and the verb is underlined twice.

With a Comma	The crocodile is hunting, it will search for frogs.
	The bear is tired, it will sleep now.
With No Comma	The orca missed its prey another orca got the seal.
	White tigers are rare they have blue eyes.

● **Practice Your Skills**

Identifying Run-on Sentences

Label each group of words **S** for *sentence* or **RO** for *run-on*.

1. Bears climb trees like cats, they sink their claws into the bark.
2. Birds use their bills for many purposes.
3. Locusts can travel three hundred miles nonstop their average air speed can reach eight miles per hour.
4. Some centipedes have 28 legs others have as many as 354 legs.
5. A trout can live in a lake for as long as four years.
6. A cheetah can reach speeds of over sixty miles per hour.
7. Humans are very seldom bitten or attacked by vampire bats these flying mammals do not like human blood.
8. Lionesses do most of the hunting lions defend the territory.
9. Cobras prey on other poisonous snakes they subdue them with very strong venom.
10. Great white sharks are the only sharks that regularly attack mammals.

Ways to Correct Run-on Sentences

The examples below show some of the approaches you can take to correct run-on sentences. For example, you can turn the run-on into separate sentences. You can also combine the sentences by using a comma and a conjunction or a semicolon and a conjunctive adverb.

Run-on Sentence	We rushed into the village, the elephant had already left.
Separate Sentences	We rushed into the village. **T**he elephant had already left.
Comma and Conjunction	We rushed into the village, **but** the elephant had already left.
Semicolon and Conjunctive Adverb	We rushed into the village**; however,** the elephant had already left.

You can fix some run-on sentences by separating them with a semicolon. You can also create a complex sentence by converting one of the sentences into a subordinate clause. You should take care, however, not to change the original meaning of the sentences.

Run-on Sentence	We rushed into the village, the elephant left.
Semicolon	We rushed into the village**;** the elephant left.
Complex Sentence	**When** we rushed into the village, the elephant left.

● Practice Your Skills

Identifying Run-on Sentences

Label each group of words **S** for sentence or **RO** for run-on. Then rewrite the run-on sentences correcting the errors.

1. In India, people and elephants compete for resources.
2. Elephants are enormous animals, they need a large amount of space.
3. India has a very large population and needs land for farming.
4. Elephants destroy vegetable crops the farmers become angry.
5. Game wardens have no choice but to capture such animals.
6. A captured elephant is transported to a refuge it gets a second chance.
7. Conservationists are looking for a better solution to the problem.
8. Some experts believe that people can learn to live with wild animals.
9. An elephant often returns to the same grazing area, when people move into these areas elephants become upset.
10. An angry elephant can cause a lot of damage it is a very big animal.

✓ Check Point: Mixed Practice

Correct each fragment or run-on sentence. Add capital letters, commas, conjunctions, and end marks where needed. If a sentence is correct, write **C**.

1. The first subway in the world opened in London. On January 10, 1863.
2. A large trench was dug a pavement was laid over it.
3. The trains were powered by steam engines, the smoke from the engines filled the tunnels with terrible fumes.
4. Ten feet of water once filled the tunnels the subway shut down briefly.
5. About thirty years later, London's first "tube tunnel" was built.
6. And instantly became a success.
7. In a tube line, a tunnel is actually bored through the ground.
8. Under the foundations of buildings.
9. The first tube line used electric power.
10. And it still runs today.
11. In 1897, Boston completed the first subway system.
12. That ran in the United States.
13. It ran only 1½ miles.
14. And used trolley cars on the subway tracks.
15. New York's subway finally opened in 1904, more than two billion people now ride it every year.

• *Connect to Speaking and Listening:* Peer Interaction

Reviewing Content

With a partner, list the types of sentence errors introduced in this chapter. Quiz each other until you know the definitions of all the new words and concepts. Then write sentences or paragraphs with sentence errors in them. Exchange papers and revise the sentences and paragraphs. Then discuss the solutions you each used to correct the problems.

Chapter Review

Assess Your Learning

Identifying Sentences, Fragments, and Run-ons

Label each group of words *S* for sentence, *F* for fragment, or *RO* for run-on.

1. Robert Louis Stevenson wrote many books, one of them was *Treasure Island*.
2. The warmth of a wool poncho on a cold day.
3. Benjamin Franklin wanted the wild turkey as our national bird.
4. Through the front door of the Mason's apartment.
5. Mavis and her sister earned their lifesaving certificates last year.
6. Corey bowed, the audience stood and cheered.
7. The horseshoe crab has two pairs of eyes.
8. Enjoyed a salad of bananas, oranges, and papayas.
9. Ostriches cannot fly they have small, weak wings.
10. The display of Indian art at the Denver Art Museum.
11. To play in the championship game.
12. Cathy reading her favorite book.
13. The bell rang the students went into class.
14. The weather has turned warmer.
15. In front of the door of the yellow house.
16. Bob Holley, the artist who painted that picture.
17. Since tomorrow is Monday.
18. The baseball player who hit the most home runs.
19. Behind the wall was a garden.
20. The dog barked, the cat ran.

■ Correcting Sentence Fragments

Write a complete sentence using each sentence fragment.

1. In the pocket of an old coat.
2. Can't find today's newspaper.
3. The parade with bands and floats.
4. Pulled over to the side of the road.
5. And ran onto the field.
6. A large school of fish beneath the boat.
7. Rock squirrels with black stripes on their backs.
8. The limb of the spruce tree.
9. Owned a red car with white stripes.
10. On the trees at the farm.

■ Correcting Sentence Errors

Rewrite the following paragraph correcting the sentence fragments and run-on sentences.

In 1844, young Elizabeth Blackwell wanted to become a doctor, medical schools did not accept women students at that time. Blackwell was very determined, however. For a while she studied. With private teachers. Then in 1846, a medical school in New York. Finally admitted her as a student. After she finished her studies, she could not find a job at any established hospital. Therefore, she founded her own hospital. For women and children. Today the Blackwell Medal is awarded to women physicians it recognizes their achievements as doctors.

Sentence Fragments and Run-ons: Posttest

Directions
Read the passage. Write the letter of the best way to write each group of underlined words. If the underlined words contain no error, write **D**.

The word *mandarin* has **(1)** several meanings all of them are interesting. There is the **(2)** mandarin orange. That originated in China. It is sweet and juicy, and it's easy to peel. **(3)** In the Chinese Empire. A mandarin is an official of rank. Also, the official spoken language in China is Mandarin. **(4)** It is based on a dialect spoken in and around Beijing. When it refers to a style of **(5)** Chinese dress, and the word *mandarin* describes a short, stand-up collar.

1. **A** several meanings, all of them
   B several meanings. All of them
   C several meanings. That all of them
   D No error

2. **A** mandarin orange, that originated in China.
   B mandarin orange and originated in China.
   C mandarin orange that originated in China.
   D No error

3. **A** In the Chinese Empire, a mandarin is
   B In the Chinese Empire a mandarin. Is
   C In the Chinese Empire, a mandarin being
   D No error

4. **A** It is based on a dialect. Spoken in and around Beijing.
   B It is based on a dialect spoken. In and around Beijing.
   C It is based. On a dialect spoken in and around Beijing.
   D No error

5. **A** Chinese dress, the word *mandarin* describes a short, stand-up collar.
   B Chinese dress. The word *mandarin* describes a short, stand-up collar.
   C Chinese dress, the word *mandarin* to describe a short, stand-up collar.
   D No error

Writer's Corner

Snapshot

23 A   A **sentence fragment** is a group of words, punctuated as a sentence, that does not express a complete thought. (pages 662–663)

23 B   A **phrase fragment** is a group of words standing alone without a subject or a verb. (pages 664–665)

23 C   A **clause fragment** is a subordinate clause punctuated as a sentence. (pages 666–667)

23 D   A **run-on sentence** is two or more sentences that are written together as a sentence by incorrectly joining them with a comma or with no mark of punctuation at all. (pages 668–670)

Power Rules

 A sentence needs to have a subject and a predicate to express a complete thought. **Fix sentence fragments by adding the missing subject or verb.** (pages 662–665)

Before Editing	After Editing
Flew in through the window.	*A bird* flew in through the window.
The neighbor next door.	The neighbor next door *had a barbecue*.

 Fix **run-on sentences** by adding a conjunction and/or appropriate punctuation. You can also fix a run-on by writing it as two sentences. (pages 669–670)

Before Editing	After Editing
Acoustic and electric guitars have six strings, bass guitars usually have four.	Acoustic and electric guitars have six strings. Bass guitars usually have four.
	Acoustic and electric guitars have six strings; bass guitars usually have four.
We rushed to catch the train, we arrived too late.	We rushed to catch the train, *but* we arrived too late.

Sentence Fragments and Run-ons

Editing Checklist

Use this checklist when editing your writing.

✓ Did I include a subject and a verb in each sentence? (See pages 662–663.)
✓ Did I make sure there were no phrase fragments? (See pages 664–665.)
✓ Did I make sure there were no clause fragments? (See pages 666–667.)
✓ Did I use the correct punctuation or conjunctions to avoid run-ons? (See pages 668–670.)

Use the Power

A sentence fragment is similar to a photo or drawing with important parts missing. It can be hard to tell what you are reading if sentence parts are missing.

A run-on sentence is similar to a picture frame with two or three images pushed together. Such sentences are hard to read because it is hard to tell where one idea stops and another starts.

Review several pieces from your portfolio, looking for run-on sentences and unwanted fragments. Revise any sentence errors you find.

Writer's Corner

Unit 5
Usage

Chapter 24	Using Verbs	678
Chapter 25	Using Pronouns	708
Chapter 26	Subject and Verb Agreement	738
Chapter 27	Using Adjectives and Adverbs	766
	A Writer's Glossary of Usage	786

AREAS HIT HARD BY FLU IN SPRING SEE LITTLE NOW

This (real) headline appeared in a metropolitan newspaper. The headline gives readers the impression that where the flu hit, widespread blindness followed. When writing to convey information, make sure your usage helps rather than hinders your cause. The words you use—the nouns, pronouns, verbs, adjectives, and adverbs—must be in agreement. Your choice of words must capture the reality of the situation and state it clearly. Consider the intended meaning of the headline above; then write a clearer headline. Check your headline against the one that is upside down below.

Areas Hit Hard by Flu See a Decrease in Cases

Areas Hit Hard by Flu in Spring See Little Now —
October 8, 2009

CHAPTER 24

Using Verbs

How can you use verbs to communicate action, the precise time of an action, and certainty or doubt?

Using Verbs: Pretest 1

Read the following first draft about the man who discovered Tutankhamen's tomb. The draft contains several errors in the use of verbs. The first error is corrected. How would you revise the draft so that all verbs are used correctly?

Howard Carter ~~is~~ *was* born in 1874. His father, an artist, learned his son how to draw. At an early age, Carter becomed interested in Egypt. He was only seventeen when he leaved home to visit Egypt for the first time. He were hired by explorers and archaeologists who teached him what he would need to know to do his own research. In 1905, the Earl of Carnarvon, who had a passion for Egyptian antiquities, wants to finance some archaeological work. Carter seem to be the best archaeologist available. He brung a lot of passion to his work, and Carnarvon admired that. Carter worked for many years. In 1922, Howard Carter's work patience will be rewarded with the discovery of King Tut's tomb—the greatest discovery in Egyptian archaeology.

Using Verbs: Pretest 2

Directions
Read the passage and write the letter of the word or group of words that belongs in each underlined space.

Baby sea turtles face many dangers. Just hatching __(1)__ a bit iffy. __(2)__ this. Some crabs __(3)__ sea turtle eggs, and adult turtles sometimes crush the nesting eggs of other turtles. Only one hatchling in one thousand __(4)__ to adulthood. Even as hatchlings scramble to the sea, predators __(5)__ to gobble them up.

Other hazards are threatening the survival of adult turtles. Pollution and poaching __(6)__ two. Actually, humans are sea turtles' greatest threat. Poachers __(7)__ turtles to meet the demand for turtle parts. Toxins __(8)__ turtles on land and in the sea. Unchecked, such problems __(9)__ sea turtles to extinction. Who __(10)__ the sea turtles' survival in the twenty-first century?

1. **A** is
   B being
   C was
   D has been

2. **A** Considers
   B Considered
   C Consider
   D Considering

3. **A** ate
   B eating
   C eats
   D eat

4. **A** has survived
   B survived
   C survives
   D is surviving

5. **A** tried
   B try
   C tries
   D have tried

6. **A** had been
   B was
   C are
   D will

7. **A** hunting
   B hunted
   C hunts
   D hunt

8. **A** harm
   B harmed
   C have harmed
   D will harm

9. **A** brings
   B could bring
   C takes
   D could take

10. **A** has assured
    B will assure
    C assures
    D assure

The Principal Parts of Verbs

You know that a verb shows action or makes a statement about the subject of a sentence. A verb also tells when the action happens.

Present Action Each day I **call** Suzanne.
Past Action Yesterday I **called** her.
Future Action Tomorrow I **will call** her again.

Notice that a verb changes its form to show the time of the action. The different forms of a verb are made from the basic parts of a verb, called principal parts.

24 A The **principal parts** of a verb are the present, the present participle, the past, and the past participle.

Following are the principal parts of the verb *call*. Notice that the present participle and the past participle must have a helping verb when they are used as verbs.

Present I often **call** my friend after dinner.
Present Participle I *am* **calling** her tonight.
Past I **called** her last week.
Past Participle I *have* **called** her six times this week.

You can learn more about helping verbs on pages 526–527.

➤ Regular Verbs

Most verbs form their past and past participle just like the verb *call*—by adding *-ed* or *-d* to the present. These verbs are called regular verbs.

24 A.1 A **regular verb** forms its past and past participle by adding *-ed* or *-d* to the present.

The principal parts of the verbs *talk, bake, stop,* and *carry* are listed on the next page. Notice that the present participle is formed by adding *-ing* to the present form. Also, as the rule says, the past is formed by adding *-ed* or *-d* to the present.

REGULAR VERBS			
Present	**Present Participle**	**Past**	**Past Participle**
talk	(is) talking	talked	(have) talked
bake	(is) baking	baked	(have) baked
stop	(is) stopping	stopped	(have) stopped
carry	(is) carrying	carried	(have) carried

When you add a word ending such as -*ing* or -*ed* to verbs such as *bake*, *stop*, and *carry*, the spelling changes. Use a dictionary if you are unsure how to spell a verb form.

You can learn more about spelling on pages 906–933.

● **Practice Your Skills**

Writing the Principal Parts of Regular Verbs

Make four columns on your paper. Label them **present, present participle, past,** and **past participle.** Then write the four principal parts of each of the regular verbs below. Use *is* when you write the present participle and *have* when you write the past participle.

1. climb
2. drag
3. suppose
4. paint
5. wish
6. stop
7. use
8. earn
9. skip
10. move

● *Connect to Writing and Speaking:* **Sentences**

Writing Sentences with Regular Verbs

Write five sentences, using the instructions below. Remember to use a helping verb with the present participle and past participle. Read your sentences aloud to a partner.

1. Write a sentence using the present form of *laugh*.
2. Write a sentence using the past form of *cry*.
3. Write a sentence using the present participle form of *play*.
4. Write a sentence using the past participle form of *hope*.
5. Write a sentence using the present participle form of *dream*.

▶ Irregular Verbs

Although most verbs form their past and past participle by adding *-ed* or *-d,* a few verbs do not. These verbs are called irregular verbs.

24 A.2 An **irregular verb** does not form its past and past participle by adding *-ed* or *-d* to the present.

Irregular verbs can be divided into groups according to the way they form their past and past participles. You should remember that the word *is* is not part of the present participle and *have* is not part of the past participle. Still, they have been added to the following lists of irregular verbs. They are there to remind you that all present and past participles must have a form of these helping verbs when they are used in a sentence.

Group 1 These irregular verbs have the same form for the present, the past, and the past participle.

Present	Present Participle	Past	Past Participle
burst	(is) bursting	burst	(have) burst
cut	(is) cutting	cut	(have) cut
let	(is) letting	let	(have) let
put	(is) putting	put	(have) put
set	(is) setting	set	(have) set

Group 2 These irregular verbs have the same form for the past and the past participle.

Present	Present Participle	Past	Past Participle
bring	(is) bringing	brought	(have) brought
buy	(is) buying	bought	(have) bought
catch	(is) catching	caught	(have) caught
leave	(is) leaving	left	(have) left
make	(is) making	made	(have) made
say	(is) saying	said	(have) said
teach	(is) teaching	taught	(have) taught

Using Verbs

● **Practice Your Skills**

Using the Correct Verb Form

Label each underlined verb form *past* or *past participle*.

1. Yesterday no one in the stadium <u>left</u> before the end of the game.
2. Jimmy's old football uniform has finally <u>burst</u> its seams.
3. Who <u>made</u> the winning touchdown last night?
4. Has everyone <u>brought</u> his playbook to today's practice?
5. Coach Lee has <u>said</u> that many times before.
6. You should have <u>put</u> your uniform in your locker at the end of practice.
7. Our coach <u>taught</u> us a new play.
8. I <u>let</u> Joe block for me.
9. Danny <u>brought</u> us each a basket of candy from the cheerleaders.
10. I have <u>made</u> the starting lineup.

● *Connect to Writing:* **Editing**

Correcting Sentences with Irregular Verbs

Rewrite the following sentences, replacing the underlined verb with the correct verb form.

1. John <u>bursted</u> through the other team's weak defense.
2. The referee <u>putted</u> the ball on the thirty-five-yard line.
3. The coach should have <u>letted</u> me play.
4. On his last run, Gary <u>brung</u> our team to within scoring distance.
5. Benjamin had <u>catched</u> the football very close to the goal line.
6. When we beat Central in the last game, we <u>maked</u> the playoffs.

● *Connect to Speaking and Listening:* **Correct a Summary**

Correcting the Use of Irregular Verbs

With a partner, take turns reading the following game summary aloud. Help one another correct any irregular verbs that have been used incorrectly.

> Last night when our team leaved the field, Coach was very proud. He say that he had never before seen such a great effort by the whole team. The local newspapers says that our team is sure to win the playoffs now. The sensational overtime win putted us in first place and brung us to the championship level.

The Principal Parts of Verbs • Lesson 1

Group 3 These irregular verbs form the past participle by adding *-n* to the past.

Present	Present Participle	Past	Past Participle
break	(is) breaking	broke	(have) broken
choose	(is) choosing	chose	(have) chosen
freeze	(is) freezing	froze	(have) frozen
speak	(is) speaking	spoke	(have) spoken
steal	(is) stealing	stole	(have) stolen

Group 4 These irregular verbs form the past participle by adding *-n* to the present.

Present	Present Participle	Past	Past Participle
blow	(is) blowing	blew	(have) blown
drive	(is) driving	drove	(have) driven
give	(is) giving	gave	(have) given
grow	(is) growing	grew	(have) grown
know	(is) knowing	knew	(have) known
see	(is) seeing	saw	(have) seen
take	(is) taking	took	(have) taken
throw	(is) throwing	threw	(have) thrown

● Practice Your Skills

Determining the Correct Verb Form

Write the correct verb form for each sentence. Remember that *have, has,* or *had* is used with the past participle.

1. Has anyone (saw, seen) the article about Tim Russell's 30th season home run?
2. Russell had (broke, broken) the college league record for the most home runs in a season.
3. By the end of the season, he had (drove, driven) thirty home runs out of the ballpark.
4. His last home run was a moment that has been (froze, frozen) in time.
5. No one in our league has (stole, stolen) Russell's record.
6. During this season, Russell's reputation (growed, grew) even more.
7. Russell has (took, taken) his record-breaking feats in stride.

8. Russell (threw, throwed) himself into playing great baseball.

9. He has (spoke, spoken) to the local press about his records.

10. He says that as a child, he never (knew, knowed) that he would be such a good hitter.

Using the Correct Verb Form

Write the past or the past participle of each verb in parentheses. Remember that *have, has,* or *had* is used with the past participle.

1. Over the past few years, bears have (drive) people to take extra precautions in national parks.

2. A grizzly bear (break) the spine of a salmon with a snap of its jaws.

3. In the past, grizzly bears have (choose) to be active at night when humans were near.

4. Bears in campgrounds (give) many groups of campers a fright.

5. Some campers have (see) bears climbing into tents in search of food.

6. The grizzly population has (grow) in mountainous areas.

7. One bear even (take) some fruit from a basket.

8. Those bears should have (know) to stay away from the ranger station.

Connect to Writing: Editing

Correcting Sentences with Irregular Verbs

Write the following sentences, replacing any incorrect verb with the correct verb form. If a sentence is correct, write **C**.

1. A bear had broke into Grandma's smokehouse.

2. Fortunately, the bear choose only the smallest piece of meat.

3. Grandma has spoke with the local game warden.

4. Last year a bear steal three of Grandma's hams.

5. She should have known that bears would want the food.

When You Speak

If you've been around young children much, you know they have difficulty using irregular verbs. They are apt to say proudly, "I **putted** my toys away," or to complain loudly, "She **drinked** my juice." You can help children learn the correct form by rephrasing their statements: "Good! You **put** your toys away," or "She **drank** your juice?"

The Principal Parts of Verbs • Lesson 1

Group 5 These irregular verbs form the past and past participle by changing a vowel. The *i* in the present changes to an *a* in the past and a *u* in the past participle.

Present	Present Participle	Past	Past Participle
begin	(is) beginning	began	(have) begun
drink	(is) drinking	drank	(have) drunk
ring	(is) ringing	rang	(have) rung
sing	(is) singing	sang	(have) sung
swim	(is) swimming	swam	(have) swum

Group 6 These irregular verbs form the past and past participle in other ways.

Present	Present Participle	Past	Past Participle
come	(is) coming	came	(have) come
do	(is) doing	did	(have) done
eat	(is) eating	ate	(have) eaten
go	(is) going	went	(have) gone
ride	(is) riding	rode	(have) ridden
run	(is) running	ran	(have) run
wear	(is) wearing	wore	(have) worn
write	(is) writing	wrote	(have) written

● Practice Your Skills

Determining the Correct Verb Form

Write the correct verb form for each sentence. Remember that *have, has,* or *had* is used with the past participle.

1. Has Patrick ever (did, done) this kind of rodeo work before?
2. The steer (ran, run) crazily into the center of the ring.
3. Have you ever (went, gone) to a rodeo?
4. I (began, begun) barrel racing when I was seven years old.
5. The starting bell (rang, rung) three minutes ago.
6. Has Nick ever (wore, worn) that blue plaid cowboy shirt?
7. Jessica (drank, drunk) three glasses of water after her barrel race.
8. Do you know who (sang, sung) the national anthem?

● **Practice Your Skills**

Using the Correct Verb Form

Write the past or the past participle of each verb in parentheses. Remember that **have, has,** or **had** is used with the past participle.

1. The three tenors (do) a second encore at the end of their performance.
2. Had those four sopranos ever (sing) together before?
3. The critics should have (eat) their words about the concert.
4. The conductor must have (ride) to rehearsal with the drummer, because they were both late.
5. The singers should have (came) an hour before the show.
6. Rehearsal had (begin) without the dancers on the stage.
7. All the musicians (wear) special jackets for the evening's first performance with the tenors.
8. Who (write) that aria?

● **Practice Your Skills**

Finding the Principal Parts in a Dictionary

Make four columns on your paper. Label them **present, present participle, past,** and **past participle.** Use a dictionary to find the principal parts of the following verbs, and write them in the correct columns.

1. think
2. fly
3. raise
4. bite
5. win
6. shake
7. lead
8. catch
9. tear
10. spring

The Principal Parts of Verbs • Lesson 1   687

● Connect to Writing: Editing

Correcting Sentences with Irregular Verbs

Rewrite each of the following sentences, replacing any incorrect verb forms with the correct verb form. If a sentence is correct, write **C**.

1. Shannon sung her first solo at the concert last night.
2. The concert almost begun without her and Samantha.
3. Shannon had wrote the song especially for her performance.
4. Marti did a dance after Shannon's solo.
5. Christina's parents come to the concert at intermission.

● Connect to Speaking: Making an Announcement

Correcting Improperly Used Verbs

Read the following intercom announcement aloud to a classmate or your teacher. As you read, correct any verb errors you see.

> We are holding auditions for the talent show on Thursday. If you have ever sang a song, please come. If you have ever did any karate performances, you are welcome too. Make sure you have wrote your name on the list. We will call and tell you the time for auditions.

✓ Check Point: Mixed Practice

Write the past or the past participle of each verb in parentheses.

1. People (write) and (say) why their city should be the nation's capital.
2. Congress finally (decide) to create a new city.
3. Congress (pass) a bill in 1790 giving permission to the president to choose a site.
4. George Washington (go) to several places and (choose) the place where the city now stands.
5. He (know) it was a good location because the Potomac River (run) deep enough for ships.
6. Maryland and Virginia (give) the land to the federal government.
7. President Washington then (bring) in a French architect to design the new city.
8. The architect (begin) to draw plans with broad avenues.

Six Problem Verbs

The following sets of verbs are called problem verbs because their meanings are often confused—causing problems.

bring and *take*

Bring indicates motion toward the speaker. *Take* indicates motion away from the speaker.

Present	Present Participle	Past	Past Participle
bring	(is) bringing	brought	(have) brought
take	(is) taking	took	(have) taken

Bring David **brings** us doughnuts every morning.
David **is bringing** us doughnuts today.
David **brought** us doughnuts yesterday.
David **has brought** us doughnuts every day this week.

Take Please **take** this chocolate cake to Mrs. Jones.
Tom **is taking** the chocolate cake to Mrs. Jones today.
Sara **took** a library book to Mrs. Jones yesterday.
I **have taken** magazines to Mrs. Jones every Saturday.

● **Practice Your Skills**

Using Bring and Take Correctly

Write the correct form of **bring** or **take**.

1. Wolf pups wait for their mother to (bring, take) them food.
2. The pups (bring, take) food from the adult wolf.
3. The pups (bring, take) the food to a corner and examine it.
4. An adult wolf (brings, takes) its pups along on hunts when the pups are about six months old.
5. Wolves were (brought, taken) to Yellowstone Park from their natural habitat.

learn and teach

Learn means "to gain knowledge." *Teach* means "to instruct" or "to show how."

Present	Present Participle	Past	Past Participle
learn	(is) learning	learned	(have) learned
teach	(is) teaching	taught	(have) taught

Learn
Sheila **learns** music very quickly.
Sheila **is learning** to play the piano.
Sheila **learned** two songs yesterday.
Sheila **has learned** some Mozart pieces already.

Teach
Teach me this overture.
Mr. Davidson **is teaching** me a new aria.
Mr. Davidson **taught** me a trumpet solo last week.
Mr. Davidson **has taught** me a concerto already.

● Practice Your Skills

Using **Learn** *and* **Teach** *Correctly*

Write the correct form of **learn** or **teach**.

1. Mozart (learned, taught) a great deal about music from his father, Leopold.
2. Before he was six years old, young Wolfgang had (learned, taught) to compose symphonies.
3. Many children have (learned, taught) one of his earliest compositions, "Twinkle, Twinkle, Little Star."
4. Mozart's father had (learned, taught) Wolfgang to play a number of instruments.
5. His music (learns, teaches) people many things about patterns of music.

leave and let

Leave means "to depart" or "go away." *Let* means "to allow" or "permit."

Present	Present Participle	Past	Past Participle
leave	(is) leaving	left	(have) left
let	(is) letting	let	(have) let

Leave
When do you **leave** for Boston?
Brenda **is leaving** for Chicago.
Sue **left** a few minutes ago on the plane to Baltimore.
Marty **has left** for San Francisco.

Let
I **let** the cat sleep on my bed.
I **am letting** the cat sleep there tonight.
I **let** the cat sleep on my bed all last week.
I **have let** the cat sleep on my bed many times before.

You can learn more about other problem verbs in *A Writer's Glossary of Usage* on pages 786–799.

Practice Your Skills

Using Leave and Let Correctly

Write the correct form of *leave* or *let*.

1. Please (leave, let) me drive you to the airport.
2. Has Judy's plane (left, let) yet?
3. Margie had (left, let) yesterday for Denver.
4. I am (leaving, letting) Jane borrow my camera for her trip to Greece.
5. What time does your plane (leave, let) the gate?

Connect to Writing: Editing

Using Problem Verbs

Rewrite each sentence, replacing any incorrect verb with the correct verb.

1. Please learn me to read the train schedule.
2. Let your suitcase with the ticket agent.
3. You should bring a jacket on your trip to Denver.
4. I taught to read an airport departure board when I was very young.
5. Kelly left me take her hair dryer on the trip, since mine was broken.

The Principal Parts of Verbs • Lesson 1

✓ Check Point: Mixed Practice

Write the correct form of each verb in parentheses.

1. The Chicago Field Museum (learned, taught) us about a dinosaur fossil.
2. The fossil (brought, took) many scientists to the museum.
3. Scientists have (learned, taught) much about dinosaurs from this fossil.
4. The fossil, named Sue, was (brought, taken) to Chicago because of the work of a paleontologist named Sue Hendricksen.
5. Once a fossil has been discovered, scientists seldom (leave, let) the site.
6. They hope to (learn, teach) about how the dinosaurs lived.
7. The Field Museum has (leave, let) the public view the bones.
8. They hope that Sue will (bring, take) many visitors to the museum.
9. The scientists will (leave, let) the excavation site as they found it.
10. Paleontologists have (learned, taught) that dinosaurs had gum disease.

Power Your Writing: ReVerberate

A **verb** conveys the action of a sentence. Ordinary verbs may get the job done, but strong, colorful verbs bring your sentences to life and reverberate in the reader's memory. Verbs not only tell your readers what happened but also give them a sense of *how* it happened. Consider the following modified examples from the article "Carved in Stone" from the *Austin American Statesman*.

Dull Verb	Weather and water affect the layers of sediment above the fossils.
Colorful Verb	Weather and water wear away the layers of sediment above the fossils.

Weather and water have affected the sediment in some way in the first sentence, but how? In the second sentence, the reader is given a more specific sense of what takes place—erosion—an image of a long-term process. The verb form *wear away* adds to the descriptive power of the sentence.

What makes the verb *cuts* stronger than the verb *runs* in the sentences below?

Dull Verb	The Colorado River runs through the land.
Colorful Verb	The Colorado River cuts through the land.

Look over a recent composition, and revise any verbs that are not strong and effective.

Verb Tense Lesson 2

24 B   The time expressed by a verb is called the **tense** of the verb.

The English language is generally considered to have at least six basic tenses: present, past, future, present perfect, past perfect, and future perfect. The basic tenses are used in the chart below.

Present	I **paint** pictures.
Past	I **painted** a picture in art class yesterday.
Future	I **will paint** another picture tomorrow.
Present Perfect	I **have painted** pictures for almost a year.
Past Perfect	I **had painted** pictures before I attended kindergarten.
Future Perfect	I **will have painted** fifteen pictures by June.

Uses of the Tenses

The tenses of a verb can be formed from the principal parts of a verb, along with the helping verbs *have, has, had, will,* and *shall*.

24 B.1   **Present tense** is used to express an action that is going on now. To form the present tense, use the present form (the first principal part of the verb) or add *-s* or *-es* to the present form.

Present Tense	I **sculpt** clay.
	Pam **begins** her art lessons with a sketch.

The present tense can also be used to express actions that recur, or happen again and again. For example, if you are a painter and someone asks what you do, you say, "I paint." You use the present tense, even though the action happens all the time.

24 B.2   **Past tense** expresses an action that already took place or was completed in the past. To form the past tense of a regular verb, add *-ed* or *-d* to the present form. To form the past tense of an irregular verb, check a dictionary, or look for it on pages 682–686.

Past Tense

I **sculpted** some clay in art class yesterday.

Pam **began** her creative art lessons last week.

24 B.3 **Future tense** is used to express an action that will take place in the future. To form the future tense, use the helping verb *shall* or *will* with the present form.

Future Tense

I **shall sculpt** more clay figures tomorrow.

Pam **will begin** an art lesson tomorrow.

You can learn more about the correct use of *shall* and *will* on page 793.

24 B.4 **Present perfect tense** expresses an action that was completed at some indefinite time in the past. It also expresses an action that started in the past and is still going on. To form the present perfect tense, add *has* or *have* to the past participle.

Present Perfect Tense

I **have sculpted** clay for two years.

Pam **has begun** art lessons this morning.

24 B.5 **Past perfect tense** expresses an action that took place before some other action. To form the past perfect tense, add *had* to the past participle.

Past Perfect Tense

I **had sculpted** clay before I took lessons.

Pam **had begun** art lessons at ten years old.

24 B.6 **Future perfect tense** expresses an action that will take place before another future action or time. To form the future perfect tense, add *shall have* or *will have* to the past participle.

Future Perfect Tense

I **will have sculpted** a new piece by Friday.

Verb Conjugation

24 B.7 A **conjugation** is a list of all the singular and plural forms of a verb in all tenses.

On the following page is the conjugation of the verb *fall*. The principal parts of *fall* are *fall, falling, fell,* and *fallen*.

694   Using Verbs

SIMPLE TENSES

Present

Singular
I fall
you fall
he, she, it falls

Plural
we fall
you fall
they fall

Past

Singular
I fell
you fell
he, she, it fell

Plural
we fell
you fell
they fell

Future

Singular
I shall/will fall
you will fall
he, she, it will fall

Plural
we shall/will fall
you will fall
they will fall

PERFECT TENSES

Present Perfect

Singular
I have fallen
you have fallen
he, she, it has fallen

Plural
we have fallen
you have fallen
they have fallen

Past Perfect

Singular
I had fallen
you had fallen
he, she, it had fallen

Plural
we had fallen
you had fallen
they had fallen

Future Perfect

Singular
I shall/will have fallen
you will have fallen
he, she, it will have fallen

Plural
we shall/will have fallen
you will have fallen
they will have fallen

The conjugation of the word *be* is very different from other irregular verbs. The principal parts of the word *be* are *am, was,* and *will be.*

SIMPLE TENSES

Present

Singular	Plural
I am	we are
you are	you are
he, she, it is	they are

Past

Singular	Plural
I was	we were
you were	you were
he, she, it was	they were

Future

Singular	Plural
I shall/will be	we shall/will be
you will be	you will be
he, she, it will be	they will be

PERFECT TENSES

Present Perfect

Singular	Plural
I have been	we have been
you have been	you have been
he, she, it has been	they have been

Past Perfect

Singular	Plural
I had been	we had been
you had been	you had been
he, she, it had been	they had been

Future Perfect

Singular	Plural
I shall/will have been	we shall/will have been
you will have been	you will have been
he, she, it will have been	they will have been

Practice Your Skills

Identifying Verb Tenses

Label the tense of each underlined verb as *present, past, future, present perfect, past perfect,* or *future perfect.*

1. A cheetah <u>becomes</u> an adult when it is only two years old.
2. In a single day, a mother cheetah <u>will have hunted</u> many times.
3. A female cheetah <u>will catch</u> live prey for her cubs to practice hunting.
4. The cheetah <u>broke</u> sixty miles per hour during the hunt.
5. After the cheetah <u>had stalked</u> its prey, it burst into a run.
6. The cheetah <u>has survived</u> in the plains of Africa for thousands of years.
7. That cheetah <u>has hunted</u> here for years.

Connect to Writing: Descriptive Paragraph

Using the Perfect Tense

Your science class is setting up a petting zoo for the children of a local day-care center. You plan to teach the students a little about each of the animals. Write a short descriptive essay about the appearance, habitat, feeding habits, and future prospects of one of the animals. Use two different verbs in which you use the present perfect, the past perfect, and the future perfect of each. Strive to use consistent tenses while writing a variety of complete sentences.

Practice Your Skills

Writing Different Tenses

Write the verbs, following the instructions below.

1. Write the present tense of *call*.
2. Write the past tense of *burst*.
3. Write the present perfect tense of *say*.
4. Write the future tense of *teach*.
5. Write the past perfect tense of *stop*.

Connect to Speaking and Writing: Play with Vocabulary

Using the Tenses

With a partner, talk about your newly acquired English vocabulary phrase *perfect tense*. Then write a two-person scene using the present perfect, past perfect, and future perfect tenses.

Shifts in Tense

When you write a story, you can tell your readers when the story takes place by the tense of the verbs you use. Keep your tenses consistent. For example, if you are telling a story that took place in the past, use the past tense of verbs. If you suddenly shift to the present, you will probably confuse your readers.

24 B.8 Avoid unnecessary shifts in tense within a sentence or within related sentences.

A shift in tense can occur within a sentence itself or within related sentences.

Inconsistent	After I **rode** my bike a few miles, the tire **goes** flat.
Inconsistent	After I **ride** my bike a few miles, the tire **went** flat.
Consistent	After I **ride** my bike a few miles, the tire **goes** flat.
Consistent	After I **had ridden** my bike a few miles, the tire **went** flat.
Inconsistent	By the time I **fixed** the flat, the clouds **pour** rain.
Inconsistent	By the time I **fix** the flat, the clouds **poured** rain.
Consistent	By the time I **fix** the flat, the clouds **pour** rain.
Consistent	By the time I **had fixed** the flat, the clouds **poured** rain.

Situations do exist where a present tense verb can correctly appear in a sentence with a past tense verb. One would be when there is a quote. The other is when a person is using the present tense to express recurring action.

"I like that painting," she said.

Yesterday, I met a woman who writes for a living.

When You Write

Professional writers often use the same verb tense to create a particular mood. The writer of the following passage uses the same tense consistently to make readers feel as if they were witnesses to what is happening.

> The lovely Miss Gomez pales. After a moment of painful hesitation, she rips the telegram open. Zzzzzt! She gasps. Aurggg! Her face goes chalky white.
> —Avi, "Who Was That Masked Man, Anyway?"

● **Practice Your Skills**

Identifying Shifts in Verb Tense

Write **S** if a sentence contains a shift in verb tense. If a sentence is correct, write **C**.

1. Before you leave for the race, check your equipment and gear.
2. When I checked my bike before the race, I find a flat rear tire.
3. Because I didn't have a patch kit, I will not ride in the race.
4. Joe says that he has a patch kit.
5. I told him that I needed a patch for my flat tire.
6. Joe gave me the kit, and I fixed the flat tire very quickly.
7. After I fix the flat tire, I left for the big bicycle race.
8. The new tire will help my performance and gave me more traction.
9. When I told the other riders about my flat tire, they shared their biking stories with me.
10. After I finished the race, I thanked Joe for his extra help.

● *Connect to Writing:* **Revising**

Correcting Shifts in Verb Tense

Rewrite the sentences in the preceding exercise that contain shifts in verb tense.

 **Progressive Verb Forms**

Each of the basic tenses has a progressive form.

24 B.9 The **progressive forms** of verbs are used to express continuing or ongoing action.

The progressive forms add a special meaning to verbs that the regular tenses do not. Notice the differences in meaning in the following examples.

Present	The groom **brushes** the horse.
	(*Brushes* shows that the groom can or does brush the horse.)
Present Progressive	The groom **is brushing** the horse.
	(*Is brushing* shows that the groom is brushing the horse right now.)

To form the progressive, add a form of the verb *be* to the present participle. Notice in the following examples that all of the progressive verb forms end in *-ing*.

Present Progressive	I am falling.
Past Progressive	I was falling.
Future Progressive	I will (shall) be falling.
Present Perfect Progressive	I have been falling.
Past Perfect Progressive	I had been falling.
Future Perfect Progressive	I will (shall) have been falling.

● **Practice Your Skills**

Identifying Progressive Verb Forms

Write each verb phrase.

1. By today's end, we will have been announcing the Kentucky Derby for twenty-five years.
2. We will be watching the entrance of the horses.
3. The horses have been prancing in anticipation of the race.
4. The favorite has been racing well all season.
5. Last year he had been placing second or third on a regular basis.
6. Today his trainer is hoping for a win.
7. The horses will be entering the post parade in a moment.

● **Connect to Writing: Revising**

Changing Verb Tenses

Rewrite each of the following sentences so that it contains a progressive verb.

1. The greatest names in thoroughbred racing have gathered in Louisville.
2. The horses have practcied for weeks.
3. The crowd roars.
4. The horses enter the starting gate.
5. The gates fly open.

✓ **Check Point: Mixed Practice**

Write each underlined verb in the tense that is indicated in parentheses.

1. Nile crocodiles <u>live</u> (present perfect progressive) in Africa for many years.
2. By the time it <u>reach</u> (present) maturity, a crocodile <u>weigh</u> (present) up to 2,220 pounds.
3. Crocodiles <u>grow</u> (present perfect) to twenty feet.
4. Some ancient people <u>believe</u> (past) that the crocodile was sly.
5. Crocodiles <u>continue</u> (future) to thrive because people <u>preserve</u> (future) their habitats.
6. The crocodile <u>survive</u> (past perfect) due to its toughness.
7. During the last wet season the crocodiles <u>live</u> (past) in rain puddles.
8. By midday a crocodile <u>wait</u> (future progressive) patiently for its prey.
9. A crocodile <u>strike</u> (future) at its prey in seconds.
10. Yesterday, a crocodile <u>lunge</u> (past perfect) for a zebra.

● **Connect to Speaking and Writing: Peer Consultation**

Using Verb Tenses

You have learned a number of important grammar terms in this chapter. Find the phrase *progressive verb forms* on page 700. Discuss with a classmate ways to remember what this phrase means and how it is used. Share ways of using it in a sentence. Then, individually, write about something you continually observe in the world around you. Use two progressive verb forms and a variety of complete sentences that include consistent tenses.

Verb Tense • Lesson 2

Emphatic Verb Forms

Every verb has an emphatic form for the present and past tense.

24 B.10 The **emphatic forms** of the present and past tenses of verbs are mainly used to show emphasis or force. To write the present emphatic, add **do** or **does** to the present tense of a verb. To write the past emphatic, add **did** to the present tense.

Present	I **fall** asleep when I'm bored.
Present Emphatic	I **do fall** asleep when I'm bored.
Past	I **fed** the cat last night.
Past Emphatic	I **did feed** the cat last night.

When You Write

Remember *Green Eggs and Ham*? One of the things that makes the story fun to listen to is the emphatic verb forms.

> **Do** you **like** green eggs and ham? I **do** not **like** them, Sam-I-am. I **do** not **like** green eggs and ham. I **do** not **like** them in a house. I **do** not **like** them with a mouse. I **do** not **like** them here or there. I **do** not **like** them anywhere.
> —Dr. Seuss, *Green Eggs and Ham*

Look over a story you are working on. Have you used the emphatic form effectively?

Practice Your Skills

Identifying Progressive and Emphatic Forms

Write the progressive or emphatic form in each sentence. Beside it write *P* for progressive or *E* for emphatic.

1. Will you be going to the rock concert?
2. I did buy my ticket last week.
3. I have been saving for this ticket for three months.
4. I did not wait a minute longer than I had to.
5. I will be the first one in line when the doors open.

Chapter Review

Assess Your Learning

Using the Correct Verb Form

Rewrite the following sentences, replacing incorrect verbs with correct verb forms. If a sentence needs no change, write **C**.

1. Julio has accidentally broke the light bulb.
2. My cousin has often sang solos with the choir.
3. I have drunk the last glass of milk.
4. They have chose Connie as the captain of the team.
5. We swum at the town beach yesterday morning.
6. Matthew done everything on the list.
7. The lake had nearly frozen by morning.
8. Who throwed the ball into our court?
9. The wind has blown the leaves around the yard.
10. The grass has already growed another inch.

Using the Correct Verb Form

Write each underlined verb in the tense that is indicated in parentheses.

1. I break (*past*) the silence with a cackling laugh.
2. Linda live (*past perfect*) in Ohio before she moved here.
3. Most bats sleep (*present*) upside down.
4. I write (*present perfect*) for a free catalog.
5. Tomorrow the sun rise (*future*) over those mountains.
6. Brian said that he mail (*past perfect*) two invitations.
7. Nancy save (*present perfect*) enough money for a new bicycle.
8. Who carry (*future*) the flag in tomorrow's parade?

Using Problem Verbs

Write the correct verb form for each sentence.

1. Margaret Hey's family (brought, took) a unique approach to clutter cleanup.
2. Here's an idea I (learned, taught) from *Family Fun*, October 1999.
3. (Leave, Let) the junk and save the collectibles.
4. The Heys' home museum (learns, teaches) visitors about family collectibles.
5. Books are available that (learn, teach) new collectors what to look for.
6. Some collectors (bring, take) their "junk" to antique road shows.
7. My friend (brought, took) his 1940s comics to have them evaluated.
8. Items (brought, taken) out of their protective wrapping lose some of their value.
9. Artists (leave, let) creative possibilities develop where they will.
10. "Heaps of junk" (left, let) in some artists' hands can become works of beauty or humor.

Using Verbs Correctly

Write five sentences that follow the directions below.
Write a sentence that . . .

1. includes the future tense of *begin*.
2. includes the past tense of *choose*.
3. includes the future perfect tense of *eat*.
4. includes the present progressive form of *race*.
5. includes the past progressive form of *throw*.

Using Verbs: Posttest

Directions
Read the passage and write the letter of the word or group of words that belongs in each underlined space.

People are living longer today! In the past, many people __(1)__ their lives in one century. My mother __(2)__ from 1907 to 1987—eighty years. My life __(3)__ two centuries. For example, my parents __(4)__ my birth in 1940. It is possible that I __(5)__ in 2040. By then, I __(6)__ sixty years in the twentieth century and forty years in the twenty-first century.

Imagine your life spanning three centuries. __(7)__ about it. It __(8)__ to others. Why not you? You __(9)__ to be 115 years old or even older. If you live to the year 2100, you __(10)__ in the twentieth, twenty-first, and twenty-second centuries.

1. **A** lives
   B live
   C lived
   D has lived

2. **A** lives
   B is living
   C have lived
   D lived

3. **A** spans
   B will span
   C is spanning
   D will span

4. **A** celebrated
   B is celebrating
   C was celebrating
   D had celebrated

5. **A** died
   B dies
   C had died
   D will die

6. **A** will have lived
   B will live
   C lives
   D had lived

7. **A** Thinks
   B Think
   C Thinking
   D Thinked

8. **A** happening
   B happens
   C has happened
   D will happen

9. **A** has lived
   B could live
   C had lived
   D will have lived

10. **A** will have lived
    B live
    C lives
    D has lived

Writer's Corner

Snapshot

24 A The **principal parts of a verb** are the present, the present participle, the past, and the past participle. (pages 680–692)

24 B The time expressed by a verb is called the **tense** of the verb. (pages 693–702)

Power Rules

Check your writing for these language patterns and make changes as needed.

Use mainstream past tense forms of regular and irregular verbs.
Memorize the forms of the most common irregular verbs. (pages 680–688)

Before Editing
The teacher *pick* me for the project.
We *growed* a plant as a class project.
After school he *run* all the way home.
She found out *I had broke* the vase.
We *was* late for the party.

After Editing
The teacher *picked* me for the project.
We *grew* a plant as a class project.
After school he *ran* all the way home.
She found out *I had broken* the vase.
We *were* late for the party.

Use a consistent verb tense except when a change is clearly necessary. (pages 693–702)

Before Editing
It *rained* yesterday, and the picnic *is* ruined.
We *visited* the lake, and we *have* a good time.
The bird *flies* out when I *opened* the cage door.

After Editing
It *rained* yesterday, and the picnic *was* ruined.
We *visited* the lake, and we *had* a good time.
The bird *flew* out when I *opened* the cage door.

Editing Checklist

Use this checklist when editing your writing.

- ✓ Did I use the correct verb tense? (See pages 693–702.)
- ✓ Did I use the correct forms of irregular verbs? (See pages 682–688.)
- ✓ Did I make the correct choice when using problem verbs? (See pages 689–692.)
- ✓ Did I avoid shifts in tenses in my sentences? (See pages 698–699.)
- ✓ Did I use the progressive form correctly? (See pages 700–701.)

Use the Power

Use verbs creatively yet precisely to construct sentences that are descriptive and interesting. Past, present, and future tenses show the reader the effects of the passage of time.

> James **ran** his race very well yesterday.
>
> James **is running** even faster in today's warm-ups.
>
> James **will run** as fast as he can in the final race tomorrow.

Choose one tense and write a paragraph about a runner training for an important race.

CHAPTER 25

Using Pronouns

William Wilberforce

How can you use pronouns in a way that makes your writing fluid and accurate?

Using Pronouns: Pretest 1

Read the draft paragraph below about William Wilberforce, a leader in the British movement to abolish the slave trade. The paragraph is hard to read because it contains several errors. The first error has been corrected as an example.

William Wilberforce is a man about ~~who~~ *whom* everyone should learn. Him is an example of what you can accomplish. He did not let difficulty stop himself. As a member of the British Parliament, Wilberforce fought against slavery. Olaudah Equiano, William Pitt, and him were among those whom joined together in this fight. After 18 years of work, he saw the slave trade outlawed. Unfortunately, this was only a partial victory, because them already held as slaves were not freed. It took nearly 25 years more for he and his friends to see their dream realized. In 1833, shortly after Wilberforce retired, slaves throughout the British Empire were finally granted they're freedom. His lifelong battle against slavery was recounted in the movie *Amazing Grace*.

Using Pronouns: Pretest 2

Directions
Read the passage and write the letter of the word or group of words that belongs in each underlined space.

Archaeology is the study of past civilizations. **(1)** involves uncovering, or excavating, clues about people and **(2)** cultures. Archaeologists study artifacts, or handmade objects, found at excavations called "digs." **(3)** are interested in **(4)** digs and artifacts. Each artifact reveals information to historians and **(5)**.

In 1922, Howard Carter and **(6)** archaeological team uncovered the entrance to King Tutankhamen's tomb. One of the greatest archaeological finds of all time was Carter's and **(7)**. For over three thousand years, this tomb and **(8)** treasures had remained undisturbed. King Tut, as he is often called today, had been buried as king of Egypt with great treasures to honor **(9)**. **(10)** could have foreseen such an amazing contribution to Egyptian culture?

1. **A** He
   B She
   C It
   D They

2. **A** their
   B my
   C his
   D our

3. **A** Them
   B Someone
   C Everybody
   D They

4. **A** these
   B her
   C this
   D we

5. **A** it
   B we
   C his
   D us

6. **A** my
   B his
   C your
   D her

7. **A** his
   B ours
   C it's
   D theirs

8. **A** it's
   B its
   C them
   D theirs

9. **A** her
   B him
   C us
   D them

10. **A** Whom
    B Who
    C He
    D Whose

The Cases of Personal Pronouns

The personal pronouns *he, him,* and *his* can all refer to the same person because pronouns have cases.

> Bob said **he** would take **his** brother with **him** to the stables.

25 A **Case** indicates a noun or pronoun's use in a sentence. Nouns and pronouns have three cases: **nominative, objective,** and **possessive.** (pages 710–723)

Following are some examples of pronouns in nominative, objective, and possessive case.

NOMINATIVE CASE
(Used for subjects and predicate nominatives)

	Singular	Plural
First Person	I	we
Second Person	you	you
Third Person	he, she, it	they

OBJECTIVE CASE
(Used for direct objects, indirect objects, and objects of prepositions)

	Singular	Plural
First Person	me	us
Second Person	you	you
Third Person	him, her, it	them

POSSESSIVE CASE
(Used to show ownership or possession)

	Singular	Plural
First Person	my, mine	our, ours
Second Person	your, yours	your, yours
Third Person	his, her, hers, its	their, theirs

● **Practice Your Skills**

Identifying the Cases of Personal Pronouns

Write the pronouns in each sentence. Label each pronoun *nominative, objective,* or *possessive.*

1. They are going to the stables.
2. That is he on the tall chestnut horse.
3. I left my saddle in the barn.
4. We like riding through the countryside.
5. That saddle belongs to me.
6. Our riding instructor taught us to groom the horses.
7. My horse kept tossing its head.
8. Justin had trouble with his horse too.
9. We tried to control our horses, but they wouldn't behave.
10. Please tell me how to keep my horse from stopping suddenly.

  The Nominative Case

The following list shows examples of personal pronouns in the nominative case.

	NOMINATIVE CASE	
	Singular	**Plural**
First Person	I	we
Second Person	you	you
Third Person	he, she, it	they

Pronouns in the nominative case are used two ways in sentences: as subjects and as predicate nominatives.

25 A.1 The **nominative case** is used both for subjects and for predicate nominatives.

Subject	**They** went to the library.
Predicate Nominative	The lady with the red book is **she.**

Pronouns Used as Subjects

A subject names the person, place, or thing the sentence is about. A pronoun used as a subject is in the nominative case.

Subjects **He** wrote his report.

Did **they** drive to the library?
(Turn a question into a statement: *They did drive to the library.* Then it is easy to find the subject.)

Sometimes a sentence has more than one subject. To determine the pronouns for a compound subject, check to make sure they are in the nominative case. There is a test you can use to check them. Say each pronoun separately.

Compound Subject Anna and (I, me) study daily.
Correct **I** study daily.
Incorrect **Me** study daily.

When you separate the choices, it becomes easy to see and hear which pronoun is correct. In this sentence, the nominative case *I* is the correct form to use.

Correct Anna and **I** study daily.

You can learn more about finding subjects on pages 479–480 and 487–490.

● Practice Your Skills

Using Pronouns as Subjects

Write the correct personal pronoun for each sentence.

1. (I, me) enjoyed reading *Born Free* by Joy Adamson.
2. (She, Her) adopted a lion cub.
3. (It, Their) was named Elsa.
4. George was Joy's husband, and (he, him) studied lions.
5. Together (they, them) learned much about these animals.
6. (We, Us) all have benefited from the Adamsons' experience.
7. Although Joy loved Elsa, (she, her) knew that the lion deserved to be free.
8. George and Joy did not want to give Elsa up, but (they, them) did.
9. George and (she, her) taught Elsa to be a wild lion.
10. Joy and (he, him) were very sad when Elsa finally set out on her own.

Pronouns Used as Predicate Nominatives

25 A.2   A **predicate nominative** is a word that follows a linking verb and identifies or renames the subject. A pronoun used as a predicate nominative is in the nominative case.

Predicate Nominative	That is **she** standing by the door.
	Is the man from the Senate **he?**
	(Turn a question into a statement. *The man from the Senate is he.* It is easy to see that *he* renames *man*.)

In a compound predicate nominative, there is an easy way to choose the correct pronoun. Turn the sentence around. Use each pronoun as a subject. Then say the sentence as if the pronoun stood alone.

Predicate Nominative	The boys on stage are Bill and (he, him).
	Bill and (he, him) are the boys on stage.
Correct	**He** is on stage.
Incorrect	**Him** is on stage.
Correct	The boys on stage are Bill and **he.**

Some of the sentences with pronouns used as predicate nominatives may *sound* wrong even though they are correct. When you write, you can avoid these awkward-sounding sentences. Simply reverse the sentences. Turn the predicate nominatives into subjects.

Awkward	My government teacher is **she.**
Better	**She** is my government teacher.
Awkward	The boys on stage are **Bill and he.**
Better	**Bill and he** are the boys on stage.

For a list of common linking verbs, see pages 528 and 584. For more about predicate nominatives, see pages 584–585.

● **Practice Your Skills**

Using Pronouns as Predicate Nominatives

Turn each sentence around to make the predicate nominative the subject. Say each pronoun aloud to find out which one is correct. Read each sentence aloud again, choosing the correct pronoun.

1. The best candidate is (she, her).
2. The two people next to Senator Jensen are Mr. Ricker and (she, her).
3. The election monitors will be the teachers or (we, us).
4. The two candidates were Carlos and (I, me).
5. The winners of the election are Tara and (he, him).

● **Practice Your Skills**

Using Pronouns as Predicate Nominatives

Write the correct personal pronoun for each sentence.

1. The best actor to play Romeo was (he, him).
2. That's (he, him) in the movie with Clare Danes.
3. My two favorite actors are Leonardo DiCaprio and (she, her).
4. That's (I, me) in the picture with the movie star.
5. The winner of the award for best actress will be Meryl Streep or (she, her).
6. The extras in the movie will be the boys from Detroit or (we, us).
7. Was that (she, her) in the hot pink dress at the movie premiere last night?
8. My favorite directors are Steven Spielberg and (he, him).

● **Practice Your Skills**

Supplying Pronouns in the Nominative Case

Complete each sentence by writing an appropriate pronoun. Do not use *you* or *it*.

1. Sandra and _____ are riding the bus to school this year.
2. It's _____ in the front seat.
3. On the night before school starts, _____ can never get any sleep.
4. Laura and _____ just got new clothes for school.
5. When did Wade and _____ leave for school?
6. Our car pool drivers will be the Samlers and _____.

Using Pronouns

● **Connect to Writing: Editing**

Correcting Nominative Case Errors

If an underlined pronoun is in the wrong case, write it correctly. If it is in the correct case, write **C**.

1. The library aides for our class this year are Grace and <u>her</u>.
2. Is that <u>he</u> by the cafeteria?
3. The twins and <u>me</u> are making plans for a special treat at lunch.
4. Bob and <u>me</u> often like to work on science projects together.
5. Rico and <u>her</u> will have the same homeroom teacher this year.
6. The teachers and <u>them</u> are looking at the new mural.
7. The driver of the first car in the pickup line is <u>she</u>.
8. Mr. Santos and <u>us</u> are going to the science museum.
9. Should Cindy and <u>me</u> wait for you?

● **Check Point: Mixed Practice**

Write the correct personal pronoun for each sentence.

1. (We, Us) are reading *Where the Red Fern Grows*.
2. (It, they) was written by Wilson Rawls.
3. I think my favorite writer is (he, him).
4. The main character works hard so that (he, him) can buy hunting dogs.
5. When the dogs arrive, (they, them) are little pups.
6. The boy and the dogs become friends, and (they, them) have many adventures together.
7. Little Ann is small, but (she, her) can think for herself.
8. I think my favorite dog is (she, her).
9. Old Dan is bigger, but (he, him) gets into trouble.
10. Little Ann and (he, him) have all sorts of adventures hunting together.

● **Connect to Writing: Friendly Letter**

Nominative Case Pronouns

Write a letter to a friend or relative telling the person about some of the new vocabulary you and your classmates have encountered while learning to use pronouns. Describe your feelings about how your class has progressed. Use pronouns in the nominative case as both subjects and predicate nominatives. Underline the nominative case pronouns you have used.

The Cases of Personal Pronouns • Lesson 1

 **The Objective Case**

The following list shows all the personal pronouns in the objective case.

	OBJECTIVE CASE	
	Singular	**Plural**
First Person	me	us
Second Person	you	you
Third Person	him, her, it	them

Pronouns in the objective case are used in three ways in sentences.

25 A.3 The **objective case** is used for direct objects, indirect objects, and objects of prepositions.

Direct Object	Barry will call **her** tonight after his flight.
Indirect Object	Mom gave **us** new suitcases.
Object of a Preposition	Is Corey going with **them** to the airport?

Pronouns Used as Direct and Indirect Objects

A pronoun used as a direct object or an indirect object is in the objective case. **A direct object** follows an action verb and answers the questions *Whom?* or *What?*

Direct Object	Tom took **us** to the station.
	(Tom took whom? *Us* is the direct object.)
	Did your dad take **you** to the station?
	(Turn a question into a statement: Your dad did take you to the station. Your dad did take whom? *You* is the direct object.)

You can learn more about direct objects on pages 581–583.

An **indirect object** comes before a direct object and answers the question *To* or *for whom?* or *To* or *for what?*

716 Using Pronouns

Indirect Object

          ⌐i.o.¬ ⌐d.o.¬
Ron gave **her** a ticket.
(Ron gave what? *Ticket* is the direct object. Ron gave a ticket to whom? *Her* is the indirect object.)

    ⌐i.o.¬ ⌐d.o.¬
Give **them** some film.
(Give what? *Film* is the direct object. Give film to whom? *Them* is the indirect object.)

          ⌐i.o.¬ ⌐———d.o.———¬
Mom wrote **her** the instructions.
(Wrote what? *Instructions* is the direct object. Wrote for whom? *Her* is the indirect object.)

You can learn more about indirect objects on pages 581–583.

To choose the correct pronoun for a compound object, just say the sentence as if the pronoun stood alone.

Direct Object	Mom called Marty and (I, me).
Incorrect	Mom called **I**.
Correct	Mom called **me**.
Correct	Mom called Marty and **me**.
Indirect Object	Gail gave Emma and (she, her) a camera.
Incorrect	Gail gave **she** a camera.
Correct	Gail gave **her** a camera.
Correct	Gail gave Emma and **her** a camera.

● **Practice Your Skills**

Using Pronouns as Direct and Indirect Objects

Write the correct personal pronoun for each sentence.

1. Joe told (we, us) the new plays for Saturday's game.
2. Give the equipment manager or (they, them) your uniform.
3. The cheerleaders sent Tom and (he, him) some goody bags before the game.
4. Did you see my neighbors or (they, them) in the stands at the game?
5. The crowd cheered Robert and (he, him) for their great team effort.
6. You should have asked (we, us) for help with the new plays.
7. Did you find Alex and (she, her) after the football game yesterday?
8. Will you throw David and (I, me) a few practice passes now?

Pronouns Used as Objects of Prepositions

A prepositional phrase begins with a preposition, such as *to, for, near,* or *by*. A prepositional phrase ends with the **object of the preposition**. A pronoun that is used as the object of a preposition is in the objective case.

Objects of Prepositions	Is the party for **me**? (*For me* is the prepositional phrase.) The video was about **him**. (*About him* is the prepositional phrase.)

An easy way to choose the correct pronoun in a compound object of a preposition is to say the sentence as if the pronoun stood alone.

Object of a Preposition	The birthday party was planned by Ian and (she, her).
Incorrect	The birthday party was planned by **she.**
Correct	The birthday party was planned by **her.**
Correct	The birthday party was planned by Ian and **her.**

When You Write and Speak

A common mistake occurs with the preposition *between*. When people try to sound formal or correct, they will often use nominative case pronouns after *between*. However, all pronouns used as objects of a preposition should be in the objective case. In this case, the more common-sounding expression is correct.

Incorrect	The cheesecake was divided between **she** and **I.**
Correct	The cheesecake was divided between **her** and **me.**

Look at a recent composition and be sure that you have used objective case pronouns correctly, particularly after the word *between*.

You can learn more about prepositions and prepositional phrases on pages 560–565 and 600–606.

● **Practice Your Skills**

Using Pronouns as Objects of Prepositions

Write the correct personal pronoun for each sentence.

1. The duet was written for Barry and (she, her).
2. The play will be financed by the Smiths and (we, us).
3. Good singers like (they, them) should audition.
4. I will share my script with you and (she, her).
5. Will someone go over the line with Ben and (I, me)?
6. Arthur's musical ability was a surprise to (we, us).
7. The play was directed by Thomas and (he, him).
8. Give these costumes to Billy and (they, them).
9. Is that prop for Will or (he, him)?
10. The play was about (she, her).

● **Practice Your Skills**

Supplying Pronouns in the Objective Case

Complete each sentence by writing an appropriate pronoun. Do not use *you* or *it*.

1. Mr. Porter gave Maureen and _____ usher uniforms.
2. Has Justin given the scripts to Doyle and _____?
3. Will you give Janine and _____ some makeup?
4. Leila ran across the stage after Rona and _____.
5. The Langs invited Cora and _____ to opening night.
6. My sister always beats Carlos and _____ to the theater after school.

● *Connect to Writing:* **Editing**

Correcting Objective Case Errors

If an underlined pronoun is in the wrong case, write it correctly. If it is in the correct case, write **C**.

1. Mr. Daniels drove Doris and I to play practice.
2. These are the scripts for the new actors and he.
3. Has Jamie given Douglas and she any lines yet?
4. Please give Amanda and he some advice on learning their lines.
5. One line is enough for Sharon and me.

✓ **Check Point: Mixed Practice**

Write the correct personal pronoun for each sentence.

1. Sheila and (I, me) were given a special classroom job.
2. I will share all of my history notes with you and (she, her).
3. Give Melinda and (he, him) some of those large index cards.
4. Sam and (I, me) want to go to the library tomorrow.
5. Carl showed (he, him) how to set up the Internet connection.
6. You should have asked (we, us) for some help with your topic.
7. Dave and (I, me) were promised an extra day for research.
8. (I, me) will teach you the correct form for an outline.
9. Give these encyclopedias to (she, her).
10. Ask Mr. Venegas about (they, them).

The Possessive Case

The following list shows all the personal pronouns in the possessive case.

POSSESSIVE CASE	Singular	Plural
First Person	my, mine	our, ours
Second Person	your, yours	your, yours
Third Person	his, her, hers, its	their, theirs

25 A.4 The **possessive case** is used to show ownership or possession.

Possessive pronouns are divided into two groups: (1) those used like adjectives to modify nouns, and (2) those used alone.

USES OF POSSESSIVE PRONOUNS	
Used Like Adjectives	my, your, his, her, its, our, your, their
Used Alone	mine, yours, his, hers, its, ours, yours, theirs

My dog is brown, but **hers** is gray.

Her dog is young, but **mine** is old.

Pronouns used as adjectives are sometimes called *possessive adjectives.*

Although apostrophes are used with possessive nouns, they are not used with possessive forms of personal pronouns.

Possessive Noun   Is this **Jill's** dog?
Possessive Pronoun Is this dog **hers?** (not *her's*)

● Practice Your Skills

Using Pronouns in the Possessive Case

Write the personal pronoun necessary to complete each sentence below.

1. Where is that dog of (your, yours)?
2. (My, Mine) is taking a nap on the couch.
3. That new bicycle is (hers, her's).
4. Which pair of skates is (your, yours)?
5. I got (my, mine) new skates last week.
6. (Our, Ours) teacher is taking a leave of absence.
7. The injured bird was dragging (its, their) wing.
8. (Their, Theirs) class is going to a competition next week.
9. That cat looks just like (our, ours) cat.
10. Please hand me (my, mine) books.

● *Connect to Writing:* Editing

Correcting Possessive Pronouns

If an underlined pronoun is incorrect, write it correctly. If it is correct, write **C.**

1. I like <u>mine</u> new skating instructor.
2. <u>Her</u> suggestions are easy to follow.
3. The first class on the ice was <u>our</u>.
4. <u>Yours</u> skates were in the locker room.
5. The team with the most first-place ribbons is <u>theirs</u>.

Possessive Pronoun or Contraction?

Because some contractions sound like personal pronouns, people sometimes confuse them in their writing.

POSSESSIVE PRONOUNS AND CONTRACTIONS	
Possessive Pronouns	its, your, their, theirs
Contractions	it's (it is), you're (you are), they're (they are), there's (there is)

The best way to separate these words in your mind is to say the two words that a contraction stands for.

Possessive Pronoun or Contraction	(You're, Your) friend is here to see you.
Incorrect	**You are** friend is here to see you.
Correct	**Your** friend is here to see you.

You can learn more about contractions on pages 746–747 and 886–887.

● Practice Your Skills

Choosing Between Possessive Pronouns and Contractions

Read each sentence aloud, trying each word separately. Remember to say the two words that make up a contraction. Then read each sentence again, choosing the correct word.

1. Where is (your, you're) apartment?
2. (Its, It's) going to rain tomorrow, so the picnic will have to be at your place.
3. (Hers, Her's) is the best place for a cookout.
4. (Their, They're) car just drove up to your apartment building.
5. (Your, You're) the perfect person to host this picnic.
6. (Theirs, There's) a surprise waiting for you after the picnic.
7. The watermelon is (ours, our's).
8. We should join them at (their, they're) house.
9. My soda lost (its, it's) fizz by the end of the picnic.
10. (Theirs, There's) is the only sugar-free dessert.

● **Connect to Writing: Drafting**

Writing Sentences with Possessive Pronouns and Contractions

Write sentences, using one of the following words in each.

1. mine
2. hers
3. its
4. your
5. they're
6. it's
7. theirs
8. ours
9. their
10. you're

✓ **Check Point: Mixed Practice**

Write the correct personal pronoun for each sentence.

1. Last week (I, me) learned about sharks in science.
2. Sharks make (their, they're) homes in the temperate oceans around the world.
3. Long teeth help the shark capture (it, its) prey.
4. The best-known shark scientists are Dr. Eugenie Clark and (he, him).
5. The shark was swimming toward (they, them).
6. When one diver was bothered by a shark, she gave (it, its) a sharp blow to the head.
7. The surprised shark left (she, her) alone.
8. We hope our teacher will give (we, us) some new information about sharks.
9. Carl and (she, her) did not know that sharks have boneless skeletons.
10. Laurie pointed out the model of the shark to Frank and (I, me).

The Cases of Personal Pronouns • Lesson 1

Pronoun Problem: Who or Whom?

In an earlier chapter you learned that some pronouns are called interrogative pronouns because they are used to ask questions. The interrogative pronouns *who* and *whom* have cases just as personal pronouns do.

THE CASES FOR WHO AND WHOM

Nominative Case	who, whoever
Objective Case	whom, whomever
Possessive Case	whose

25 B A common problem with pronouns concerns whether to use **who** or **whom**.

Because *who* is in the nominative case, it is used as a subject.

> **Subject**   **Who** wrote that book?

Because *whom* is in the objective case, it is used as a direct object or an object of the preposition.

> **Direct Object**   **Whom** did you suspect?
> (Turn a question into a statement: *You did suspect whom? Whom* is the direct object.)
>
> **Object of the Preposition**   From **whom** did you get that information?
> (*From whom* is a prepositional phrase.)

Whose can also be used as an interrogative pronoun. It always shows possession.

> **Whose** books are these? (*whose* used as an adjective)
>
> Looking at both stacks of books, we didn't know **whose** were **whose!**
> (*whose* used as a pronoun)

Be careful not to confuse the pronoun *whose* with the contraction *who's*. *Who's* stands for *who is*.

You can learn more about interrogative pronouns on page 513.

When You Write

When talking with friends, you might hear someone say, "Who did you see?" This use of *who* is generally accepted in informal situations, but "*Whom* did you see?" should be used in formal situations, such as on a resumé or in a job interview.

Look over a recent composition, and check to be sure you have used the words *who, whom, who's,* and *whose* correctly.

● Practice Your Skills

Using Who and Whom Correctly

Write the correct word in parentheses for each sentence.

1. (Whose, Who's) is this mystery book?
2. (Who, Whom) is your favorite character in the book?
3. About (who, whom) was the novel written?
4. (Who, Whom) is the author?
5. (Who, Whom) did you believe was really telling the truth?
6. (Whose, Who's) was the best alibi?
7. From (who, whom) did you pick up most of your clues?
8. (Who, Whom) did the detective question about the crime?
9. (Who, Whom) committed the crime?
10. (Whose, Who's) giving the book report on the next mystery story?

● *Connect to Writing:* Drafting

Writing Sentences with Interrogative Pronouns

Write five sentences, following the instructions below.

1. Use *who* as a subject.
2. Use *whose* as a possessive pronoun.
3. Use *whom* as the object of a preposition.
4. Use *whom* as a direct object.
5. Use *who's* as a subject and verb.

Pronouns and Their Antecedents

The word that a pronoun refers to, or replaces, is called the pronoun's **antecedent.**

Pronouns and Antecedents	**Ruth** left **her** ticket at the house.
	The **McGanns** are selling **their** cottage.

In the preceding sentences, *Ruth* is the antecedent of *her,* and *McGanns* is the antecedent of *their*. A pronoun and its antecedent must agree because they refer to the same person, place, or thing.

25 C A pronoun and its **antecedent,** the word that a pronoun refers to or replaces, must agree in number and gender.

Number is the term that indicates whether a noun or a pronoun is singular (one) or plural (more than one). A pronoun must be singular if its antecedent is singular. It must be plural if its antecedent is plural.

Singular	**James** can't find **his** camera.
Plural	The **girls** can't find **their** cameras.

A pronoun must also agree with its antecedent in gender. **Gender** tells whether a noun or a pronoun is masculine, feminine, or neuter. *He, him*, and *his* are masculine. *She, her,* and *hers* are feminine. *It* and *its* are neuter.

GENDER			
Masculine	he	him	his
Feminine	she	her	hers
Neuter	it	its	

Masculine	**Andrew** said that **he** wasn't feeling well.
Feminine	**Judy** finished **her** vacation early.
Neuter	The **car** blew **its** tire.

Plural pronouns such as *them* and *their* can refer to masculine, feminine, or neuter antecedents.

> The girls discussed **their** tennis game while the boys discussed **their** golf handicaps.
>
> I searched all day for my new gloves, and I finally found **them.**

● **Practice Your Skills**

Making Pronouns and Their Antecedents Agree

Complete each sentence by writing an appropriate pronoun.

1. Janice is going on vacation with ____ best friend.
2. Mom and Dad packed ____ bags for the trip.
3. Thomas packed ____ suitcase yesterday.
4. Susan forgot to pack ____ bathing suit.
5. My brothers brought ____ sleeping bags to the car this morning.
6. Did the girls bring ____ hair dryers?
7. The car lost ____ left rear tire.
8. Ellen signed ____ name to the card.
9. Peter took ____ binoculars on the hike.
10. Three raccoons ate ____ dinner on the hotel doorstep.

● *Connect to Writing:* **Editing**

Correcting Errors with Pronouns and Their Antecedents

Rewrite the following sentences, making sure each pronoun agrees with its antecedent. If a sentence is correct, write **C**.

1. Michelle found her camera on the sofa.
2. Jane finished his hamburger.
3. A pigeon flapped her wings and begged for food.
4. The boys took his video games on the trip to Alaska.
5. The Smiths are sending their children to camp for the summer.

Indefinite Pronouns as Antecedents

Sometimes an **indefinite pronoun** can be the antecedent of a personal pronoun. Some indefinite pronouns are singular and some are plural.

COMMON INDEFINITE PRONOUNS	
Singular	anybody, anyone, another, anything, each, either, everybody, everyone, everything, neither, nobody, nothing, no one, one, somebody, someone, something
Plural	both, few, many, several

A personal pronoun must be singular if its antecedent is one of the singular indefinite pronouns.

Singular   **One** of the girls can't find **her** shoes.

Somebody in the boys' gym lost **his** sneakers.

When the gender of a singular indefinite pronoun is not known, use *his* or *her* to refer to the indefinite pronoun.

Singular   **Everyone** must practice **his or her** sprints.

Although the previous sentence is correct, it might still sound awkward. You can often eliminate an awkward sentence by rewriting it in the plural form.

Plural   All track team **members** must practice **their** sprints.

● Connect to Writing: Diary Entry

Using Indefinite Pronouns as Antecedents

Write a diary entry that covers your day at school. Describe all the people you observed, including your teachers. Use indefinite pronouns as antecedents as often as you can. Count up the indefinite pronouns you have used and compare your total to those of your classmates.

A personal pronoun must be plural if its antecedent is one of the plural indefinite pronouns.

Plural	**Several** of the girls can't find **their** coats in the locker room.
	Many of the boys forgot **their** towels.

● **Practice Your Skills**

Making Pronouns and Their Antecedents Agree

Complete each sentence by writing an appropriate personal pronoun.

1. Each of the girls on the track team wore ___ school sweater to the game.
2. Only one of the other school teams carried ___ coach off the field.
3. Both of my sisters like ___ track coach very much.
4. Neither of my brothers remembered ___ equipment for the meet today.
5. Several of the shoes in the locker room do not have ___ laces.
6. Everyone on the boys' team wore ___ jacket in honor of the victory.
7. Many of the boys on the team take ___ equipment home with them.
8. Someone in the girls' locker room left ___ locker open.
9. Either of my brothers will give you ___ advice about your performance.
10. Few of the girls on the team had ___ physical examinations yet.

● *Connect to Writing:* **Editing**

Correcting Errors with Pronouns and Their Antecedents

Rewrite the following sentences, making sure each pronoun agrees with its antecedent. If a sentence is correct, write **C**.

1. Everybody on the girls' teams tried his best.
2. Many of the spectators brought its cameras.
3. The city has improved his track fields.
4. Did anyone on the boys' team lose his key?
5. Each of the team members has their own locker.

Pronouns and Their Antecedents • Lesson 3

Unclear, Missing, or Confusing Antecedents — Lesson 4

When you edit your written work, be sure your pronouns are in the correct case and have clear antecedents. If some antecedents are missing or not clear, the meaning of your words will be confusing or misleading.

25 D **Personal pronouns** should clearly refer to a **specific antecedent**.

➤ Unclear Antecedents

Someone reading your written work should never have to stop to figure out your meaning because some pronouns—such as *it, they, this,* and *that*—only vaguely refer to their antecedents. Always replace any such pronouns with specific antecedents to avoid any possible confusion or misunderstanding.

Unclear	I don't like the ski lift because **you** might get stuck. (*You* is incorrectly used because it refers to the person being spoken to rather than the speaker. *You* should not be used in place of the third person in formal writing.)
Clear	I don't like the ski lift because **I** might get stuck.
Missing	After a long day of skating, **it** felt good. (What does *it* refer to in this sentence? The antecedent is missing.)
Clear	After a long day of skating, the **fire** felt good.
Missing	My suitcase was on the plane, but now **it's** gone. (What does *it* refer to in this sentence, the suitcase or the plane? The antecedent is unclear.)
Clear	My suitcase was on the plane, but now **my suitcase is** gone.
	My suitcase was on the plane, but now **the plane is** gone.

● Practice Your Skills

Recognizing Unclear Antecedents

Write *I* for each antecedent that is unclear or missing and **C** for each antecedent that is used correctly.

1. Jimmy likes the winter because he can drink hot cocoa.
2. At the end of a long day of skiing, it tastes delicious.

3. I knew Em was a good skier, but I had never seen her skiing until yesterday.
4. I like skiing because you get to be outside.
5. Mom got a new ski pole so that she can ski better.

Missing Antecedents

Occasionally pronouns are written without any antecedent. To correct this kind of mistake, you often have to rewrite the sentence.

Missing	In the diagram **it** explains how to wire a lamp.
	(The antecedent of *it* is missing.)
Clear	The **diagram** shows how to wire a lamp.
Missing	In Hollywood **they** have many young actors.
	(The antecedent of *they* is missing.)
Clear	**Hollywood** has many young actors.

Practice Your Skills

Recognizing Missing Antecedents

Write *I* for each antecedent that is unclear or missing and *C* for each antecedent that is used correctly.

1. Sue's ankle was swollen, but now it has disappeared.
2. At the end of a school day, that is happiness.
3. Writers are my favorite people; that's what I want to do.
4. Texas has a number of exceptional universities.
5. Ken emptied his pockets and let them fall to the floor.

Connect to Writing: Team Profile

Using Pronouns and Their Antecedents

You have been asked to write a profile of each member of your track team for the school paper. Write a short description of each teammate. Use a variety of complete sentences that include correctly identified antecedents.

Confusing Antecedents

The problem with other pronouns is that they have more than one possible antecedent. As a result, readers can easily confuse the meaning of the sentence.

Confusing	Separate the wrapper from the cartridge and place **it** in the printer. (What should be placed in the printer, the cartridge or the wrapper?)
Clear	Remove the wrapper from the cartridge and place **the cartridge** in the printer.
Confusing	If the deer eat the plants, place chicken wire over **them**. (Should the deer or the plants be put under wire?)
Clear	Place chicken wire over the **plants** if the deer eat them.

Practice Your Skills

Identifying Pronoun-Antecedent Errors

Write *I* if the sentence contains a pronoun-antecedent error and *C* if the sentence is correct.

1. If golfers do not wear sunscreen on the course, it can cause sunburn.
2. In our school they play hopscotch all year long.
3. Alice told Sal, "You have won the 'Cookie of the Month' award."
4. I was nervous about sledding down that steep hill because you're afraid of breaking a leg.
5. After hiking in the woods, I had mosquito bites on my legs and arms, but they soon healed.

Check Point: Mixed Practice

Correct each underlined pronoun that is used incorrectly. If the pronoun is correct, write **C**.

1. <u>Whom</u> is cooking the dinner tomorrow night?
2. Everyone says John is a good cook, but I have never tasted any of <u>it</u>.
3. Each of the people in my group will bring <u>our</u> favorite dessert to the dinner.
4. From <u>whom</u> did you get this recipe?
5. Most of the recipe books in my house do not have <u>its</u> covers.

Chapter Review

Assess Your Learning

Using Pronouns in the Correct Case

Write the correct personal pronoun for each sentence.

1. The coach put James and (I, me) in the game in the last quarter.
2. Michael went to the basketball game with Rebecca and (she, her).
3. Did Eli or (he, him) make this bread?
4. Joan snapped a picture of Lana and (I, me).
5. Ron didn't know for (who, whom) the invitation to the party was intended.
6. Uncle George told Dad and (we, us) some good jokes.
7. That climb won't be hard for Sam and (she, her).
8. It must be (they, them) on the dock.
9. Did (he, him) and Rudy study their Spanish notes at the library today?
10. (Who, Whom) went to the store for potatoes earlier today?

Correcting Pronoun Errors

Write each sentence using the correct pronoun form. If a sentence needs no change, write **C**.

1. Mr. Daniels drove Doris and I to the stadium.
2. The cooks tonight are Grace and her.
3. For whom was the money intended?
4. Mom gave Megan and he the good news.
5. The Wongs and us are having a barbecue on the Fourth of July weekend.
6. Whom could that be in the plaid shirt?
7. Joyce went canoeing with Ginnie and we.
8. May Allie and me go for a swim after lunch?
9. The invitation is for Martha and me.
10. Rico and him live on the same street.

Making Pronouns Agree with Antecedents

Write a personal pronoun that correctly completes each sentence.

1. Neither of the boys could finish _____ dinner.
2. Julie hasn't found _____ glasses yet.
3. Many of the members have paid _____ club dues.
4. Somebody has left the lights on in _____ car.
5. A few of the fathers played soccer with _____ daughters.
6. Should Carlos bring _____ sunscreen to the beach?
7. Each of my sisters is looking for a job during _____ summer vacation.
8. A turtle must carry _____ home all the time.
9. One of the girls left _____ sweater on the bus.
10. All of the students must turn in _____ homework.

Using Pronouns Correctly

Write sentences that follow the directions below.

Write a sentence that . . .

1. includes *Bill and I* as the subject.
2. includes *him and her* as the indirect object.
3. includes the words *your* and *you're*.
4. includes the word *who*.
5. includes *everyone* as the subject.

Using Pronouns: Posttest

Directions
Read the passage and write the letter of the word or group of words that belongs in each underlined space.

⎯(1)⎯ on ⎯(2)⎯ tour bus is fascinated with the history of ancient Egypt. ⎯(3)⎯ are learning much about Egyptian culture on this tour. The tour guide explained that ancient Egyptians cared very much about ⎯(4)⎯ appearance. An Egyptian woman, for example, would paint ⎯(5)⎯ nails red with henna and wear large, round earrings. An Egyptian man would shave ⎯(6)⎯ beard and head with a razor.

⎯(7)⎯ have learned other interesting facts about Egypt on this tour as well. As early as 5000 B.C., writing in the form of hieroglyphs appeared. ⎯(8)⎯ could have taken our first chariot ride in Egypt in 1600 B.C. ⎯(9)⎯ also learned that between 1567 B.C. and 1070 B.C., Egypt had ⎯(10)⎯ first female pharaoh, Queen Hatshepsut, and later a boy king, Tutankhamen.

1. A Many
   B All
   C Everyone
   D Few

2. A its
   B mine
   C our
   D them

3. A Us
   B It
   C I
   D We

4. A their
   B his or her
   C his or hers
   D theirs

5. A your
   B my
   C his
   D her

6. A my
   B his
   C her
   D their

7. A Me
   B Us
   C You
   D We

8. A You and me
   B You and I
   C You and my
   D You and him

9. A She
   B We
   C They
   D Them

10. A their
    B its
    C his
    D my

Writer's Corner

Snapshot

25 A **Case** indicates a noun or pronoun's use in a sentence. Nouns and pronouns have three cases: **nominative, objective,** and **possessive.** (pages 710–723)

25 B A common problem with pronouns concerns whether to use **who** or **whom**. (pages 724–725)

25 C A pronoun and its **antecedent**, the word that a pronoun refers to or replaces, must agree in number and gender. (pages 726–729)

25 D **Personal pronouns** should clearly refer to a **specific antecedent.** (pages 730–732)

Power Rules

 Use **subject forms of pronouns** in subject position. (pages 711–712) Use **object forms of pronouns** in object position. (pages 716–719)

Before Editing	**After Editing**
Cornell and *him* are good friends.	Cornell and *he* are good friends.
They will meet Tim and *we* at the airport.	They will meet Tim and *us* at the airport.
Mom sent a package to you and *I*.	Mom sent a package to you and *me*.

 For **sound-alikes** and certain words that sound almost alike, choose the word with your intended meaning. (pages 722–723)

Before Editing	**After Editing**
Its beginning to look like it might rain.	*It's* beginning to look like it might rain.
Do you think *your* ready for the test?	Do you think *you're* ready for the test?
I left my bicycle in *they're* yard.	I left my bicycle in *their* yard.

Editing Checklist

Use this checklist when editing your writing.

✓ Did I use the right case of pronoun? (See pages 710–723.)
✓ Do my pronouns agree in number and gender with their antecedents? (See pages 726–729.)
✓ Did I use *who* and *whom* correctly? (See pages 724–725.)
✓ Did I use possessive pronouns and contractions correctly? (See pages 722–723.)
✓ Are the antecedents for each pronoun clear? (See pages 730–732.)

Use the Power

Use this chart to help you remember how each pronoun case is used.

What the pronoun does	Where this happens	The case to use
It names	Subject, Predicate Nominative	Nominative
It identifies an object	Direct Object, Indirect Object, Object of a Preposition	Objective
It shows possession	Whenever you're describing something that belongs to someone or something	Possessive

Write a paragraph or two about something you enjoy doing. Use pronouns in the nominative, objective, and possessive case.

CHAPTER 26

Subject and Verb Agreement

How can you make your subjects and verbs work together so that your ideas are clear?

Subject and Verb Agreement: Pretest 1

Read the following first draft about the Adler Planetarium. The first sentence has an error in subject and verb agreement, which has been corrected. How would you revise the remaining sentences so that subjects and verbs agree?

Chicago's Adler Planetarium ~~were~~ *was* the first planetarium in the United States. Opened in 1930, the Adler continue to grow and change. The experts at the Adler offers amazing opportunities to learn about the universe around us. Who don't love stars? In the Sky Theater, you can lean back in a comfy reclining chair as you and the rest of the audience watches a changing nighttime sky or rapidly forming star cluster. In the StarRider Theater, vistors explores new galaxies in the world's first interactive computer graphics theater. There's also many exhibits. Everyone have a chance to learn how to steer by the stars as the ancients did. In other exhibits, you drives a rover on Mars or learn your weight on Jupiter. You can even take a 3-D tour of the Milky Way.

Subject and Verb Agreement: Pretest 2

Directions
Read the passage and write the letter of the word or group of words that belongs in each underlined space.

Natural resources and wildlife often __(1)__ easy to identify. Regional environmental education centers are great resources. They __(2)__ hands-on experience. __(3)__ you have a center near you? The center near me __(4)__ programs year-round. One program about the history and methods of making maple syrup __(5)__ for this month. Another, Animal Tracking Techniques, draws some amateur detectives every time it is offered.

In northeastern Pennsylvania, white-tailed deer and red foxes __(6)__ familiar backyard visitors. A gaggle of geese __(7)__ temporarily on small ponds. Groundhogs, on the other hand, __(8)__ housekeeping. They __(9)__ underground homes and make huge holes in the yard. Either woodpeckers or sapsuckers __(10)__ the biggest nuisance award because they drill holes in houses.

1. **A** has been
   B am
   C is
   D are

2. **A** provides
   B provide
   C was providing
   D providing

3. **A** Doing
   B Doesn't
   C Do
   D Does

4. **A** have offered
   B offer
   C offers
   D offering

5. **A** is scheduled
   B are scheduled
   C were scheduled
   D have been scheduled

6. **A** are
   B is
   C am
   D was

7. **A** lands
   B have landed
   C were landed
   D do land

8. **A** does set up
   B has set up
   C sets up
   D set up

9. **A** has built
   B build
   C is building
   D builds

10. **A** win
    B wins
    C winning
    D has win

Agreement of Subjects and Verbs

Something is wrong with these sentences.

> He don't like spaghetti.
> Is you taking Spanish this year?

Read the following sentences. This time the form of the verbs has been changed.

> He **does**n't like spaghetti.
> **Are** you taking Spanish this year?

Now the sentences are correct because there is agreement between each verb and its subject. One basic agreement rule applies to all subjects and verbs.

26 A A verb must agree with its subject in **number**.

 Number

Number is the term used to indicate whether a word is singular or plural. In this chapter you will see that nouns, pronouns, and verbs all have number and that the number of a subject and a verb must agree.

The Number of Nouns and Pronouns

The plural of most nouns is formed by adding *-s* or *-es* to the singular form.

REGULAR NOUNS		
Singular	truck	potato
Plural	trucks	potato**es**

A few nouns form their plurals in other ways. A dictionary always lists an irregular plural.

IRREGULAR NOUNS		
Singular	mouse	child
Plural	mice	children

Pronouns can also be singular or plural. *I, he, she*, and *it* are singular, and *we* and *they* are plural. *You* can be singular or plural.

You can learn about spelling plural nouns on pages 914–921.

● **Practice Your Skills**

Determining the Number of Nouns and Pronouns

Label each word *singular* or *plural.*

1. Ohio
2. they
3. glove
4. flower
5. test
6. lamps
7. she
8. it
9. boxes
10. shoe
11. we
12. flags
13. vases
14. men
15. horse
16. car

The Number of Verbs

In the present tense, most verbs add *-s* or *-es* to form the singular. Plural forms in the present tense do not end in *-s* or *-es*.

SINGULAR	PLURAL
The boy { sing**s**. laugh**s**. catch**es**.	The boys { sing. laugh. catch.

Be, have, and *do*, however, have special singular and plural forms in the present tense. *Be* also has special forms in the past tense.

FORMS OF *BE, HAVE,* AND *DO*

	Singular	Plural
be	am, is (present) was (past)	are (present) were (past)
have	has	have
do	does	do

Agreement of Subjects and Verbs • Lesson 1

In the following examples, each subject is underlined once, and each verb is underlined twice.

Singular She is my best friend.
Patty was my best friend.
Lance has a new friend.

Plural They are my friends also.
Tim and my cousin were good friends.
The Morrisons have some nice friends.

● **Practice Your Skills**

Determining the Number of Verbs

Write each verb and label it *singular* or *plural*.

1. Alvin enjoys
2. twins have
3. students play
4. he was
5. truck has
6. we do
7. it is
8. they drive
9. pictures are
10. Pauline does

 Singular and Plural Subjects

The number of a verb must agree with the number of its noun or pronoun subject.

26 A.1 A singular subject takes a singular verb. A plural subject takes a plural verb.

To make a verb agree with its subject, ask yourself two questions: *What is the subject?* and *Is the subject singular or plural?* Then choose the correct verb form. In the following sentences, each subject is underlined once, and each verb is underlined twice.

Singular Kristen dances gracefully.
Plural They dance gracefully.
Singular Matt was in a hurry.
Plural They were in a hurry.

742   Subject and Verb Agreement

● **Practice Your Skills**

Making Subjects and Verbs Agree

Write each subject and label it *singular* or *plural*. Then write the form of the verb in parentheses that agrees with the subject.

1. Brown pelicans (dives, dive) into the ocean for fish.
2. A white pelican (scoops, scoop) fish out of the water just below the surface.
3. Mockingbirds (eats, eat) insects.
4. Owls (flies, fly) almost noiselessly.
5. The short-eared owl (helps, help) control rodents.
6. All birds (has, have) special colors and songs.
7. Male blue jays (is, are) a different color than female blue jays.
8. An average condor (have, has) a wingspan of more than nine feet.
9. A duck's webbed feet (acts, act) as paddles.
10. The trumpeter swan (is, are) the largest of all water birds.

● *Connect to Writing:* **Editing**

Correcting for Subject and Verb Agreement

Write correctly each sentence in which the subject and verb do not agree. If a sentence is correct, write **C**.

1. Ravens are very clever birds.
2. The bald eagle are the symbol of the United States and its national bird.
3. The mockingbird imitate the calls of many different kinds of birds.
4. Cardinals likes evergreen trees for their nests.
5. Urban pigeons lives in towns and cities.

✓ Check Point: Mixed Practice

Write each subject and label it *singular* or *plural.* Then write the form of the verb in parentheses that agrees with the subject.

1. Big cats (is, are) predators.
2. The lion (is, are) the king of beasts.
3. Lions (lives, live) in the African grassland.
4. They (eats, eat) gazelles, antelopes, and zebras.
5. A male lion (weighs, weigh) almost 550 pounds.
6. Lionesses (do, does) most of the hunting for the pride.
7. All the lions (cares, care) for the lion cubs.
8. A lion cub (loves, love) to play.
9. Lions (sleeps, sleep) most of the day.
10. The lion (creeps, creep) up on its unsuspecting prey.

• Connect to Writing: Descriptive Paragraph

Using Subject and Verb Agreement

A local biologist is preparing a presentation about wild mammals living in your town. She will be making a presentation to the city council so that they can make decisions about future land development. Your class has been asked to write a descriptive paragraph about mammals (such as squirrels, rabbits, deer, and skunks) that you have seen in your area. Include an accurate description of the animal you choose. Also write about its habitat, behavior, and any other interesting observations. Be sure that subjects and verbs agree in your description.

Common Agreement Problems — Lesson 2

Making certain subjects and verbs agree can sometimes present a challenge. Some of the more common problems are explained in the following section.

26 B Helping verbs, contractions, interrupting words, and inverted order can lead to agreement problems.

➤ Verb Phrases

You may recall that the main verb plus one or more helping verbs is called a **verb phrase.** If a sentence has a verb phrase, the first helping verb must agree in number with the subject. In all of the following examples, the subject is underlined once, the verb phrase is underlined twice, and the first helping verb is in bold type.

Singular	Chris **is** looking for Coach.
	(*Chris* and the helping verb *is* agree because they are both singular.)
Plural	They **have** been waiting for the coach.
	(*They* and the first helping verb *have* agree because they are both plural.)

26 B.1 The first helping verb must agree in number with the subject.

The following list shows the singular and plural forms of common helping verbs.

COMMON HELPING VERBS	
Singular	am, is, was, has, does
Plural	are, were, have, do

Singular	The player **is** throwing the ball now.
	Your team **does** practice hard once or twice a day.
Plural	Many teams **are** being honored every year.
	Your teammates **are** going too.

● **Practice Your Skills**

Making Subject and Verb Phrases Agree

Write each subject and label it singular or plural. Then write the helping verb in parentheses that agrees with the subject.

1. The first football game (was, were) played between Rutgers and Princeton.
2. Downhill skiers (has, have) raced at over 120 miles per hour.
3. Helmets (was, were) first introduced to the major baseball league in 1941.
4. Soccer (does, do) require a lot of skill.
5. Basketball (was, were) invented by James Naismith.
6. Ice hockey (is, are) played mostly in the northern states.
7. Cyclists (has, have) raced through France for many years.
8. Runners (do, does) practice for many hours.
9. The first marathon (was, were) held in Greece.
10. Tennis (was, were) played in the Middle Ages.

● *Connect to Writing:* **Editing**

Correcting Subject and Verb Agreement

Rewrite each sentence in which the subject and verb do not agree. If a sentence is correct, write **C**.

1. Table tennis are becoming a popular indoor sport.
2. Jerry is playing today.
3. Floyd do like tennis.
4. Anna was introduced to cricket in England.
5. Bill were practicing hard yesterday.

➤ *Doesn't or Don't?*

When contractions are used, agreement with a subject can be confusing. When you check for agreement, always say the individual words of a contraction.

26 B.2 The verb part of a contraction must agree in number with the subject.

Incorrect	That ant **do**n't look good on the kitchen counter.
Correct	That ant **does** not look good on the kitchen counter.
	That ant **does**n't look good on the kitchen counter.

Incorrect	Tim and his father **does**n't like ants in the kitchen.
Correct	Tim and his father **do** not like ants in the kitchen.
	Tim and his father **do**n't like ants in the kitchen.

The preceding rule applies to all other contractions as well. Keep in mind which contractions are singular and which are plural.

CONTRACTIONS	
Singular	**does**n't, **has**n't, **is**n't, **was**n't
Plural	**do**n't, **have**n't, **are**n't, **were**n't

● Practice Your Skills

Making Subject and Verb Phrases Agree

Write each subject. Then write the contraction in parentheses that agrees with the subject.

1. Scientists (doesn't, don't) ignore the importance of ants.
2. Ants (wasn't, weren't) crawling on that plant.
3. Weaver ants (doesn't, don't) live on the ground.
4. Those ants (wasn't, weren't) unusual.
5. Some ants (doesn't, don't) live underground.
6. Some of the ants (isn't, aren't) leaving the nest.
7. I (hasn't, haven't) ever seen a herdsman ant.
8. The queen and the workers (hasn't, haven't) arrived yet.
9. That ant (isn't, aren't) crawling very fast along the garden path.
10. Aphids and mealy bugs (doesn't, don't) like any kind of ants.

● *Connect to Writing:* Editing

Correcting for Subject and Verb Agreement

Rewrite each sentence in which the subject and verb do not agree. If a sentence is correct, write **C**.

1. Herdsman ants doesn't like to stay in one place.
2. Plants aren't always homes for ants.
3. Some ants hasn't been studied yet.
4. Ants and plants doesn't always support each other.
5. Those ants weren't very large

Interrupting Words

Sometimes words—a prepositional phrase, for example—can come between a subject and its verb. When this happens, you must be sure that your subject and verb agree no matter how far apart they are.

26 B.3 The agreement of a verb with its subject is not changed by any interrupting words.

In the following examples, each subject and verb agree in number in spite of the words that come between them. The best way to find the correct agreement in these sentences is to mentally take out all of the prepositional phrases. When revising, you might imagine parentheses around them. Then it is easy to see the subject and verb.

Singular A list of new drivers is available.
(*Is* agrees with the subject *list,* not with the object of the preposition *drivers*—even though *drivers* is closer to the verb.)

Plural The drivers in that room are winners.
(*Are* agrees with the subject *drivers,* not with the object of the preposition *room*—even though *room* is closer to the verb.)

Compound prepositions—such as *in addition to, as well as,* and *along with*—often begin interrupting phrases. Make sure the verb always agrees with the subject, not the object of the preposition.

My sister as well as many other race fans was visiting the NASCAR Museum.
(*Was* agrees with the subject *sister*—not with *fans,* the object of the preposition *as well as.*)

● **Practice Your Skills**

Making Interrupted Subjects and Verbs Agree

Write each subject and label it *singular* or *plural.* Then write the form of the verb in parentheses that agrees with the subject.

1. The car with the rainbow on its door (sits, sit) on the pit road.
2. The drivers at the track (seems, seem) friendly.
3. Throughout the years the friendship among the drivers (has, have) remained strong.
4. The TV announcers, along with the fans, (enjoys, enjoy) a good race.
5. People like Jeff Gordon (appears, appear) self-confident.

Connect to Speaking and Writing: Grammar Vocabulary

Understanding Interrupting Prepositions

With a partner, discuss what you have learned about the influence of prepositions and prepositional phrases on subject-verb agreement. Share an example with each other. Then say the sentences below aloud and discuss how you would make each subject and verb agree. Write your corrected sentences, and read them aloud.

1. The announcers from the TV station at the track is preparing for the race.
2. The drivers in the red and white cars is on the same winning team.
3. The driver with the fewest wrecks on their record are Martin.
4. The track with the most dangerous turns are in New York.

Inverted Order

In most sentences the subject comes before the verb. This is a sentence's **natural order.** In some sentences, however, the verb or part of a verb phrase comes before the subject. Such a sentence has **inverted order.** A verb always agrees with its subject, whether the sentence is in its natural order or in inverted order.

26 B.4 The subject and verb of an inverted sentence must agree in number.

There are several types of inverted sentences. When you are looking for the subject in an inverted-order sentence, turn the sentence around to its natural order.

Inverted Order	In the supply closet is some gum.
Natural Order	Some gum is in the supply closet.
Question	Has Coach answered your request?
Natural Order	Coach has answered your request.
Sentence Beginning With *Here*	Here is my favorite catcher's mitt.
Natural Order	My favorite catcher's mitt is here.
Sentence Beginning With *There*	There were six members at the meeting.
Natural Order	Six members were at the meeting.
	(Sometimes *here* or *there* must be dropped for the sentence to make sense.)

The words *here* and *there* are never the subject of a sentence.

Common Agreement Problems • Lesson 2

● **Practice Your Skills**

Making Subjects and Verbs in Inverted Order Agree

Write each subject and label it *singular* or *plural.* Then write the form of the verb in parentheses that agrees with the subject.

1. There (is, are) only one baseball game after school this week.
2. When (does, do) your sister Maria pitch?
3. (Has, Have) your practices for games been challenging this year?
4. Here (is, are) my glove for the catcher.
5. In the dugout there (was, were) two heavy bags full of bats.
6. Where (was, were) the catcher at four o'clock yesterday afternoon?
7. On top of the pitcher's mound (stands, stand) a strong pitcher.
8. (Does, Do) Tito and his brother stay after practice?
9. Here (is, are) some socks from my bag.
10. (Was, Were) there any foul balls in the game last night?

● *Connect to Writing:* **Drafting**

Writing Sentences Using Subject and Verb Agreement

Write four sentences, following the instructions below.

1. Write a sentence that begins with the word *here.*
2. Write a question.
3. Write a sentence that begins with the word *there.*
4. Write a sentence that begins with a prepositional phrase and is in inverted order.

● *Connect to Writing:* **Editing**

Correcting Subject and Verb Agreement

Write correctly each sentence in which the subject and verb do not agree. If a sentence is correct, write **C.**

1. When does the players arrive?
2. On the bus were two of my favorite gloves.
3. Here are the umpire.
4. There was two mascots for our team last year.
5. By the pitcher's mound was a small glove.
6. Do that glove belong to one of the infielders?

Check Point: Mixed Practice

Write each subject. Then write the form of the verb in parentheses that agrees with the subject.

1. The largest cat in the Americas (is, are) the jaguar.
2. Elephants in Africa (has, have) large ears and flat heads.
3. In the jungle (roam, roams) many wild animals.
4. A queen ant in a colony (lives, live) about ten to twenty years.
5. There (was, were) two alligators in the mud at the edge of the lake.
6. A jellyfish (has, have) little or no color.
7. Bees (doesn't, don't) want to be disturbed.
8. When (do, does) the birds migrate?
9. (Wasn't, Weren't) those birds unusual?
10. The wolf (is, are) known for its instinct to form packs.

Power Your Writing: Who or What?

An **appositive phrase** is a group of words with no subject or verb that adds information about a preceding noun in the sentence. An appositive phrase gives your reader insight into who someone is or what something is like. In the following sentence from Jean Craighead George's *Julie of the Wolves* (pages 151–155), for example, readers are given a further glimpse into Julie through an appositive phrase, which comes between the subject (the noun *life*) and the verb phrase (*depended upon*). Notice that the appositive phrase is set off by commas.

Appositive Phrase	Somewhere in this cosmos was Miyax; and the very life in her body, **its spark and warmth,** depended upon these wolves for survival.

You can use appositive phrases to give deeper meaning to who is experiencing an event and what those feelings entail.

Common Agreement Problems • Lesson 2

Other Agreement Problems

26 C **Compound subjects** and **collective nouns** can cause agreement problems.

➤ Compound Subjects

A **compound subject** is two or more subjects that have the same verb. A compound subject is usually joined by a single conjunction, such as *and* or *or*, or by a pair of conjunctions, such as *either/or* or *neither/nor*.

26 C.1 When subjects are joined by *and*, the verb is usually plural.

When a subject is more than one, it is plural. The verb, therefore, must also be plural to agree with the subject. In all of the following examples, the subject is underlined once and the verb is underlined twice.

Plural Verbs	Cathy **and** Beth take the early bus to work.
	This trunk **and** those suitcases have traveled many miles.
	Breakfast **and** lunch are served in the dining car.

Agreement between the subject and the verb follows a different rule when a compound subject is joined by *or*, *either/or*, or *neither/nor*.

26 C.2 When subjects are joined by *or*, *either/or*, or *neither/nor*, the verb agrees with the closer subject.

Singular Verb	**Either** Mercury **or** Venus **is** very small.
	(The verb is singular because *Venus*, the subject closer to it, is singular.)
Plural Verb	**Neither** the moon **nor** the planets **have** risen yet.
	(The verb is plural because *planets*, the subject closer to it, is plural.)
Singular Verb	**Either** those high buildings **or** that tree **is** blocking the telescope.
	(The verb is singular because *tree*, the subject closer to it, is singular.)
Plural Verb	**Either** that tree **or** those buildings **are** blocking the telescope.
	(The verb is plural because *buildings*, the subject closer to it, is plural.)

● **Practice Your Skills**

Making Verbs Agree with Compound Subjects

Write the correct form of the verb in parentheses.

1. Sopranos and tenors (sings, sing) the high parts.
2. Either the altos or the basses (has, have) the harmony.
3. Neither the sopranos nor the altos (remembers, remember) their cues.
4. The piano and the flutes (plays, play) the introduction.
5. The drums and the oboe (starts, start) the second section.
6. The piano and the drums (is, are) considered percussion instruments.
7. Neither the trumpets nor the trombones (has, have) the melody.
8. Either the soloist or the conductor (bows, bow) after the music is over.
9. The clarinets and the oboes (sounds, sound) similar.
10. Neither the saxophones nor the piccolo (has, have) a part in this song.

● *Connect to Writing:* **Drafting**

Writing Sentences with Compound Subjects

Write the correct form of the verb in parentheses.

1. Juan and his brothers (was, were) musicians.
2. The basses or the tenors (has, have) the practice rooms now.
3. The chimes and the triangle often (ring, rings) together.
4. That old, broken piano and those new flutes (was, were) given away.
5. Sopranos and altos (is, are) going to practice tomorrow.
6. The guitarist and the brass players (is, are) working up a new number.
7. The director and the jazz band (has, have) been practicing.
8. My sister and I (plans, plan) to attend the concert.

● *Connect to Writing:* **Editing**

Correcting Subject and Verb Agreement

Rewrite the sentences in which the subject and verb do not agree. If a sentence is correct, write **C**.

1. My flute and the twins' clarinets is out of tune again.
2. The woodwinds and the brass horns have the best parts in the concert.
3. The soloist and the altos likes to sing harmony together.
4. Neither Katharine's reed nor Michael's keys was broken in practice.
5. Either the bassoons or the tuba were flat during the recital.

Other Agreement Problems • Lesson 3

➤ Collective Nouns

A **collective noun** names a group of people or things. The words in the box below are examples of collective nouns.

COMMON COLLECTIVE NOUNS			
band	committee	flock	orchestra
bunch	congregation	gang	school
class	crew	group	swarm
cluster	crowd	herd	team
colony	family	league	tribe

The way you use a collective noun determines what verb to use.

26 C.3   Use a singular verb with a collective noun subject that is thought of as a unit.

You may on occasion use a plural verb with a collective noun to emphasize the role of the individuals in the sentence.

> The crew **is** sailing in the Memorial Day race next weekend.
> (The crew as a whole, as one unit, is sailing. Therefore, the verb is singular.)
>
> The crew **are** not agreeing on the color of the new uniforms.
> (The individuals on the crew are acting separately because they are not agreeing with one another. Therefore, the verb is plural.)

To make the second sentence even clearer, you could add the word *members* after *crew*. Then the agreement between *members* and *are* would be clear.

> The crew members **are** not agreeing on the color of the new uniforms.

● Practice Your Skills

Making Verbs Agree with Collective Nouns

Write the correct form of the verb in parentheses.

1. A large and curious crowd (has, have) gathered at the dock.
2. The ship's crew (is, are) arguing over the type of sails to use.
3. A flock of seagulls (flies, fly) low in the sky.
4. The band (tunes, tune) their instruments before they play for the sailors.
5. The judging committee (makes, make) a final inspection of the ship.
6. The captain's family (wishes, wish) him good luck.
7. The sailors' league (checks, check) the boat carefully.

8. The team (disagrees, disagree) over the official start time for the race.
9. This class of boats (is, are) very fast.
10. A pod of dolphins (swims, swim) with the boat during part of the race.

Connect to Writing: Editing

Correcting Subject and Verb Agreement

Rewrite each sentence in which the subject and verb do not agree. If a sentence is correct, write **C**.

1. The orchestra plays every night on the cruise ship.
2. A flock of gulls land on the deck of the big ship every afternoon.
3. My family like sailing.
4. The enthusiastic crowd cheers loudly for its favorite boat.
5. The crew prepare for a long race.

✓ Check Point: Mixed Practice

Write the form of the verb in parentheses that agrees with the subject.

1. An ant colony (is, are) very complex.
2. Termites and ants (does, do) a lot of damage to homes and lawns.
3. In Texas, bees and ants (is, are) considered pests by many people.
4. A swarm (flies, fly) to find its new home.
5. People and animals (has, have) been disturbed by ants.
6. Either ants or bees (stings, sting) people.
7. The cattle herd (avoids, avoid) ant mounds.
8. Neither fleas nor ticks (are, is) very pleasant to encounter.
9. A termite colony (does, do) need to be watched carefully.
10. Fire ants (has, have) particularly painful stings.
11. (Doesn't, Don't) hungry termites silently eat away at all the wood in homes?
12. Warm areas of the country (has, have) more problems with ants and termites than cooler areas.

Connect to Writing and Speaking: Writing a Short Essay

A Collective of Animals

Talk to a partner about the many nouns used to identify groups of animals, such as "a herd of antelope" or "an army of ants." Do some research, and make a list of collective names for animals. Then write a short essay that describes some of these groups. Use their collective names.

Agreement Problems with Pronouns

26 D When certain pronouns are used as subjects, they can present subject-verb agreement problems.

▶ *You* and *I* as Subjects

The singular pronouns *you* and *I* are exceptions to the two rules for agreement between subjects and verbs.

26 D.1 *You* is always used with a plural verb even when *you* refers to one person.

In the examples below, the subject is underlined once and the verb is underlined twice.

| **Plural Verbs** | Anne, you are always very organized. |
| | Boys, you work very hard. |

26 D.2 *I* takes a plural verb unless it is used with the verbs *am* or *was*.

Plural Verbs	I study models of ships.
	I have a new math teacher.
Singular Verbs	I am ready to study.
	I was sick yesterday.

When You Write

Writers may ignore the rules for subject-verb agreement to create authentic dialogue, as in the passage below.

> "What are you getting up so soon for, Sam?" asked Bill.
>
> "Me?" says I. "Oh, I got a kind of pain in my shoulder. I thought sitting up would rest it."
>
> "You're a liar!" says Bill. "You're afraid. You was to be burned at sun-rise, and you was afraid he'd do it. And he would, too, if he could find a match."
>
> —O. Henry, "The Ransom of Red Chief"

Write a scene between two people that uses *You* and *I* with correct subject-verb agreement. Use the format above to write quotation marks properly.

● **Practice Your Skills**

Making Verbs Agree with You and I

Write the correct form of the verb in parentheses.

1. I (likes, like) history class.
2. You (is, are) the best student in our mathematics class.
3. I (has, have) some homework.
4. You (has, have) a report to prepare for geography class tomorrow.
5. We (was, were) in English class.
6. You (needs, need) Internet access to finish your report.
7. You (was, were) very amusing in this year's school play.
8. This year you should (studies, study) hard.
9. I always (wears, wear) this old shirt to gym class.
10. You (has, have) a lot of homework to do this weekend.

● *Connect to Writing:* **Editing**

Correcting Subject and Verb Agreement

Rewrite each sentence in which the subject and verb do not agree. If a sentence is correct, write **C**.

1. I likes my math class this year.
2. You reads many nonfiction books.
3. I enjoy science.
4. You finish your math homework quickly.
5. I types faster than you.

 **Indefinite Pronouns**

An **indefinite pronoun**—such as *someone, many,* and *all*—can be the subject of a sentence. Indefinite pronouns have number. Some are singular and some are plural.

26 D.3 A verb must agree in number with an indefinite pronoun used as a subject.

The following list shows the number of common indefinite pronouns.

COMMON INDEFINITE PRONOUNS	
Singular	anybody, anyone, each, either, everybody, everyone, neither, nobody, no one, one, somebody, someone
Plural	both, few, many, several

Singular indefinite pronouns used as subjects always take a singular verb. Plural indefinite pronouns used as subjects always take a plural verb. Interrupting words do not affect this agreement.

Singular Everyone is ready.
(*Is* agrees with the singular indefinite pronoun *everyone.*)

One of my sisters was there.
(*Was* agrees with the singular indefinite pronoun *one,* not with the object of the preposition *sisters.*)

Plural Many play at this field each day.
(*Play* agrees with the plural indefinite pronoun *many.*)

Several in the group go to soccer camp each summer.
(*Go* agrees with the plural indefinite pronoun *several,* not the object of the preposition *group.*)

You can learn more about indefinite pronouns on pages 728–729.

Practice Your Skills

Making Verbs Agree with Indefinite Pronouns

Write each subject and label it singular or plural. Then write the form of the verb in parentheses that agrees with the subject.

1. One of the suitcases (has, have) a hole in it.
2. Each of the tourists (has, have) eaten some dinner in the small café.
3. Several of my friends (takes, take) pictures.
4. (Has, Have) everyone slept well?
5. Neither of the twins (has, have) ever gone to the beach.
6. Both of the tickets (has, have) been ordered.
7. Nobody (was, were) waiting at the train station.
8. Many of the students on our bus (listens, listen) using headphones.
9. Everybody on the plane (cheers, cheer) loudly when we arrive.
10. Somebody in our hotel (is, are) a singer.

Connect to Writing: Drafting

Writing Sentences with Indefinite Pronouns

Write five sentences using the following indefinite pronouns as subjects.

1. many
2. few
3. both
4. nobody
5. someone

Connect to Writing: Editing

Correcting Subject and Verb Agreement

Rewrite each sentence in which the subject and verb do not agree. If a sentence is correct, write **C**.

1. A few of the suitcases is missing.
2. Several of the tourists are tired.
3. No one like our hotel.
4. Many of the sightseers does enjoy travel.
5. Few want to return home.

● **Connect to Writing: Club Brochure**

Using Subject-Verb Agreement Creatively

You are creating a brochure for your travel club. The brochure will help new students understand what your club is all about. Detail the trips your club has taken in the brochure, and be sure that your subjects and verbs agree.

✓ **Check Point: Mixed Practice**

Write the correct form of the verb in parentheses.

1. Coins (has, have) been around for more than 2,500 years.
2. Once only kings and rich people (was, were) coin collectors.
3. Now more than five million people throughout the world (takes, take) part in this hobby.
4. Many of the collectors (does, do) it as an investment.
5. This hobby (is, are) often begun with just a handful of pennies.
6. There (is, are) a few pennies with a value of $115!
7. A Jefferson nickel or a Roosevelt dime (is, are) also a good addition to a collection.
8. The condition of rare coins (is, are) very important to buyers.
9. Collectors (doesn't, don't) hold any of the coins in their hands.
10. The moisture from hands (has, have) stained many valuable coins.
11. Coin dealers across the country (rates, rate) coins.
12. One of the best ratings (is, are) "extremely fine."
13. The surfaces of these coins (shows, show) little or no wear.
14. Pennies in "extremely fine" condition (is, are) worth twenty-five cents.
15. (Has, Have) you ever wanted to start a coin collection?

Subject and Verb Agreement

Chapter Review

Assess Your Learning

Selecting Subjects and Verbs That Agree

Write the form of the verb in parentheses that agrees with each subject.

1. The canals on Mars (is, are) probably dry riverbeds.
2. Many of my friends (was, were) at the mall today.
3. Here (is, are) five quarters from my allowance.
4. (Does, Do) a normal caterpillar have sixteen legs?
5. A trumpeter and a drummer (is, are) needed tonight.
6. In the small pond (was, were) several goldfish.
7. One of those oranges (is, are) enough for me.
8. (Has, Have) you noticed the school's new flag?
9. A boxer or a collie (is, are) a good pet.
10. The orchestra (does, do) not have a violin section.

Making Subjects and Verbs Agree

Find and write the verbs that do not agree with their subjects. Then write each sentence correctly. If a sentence needs no change, write **C**.

1. The herd is easily quieted on warm nights.
2. One of the books have a funny title.
3. Haven't Lou or Max mowed the lawn yet?
4. There is many tiny creatures in a drop of water.
5. Behind the garage is three grapevines.
6. Was you afraid of that Doberman?
7. Stacy and I have been friends since fifth grade.
8. Each of those flowers have its own special scent.

Editing for Subject and Verb Agreement

Write the following paragraphs, correcting each verb that does not agree with its subject.

One of the world's greatest masterpieces are the Great Sphinx at Giza, Egypt. A sphinx is a mythical animal with the head of a human and the body of a lion. Many sphinxes was built in Egypt, but the Great Sphinx are the oldest of its kind. The features of the sphinx resembles King Khafre, the king at that time.

The body and the head is carved from a natural cliff in the center of a large stone quarry. However, the outstretched paws of the sphinx was added. The figure were originally covered with painted plaster, and there is still some traces of the plaster. The Great Sphinx is 66 feet high and 240 feet long. Its nose alone measure 5 feet 7 inches. The crew at the dig were astounded by its size.

Using Subject and Verb Agreement

Write a sentence that . . .

1. includes *doesn't* at the beginning.
2. includes *there* at the beginning.
3. includes *my dog and cat* as the subject.
4. includes *either Tim or his brothers* as the subject.
5. includes *anyone* as the subject.

Subject and Verb Agreement: Posttest

Directions
Read the passage and write the letter of the word or group of words that belongs in each underlined space.

Opportunities for students to learn about their environment __(1)__ many. Topics __(2)__ seasonal changes, animals, and endangered species, to name just a few. Projects and field trips __(3)__ hands-on experience. A class visiting local recycling centers, wetlands, farms, or fisheries __(4)__ first hand about local resources. __(5)__ you want to sample freshly made maple syrup at the end of a program on methods of collecting maple syrup?

Vacations are a super way to learn about the environment. People __(6)__ more interesting vacations! Whale-watch weekends __(7)__ more popular in recent years. Recently friends and I __(8)__ a humpback whale as she reeled in schools of sun eels. First, she __(9)__ bubbles under the water to get the sun eels into one spot. Then she opened her mouth and __(10)__ hundreds of them.

1. **A** are
   B is
   C was
   D be

2. **A** does include
   B including
   C includes
   D include

3. **A** offers
   B offer
   C offering
   D is offering

4. **A** learns
   B were learning
   C are learning
   D learn

5. **A** Doing
   B Do
   C Done
   D Does

6. **A** looks for and finds
   B has look for and has find
   C are looking for and are finding
   D is looking for and finding

7. **A** has becoming
   B have become
   C becomes
   D has become

8. **A** were watching
   B was watching
   C have watch
   D has watch

9. **A** blow
   B have blown
   C blew
   D is blown

10. **A** am scooping
    B have scooped up
    C scoop up
    D scooped up

Writer's Corner

Snapshot

26 A   A verb must agree with its subject in **number**. (pages 740–744)

26 B   **Helping verbs, contractions, interrupting words,** and **inverted order** can lead to agreement problems. (pages 745–751)

26 C   **Compound subjects** and **collective nouns** can cause agreement problems. (pages 752–755)

26 D   When certain **pronouns** are used as subjects, they can present subject-verb agreement problems. (pages 756–760)

Power Rules

Check your writing for these language patterns and make changes as needed.

 Use **verbs** that agree with the subject. (pages 738–760)

Before Editing	After Editing
Jorge and Stan *is* going to a movie.	Jorge and Stan *are* going to a movie.
Everybody *were* invited.	Everybody *was* invited.
A book of rules *are* available.	A book of rules *is* available.

 Use **subject forms** of pronouns in the subject position. (pages 712–715)

Before Editing	After Editing
Vanessa and *her* are studying together.	Vanessa and *she* are studying together.
Bill and *him* were late for school.	Bill and *he* were late for school.
Sondra and *me* have the same birthday.	Sondra and *I* have the same birthday.

Editing Checklist

Use this checklist when editing your writing.

✓ Do subjects and verbs agree, including those in sentences with compound subjects? (See pages 740–760.)
✓ Did I check for agreement in sentences with inverted order or interrupting phrases? (See pages 748–751.)
✓ Does the verb part of each contraction agree in number with the subject? (See pages 746–747.)
✓ Did I use verbs correctly with collective nouns? (See pages 754–755.)
✓ Do verbs agree with indefinite pronouns used as subjects? (See pages 758–760.)

Use the Power

When subjects and verbs in a sentence don't agree, the reader feels as though square pegs are being jammed into round holes. The words—and the thoughts— just don't fit together properly. Always check for subject-verb agreement in your writing.

Write a short description of a toy you enjoyed playing with as a child. Use two or three compound subjects and one collective noun. Be sure that interrupting prepositional phrases do not hinder subject and verb agreement.

CHAPTER 27

Using Adjectives and Adverbs

How can you use adjectives and adverbs to show precise relationships among your ideas?

Using Adjectives and Adverbs: Pretest 1

The following draft is hard to read because it contains errors in the use of adjectives and adverbs. Revise the passage so that all comparisons are correct. The first error has been corrected as an example.

John Colter was good at exploring, but he was ~~more~~ better at trapping. He had been traveling with the Lewis and Clark expedition, but his most biggest adventures came after he left to join two other trappers. Colter wandered into an area that was weirder than anything. He didn't know nothing about geysers and other geothermal activities. When he returned home, he described boiling mud and steaming water shooting into the air. These were the curiousest stories people had ever heard, and many thought Colter had gone crazy. However, settlers heading west avoided "Colter's Hell." Sixty years later, Ferdinand Hayden led a new expedition into the area, which had remained unexplored. His team of scientists and artists returned with the wonderfulest reports. As a result, in 1872, the area became the country's first national park. Today, thousands of people visit Yellowstone National Park every year.

766 Using Adjectives and Adverbs

Using Adjectives and Adverbs: Pretest 2

Directions
Read the passage and write the letter of the modifier that belongs in each underlined space.

Hiking is growing __(1)__ each day. In 1999, about 50 million Americans went hiking. That's 100 percent __(2)__ than the number of hikers during the 1980s. It is one of the __(3)__ expensive of all recreational activities. In addition, trails are __(4)__. If you're interested, check the state parks in your area. If there are several parks in your state, one of them may be __(5)__ to you than the others.

Trails in state parks are __(6)__ well marked. Also, trail maps provide __(7)__ information about landmarks along the trail itself. Hikers are __(8)__ cautioned to stay on marked trails. The __(9)__ trails in the park may become crowded. However, experienced hikers don't stray from the trails as __(10)__ as inexperienced ones.

1. **A** popularer
   B most popular
   C more popular
   D popularly

2. **A** most
   B more
   C much
   D much more

3. **A** little
   B less
   C littler
   D least

4. **A** availabler
   B available
   C availablely
   D most available

5. **A** closer
   B more closer
   C closest
   D close

6. **A** usually
   B usual
   C most usual
   D more usual

7. **A** more useful
   B useful
   C usefuler
   D usefulest

8. **A** regular
   B regularly
   C more regular
   D most regularly

9. **A** most popular
   B popularest
   C popularer
   D more popular

10. **A** most often
    B more often
    C oftener
    D often

Comparison of Adjectives and Adverbs

Adjectives and adverbs usually change form when they are used to compare two or more people or things. Most adjectives and adverbs have three forms to show differences in the degree of comparison.

27 A Most adjectives and adverbs have three degrees of comparison: the **positive,** the **comparative,** and the **superlative.**

The **positive degree** is used when no comparison is being made.

> **Adjective** This bear is **big.**
> **Adverb** The bee works **quickly.**

The **comparative degree** is used when two people, things, or actions are being compared.

> **Adjective** This black bear is **bigger** than the other black bear.
> **Adverb** The bees work **more quickly** than the snails.

The **superlative degree** is used when more than two people, things, or actions are being compared.

> **Adjective** This black bear is the **biggest** bear in the entire forest.
> **Adverb** Of all the insects, I think bees work **most quickly.**

You can learn more about adjectives and adverbs on pages 536–557.

● Practice Your Skills

Identifying the Degree of Comparison

Label each underlined adjective or adverb *P* for positive, *C* for comparative, or *S* for superlative.

1. Of the mammals on both land and sea, the blue whale is the <u>largest</u>.
2. Scientists have recently discovered the <u>smallest</u> mammal.
3. The <u>tiny</u> rodent is less than an inch long.
4. A cheetah can run <u>faster</u> than a lion.

768 Using Adjectives and Adverbs

5. A baby orca <u>rapidly</u> puts on weight.
6. A pack of wolves will hunt <u>larger</u> prey than a single wolf will hunt.
7. A peacock has the <u>most impressive</u> display of feathers of all the pheasants.
8. Does the snail crawl <u>more slowly</u> than the turtle?
9. Of all the fish in the river, that salmon jumps <u>highest</u>.
10. A cobra's venom is <u>poisonous</u>.

▶ Regular Comparison

Almost all adjectives and adverbs form the comparative and superlative degrees in the same manner. These forms depend on the number of syllables in the modifier.

One-Syllable Modifiers

27 A.1 Add *-er* to form the comparative degree and *-est* to form the superlative degree of most one-syllable modifiers.

ONE-SYLLABLE MODIFIERS

	Positive	Comparative	Superlative
Adjective	smart	smart**er**	smart**est**
	hot	hot**ter**	hot**test**
Adverb	near	near**er**	near**est**
	fast	fast**er**	fast**est**

Sometimes a spelling change occurs when *-er* or *-est* is added to certain modifiers, such as *hot*. Look in a dictionary to check the spelling of such words.

Two-Syllable Modifiers

Many two-syllable adjectives or adverbs are formed exactly like one-syllable adjectives and adverbs—by adding *-er* or *-est*. Some two-syllable modifiers, however, are difficult to say with those endings, such as *usefuller* and *usefullest*. For such two-syllable modifiers, *more* and *most* should be used to form the comparative and superlative degrees. *More* and *most* are generally used with adverbs that end in *-ly*.

27 A.2 Use *-er* or the word *more* to form the comparative degree and *-est* or the word *most* to form the superlative degree of two-syllable modifiers.

TWO-SYLLABLE MODIFIERS			
	Positive	Comparative	Superlative
Adjective	narrow	narrow**er**	narrow**est**
	happy	happi**er**	happi**est**
	helpless	**more** helpless	**most** helpless
Adverb	soon	soon**er**	soon**est**
	slowly	**more** slowly	**most** slowly

Notice that a spelling change occurs in many modifiers that end in *y*, such as *happy*. The *y* changes to *i* before *-er* or *-est* is added.

Modifiers with Three or More Syllables

All modifiers with three or more syllables form their comparative and superlative degrees by using *more* and *most*.

27 A.3 Use *more* to form the comparative degree and *most* to form the superlative degree of modifiers with three or more syllables.

THREE-SYLLABLE MODIFIERS			
	Positive	Comparative	Superlative
Adjective	horrible	**more** horrible	**most** horrible
Adverb	eagerly	**more** eagerly	**most** eagerly

- **Practice Your Skills**

    Forming the Comparison of Modifiers

    Copy each modifier. Then write its comparative and superlative forms.

    1. quick
    2. quiet
    3. slowly
    4. great
    5. merrily
    6. dangerous
    7. rapidly
    8. dry
    9. cold
    10. neatly
    11. careful
    12. big
    13. curious
    14. early
    15. weakly

- *Connect to Writing:* **Describing a Scene**

    Using Modifiers

    Write a paragraph that describes a place you enjoy. Use a variety of complete sentences that include properly placed modifiers such as those on this page.

Using Adjectives and Adverbs

● **Practice Your Skills**

Using the Correct Form of Modifiers

Write the correct modifier in each sentence.

1. Marty wasn't sure which was (easier, easiest), rowing or paddling.
2. Does the canoe or the rowboat glide (faster, fastest)?
3. Juan faced the situation (more bravely, most bravely) than I did.
4. Of the two boats, which do you think is (bigger, biggest)?
5. Of the five rowers, Barry rows the (more skillfully, most skillfully).
6. Which of the two rowing teams is (more powerful, most powerful)?
7. Of the ten races I've seen, this was the (more enjoyable, most enjoyable).
8. Joe is the (stronger, strongest) member of the rowing team.
9. A canoe can move (more quickly, most quickly) than a barge.
10. Which race was the (shorter, shortest), the first or the last?

Irregular Comparison

A few adjectives and adverbs are compared in an irregular manner.

IRREGULAR MODIFIERS

Positive	Comparative	Superlative
bad/badly	worse	worst
good/well	better	best
little	less	least
much/many	more	most

Positive   The salad was **good.**
Comparative It was **better** than yesterday's salad.
Superlative   It was the **best** salad we have ever had.

● *Connect to Speaking, Listening, and Writing:* **Peer Interaction**

Using Irregular Comparisons

With a partner, brainstorm five sentences for each irregular modifier charted above. Be sure your modifiers are properly placed. Use the positive, comparative, and superlative forms, and be creative. Then use these sentences to write a cohesive paragraph.

● **Practice Your Skills**

Forming Comparisons of Modifiers

Read the following sentences aloud, trying out each word in parentheses. Then read each sentence aloud again, choosing the correct word.

1. This is the (goodest, best) place for a picnic.
2. Did you do (weller, better) in the potato sack races than Sita?
3. Sue ate the (less, least) amount of food of anyone at the picnic.
4. Margaret had (mucher, more) chicken than Sharlene had.
5. That was the (baddest, worst) potato salad I have ever eaten.
6. The games were the (best, better) we have ever had.
7. The planning of the picnic went (well, good).
8. The food preparation was (easiest, easier) than last year.
9. There were (more, most) vegetarians this year.
10. There was (less, lesser) food left over.

● **Practice Your Skills**

Supplying the Correct Form of Modifiers

Read the first sentence in each group. Then write the comparative and superlative forms of the underlined modifier that should go in the two sentences below it.

1. I have <u>little</u> interest in science fiction.
   I have _____ interest in fables.
   I have the _____ interest in biographies.
2. You read quite <u>well</u>.
   You read _____ than my sister.
   You read the ____ of all the students in my class.
3. The book this week is <u>good</u>.
   I think it is _____ than last week's book.
   In fact, it is the _____ book I have read so far this month.
4. <u>Many</u> people in my class buy books.
   _____ people use the library.
   However, _____ people prefer to borrow books from one another.
5. I feel <u>bad</u> about the ending of this book.
   I felt even ___ about the ending of last week's book.
   Two weeks ago, I felt ____ of all.

● **Connect to Writing: Editing**

Using the Correct Form of Modifiers

Write **C** if the modifiers in each sentence are used correctly. If a modifier is used incorrectly, rewrite the sentence.

1. Which do you like goodest, animal stories or science fiction?
2. That book is definitely the worst one I have read all year.
3. Leslie couldn't decide which book she liked most, the mystery or the fairy tale.
4. Who reads fastest, Lee or Shirley?
5. That science encyclopedia is the bigger book in the whole library.

✓ **Check Point: Mixed Practice**

Find and write each incorrect modifier. Then write it correctly.

1. Which type of music do you like best, classical or jazz?
2. Of the three composers, Mozart is the more challenging.
3. Is jazz, classical, or pop the harder to play on the guitar?
4. Who wrote the best music, Ludwig van Beethoven or Johann Sebastian Bach?
5. That composition was the more difficult piece I have ever played.
6. That song was without a doubt the worse song I've heard all year!
7. Which instrument plays most loudly, the tuba or the piccolo?
8. Of all the instruments my brother can play, I like the viola the less.
9. In our many concerts we have played the Mozart piece more recently.
10. Which composition came earliest in the program, "Für Elise" or the *Moonlight Sonata?*
11. I am least eager to hear the symphony than Cynthia is.
12. He couldn't decide which he liked most, the trumpet or the flute.

Problems with Modifiers  Lesson 2

In addition to knowing the comparative and superlative forms of modifiers, you also need to be aware of a few other possible problems when you use adjectives and adverbs.

27 B   Avoid comparing something to itself and using **double comparisons** and **double negatives**.

 ## *Other* and *Else*

When you compare one thing to the others in a group, do not make the mistake of comparing the first thing with itself. Instead add the word *other* or *else* to your comparison.

27 B.1   Add *other* or *else* when comparing a member of a group to the rest of the group.

Incorrect	David sings louder than any boy in the chorus. (David is being compared to all boys in the chorus, which means that he is also being compared to himself because he is in the chorus.)
Correct	David sings louder than any **other** boy in the chorus. (Now David is being compared only to the other boys, not to himself.)
Incorrect	Kay dances better than anyone in the play. (Because Kay is in the play, she is being compared to herself.)
Correct	Kay dances better than anyone **else** in the play. (Now Kay is being compared only to other students, not to herself.)

When You Speak or Write

When you speak and write, be sure that your comparisons are logical. Notice the difference between these two sentences.

Seventh graders' math assignments are more difficult than sixth graders.
Seventh graders' math assignments are more difficult than sixth graders' assignments.

Although the first sentence may sound logical when you speak, it becomes illogical when you write. The first sentence incorrectly compares math assignments to sixth grade students. The second correctly compares math assignments to math assignments.

● **Practice Your Skills**

Identifying Problems with Other or Else

Read the following sentences, looking for problems with *other* or *else*. Write **C** if the sentence is correct and **I** if the sentence is incorrect.

1. Harry learned his lines more quickly than anyone in the play.
2. Our play was better than any other play performed by seventh graders.
3. Sally sings better than any singer in the play.
4. Mrs. Constanza dedicated more of her time to the production than anyone else at our school.
5. My mom took more pictures of the dress rehearsal than anyone did.
6. Sharon had stage fright worse than anyone in the cast.
7. No one was as calm as Juan.
8. Jori got the part because she is taller than any other student who auditioned.
9. Mrs. Constanza was more nervous than the other teachers.
10. Sam sang louder than any other performer in the cast.
11. Barry recited more lines of dialogue than any other cast member.
12. Chen practiced his lines for this play harder than anyone.

● *Connect to Writing:* **Editing**

Correcting Errors with Other or Else

Rewrite the incorrect sentences from the preceding exercise, using *other* or *else* correctly.

Double Comparisons

Use only one method of forming the comparative or the superlative form of a modifier. Using both methods together—for example -er and *more*—results in a **double comparison,** which is incorrect.

27 B.2 Do not use both *-er* and *more* to form the comparative degree or both *-est* and *most* to form the superlative degree.

Double Comparison	Our winter weather comes **more earlier** than yours.
Correct	Our winter weather comes **earlier** than yours.
Double Comparison	We drove through the **most foggiest** area in the valley.
Correct	We drove through the **foggiest** area in the valley.

● **Practice Your Skills**

Identifying Double Comparisons

Read the following sentences, looking for problems with double comparisons. Write **C** if the sentence is correct and **I** if the sentence is incorrect.

1. The weather in Texas is more drier than the weather in Pennsylvania.
2. Some people think the hills of Austin are prettier than the hills of Pittsburgh.
3. The terrain west of Austin becomes more steeper than the terrain east of Austin.
4. Spanish explorers arrived in Texas earlier than the French arrived in Pennsylvania.
5. People in Texas can swim outside for a more longer time than people in Pennsylvania.
6. Many agree that sunrises on the Gulf Coast are the prettiest they have ever seen.
7. Most Texans believe that their chili is more tastier than Northern chili.
8. Texas is the most biggest state in the continental United States.
9. Some of the most interesting architecture in the state can be seen in the city of Austin.
10. Winter in Texas is warmer than in Pennsylvania.

● **Connect to Writing: Editing**

Correcting Errors with Double Comparisons

Rewrite the incorrect sentences from the preceding exercise so that there are no double comparisons.

➤ Double Negatives

The following is a list of common negative words. Notice that all of these words begin with *n*.

COMMON NEGATIVES	
never	none
no	not (and its contraction *n't*)
no one	nothing

Two of these words should never be used together to express the same idea. When they are, the result is a **double negative,** which is incorrect.

27 B.3 Avoid using double negatives: two negatives used to express the same thought.

Double Negative	Ken does**n't** know **nothing** about animals.
Correct	Ken does**n't** know anything about animals.
Correct	Ken knows **nothing** about animals.

Problems with Modifiers • Lesson 2   777

- **Practice Your Skills**

    Identifying Double Negatives

    Read each of the following sentences, looking for double negatives. Write **C** if the sentence is correct and **I** if the sentence is incorrect.

    1. Porpoises don't have no gills.
    2. Some salamanders don't have no lungs, so they breathe through their skin.
    3. Most people didn't know anything about dodo birds until they became extinct.
    4. Some squirrels can't never find the acorns they bury.
    5. An eagle won't let anything harm its chicks.
    6. That mongoose has not done nothing about the cobra in the garden.
    7. The scientists have never seen that species before.
    8. There is no way to protect endangered species without educating the public.
    9. That caterpillar hasn't never stopped eating parsley.
    10. A newly hatched hornbill cannot leave the nest until its feathers grow.

- *Connect to Speaking and Listening:* **Peer Interaction**

    Reviewing Content

    With a partner, review the vocabulary you have learned in this chapter. (Hint: new terms are printed in purple.) Quiz each other until you understand the definitions of all the new words and concepts.

Power Your Writing: Scene Setters

In the sentence below from "Cleopatra," the adjectival phrases highlighted in yellow provide added meaning. Such scene-setting phrases can indicate time or place, as they do in this example, or they can explain how or why something is said or done. Notice that the adjectival phrase is set between commas.

> A host of writers, **from her time to the present,** have found inspiration in the colorful life of the Egyptian queen.
>
> William A. DeWitt, "Cleopatra"

This scene-setting information is often most helpful at the beginning of a sentence. It can lose its effectiveness when placed at the end of the sentence. Below, the adjectival phrase is followed by a comma.

> **From her time to the present,** a host of writers have found inspiration in the colorful life of the Egyptian queen.

Using Adjectives and Adverbs

 Good or Well?

Good is always an adjective. *Well* is usually an adverb. However, when *well* means "in good health," it is used as an adjective.

Adjective	The music sounded **good**.
	(*Good* is a predicate adjective that describes *music*.)
Adverb	He always plays **well**.
	(*Well* is an adverb that tells how he plays.)
Adjective	The conductor doesn't feel **well** today.
	(*Well* means "in good health.")

You can learn more about predicate adjectives and linking verbs on pages 528–530 and 584–587.

● Practice Your Skills

Using Good or Well

Write *good* or *well* to correctly complete each sentence.

1. Vacuum the rug _____.
2. Janice dances _____.
3. I feel quite _____.
4. The juicy steak looks _____.
5. It's running _____.
6. The lunch tasted _____.
7. The Lions played _____.
8. That rain feels _____.
9. Sandra dives _____.
10. Tim's voice is _____.

● *Connect to Writing:* Editing

Correcting Errors with Good or Well

Rewrite the following sentences if they contain errors with *good* or *well*. If a sentence is correct, write **C**.

1. The new band sounds good.
2. They played good at their first concert.
3. The conductor was not feeling well.
4. The flute section did well with the solo.

✓ Check Point: Mixed Practice

Rewrite the following paragraphs, correcting the use of modifiers.

1. Which is most famous, a rabbit or a hare? There's no question about it. Rabbits win every time. After all, who hasn't never read about Bugs Bunny, Peter Rabbit, or Brer Rabbit?

2. A rabbit is different from a hare. Of the two animals, the rabbit is smallest. A rabbit has more shorter ears and legs than a hare has. Rabbits build their nests in burrows. Their young are born blind. A newly born hare, on the other hand, has fully opened eyes. In addition, a rabbit doesn't have no hair when it is born, but a newborn hare has a full coat of hair. Newborn hares are able to hop more earlier than baby rabbits can. Young hares are born in an open field. As a result, they can take better care of themselves sooner than young rabbits can.

3. All rabbits and hares run and jump good. They jump faster than any animal in the forest. A running jackrabbit takes a more higher leap every sixth stride. By doing this, it is able to look around for any possible danger. The strong hind legs of rabbits make them fast runners.

4. Both kinds of animals are more activer at night than in the day. Rabbits and hares eat plants, but they don't eat no meat.

• Connect to Speaking, Listening, and Writing: Peer Interaction

Comparing Sports

With a partner, talk about your favorite sports. Take notes, using a graphic organizer like the one below. Then develop a list of qualities that you believe define the good, better, and best aspects of a particular sport. If you want to pursue the subject further, create another chart defining the bad, worse, and the worst aspects of particular sports. Write a report based on your ideas.

Soccer		
Good	**Better**	**Best**
good exercise		

780 Using Adjectives and Adverbs

Chapter Review

Assess Your Learning

Using the Correct Forms of Modifiers

Write the correct modifier in parentheses for each sentence.

1. This is the (heavier, heaviest) crate I have ever lifted.
2. Of my two uncles, I think Uncle Pete is (older, oldest).
3. Our young chickens are coming along (good, well).
4. Of all the people at the tryouts for the play, Ned was the (more, most) talented.
5. Sandy types (more, most) accurately than Eric.
6. Both pieces of meat look good, but this piece tastes (better, best).
7. There aren't (no, any) erasers for the chalkboard in homeroom.
8. Because Rico didn't sing (good, well) at rehearsal, he is nervous about the concert.
9. Your skates are (newer, more newer) than mine.
10. Mr. Lyons looks (good, well) in a three-piece suit.

Correcting Errors with Modifiers

Write the following sentences, correcting each error. If the sentence needs no change, write C.

1. This bread is more fresher than those rolls.
2. Doesn't no one have a flashlight?
3. I think a panther looks more fiercer than a tiger.
4. He learned his lesson good.
5. I play basketball more better than soccer.
6. Which do you like better, swimming in the ocean or swimming in a lake?
7. We didn't have no practice for three days.
8. Tim's was the most biggest trout caught today.
9. You can't ever depend on the weather in New England.
10. The lost notebook doesn't have no name on it.

■ Forming the Comparison of Modifiers

Write the correct form of each modifier indicated below. Then use each word in a sentence.

1. the comparative of *quickly*
2. the superlative of *long*
3. the comparative of *little*
4. the superlative of *fast*
5. the comparative of *bad*
6. the comparative of *energetic*
7. the superlative of *helpful*
8. the superlative of *good*
9. the comparative of *clear*
10. the comparative of *bravely*

■ Using Adjectives and Adverbs

Write five sentences that follow the directions below.

Write a sentence that . . .

1. uses a form of *little* to compare three pets.
2. uses the word *other* in a comparison.
3. uses the word *else* in a comparison.
4. includes the word *good*.
5. includes the word *bad*.

Using Adjectives and Adverbs: Posttest

Directions
Read the passage and write the letter of the modifier that belongs in each underlined space.

Backpacks include items that are nice to have as well as items that are __(1)__. For example, a brush is nice to have, but you might need snacks __(2)__. Forgetting a swimsuit may be bad, but having no dry clothes may be __(3)__. In some areas, the possibility of __(4)__ temperature changes makes lightweight layered clothing preferable. Your __(5)__ supply of all, however, is good, clean water.

Experienced hikers are __(6)__ kind to their feet. They choose footwear that is __(7)__ for their feet. Many people find low-cut lightweight boots the __(8)__. These day-hiking boots offer less protection than the __(9)__ boots worn by weekend hikers. There is not __(10)__ worse than sore feet at the end of a long day.

1. A importantly
   B more importantly
   C most importantly
   D more important

2. A many
   B much
   C more
   D most

3. A badder
   B worse
   C worst
   D more bad

4. A suddener
   B sudden
   C suddenly
   D suddenest

5. A most necessary
   B more necessary
   C necessariest
   D most necessariest

6. A especial
   B most especial
   C more especially
   D especially

7. A appropriate
   B appropriately
   C more appropriately
   D appropriatest

8. A goodest
   B better
   C best
   D wellest

9. A heaviest
   B more heavy
   C heavier
   D more heavily

10. A nothing
    B anything
    C no
    D none

Writer's Corner

Snapshot

27 A Most adjectives and adverbs have three degrees of **comparison:** the **positive,** the **comparative,** and the **superlative.** (pages 768–773)

27 B Avoid comparing something to itself and using **double comparisons** and **double negatives**. (pages 774–778)

Power Rules

Use only one **negative** form for a single negative idea. (pages 777–778)

Before Editing	After Editing
I do*n't* have *nothing* to wear to the party.	I have *nothing* to wear to the party.
Mom *never* got us *none* of those unhealthy foods.	Mom *never* got us *any* of those unhealthy foods.
Our teachers *don't never* allow us to text message during class.	Our teachers *don't* allow us to text message during class.
	Our teachers *never* allow us to text message during class.

Editing Checklist

Use this checklist when editing your writing.

- ✓ Did I use the correct degree of comparison? (See pages 768–773.)
- ✓ Did I use the correct form of irregular modifiers? (See pages 771–773.)
- ✓ Did I add *other* or *else* when comparing a member of a group to the rest of the group? (See pages 774–775.)
- ✓ Was I careful not to use both *-er* and *more* or *-est* and *most?* (See pages 776–777.)
- ✓ Was I careful not to use two negative words together? (See pages 777–778.)
- ✓ Did I use *well* and *good* correctly? (See pages 779–780.)

Use the Power

Comparisons are essential writing tools when you are organizing your ideas in order of importance or degree. Transitional phrases such as *more important* and *most important* are guideposts that can help your reader understand the structure of your composition and the relationship of your ideas.

Think about ways you have used transitional words in your writing. Look over compositions you are working on and find how you've used comparatives in your transitions. Then revise your writing to make effective use of transitions.

The horse is a large mammal.

The elephant is a larger mammal.

The whale is the largest mammal of all.

A Writer's Glossary of Usage

The basic elements of usage appeared in the last four chapters. In this section, you will find specific areas that often cause difficulty for students of English. To make it easier for you to use this guide as a reference, entries are arranged alphabetically.

When you examine "A Writer's Glossary of Usage," notice the variety in language levels, two of which are standard English and nonstandard English. **Standard English,** used by the majority of English-speaking people around the world, has a set pattern of rules and conventions. On the other hand, **nonstandard English** is used by people of varying regions and dialects. It has many differences and includes slang words. Using nonstandard English with friends is not necessarily incorrect; however, it is not acceptable in certain situations. When you write or speak in formal situations, such as in school assignments, you should use standard English.

Examples of both formal and informal English are shown in the glossary. **Formal English** conforms to the accepted rules for grammar, usage, and mechanics in writing. Some typical examples of formal English include business letters, technical reports, and well-written essays. Although **informal English** follows most of the conventional rules of standard English, it contains words and phrases that may not sound appropriate in formal writing. Informal English is frequently used in magazines, newspapers, fiction, and personal writing aimed at general audiences.

a, an Use *a* before words beginning with consonant sounds and *an* before words beginning with vowel sounds.

> It was **an** evening filled with excitement.
>
> After the movies, we went to **a** restaurant.

accept, except *Accept* is a verb that means "to receive with consent." *Except* is usually a preposition that means "but" or "other than."

> **Except** for an emergency, the teacher will not **accept** any late papers.

affect, effect *Affect* is usually a verb that means "to influence" or "to act upon." *Effect* is usually a noun that means "a result" or "an influence." As a verb, *effect* means "to accomplish" or "to produce."

The lively debate **affected** the audience in different ways.

On most, the **effect** was a positive one.

At least it **effected** a needed change in policy.

all ready, already *All ready* means "completely ready." *Already* means "previously."

Are you surprised that my suitcase is **all ready** to be taken to the car?

Because you wanted to leave early, I had **already** packed it.

When You Speak and Write

To avoid confusion between *all ready* and *already,* remember that the word *all* can mean "everything" or "everyone." For example, if you say or write that something is *all ready* or that a group is *all ready,* you are actually saying that everything is ready or that everyone is ready.

a lot People very often write these two words incorrectly as one. There is no such word as "alot." *A lot,* even as two words, should be avoided in formal writing.

Informal	**A lot** of people gathered to honor the graduates.
Formal	**A large number** of people gathered to honor the graduates.

among, between These words are both prepositions. *Among* is used when referring to three or more people or things. *Between* is used when referring to two people or things.

You should be able to find one pair of shoes **among** the many that are on display.

I cannot choose **between** the sandals and the sneakers.

amount, number *Amount* refers to a singular word. *Number* refers to a plural word.

The large **amount** of help probably accounts for the **number** of happy people.

anywhere, everywhere, nowhere, somewhere Do not add *s* to any of these words.

You will find the book you lost **somewhere.**

A Writer's Glossary of Usage

at Do not use *at* after *where*.

> **Nonstandard** Do you know **where** the new stadium is **at?**
> **Standard** Do you know **where** the new stadium is?

● **Practice Your Skills**

Finding the Correct Word

Write the word in parentheses that correctly completes each sentence.

1. (Among, Between) the skills to master, none is more important than reading.
2. You have (all ready, already) learned some reading strategies.
3. The ability to read well (affects, effects) your life.
4. It has a direct (affect, effect) on whether you enjoy reading.
5. It also can (affect, effect) your comprehension.
6. That cat is (somewhere, somewheres) around the house I'm sure.
7. A varied (amount, number) of strategies are available to help you.
8. When you read, you create (a, an) interaction (among, between) yourself and the text.
9. (A, An) reading log allows you to record (many, a lot) of your thoughts.
10. With an open mind and your reading log, you are (all ready, already) to start an exciting journey.

When You Use Technology

The spell check feature on your word processing or e-mail software can be very helpful. It can help you check your spelling as you compose or edit your writing. Be careful, however, because a spelling check will not edit your work. For example, spell check will not flag your writing when you incorrectly use *affect* when *effect* is the right choice.

You can usually find the spelling feature in the Edit or the Tools menu of your software. You can also set most current programs to mark misspelled words as you type. Look in the Preferences menu to activate this feature.

● **Connect to Writing: Editing**

Recognizing Correct Usage

Write the underlined words from the following paragraph. If a word is used correctly, write *C* beside it. If a word is used incorrectly, write the correct form of the word.

Most teachers will **(1)** except any reading log response to the text **(2)** except a plot summary. Any place in the text where you find a problem **(3)** at, you should list possible questions. If a certain character **(4)** effects you, you can describe your feelings. **(5)** Anywheres you find a line or passage you especially like, explain the **(6)** effect it has on you. If a situation reminds you of a book you have **(7)** all ready read, compare the similarities **(8)** between the two. With these strategies, you can gain a large **(9)** amount of practice. You should then be **(10)** all ready for an intelligent class discussion.

bad, badly *Bad* is an adjective and often follows a linking verb. *Badly* is used as an adverb. In the first two examples, *sounds* is a linking verb.

Nonstandard	Do you think the speech sounds **badly?**
Standard	Do you think the speech sounds **bad?**
Standard	I very **badly** wanted to be the last to speak.

You can learn more about using adjectives and adverbs on pages 766–785.

because, since Don't use the subordinating conjunction *since* when you should use *because*. *Since* indicates time. *Because* means "for the reason that."

Since I've been home I've been helping out **because** my parents aren't well.

bring, take *Bring* indicates motion toward the speaker. *Take* indicates motion away from the speaker.

If you **bring** me an application, I'll **take** it to the office.

You can learn more about using problem verbs on pages 689–692.

can, may *Can* expresses ability. *May* expresses possibility or permission.

None of my friends **can** write as well as Eddie.

May I see some of his writing?

A Writer's Glossary of Usage

doesn't, don't *Doesn't* is singular and must agree with a singular subject. *Don't* is plural and must agree with a plural subject or with the singular pronouns *I* and *you*.

> A cat **doesn't** usually like dogs.
>
> Cats **don't** usually like dogs.

double negative Words such as *but* (when it means "only"), *hardly, never, no, none, no one, nobody, not* (and its contraction *n't*), *nothing, nowhere, only, barely,* and *scarcely* are all negatives. Do not use two negatives to express one negative meaning.

> | **Nonstandard** | **Hardly no one** failed the test. |
> | **Standard** | **Hardly anyone** failed the test. |
> | **Standard** | **No one** failed the test. |

You can learn more about the use of negatives on pages 777–778.

fewer, less *Fewer*, the comparative of *few*, is plural and refers to things that can be counted. *Less* is a singular adjective or adverb that refers to quantities and qualities that cannot be counted.

> The **fewer** exercises you do, the **less** chance you have of passing your final exam.

good, well *Good* is an adjective and often follows a linking verb. *Well* is an adverb and often follows an action verb. However, when *well* means "in good health" or "satisfactory," it is used as an adjective.

You can learn more about using *good* and *well* on pages 779–780.

> The team looked **good** in practice.
> (adjective)
>
> Our new quarterback threw **well** in practice.
> (adverb)
>
> Let's hope he feels **well** for the first game.
> (adjective meaning "in good health")

You can learn more about using adjectives and adverbs on pages 766–785.

have, of Never substitute *of* for the verb *have*. When speaking, many people make a contraction of *have*. For example, they might say, "We should've gone." Because *'ve* sounds like *of, of* is often mistakenly substituted for *have* in writing.

Nonstandard	I know that I should **of** gone.
Standard	I know that I should **have** gone.
Nonstandard	I could **of** joined the team, but I didn't want to.
Standard	I would **have** called you, but I lost my cell phone.

in, into Use *in* when you are referring to a place. Use *into* when you want to express motion from one place to another.

Is your towel **in** the locker?

Don't forget to put it **into** your backpack when you leave.

When You Speak and Write

Unlike the word *into*, the word *in* does not suggest that a motion is taking place.

> We were *in* science class when the fire began.
> I had a a great time *in* Minneapolis.

its, it's *Its* is a possessive pronoun and means "belonging to it." *It's* is a contraction for *it is*.

When we find **its** entrance, let's explore the cave.

I think **it's** too dangerous until we know more about **its** tunnels.

Connect to Writing: Editing

Recognizing Correct Usage

Write the underlined words from the following paragraph. If a word is used correctly, write **C** beside it. If a word is used incorrectly, write the correct form of the word.

Kayaks **(1)** can be navigated through the canals in the city of Ketchikan. **(2)** Its also known as "the Salmon Capital of the World." You might feel **(3)** badly about missing a feast if you don't go to a salmon bake. One spectacular sight is the rain forest with **(4)** its collection of totem poles. In Juneau you **(5)** can find it difficult to walk on the steep streets. If you **(6)** badly want to walk on ice, take a helicopter ride to Mendenhall Glacier. After most cruise ships leave Juneau, they travel **(7)** into Glacier Bay. The glaciers, which gleam like diamonds, **(8)** don't hardly seem real. Although Sitka has **(9)** less people than Ketchikan and Juneau, it is a historic place. You **(10)** doesn't want to miss seeing the icons **(11)** in St. Michael's Cathedral.

A Writer's Glossary of Usage

Connect to Writing: Composing a Description

Avoiding Word Usage Problems

Jack London, a well-known American author, rose to fame when he published *The Call of the Wild,* a novel about Buck. Buck is a dog who fights for survival in the rugged but beautiful territory of Alaska. In the following excerpt from his novel, London paints a vivid picture of spring emerging in the wilderness. Read the description carefully, and then follow the instructions.

> Each day the sun rose earlier and set later. It was dawn by three in the morning, and twilight lingered till nine at night. The whole long day was a blaze of sunshine. The ghostly winter silence had given way to the great spring murmur of awakening life. . . . The sap was rising in the pines. The willows and aspens were bursting out in young buds. Shrubs and vines were putting on fresh garbs of green.
>
> Jack London, *The Call of the Wild*

Imagine that the school newspaper editor has asked you to write a description of a nature scene to include in its next edition. Use any five of the glossary entries from *a/an* through *its/it's,* and write a description of an outdoor scene that you remember. Be sure to use the correct forms of the words.

---

lie, lay *Lie* means "to rest or recline." *Lie* is never followed by a direct object. Its principal parts are *lie, lying, lay,* and *lain. Lay* means "to put or set (something) down." *Lay* is usually followed by a direct object. Its principal parts are *lay, laying, laid,* and *laid.*

Lie If I **lie** down now, I'll feel like going with you later.

I was **lying** on the sofa when the phone rang.

I **lay** there yesterday.

In fact, I have **lain** there many times before.

Lay **Lay** the directions on the table before you leave.

(*Directions* is the direct object.)

Are you **laying** the directions on the seat of my car?

Isn't that where you **laid** the grocery list yesterday?

When I have **laid** reminders on the table, you never could find them.

learn, teach *Learn* means "to gain knowledge." *Teach* means "to instruct" or "to show how."

After the students **learn** about ratios, you can **teach** them about proportions.

leave, let *Leave* means "to depart" or "to go away from." *Let* means "to allow" or "to permit."

Nonstandard	I wish you would **leave** me do my job.
Standard	I wish you would **let** me do my job.
Standard	If you feel that way about it, I'll **leave** now.

passed, past *Passed* is the past tense of the verb *pass*. As a noun *past* means "a time gone by." As an adjective *past* means "just gone" or "elapsed." As a preposition *past* means "beyond."

- The way he **passed** the football reminded me of a play in the **past.** (*past* as a noun)
- Our quarterback has thrown the football **past** his receiver twice in the **past** two games. (*past* as a preposition and then as an adjective)

rise, raise *Rise* means "to move upward" or "to get up." *Rise* is never followed by a direct object. Its principal parts are *rise, rising, rose,* and *risen. Raise* means "to lift (something) up," "to increase," or "to grow something." *Raise* is usually followed by a direct object. Its principal parts are *raise, raising, raised,* and *raised*.

- If you want to **rise** early, be sure to set your alarm.
- Then I won't have to **raise** my voice to make sure you're up on time.
- (*Voice* is the direct object.)

shall, will Formal English uses *shall* with first-person pronouns and *will* with second- and third-person pronouns. Today *shall* and *will* are often used interchangeably with *I* and *we,* except that *shall* is used with *I* and *we* for questions.

- **Shall** I ask permission to leave?
- No, they **will** dismiss us soon.

sit, set *Sit* means "to rest in an upright position." *Sit* is never followed by a direct object. Its principal parts are *sit, sitting, sat,* and *sat. Set* means "to put or place (something)." Set is usually followed by a direct object. Its principal parts are *set, setting, set,* and *set*.

- Please **set** your book down before we **sit** down for dinner. (*Book* is the direct object.)

A Writer's Glossary of Usage

suppose to, supposed to Be sure to add the *d* to *suppose* when it is followed by *to*.

> **Nonstandard** She was **suppose to** return the movie last night.
> **Standard** She was **supposed to** return the movie last night.

than, then *Than* is a subordinating conjunction and is used for comparisons. *Then* is an adverb and means "at that time" or "next."

> **Nonstandard** I can't believe you're older **then** your sister.
> **Standard** When the others found out that I was older **than** she, they **then** let me go with them.

that, which, who As relative pronouns, *that* refers to animals, things, or a class of people; *which* refers to animals or things; and *who* refers to people.

> Our class enjoyed the art exhibit **that** we attended.
> Several of the paintings, **which** were located upstairs, were portraits of famous people.
> The guide **who** directed the tour provided us with useful information.

● Practice Your Skills

Finding the Correct Word

Write the word in parentheses that correctly completes each sentence.

1. Classroom expectations receive more attention now (than, then) in the (passed, past).
2. When teachers (raise, rise) their expectations, students usually respond.
3. This concept results in (learning, teaching) students to (set, sit) higher goals.
4. When students (raise, rise) to a new level, (than, then) they are often rewarded.
5. As a result, students (learn, teach) the connection that (lays, lies) between success and recognition.
6. The recognition (that, which, who) students receive comes in a variety of forms.
7. Some teachers (shall, will) display superior assignments on the bulletin board.
8. This reward (leaves, lets) students enjoy peer recognition also.

9. Students (that, who) have (passed, past) certain goals receive certificates.
10. Complimentary postcards, (which, who) praise a student's efforts, may be sent to parents.

Connect to Writing: Editing

Using Correct Forms of Verbs

Write the underlined verbs. If the verb is used correctly, write C. beside it. If the verb is used incorrectly, write the correct form of the verb.

The teacher informed the students that if they <u>lay</u> down on the job, this failure might <u>lay</u> in a lack of effort. The students <u>set</u> attentively through the class. They are <u>sitting</u> their goals for success. The teacher further explained that they should be <u>setting</u> their minds on their goals. A goal helps <u>sit</u> the tone for achievement. As a result, the teacher who <u>raised</u> the issue saw a sharp <u>raise</u> in students' attitudes. success. At the end of the year, students had <u>raised</u> their grades. Their self-esteem had <u>raised</u> also.

their, there, they're *Their* is a possessive pronoun. *There* is usually an adverb, but sometimes it begins an inverted sentence. *They're* is a contraction for *they are.*

- The students will have **their** class pictures taken tomorrow.
- **There** is a mirror **there** in case it's needed.
- **They're** going to have retakes in a few weeks.

theirs, there's *Theirs* is a possessive pronoun. *There's* is a contraction for *there is.*

- If **theirs** isn't ready, ask if they want a bite of ours.
- **There's** enough to share with them.

A Writer's Glossary of Usage

them, those Never use *them* as a subject or a modifier.

Nonstandard	**Them** are the skates I bought. (subject)
Standard	**Those** are the skates I bought.
Nonstandard	**Them** skates are like mine. (adjective)
Standard	**Those** skates are like mine.

this here, that there Avoid using *here* or *there* alongside *this* or *that*.

Nonstandard	Have you and Jason been to **that there** new restaurant?
Standard	Have you and Jason been to **that** new restaurant?

When You Speak and Write

The word *this* indicates that a person or thing is nearby, or here. *That* indicates that a person or thing is far away, or there. When you say *this here* or *that there*, what you are really saying is "this here here" or "that there there."

to, too, two *To* is a preposition. *To* also begins an infinitive. *Too* is an adverb that modifies a verb, an adjective, or another adverb. *Two* is a number.

- Are they going **to** the beach **to** play volleyball?
- If it's not **too** hot, the **two** of them will play there.
- Can I go **too** if I want **to** watch?

use to, used to Be sure to add the *d* to *use*.

Nonstandard	She **use to** have a miniature doll collection.
Standard	She **used to** have a miniature doll collection.

way, ways Do not substitute *ways* for *way* when referring to a distance.

Nonstandard	The rocket went a **long ways** over the ocean.
Standard	The rocket went a **long way** over the ocean.

where Do not substitute *where* for *that*.

> **Nonstandard** I noticed **where** the days are getting longer.
> **Standard** I noticed **that** the days are getting longer.

who, whom *Who,* a pronoun in the nominative case, is used as either a subject or a predicate nominative. *Whom,* a pronoun in the objective case, is used as a direct object, an indirect object, or an object of a preposition.

> **Who** will take your place in the play?
> (subject)
> **Whom** did the director suggest?
> (direct object)

whose, who's *Whose* is a possessive pronoun or an adjective. *Who's* is a contraction for *who is*.

> **Whose** presentation was the best?
> **Who's** the winner?

your, you're *Your* is a possessive pronoun. *You're* is a contraction for *you are*.

> After the dance, we're all going to **your** house.
> **You're** sure we'll have enough time?

● Practice Your Skills

Finding the Correct Word

Write the word in parentheses that correctly completes each sentence.

1. (Their, There, They're) will likely be a variety of assignments for special credit in (your, you're) geography class.
2. Map drawing allows students (to, too, two) visualize the shape of (that, that there) particular country.
3. Filling in names of important cities helps with learning (to, too, two).
4. (Them, Those) maps are both informative and creative.
5. Frequently, guest speakers who (use to, used to) live in another country give interesting and valuable talks.
6. (Those, Them) interested in a particular country might do more research.

A Writer's Glossary of Usage

7. Students (who, whom) enjoy cooperative learning might prefer to work in groups of (to, too, two) or more.
8. Students have great fun when they plan a trip to the country of (their, there, they're) choice.
9. (Their, There, They're) required to calculate the mileage of the trip (their, there, they're).
10. When (your, you're) deciding what clothes to pack for (this, this here) trip, think about the climate of the country you are visiting.

Connect to Writing: Editing

Recognizing Correct Usage

Write the underlined words. If a word is used correctly, write *C* beside it. If a word is used incorrectly, write the correct form of the word.

Learning about other people's cultures is exciting because **(1)** theirs is different from your own. A cultural-awareness day serves **(2)** too purposes. **(3)** Them purposes are the enjoyment and involvement of everyone in class. Advance planning is necessary to decide **(4)** whose responsible for different projects. One group, **(5)** whose focus is language, might learn key phrases to teach **(6)** too the class. Another might concentrate on the food of **(7)** that there country. Students **(8)** who like to cook could prepare native dishes. Others **(9)** whom are artistic might design costumes worn in **(10)** that country. **(11)** Them games that are popular **(12)** they're could be played too. At the end of the project, **(13)** your certain to have come a long **(14)** ways in understanding another culture.

Connect to Writing: Composing Sentences

Using Pronouns

The words *who, whom, whose,* and *who's* can be very confusing to use. Suppose your teacher asked you to help another student who is having difficulty using these pronouns. To help the student, write an original sentence for each word. Briefly explain the reason for each word choice.

✓ Check Point: Mixed Practice

Write the word in parentheses that correctly completes each sentence.

1. (Shall, Will) we take a glimpse (in, into) the center of Europe?
2. One fascinating country (whose, who's) neutrality is known (everywhere, everywheres) is Switzerland.
3. Switzerland is (good, well) known for its mountains.
4. The Swiss Alps, (that, which, who) are one of three geographical regions in the country, are also (among, between) the world's most famous mountain ranges.
5. (Their, There, They're) also part of the literary (passed, past) in Johanna Spyri's story of Heidi.
6. If you travel to Mount Titlis, you (can, may) eat in a mountaintop restaurant.
7. (Theirs, There's) (not any, not no) better dining experience (than, then) fondue.
8. (Fewer, Less) than ten cows can stop traffic as they descend from the mountains.
9. The cows have large cowbells around (their, there, they're) necks and are often decorated with ribbons and flowers.
10. In no place (accept, except) Bern, the capital of Switzerland, (shall, will) you find a bear pit in the middle of the city!

● *Connect to Writing:* Writing a Narrative

Using Glossary Words

Read over this writer's glossary, paying particular attention to any items that give you trouble in your writing. Then write a short account of an interesting day you spent with a friend. Write about what you did and why it was interesting. Describe the setting and recreate the action of the day. Try to use as many of the words you find troublesome as you can. Read your narrative aloud for your class.

A Writer's Glossary of Usage

Unit 6
Mechanics

Chapter 28 Capital Letters   802

Chapter 29 End Marks and Commas   828

Chapter 30 Italics and Quotation Marks   858

Chapter 31 Other Punctuation   878

Chapter 32 Spelling Correctly   906

Like Winnie-the-Pooh, your spelling may be wobbly when writing certain words. You have probably had the experience of writing so intensely that spelling is secondary to getting the ideas down on the page. When you are knee-deep in writing, this makes sense. Your work is far from complete when you finish that first draft, however. The process of checking punctuation, capitalization, and spelling is absolutely necessary if you expect your readers to step into your writing and respect your ideas. Wobble away when you compose, but remain unswerving when you revise.

My spelling is Wobbly. It's good spelling but it Wobbles, and the letters get in the wrong places.

— *Pooh asking Owl to spell "A Happy Birthday,"* Winnie-the-Pooh *by A.A. Milne*

CHAPTER 28

Capital Letters

How can you use capital letters to clarify your writing?

Capital Letters: Pretest 1

The following first draft is difficult to read because it contains errors in capitalization. The first error has been corrected by indicating that the *c* in Chicago should be capitalized. How would you revise this draft to be sure that capital letters are used correctly?

> The skyscraper was born in chicago, illinois, in the late 1800s. The bessemer process for producing strong steel had been brought to the United states by Andrew carnegie in the 1870s. Elisha graves otis had recently created safety elevators. with the use of steel and elevators, buildings could be taller. When the great chicago fire destroyed a huge section of the city, the stage was set. Famous architects were drawn to Chicago. William Le Baron Jenney came from france, where he had been classmates with the creator of the eiffel Tower in paris. It was Jenney who designed the first skyscraper, the Home insurance Building. completed in 1885, it was the tallest building in the country—an impressive ten stories high. with the success of this building, skyscrapers began to appear all over chicago, and soon were seen in other cities.

Capital Letters: Pretest 2

Directions
Read the passage and decide which underlined word or words should be capitalized. Write the letter of the correct answer. If the underlined word or words contain no error, write **D**.

The early 1900s was a period of exciting "firsts." In 1901, **(1)** baseball's American league was formed to compete with the National League. American **(2)** explorer robert e. peary reached the North Pole in 1909. The year 1916 brought Jeannette Rankin to the **(3)** U.S. house of representatives as its first female member. By 1921, mystery writer Agatha Christie had published her **(4)** first hercule poirot story. In 1928, *Steamboat Willie*, the first sound cartoon, featured **(5)** walt disney's Mickey Mouse.

1. **A** baseball's American League
   B Baseball's American league
   C Baseball's American League
   D No error

2. **A** explorer Robert e. peary
   B explorer Robert E. Peary
   C Explorer Robert E. Peary
   D No error

3. **A** u.s. house of representatives
   B U.S. House of representatives
   C U.S. House of Representatives
   D No error

4. **A** first Hercule Poirot story
   B First Hercule Poirot story
   C First Hercule Poirot Story
   D No error

5. **A** walt Disney's mickey mouse
   B Walt Disney's mickey mouse
   C Walt Disney's Mickey Mouse
   D No error

Rules of Capital Letters

Capital letters and punctuation marks were not used when writing first began. They were developed over the years to indicate the structure and organization of writing, as well as to indicate pauses and tone of voice when reading aloud.

28 A Capitalize **first words**, the pronoun *I*, and **proper nouns**.

➤ First Words

Without capital letters and end marks, one sentence would run into another.

Sentences

A capital letter always begins a new sentence.

28 A.1 Capitalize the first word in a sentence.

Statement	**L**ast night's frost threatened the delicate flowers.
Question	**W**ere your roses damaged in last night's frost?

Lines of Poetry

A capital letter also signals the beginning of a new line of poetry in most poems.

28 A.2 Capitalize the first word in a line of poetry.

Lines of Poetry
   I dwell in a lonely house I know
   That vanished many a summer ago
      And left no trace but the cellar walls,
      And a cellar in which the daylight falls,
   And the purple-stemmed wild raspberries grow.

   Robert Frost, "Ghost House"

When You Write

A few modern poets purposely misuse capital letters or do not use any capital letters at all in their poetry. If you are quoting such a poem, copy it exactly as the poet wrote it. Notice the lack of capital letters in the following fragment of a poem by e. e. cummings.

> who knows if the moon's
> a balloon, coming out of a keen city
> in the sky—filled with pretty people?
>   *e. e. cummings*, "who knows if the moon's"

Parts of Letters

Capital letters bring attention to certain parts of a letter.

28 A.3   Capitalize the first word in the greeting of a letter and the first word in the closing of a letter.

GREETINGS AND CLOSINGS

Greeting	**D**ear Terri,	**G**entlemen:
Closing	**S**incerely,	**V**ery truly yours,

Outlines

The main points of an outline begin with a capital letter. The capital letters help draw attention to the important points in the outline.

28 A.4   Capitalize the first word of each item in an outline and the letters that begin major subsections of the outline.

    I. **S**evere weather storms
        A. Tornadoes
        B. Hurricanes (cyclones)
        C. Thunderstorms

   II. **M**ild weather storms
        A. Snow
        B. Rain
        C. Sleet
        D. Wind

The Pronoun *I*

The pronoun *I* is always capitalized, whether it stands alone or is part of a contraction.

28 A.5 Capitalize the pronoun *I*, both alone and in contractions.

Alone	Did you see the enormous snowball that **I** made?
Contractions	Next winter **I**'m going to visit San Antonio, Texas.
	Everyone says **I**'ll like the sights in San Antonio.

You can learn about capital letters with direct quotations on page 866.

● Practice Your Skills

Capitalizing First Words and *I*

Write correctly each word that should be capitalized.

1. before snowy Canada converted to the metric system, my family took a trip to Montreal.
2. montreal is a beautiful city.
3. it has incredible museums.
4. consumer goods in Montreal were measured by the Canadian system.
5. for example, gasoline was sold by the imperial gallon.
6. an imperial gallon is equal to approximately five U.S. quarts.
7. the imperial gallon sold for about $1.50, but the U.S. gallon cost about $1.15.
8. my father asked me to calculate the relative cost of gasoline in Canada and the United States.
9. furthermore, i had to figure which price was the better bargain.
10. i'll never forget how long it took me to calculate the costs.

● *Connect to Writing:* Writing a Thank-you Note

Using Capital Letters

Write a thank-you note to someone at your school who has helped you in some way. Be sure to tell the person what services he or she provided and why you appreciate it. Use capital letters for your greeting and closing, to begin sentences, and for the pronoun *I*.

● *Connect to Writing:* Editing

Using Capital Letters

Rewrite the following letter, adding capital letters where needed.

(1) dear Mr. Grieb,

(2) now that English class is over, i wish to thank you for talking to our class about poetry. (3) your information was appreciated by the whole class. (4) i found this quotation that i think you'll enjoy. (5) Algernon Charles Swinburne wrote:

(6) sleep; and if life were bitter to thee, pardon,
(7) if sweet, give thanks; thou hast no more to live;
(8) and to give thanks is good, and to forgive.

(9) i hope that you are able to visit our English class again soon.
(10)   sincerely,

(11)   Monica

Proper Nouns

28 A.6 Capitalize proper nouns and their abbreviations.

A noun is the name of a person, a place, a thing, or an idea. A proper noun is the name of a particular person, place, thing, or idea.

COMMON AND PROPER NOUNS	
Common Nouns	**Proper Nouns**
girl	Serena
city	Seattle
road	Evergreen Road
school	Teague Middle School
law	the United States Constitution
team	Texas Rangers
mountain	Pike's Peak
language	English

Study the groups of rules for capitalizing proper nouns. Refer to them when you edit your writing.

You can learn more about nouns on pages 504–508.

Names of persons and animals should be capitalized. Also capitalize the initials that stand for people's names.

NAMES OF PERSONS AND ANIMALS	
Persons	Marianne, M. W. Raymond, Jon Davies, Jr.
Animals	Arnold, Bambi, Maggie, Rover, Spot, Willie

You can learn more about the capitalization of people's titles on pages 817–820.

● **Practice Your Skills**

Capitalizing Proper Nouns

Write correctly each word that should be capitalized.

1. Rita likes American colonial history more than her friend fred does.
2. Planter james madison called for a Constitutional Convention.
3. Back in 1786, madison wanted to revise the Articles of Confederation.
4. At first george washington was not enthusiastic.
5. Finally washington agreed with james madison and alexander hamilton that changes were needed.
6. Fifty-five delegates went to ben franklin's hometown.
7. They were to work with madison, hamilton, and franklin on the United States constitution.
8. The delegates chose washington as presiding officer.
9. james madison's plan called for a two-house Congress.
10. On the other hand, william patterson favored a one-house plan.

● *Connect to Writing:* **Historical Caption**

Using Capitals

Find an interesting photograph or drawing of an important moment in American history. Write a two- or three-sentence caption for the photograph. Capitalize all proper nouns.

See page 810 for more information on capitalizing events.

808   Capital Letters

Geographical names and their abbreviations, initials, and acronyms are capitalized.

GEOGRAPHICAL NAMES	
Streets and Highways	Preston Road (Rd.), New Jersey Turnpike, Thirty-third Street (St.) (The second part of a hyphenated numbered street is *not* capitalized.)
Cities, States	Austin, Texas (TX), Orlando, Florida (FL)
Counties, Parishes, and Townships	Orange County, Louisiana Parish, Washington Township
Countries	France, Mexico, Greece, India, United States of America (U.S.A.)
Continents	Australia, South America, Europe
World Regions	Northern Hemisphere, South Pole
Islands	Virgin Islands, Galveston Island
Mountains	Rocky Mountains, Mount (Mt.) Ida
Forests and Parks	Ocala National Forest, Little Brown Park, Yellowstone National Park
Bodies of Water	Lake Michigan, the Pacific Ocean, the Po River, Hudson Bay
Sections of the Country	the South, the West, New England, the Midwest (Simple compass directions are not capitalized. *Go south on Center Street.*)

Words such as *city, street, lake, ocean,* and *mountain* are capitalized only when they are part of a proper noun.

> We live near some lakes, but they are small compared to the Great Lakes.

● *Connect to Speaking and Writing:* **Travel Brochure**

Capitalizing Geographical Names

With your classmates, talk about the names listed on the chart above. Have you visited any of these places? Share information about the places and what they are like. Then collaborate on a four-page travel brochure that tells about one of these interesting locations. Finally, proofread your brochure to be sure that you have capitalized all the proper nouns.

Rules of Capital Letters • Lesson 1

● **Practice Your Skills**

Capitalizing Geographical Names

Write correctly each word that should be capitalized.

   (1) In 1840, the united states had 3,000 miles of railroad track. **(2)** By 1850, workers were constructing railroads in all of the states east of the mississippi river. **(3)** One of these railroads linked new york city and buffalo, new york. **(4)** Others linked such cities as baltimore, maryland, and wheeling, west virginia. **(5)** Railway builders linked these eastern lines with lines in ohio, indiana, and illinois. **(6)** Railway lines went around both lake erie and lake michigan. **(7)** Before the railroads many depended on the mississippi river to transport goods. **(8)** The goods were put on ships in new orleans, louisiana. **(9)** The ships sailed around florida to cities in the east. **(10)** From the east to past the rocky mountains, north america was opened up by the railroad.

Names of historical importance should be capitalized. Capitalize the names of historical events, periods, and documents and associated initials and acronyms. (Prepositions, such as the *of* in *Bill of Rights*, are not capitalized.)

HISTORIC NAMES	
Events	World War II (**WWII**), the **B**oston **T**ea **P**arty, the **T**reaty of **V**ersailles
Periods of Time	the **M**iddle **A**ges, the **I**ndustrial **R**evolution, the **E**nlightenment, the **J**azz **A**ge
Documents	the **C**onstitution, the **B**ill of **R**ights, the **E**mancipation **P**roclamation

Names of groups and businesses begin with capital letters. Capitalize the names of organizations, businesses, institutions, teams, and government bodies.

NAMES OF GROUPS	
Organizations	the **U**nited **N**ations (**UN**), **H**abitat for **H**umanity, the **N**ational **A**ssociation for the **A**dvancement of **C**olored **P**eople (**NAACP**)
Businesses	**R**oberto & **S**ons, **B&M P**lumbing
Institutions	**U**niversity of **S**outhern **C**alifornia (**USC**)
Teams	the **D**allas **C**owboys, the **O**akland **R**aiders
Government Bodies	**C**ongress, the **H**ouse of **R**epresentatives, the **F**ederal **B**ureau of **I**nvestigation (**FBI**)

● **Practice Your Skills**

Using Capital Letters

Write correctly each word that should be capitalized.

(1) A major peacekeeping organization was created after world war II. (2) The united nations (un) was established to ensure peace. (3) It was an effort to improve on the league of nations. (4) The league of nations was formed after wwI. (5) Almost 200 member nations support the un financially. (6) The united states senate and the house of representatives must pass the budget for the un each year. (7) The united nations supports the world health organization and unicef. (8) The security council guides all activities of the un. (9) The general assembly includes all members of the organization. (10) The offices of the un are located in new york city.

● *Connect to Writing:* **Editing**

Using Capital Letters

Rewrite the following sentences, adding capital letters where needed.

(1) On June 28, 1919, the allies and Germany signed a treaty to end world war I. (2) The agreement was called the treaty of versailles. (3) With the support of congress, the treaty would divide the German empire into nine nations. (4) President Wilson managed to get the league of nations included as part of the treaty. (5) This accomplishment was one of Wilson's famous fourteen points. (6) The American president hoped that the league would help lessen the impact of the treaty of versailles on Germany.

Specific time periods and events begin with capital letters. Capitalize the days of the week, the months of the year, civil and religious holidays, and special events. Also capitalize the abbreviations A.D., B.C., and B.C.E. (Before the Common Era).

TIME PERIODS AND EVENTS	
Days, Months	Sunday (Sun.), Saturday (Sat.), January (Jan.), May
Holidays	Fourth of July, Presidents' Day
Special Events	Rose Bowl Parade, Olympics
Time Abbreviations	A.D. B.C. B.C.E. AM or a.m. PM or p.m. (Confucius lived during the years 551 to 487 B.C.)

Rules of Capital Letters • Lesson 1

Do not capitalize the seasons of the year unless they are part of a specific name.

> My favorite **s**pring event is the **S**pring Jamboree.

You can learn more about the punctuation of abbreviations on pages 831–834.

Names of nationalities and ethnicities should be capitalized.

NATIONALITIES AND ETHNIC GROUPS	
Nationalities	an **A**rgentinian, a **S**eminole, a **C**anadian
Ethnic Groups	**K**hmer, **B**asque, **H**ispanic

Religions, religious references, and religious holidays begin with capital letters.

RELIGIOUS NAMES	
Religions	**C**hristianity, **J**udaism, **B**uddhism, **I**slam
Religious Holidays	**H**anukkah, **C**hristmas, **R**amadan, **E**piphany, **P**urim, **E**aster, **P**assover
Religious References	**G**od, the **L**ord, the **C**reator, the **B**ible, the **T**orah, the **K**oran, the **N**ew **T**estament

The word *god* is not capitalized when it refers to gods in polytheistic religions. Do capitalize their names, however.

> The Vikings said that **T**hor was the **g**od of thunder.

● **Practice Your Skills**

Using Capital Letters

Write correctly each word that should be capitalized. If the sentence is correct, write C.

(1) The fall of the school year is full of both religious and secular holidays. (2) Just as september begins, there is labor day. (3) Also in september, jews celebrate rosh hashanah. (4) The second monday of october is columbus day. (5) United nations Day is october 24. (6) By late october halloween is upon us. (7) On November 11 we celebrate veterans day. (8) On a thursday in november is thanksgiving. (9) December brings the christian season of christmas. (10) In some years during the same period, muslims begin observing ramadan.

● **Connect to Writing: Editing**

Using Capital Letters

Rewrite the following paragraph, adding capital letters.

(1) After christmas, new year's day, and martin luther king, jr., day, what is there to look forward to in february? (2) What the winter needs is another holiday! (3) It should be a holiday that appeals to many groups—Chinese, West Indian, Latino, and Pakistani—to name a few. (4) Perhaps we should celebrate it on a tuesday or a thursday. (5) It should not conflict with the days of worship for christianity, judaism, islam, and other faiths. (6) Could it be a mixture of a fiesta and the fourth of july? (7) The activities would start at four p.m. (8) There would be tasty food, fun, and games. (9) Let's have it on february 4. (10) We'll call it february's festival day!

Names of planets, stars, and constellations are capitalized.

ASTRONOMICAL NAMES	
Planets	Jupiter, Venus, Mars, Saturn
Stars	the North Star, Sirius, Vega
Constellations	Little Dipper, Taurus, Ursa Minor

Do not capitalize *sun* or *moon*. Do not capitalize *earth* if the word *the* comes in front of it.

Capital	Is it rare that Venus lines up with Earth?
No Capital	It depends on how many times the earth travels around the sun in a given time.

Languages and specific school courses followed by a number are capitalized.

LANGUAGES AND SCHOOL COURSES	
Languages	English, Latin, Russian, Spanish
Computer Languages	Java, Cobol, Visual Basic
Numbered Courses	Art II, Typing I, Chorus II

Except for language courses, course names without a number such as *history, math, science,* and *physical education* are not capitalized.

Other proper nouns should also begin with capital letters.

OTHER PROPER NOUNS	
Awards	Academy Awards®, Heisman Trophy
Brand Names	Klean soap, Kone cheese, Verdon chicken (The product itself—such as *soap, cheese,* and *chicken*—is not capitalized.)
Bridges and Buildings	Fargo Building, Tower of London
Monuments and Memorials	Washington Monument, Jefferson Memorial, Statue of Liberty
Technological Terms	Internet, Web, World Wide Web, Web site, Web page
Vehicles	Apollo 17, Columbia, Old Ironsides

● **Practice Your Skills**

Using Capital Letters

Write correctly each word that should be capitalized.

1. Can you imagine what the public thought in the old days about traveling to mars or other planets?
2. Was the spaceship the size and the shape of the washington monument?
3. Did the crew fill up the tank with pell gasoline?
4. Who besides nasa could try space travel?
5. How does a person get a road map to saturn?
6. You can't exactly go north and turn right at the planet mercury.
7. Did the astronauts travel in the *voyager* spacecraft?
8. Would the astronauts have to be able to speak russian, spanish, and computer languages?
9. They would need to have passed more science courses than physics IV.
10. Do you think astronauts should be given the congressional medal of honor?

● *Connect to Writing:* **Personal Journal**

Using Capital Letters Every Day

Do you ever have trouble deciding whether to capitalize certain words you use in school every day? Should you capitalize *Student Council,* for example? You capitalize *Principal Cortez,* but what about *Mr. Cortez, our principal?* Keep a journal that answers these and other questions, and then use them correctly in sentences.

● **Connect to Writing: Editing**

Using Capital Letters

Rewrite the following paragraph, adding capital letters where needed.

(1) Plu is from pluto. (2) His eyes are the size of the pancakes from the tasty maple brand of pancakes. (3) His skin is as smooth as the ice at the metro skating rink. (4) Toothless, he stands as tall and as bony as the eiffel tower in Paris. (5) Plu from pluto has no arms or legs. (6) Rapid german-like sounds come out of his toothless mouth. (7) Through an instant translation machine borrowed from nasa, Plu asked me if I owned a fire-engine red automobile. (8) When I told him I was too young to drive a car, he said he would settle for a ride in the *discovery* space shuttle. (9) From what I could tell, I would have to take german I, II, and III to understand his language and physics IV to figure out how he got to earth. (10) Unfortunately, Plu broke my computer when he tried to put his own web page on the internet.

✓ **Check Point: Mixed Practice**

Write each sentence, adding capital letters where needed. Then answer each question—if you can!

1. who was the first person to sign the declaration of independence?
2. who used a middle initial that did not stand for a middle name—harry s. truman or franklin d. roosevelt?
3. who built their empire first, the mayas or the aztecs?
4. who was raised in the midwest, jefferson or lincoln?
5. who, little orphan annie or mickey mouse, owned a dog named pluto?
6. who was the first person to walk on the moon, michael collins or neil armstrong?
7. who sold louisiana to the americans in 1803, the english or the french?
8. who was the captain of the starship *enterprise*, james kirk or alan shepard?

● **Connect to Speaking and Writing: Editorial**

Capitalizing

With a partner, write an editorial for your school newspaper in which you address an issue that you feel should be resolved. Briefly describe the issue and offer ideas for taking action. Use capital letters where needed to identify school personnel and organizations and community groups who might be involved.

Rules of Capital Letters • Lesson 1

Other Uses of Capital Letters

You have learned the most common uses for capital letters. There are, however, a few other uses that you should remember to use in your writing.

28 B Capitalize **proper adjectives** and the **titles of people and works of art**.

 Proper Adjectives

You just finished reviewing proper nouns, words that name specific people, places, and things. Like proper nouns, most proper adjectives begin with a capital letter.

28 B.1 Capitalize proper adjectives.

PROPER NOUNS	PROPER ADJECTIVES
Europe	European history
North America	North American countries
the South	Southern states
Africa	an African company
France	French dressing

● **Practice Your Skills**

Capitalizing Proper Adjectives

Write correctly each word that should be capitalized.

1. Political candidates collect different experiences during a tour of the north american continent.
2. They travel north to the canadian border.
3. They go south as far as the mexican border.
4. They might collect swedish recipes from chefs in Minnesota.
5. They dine on chinese food in San Francisco.
6. Cheeses are given to them by the pennsylvania dutch population.
7. Samples of texas barbecue sauce are plentiful.
8. In the Empire State Building, they can feast on italian food.
9. In the South, they get bags of georgia peanuts.
10. They can sample irish stew on St. Patrick's Day.

● **Connect to Writing: Editing**

Capitalizing Proper Adjectives

Rewrite the following paragraph, adding capital letters where needed.

(1) The european railway system is vital to the economy. (2) An american traveler can see all of Europe from the trains. (3) One day an american tourist can join in the scottish dances. (4) The next day he or she can zip south to english soil and take in a Shakespearean play. (5) However, a real shopper will use the railroad to find goods in other countries. (6) With a longer journey, the traveler can buy the products of spanish merchants. (7) Many seek french fashions and italian shoes. (8) Others want german automobiles. (9) No one wants to miss the european sights. (10) The buildings themselves are evidence of events from roman history.

➡ Titles

Capital letters are used in the titles of people, of written works, and of other works of art.

28 B.2 Capitalize the titles of people and works of art.

Titles Used with Names of Persons

Capitalize a title showing office, rank, or profession when it comes before a person's name. The same title is usually not capitalized when it follows a name.

Before a Name	Have you met **S**enator Caldwell? (capital letter)
After a Name	Is Max Caldwell a **s**enator from your state? (no capital letter)
Before a Name	Did you consult **C**hairperson Brooks? (capital letter)
After a Name	Adam Brooks is **c**hairperson of the special committee on education. (no capital letter)

Other titles or their abbreviations such as *Ms., Dr.,* and *Lt.* should be capitalized when they come before a person's name.

This message is for **M**r. Jordan.

An official letter from the committee has arrived for **S**gt. Shaw.

Titles Used in Direct Address

A noun of direct address is used to call someone by name. Capitalize a title used instead of a name in direct address.

Direct Address   When will you be free, **S**enator?
I think, **G**overnor, the bill will pass.

You can learn more about using commas with direct address on pages 846–847.

Titles Showing Family Relationships

Capitalize titles showing family relationships when the titles come before people's names. Capitalize the titles also when they are used instead of names or in direct address.

Before a Name   Is **U**ncle **J**eb running for Congress?

Used as a Name   Tell **D**ad that I'm leaving soon.
Where did **G**ramma get the yellow Jaguar?

In Direct Address   Are you leaving, **S**is?

Do not capitalize a title showing a family relationship when it is preceded by a possessive noun or pronoun unless it is considered part of a person's name.

No Capital   My **d**ad works at the legislature.
(The word *dad* is preceded by a possessive pronoun, *my*.)

Capital   The press interviewed my **U**ncle **J**eb.
(*Uncle* is part of the person's name.)

You can learn about using apostrophes with possessive nouns and pronouns on pages 880–885.

● **Practice Your Skills**

Capitalizing Titles of People

Write correctly each word that should be capitalized. If the sentence is correct, write **C**.

1. Have you been to mr. Brook's new chemistry laboratory?
2. Yes, mr. Brook is my sister's chemistry teacher this year.
3. He is the nephew of principal Balinger.
4. There is a huge chart hanging on the wall in the chemistry lab.
5. In the late 1800s, dr. Dimitri Mendeleev did important work.
6. Indeed, doctor, you made the study of chemistry much easier.
7. The doctor from Russia created a table for the elements.
8. dr. Mendeleev's table arranged the elements according to atomic mass.
9. In 1913, professor Henry G. J. Moseley improved on the table.
10. The professor improved on the doctor's analysis of elements.

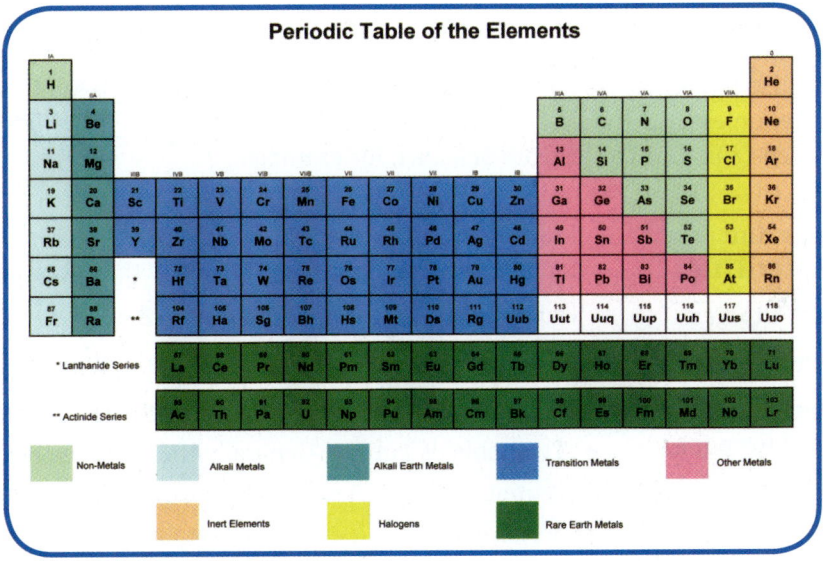

● *Connect to Writing:* **Proposal**

Capitalizing Titles

Write a proposal to your principal about what should be included in a time capsule to represent your generation. You can propose images, books, movies, music, or other forms of art that you feel represent young people today. Use capital letters where needed.

● **Connect to Writing: Editing**

Using Capital Letters

Rewrite the following paragraph, adding capital letters where needed.

(1) After many medical tests on governor salem, Dr. Harry Rose found a tumor in his patient's thyroid. (2) The doctor told the governor immediately. (3) medical chief of staff Rose decided to treat the tumor with a radioactive isotope. (4) Our governor asked about the treatment. (5) As expected, dr. Rose was very informative. (6) The doctor explained that he had used the isotope on his aunt the week before. (7) The isotope is called iodine-131 and is very unstable. (8) That instability helped aunt Mildred because it released radiation into her tumor. (9) As it did for the doctor's aunt, the isotope would help shrink or destroy governor salem's tumor. (10) The isotope of iodine, according to dr. Rose, is a doctor's friend.

Titles of Written Works and Other Works of Art

Capitalize the first word, the last word, and all important words in titles of books, newspapers, magazines, stories, poems, movies, plays, musical compositions, and other works of art. Do not capitalize a preposition, a coordinating conjunction, or an article (*a, an,* or *the*) unless it is the first or last word in a title. Prepositions of five letters or more are often capitalized—the word *between*, for example.

Books and Chapter Titles	I looked up some information in *History of Russia* and found a good quotation in "The Growth of Russia."
Short Stories	Have you read the story "The Stone Boy"?
Poems	My favorite poem is "Who Has Seen the Wind?"
Newspapers and Newspaper Articles	Today the *New York Daily News* published the article "Turntable of Tunes." (Generally the word *the* before the first word of a newspaper or magazine title is not capitalized.)
Magazines and Magazine Articles	*Sports Illustrated* did an article "The Spurs Win, the Spurs Win!"
Musical Compositions	I like the song "Leaving the Promised Land" from George Gershwin's *Porgy and Bess*.

You can learn about punctuating titles on pages 860–864.

Practice Your Skills

Capitalizing Titles

Write correctly each word that should be capitalized.

(1) Helen is an old-fashioned teenager right out of Thornton Wilder's play *our town*. (2) Her favorite song is Katherine Lee Bates's "america the beautiful." (3) She enjoys reading articles like "essentials of good citizenship" in *reader's digest*. (4) She prefers animated films such as *the lion king* and *bambi*. (5) The fable "the tortoise and the hare" is a good example of how she leads her life. (6) She subscribes to the *new york times*. (7) It is a newspaper without comics like *for better or worse*. (8) Her idea of a romantic song is "moon river." (9) Her favorite book is *the summer of my german soldier*. (10) She wants to play Juliet in Shakespeare's *romeo and juliet*.

Connect to Writing: Editing

Using Capital Letters

Rewrite the following paragraphs, adding capital letters where needed.

(1) More than 350 years ago, the inca indians of south america controlled an empire of almost 2,500 miles, from colombia to chile. (2) In approximately a.d. 1400, this tribe conquered some 10 million people living in present-day peru, ecuador, bolivia, western argentina, and the northern part of chile.

(3) Across the many miles of the empire, the incas built a network of roads. (4) The roads, however, had to run through and around the andes mountains. (5) This feat would be difficult even for modern engineers.

(6) Often the incas tunneled through the mountain cliffs, but they also built bridges. (7) The longest of the inca bridges was made famous in the novel *the bridge of san luis rey*. (8) This 148-foot suspension bridge crossed a deep ravine of the apurimac river. (9) Until the bridge fell early in the twentieth century, it had been in use longer than any other bridge in south america.

(10) Because of an internal civil war in their empire, these mighty indians were conquered by a handful of spaniards led by francisco pizarro. (11) Information about their art, culture, and village life is contained in spanish chronicles.

✓ Check Point: Mixed Practice

Write each sentence, adding capital letters where needed. Then answer each question—if you can!

1. which is closer to the sun, mercury or venus?
2. what is the name of clark kent's newspaper, the *daily news* or the *daily planet*?
3. what river begins in new hampshire but is named for another state—the connecticut or the delaware?
4. what famous indian princess rescued john smith from death?
5. in what year did columbus sight land in what is now the bahamas?
6. what group first recorded the song "with a little help from my friends"?
7. what is the first monday in september called?
8. what manned rocket launch facility is near cape canaveral in florida?
9. what state is directly north of Oregon?
10. what city is sacred to jews, christians, and muslims?

Chapter Review

Assess Your Learning

Using Capital Letters

Correctly write each word that should begin with a capital letter.

1. five states border the gulf of mexico.
2. for more than 150 years, american colonists lived under british rule.
3. i love the poem "the road not taken."
4. the capital of arkansas is little rock.
5. a painting titled *lady musician and young girl* was painted in the first century b.c.
6. which is larger, jupiter or earth?
7. after moving to the northeast from oregon, my brother settled in connecticut.
8. get on venton road and go north for two miles.
9. my favorite aunt and uncle will visit us soon.
10. lyndon b. johnson, who was president in the mid-1960s, signed a document called the education bill.
11. is the sun farther from earth in summer or in winter?
12. is your computer connected to the internet?
13. every morning my mom reads the *washington post*.
14. the last of the thirteen english colonies to be settled was georgia.
15. uncle david is president of the ridley golf league.
16. one american signed the declaration of independence in very large letters.
17. tell us, officer, were there any witnesses?
18. which do you enjoy more, science or european history?
19. the name of the first space shuttle was *columbia*.
20. have you ever been to walker lake in nevada?

◼ Editing for Proper Capitalization

Read the following paragraphs. Find the twenty-five words that should begin with a capital letter. Then rewrite the paragraphs correctly.

   (1) the battle of new orleans was one of the greatest victories in united states history. **(2)** leading a force of frontiersmen, general andrew jackson of tennessee confronted troops of british soldiers who had just defeated napoleon's great french army.

   (3) the battle took place on january 8, 1815—just fifteen days after a treaty ending the war of 1812 had been signed in europe. **(4)** unfortunately, the news of the treaty had not reached andrew jackson or the british. **(5)** in fact, jackson's superiors in washington were unaware of either the battle or the treaty.

◼ Writing Sentences

Write sentences that follow the directions.

Write a sentence that includes . . .
   1. the name of your city and state.
   2. today's date with the day, month, and year.
   3. the name of a South American country.
   4. the brand name of a product you use.
   5. a proper adjective.

Capital Letters: Posttest

Directions
Read the passage and decide which underlined word or words should be capitalized. Write the letter of the correct answer. If the underlined word or words contain no error, write **D**.

The decades of the 1950s and 1960s brought innovations and new milestones. In 1952, the first automatic pinsetter was installed in a **(1)** <u>bowling alley in Brooklyn, NY</u>. The following year James Baldwin published his first novel, **(2)** <u>*Go tell it on the mountain*</u>. Soviet cosmonaut **(3)** <u>Yuri gagarin orbited earth</u> in 1961. That same year, astronaut John Glenn became the first **(4)** <u>American to orbit Earth</u>. The U.S. **(5)** <u>civil rights act</u> of 1965 prohibited discrimination in employment.

1. **A** Bowling Alley in Brooklyn, NY.
   B Bowling alley in Brooklyn, NY.
   C bowling alley in Brooklyn, Ny.
   D No error

2. **A** *Go Tell It on The Mountain*
   B *Go Tell It on the Mountain*
   C *Go Tell it on the Mountain*
   D No error

3. **A** yuri gagarin orbited earth
   B Yuri Gagarin orbited Earth
   C Yuri Gagarin orbited earth
   D No error

4. **A** American To Orbit Earth
   B american to orbit earth
   C American to orbit earth
   D No error

5. **A** civil Rights act
   B Civil rights act
   C Civil Rights Act
   D No error

Writer's Corner

Snapshot

28 A Capitalize **first words**, the pronoun **I**, and **proper nouns**. (pages 804–815)

28 B Capitalize **proper adjectives** and the **titles of people and works of art**. (pages 816–822)

Power Rules

 Use **sentence fragments** only the way professional writers do. Fix sentence fragments that occur before the sentence they refer to and ones that occur in the middle of a sentence. (pages 662–667)

Before Editing

In the woods. My friends and I looked for colorful leaves.

After the movie. We can go out for dinner.

After Editing

In the woods my friends and I looked for colorful leaves.

After the movie we can go out for dinner.

 Use the best conjunction for the meaning and/or use appropriate punctuation to separate sentences in a **run-on sentence.** (pages 668–670)

Before Editing

Our class went to the zoo, we saw a polar bear.

The little boat was in trouble, the waves were coming over the sides.

After Editing

Our class went to the zoo, and we saw a polar bear.

The little boat was in trouble. The waves were coming over the sides.

Editing Checklist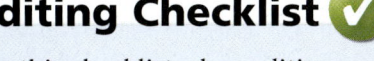

Use this checklist when editing your writing.

✓ Did I use capital letters correctly for first words in sentences, poetry, outlines, and parts of letters? (See pages 804–805.)
✓ Is the pronoun *I* capitalized everywhere? (See pages 806–807.)
✓ Did I capitalize all the proper nouns? (See pages 807–815.)
✓ Did I capitalize all the proper adjectives? (See pages 816–817.)
✓ Did I capitalize titles correctly ? (See pages 817–822.)

Use the Power

Capital letters can make a big difference in how readers perceive your words. Capitals signal where things belong and let your reader know when something is a proper name. You wouldn't know, for example, that Salt River Bay is a specific place without the capital letters.

Without capital letters, what you write could have more than one meaning—leaving your reader very confused.

Write a review of a book or short story you read recently. Name the title and author and give a short description of the plot, setting, and characters. Then explain why you liked or didn't like the work.

CHAPTER 29

End Marks and Commas

How can you create meaning through the careful use of end marks and commas?

End Marks and Commas: Pretest 1

The following first draft has a number of errors in the use of end marks and commas. The first sentence, which calls for a question mark instead of a period, has been corrected. How would you revise the remaining sentences so that commas and end marks are used properly?

Have you ever been to Morocco? It is a country in the western part of North Africa! In Morocco you can visit ancient Arab cities Roman ruins burning desert snow-capped mountains and seaside villages. Morocco is very green in the north where it faces the Atlantic Ocean and the Mediterranean Sea. In the south however the weather is hot? In fact the great desert called the Sahara covers the southern part of Morocco. Even in the desert if you come to an oasis you will find date palms farms gardens and people grazing animals. The Berbers have lived in this area since before the rise of the Roman Empire but they now share the land with Arabs who arrived hundreds of years later. Don't you think Morocco sounds astonishing. It is.

End Marks and Commas: Pretest 2

Directions
Read the passage and choose the punctuation mark that belongs in each underlined space. Write the letter of the correct answer. If no punctuation is needed, write D.

Dear Mom __(1)__

    I am having a lot of fun with Aunt Jo. We rented mountain bikes __(2)__ and went to Mt __(3)__ Shasta. Did you know that Aunt Jo used to compete in downhill races __(4)__ Wow __(5)__ That sounds really scary to me.

    After an hour or so __(6)__ Aunt Jo and I were hungry. We ate dinner at Jenny's Cafe. We met Ms. __(7)__ Jenny and her brother __(8)__ Slim. They cook yummy food! We had appetizers, dinner __(9)__ and dessert. It was getting late __(10)__ and we decided to go home.

Love,
Miguel

1. A colon
   B comma
   C period
   D No punctuation needed

2. A exclamation point
   B comma
   C period
   D No punctuation needed

3. A question mark
   B comma
   C period
   D No punctuation needed

4. A question mark
   B comma
   C period
   D No punctuation needed

5. A exclamation point
   B comma
   C period
   D No punctuation needed

6. A question mark
   B comma
   C period
   D No punctuation needed

7. A colon
   B comma
   C period
   D No punctuation needed

8. A exclamation point
   B comma
   C period
   D No punctuation needed

9. A question mark
   B comma
   C period
   D No punctuation needed

10. A exclamation point
    B comma
    C period
    D No punctuation needed

End Marks — Lesson 1

End marks and capital letters signal to a reader that one sentence has ended and another has started.

29 A Depending on the purpose, different sentences have different end marks.

29 A.1 Place a **period** after a statement, after an opinion, and after a command or request made in a normal tone of voice.

Periods
I have some Russian heritage**.**
(statement)

Russians have an interesting culture**.**
(opinion)

Give all cultures your respect**.**
(command)

29 A.2 Place a **question mark** after a sentence that asks a question.

Question Mark What is your heritage**?**

29 A.3 Place an **exclamation point** after a sentence that states strong feeling, after a command or request that expresses great excitement, and after an interjection.

Exclamation Points
My aunt won the blue ribbon**!**
(a sentence expressing strong feeling)

Hey**!** Don't touch that lever**!**
(a sentence giving a command with great excitement)

You can learn about end marks and quotations on pages 868–869.

● Practice Your Skills

Using End Marks

Read each sentence and then write the correct end mark.

1. Who were the first people to settle in North America
2. The Europeans found Native Americans already there in the 1400s
3. Where had the Native Americans come from

4. Some thought the first Americans came from Asia
5. Others said that they came from Atlantis, an island that sank into the ocean
6. Science has another theory
7. Look at a current map of the world
8. The continents' shapes suggest a missing link between America and Asia
9. Do you think the land between the two sank into the ocean

● *Connect to Writing:* **Editing**

Using End Marks

Rewrite the following paragraph, adding or changing end marks where needed.

> Have you ever heard of Beringia. According to scientists, that is the stretch of land that once was between Asia and America Can you imagine that. Our Earth has passed through many Ice Ages! Do you know when the last Ice Age was it occurred about 12,000 years ago, the frozen period lowered the sea levels? When the ice melted, land was exposed! Does that theory seem believable to you.

● *Connect to Writing and Speaking:* **Travel Article**

Using End Marks

You have just visited the most beautiful place that you've ever seen. Write a description of this place for a travel magazine. Use a variety of complete sentences that include consistent tenses and that require periods, question marks, and exclamation points. Read your description to the class.

➤ Other Uses of Periods

Periods are used in places other than at the ends of sentences.

Periods with Abbreviations

Abbreviations are shortened words. Most abbreviations do not belong in business letters, research reports, or other formal writing. You can use them when writing an e-mail or note.

29 A.4   Use a period with most abbreviations.

The box on the next page contains some common abbreviations.

COMMON ABBREVIATIONS

Days	Sun.	Mon.	Tues.	Wed.	
	Thurs.	Fri.	Sat.		
Months	Jan.	Feb.	Mar.	Apr.	Aug.
	Sept.	Oct.	Nov.	Dec.	
	(Do not abbreviate *May, June,* or *July.*)				
Addresses	Ave.	Blvd.	Hwy.	Pl.	
	Rd.	Rt.	St.	Apt.	
Titles with Names	Mr.	Ms.	Rev.	Sgt.	Jr.
	Mrs.	Dr.	Gen.	Sen.	Sr.
	(These titles appear before a person's name except for *Jr.* and *Sr.*)				
Initials for Names	R. L. Rosen		Karen A. Breen		
	T. S. Eliot		H. L. March		
	R. Eric Madison		M. Ellen Zink		
Times with Numbers	2:30 AM or a.m.	7:00 PM or p.m.	47 B.C.	47 B.C.E.	A.D. 200
	(A colon [:] goes between the hours and the minutes when time is written in numbers.)				
Companies	Assoc.	Co.	Corp.	Dept.	Inc.

Some organizations and companies are known by abbreviations that stand for their full names. The majority of these abbreviations do not use periods. A few other common abbreviations also do not include periods.

ABBREVIATIONS WITHOUT PERIODS

ATM = automatic teller machine	FBI = Federal Bureau of Investigation
CD = compact disc	IQ = intelligence quotient
CIA = Central Intelligence Agency	km = kilometers
DVD = digital video disc	SAT = Scholastic Aptitude Test
e-mail = electronic mail	UN = United Nations
fax = facsimile	

For the spelling and punctuation of other abbreviations, look in a dictionary. Most dictionaries have a special section (often in the back) that lists abbreviations.

The post office's two-letter state abbreviations are used by most people today. These abbreviations do not include periods. A list of these state abbreviations can be found in the front of most telephone books. The following are a few examples.

STATE ABBREVIATIONS		
AL = Alabama	MD = Maryland	OH = Ohio
CT = Connecticut	NV = Nevada	TX = Texas
HI = Hawaii	NY = New York	UT = Utah

If a sentence ends with an abbreviation that ends with a period, only one period is used. It serves both as the period for the abbreviation and as the end mark for the sentence.

> The train arrives at 7:30 p.m.

Periods with Outlines

29 A.5 Use a period after each number or letter that shows a division in an outline.

> I. Professional Sports
>   A. Baseball
>   1. Minor League
>   2. Major League
>   B. Football
>   1. Arena Football League
>   2. National Football League
> II. Coaching

You can learn more about using capital letters in outlines on page 805.

● *Connect to Writing:* **Narrative**

End Marks

Using the example above as your model, create an outline that details what you do to get ready for school each day. Include specific examples. Then write a short narrative telling about your pre-school preparations.

Practice Your Skills

Using End Marks

Write the abbreviations that stand for the following items. Be sure to use a period when appropriate. Use a dictionary if you are not sure of an abbreviation.

1. pounds
2. Celsius
3. road
4. longitude
5. street
6. doctor
7. March
8. junior
9. meter
10. Friday

Connect to Speaking and Listening: Peer Interaction

Speaking with Inflections

Play an inflection game with a partner. *Inflection* means "changing the pitch or loudness of your voice." Each of you writes three or four statements, such as the following: "That is good news" or "She said that" or "You don't agree." Now, say each statement in one of three ways: as a statement with no inflection, as a question with inflection at the end, and as an exclamation with excitement in your voice. Your partner's job is to decide which end mark to use with each sentence.

Connect to Writing: Editing

Using End Marks

Write each sentence, using periods where needed.

1. It was an emergency
2. At 8:45 am, Dr Harriet L Sackel rushed from 2422 Forest St
3. The patient was being given CPR by a Lt J W Snow
4. The lieutenant worked for the Orange County Sheriff's Department
5. Dr Sackel asked the officer about the man's condition
6. He gave the patient's blood pressure and pulse
7. No one knew what had happened
8. Mr Gary L Martin had been found unconscious
9. His home state on his driver's license was listed as Texas
10. Dr Sackel asked Lt Snow to call for an ambulance

End Marks and Commas

Commas That Separate

A comma is used in two ways: to separate and to enclose. We will look at commas that separate first. Just as an end mark keeps sentences from running together, a comma keeps items within a sentence from running together.

29 B **Use commas to separate,** as with items in a series, adjectives before a noun, compound sentences, introductory structures, and in dates, addresses, and letters.

▶ Items in a Series

A series is three or more similar items listed one after another. When words and groups of words are written in a series, commas should separate them.

29 B.1 Use commas to separate items in a series.

Words

Nouns	Paper, pencils, and markers were our supplies.
Verbs	We sketched, painted, and labeled our drawings of the atom.
Adjectives	Our science classroom looked bright, colorful, and interesting.

Some people make the mistake of adding a third comma after the word *markers* above, but remember: only the first two commas are needed to separate the items.

Groups of Words

Complete Subject	My friend, his cousin, and a neighbor went to the store.
Complete Predicate	We checked the list, packed our supplies, and set off.
Prepositional Phrase	He walked to school, across the campus, and into class.

If a conjunction such as *and* or *or* connects all the items in a series, no commas are needed.

He walked to school **and** across the campus **and** into class.
(no commas)

I will take a class in music **or** art **or** gymnastics next semester.
(no commas)

You can learn about commas with direct quotations on page 867.

When You Write

When listing groups of word in series, use parallel structure. **Parallel structure,** also known as *parallelism,* is the repetition of a pattern of words to show that ideas have the same importance. Parallel structure makes writing flow more smoothly and gives punch and impact to otherwise dull prose.

Mixed Verb Forms	We hiked, went looking at leaves, and had a canoe ride on the lake.
Parallel	We hiked, looked at leaves, and canoed on the lake.
Mixed Verb Phrase Forms	If you are interested, have talent, and you want something to do in your free time, audition for the spring play.
Parallel	If you have the interest, the talent, and the free time, audition for the spring play.

● Practice Your Skills

Using Commas in a Series

Write *C* if a sentence uses commas correctly. If a sentence uses commas incorrectly, write *I*.

(1) An atom contains electrons protons and neutrons. **(2)** The nucleus is the center of the atom, is positively charged, and is made of protons and neutrons. **(3)** A neutron is located in the nucleus has no charge, and has a relative mass of 1. **(4)** Electrons are negatively charged, small in mass and outside the nucleus. **(5)** The mass of the electron is about 1/2000 of the proton and of the neutron.

● *Connect to Writing:* Parallelism

Using Commas with Verb Forms

Write a story telling about various things you did on a field trip or on your summer vacation. Use parallel structure.

● **Connect to Writing: Editing**

Using Commas in a Series

Write each sentence, adding commas where needed. If a sentence is correct as written, write **C**.

1. The home of Thomas Edison in Fort Myers was painted in 1994 1996 and 1998.
2. White is used for the exterior walls the porch and the gables.
3. The painters wash scrape and sand the surface before painting.
4. The windows and the fixtures are more difficult to paint.
5. They require small tools delicate work and careful attention.
6. Are the windows painted a robin's egg blue a navy blue or turquoise?
7. The fixtures on the gables the doors and the roof are red.
8. The Thomas Edison home in Fort Myers is simple, elegant, and inviting.

Adjectives Before a Noun

If you have three or more adjectives before a noun, you will probably need a comma to separate each item in the series. If you have only two adjectives before a noun, you may or may not need a comma. Use the test below to help you decide if a comma is needed.

Read the sentence with the word *and* between the two adjectives. If the sentence makes sense, a comma is needed. If the sentence sounds awkward, no comma is needed.

Comma	That movie is a bright, cheerful production.
	(*A bright and cheerful production* reads well; use a comma.)
	Shania is the tallest, most graceful person on stage.
	(*The tallest and most graceful person* reads well; use a comma.)
No Comma	That old movie is a dark murder mystery.
	(*A dark and murder mystery* sounds awkward; no comma is needed.)

29 B.2 Use a comma to separate two adjectives that precede a noun and that would read well with the word *and* between them.

Usually no comma is needed after a number or after an adjective that refers to size, shape, color, or age. For example, no commas are needed in the following expressions.

ADJECTIVE EXPRESSIONS	
ten e-mail messages	a small hooded sweater
four square boxes	a ripe green apple

Commas That Separate • Lesson 2

● **Practice Your Skills**

Using Commas Before a Noun

Write the underlined words in each sentence, adding commas where needed. If no commas are needed, write **C**.

1. The classic movie *Field of Dreams* is based on a <u>short readable novel</u> by W. P. Kinsella.
2. The book *Shoeless Joe* is told by a <u>young idealistic dreamer.</u>
3. A <u>deep mysterious</u> voice tells him to build a baseball field.
4. "Build it and he will come" is the <u>vague and abstract instruction.</u>
5. Ray plows under his <u>fertile Iowa farmland.</u>
6. In the novel the field first includes only a <u>shabby left field.</u>
7. One day the ghost of a <u>gifted handsome outfielder</u> appears.
8. Shoeless Joe Jackson had played for a <u>disgraced baseball team</u>, the 1919 Chicago White Sox.
9. Several players had taken <u>large illegal bribes</u> to lose the World Series.
10. Regardless of the charges, Shoeless Joe had been a <u>great hero</u> of Ray's dead father.

● *Connect to Writing:* **Editing**

Using Commas with Adjectives

Write each sentence, adding commas where needed. If no commas are needed, write **C**.

1. The United States is generally thought to contain the Northeast Mid-Atlantic Midwest Southwest Southeast and West regions.
2. The state of Florida is part of the hot sunny Southeast region.
3. The state has a low flat elevation.
4. Lake Okeechobee is one of the largest lakes in the United States and is filled with shallow fresh water.
5. Florida's delightful winter weather attracts many tourists.
6. I looked around the small crowded room for an exit.
7. The difficult lengthy exam tested all our knowledge about the Civil War.
8. The surgeon's knot is useful in tying large, bulky packages.

● *Connect to Writing:* **Drafting**

Writing Sentences with Adjectives

Write five sentences, following the instructions below. Use at least two adjectives before the noun in each sentence.

1. Describe the geography of your region.
2. Describe the geography of your state.
3. Describe a natural resource found in your area.
4. Describe the crops grown in your area.
5. Describe the climate of your area.

● *Connect to Writing:* **Description**

Using Commas

Read over the sentences you wrote in the drafting exercise above. Use these sentences to write a descriptive paragraph of your region of the country. Use adjectives before nouns and items in a series.

✓ Check Point: Mixed Practice

Write the following paragraph, adding commas where needed.

(1) Andrew Wyeth, an American painter, is part of a famous family of artists. (2) Wyeth drew sketched and painted at a very young age. (3) He was encouraged by his father his sisters and family friends. (4) The long difficult study of art began with his famous father at home. (5) Andrew painted people places and experiences familiar to him. (6) His work includes images of Pennsylvania and Maine. (7) The paintings show the faces of his neighbors their houses and their land. (8) The paintings generally are not portraits of the people but show them in their everyday ordinary surroundings.

➤ Compound Sentences

A compound sentence is made up of two or more simple sentences. When the parts of a compound sentence are joined by a coordinating conjunction—*and, or, but,* or *yet*—a comma is usually placed before the conjunction.

29 B.3 Use a comma before a coordinating conjunction that joins the parts of a compound sentence.

You can polish the saddles**,** and I will clean the stalls.

The king's three horses jumped the fence**,** but we caught them within half an hour.

Do not confuse a compound sentence with a simple sentence that has a compound verb.

Compound Sentence Queen Kate rides well**,** and everyone wants her for a partner.
(A comma is needed.)

Compound Verb Queen Kate sits straight in the saddle and holds the horse steady.
(No comma is needed.)

You can learn more about compound sentences on pages 647–650.

● Practice Your Skills

Using Commas with Compound Sentences

Write *I* if a sentence needs a comma. Write *C* if a sentence is correct.

(1) King Midas loved gold very much and a god granted him the "golden touch." **(2)** Midas touched his throne and turned it into gold. **(3)** He was very happy with his new power and soon almost everything in his palace became gold. **(4)** One day the king called for his dinner and a fine meal was set before him. **(5)** He picked up a goblet and raised it to his lips. **(6)** His drink instantly hardened to gold and he could not drink it. **(7)** Then Midas quickly crammed a piece of bread into his mouth but it turned into a lump of hot gold. **(8)** Sometime later he walked through his garden and forgot about his power. **(9)** The beautiful roses made the air sweet and Midas loved them. **(10)** He gently touched one red rose and it instantly turned to gold. **(11)** Just then the king's daughter entered the garden and Midas drew back in horror. **(12)** The little girl put her hand on his arm and was turned into a golden statue! **(13)** Midas prayed very hard and finally the god heard his pleas. **(14)** The king followed the god's instructions and soon the golden touch was gone. **(15)** Midas happily threw his arms around his precious daughter and thanked the god for bringing her back to life.

● *Connect to Writing:* Editing

Using Commas in Compound Sentences

Rewrite the incorrect sentences from the preceding exercise, adding commas where needed.

● **_Connect to Writing:_ Drafting**

Using Commas with Compound Sentences

Write one compound sentence about each of the following topics. Make sure the clauses in each sentence are related and punctuated correctly.

1. a fantasy
2. three wishes
3. a hero
4. an important ideal
5. a fear or fears

▶ Introductory Structures

A comma follows certain words, phrases, or clauses when they begin a sentence.

29 B.4 Use a comma after certain introductory words, phrases, or clauses.

Usually a comma follows words such as *no, oh, well,* or *yes* when they begin a sentence.

Words   **Oh,** that lightning was close.

Well, the weather turned cool after the storm.

Words such as *oh* and *well* can also be interjections. When they are, they are followed by an exclamation point.

Oh! Our electricity went out.

You can learn more about interjections and exclamation points on pages 569–571 and 830.

When two or more prepositional phrases or one prepositional phrase of four words or longer comes at the beginning of a sentence, a comma should separate them from the rest of the sentence.

Prepositional Phrases   **From the dark clouds in the east,** we heard a loud clap of thunder. (two prepositional phrases)

Throughout the long storm, the children sat quietly. (one prepositional phrase with four words)

You can learn more about prepositional phrases on pages 600–606.

A comma follows a participial phrase that comes at the beginning of a sentence. A participial phrase is a group of words used as an adjective that begins with a verb form.

> **Participial Phrases**
> **Alerted by the siren,** the students gathered in the building.
> **Sitting in the gym,** the group talked quietly.

You can learn more about participial phrases on pages 618–625.

A comma follows an adverbial clause when it comes at the beginning of a sentence. An adverbial clause is a subordinate clause that begins with a subordinating conjunction such as *after, because, if, since,* and *when*.

> **Adverbial Clause**
> **If you can't get through the storm,** please call Megan and tell her.
> **When we left,** the storm was just beginning.

You can learn more about adverbial clauses on pages 640–642.

● Practice Your Skills

Using Commas with Introductory Elements

Write *I* if a sentence needs a comma. Write *C* if a sentence is correct.

1. To the Europeans' surprise many Native American tribes rose, flourished, and disappeared before the settlers came.
2. Adapting to the hot desert the Hohokam came to Arizona.
3. From A.D. 300 to A.D. 1200 they flourished between the Gila River and Salt River valleys.
4. Their way of life depended heavily on irrigation channels.
5. In addition to miles of irrigation channels the Hohokam left behind stone pottery and shells.
6. Historians believe the shells were received from coastal tribes.
7. Oh the etchings on the shells were done with a kind of acid.
8. In the area of Utah, Colorado, Arizona, and New Mexico, the Anasazi tribe lived during the same time as the Hohokam.
9. According to the Spanish conquerors they lived in great stone pueblos because of the heat.
10. Because drought threatened their large cities the Anasazi disbanded into small communities.

● **Connect to Writing and Speaking: Peer Consultation**

Writing and Telling a Story

With a partner, research legends from North America. Together, write a modern story based on a legend that you find powerful and instructive. Use introductory words or phrases—always following these words or phrases with a comma. Use compound sentences also, and remember to use commas before coordinating conjunctions. Read your story to the class.

● **Connect to Writing: Drafting**

Using Commas with Introductory Elements

Write five sentences, using each of the following introductory words or phrases. Add commas where needed.

1. After the long summer vacation
2. As August turned into September
3. Well
4. Fearing the worst from the new situation
5. By the first day

Commonly Used Commas

The following are examples of some other commonly used commas.

Commas with Dates and Addresses

Commas between the parts of a date or an address are probably the most often used commas.

29 B.5 Use commas to separate elements in dates and addresses.

When a date or an address comes within a sentence, another comma goes at the end to separate it from the rest of the sentence.

Dates On July 20, 1969, Neil Armstrong took the first human step on the moon.
(No comma goes between the month and day, but a comma goes after the year to separate the date from the rest of the sentence.)

In July 1989, Annemarie's youngest brother was born.
(No comma goes between the month and the year if no day is given.)

Addresses   Write to Rockland Crafts, 420 Woodbriar Drive, DeLand, Florida 32720, for a catalog.
(No comma goes between the state and the ZIP code, but a comma goes after the ZIP code to separate the address from the rest of the sentence.)

I live at 12 Richmond Street **in** Dallas, Texas.
(A preposition can take the place of a comma between parts of an address.)

Commas in Letters

29 B.6   Use a comma after the salutation of a friendly letter and after the closing of all letters.

SALUTATIONS AND CLOSINGS	
Salutations	Dear Dad, Dearest Gram, Dear Ali,
Closings	Sincerely, Love, Yours truly, As always,

When You Write

Deciding when to use a comma makes some writers nervous. They then use a comma to indicate a pause or if the sentence seems too long without one. Misplacing or overusing commas can be confusing to a reader. Use commas only where a rule states you should.

● Practice Your Skills

Using Commas in Dates and Addresses

Write *a* or *b* to indicate the item that is correctly written in each of the following pairs.

1. a. Sunday, May 14 2010
   b. Sunday, May 14, 2010
2. a. Dear Maury
   b. Dear Maury,
3. a. Mary New, 129 Jones Street, Los Angeles, CA 90068
   b. Mary New, 129 Jones Street, Los Angeles, CA, 90068
4. a. Thursday August 10, 2010
   b. Thursday, August 10, 2010

End Marks and Commas

5. a. Sincerely
   b. Sincerely,

6. a. Dear John,
   b. Dear John

7. a. Thursday, July 9 1946
   b. Thursday, July 9, 1946

8. a. Dr. John Jahr, Box 456 Farmington, NM 87401
   b. Dr. John Jahr, Box 456, Farmington, NM 87401

9. a. Corpus Christi Texas
   b. Corpus Christi, Texas

10. a. Very truly yours,
   b. Very truly yours

Connect to Writing: Drafting

Using Commas

Follow the directions to write sentences. Be sure to use commas correctly.

1. Write a sentence that includes the city and state in which you live.
2. Write a sentence that includes the month and year that you were born.
3. Write a sentence that includes the address of your school.
4. Write a sentence that includes the city, state, and ZIP code of someone you know.

Connect to Writing: Revising

Adding Commas to Sentences

Write each sentence, using commas correctly.

1. The United States capital city was Philadelphia Pennsylvania before the capital was moved to Washington D.C.
2. The White House is located at 1600 Pennsylvania Avenue Washington D.C. 20003.
3. John Adams and his wife hosted the first reception at the White House on January 1 1801.
4. In 1864 Abraham Lincoln sat for Vinnie Ream so that the talented 16-year-old girl could sculpt his image.
5. On July 27 1866 Ream was the first woman to receive a commission for sculpture from the United States Congress.

Commas That Enclose — Lesson 3

Any group of words that interrupts a sentence can be removed without changing the meaning of the sentence. Commas are used to enclose these expressions. The word *enclose* means that a comma comes at the beginning and at the end of each expression.

29 C Use commas to enclose groups of words that interrupt a sentence.

Direct Address

Sometimes when you talk, you call another person by name. This kind of sentence interrupter is called a **noun of direct address.**

29 C.1 Use a comma or commas to set off **nouns of direct address**.

Please**,** **Coach Curtis,** put me in the game.

In the following examples, only one comma is needed because the noun of direct address comes at the beginning or at the end of the sentence.

Coach Curtis, your strategy is good.

I would give you a sportsmanship award**,** **Coach Curtis**.

● Practice Your Skills

Using Commas with Direct Address

Write *I* if commas are used incorrectly in or are missing from the following sentences. Write *C* if a sentence is correct.

1. Quick, Coach the pitcher needs your help!
2. Christine don't you bat after, Siela?
3. On your way to first base Carla, be sure to turn toward second.
4. Do you like to steal bases, Anna?
5. Look over at the third-base coach, Keisha, for the signs.
6. Josie there is only one out in the inning.
7. Yes, Karen we need to score some runs.
8. Where is your batter's helmet, Elaine?
9. Cora you bat, for Betty.
10. You're our last chance Nancy.

• **_Connect to Writing:_ Editing**

Correcting Commas with Direct Address

Write the incorrect sentences from the preceding exercise, adding or deleting commas where needed.

➤ Parenthetical Expressions

A **parenthetical expression** provides additional or related ideas. Below is a list of common parenthetical expressions. In sentences these words usually are enclosed by commas.

COMMON PARENTHETICAL EXPRESSIONS		
after all	for instance	on the contrary
at any rate	generally speaking	on the other hand
by the way	I believe (guess, hope, know)	moreover
consequently	in fact	nevertheless
however	in my opinion	to tell the truth
for example	of course	furthermore

29 C.2 Use commas to set off parenthetical expressions.

A sonnet normally has fourteen lines**, for example,** not sixteen.

Only one comma is needed when a parenthetical expression comes at the beginning or at the end of a sentence.

In fact, a traditional sonnet should have fourteen lines.

A sonnet is sometimes changed**, nevertheless**.

• **Practice Your Skills**

Using Commas with Parenthetical Expressions

Write **I** if commas are used incorrectly in or are missing from a sentence. Write **C** if a sentence is correct.

1. By the way poetry offers an interesting challenge.
2. Poetry generally, speaking, is the oldest form of literature.
3. Poems, I believe, were sung or repeated around the first campfires.
4. At any rate poems require careful attention.

5. The most important part of a poem in my opinion, is the meaning of each word.
6. For example many kinds, of words, can be used.
7. The words, after all, create feelings and meaning.
8. Of course poems, also, depend on sound.
9. I, however like rhyming poems.
10. Nevertheless, many famous poems do not rhyme.

● *Connect to Writing:* **Editing**

Correcting Commas in Parenthetical Expressions

Write the incorrect sentences from the preceding exercise, adding or deleting commas where needed.

Appositives

Another interrupter, the **appositive,** is a word or group of words that further explains a noun or a pronoun. An appositive or **appositive phrase** interrupts the flow of a sentence. For that reason, appositives usually require commas.

29 C.3 Use commas to set off most appositives and appositive phrases.

Two Commas Alaska**, the largest state,** was once owned by Russia.

Only one comma is needed when the appositive comes at the end of the sentence. Sometimes commas are not used if an appositive is a name.

One Comma Have you read about William H. Seward**, the secretary of state**?

No Commas Have you read the book *The History of Russia*?

My cousin **Bill** is reading a book about the wilderness.

You can learn more about appositive and appositive phrases and when to use commas with them on pages 607–608.

Practice Your Skills

Using Commas with Appositives

Write *I* if commas are used incorrectly or are missing from a sentence. Write *C* if a sentence is correct. Write each incorrect sentence correctly.

(1) Over the years the legend of Paul Bunyan, the most famous lumberjack of all, grew and grew. (2) Paul Bunyan a huge man towered above the trees. (3) His voice once caused a landslide near Pikes Peak a mountain, in Colorado. (4) His mighty blue ox Babe straightened the course of the Whistling River. (5) Hot Biscuit Slim, the cook, was an important member of his logging crew. (6) Cream puffs, the favorite dessert of the crew were baked by the camp cook. (7) Big Swede one of Paul's workers, was known for his accidents. (8) Johnny Inkslinger, the first bookkeeper in the legend, did all the figuring for Paul. (9) It took a bucket brigade of thirty men to fill Johnny's pen a giant rubber hose. (10) The Paul Bunyan legends stories about life in the forest are a big part of American folklore.

Connect to Writing: Movie Genres

Using Appositives

Your class is helping to put together a guide to movies for younger students. You and a partner will cover your favorite genres: action-adventure films and comedies. Use the appositive phrases below in your descriptions.

- an excellent example of slapstick
- the best chase scene since *Transformers*
- a perfect film for lovers of broad comedy
- a film starring two young actors

✓ Check Point: Mixed Practice

Write each sentence, adding commas where needed. If no commas are needed, write *C*.

1. Ellen does your school have a writers' workshop?
2. A writers' workshop a group of five to seven students meets regularly.
3. In fact in the group they discuss their own writing.
4. Most workshops generally speaking focus on one type of writing.
5. This for example might be fiction or poetry or plays.
6. However some workshops can be unusual.
7. One workshop the Fourteen Liners concentrates just on sonnets.
8. That is correct Ellen.
9. Other workshops may focus on science fiction, horror, or mysteries.

Commas That Enclose • Lesson 3

Nonrestrictive and Restrictive Elements

Entire phrases and clauses can interrupt a sentence the same way a parenthetical expression does. Moreover, some of these phrases and clauses are not necessary to the sentence.

A nonrestrictive phrase or clause could actually be removed from a sentence, and the sentence would still make complete sense. A comma goes before and after a nonrestrictive phrase or clause to show that the words in between the commas could be removed from the sentence.

29 C.4 Use commas to set off **nonrestrictive participial phrases** and **nonrestrictive clauses.**

If a participial phrase provides extra, unnecessary information, it is a **nonrestrictive phrase.** A nonrestrictive phrase simply comments on the subject.

Nonrestrictive Participial Phrases	Computers**, used at home and at work,** provide access to the Internet.
	The Internet**, created mostly for data transfer,** is very popular.
	Chen Li**, searching the Internet day and night,** learns much about the world.

If the nonrestrictive participial phrase were dropped, the main idea of each sentence would not be changed in any way.

Computers provide access to the Internet.

The Internet is very popular.

Chen Li learns much about the world.

You can learn more about participial phrases on pages 618–625.

An adjectival clause is nonessential if it provides extra, unnecessary information.

Nonrestrictive Adjectival Clauses	The hard drive is the primary information storage device in a computer**, which processes binary data.**
	The hard drive**, which is less accessible than CDs,** usually stores the computer's operating systems.

If the nonessential adjectival clause were dropped, the basic meaning of each sentence would not be changed at all.

> The hard drive is the primary information storage device in a computer.
>
> The hard drive usually stores the computer's operating systems.

You can learn more about adjectival clauses on pages 643–646.

29 C.5 If a **participial phrase** or a clause is restrictive, or necessary, to the meaning of a sentence, no commas are used.

Many participial phrases and adjectival clauses, of course, are necessary. The information in them is necessary to fully understand the sentence in which they appear. If such a phrase or clause is dropped, the meaning of the sentence will be incomplete. Restrictive phrases and clauses usually identify a person, place, or thing and answer the question *Which one?* When a phrase or clause is essential, no commas are used.

Restrictive Participial Phrase	We like computer games **imitating car races.** (Without the phrase, the sentence would read, *We like computer games.* The reader would not know which games.)
Restrictive Adjectival Clause	The game **that has the best car race** is on Tom's computer. (Without the clause, the sentence would read, *The game is on Tom's computer.* No one would know which game.)
	Tom is the student **who has computer experience.** (Without the clause, the sentence would read, *Tom is the student.* No one would know which student Tom is.)

Since the phrase and the clauses in these examples are restrictive, no commas are used.

● Practice Your Skills

Using Commas with Restrictive Elements

Write **C** if a sentence is correctly punctuated. Write **I** if a sentence is incorrectly punctuated.

1. People who help other people are heroes.
2. Volunteer work which happens all over the world is good citizenship.
3. In fact, there is a computer database that lists willing volunteers in a community.
4. This computer program, which is easily downloaded, also keeps track of the people, being served.
5. It also does accounting which is important for state funding.

6. Often volunteers work in shelters that feed homeless people.
7. These volunteers who come from all walks of life serve food.
8. Some heroes visit hospital patients who have no families.
9. The "candy stripers" who wear uniforms with stripes help the nurses.

● *Connect to Writing:* **Editing**

Correcting Commas with Nonrestrictive Elements

Write the incorrect sentences from the preceding exercise, adding or deleting commas where needed.

● *Connect to Writing:* **Character Sketch**

Correcting Commas with Restrictive and Nonrestrictive Elements

There is probably a person in your life more interesting and unusual than any other. What makes this person different? How does he or she act, dress, move, and speak? How does the person approach life and discuss issues? Write a character sketch that will have readers seeing this person just as you do. Use commas as needed.

✓ Check Point: Mixed Practice

Write each sentence, adding commas where needed. If the sentence is correct, write **C**.

1. Pee Wee Reese the Brooklyn Dodger shortstop was inducted into the Baseball Hall of Fame in 1984.
2. Reese who helped Jackie Robinson adjust to major league baseball was born in Kentucky.
3. Roger Kahn's book *The Boys of Summer* tells how Reese helped baseball integration.
4. Reese however was also a great baseball player.
5. The well-liked man was an eight-time All-Star hitting 126 home runs with 885 RBI.
6. Reese the heart and soul of the Dodgers stole thirty bases in 1930.
7. In 1947, Reese who battled cancer late in life led his league in runs scored.
8. Reese a man of many nicknames was also called "The Little Colonel."

Chapter Review

Assess Your Learning

Using End Marks Correctly

Write each sentence, adding period(s), exclamation point(s), or question mark(s) where needed. If a sentence does not need any marks, write **C**.

1. Are we meeting at 8 am or 8 pm
2. Some kittens do not like catnip
3. Look out for that car
4. My big sister gave me a CD for my birthday.
5. I wondered why the two countries were at war
6. T S Eliot was a poet and a literary critic.
7. I moved from Forty-fourth St to Ivy Dr
8. How dare he say that Georgia O'Keeffe could not paint
9. Tania volunteers after school every Monday.
10. Did you see that manatee

Using Commas Correctly

Write each sentence, adding a comma or commas where needed. If a sentence does not need commas, write **C**.

1. My neighbor Ellen, who attends Carleton College, came home today.
2. The trunk in our attic is old large and heavy.
3. Greenland the largest island on this planet is about sixteen hundred miles in length.
4. For an hour all the lights were out.
5. Your dental appointment David is on Monday.
6. The magician is good but the mime is better.
7. We walked for two miles and then took a rest.
8. The ladybird on the other hand is actually a beetle.

Using Commas Correctly

Write the following paragraphs, adding commas where needed.

Are you interested in the outdoors animals or science? There are magazines about each of these subjects. *Ranger Rick* for example tells you about the wonders of nature. The articles will keep you up to date on all the latest environmental news and each issue includes games stories, puzzles and projects.

Odyssey a magazine about science covers interesting topics from cooking to ring tones. Each month there is a new experiment and each issue has some regular columns. One column for instance gives helpful facts about triangles.

Using Commas

Write sentences that follow the directions below. (The sentences may come in any order.) Write about your family tree, a historical event, or a topic of your own choosing.

Write a sentence that...

1. includes a series of nouns.
2. includes two adjectives before a noun.
3. has two independent clauses joined by a coordinating conjunction.
4. includes a participial phrase at the beginning.
5. includes an adverbial clause at the beginning.
6. includes direct address.
7. includes a parenthetical expression.
8. includes an appositive.
9. includes a nonessential adjectival clause.
10. includes your street number and name, city, state, and ZIP code.

End Marks and Commas: Posttest

Directions
Read the passage and write the letter of the best way to write each underlined word or words. If the underlined word or words contain no error, write D.

(1) <u>In science class today</u> we studied bromeliads. They are native to the (2) <u>Americas and grow</u> as far (3) <u>north as the Virginia</u> coast. They are known for (4) <u>their large colorful stalks.</u>
(5) <u>Spanish moss or</u> "old man's beard," is a common bromeliad in the southeastern United States. Like many other bromeliads, it (6) <u>grows on trees</u> The trees (7) <u>are not harmed and such</u> bromeliads are called airplants.
(8) <u>Bromeliads whether</u> they grow in trees or in the ground, usually collect water in a central cup or in their leaves. (9) <u>Insects, snakes and frogs</u> make their homes in these moist shelters. Fertilizing the bromeliads with (10) <u>decaying organic matter</u> the organisms provide as large a benefit as they receive.

1. **A** In science class, today
   B In science class today,
   C In science, class today
   D No error

2. **A** Americas, and grow
   B Americas and, grow
   C Americas and grow,
   D No error

3. **A** north, as the Virginia
   B north as the Virginia.
   C north as the Virginia,
   D No error

4. **A** their large colorful, stalks.
   B their large, colorful stalks.
   C their, large colorful stalks.
   D No error

5. **A** Spanish moss, or
   B Spanish, moss or
   C Spanish moss or,
   D No error

6. **A** grows, on trees.
   B grows on trees!
   C grows on trees.
   D No error

7. **A** are not harmed, and such
   B are not harmed and such,
   C are not harmed. And such
   D No error

8. **A** Bromeliads, whether
   B Bromeliads! Whether
   C Bromeliads whether,
   D No error

9. **A** Insects, snakes and frogs,
   B Insects snakes and frogs
   C Insects, snakes, and frogs
   D No error

10. **A** decaying, organic matter
    B decaying organic, matter
    C decaying organic matter,
    D No error

Writer's Corner

Snapshot

29 A Depending on the purpose, **different sentences have different end marks.** (pages 830–834)

29 B **Use commas to separate,** as with items in a series, adjectives before a noun, compound sentences, introductory structures, and in dates, addresses, and letters. (pages 835–845)

29 C **Use commas to enclose** groups of words that interrupt a sentence. (pages 846–852)

Power Rules

 Use **sentence fragments** only the way professional writers do. Fix sentence fragments that occur before the sentence they refer to and ones that occur in the middle of a sentence. (See pages 662–667.)

Before Editing

Before it rains. We need to get our equipment inside.

When your father gets home. We'll go to the store.

After Editing

Before it rains, we need to get our equipment inside.

When your father gets home, we'll go to the store.

 Avoid run-on sentences. Use the best conjunction for the meaning and/or use appropriate punctuation to separate sentences in a run-on sentence. (See pages 668–670.)

Before Editing

I love spring, the trees are budding and the flowers are growing.

When summer is here we'll have vacation, I'll go to camp.

After Editing

I love spring. The trees are budding, and the flowers are growing.

When summer is here, we'll have vacation, and I'll go to camp.

Editing Checklist

Use this checklist when editing your writing.

✓ Did I use the correct end mark for the type of sentence? (See pages 830–831.)
✓ Did I use periods correctly for abbreviations or in an outline? (See pages 831–834.)
✓ Did I separate items in a series with commas? (See pages 835–839.)
✓ Are commas used correctly when separating phrases and clauses? (See pages 841–843.)
✓ Are commas used correctly for dates and letters? (See pages 843–845.)
✓ Did I use commas to correctly enclose nouns of direct address, appositives, and parenthetical expressions? (See pages 846–849.)
✓ Are nonessential phrases and clauses set off by commas? (See pages 850–852.)

Use the Power

The sentence pairs below demonstrate how end marks can change the meaning of a sentence.

Statement	Sharon won the achievement award**.**
Exclamation	Sharon won the achievement award**!**

Statement	She won the award for her science project**.**
Question	She won the award for her science project**?**

Exclamation	Hurry! We have to protest this**!**
Command	Protest this**.**

Use end marks to create a dramatic scene between two friends. In the dialogue, use end marks to your advantage. Question marks can be used to show surprise or disbelief, for example. Don't overuse question marks and exclamation points, however, as doing so may annoy your readers.

CHAPTER 30

Italics and Quotation Marks

How can italics and quotation marks help you communicate clearly, make characters believable, and provide expert support for your ideas?

Italics and Quotation Marks: Pretest 1

The first draft below contains errors in italics and quotation marks. One item has been corrected. How would you edit the rest of the draft by adding underlining (to represent italics) and quotation marks?

> Have you ever seen the movie <u>Star Trek II: The Wrath of Khan</u>? There is a lot of action, but there are also lots of references to literature. Spock gives Kirk a copy of Dickens's novel A Tale of Two Cities as a gift. Kirk opens the book and reads the first line aloud: It was the best of times, it was the worst of times. Near the end of the movie, as Kirk reflects on Spock's sacrifice, we hear another famous quote from the same book: It is a far, far better thing that I do, than I have ever done. But that's not the only book that gets quoted. When Chekov first stumbles upon the the remains of Khan's ship, he sees a copy of the book Moby Dick. Khan quotes from this as he's dying, saying, To the last I grapple with thee; from hell's heart I stab at thee; for hate's sake I spit my last breath at thee. This was the perfect quote because Khan was as obsessed with destroying Kirk as Ahab in Moby Dick was obsessed with destroying the white whale.

Italics and Quotation Marks: Pretest 2

Directions
Read the passage and write the letter of the word or group of words that belongs in each underlined space.

  Fran showed Theo a book __(1)__ She explained that the __(2)__ is taken from the word *magazine*. "Unlike magazines," __(3)__ are usually homemade."
  Theo asked __(4)__ __(5)__ "a lot of kids our age or in high school write zines."
  Theo __(6)__ you have to be rich to publish something?"
  "Zines are usually short, photocopied booklets that are stapled __(7)__ usually trade them for one another's zines," said Fran.
  "What are zines __(8)__ asked.
  Fran explained that zines can include poetry, comic strips, journal entries, music reviews, even articles on the latest episode of "The Prisoner."

1. A called "Zine Scene".
   B called "Zine Scene."
   C called *Zine Scene*.
   D called, Zine Scene.

2. A word "zine"
   B word *zine*
   C "word" zine
   D word zine

3. A Fran began "Zines
   B Fran began, "Zines
   C Fran began, "zines
   D Fran began "zines

4. A what Fran meant.
   B "What Fran meant?"
   C what Fran meant?
   D "what Fran meant."

5. A "Well, Fran said,
   B "Well" Fran said,
   C "Well," Fran said,
   D "Well," Fran said

6. A asked. "don't
   B asked, "Don't
   C asked? "Don't
   D asked? "don't

7. A together." "Kids
   B together." Kids, "
   C together. Kids
   D together." Kids

8. A about"? Theo
   B about?", Theo
   C about," Theo
   D about?" Theo

Italics and Quotation Marks: Pretest

Italics (Underlining)  Lesson 1

Words printed in italics slant to the right *like this*. When you are writing in longhand, use underlining to show italics. To italicize when using a computer, highlight the words and then use the command for italics (often command plus *i*).

Italics with Titles

30 A   **Italics** (underlining) are used to set off titles and certain numbers, words, and letters.

Italics	Have you ever read the book *Stuart Little* by E. B. White?
Underlining	Have you ever read the book Stuart Little by E. B. White?

Certain letters, numbers, words, and titles should be italicized or underlined.

30 A.1   Italicize (underline) letters, numbers, and words when they are used to represent themselves.

Letters	Does that word have three *t*'s?
Numbers	Austin's ZIP code begins with a *7*.
Words	The word *Mississippi* is hard to spell.

Only the *t* is italicized in *t*'s, not the apostrophe and the *s* that makes it plural.

30 A.2   Italicize (underline) the titles of long written or musical works that are published as a single unit, titles of paintings and sculptures, and the names of vehicles.

This rule includes books, magazines, newspapers, full-length plays, movies, television series, and very long poems. Long musical works include operas, symphonies, ballets, albums, and CDs. Vehicles include airplanes, ships, trains, and spacecraft.

Books	After I finish *Tom Sawyer*, I am definitely going to read *Huckleberry Finn*.
Magazines	My uncle reads *National Geographic*.
Newspapers	Our neighbor has the Wall Street Journal mailed to his house every day. (The word *the* is not usually considered part of the title of a newspaper or magazine.)

Plays and Movies	The play *Our Town* by Thornton Wilder is set in a small New England town.
Works of Art	Andrew Wyeth's *Christina's World* shows a woman on a New Hampshire farm.
Musical Works	We saw the opera *The Barber of Seville*.
Names of Vehicles	One of the early space shuttles was the *Challenger*. (The word *the* is not considered part of the title of a vehicle.)

You can learn about the capitalization of titles on pages 817–822.

Practice Your Skills

Using Italics (Underlining)

Write *a* or *b* to indicate the item that is correctly underlined in each of the following pairs. For the names of newspapers, magazines, and vehicles, remember that the word *the* is not part of the title.

1. **a.** the nonfiction <u>book</u> <u>Profiles in Courage</u> by John F. Kennedy
   b. the nonfiction book <u>Profiles in Courage</u> by John F. Kennedy
2. **a.** a steamboat called the <u>Clermont</u>
   b. a steamboat called the <u>Clermont</u>
3. **a.** the letters <u>g</u> and <u>q</u>
   b. the letters <u>g</u> and <u>q</u>
4. **a.** the newspaper the <u>Nashville Banner</u>
   b. the newspaper the <u>Nashville Banner</u>
5. **a.** the movie <u>The Iron Giant</u>
   b. the movie The <u>Iron Giant</u>
6. **a.** the Broadway play <u>Cats</u>
   b. the <u>Broadway play Cats</u>
7. **a.** the famous painting The <u>Starry Night</u>
   b. the famous painting <u>The Starry Night</u>
8. **a.** the space shuttle <u>Discovery</u>
   b. the <u>space shuttle Discovery</u>
9. **a.** the movie <u>Flubber</u> with Robin Williams
   b. the movie <u>Flubber with Robin Williams</u>
10. **a.** the magazine American <u>Girl</u>
    b. the magazine <u>American Girl</u>

Connect to Writing: Editing

Using Underlining Correctly

Rewrite each sentence, underlining where needed.

1. The Los Angeles Times is a big newspaper.
2. Readers can read a review of a book such as Richard Peck's A Long Way from Chicago.
3. The reviews are longer than those in Newsweek.
4. The letter i comes before e in the word review.
5. A newspaper will announce the showing of paintings such as Van Gogh's Sunflowers.
6. The theater page will review a play such as Beauty and the Beast.
7. A feature article might give the history of the space station Mir.
8. Every newspaper in the country reviewed the movie Star Wars: Episode One.
9. Music critics review operas such as Carmen.
10. Write your 7s so that they do not look like 9s.

Connect to Writing: Opinion Paragraph

Italics (Underlining)

In a newspaper or magazine, find a review of a movie you have seen. Explain the reviewer's opinion in a paragraph for your classmates, and then tell why you agree or disagree with it. Use italics (underlining) when you write the name of the movie and the name of the newspaper or magazine where the review appeared.

Connect to Speaking, Listening, and Writing: Peer Consultation

Using Italics in Writing

Write a paragraph about the books, magazines, films, and music you most admire. Then consult with a partner about your preferences. Together, write a new paragraph that combines examples that you both agree are the most admirable. Be sure your examples are correctly italicized. Read your paragraph for the class.

Quotation Marks

You can enhance your writing by using quotation marks (" ") correctly. Your stories, for example, will be more realistic if you include conversations among your characters. Your reports also will be read with greater interest if they include quoted statements from experts.

30 B **Quotation marks** are used to enclose the titles of short works and parts of longer works and to set off a speaker's exact words.

▶ Quotation Marks with Titles

Not all titles are underlined. The titles of smaller parts of long works are enclosed in quotation marks.

30 B.1 Use quotation marks to enclose the titles of chapters, articles, stories, one-act plays, short poems, and songs.

Book Chapters	After reading "Eastward," the first chapter of *Blue Highways*, Tom was inspired.
Magazine Articles	Dad read the article "Travel Trends in the New Year" in the magazine *Going Places*.
Short Stories in Books	Harriet enjoyed the short story "The Cat That Walked by Itself" in *Just So Stories*.
Short Poems in Books	The short poem "Color" appears in the book *Make a Joyful Sound*.
Songs	Kathy sings "My Heart Will Go On" all the time.

● Practice Your Skills

Punctuating Titles Correctly

Read the following sentences. Write **C** if the quotation marks and underlining in a sentence are used correctly. Write **I** if the quotation marks and underlining are used incorrectly. Rewrite sentences you have marked **I** so that they are correct.

1. The song Guinevere is from the musical "Camelot."
2. I read the poem "Paul Revere's Ride" in speech class.
3. The Buck in the Hills is a short story about hunting.
4. We are studying the chapter "The Colonies Win Freedom" in our history book, The Heritage of America.

Quotation Marks • Lesson 2 863

5. The article <u>A Lost Son Is Found</u> was published in Newsweek.
6. "The Ugly Duckling" is a one-act play.
7. I copied Helen Hunt Jackson's short poem "September."
8. Julie loves the song Tomorrow from the musical <u>Annie</u>.
9. <u>Sponges</u> is the name of a chapter in our textbook Life Science.
10. We read the article "India Today" in this week's Time.

Connect to Writing: Bibliography

Using Correct Punctuation with Titles

Imagine that you are writing a report on a recent scientific development. In your library, find two magazine articles and two book chapters that you could use for your report. List the titles as well as the magazines and books you found them in. Use quotation marks and underlining correctly.

Quotation Marks with Direct Quotations

A person's exact words are quoted in a **direct quotation.** Quotation marks are used before and after any words the person says.

30 B.2 Use quotation marks to enclose a person's exact words.

A one-sentence direct quotation can be written in several ways. You can place it before or after a **speaker tag,** words such as *she said* or *he asked*. You can also place a speaker tag in the middle of a direct quotation. Place all quotation marks only before and after the person's exact words.

Exact Words Before Speaker Tag	"A person's normal body temperature is 98.6°F," said the nurse.
Exact Words After Speaker Tag	The nurse said, "A person's normal body temperature is 98.6°F."
Exact Words Interrupted by Speaker Tag	"A person's normal body temperature," the nurse said, "is 98.6°F." (Two sets of quotation marks are needed because the speaker tag interrupts the direct quotation.)

A person's exact words are not quoted in an **indirect quotation.** Quotation marks, therefore, are not used.

Indirect Quotations   Mark said that he had practice after school. He added he would probably finish by six o'clock.

The word *that* is often used with an indirect quotation. In the second sentence above, *that* is understood.

He added (that) he would probably finish by six o'clock.

When You Write

To describe exactly how someone spoke, writers often use a variety of verbs in speaker tags. Consider using vivid verbs such as those listed here when you use direct quotations:

he **mumbled**	he **agreed**	she **pleaded**
he **stammered**	she **boasted**	he **teased**
she **wondered**	he **complained**	she **demanded**

Write a short dialogue between a child and a parent using direct quotations. You may use any of the verbs above, but don't overdo them. There is nothing wrong with the standard speaker tags *he said* or *she said*.

Practice Your Skills

Using Quotation Marks with Direct Quotations

Read the following sentences. Write **C** if a sentence is punctuated correctly. Write **I** if a sentence is punctuated incorrectly. Write incorrect sentences correctly.

1. "I once had a temperature of 103°F, said Devon."
2. The nurse said that a temperature that high was a sign of infection.
3. "Sometimes, she added," "a lukewarm bath can bring down a temperature."
4. Kayla said, "My mom gives me medicine when I have a fever."
5. "If a fever lasts more than a few days, the nurse continued, you should probably see a doctor.
6. "The doctor may be able to tell what kind of infection you have," she explained.
7. She said "that the infection could be caused by bacteria."
8. In that case, "she went on," you might need to take antibiotics.
9. "Don't ask for antibiotics if you don't need them," the nurse urged.
10. "If you do, she explained, your body might eventually develop germs that are stronger than the antibiotics."

Capital Letters with Direct Quotations

30 B.3 Capitalize the first word of a direct quotation.

"**T**he meeting will be held in the gym," she said.

She said, "**T**he meeting will be held in the gym."

"**T**he meeting," she said, "will be held in the gym."
(The word *will* does not begin with a capital letter because it is in the middle of a one-sentence direct quotation.)

"**T**he meeting will be held in the gym," she said. "**I**t begins at four o'clock."
(The word *it* begins with a capital letter because it starts a new sentence.)

● **Practice Your Skills**

Using Capital Letters with Direct Quotations

Write **C** if capital letters are used correctly in a sentence. Write **I** if capital letters are used incorrectly in a sentence. Write incorrect sentences correctly.

1. The Boy Scout leader said, "we are here to discuss how to help our community."
2. He continued, "Our community has many different needs."
3. "We can identify these needs," he went on, "by listing the groups who have asked for our help."
4. "first, there are those who need food and shelter," he said.
5. "Among the other groups," he added, "Are the young, the elderly, and the disabled."
6. "Remember," he said, "this help is community service and not charity."
7. "Volunteers make our whole community stronger," He claimed.
8. "By helping others," he insisted, "You also help yourself."
9. "It is your community," he said. "It is your responsibility."
10. The Boy Scout leader concluded, "come join your community."

● *Connect to Writing:* **Interview**

Using Direct Quotations

Interview a classmate about the kind of job he or she would like to have in the future. Take notes or record the interview. Write a summary of what the person said. Use some of the speaker's exact words. Be sure you have used punctuation and capital letters correctly in direct quotations.

Commas with Direct Quotations

30 B.4 Use a comma to separate a direct quotation from a speaker tag.

"Ms. Poe is an expert on desert animals**,**" he said.
(The comma is *inside* the closing quotation marks.)

He said**,** "Ms. Poe is an expert on desert animals."
(The comma comes *before* the quotation marks.)

"Ms. Poe**,**" he said**,** "is an expert on desert animals."
(Two commas are needed to separate the speaker tag from the direct quotation. The first comma goes *inside* the closing quotation marks.)

● **Practice Your Skills**

Using Commas with Direct Quotations

Write *C* if commas are used correctly in a sentence. Write *I* if commas are used incorrectly.

1. "Chuckwallas are playful lizards", Ms. Poe said.
2. "They live in the desert," she added.
3. She continued ",Chuckwallas play hide-and-seek."
4. "They run to a hiding place," she explained "and then peep out to spy on the others."
5. Ms. Poe went on, "Sometimes a chuckwalla will jump out and grab another's tail just for fun."
6. "Snakes and birds" Ms. Poe added, "sometimes attack them."
7. She added, "A chuckwalla can easily protect itself."
8. "It crawls in between rocks", she explained "and blows up like a balloon."
9. She added "An enemy cannot pull it loose."
10. "When the attacker gives up," she concluded, "the chuckwalla lets out the air and scurries off."

● *Connect to Writing:* **Editing**

Using Commas in Direct Quotations

Rewrite the incorrect sentences from the preceding exercise, using commas correctly.

End Marks with Direct Quotations

When a quotation ends with a period, the period goes inside the closing quotation marks.

30 B.5 Place a period inside the closing quotation marks when the end of the quotation comes at the end of a sentence.

The bandleader said, "The parade begins in two minutes."

"The parade begins," the bandleader said, "in two minutes."

The same is true of question marks and exclamation points that end a quotation.

She yelled, "Let's get started!"
(The exclamation point belongs inside the closing quotation marks.)

"When," he asked, "did you find time to organize this parade?"
(The question mark goes inside the closing quotation marks.)

When a question or an exclamation comes before a speaker tag, the question mark or the exclamation point is still placed inside the closing quotation marks, in place of the usual comma.

"Please hurry!" Margo pleaded.
(The exclamation point belongs inside the closing quotation marks.)

"Do you want to bring a water bottle?" Peg asked.
(The question mark goes inside the closing quotation marks.)

● **Practice Your Skills**

Using End Marks with Direct Quotations

Write *C* if the end marks in a sentence are used correctly. Write *I* if end marks are used incorrectly.

1. "Have you ever hunted for pearls," asked Linda?
2. "No," Mr. Quinn answered, "but I would like to find one sometime".
3. "Is diving for pearls dangerous?" Hector asked.
4. "It can be extremely dangerous!" Mr. Quinn exclaimed.
5. Taylor asked, "Do pearl divers know which oysters contain pearls"?
6. "They can't tell," Mr. Quinn replied, "until they look inside the shell."

7. "What happens to the oyster once the pearl is removed?" she asked.
8. Mr. Quinn explained, "A diver returns the oyster to the water?"
9. "The diver hopes," Mr. Quinn continued, "the oyster will make a new pearl."
10. "What a job," Linda exclaimed, "No wonder pearls are so expensive!"

Connect to Writing: Editing

Using End Marks in Quotations Correctly

Rewrite the incorrectly punctuated quotations from the preceding exercise, using end marks correctly.

Connect to Writing, Speaking, Listening: Peer Collaboration

Coloring and Voicing Punctuation

Get together with classmates and write sentences that require quotation marks and other punctuation. Then, use marker colors to write in the punctuation needed for your sentences. When you are satisfied that your sentences are punctuated properly, read them out loud, saying the names of all the punctuation, such as "Open quotation, Stop comma thief, exclamation point, close quotation, yelled Clare when her bag was stolen, period."

✓ Check Point: Mixed Practice

Rewrite the direct quotations below, adding quotation marks, commas, end marks, and capital letters where needed.

1. many people do not realize that the crow is a very smart bird Mr. Adams said
2. he added a crow can outwit hawks and most people
3. does putting a scarecrow in a cornfield really help Andrea asked
4. that is a big mistake exclaimed Mr. Adams.
5. many crows he explained use the scarecrows as lookout posts
6. one crow he continued will act as a guard for a flock of crows in a cornfield
7. Sam asked what does the crow do if it senses danger
8. it caws a danger signal to the others Mr. Adams said and they all fly away
9. a team of three crows will also work together to get food from an animal Mr. Adams added
10. how do they do that Beth asked
11. a crow lands on each side of the animal Mr. Adams answered and pretends to steal the animal's food.
12. then the third crow he continued swoops down and snatches the food.

Other Uses of Quotation Marks

Now that you understand how to punctuate direct quotations, you can apply this knowledge to the following situations.

Writing Dialogue

A conversation between two or more persons is called a **dialogue.** Dialogue is an efficient way to let the reader know who is speaking.

30 B.6 When writing dialogue, begin a new paragraph each time the speaker changes.

In the following dialogue between Gina and Connie, a new paragraph begins each time the speaker changes.

> "When is your appointment with the guidance counselor?" Gina asked Connie, who was sitting on the bench outside the office.
>
> "I see her after lunch," Connie answered. "We are going to talk about my doing some volunteer work."

● *Connect to Speaking and Listening:* **Peer Interaction**

Using Dialogue

With a classmate, read aloud the following dialogue between Pat Picasso and Morgan Monet. Point out each place where a new paragraph should begin.

> Morgan exclaimed, "What a brilliant painting, Pat! I should also use that perspective." "I hope the art critics are as responsive to my work as you are, Morgan," Pat responded. "I'm not sure that my cerulean blue is living up to its name." "I disagree," replied Morgan. "It has just the depth of blueness required—like a brilliant answer to a puzzling question." "You are too kind," Pat responded. "But you are right. Where would the world be without cerulean blue?"

● *Connect to Writing:* **A Short Dialogue**

Using Quotes and New Paragraphs

Continue the dialogue between Pat Picasso and Morgan Monet above. This time, have Pat comment on Morgan's artwork. Be sure to use quotation marks correctly, and remember to begin a new paragraph with each new speaker.

Quoting Long Passages

30 B.7 When quoting a passage of more than a paragraph, place quotation marks at the beginning of each paragraph—but at the end of only the last paragraph.

Do not put closing quotation marks at the end of each paragraph, except the last one. This tells the reader that the quotation continues.

The following example is a long quotation that a student used in a report about building affordable housing in the United States.

> **"**Here, then, is the idea to set loose in the land: *Everyone should have a simple, decent place to live.* (no quotation marks)
> **"**We have the know-how in the world to house everyone. We have the resources in the world to house everyone. All that's missing is the will to do it. (no quotation marks)
> **"**Make no small plans. (no quotation marks)
> **"**Can we build houses for a million people? Why not? Why not a million houses for five million people? Why not even more?**"**
> (closing quotation marks)
>
> —Millard Fuller, *A Simple, Decent Place to Live*

When You Write

Another way to quote a long passage is to set it off from the rest of the text by indenting both side margins. This method, the block quote, requires no quotation marks.

Practice Your Skills

Quoting Long Passages

Where would you add quotation marks in the passage below?

> How good really is a house built by volunteers?
> Hurricane Andrew, which destroyed thousands of houses, didn't take down a single Habitat house. *That's* how good.
> All twenty-seven houses built by Habitat for Humanity in south Florida were still standing with only the slightest of damage. And some were right in the hurricane's path. On Guava Street in west Perrine, all that was left of the neighborhood were splintered trees, trashed cars, headless palms, and yards full of debris, which once had been houses . . . except for four Habitat houses standing side-by-side in a sea of devastation.
>
> —Millard Fuller, *A Simple, Decent Place to Live*

✓ Check Point: Mixed Practice

Rewrite each sentence, adding underlining, quotation marks, commas, and end marks where needed. Remember that only a sentence with a speaker tag should be considered a direct quotation.

1. Theodore H. White was a reporter for Time magazine
2. He is different from the T. H. White who wrote the book The Once and Future King
3. White wrote an article called The American Idea for the New York Times
4. In his article White wrote Americans are a nation born of an idea
5. All men are created equal Thomas Jefferson wrote in 1776
6. Theodore White said Jefferson himself could not have imagined the reach of his call across the world in times to come
7. Why did Jefferson use the word men instead of the word people
8. In 1848 Elizabeth Cady Stanton said All men and women are created equal
9. Along with Susan B. Anthony, Stanton coedited three volumes of a book called History of Woman Suffrage.
10. Anthony published a weekly journal called The Revolution
11. Charlotte Perkins Gilman also argued for women's rights in her magazine called the Forerunner.
12. The word suffragette was used to describe a woman who fought for the right to vote.

• *Connect to Writing:* Dialogue

Writing Dialogue

You have many conversations each day. Some conversations are serious and others are fun. You talk to your friends, family members, teachers, and clerks in stores. Recall a recent conversation you had with someone. Write a dialogue, showing each speaker's exact words. If you cannot remember the exact words, paraphrase them. Be sure to punctuate the dialogue correctly and start a new paragraph every time the speaker changes.

Chapter Review

Assess Your Learning

Punctuating Titles

Write each sentence, adding quotation marks or underlining to the titles. (These sentences are not direct quotations.)

1. The Honeymooners once was a popular TV series.
2. Catalogue is a delightful short poem about cats.
3. Ani DiFranco was featured on the covers of Spin and Ms.
4. I finished reading the short story The Pacing Goose.
5. The painting Twittering Machine is by Paul Klee.
6. I loved the movie Planet of the Apes.
7. Charles Lindbergh flew the Spirit of St. Louis on the first nonstop solo flight from New York to Paris.
8. Education in America was an article in Newsweek.
9. The American troops once marched to Yankee Doodle.
10. Read the chapter Animal Behavior in the magazine Science Today.

Punctuating Direct Quotations

Write each sentence, adding capital letters, quotation marks, and other punctuation marks where needed.

1. the Yukon is the largest river in Alaska he stated
2. why are you leaving so early Mandy asked
3. Vickie remarked fish is a good source of protein
4. the travel guide asked have you ever been to Spain
5. wow he exclaimed look at that wave
6. an earthquake can create huge sea waves she stated
7. you can't have everything Steven Wright said
8. watch out for that falling ladder she screamed

Writing Dialogue

Rewrite the following dialogue between Kenneth and Shirley. Add capital letters, quotation marks, and other punctuation marks. Begin a new paragraph each time the speaker changes.

Kenneth began our report is about the discovery of the Americas by the European world. Shirley added as everyone knows, Columbus discovered America by accident because he was really looking for a faster route to the Far East. Why was a faster route so important Kenneth asked. A shipload of spices Shirley replied could make a person rich for life. Kenneth continued the nation that controlled the spice trade to a great extent controlled the commerce of Europe. Why were spices so important in the fifteenth and sixteenth centuries Shirley asked. They were needed for everyday life Kenneth replied. In the days before refrigeration, spices were needed to preserve food and make medicines.

Using Quotation Marks

Follow the directions below.

1. Write an imaginary dialogue between you and your great-great-grandparents. Punctuate the dialogue correctly.
2. After an introductory paragraph, quote a long passage from a nonfiction book.

Italics and Quotation Marks: Posttest

Directions
Read the passage and write the letter of the word or group of words that belongs in each underlined space.

    I told Ian that __(1)__ Ian agreed but said that he likes scary stories such as Edgar Allan Poe's __(2)__
    "That was so __(3)__
    Derek said that Poe was one of his favorites and asked if we knew that poem __(4)__ We all agreed that it was a very spooky poem.
    "Don't you like funny __(5)__ than scary stories?"
    Then we all laughed and talked about last week's episode of __(6)__ The word __(7)__ doesn't really do it justice.
    "Okay, who's brave enough to admit that they like sad __(8)__
    __(9)__ I confessed.
    Our short story that day in English had been __(10)__ We all looked rather glum.

1. **A** "I hate scary movies"
   B "I hate scary movies."
   C *I hate scary movies.*
   D I hate scary movies.

2. **A** *Tell-Tale Heart.*
   B "Tell-Tale Heart".
   C "Tell-Tale Heart."
   D Tell-Tale Heart.

3. **A** scary," Maria piped up!
   B scary!" Maria piped up.
   C scary!", Maria piped up.
   D scary!" Maria piped up

4. **A** "The Raven."
   B "The Raven"?
   C *The Raven.*
   D The Raven?

5. **A** stories," I asked, "better
   B stories?" I asked, "better
   C stories," I asked "better
   D stories" I asked "better

6. **A** "The Simpsons".
   B "The Simpsons."
   C *The Simpsons.*
   D "the Simpsons."

7. **A** *hilarious*
   B "hilarious"
   C "hilarious,"
   D hilarious,

8. **A** stories?" Ian asked.
   B "stories," Ian asked?
   C stories"? Ian asked.
   D stories" Ian asked.

9. **A** I admit "Babe" made me cry"
   B "I admit *Babe* made me cry,"
   C "I admit Babe made me cry,
   D "I admit Babe made me cry."

10. **A** "The Scarlet Ibis".
    B The Scarlet Ibis.
    C "The Scarlet Ibis."
    D *The Scarlet Ibis.*

Writer's Corner

Snapshot

30 A **Italics (underlining)** are used to set off titles and certain numbers, words, and letters. (pages 860–862)

30 B **Quotation marks** are used to enclose the titles of short works and parts of longer works and to set off a speaker's exact words. (pages 863–872)

Power Rules

 Use **sentence fragments** only the way professional writers do. Never use them in formal or academic writing. Fix sentence fragments that occur before the sentence they refer to and ones that occur in the middle of a sentence. (See pages 662–667.)

Before Editing

After band practice. We can go to the park.

If the doorbell rings. Please see who's there.

After Editing

After band practice we can go to the park.

If the doorbell rings, please see who's there.

 Use only **one negative form** for a single negative idea. (See pages 777–778.)

Before Editing

For gardening, you shouldn't wear *nothing* you can't get dirty.

Our teacher *never* gave us *none* of those kinds of assignments.

After Editing

For gardening, you shouldn't wear *anything* you can't get dirty.

Our teacher *never* gave us *any* of those kinds of assignments.

Our teacher gave us *none* of those kinds of assignments.

Editing Checklist

Use this checklist when editing your writing.

✓ Did I underline or italicize words, numbers, or letters used to represent themselves? (See pages 860–862.)
✓ Did I underline or use italics correctly for the titles of longer works? (See pages 860–862.)
✓ Did I use quotation marks for titles of chapters, articles, stories, poems, and songs? (See pages 863–864.)
✓ Did I use quotation marks when quoting someone exactly? (See pages 864–865.)
✓ Did I capitalize the first word of a direct quote? (See page 866.)
✓ Did I use commas to separate speaker tags from quotes? (See page 867.)
✓ Did I put punctuation in the correct position inside or outside the quotation marks? (See pages 868–869.)
✓ Did I start a new paragraph when the speaker changed in a dialogue? (See page 870.)
✓ Did I use quotation marks in longer passages correctly? (See pages 871–872.)

Use the Power

Quotation marks are like the speech bubbles in cartoons. They show us what is being said. The speaker tags (*he said, she whispered, they yelled*) in writing are like the tails on the speech bubbles, connecting the words to the speaker.

Write a synopsis of a movie you enjoyed, integrating quotations from the film into your written text. Also share quotations from others who enjoyed the film as you present your own ideas.

CHAPTER 31

Other Punctuation

How can you use apostrophes, semicolons, colons, hyphens, and other punctuation to communicate precisely and to enhance your writing style?

Other Punctuation: Pretest 1

The following first draft about Francis Marion, pictured above on the right, contains errors in punctuation. The first error has been corrected. How would you edit the remaining sentences so that all punctuation is correct?

The American Revolution had many heroes. Francis Marion was one of them. After South Carolinas capture by the British, Marion and his band of men slipped away into the swamps. Marion had several elements that gave him an advantage over the British surprise, speed, and his men's knowledge of the swampy terrain. This often enabled Marions forces to defeat larger British forces. The ruthless British officer Banastre Tarleton couldnt capture him. It was Tarleton who first called Marion the "Swamp Fox" because Marion remained elusive despite being almost constantly hunted. Living off the land, Marion and his men moved easily amid the often dangerous Carolina swamps they left their hideout only to attack. They successfully sabotaged communication and supply lines, captured British soldiers, and rescued American prisoners. After these attacks Marion and his band vanished back into the swamps.

Other Punctuation: Pretest 2

Directions
Read the sentences and write the letter of the correct way to write each group of underlined words. If the underlined word or words contain no error, write **D**.

(1) This won't be your standard field trip we aren't going to the zoo or to a museum. (2) We're going on a scientists trip into the field. (3) Well study the coast redwood of California. (4) Lets pack a camera. (5) Bring the textbook, a tape measure, and a pen. (6) There are three kinds of redwoods the coast redwoods, the giant sequoias, and the dawn redwoods. (7) Your necks will be sore tomorrow the coast redwoods are tall! (8) In the 1930s, a 2,200-year-old coast redwood was logged, and its height was amazing.

1. **A** field-trip we aren't
   B field trip; we aren't
   C field trip-we aren't
   D No error

2. **A** scientists' trip
   B scientists trip:
   C scientists trip;
   D No error

3. **A** Well study the coast-redwood
   B Well study: the coast redwood
   C We'll study the coast redwood
   D No error

4. **A** Lets pack:
   B Lets pack;
   C Let's pack
   D No error

5. **A** text-book, a tape measure
   B textbook, a tape-measure
   C textbook, a tape measure;
   D No error

6. **A** redwoods: the coast
   B redwood's the coast
   C redwoods; the coast
   D No error

7. **A** be: sore tomorrow
   B be sore; tomorrow
   C be sore tomorrow;
   D No error

8. **A** it's height was
   B its height was:
   C its' height was
   D No error

Apostrophes Lesson 1

31 A Use an **apostrophe** (**'**) to show ownership and to represent missing letters in contractions. Also use it with certain plurals.

➤ Apostrophes to Show Possession

The most common use of apostrophes is to show that someone or something owns something else.

> Rick**'s** dinosaur book = the dinosaur book of Rick
> the dinosaurs**'** names = the names of the dinosaurs
> the cavemen**'s** fossils = the fossils of the cavemen

The Possessive Form of Singular Nouns

Before writing the possessive form of a singular noun, write just the noun itself. Then add an apostrophe and an *s*.

31 A.1 Add **'s** to form the possessive of a singular noun.

> Clemens + **'s** = Clemens**'s**   Samuel Clemens**'s** pen name is Mark Twain.
> Seth + **'s** = Seth**'s**   Is this Seth**'s** personal copy of *Tom Sawyer?*
> library + **'s** = library**'s**   It is the library**'s** copy.
> computer + **'s** = computer**'s**   The computer**'s** database shows one copy.
> shelf + **'s** = shelf**'s**   Find the shelf**'s** location.

● Practice Your Skills

Forming Possessive Singular Nouns

Rewrite each of the following phrases, using the possessive form.

1. the fields of the farmer
2. the tires of the bus
3. the whiskers of the cat
4. the skill of the typist
5. the role of the actor
6. muffins belonging to Sue

> ● **Connect to Writing: Drafting**
> **Using Apostrophes with Singular Possessive Nouns**
> Write three sentences, using five of the possessive phrases you formed in the preceding exercise.

The Possessive Forms of Plural Nouns

Most plural nouns end in *s*: *tomatoes, papers*. A few plural nouns, such as *children* and *mice*, do not end in *s*. The possessive form of a plural noun depends on its ending.

31 A.2 Add only an apostrophe to form the possessive of a plural noun that ends in *s*.

girls + **'** = girls**'**	The girls**'** book reports are due.
books + **'** = books**'**	The books**'** titles were similar.

31 A.3 Add **'**s to form the possessive of a plural noun that does not end in *s*.

men + **'**s = men**'**s	The men**'**s choice was a poem.
children + **'**s = children**'**s	It was "The Children**'**s Hour."

When you write the possessive of a plural noun, take two steps. First, write the plural of the noun. Second, look at the ending of the word. If the word ends in *s*, add only an apostrophe. If it does not end in *s*, add an apostrophe and an *s*.

FORMING THE POSSESSIVE OF NOUNS

Plural	Ending	Add	Possessive
teachers	s	**'**	teachers**'** lounge
lawyers	s	**'**	lawyers**'** office
women	no s	**'**s	women**'**s class
children	no s	**'**s	children**'**s toys

Do not use an apostrophe just to make a noun plural.

Incorrect	The **boys'** were improving their grades.
Correct	The **boys** were improving their grades.
Correct	The **boys'** grades were improving.

Practice Your Skills

Forming Possessive Plural Nouns

Rewrite each of the following phrases, using the possessive form.

1. playground of the children
2. feathers of the turkeys
3. lids of the boxes
4. mealtimes of the puppies
5. howls of the wolves
6. nest of the birds
7. migration of the geese
8. sizes of the shoes
9. suits of the women
10. claws of the tigers

Practice Your Skills

Forming Possessive Nouns

Rewrite each of the following phrases, using the correct possessive form. Notice that some nouns are singular and some are plural.

1. the ringing of the alarm clock
2. the rising of the sun
3. the aroma of the coffee
4. the crackling of cereal
5. the sounds of appliances
6. the yawns of slow risers
7. the arrival of the newspaper
8. the schedules of the buses
9. the conversations of the children
10. the laughter of the women

Connect to Writing: Narrative

Using Possessive Nouns

Write a paragraph describing a typical Saturday morning in your home. Use as many of the possessive phrases you formed in the preceding exercise as you can, but don't feel restricted by them. Rather, let these phrases be a jumping-off place for an entertaining and perceptive account of your Saturday morning routine.

● *Connect to Writing:* **Revising**

Replacing Phrases with Possessive Nouns

Rewrite each sentence, replacing the underlined phrases with possessive nouns.

1. The <u>desks of the students</u> await their arrival.
2. The <u>heat of the building</u> is turned on.
3. The <u>hands of the clock</u> inch toward eight o'clock.
4. The <u>coats of the girls</u> are hung up.
5. The <u>briefcases of the teachers</u> are opened.
6. The <u>music of the band</u> floats across the room.

Possessive Forms of Pronouns

Personal pronouns do not use an apostrophe to show possession the way nouns do. Instead, they change form.

POSSESSIVE PERSONAL PRONOUNS	
Singular	my, mine, your, yours, his, her, hers, its
Plural	our, ours, your, yours, their, theirs

31 A.4 Do not add an apostrophe to form the possessive of a personal pronoun.

Personal Pronouns
The book bag is **hers.**
The heat cracked **its** leather.
Our new books are still in the classroom.

Indefinite pronouns form the possessive by adding *'s* just the way singular nouns do.

COMMON INDEFINITE PRONOUNS	
Singular	anybody, anyone, each, either, everybody, everyone, neither, nobody, no one, one, somebody, someone
Plural	both, few, many, several

Apostrophes • Lesson 1

31 A.5 Add **'s** to form the possessive of an indefinite pronoun.

Indefinite Pronouns

This seems to be everyone**'s** library time.

Someone**'s** library assignment is on the floor.

Nobody**'s** books were turned in to the office.

● **Practice Your Skills**

Using Possessive Pronouns

Write **C** if the correct possessive form is used in a sentence. Write **I** if the incorrect form is used. Write the incorrect sentences correctly on a separate sheet of paper.

1. Everyone's report must include library research.
2. Is your's about computers?
3. Jason and I worked on our's together.
4. Its title is "Medical Miracles."
5. Does your report list all of your sources?
6. Is this library book hers'?
7. Is anyones report finished yet?
8. Hector finished his's on Monday.
9. Kayla and Erin have finished theirs, too.
10. I hope no one's grade depends on this one assignment.

● *Connect to Writing:* **Dialogue**

Using Possessive Nouns and Pronouns

Imagine that you are listening to a conversation between two friends who are discussing their favorite books. Write a brief dialogue between the characters. In your dialogue, use at least three possessive pronouns and three possessive nouns. Underline them.

✓ Check Point: Mixed Practice

Write the correct form of any incorrect possessive nouns and pronouns in the following sentences. If a sentence is correct, write **C**.

1. Eleanor Roosevelt was President Franklin Roosevelts' wife.
2. She took her job as the nation's first lady very seriously.
3. Mrs. Roosevelt visited battlefields and raised many soldiers spirits.
4. She visited coal miners and tried to improve they're lives.
5. Mrs. Roosevelt spoke up for womens' rights.
6. She also supported African Americans' rights.
7. Many ideas that the President suggested were actually her's.
8. She believed that doing useful work was everyone's responsibility.
9. After World War II, she helped the United Nations with its work on human rights.

Connect to Writing: Newspaper Article

Possessive Pronouns

Write an article for the school newspaper about one of the musical groups at your school. Describe the accomplishments of the whole group, as well as those of individual members. Use a variety of possessive nouns and pronouns in your article.

Apostrophes • Lesson 1

Apostrophes with Contractions

A contraction is formed by combining two or more words. An apostrophe replaces one or more missing letters.

31 A.6 Use an apostrophe in a contraction to show where one or more letters have been omitted.

The following examples show how some contractions are formed.

CONTRACTIONS	
does n~~o~~t = doesn'**t**	let ~~us~~ = let'**s**
he w~~oul~~d = he'**d**	that ~~i~~s = that'**s**
who ~~i~~s = who'**s**	~~of the~~ clock = o'**clock**

When a contraction is written, no letters should be added or moved around. There is one common exception to this rule: *will + not = won't.*

Contraction or Possessive Pronoun?

Do not confuse a contraction with a possessive pronoun.

Contractions it'**s** = it is, you'**re** = you are, they'**re** = they are

there'**s** = there is or there has

who'**s** = who is or who has

Possessives its (belonging to it)

your/yours (belonging to you)

their/theirs (belonging to them)

whose (belonging to whom)

When You Write

When you are writing and you are not sure whether to add an apostrophe, ask yourself if the word could be replaced with two individual words. If the answer is yes, use an apostrophe. If the answer is no, do not use an apostrophe.

It'**s** a lovely day. (*It's* could be replaced with *It is.* Use an apostrophe.)

Its tires were flat. (*Its* could not be replaced with *It is.* Do not use an apostrophe.)

Practice Your Skills

Forming Contractions

Write the contractions for each pair of words.

1. there is
2. would not
3. they are
4. will not
5. we have
6. were not
7. had not
8. who is
9. do not
10. are not
11. let us
12. you are
13. I have
14. I am
15. I will
16. it is

Practice Your Skills

Distinguishing Between Contractions and Possessive Pronouns

Write the correct word in parentheses.

1. (There's, Theirs) a snake!
2. Did (your, you're) science class ever study snakes?
3. That snake was once rattling (it's, its) tail.
4. (Who's, Whose) going to touch it?
5. I think (you're, your) interested in snakes.
6. (It's, Its) going to be an interesting class.
7. Did you see (they're, their) lab manual?
8. I don't know (who's, whose) rubber gloves these are.
9. (There's, Theirs) are on the table.
10. (They're, Their) starting (they're, their) experiment.

Connect to Speaking, Listening, and Writing: Peer Consultation

Using Contractions and Possessive Pronouns

With a small group, take turns reading each sentence below aloud. Then work together to decide how to correct any sentences that use incorrect contractions or possessive pronouns. Read the sentences again, this time spelling the word in question.

1. Whose picking you up after school today?
2. I hope your ready because your bus is here.
3. It's too late for them to check their lockers now.
4. Who's notebook is this?
5. There's a backpack on that desk.
6. It's zipper is broken.

Apostrophes with Certain Plurals

To prevent confusion, certain items form their plurals by adding **'s**.

31 A.7 Add **'s** to form the plural of lowercase letters, some capital letters, and some words used as words that people might otherwise misread.

Lowercase Letters Are these letters *i*'**s** or *e*'**s**?
(Without the apostrophe, you might misread *i*'s as the word *is*.)

Capital Letters How many *U*'**s** did you write?
(Without the apostrophe, you might misread *U*'s as the word *Us*.)

Words Used as Words That little girl uses a lot of *no*'**s** when she talks to her brothers.
(Without the apostrophe, you might think that *nos* was a word.)

The plurals of most other letters, symbols, numerals, dates, and words used as words can be formed by just adding *s*.

Capital Letters How many *B***s** did you get on your report card?

Symbols Don't use those *&***s** in your report.

Numerals Her *7***s** look like *9***s**.

Dates The Internet became very popular in the 1990**s**.

Words Used as Words Replace some of the *but***s** in your sentences.

Notice that each number, letter, symbol, and word used as a word is italicized (underlined), but the apostrophe and the *s* are not.

You can learn more about italics on pages 860–862.

● **Practice Your Skills**

Using Apostrophes

Write the plural form of each of the following letters, symbols, or words used as words.

1. a
2. c
3. B
4. I
5. +
6. #
7. 2
8. 1960
9. and
10. hi

● *Connect to Writing:* **Drafting**

Writing Sentences Using Plurals

Write five sentences using five of the plurals you formed in the preceding exercise.

✓ **Check Point:** **Mixed Practice**

Write the underlined word in each sentence correctly, adding an apostrophe where needed. If no apostrophe is needed, write **C**.

1. By the 1700s, both France and Great Britain were powerful nations.
2. In North America both nations wanted to make the colonies theirs.
3. Each side sought the Native Americans help.
4. Frances goal was to build trade in North America.
5. Great Britains objective was different.
6. It wanted to add territory to its empire.
7. The is were dotted in each treaty with the Native Americans.
8. Everyones life was changed in the colonies because of both European nations greed.
9. The mens lives were changed because they became soldiers.
10. Womens and childrens lives were changed because they didn't know whether their husbands and fathers were coming home.

Semicolons

31 B Use a **semicolon** (**;**) to separate independent clauses of a compound sentence and to avoid confusion in certain sentences.

➡ Semicolons with Compound Sentences

A **compound sentence** has two or more independent clauses. These clauses can be joined by a comma and a coordinating conjunction or by a semicolon. Coordinating conjunctions include *and, but, or,* and *yet*.

31 B.1 Use a semicolon between the clauses of a compound sentence that are not joined by a coordinating conjunction.

Comma and Conjunction	We went to Colorado, **and** everyone enjoyed the trip.
	My mom loved Pike's Peak, **but** my favorite place was Mesa Verde.
	I am going fishing on the lake, **yet** I'd prefer to go whitewater rafting on the Colorado River.
Semicolon	We went to Colorado; everyone enjoyed the trip.
	My mom loved Pike's Peak; my favorite place was Mesa Verde.
	I am going fishing on the lake; I'd prefer to go whitewater rafting on the Colorado River.

You can learn more about compound sentences on pages 647–650.

When You Write

When you edit your writing, look for sentences that are incorrectly joined by commas. Revise them by adding a semicolon or a coordinating conjunction.

Run-on	Mesa Verde has ancient Native American cliff houses, they are at least seven hundred years old.
Correct	Mesa Verde has ancient Native American cliff houses, **and** they are at least seven hundred years old.
Correct	Mesa Verde has ancient Native American cliff houses; they are at least seven hundred years old.

Look at a recent composition, and check to be sure you've used commas and semicolons correctly.

● **Practice Your Skills**

Using Commas and Semicolons with Compound Sentences

Write **C** if a sentence is punctuated correctly. Write **I** if a sentence is punctuated incorrectly.

1. Mesa Verde is located in southwestern Colorado, it is near the city of Cortez.
2. The Anasazi people built the cliff houses; some of the buildings are four stories high.
3. The Anasazi people lived at Mesa Verde for almost one hundred years, then the people disappeared from the area.
4. Centuries later the Ute Indians moved into the area, but they stayed away from the deserted cliff houses.
5. Spanish settlers explored the area; but they never saw the forsaken dwellings.
6. Two ranchers discovered the buildings in 1888 and in the 1890s, curious visitors flocked to the ancient settlement.
7. Many visitors stole precious souvenirs from the area, then an angry newspaper reporter complained.
8. In 1906, Congress decided to protect the ancient dwellings; it passed legislation that created Mesa Verde National Park.
9. The Cliff Palace is the park's most popular attraction, and we decided to take a tour of it.
10. Visitors to the Balcony House must climb a 32 foot ladder to get inside, I decided to try it.

● *Connect to Writing:* **Editing**

Punctuating Compound Sentences

Rewrite the incorrectly punctuated sentences from the preceding exercise, using commas and semicolons correctly.

● *Connect to Speaking and Listening:* **Peer Interaction**

Listening for Semicolons

One of the best ways to learn when to use a semicolon is to acquire an ear for its use. With a partner, practice reading some of the examples in this lesson. Then give each other pairs of closely related sentences to join with semicolons. Read your new sentences aloud, including the word *semicolon* where it appears: *I'm looking forward to studying Spanish [semicolon] this year I am going to do my best to become fluent in the language.*

Semicolons to Avoid Confusion

Occasionally a semicolon will be used in place of a comma to eliminate confusion in a sentence.

31 B.2   Use a semicolon instead of a comma between the clauses of a compound sentence if there are already commas within one of the clauses.

In the following sentences, a semicolon takes the place of a comma between the two independent clauses because the first clause already has commas in it. The semicolon is used even though a coordinating conjunction connects the clauses.

> Colombia, Brazil, and Ecuador are three nations in northern South America; and all three lie along the equator.
>
> All three countries have rain forests, lush, tropical areas crowded with tall, fast-growing trees; but Ecuador also has a cold, mountainous area.

When You Write

When you revise your writing, check long sentences to make sure they are not confusing. If necessary, break up some long compound sentences into simple sentences.

> Colombia, Brazil, and Ecuador are three nations in northern South America. All three lie along the equator.

31 B.3   Use a semicolon instead of a comma between the items in a series if the items contain commas.

In the examples below, semicolons take the place of the commas between the items in the series. Because the items themselves contain commas, the sentences would become confusing to read without the semicolons.

> The capitals of these nations are Quito, Ecuador; Bogotá, Colombia; and Brasília, Brazil.
>
> Other cities in Brazil include Sao Paulo, the largest city in South America; Rio de Janeiro, a popular beach resort; and Salvador, another city on the Atlantic coast.

You can learn more about items in a series on pages 835–839.

Practice Your Skills

Using Semicolons

Write **C** if a sentence is punctuated correctly. Write **I** if a sentence is punctuated incorrectly. Rewrite the incorrectly punctuated sentence using commas and semicolons correctly.

(1) South American nations include Chile, located on the South Pacific coast, Argentina, reaching down to the continent's tip, and Uruguay, located on the South Atlantic coast. **(2)** The three nations' capitals are Santiago, Chile, Buenos Aires, Argentina, and Montevideo, Uruguay. **(3)** Chile's population includes people of European, Indian, and other backgrounds; and its primary language is Spanish. **(4)** Chile's crops include wheat, corn, and grapes, but its main export is copper. **(5)** Argentina's major cities include Buenos Aires, with thirteen million people, Cordoba, with more than a million people, and Moron, with at least half a million people. **(6)** Languages spoken in Argentina include Spanish, English, Italian, German, and French; and most of the country's population is of the Roman Catholic faith. **(7)** Argentina exports meat, wheat, and corn; and it imports machinery, chemicals, fuel, and other industrial products. **(8)** Uruguay's major cities include Montevideo, Salto, and Paysandu, but Montevideo is much larger than any of the other cities.

Power Your Writing: Catch and Release

In the following passage from *Learning English: My New Found Land* (pages 35–37), Julia Alvarez uses the semicolon to combine (catch) and to separate (release) two independent clauses. She also uses the comma and parallel wording effectively to give the passage a rhythm and sense of urgency.

> I learned not to hear it as English, but as sense. I no longer strained to understand; I understood.

These sentences are related yet each can stand alone. Alvarez could have written:

> I learned not to hear it as English. I heard it as sense. I no longer strained to understand. I understood.

Instead, Alvarez uses a comma in the first sentence and a semicolon in the second, inviting the reader to become actively engaged in the reading and to experience her thought processes as they occurred.

Go back to a composition you have worked on recently. Revise two closely related sentences by using a semicolon.

Colons — Lesson 3

31 C Use a **colon** (:) before lists of items. Also use a colon between hours and minutes, between Biblical chapter and verse, and in the salutation of some letters.

31 C.1 Use a colon before most lists of items, especially when the list comes after an expression like *the following*.

Notice that commas go between the items in each series.

> We have packed the following items: first-aid kit, sunscreen lotion, and insect repellent.

A colon is not needed between a verb and its complements or directly after a preposition.

> **Incorrect**   Three hiking friends of mine are: Mary, Bob, and Tad.
> **Correct**   I have three hiking friends: Mary, Bob, and Tad.
> **Incorrect**   On our vacation we will be going to: Texas, Utah, and Idaho.
> **Correct**   On our vacation we will be going to the following states: Texas, Utah, and Idaho.

There are a few other special situations that also require a colon.

COLON USAGE	
Hours and Minutes	7:10 p.m. or 7:10 P.M.
Biblical Chapter and Verse	Matthew 7:7
Salutations in Business Letters	Dear Sir:

894 Other Punctuation

● **Practice Your Skills**

Using Colons

Write **C** if a sentence is punctuated correctly. Write **I** if a sentence is punctuated incorrectly. Rewrite each incorrect sentence using colons correctly.

1. Some popular vacations include the following luxury cruises, adventure trips, and European travel.
2. Travel agencies recommend three cruise destinations: Alaska, the Caribbean, and the Mediterranean.
3. Some popular cruise ships are the *Silver Cloud*, the *Wind Song*, and the *Whisper Spirit*.
4. The great thing about a cruise is that no one has to get up at 6 30 a.m.
5. Travel brochures offer the following adventures motorcycle trips in Costa Rica, polar bear viewing in Canada, or an island tour of Hawaii.
6. If you go on an adventure vacation, be sure to take a camera, sunscreen, insect repellent, and a first-aid kit.
7. There are three popular vacation cities in Europe Paris, London, and Amsterdam.
8. Travelers' favorite American cities include New York City, Orlando, and Las Vegas.
9. A South American vacation could include adventures in: Ecuador, Venezuela, Colombia, or Peru.
10. Dear Sir,
    Please send me the following forms A2, A12, B12, and B18.

● *Connect to Writing:* **Visitor's Guide and Letter**

Using Colons

Research facts about one of America's national parks. You can find a list on the Internet. Write a visitor's guide to the park. Include interesting information about the park's history and attractions and items people might want to bring along when visiting the park. Then write a letter to a magazine offering your guide for publication. Use a colon for your salutation.

✓ Check Point: Mixed Practice

Rewrite each sentence, using commas, semicolons, and colons correctly. If a sentence is correct, write **C**.

1. Meriwether Lewis and William Clark were important explorers, they opened up the West for expansion.
2. Their expedition set off from St. Louis, Missouri, in the spring of 1804, and they reached the Pacific Ocean in November of 1805.
3. The long trip was a success, and President Jefferson was delighted with their discoveries.
4. The two adventurers collected information on the following the people, plants, animals, and geography of the West.
5. Their crew included: soldiers, interpreters, and one slave.
6. The list of obstacles was endless: rivers, mountains, weather, and animals.
7. In a village in North Dakota, they met a Shoshone Indian woman named Sacagawea, she became their guide.
8. Sacagawea knew the land and the local tribes; and her knowledge saved the expedition.
9. Lewis and Clark explored: the Missouri River, the Columbia River, and the Snake River.
10. Afterward, they returned to the East and reported on the wonders they had seen; their reports inspired settlers to move farther westward.

● *Connect to Writing:* Descriptive Paragraph

Using Apostrophes, Semicolons, and Colons

Your class took a field trip to an art museum, but your best friend was unable to go. You saw the image below while there, and you want to describe it to your friend. Write a paragraph that uses descriptive phrases as well as apostrophes, semicolons, and colons to help create the image in your friend's mind.

Hyphens — Lesson 4

31 D Use a **hyphen** (-) to divide a word and to separate certain numbers, fractions, and compound nouns.

You will use hyphens most often to divide a word at the end of a line. Avoid dividing words if possible because doing so can slow a reader down or cause misunderstanding. When you must divide a word to keep your margin, divide the word at the proper place using a hyphen.

31 D.1 Use a hyphen to divide a word at the end of a line.

The following guidelines show how to divide a word at the end of a line. If you are not certain about where each syllable in a word ends, look the word up in a dictionary. Each entry word is divided into syllables.

GUIDELINES FOR DIVIDING WORDS

1. Divide words only between syllables.
gym·nas·tics: gym-nastics or gymnas-tics

2. Never divide a one-syllable word.
DO NOT BREAK   stay   laugh   called

3. Do not divide a word so that one letter stands alone.
DO NOT BREAK   a·round   e·mit   o·bey   sleep·y

4. Divide hyphenated words only after the hyphens.
brother-in-law   face-to-face   maid-of-honor

● **Practice Your Skills**

Using Hyphens

Write each word, adding a hyphen or hyphens to show where it can be correctly divided. If a word should not be divided, write **NO** after the word.

1. hamster
2. among
3. galaxy
4. make
5. about
6. liquid
7. item
8. single
9. surprise
10. strong
11. captain
12. build
13. action
14. opal
15. trespass

● **_Connect to Writing:_ Editing**

Correcting Sentences with Hyphens

Rewrite the following paragraphs, correcting the use of hyphens wherever they are misused. If a word can be hyphenated, move the hyphen to an appropriate place. If a word cannot be hyphenated, write it as one word.

> Jonas Salk was a scient-ist who studied bacteria at the U-niversity of Pittsburgh. In 1955, he made a discovery that changed the wor-ld. He had made a vaccine that could protect children from a disea-se called polio.
>
> In the early 1900s, polio had cri-ppled or killed nearly a million Americ-ans. Salk's vaccine was soon being give-n to America's children as an injec-tion. It was very effective, but soon an e-ven better polio vaccine was discovered. A scientist named Albert Sabin created a poli-o vaccine that children could take oral-ly. Now children can be protected from polio without even having a shot.

➤ Other Uses of Hyphens

Although used most often to divide words, a hyphen has other uses.

Hyphens with Certain Numbers

When you write numbers out in a story or report, use a hyphen to spell most numbers correctly.

31 D.2   Use a hyphen when writing out the numbers *twenty-one* through *ninety-nine*.

> They counted fifty-six rooms in the school.
> Twenty-one rooms in the school have computers.

If a number is the first word of a sentence, it must always be written out.

Hyphens with Certain Fractions

Fractions used as adjectives are hyphenated.

31 D.3 Use a hyphen when writing out a fraction used as an adjective.

Hyphen	A **three-fourths** majority of the teachers did not have computers in school.
	(*Three-fourths* is an adjective that describes *majority*.)
No Hyphen	**Three fourths** of the class is computer literate.
	(The noun *three fourths* is the subject.)
Hyphen	A **two-thirds** vote by the school board approved the purchase of new computers.
No Hyphen	**Two thirds** of their computers are old.

You can learn more about adjectives on pages 538–546 and 766–785.

Hyphens with Some Compound Nouns

A **compound noun** is a noun made up of two or more words. The words in a compound noun may be written in one of three ways: (1) together, as one word; (2) as two separate words; or (3) as two words joined with a hyphen.

31 D.4 Use a hyphen to separate the parts of some compound nouns.

COMPOUND NOUNS	
One Word	handbook, housewife, toothache, northeast
Two Words	coffee table, home run, dream world
Hyphenated	tractor-trailer, cross-country, drive-in

If you are unsure of the spelling of a compound noun, check it in a dictionary.

You can learn more about compound nouns on pages 506–507 and 918.

● **Practice Your Skills**

Using Hyphens

Write **C** if a sentence is punctuated correctly. Write *I* if a sentence is punctuated incorrectly. Write the incorrect sentences correctly on a separate sheet of paper.

1. The student council met in the home economics room yesterday afternoon.
2. Twenty two students attended the meeting.
3. Three fourths of the members answered the roll.
4. Four-teen members offered suggestions from the student body.
5. Many suggestions were about improving school lunches by offering more hamburgers, hot-dogs, and french-fries.
6. The secretary wrote minutes in her note-book.
7. A motion was made to spend thirty-three dollars for decorations for the homecoming dance.
8. The motion passed with a three fourths majority.
9. One-fourth of the council voted against the idea.
10. At the end of the meeting, the members posed for their yearbook picture.

● *Connect to Writing:* **Meeting Report**

Using Hyphens

Write a brief hand-written report about an imaginary meeting of the Interstellar Brainstorming Club. Describe who attended, what was discussed, what votes were taken, and the results of the votes. Use hyphens where needed.

✓ **Check Point:** **Mixed Practice**

Rewrite each sentence, adding apostrophes, semicolons, colons, and hyphens where needed.

1. Todays school lunch includes the following turkey, green beans, mashed potatoes, apple pie, and milk.
2. Good nutrition is vital to a teenagers health and well being.
3. One third of the student body does not eat the meal offered in our schools lunchroom.
4. Everyones appetite is different, but balanced nutrition is important to success in school.
5. Some students eat only "junk food" cake, candy, and soda.

Chapter Review

Assess Your Learning

Punctuating Correctly

Write each sentence, adding apostrophes, semicolons, colons, and hyphens where needed.

1. Pineapples are not native to Hawaii they were first planted there in 1790.
2. A mosquitos wings can move 1,000 times a second.
3. Well meet you for lunch at 1230.
4. New York Citys population is greater than that of the following countries Denmark, Austria, and Norway.
5. Six photographers studios are on the sixth floor.
6. Thirty six members were present at the meeting.
7. I cant believe this mess is yours!
8. Texas has 154 counties Alaska has none.
9. Why isnt Mr. Browns dog inside tonight?
10. I have lived in Pittsburgh, Pennsylvania Orlando, Florida and San Francisco, California.

Using Punctuation

Write each sentence, adding apostrophes, semicolons, colons, and hyphens where needed.

1. Are there more *a*s or *i*s in your name?
2. Eighty four people entered the contest.
3. That brand of mens sweaters runs small.
4. There are three small eyes on top of a bees head two larger ones are in the front.
5. In 1841, the United States had three presidents Martin Van Buren, William Harrison, and John Tyler.

Punctuating Correctly

Write each sentence, adding apostrophes, semicolons, colons, and hyphens where needed. If a sentence needs no change, write **C**.

1. The sun is an average star it is not a huge one.
2. Because its so close to Earth, the sun seems much brighter than other stars.
3. Seventy five percent of the sun consists of hydrogen.
4. The suns interior temperature is about 27 million degrees Fahrenheit.
5. Its energy comes from nuclear reactions.
6. The following are all caused by the suns energy plant growth, ocean currents, and tides.
7. Without the sun there wouldnt be any life on Earth.
8. The sun is the center of the solar system there are eight planets orbiting the sun.
9. The planets orbits are determined by gravity.
10. The sun rotates on its axis each rotation takes a month.

Using Punctuation Marks

Write sentences that follow the directions below.

Write a sentence that ...

1. includes the possessive form of the noun *dog*.
2. includes the possessive form of the noun *friends*.
3. includes the possessive form of the noun *women*.
4. includes the possessive form of the pronoun *someone*.
5. includes the words *they're* and *their*.
6. includes the plural of *yes*.
7. includes two independent clauses joined by only a semicolon.
8. includes *two thirds* as an adjective.

Other Punctuation: Posttest

Directions
Read the passage and write the letter of the correct way to write each group of underlined words. If the underlined word or words need no change, write **D.**

People use many activities to **(1)** stay healthy jogging, aerobics, or rollerblading. One activity predates the **(2)** Western worlds interest in **(3)** fitness and is referred to as an *art*—the martial arts.

(4) Peoples misconceptions about the martial arts are surprising to me. For people **(5)** who devote a lifetime to a martial art, it's not about **(6)** violence the goal is not to hurt others. **(7)** The *do*s at the end of *judo* and *aikido* mean "the way" **(8)** to the following goals enlightenment, self-realization, and understanding. **(9)** Students goals should be to train their minds and energize their bodies. This focus **(10)** lets students connect with the true spirit of martial arts.

1. **A** stay: healthy
   B stay healthy:
   C stay healthy;
   D No error

2. **A** Western world's interest
   B Western worlds' interest
   C Western-worlds interest
   D No error

3. **A** fitness: and
   B fitness; and
   C fitness-and
   D No error

4. **A** Peoples' misconceptions
   B People's misconceptions
   C Peoples misconception's
   D No error

5. **A** who devote a lifetime:
   B who de-vote a lifetime
   C who devote a life-time
   D No error

6. **A** violence the goal is:
   B violence; the goal is
   C violence the goal is;
   D No error

7. **A** The *do's* at the end
   B The *dos* at the end;
   C The *do-s* at the end
   D No error

8. **A** to: the following goals
   B to the following goals;
   C to the following goals:
   D No error

9. **A** Students' goals should be
   B Student's goals should be
   C Students goals should be:
   D No error

10. **A** let's students connect
    B lets student's connect
    C lets students connect:
    D No error

Writer's Corner

Snapshot

31 A Use an **apostrophe** (') to show ownership and to represent missing letters in contractions. Also use it with certain plurals. (pages 880–889)

31 B Use a **semicolon** (;) to separate independent clauses of a compound sentence and to avoid confusion in certain sentences. (pages 890–893)

31 C Use a **colon** (:) before lists of items. A colon is also used between hours and minutes, between Biblical chapter and verse, and in the salutation of some letters. (pages 894–896)

31 D Use a **hyphen** (-) to divide a word and to separate certain numbers, fractions, and compound nouns. (pages 897–900)

Power Rules

 Use standard ways to make nouns possessive. (pages 880–882)

Before Editing	**After Editing**
I need the *teachers* advice on this.	I need the *teacher's* advice on this.
Is that *Charles'* book?	Is that *Charles's* book?
How many *states's* capitals can you name?	How many *states'* capitals can you name?

 A **semicolon** can be used to separate sentences in a run-on sentence. (pages 669–670)

Before Editing	**After Editing**
We'll be home tomorrow night, I can't wait to sleep in my own bed.	We'll be home tomorrow night; I can't wait to sleep in my own bed.

Editing Checklist

Use this checklist when editing your writing.

- ✓ Did I create possessive forms correctly? (See pages 880–885.)
- ✓ Did I use apostrophes to replace missing letters in contractions? (See pages 886–887.)
- ✓ Did I use semicolons to connect related sentences? (See pages 890–891.)
- ✓ Did I use semicolons to connect clauses that contain commas? (See pages 892–893.)
- ✓ Did I correctly use colons before lists of items? (See pages 894–896.)
- ✓ Did I use colons correctly when showing time, writing letters, or noting Biblical passages? (See pages 894–896.)
- ✓ Did I use hyphens to divide a word at the end of a line? (See pages 897–898.)
- ✓ Did I use hyphens correctly in numbers, fractions, and compound nouns? (See pages 898–900.)

Use the Power

Apostrophes show where one or more letters have been omitted in a contraction. If letters are removed from more than one place—for example, both the beginning and end of a word—there needs to be an apostrophe in each place. But if letters are removed from only one place, even if it's many letters, you need only one apostrophe.

Write a poem about the apostrophe using as many words with apostrophes as you can conjure up.

CHAPTER 32

Spelling Correctly

How can you communicate your message effectively by using accurate spelling?

Spelling Correctly: Pretest 1

The first draft below contains spelling errors. The first error has been corrected. How would you edit the draft so that all words are spelled correctly?

    I ~~beleive~~ *believe* my school is the best one in the state. That's a good thing because we spend half our lives here. We lern important lessons that will help us secseed once we have graduated. Their are lessins about history, which help you understand the world. Math is good four just about everything. We study wrihting and spelling so we can communicate well. We also have clubs, where we can join with others who share our hobbys. There are so many ways we can develop ourselfs. The teachers are mostly likable, and many have a lot of wisedom to share. Our sports teams are often wining, but even when there not, we learn sportsmanship. Its a good place to be.

Spelling Correctly: Pretest 2

Directions
Read the passage and write the letter of the choice that correctly respells each underlined word. If the underlined word needs no change, write **D**.

Camping combines work and **(1)** plesure. It is **(2)** usefull to know how to pitch a tent and how to cook outdoors. It takes teamwork to pitch a tent **(3)** successfully. Meal **(4)** preperation requires menu planning, cooking, and cleaning. **(5)** Divideing the work leaves time for fun. Campgrounds have a **(6)** variety of activities. **(7)** Swiming pools are common. The nature trail provides **(8)** peaceful scenery. A sharp eye **(9)** usually reveals insects, birds, and animals. At day's end, campers gather with **(10)** egerness around a roaring campfire.

1. **A** pleasure
   B pleasyre
   C pleassure
   D No error

2. **A** yousful
   B usful
   C useful
   D No error

3. **A** sucessfully
   B sucesfully
   C successfuly
   D No error

4. **A** preparation
   B preperration
   C preparashun
   D No error

5. **A** Deviding
   B Dividing
   C Dividding
   D No error

6. **A** vareity
   B veriety
   C varietie
   D No error

7. **A** Swimming
   B Sweming
   C Swimmin
   D No error

8. **A** peacefull
   B peaseful
   C peacful
   D No error

9. **A** usualy
   B usualie
   C useally
   D No error

10. **A** eagrness
    B eagernes
    C eagerness
    D No error

Strategies for Learning to Spell

Your senses of hearing, sight, and touch help you learn to spell words correctly. Many people successfully spell unfamiliar words by using the following five-step strategy.

1 Auditory

Say the word aloud. Answer these questions.

- Where have I heard or read the word before?
- What was the context in which I heard or read the word?

2 Visual

Look at the word. Answer these questions.

- Does this word divide into parts? Is it a compound word? Does it have a prefix or a suffix?
- Does this word look like any other word I know? Could it be part of a word family I would recognize?

3 Auditory

Spell the word to yourself. Answer these questions.

- How is each sound spelled?
- Are there any surprises? Does the word follow spelling rules I know, or does it break the rules?

4 Visual/Kinesthetic

Write the word as you look at it. Answer these questions.

- Have I written the word clearly?
- Are my letters formed correctly?

5 Visual/Kinesthetic

Cover up the word. Visualize it. Write it. Answer this question.

- Did I write the word correctly?

If the answer is no, return to step 1.

Spelling Strategies

Spelling errors are distracting and confusing. Readers may not be able to understand what you've written, or they may just give up if spelling errors make reading difficult. Making sure that your writing is free of spelling errors takes just a few extra minutes and makes a world of difference. Use these strategies to check for spelling mistakes.

Use a dictionary. If you are not sure how to spell a word, check its spelling in a dictionary. If good spelling doesn't come easily to you, you can make up for it by keeping a dictionary close at hand and using it automatically.

Proofread your writing carefully. It is often easiest to look for one kind of error at a time. Use your computer's spell-checking program by all means, but be aware that it doesn't catch everything, such as misspelling *which* as *witch*.

Be sure you are pronouncing words correctly. "Swallowing" syllables or adding extra syllables can cause you to misspell a word.

Make up mnemonic devices. A sentence like "**Je**nnie **wel**comed **Ry**an's ring" can help you remember how to spell *jewelry*. (Using a dictionary or word list makes it easier to create your own mnemonics.) Also, look for memorable spelling patterns: "It's a *coincidence* that three *c + vowel* combinations appear in *coincidence* and that the vowels are in reverse alphabetical order—*o, i,* and *e*!"

Keep a spelling journal. Use a journal to record the words you have had trouble spelling. Here are some suggestions for organizing your spelling journal.

- Write the word correctly.
- Write the word again, underlining the part of the word that gives you trouble.
- Write a tip that will help you remember how to spell the word in the future.

dessert	de**ss**ert	The de**ss**ert you eat has 2 *s*'s in it—just like **s**trawberry **s**hortcake!
knowledge	knowl**edge**	If I want to gain an **edge** in the job market, I need to invest in knowl**edge**.
gnaw	**gn**aw	The **gn**u at the zoo likes to **gn**aw on its food.

Practice Your Skills

Recognizing Misspelled Words

Write the letter of the misspelled word in each set. Then write the word correctly.

1. (a) disease   (b) benifits   (c) height
2. (a) vegetable   (b) grammar   (c) exsercise
3. (a) seize   (b) allready   (c) similar
4. (a) scenrey   (b) acquire   (c) visible
5. (a) lovable   (b) interrupt   (c) embarass
6. (a) pursue   (b) excape   (c) fascinate
7. (a) reccommend   (b) emigrate   (c) heroes
8. (a) opinion   (b) existance   (c) license
9. (a) occassion   (b) debtor   (c) sincerely
10. (a) seperate   (b) eighth   (c) definite

Practice Your Skills

Pronouncing Words

Practice saying each syllable in the following words to help you spell the words correctly.

1. pos•si•bil•i•ty
2. ab•bre•vi•ate
3. a•lu•mi•num
4. per•spire
5. in•ter•est•ing
6. co•in•ci•dence
7. soph•o•more
8. jew•el•ry
9. car•a•mel
10. par•tic•u•lar

When You Write

When you're creating a draft, try to spell words correctly, just so you don't reinforce incorrect spelling. If the ideas are flowing, and you don't want to stop to pick up the dictionary, underline or circle a word of which you are unsure. You can then go back to check it later. While a computer with a spell-checking program is helpful, always check a dictionary as well (the computer may have one built in). Make sure that the spelling the computer suggests is for the word you really wanted to use. Words that are different by one or two letters can have vastly different meanings. For example, *tortuous* means "with many turns or bends; complex," while *torturous* means "causing severe physical pain." That *r* makes a big difference.

Spelling Correctly

Spelling Patterns — Lesson 1

The English language contains at least 500,000 words. If you tried to memorize the spellings of 10 words a day, it would take you more than 130 years to memorize them all! A far easier way to become a good speller is to learn spelling generalizations and to look for patterns in the words you use most often.

32 A Some spelling generalizations are based on the **patterns of letters** in words. You can find certain common patterns in words spelled with *ie* or *ei* and in words that end with the *seed* sound.

Words with *ie* and *ei*

Many generations of students have used the following rhyme to help them spell words with *ie* and *ei*.

> Write *i* before *e*
> Except after *c*
> Or when the sound is long *a*
> As in *neighbor* and *weigh*.

32 A.1 When you spell words with *ie* or *ei*, *i* comes before *e* except when the letters follow *c* or when they stand for the long *a* sound.

IE AND EI				
I Before E	believe	mischief	niece	piece	thief
Except After C	ceiling	conceit	deceive	perceive	receive
Sounds Like A	eight	freight	sleigh	veil	weight

These words do not follow the pattern.

EXCEPTIONS					
ancient	either	height	neither	seize	their
conscience	foreign	leisure	protein	species	weird

WORD ALERT

Unfortunately, sometimes there are a lot of exceptions to a generalization. To make them easier to remember, create a mnemonic sentence using words with the same spelling. For example, if you know how to spell *their*, you can spell every word in this sentence.

The for**ei**gn h**ei**rs must s**ei**ze the sh**ei**kdom or forf**ei**t th**ei**r claims.

Words Ending in *–cede*, *–ceed*, and *–sede*

Some other words that cause problems are those that end with a "seed" sound. This sound can be spelled *–cede*, *–ceed*, or *–sede*. By far the greatest number of words that end with this sound are spelled with *–cede*.

32 A.2 In all but four words that end with the "seed" sound, this sound is spelled *–cede*.

–CEDE				
Examples	precede	recede	concede	intercede

You'll have no trouble spelling these words if you memorize the four exceptions.

EXCEPTIONS			
exceed	proceed	succeed	supersede

● Practice Your Skills

Using Spelling Patterns

Write each word correctly, adding *ie* or *ei*.

1. r☐ndeer
2. ach☐ve
3. rel☐ve
4. anc☐nt
5. n☐ghbor
6. v☐n
7. w☐rd
8. th☐r
9. f☐ld
10. w☐gh
11. f☐rce
12. conc☐t
13. s☐ve
14. l☐sure
15. n☐ther
16. h☐ght
17. dec☐t
18. ☐ther
19. p☐ce
20. s☐ze
21. th☐f
22. bel☐f
23. ☐ghteen
24. s☐smic
25. fr☐nd
26. v☐l

912 Spelling Correctly

Practice Your Skills

Using Spelling Patterns

Write each word correctly, adding *–sede, –ceed,* or *–cede.*

1. re
2. ex
3. ac
4. se
5. suc
6. con
7. pre
8. pro
9. super
10. inter

Connect to Writing: Editing

Using Spelling Patterns

Find and rewrite the nine words that have been spelled incorrectly.

In medeval times wealthy lords often made war against one another over small greivances or to acquire their nieghbor's property. Outright theivery did not bother some if they thought they could succede in adding to their wealth. Most nobles had so few trained soldiers that they did not wage war on the battlefield. Instead, the attacker proceded to surround the castle with the knights and peasants who owed allegience to him. They shot arrows and lobbed rocks over the wall to persuade their enemies to yeild. However, what usually caused one side to conceed defeat was a lack of food.

Spelling Patterns • Lesson 1

Plurals — Lesson 2

32 B A few generalizations will help you spell the **plurals** of nouns correctly. When you're in doubt about an exception, look up the word in a dictionary.

Regular Nouns

32 B.1 To form the plural of most nouns, simply add *s*.

MOST NOUNS				
Singular	computer	book	bath	plane
Plural	computers	books	baths	planes

32 B.2 If a noun ends in *s, ch, sh, x,* or *z*, add *es* to form the plural.

S, CH, SH, X, OR Z				
Singular	boss	match	dash	box	blitz
Plural	bosses	matches	dashes	boxes	blitzes

Follow the same generalizations when you write the plural forms of proper nouns.

- the Lynch family = the Lynch**es**
- the Martinez family = the Martinez**es**

The apostrophe is never used to make the plural form of proper nouns. It is used only to show possession.

You can learn about using the apostrophe with nouns on pages 880–883.

Nouns Ending in *y*

32 B.3 Add *s* to form the plural of a noun ending in a vowel and *y*.

VOWELS AND Y				
Singular	boy	tray	buoy	valley
Plural	boys	trays	buoys	valleys

Spelling Correctly

32 B.4 Change the *y* to *i* and add *es* to a noun ending in a consonant and *y*.

CONSONANTS AND Y				
Singular	li**ly**	hob**by**	dia**ry**	courte**sy**
Plural	li**lies**	hob**bies**	dia**ries**	courte**sies**

● **Practice Your Skills**

Forming Plurals

Write the plural form of each noun.

1. berry
2. radish
3. fox
4. day
5. kiss
6. maze
7. topaz
8. ash
9. cross
10. company
11. tax
12. anxiety
13. stick
14. stitch
15. volley
16. discovery
17. whisper
18. century
19. speech
20. Harris

● *Connect to Writing:* **Editing**

Spelling Plural Nouns

Rewrite this paragraph, changing the underlined nouns from singular to plural.

From rolling field to woodland valley, red fox make their homes in most parts of North America. These shy creatures have body that are about thirty-six inch long and weigh ten to fifteen pound. All red fox have white-tipped brush, or tails, and black leg, but their coat may be different color. There are yellowish-red fox with white belly, black one with white-tipped fur, and red one with black cross on their back. All three variation may be seen among the baby in a single litter.

Nouns Ending in *o*

32 B.5 Add *s* to form the plural of a noun ending with a vowel and *o*.

VOWELS AND O				
Singular	ratio	video	shampoo	igloo
Plural	ratios	videos	shampoos	igloos

Plurals • Lesson 2

32 B.6 Add *s* to form the plural of musical terms ending in *o*.

MUSICAL TERMS ENDING WITH *O*				
Singular	alto	cello	piano	crescendo
Plural	altos	cellos	pianos	crescendos

32 B.7 Add *s* to form the plural of words that were borrowed from the Spanish language.

SPANISH WORDS WITH *O*				
Singular	burro	burrito	pueblo	patio
Plural	burros	burritos	pueblos	patios

32 B.8 The plurals of nouns ending in a consonant and *o* do not follow a regular pattern.

CONSONANTS AND *O*				
Singular	auto	rhino	tomato	motto
Plural	autos	rhinos	tomato**es**	motto**es**

When you are not sure how to form the plural of a word that ends in *o*, consult a dictionary. Sometimes you will find that either spelling is acceptable. In these cases, use the first form given. If the dictionary does not give a plural form, the plural is usually formed by adding *s*.

Nouns Ending in *f* or *fe*

32 B.9 To form the plural of some nouns ending in *f* or *fe*, just add *s*.

F AND *FE*				
Singular	chief	gulf	safe	giraffe
Plural	chiefs	gulfs	safes	giraffes

32 B.10 For some nouns ending in *f* or *fe*, change the *f* to *v* and add *es*.

F AND *FE* TO *V*				
Singular	half	self	life	knife
Plural	halves	selves	lives	knives

Because there is no way to tell which generalization applies, consult a dictionary for plural forms of words that end in *f* or *fe*.

WORD ALERT

Watch out! Your computer spell-check will not inform you that you have misspelled the plurals of some nouns. That's because they can also be used as verbs. For example, someone *loafs* around or bakes *loaves* of bread.

● **Practice Your Skills**

Forming Plurals

Write the plural form of each noun. Check a dictionary to be sure you have formed the plural correctly.

1. potato
2. café
3. echo
4. whiff
5. hero
6. leaf
7. cameo
8. scruff
9. studio
10. belief
11. cello
12. wolf
13. wife
14. sheriff
15. bronco
16. tattoo
17. handkerchief
18. radio
19. hoof
20. soprano

● *Connect to Writing:* **Editing**

Spelling Plural Nouns

Rewrite this paragraph, changing the underlined nouns to plural from singular.

Have you seen any of the **(1)** video of the State Championship **(2)** Cook-off? I watched the one in which the **(3)** chef had to create main courses using local produce like **(4)** tomato and **(5)** avocado. They had many **(6)** shelf full of fresh vegetables and other **(7)** foodstuff to work with. One creatively made some hen-shaped **(8)** meatloaf surrounded by potato **(9)** puff in a nest of cabbage **(10)** leaf. Another made delicious-looking **(11)** taco that had chopped-up **(12)** potato in them.

Plurals • Lesson 2

Compound Words

Most compound nouns are made plural in the same way as other nouns, by adding an *s* or *es* at the end. However, sometimes it makes more sense to add the ending to the first word in the compound.

32 B.11 The letters *s* or *es* are added to the end of most compound nouns to make them plural.

MOST COMPOUND NOUNS				
Singular	classmate	headdress	flare-up	wristwatch
Plural	classmate**s**	headdress**es**	flare-up**s**	wristwatch**es**

32 B.12 When the main word in a compound noun appears first, that word is made plural.

COMPOUND NOUN EXCEPTIONS			
Singular	sister-in-law	runner-up	standard of living
Plural	sister**s**-in-law	runner**s**-up	standard**s** of living

Numerals, Letters, Symbols, and Words as Words

32 B.13 To form the plurals of many numerals, letters, symbols, and words used as words, add an *s*.

> Are those *G***s** or *6***s**?
>
> The Great Depression occurred during the early 1930**s**.
>
> Good writers use *!***s** very seldom.
>
> She wanted to know the *why***s** and *wherefore***s**.

To prevent confusion, it's best to use an apostrophe and *s* with lowercase letters, some capital letters, and some words used as words. When you use this method to create the plural of italicized letters or words, you do not italicize the apostrophe and *s*.

> The *y***'s** in old English writing stand for the *th* sound.
>
> The arches were like upside-down *U***'s**.
>
> There are too many *so***'s** in this paragraph.

You can learn about the use of italics on pages 860–862.

Practice Your Skills

Forming Plurals

Write the plural form of each noun.

1. *9*
2. *1900*
3. take-off
4. *o*
5. right-of-way
6. cost of living
7. bowling alley
8. *G*
9. *'20*
10. lookout
11. *!*
12. *yes* and *no*
13. brother-in-law
14. ooh and ah
15. prisoner of war
16. hand-me-down
17. queen of hearts
18. commander in chief
19. boot camp
20. coat of arms

Connect to Writing: Editing

Spelling Plural Nouns

Rewrite each sentence, changing the underlined items from singular to plural.

1. Chiffoniers are <u>chest of drawers</u>.
2. Don't forget to dot your *i*.
3. The Enlightenment refers to the <u>1600</u> and <u>1700</u>.
4. We prefer the word *menu* to *bill of fare*.
5. When the British make *naught*, they are making *0*.
6. <u>Man-of-war</u> are ships, not soldiers.
7. Some <u>lily-of-the-valley</u> are known as *convallaria*.
8. Do you have any <u>brother-in-law</u>?
9. <u>Curtain-raiser</u> are short plays.
10. Who are your first <u>cousin once removed</u>?

Other Plural Forms

32 B.14 Irregular plurals are not formed by adding *s* or *es*.

IRREGULAR PLURALS		
tooth, t**eeth**	man, m**en**	ox, ox**en**
foot, f**eet**	woman, w**omen**	child, child**ren**
goose, g**eese**	mouse, m**ice**	person, pe**ople**

32 B.15 Some nouns have the same form for singular and plural.

SAME FORM SINGULAR AND PLURAL			
Chinese	sheep	scissors	Portuguese
moose	headquarters	politics	surf
Swiss	salmon	series	corps

● **Practice Your Skills**

Forming Plurals

Write the plural form of each noun.

1. clergywoman
2. webfoot
3. field mouse
4. Japanese
5. shorts
6. Canada goose
7. countryman
8. news
9. catfish
10. mail
11. childhood
12. clothing
13. ox
14. rabies
15. moose
16. knowledge
17. canine tooth
18. pliers
19. child
20. Canadian

● *Connect to Writing:* **Editing**

Spelling Plural Nouns

Rewrite each sentence, changing the underlined items to plurals.

1. New England blue plate specials often feature <u>shrimp</u> or <u>codfish</u>.
2. Blue-collar <u>worker</u> got that name because <u>man</u> who did hard labor often wore blue shirts.
3. The <u>child</u> of <u>royalty</u> were "born to the purple."
4. Family <u>member</u> who don't conform may be called black <u>sheep</u>.
5. Blue <u>doe</u> are not <u>deer</u> but female <u>kangaroo</u>.
6. Indigo <u>snake</u> are black and may grow to nearly nine <u>foot</u> long.

Check Point: **Mixed Practice**

Write *a* or *b* to indicate the letter of the word that is spelled correctly in each of the following pairs.

1. a. cieling
   b. ceiling
2. a. height
   b. hieght
3. a. weird
   b. wierd
4. a. dishs
   b. dishes
5. a. canarys
   b. canaries
6. a. radioes
   b. radios
7. a. knives
   b. knifes
8. a. mouses
   b. mice
9. a. teeth
   b. teeths
10. a. sheeps
    b. sheep

Prefixes and Suffixes

32 C A **prefix** is placed in front of a base word to form a new word. A **suffix** is placed after a base word to create a new word.

When you add a prefix, the base word does not change. The new word has a different meaning.

PREFIXES

in + complete = **in**complete	**im** + possible = **im**possible
pre + judge = **pre**judge	**over** + rule = **over**rule
dis + obey = **dis**obey	**mis** + step = **mis**step
re + appear = **re**appear	**un** + natural = **un**natural
ir + regular = **ir**regular	**il** + literate = **il**literate

In a few cases, you must add a hyphen after a prefix to avoid confusing your reader, as when the prefix ends with the same letter the word begins with. Check a dictionary if you are in doubt.

WORDS WITH HYPHENATED PREFIXES

anti-intellectual	**semi**-independent	**re**-evaluate

WORD ALERT

You will never misspell *misspell* if you do not change the base word when you add a prefix. Words like *misshapen, dissatisfy, illogical,* and *irresponsible* should be easier to spell too.

A **suffix** is one or more syllables placed after a base word to change its part of speech and possibly also its meaning. In many cases, especially when the base word ends in a consonant, you simply add the suffix.

SUFFIXES WITH CONSONANTS

thick + **ness** = thick**ness**	mild + **ly** = mild**ly**
content + **ment** = content**ment**	pain + **ful** = pain**ful**

In other cases you must change the spelling of the base word before you add the suffix.

Words Ending in *e*

32 C.1 Drop the final *e* before a suffix that begins with a vowel.

SUFFIXES WITH VOWELS

culture + **al** = cultur**al**
like + **able** = lik**able**
locate + **ion** = locat**ion**
struggle + **ing** = struggl**ing**

32 C.2 Keep the final *e* in words that end in *ce* or *ge* if the suffix begins with an *a* or *o*. The *e* keeps the sound of the *c* or *g* soft before these vowels.

CE AND GE

knowledge + **able** = knowledge**able**
notice + **able** = notice**able**
outrage + **ous** = outrage**ous**
replace + **able** = replace**able**

32 C.3 Keep the final *e* when adding a suffix that begins with a consonant.

SUFFIXES WITH FINAL *E*

Examples
- amuse + **ment** = amuse**ment**
- hope + **less** = hope**less**
- peace + **ful** = peace**ful**
- wise + **ly** = wise**ly**

Exceptions
- argue + **ment** = argu**ment**
- judge + **ment** = judg**ment**
- true + **ly** = tru**ly**
- wise + **dom** = wis**dom**

WORD ALERT

Remind yourself that you're <u>likely</u> to remember the *e* in *likely* but that *truly* has a <u>truly</u> unusual spelling.

Practice Your Skills

Adding Suffixes

Combine the base words and suffixes. Remember to make any necessary spelling changes.

1. erase + er
2. nature + al
3. move + able
4. grace + ful
5. imitate + ion
6. value + able
7. agree + ment
8. confuse + ion
9. true + ly
10. secure + ity
11. continue + al
12. pale + ness
13. operate + ion
14. grave + ly
15. mule + ish
16. resemble + ance
17. judge + ment
18. peace + able
19. supply + ing
20. notice + ing

Connect to Writing: Editing

Spelling Words with Prefixes and Suffixes

Rewrite the underlined words in the following paragraph, correctly spelling those that are incorrect. There are 22 words.

Artist Clayton Turner's <u>drawings</u> of the Old West show <u>truely</u> <u>remarkable</u> <u>creativeity</u> and <u>sensitiveity</u>. Turner had little formal art <u>educateion</u>, but he concentrated on <u>refining</u> his skills for decades. His Western scenes show such things as cowboys <u>batheing</u> in a river or <u>couragous</u> pioneers <u>traveling</u> westward. He depicts cowboys <u>angling</u> out their knees as they ride, indicating he clearly was a <u>knowledgable</u> horseman himself.

However, his pictures are based on his <u>recollections</u> of a distant past. As the result of an <u>unfortuneate</u> diving accident in his teens, his hands and legs were <u>unuseable</u>. He painted by clamping a brush between his teeth and <u>moving</u> his head. His <u>perseverance</u> made him not only a <u>noteable</u> artist but a <u>valuable</u> political spokesperson. He <u>tirelessly</u> lobbied for <u>architectureal</u> reforms to make public places more <u>accessible</u> to anyone with a disability. Clayton Turner died in November of 2009.

Words Ending with *y*

32 C.4 To add a suffix to most words ending in a vowel and *y*, keep the *y*.

VOWELS AND *Y*	
Examples	annoy + **ance** = annoy**ance**
	employ + **able** = employ**able**
	fray + **ed** = fray**ed**
	prey + **ing** = prey**ing**
Exceptions	day + **ly** = dai**ly**
	gay + **ly** = gai**ly**

WORD ALERT

Use mnemonic devices, such as phrases or short poems, to help remember how to spell exceptions to the rules.

Jay changes the *y* <u>daily</u>
And adds the *i* <u>gaily</u>.

32 C.5 To add certain suffixes to most words ending in a consonant and *y*, change the *y* to *i* before adding the suffix. However, do not drop the *y* when adding the suffix *–ing*.

CONSONANTS AND *Y*	
Examples	clumsy + **ly** = clumsi**ly**
	dry + **ing** = dry**ing**
	duty + **ful** = duti**ful**
	ready + **ness** = readi**ness**
	rely + **able** = relia**ble**
Exceptions	dry + **ness** = dry**ness**
	shy + **ness** = shy**ness**

Doubling the Final Consonant

Sometimes the final consonant in a word is doubled before a suffix is added.

32 C.6 Double the final consonant in a word before adding a suffix when *all three* of the following are true:

(1) The suffix begins with a vowel.
(2) The base word has only one syllable or is stressed on the last syllable.
(3) The base word ends in one consonant preceded by a vowel.

DOUBLE CONSONANTS

One-syllable Words	win + **ing** = wi**nn**ing	drum + **er** = dru**mm**er
	shop + **ed** = sho**pp**ed	hot + **est** = ho**tt**est
Final Syllable Stressed	begin + **ing** = begi**nn**ing	refer + **al** = refe**rr**al
	allot + **ed** = allo**tt**ed	occur + **ence** = occu**rr**ence

You do not double the final *r* in words that end in *fer* when you add the suffix *–ence* or *–able*. You can recognize these words because the pronunciation of the base word changes when the suffix is added.

FINAL *R*

refer + ence = reference	infer + ence = inference
defer + ence = deference	transfer + able = transferable

Be sure *not* to double the final letter if it is preceded by *two* vowels.

TWO VOWELS

float + **ing** = floating	shout + **ed** = shouted
speak + **er** = speaker	neat + **est** = neatest

Practice Your Skills

Adding Suffixes

Combine the base words and suffixes. Remember to make any necessary spelling changes.

1. mislay + ing
2. whip + ed
3. enjoy + ed
4. survey + ing
5. occur + ing
6. transfer + ed
7. heat + er
8. day + ly
9. read + able
10. knit + ing
11. mad + est
12. defy + ance
13. red + en
14. pity + ful
15. shy + ly
16. prefer + ed
17. rely + able
18. soap + y
19. journey + ed
20. unlucky + ly

Connect to Writing: Editing

Spelling Words with Prefixes and Suffixes

Look at all the underlined words in the following paragraph. Correctly spell any that are spelled incorrectly. There are 25 words.

I visited Waitomo Cave when I was staying in New Zealand. It was one of the most enjoiable things I did on my trip. Accompanyed by other tourists, I stepped into the murkyness of the cave. The limestone decorateions in the forms of stalactites, stalagmites, and sculptures made the cave look like a natureal cathedral. We followed our guide to a demonstration platform. There she identified some colonys of glowworms on the walls of a small grotto. She also explainned how they live. Next we were taken to a woodden dock and loaded into a flat-bottomed boat. The boat carryied us down a gloomy underground river to a large grotto. Overhead and reflected in the water, stary blue-green lights were shining eerily. The otherwise black cavern was occupied by tens of thousands of glowworms. I would have prefered to study them dreamily for hours. I regreted being ferryed back to the dock and leaving that stuning spectacle behind. That cavern was easly one of the loveliest sights I have ever seen.

✓ Check Point: Mixed Practice

Add the prefix or suffix to each base word and write the new word.

1. raid + ers
2. icy + ness
3. prefer + able
4. over + ripe
5. crafty + ly
6. judge + ment
7. unfit + ed
8. pay + able
9. false + ity
10. confuse + ion
11. deter + ed
12. regret + able
13. fly + er
14. destroy + ing
15. active + ity
16. love + able
17. pronounce + able
18. soap + y
19. slim + est
20. move + ing
21. occur + ence
22. annoy + ance
23. clumsy + ly
24. ready + ness
25. study + ing
26. under + estimate
27. un + event + ful
28. excel + ence
29. anti + inflate + ion
30. balance + ing
31. fatigue + ing
32. taste + less
33. dedicate + ion
34. persuasive + ly
35. opposite + ness
36. re + assure + ance
37. dis + loyal
38. courage + ous
39. empty + ness
40. magnify + ing

● *Connect to Writing:* Friendly Letter

Using Words with Prefixes and Suffixes

The Carlsbad Caverns and the hoodoos of Bryce Canyon are two places that seem almost otherworldly to the average visitor. Think of an unusual or mystical place that you have visited or read about. How would you describe it? Write a letter to a friend in which you tell him or her all about your feelings for this place. Use two words with prefixes and two words with suffixes, and proofread your letter to be sure all words are spelled correctly.

Words to Master

Make it your goal to learn to spell these fifty words this year. Use them in your writing and practice writing them until spelling them comes automatically.

accompany
acquaint
altogether
argument
assistance
bargain
boulevard
campaign
chauffeur
condemn
convenient
cooperate
courtesy
deceive
definition
dependent
drought

environment
fascinate
fiery
foreign
heiress
immigrant
inference
irregular
jealous
lieutenant
mileage
occasion
opponent
pamphlet
preferred
professional
pronounceable

pursuit
receipt
reference
referral
regrettable
reign
remembrance
responsibility
scenery
separation
sufficient
supersede
undeniable
unique
unmanageable
weight

Chapter Review

Assess Your Learning

Applying Spelling Generalizations

Write the letter of the misspelled word in each group. Then write the word, spelling it correctly.

1. (a) piece　　(b) radioes　　(c) merriment
2. (a) supersede　　(b) weight　　(c) inconsistant
3. (a) harass　　(b) niether　　(c) entertainment
4. (a) suffered　　(b) harmonize　　(c) mathmatics
5. (a) deceit　　(b) churchs　　(c) conscientious
6. (a) practically　　(b) thickness　　(c) rights-of-ways
7. (a) pridefull　　(b) wisely　　(c) misbehave
8. (a) thirtieth　　(b) sideing　　(c) amusement
9. (a) companes　　(b) trained　　(c) exceed
10. (a) strapped　　(b) knaves　　(c) alloted
11. (a) mistake　　(b) believe　　(c) sombreroes
12. (a) imoveable　　(b) curing　　(c) portrayal
13. (a) indelable　　(b) frying　　(c) judgment
14. (a) amused　　(b) sovereign　　(c) courteus
15. (a) chilly　　(b) triping　　(c) galleys
16. (a) runners-up　　(b) reefs　　(c) *yesses*
17. (a) carving　　(b) releive　　(c) partying
18. (a) leisure　　(b) chiefs　　(c) noisyly
19. (a) cameos　　(b) tooths　　(c) mispronounce
20. (a) playful　　(b) seprate　　(c) king

Spelling Correctly: Posttest

Directions
Read the passage and write the letter of the choice that correctly respells each underlined word. If the underlined word needs no change, write **D**.

Bangkok, the capital of Thailand, offers a **(1)** mickture of the old and the new. Tall skyscrapers dot the **(2)** horizen. In contrast lie hundreds of **(3)** beautiful, aged Buddhist temples. Large **(4)** factorys and small family-owned shops operate side by side. Individual vendors **(5)** peddling their goods compete with modern department stores. Broad streets have **(6)** reeplaced many narrow roads. **(7)** Espressways have been constructed over some filled-in canals. Bicycles and carts are no competition for cars, trucks, and three-wheeled **(8)** taxies. The bicyclists and cart-pushers are a **(9)** daily reminder of the past. **(10)** Hopefulley, the old ways will never be completely lost.

1. **A** mixshur
   B micksure
   C mixture
   D No error

2. **A** herizen
   B horizon
   C herizon
   D No error

3. **A** beutiful
   B beautifull
   C beauteeful
   D No error

4. **A** factories
   B factorees
   C facteries
   D No error

5. **A** peddeling
   B pedaling
   C peddleing
   D No error

6. **A** replaced
   B replased
   C reeplased
   D No error

7. **A** Expresworys
   B Expressweighs
   C Expressways
   D No error

8. **A** taxees
   B tackcees
   C taxis
   D No error

9. **A** daylee
   B dailey
   C dayly
   D No error

10. **A** Hopefuly
    B Hopefully
    C Hopfully
    D No error

Writer's Corner

Snapshot

32 A Some spelling generalizations are based on the **patterns of letters** in words. You can find certain common patterns in words spelled with *ie* or *ei* and in words that end with the *seed* sound. (pages 911–913)

32 B A few generalizations will help you spell the **plurals** of nouns correctly. (pages 914–921)

32 C A **prefix** is placed in front of a base word to form a new word. A **suffix** is placed after a base word to create a new word. (pages 922–928)

Power Rules

Homophones are words that sound alike but have different meanings. When you write, be sure you use the word with your intended meaning. It often helps to say contractions as two words. (pages 722–723 and 886–887)

Before Editing	**After Editing**
Is *you're* sister coming to the play?	Is *your* sister coming to the play?
We borrowed *there* shovel last week.	We borrowed *their* shovel last week.
Their from a family of musicians.	*They're* from a family of musicians.
A snake sheds *it's* skin.	A snake sheds *its* skin.
Its four o'clock in the afternoon.	*It's* four o'clock in the afternoon.

Avoid misusing or misspelling commonly confused words. (pages 786–794)

Before Editing	**After Editing**
Did you *brake* the glass?	Did you *break* the glass? (*break* means "to smash or shatter")
Are class is going on a field trip.	*Our* class is going on a field trip. (*our* is a possessive pronoun)
Al *past* the test with a high score.	Al *passed* the test with a high score. (*passed*—a past tense form of the verb *pass*—means "to move forward or through")

Editing Checklist ✓

Use this checklist when editing your writing.

- ✓ Did I pay attention to spelling patterns? (See pages 911–913.)
- ✓ Did I correctly form regular and irregular plurals of nouns? (See pages 914–921.)
- ✓ Did I alter base words as necessary when adding prefixes and suffixes? (See pages 922–928.)
- ✓ Did I use a dictionary to check the spelling of words of which I was unsure? (See pages 405–410 and 909.)
- ✓ Was I careful when using sound-alike words to choose the correct word? (See pages 722–723.)

Use the Power

Some words or word parts sound the same but are spelled differently. Use a mnemonic device to help you remember how to spell difficult words.

WORD	MNEMONIC DEVICE
piece / peace	I'd love a **PIE**ce of **PIE**.
capital / capitol	The *capit**Al*** letters begin with capital **A**.
loose / lose	**LOOSE** rhymes with m**OOSE**.
fourth / forth	**FOUR**th grade = grade **FOUR** (4)
who's / whose	who + is = **who's**
advice / advise	It's n**ICE** to get ad**VICE**; you must be w**ISE** to ad**VISE**.

Language QuickGuide

The Power Rules	935
Ten Tools for Powerful Writing	938
Grammar QuickGuide	940
14. The Sentence	940
15. Nouns and Pronouns	941
16. Verbs	942
17. Adjectives and Adverbs	943
18. Other Parts of Speech and Review	943
19. Complements	944
20. Phrases	944
21. Verbals and Verbal Phrases	945
22. Clauses	945
23. Sentence Fragments and Run-ons	946
Usage QuickGuide	948
24. Using Verbs	948
25. Using Pronouns	949
26. Subject and Verb Agreement	950
27. Using Adjectives and Adverbs	951
Mechanics QuickGuide	953
28. Capital Letters	953
29. End Marks and Commas	953
30. Italics and Quotation Marks	955
31. Other Punctuation	956
32. Spelling Correctly	957

The Power Rules

Researchers have found that certain patterns of language use offend educated people more than others and therefore affect how people perceive you. Since these patterns of language use have such an impact on future success, you should learn how to edit for the more widely accepted forms. The list below identifies ten of the most important conventions to master, the Power Rules. Always check for them when you edit.

1. **Use only one negative form for a single negative idea.** (See pages 258, 777–778 and 784.)

   Before Editing
   We *didn't* do *nothing* last night.
   I *didn't* have *nothing* to eat.

   After Editing
   We *didn't* do *anything* last night.
   I *didn't* have *anything* to eat.

2. **Use mainstream past-tense forms of regular and irregular verbs.**
   (See pages 680–686.) You might try to recite and memorize the parts of the most common irregular verbs.

   Before Editing
   I already *eat* the cheesecake.
   They *been* happy.
   Chester *come* to my house yesterday.
   We *brang* the salad to the potluck.
   You should have *went* to the game!

   After Editing
   I already *ate* the cheesecake.
   They *were* happy.
   Chester *came* to my house yesterday.
   We *brought* the salad to the potluck.
   You should have *gone* to the game!

3. **Use verbs that agree with the subject.** (See pages 740–743 and 752–760.)

   Before Editing
   It *don't* make a difference.
   Bruno always *study* for the test.
   The cat and the dog *gets* along well.
   Either the knights or the princess *rescue* the king.
   Neither Hank nor his friends *feels* terrible about the accident.

   After Editing
   It *doesn't* make a difference.
   Bruno always *studies* for the test.
   The cat and the dog *get* along well.
   Either the knights or the princess *rescues* the king.
   Neither Hank nor his friends *feel* terrible about the accident.

The Power Rules

4. Use subject forms of pronouns in subject position. Use object forms of pronouns in object position. (See pages 712–719.)

Before Editing
Her and her mom look alike.
Him and his brothers live in different houses.
Marie wants to start a business with Frank and *I*.

After Editing
She and her mom look alike.
He and his brothers live in different houses.
Marie wants to start a business with Frank and *me*.

5. Use standard ways to make nouns possessive. (See pages 880–882.)

Before Editing
Where is the *rabbit* foot?
Where are all the *kings* men?
Buffy repainted the *houses* exterior.
The *trees* leaves are starting to fall.
The *soldiers* rifles all shot in unison.

After Editing
Where is the *rabbit's* foot?
Where are all the *king's* men?
Buffy repainted the *house's* exterior.
The *trees'* leaves are starting to fall.
The *soldiers'* rifles all shot in unison.

6. Use a consistent verb tense except when a change is clearly necessary. (See pages 698–699.)

Before Editing
The rooster *crows* when the sun *rose*.
When the show *ended*, he *stands* up and cheered.

After Editing
The rooster *crows* when the sun *rises*.
When the show *ended*, he *stood* up and cheered.

7. Use sentence fragments only the way professional writers do, after the sentence they refer to and usually to emphasize a point. Fix all sentence fragments that occur before the sentence they refer to and ones that occur in the middle of a sentence. (See pages 662–667.)

Before Editing
One day. The cat let me pet her.
Trying to sail is hard. *During a typhoon.* So we try to avoid it.
I let my plants die. *The reason being that I forgot to water them.*

After Editing
One day the cat let me pet her.
Trying to sail *during a typhoon is hard,* so we try to avoid it.
I let my plants die *because* I forgot to water them.

8. Use the best conjunction and/or punctuation for the meaning when connecting two sentences. Revise run-on sentences. (See pages 668–669.)

Before Editing
We dropped by the elementary school we visited with our favorite teacher.
The private saluted improperly, the sergeant told him to do 50 pushups.
I adjusted the speakers, they sounded better.

After Editing
When we dropped by the elementary school, we visited with our favorite teacher.
After the private saluted improperly, the sergeant told him to do 50 pushups.
I adjusted the speakers, *and* they sounded better.

9. Use the contraction *'ve* (not *of*) when the correct word is *have*, or use the full word *have*. Use *supposed* instead of *suppose* and *used* instead of *use* when appropriate. (See pages 291, 790, 794, and 796.)

Before Editing
They should *of* turned left instead of right.
We might *of* added the ingredients In the wrong order.
The car could *of* started if we'd had the key.
We were *suppose* to read chapter 6 for homework.
Pedro *use* to live on a farm.

After Editing
They should *have* turned left instead of right.
We might *have* added the ingredients in the wrong order.
The car could *have* started if we'd had the key.
We were *supposed* to read chapter 6 for homework.
Pedro *used* to live on a farm.

10. For sound-alikes and certain words that sound almost alike, choose the word with your intended meaning. (See pages 291, 722–723, and 736.)

Before Editing
I am going *too* save money for a rainy day. (*too* means "also" or "in addition")
I will shoot *to* free throws. (*to* means "in the direction of")
Was that *you're* meal I ate? (*you're* is a contraction of *you are*)
They're commute is very long. (*they're* is a contraction of *they are*)
Let's have a seat over *their*. (*their* is the possessive form of *they*)
Its a great day to be alive! (*its* is the possessive form of *it*)

After Editing
I am going *to* save money for a rainy day. (*to* is part of the infinitive of the verb *save*)
I will shoot *two* free throws. (*two* is a number)
Was that *your* meal I ate? (*your* is the possessive form of *you*)
Their commute is very long. (*their* is the possessive form of *they*)
Let's have a seat over *there*. (*there* means "in that place")
It's a great day to be alive! (*it's* is a contraction of *it is*)

The Power Rules

Ten Tools for Powerful Writing

Besides using the Power Rules to help you avoid errors, you can also use the following ten tools to turn good writing into powerful writing.

1. Write **in living color** with strong verbs. (See page 224.)

Here's how a statement might look in "black and white."

　The pitcher threw the ball.

Strengthen the verb, though, and suddenly the scene takes on color.

　The pitcher **hurled** the ball.

2. Add variety to your sentences by using **modifiers come lately.** (See page 278.)

You use adjectives to elaborate, to add descriptive detail. In the usual word order, you would put the adjectives that modify *pitcher* before the word *pitcher*.

　The **agile and powerful** pitcher hurled the ball.

Let your adjectives "come lately," though, and the sentence becomes more graceful and grown up.

　The pitcher, **agile and powerful,** hurled the ball.

3. **Set the scene** with adverbs and phrases. (See page 112.)

While you might want your adjectives to come lately, you might want your adverbs and phrases to come early so they can set the scene.

　The pitcher hurled the ball.

　Fluidly, the pitcher hurled the ball.

　After the long wind-up, the pitcher hurled the ball.

4. **Get into the action** with participial phrases. (See page 189.)

You can pack a lot of action into your sentences if you include an *–ing* verb, or "*–ing* modifier." Formally called *present participial phrases*, these *–ing* modifiers describe a person, thing, or action in a sentence.

　Keeping his eye on the target, the pitcher hurled the ball, sensing nothing but the motion of his own body, his own breath.

5. Elaborate by **explaining who or what with appositives.** (See page 67.)

Details that elaborate on a person, place, or thing will strengthen your writing. You can add such details in the form of an appositive. An appositive is a noun or pronoun phrase that identifies or adds identifying information to the preceding noun.

　Keeping his eye on the target, the pitcher, **a young left-hander,** hurled the ball.

6. **Catch and release** related sentences with a semicolon. (See page 93.)

The semicolon combines a comma and a period. The period "catches" the idea in the words before the semicolon, signaling its end. The comma "releases" it and relates it to another idea. Semicolons invite the reader to supply the words or idea that connects what could be two separate sentences.

> The pitcher, a young left-hander, hurled the ball; **less than a second later, it smacked into the catcher's glove.**

7. Don't forget the **fine points;** use descriptive adverbs to sharpen the focus. (See page 138.)

Adverbs describe the fine details about an action. Help your reader understand exactly how or when an action occurred by adding precise adverbs. Adverbs can show the passage of time and provide transitions.

> **Finally,** the pitcher hurled the ball.

> The pitcher threw the ball **skillfully yesterday.**

8. Use the **power of 3s** to add style and emphasis with **parallelism.** (See page 164.)

One way to add power is to use a writing device called parallelism. Parallelism is the use of the same kind of word or group of words in a series of three or more.

> **Focusing on his target, concentrating his energy,** and **ignoring the crowd's deafening cheers for his opponent,** the pitcher hurled the ball.

9. Emphasize your ideas by **using repetition.** (See page 256.)

Call attention to important ideas by setting up a pattern of repetition.

> **Focus** is everything in baseball. The catcher must **focus** on choosing the pitch the batter least expects. The pitcher must **focus** on delivering that pitch with power and precision. The batter must then **focus** on hitting the pitched ball, which can hurtle toward him at ninety miles per hour.

10. Write with variety and coherence and **let it flow.** (See page 346.)

Vary the length, structure, and beginnings of your sentences and use connecting words to help your writing flow smoothly.

> The pitcher, a young left-hander, leaned forward on the mound. Peering at his catcher, he shook off several signs. Finally, he nodded. The wind-up, fluid and quick, followed. Focusing on his target, concentrating his energy, and ignoring the crowd's deafening cheers for his opponent, the pitcher hurled the ball toward the plate; less than a second later, it smacked into the catcher's glove. The inning was over.

Ten Tools for Powerful Writing

Grammar QuickGuide

This section presents an easy-to-use reference for the definitions of grammatical terms. The number on the colored tab tells you the chapter covering that topic. The page number to the right of each definition refers to the place in the chapter where you can find additional instruction, examples, and applications to writing.

14 The Sentence

How can you create fluency in your writing by using a variety of sentence types?

A Sentence

14 A   A **sentence** is a group of words that expresses a complete thought.   478

14 A.1   A group of words that expresses an incomplete thought is called a **sentence fragment.**   478

Complete and Simple Subjects

14 B   The **subject** of a sentence names the person, place, thing, or idea that the sentence is about.   479

14 B.1   A **complete subject** includes all the words used to identify the person, place, thing, or idea that the sentence is about.   479

14 B.2   A **simple subject** is the main person, place, or thing in a complete subject.   480

Complete and Simple Predicates

14 C   The **predicate** tells what the subject is or does.   481

14 C.1   A **complete predicate** includes all the words that tell what the subject is doing or that tell something about the subject.   481

14 C.2   A **simple predicate,** or **verb,** is the main word or phrase in the complete predicate.   482

14 C.3   The main verb and any helping verbs make up a **verb phrase.**   484

Different Positions of Subjects

14 D   The subject of a sentence can appear in different positions or be understood.   487

14 D.1   When the subject appears before the verb, a sentence is said to be in **natural order.**   487

14 D.2	When the verb comes before the subject, the sentence is in **inverted order.**	487
14 D.3	The unstated *you* in a command or request is called the **understood subject.**	488

Compound Subjects and Verbs

14 E	Sentences can contain **compound subjects** and **compound verbs.**	490
14 E.1	A **compound subject** is two or more subjects in one sentence that have the same verb and are joined by a conjunction.	490
14 E.2	A **compound verb** is two or more verbs that have the same subject and are joined by a conjunction.	491

Kinds of Sentences

14 F	There are four different kinds of sentences, each with a different purpose.	493
14 F.1	A **declarative sentence** makes a statement or expresses an opinion and ends with a period.	493
14 F.2	An **interrogative sentence** asks a question and ends with a question mark.	493
14 F.3	An **imperative sentence** makes a request or gives a command and ends with either a period or an exclamation point.	493
14 F.4	An **exclamatory sentence** expresses strong feeling and ends with an exclamation point.	493

15 Nouns and Pronouns

Why is it important to use nouns and pronouns correctly?

Nouns

15 A	A **noun** is a word that names a person, a place, a thing, or an idea.	504
15 A.1	**Concrete nouns** name things that can be seen or touched; **abstract nouns** name things that cannot be seen or touched.	504
15 A.2	A noun that includes more than one word is called a **compound noun.**	506
15 A.3	A **common noun** names any person, place, or thing. A **proper noun** names a particular person, place, or thing.	507

Pronouns

15 B A **pronoun** is a word that takes the place of one or more nouns. — 509

    15 B.1 The noun that a pronoun replaces, or refers to, is called its **antecedent.** — 509

    15 B.2 There are several kinds of pronouns, including personal, reflexive, intensive, and indefinite. **Personal pronouns** are used as substitutions for proper or common nouns. — 510

    15 B.3 **Reflexive** and **intensive pronouns** refer to or emphasize a noun or another pronoun. — 510

    15 B.4 **Indefinite pronouns** refer to unnamed people, places, things, or ideas. — 512

    15 B.5 **Demonstrative pronouns** point out a specific person, place, thing, or idea. — 512

    15 B.6 **Interrogative pronouns** are used to ask questions. — 513

    15 B.7 **Relative pronouns** are used to relate an adjective clause to the noun or the pronoun that the clause describes. — 513

16 Verbs

How can you add color to your writing by using just the right verbs?

Action Verbs

16 A A **verb** is a word used to express an action or a state of being. — 522

    16 A.1 An **action verb** tells what action a subject is performing. — 522

Transitive and Intransitive Verbs

16 B A **transitive verb** expresses action directly toward a person or a thing. An **intransitive verb** expresses action that is not directed at a person or a thing. — 524

Helping Verbs

16 C A **helping verb,** or auxiliary verb, is a verb that is combined with a main verb to form a verb phrase. — 526

    16 C.1 A **verb phrase** is made up of a main verb and one or more helping verbs. — 526

Linking Verbs

16 D   A **linking verb** links the subject with another word that renames or describes the subject.   528

17 Adjectives and Adverbs

How can you add interest and detail to your writing with adjectives and adverbs?

Adjectives

17 A   An **adjective** is a word that modifies a noun or pronoun.   538

     17 A.1   The words *a*, *an*, and *the* form a special group of adjectives called **articles**.   541

     17 A.2   A **proper adjective** is used to describe a noun or a pronoun and always begins with a capital letter.   541

Adverbs

17 B   An **adverb** is a word that modifies a verb, an adjective, or another adverb.   547

18 Other Parts of Speech and Review

How can you create fluency in your writing by using prepositions, conjunctions, and interjections?

Prepositions

18 A   A **preposition** is a word that shows the relationship between a noun or a pronoun and another word in the sentence.   560

     18 A.1   A **prepositional phrase** is a group of words made up of a preposition, its object, and any words that modify the object.   561

Conjunctions and Interjections

18 B   A **conjunction** connects words or groups of words; an **interjection** shows strong feeling.   566

     18 B.1   Both **coordinating conjunctions** and **correlative conjunctions** connect words or groups of words.   566

     18 B.2   A **conjunctive adverb** is an adverb that acts as a conjunction connecting complete ideas.   567

18 B.3	**Parallelism** refers to the use of similar grammatical constructions for similar ideas.	568
18 B.4	A **transition** is a word or phrase that shows how two subjects or ideas are related.	568
18 B.5	An **interjection** is a word that expresses strong feeling.	569

19 Complements

How can you use complements to focus your writing?

Kinds of Complements

19 A	A **complement** is a word that is necessary to complete the meaning of a sentence.	580

Direct and Indirect Objects

19 B	A **direct object** is a noun or pronoun that answers the question *What?* or *Whom?* after an action verb. An **indirect object** is a noun or pronoun that answers the question *To or for whom?* or *To or for what?* after an action verb.	581

Predicate Nominatives and Predicate Adjectives

19 C	A **predicate nominative** is a noun or a pronoun that follows a linking verb and identifies, renames, or explains the subject. A **predicate adjective** is an adjective that follows a linking verb and modifies the subject.	584

20 Phrases

How can you add precision and variety to your writing with phrases?

Prepositional Phrases

20 A	A **prepositional phrase** is a group of words that begins with a preposition, ends with a noun or a pronoun, and is used as an adjective or adverb.	600
20 A.1	An **adjectival phrase** is a prepositional phrase that modifies a noun or pronoun.	601
20 A.2	When an adjectival phrase is placed too far from the word it describes, it is called a **misplaced modifier.** A misplaced modifier can confuse readers.	603

944 Language QuickGuide

20 A.3 An **adverbial phrase** is a prepositional phrase that is used mainly to modify a verb. — 604

Appositives and Appositive Phrases

20 B An **appositive** is a noun or pronoun that identifies or explains another noun or pronoun in the sentence. — 607

21 Verbals and Verbal Phrases

How can you use verbals and verbal phrases to add fluency to your writing?

Participles and Participial Phrases

21 A A **participle** is a verb form that is used as an adjective. — 618

21 A.1 A **participial phrase** is a participle joined with related words. The related words in a participial phrase often include a complement, an adverb, or a prepositional phrase. — 621

Infinitives and Infinitive Phrases

21 B An **infinitive** is a verb form that usually begins with *to*. It is used as a noun, an adjective, or an adverb. — 626

21 B.1 An **infinitive phrase** is an infinitive with its modifiers and complements—all working together as a noun, an adjective, or an adverb. — 627

Parallelism with Verbals

21 C **Parallelism** refers to the use of similar grammatical constructions for similar ideas. — 628

22 Clauses

How can you use clauses to create a smooth flow and express ideas precisely?

Independent and Subordinate Clauses

22 A A **clause** is a group of words that has a subject and a verb. — 638

22 A.1 An **independent, or main, clause** can stand alone as a sentence because it expresses a complete idea. — 638

22 A.2 A **subordinate, or dependent, clause** cannot stand alone as a sentence because it does not express a complete thought. — 638

Grammar QuickGuide **945**

Uses of Subordinate Clauses

22 B   A **subordinate clause** can be used as an adverb or as an adjective. — 640

22 B.1   An **adverbial clause** is a subordinate clause used mainly to modify a verb. — 640

22 B.2   An **adjectival clause** is a subordinate clause that is used to modify a noun or a pronoun. — 643

22 B.3   Most adjectival clauses begin with a relative pronoun. A **relative pronoun** relates an adjective clause to the noun or the pronoun that the clause describes. — 643

22 B.4   A **misplaced adjectival clause** is placed so far from the word it modifies that it creates unintended meaning. — 646

Kinds of Sentences

22 C   There are three basic kinds of sentences: **simple, compound,** and **complex.** — 647

22 C.1   A **simple sentence** has one subject (or a compound subject) and one verb. — 647

22 C.2   A **compound sentence** is made up of two or more simple sentences, usually joined by a comma and a coordinating conjunction: *and, but, or,* or *yet.* — 647

22 C.3   A **complex sentence** consists of one main, or independent, clause and one or more subordinate clauses. — 650

23 Sentence Fragments and Run-ons

How can you clarify your meaning and add sentence variety by fixing unintended sentence fragments and run-ons?

Sentence Fragments

23 A   A **sentence fragment** is a group of words punctuated as a sentence that does not express a complete thought. — 662

Phrase Fragments

23 B   A **phrase fragment** is a group of words standing alone without a subject or a verb. — 664

Clause Fragments

23 C A **clause fragment** is a subordinate clause punctuated as a sentence. 666

Run-on Sentences

23 D A **run-on sentence** is two or more sentences that are written together as one sentence by incorrectly connecting them with a comma or with no mark of punctuation at all. 668

Usage QuickGuide

This section presents an easy-to-use reference for the explanations of how various grammatical elements are and should be used. The number on the colored tab tells you the chapter covering that topic. The page number to the right of each definition refers to the place in the chapter where you can find additional instruction, examples, and applications to writing. You can also refer to the Writer's Glossary of Usage (pages 786–799) for help with commonly confused usage items.

24 Using Verbs

How can you use verbs to communicate action, the precise time of an action, and certainty or doubt?

The Principal Parts of Verbs

24 A The **principal parts** of a verb are the present, the present participle, the past, and the past participle. — 680

24 A.1 A **regular verb** forms its past and past participle by adding *–ed* or *–d* to the present. — 680

24 A.2 An **irregular verb** does not form its past and past participle by adding *–ed* or *–d* to the present. — 682

Verb Tense

24 B The time expressed by a verb is called the **tense** of the verb. — 693

24 B.1 **Present tense** is used to express an action that is going on now. To form the present tense, use the present form (the first principal part of the verb) or add *–s* or *–es* to the present form. — 693

24 B.2 **Past tense** expresses an action that already took place or was completed in the past. To form the past tense of a regular verb, add *–ed* or *–d* to the present form. To form the past tense of an irregular verb, check a dictionary, or look for it on pages 682–692. — 693

24 B.3 **Future tense** is used to express an action that will take place in the future. To form the future tense, use the helping verb *shall* or *will* with the present form. — 694

24 B.4	**Present perfect tense** expresses an action that was completed at some indefinite time in the past. It also expresses an action that started in the past and is still going on. To form the present perfect tense, add *has* or *have* to the past participle.	694
24 B.5	**Past perfect tense** expresses an action that took place before some other action. To form the past perfect tense, add *had* to the past participle.	694
24 B.6	**Future perfect tense** expresses an action that will take place before another future action or time. To form the future perfect tense, add *shall have* or *will have* to the past participle.	694
24 B.7	A **conjugation** is a list of all the singular and plural forms of a verb in all tenses.	694
24 B.8	Avoid unnecessary shifts in tense within a sentence or within related sentences.	698
24 B.9	The **progressive forms** of verbs are used to express continuing or ongoing action.	700
24 B.10	The **emphatic forms** of the present and past tenses of verbs are mainly used to show emphasis or force. To write the present emphatic, add *do* or *does* to the present tense of a verb. To write the past emphatic, add *did* to the present tense.	702

25 Using Pronouns

How can you use pronouns in a way that makes your writing fluid and accurate?

The Cases of Personal Pronouns

25 A	**Case** indicates a pronoun's use in a sentence. Pronouns have three cases: **nominative, objective,** and **possessive.**	710
25 A.1	The **nominative case** is used both for subjects and for predicate nominatives.	711
25 A.2	A **predicate nominative** is a word that follows a linking verb and identifies or renames the subject. A pronoun used as a predicate nominative is in the nominative case.	713
25 A.3	The **objective case** is used for direct objects, indirect objects, and objects of prepositions.	716
25 A.4	The **possessive case** is used to show ownership or possession.	720

Pronoun Problem: *Who* or *Whom?*

25 B A common problem with pronouns concerns whether to use *who* or *whom.* 724

Pronouns and Their Antecedents

25 C A pronoun and its **antecedent,** the word that a pronoun refers to or replaces, must agree in number and gender. 726

Unclear, Missing, or Confusing Antecedents

25 D **Personal pronouns** should clearly refer to a **specific antecedent.** 730

26 Subject and Verb Agreement

How can you make your subjects and verbs work together so that your ideas are clear?

Agreement of Subjects and Verbs

26 A A verb must agree with its subject in **number.** 740

    26 A.1 A singular subject takes a singular verb. A plural subject takes a plural verb. 742

Common Agreement Problems

26 B Helping verbs, contractions, interrupting words, and inverted order can lead to agreement problems. 745

    26 B.1 The first helping verb must agree in number with the subject. 745

    26 B.2 The verb part of a contraction must agree in number with the subject. 746

    26 B.3 The agreement of a verb with its subject is not changed by any interrupting words. 748

    26 B.4 The subject and verb of an inverted sentence must agree in number. 749

Other Agreement Problems

26 C **Compound subjects** and **collective nouns** can cause agreement problems. 752

    26 C.1 When subjects are joined by *and*, the verb is usually plural. 752

26 C.2	When subjects are joined by *or, either/or,* or *neither/nor,* the verb agrees with the closer subject.	752
26 C.3	Use a singular verb with a collective noun subject that is thought of as a unit.	754

Agreement Problems with Pronouns

26 D When certain pronouns are used as subjects, they can present subject-verb agreement problems. — 756

    26 D.1 *You* is always used with a plural verb even when *you* refers to one person. — 756

    26 D.2 *I* takes a plural verb unless it is used with the verbs *am* or *was.* — 756

    26 D.3 A verb must agree in number with an indefinite pronoun used as a subject. — 758

27 Using Adjectives and Adverbs

How can you use adjectives and adverbs to show precise relationships among your ideas?

Comparison of Adjectives and Adverbs

27 A Most adjectives and adverbs have three degrees of comparison: the **positive,** the **comparative,** and the **superlative.** — 768

    27 A.1 Add *–er* to form the comparative degree and *–est* to form the superlative degree of most one-syllable modifiers. — 769

    27 A.2 Use *–er* or the word *more* to form the comparative degree and *–est* or the word *most* to form the superlative degree of two-syllable modifiers. — 769

    27 A.3 Use *more* to form the comparative degree and *most* to form the superlative degree of modifiers with three or more syllables. — 770

Problems with Modifiers

27 B Avoid comparing something to itself and using **double comparisons** and **double negatives.** — 774

    27 B.1 Add *other* or *else* when comparing a member of a group to the rest of the group. — 774

Usage QuickGuide   **951**

| 27 B.2 | Do not use both *-er* and *more* to form the comparative degree or both *-est* and *most* to form the superlative degree. | 776 |
| 27 B.3 | Avoid using double negatives: two negatives used to express the same thought. | 777 |

Mechanics QuickGuide

This section presents an easy-to-use reference for the mechanics of writing: capitalization, punctuation, and spelling. The number on the colored tab tells you the chapter covering that topic. The page number to the right of each definition refers to the place in the chapter where you can find additional instruction, examples, and applications to writing.

28 Capital Letters

How can you use capital letters to clarify your writing?

Rules of Capital Letters

28 A	Capitalize first words, the pronoun *I*, and proper nouns.	804
28 A.1	Capitalize the first word in a sentence.	804
28 A.2	Capitalize the first word in a line of poetry.	804
28 A.3	Capitalize the first word in the greeting of a letter and the first word in the closing of a letter.	805
28 A.4	Capitalize the first word of each item in an outline and the letters that begin major subsections of the outline.	805
28 A.5	Capitalize the pronoun *I*, both alone and in contractions.	806
28 A.6	Capitalize proper nouns and their abbreviations.	807

Other Uses of Capital Letters

28 B	Capitalize proper adjectives and the titles of people and works of art.	816
28 B.1	Capitalize proper adjectives.	816
28 B.2	Capitalize the titles of people and works of art.	817

29 End Marks and Commas

How can you create meaning through the careful use of end marks and commas?

End Marks

29 A	Depending on the purpose, different sentences have different end marks.	830

29 A.1	Place a **period** after a statement, after an opinion, and after a command or request made in a normal tone of voice.	830
29 A.2	Place a **question mark** after a sentence that asks a question.	830
29 A.3	Place an **exclamation point** after a sentence that states strong feeling, after a command or request that expresses great excitement, and after an interjection.	830
29 A.4	Use a period with most abbreviations.	831
29 A.5	Use a period after each number or letter that shows a division in an outline.	833

Commas That Separate

29 B	Use commas to separate, as with items in a series, adjectives before a noun, compound sentences, introductory structures, and in dates, addresses, and letters.	835
29 B.1	Use commas to separate items in a series.	835
29 B.2	Use a comma to separate two adjectives that precede a noun and that would read well with the word *and* between them.	837
29 B.3	Use a comma before a coordinating conjunction that joins the parts of a compound sentence.	839
29 B.4	Use a comma after certain introductory words, phrases, or clauses.	841
29 B.5	Use commas to separate elements in dates and addresses.	843
29 B.6	Use a comma after the salutation of a friendly letter and after the closing of all letters.	844

Commas That Enclose

29 C	Use commas to enclose groups of words that interrupt a sentence.	846
29 C.1	Use a comma or commas to set off nouns of direct address.	846
29 C.2	Use commas to set off parenthetical expressions.	847
29 C.3	Use commas to set off most appositives and appositive phrases.	848
29 C.4	Use commas to set off **nonrestrictive participial phrases** and **nonrestrictive clauses**.	850
29 C.5	If a **participial phrase** or a clause is restrictive, or necessary, to the meaning of a sentence, no commas are used.	851

30 Italics and Quotation Marks

How can italics and quotation marks help you communicate clearly, make characters believable, and provide expert support for your ideas?

Italics (Underlining)

30 A	Italics (underlining) are used to set off titles and certain numbers, words, and letters.	860
30 A.1	Italicize (underline) letters, numbers, and words when they are used to represent themselves.	860
30 A.2	Italicize (underline) the titles of long written or musical works that are published as a single unit, titles of paintings and sculptures, and the names of vehicles.	860

Quotation Marks

30 B	Quotation marks are used to enclose the titles of short works and parts of longer works and to set off a speaker's exact words.	863
30 B.1	Use quotation marks to enclose the titles of chapters, articles, stories, one-act plays, short poems, and songs.	863
30 B.2	Use quotation marks to enclose a person's exact words.	864
30 B.3	Capitalize the first word of a direct quotation.	866
30 B.4	Use a comma to separate a direct quotation from a speaker tag.	867
30 B.5	Place a period inside the closing quotation marks when the end of the quotation comes at the end of a sentence.	868
30 B.6	When writing dialogue, begin a new paragraph each time the speaker changes.	870
30 B.7	When quoting a passage of more than a paragraph, place quotation marks at the beginning of each paragraph—but at the end of only the last paragraph.	871

31 Other Punctuation

How can you use apostrophes, semicolons, colons, hyphens, and other punctuation to communicate precisely and to enhance your writing style?

Apostrophes

31 A Use an **apostrophe** (') to show ownership and to represent missing letters in contractions. Also use it with certain plurals. — 880

- **31 A.1** Add 's to form the possessive of a singular noun. — 880
- **31 A.2** Add only an apostrophe to form the possessive of a plural noun that ends in *s*. — 881
- **31 A.3** Add 's to form the possessive of a plural noun that does not end in *s*. — 881
- **31 A.4** Do not add an apostrophe to form the possessive of a personal pronoun. — 883
- **31 A.5** Add 's to form the possessive of an indefinite pronoun. — 884
- **31 A.6** Use an apostrophe in a contraction to show where one or more letters have been omitted. — 886
- **31 A.7** Add 's to form the plural of lowercase letters, some capital letters, and some words used as words that people might otherwise misread. — 888

Semicolons

31 B Use a **semicolon** (;) to separate independent clauses of a compound sentence and to avoid confusion in certain sentences. — 890

- **31 B.1** Use a semicolon between the clauses of a compound sentence that are not joined by a coordinating conjunction. — 890
- **31 B.2** Use a semicolon instead of a comma between the clauses of a compound sentence if there are already commas within one of the clauses. — 892
- **31 B.3** Use a semicolon instead of a comma between the items in a series if the items contain commas. — 892

Colons

31 C Use a **colon** (**:**) before lists of items. Also use a colon between hours and minutes, between Biblical chapter and verse, and in the salutation of some letters. — 894

> **31 C.1** Use a colon before most lists of items, especially when the list comes after an expression like *the following*. — 894

Hyphens

31 D Use a **hyphen** (**-**) to divide a word and to separate certain numbers, fractions, and compound nouns. — 897

> **31 D.1** Use a hyphen to divide a word at the end of a line. — 897
>
> **31 D.2** Use a hyphen when writing out the numbers *twenty-one* through *ninety-nine*. — 898
>
> **31 D.3** Use a hyphen when writing out a fraction used as an adjective. — 899
>
> **31 D.4** Use a hyphen to separate the parts of some compound nouns. — 899

32 Spelling Correctly

How can you communicate your message effectively by using accurate spelling?

Spelling Patterns

32 A Some spelling generalizations are based on the patterns of letters in words. You can find certain common patterns in words spelled with *ie* or *ei* and in words that end with the *seed* sound. — 911

> **32 A.1** When you spell words with *ie* or *ei*, *i* comes before *e* except when the letters follow *c* or when they stand for the long *a* sound. — 911
>
> **32 A.2** In all but four words that end with the "seed" sound, this sound is spelled *–cede*. — 912

Plurals

32 B A few generalizations will help you spell the plurals of nouns correctly. When you're in doubt about an exception, look up the word in a dictionary. — 914

> **32 B.1** To form the plural of most nouns, simply add *s*. — 914

32 B.2	If a noun ends in *s, ch, sh, x,* or *z,* add *es* to form the plural.	914
32 B.3	Add *s* to form the plural of a noun ending in a vowel and *y.*	914
32 B.4	Change the *y* to *i* and add *es* to a noun ending in a consonant and *y.*	915
32 B.5	Add *s* to form the plural of a noun ending with a vowel and *o.*	915
32 B.6	Add *s* to form the plural of musical terms ending in *o.*	916
32 B.7	Add *s* to form the plural of words that were borrowed from the Spanish language.	916
32 B.8	The plurals of nouns ending in a consonant and *o* do not follow a regular pattern.	916
32 B.9	To form the plural of some nouns ending in *f* or *fe,* just add *s.*	916
32 B.10	For some nouns ending in *f* or *fe,* change the *f* to *v* and add *es.*	916
32 B.11	Add *s* or *es* to the end of most compound nouns to make them plural.	918
32 B.12	When the main word in a compound noun appears first, that word is made plural.	918
32 B.13	To form the plurals of many numerals, letters, symbols, and words used as words, add an *s.*	918
32 B.14	Irregular plurals are not formed by adding *s* or *es.*	919
32 B.15	Some nouns have the same form for singular and plural.	920

Prefixes and Suffixes

32 C	A **prefix** is placed in front of a base word to form a new word. A **suffix** is placed after a base word to create a new word.	922
32 C.1	Drop the final *e* before a suffix that begins with a vowel.	923
32 C.2	Keep the final *e* in words that end in *ce* or *ge* if the suffix begins with an *a* or *o.* The *e* keeps the sound of the *c* or *g* soft before these vowels.	923
32 C.3	Keep the final *e* when adding a suffix that begins with a consonant.	923
32 C.4	To add a suffix to most words ending in a vowel and *y,* keep the *y.*	925

32 C.5 To add certain suffixes to most words ending in a consonant and *y*, change the *y* to *i* before adding the suffix. However, do not drop the *y* when adding the suffix *–ing*. 925

32 C.6 Double the final consonant in a word before adding a suffix when *all three* of the following are true: (1) The suffix begins with a vowel. (2) The base word has only one syllable or is stressed on the last syllable. (3) The base word ends in one consonant preceded by a vowel. 926

Glossary

English

abbreviation shortened form of a word that generally begins with a capital letter and ends with a period.

abstract noun noun naming something that cannot be seen or touched, such as an idea, quality, or characteristic.

acronym an abbreviation formed by using the initial letters of a phrase or name (RADAR—radio detecting and ranging).

action verb verb that tells what action a subject is performing.

active voice voice the verb is in when it expresses that the subject is performing the action.

adjective word that modifies a noun or a pronoun.

adjectival clause subordinate clause used to modify a noun or pronoun.

adjectival phrase prepositional phrase that modifies a noun or a pronoun.

adverb word that modifies a verb, an adjective, or another adverb.

adverbial clause subordinate clause used mainly to modify a verb.

Español

abreviatura forma reducida de una palabra que generalmente comienza con mayúscula y termina en punto.

austantivo abstracto sustantivo que no puede verse ni tocarse, como una idea, una cualidad o una característica.

acrónimo abreviatura que se forma al usar las letras iniciales de una frase o de un nombre (ALICE—America Latina Interconectada Con Europa).

verbo de acción verbo que indica qué acción realiza el sujeto.

voz activa voz en que está el verbo cuando expresa que el sujeto está realizando la acción.

adjetivo palabra que modifica a un sustantivo o a un pronombre.

cláusula adjetiva cláusula subordinada utilizada para modificar a un sustantivo o a un pronombre.

frase adjetiva frase preposicional que modifica a un sustantivo o a un pronombre.

adverbio palabra que modifica a un verbo, a un adjetivo o a otro adverbio.

cláusula adverbial cláusula subordinada que se utiliza principalmente para modificar a un verbo.

English	Español
adverbial phrase prepositional phrase that is used mainly to modify a verb.	**frase adverbial** frase preposicional que se utiliza principalmente para modificar a un verbo.
analogy logical relationship between a pair of words.	**analogía** relación lógica entre una pareja de palabras.
antecedent word or group of words to which a pronoun refers.	**antecedente** palabra o grupo de palabras a que hace referencia un pronombre.
antonym word that means the opposite of another word.	**antónimo** palabra que significa lo opuesto de otra palabra.
appositive noun or pronoun that identifies or explains another noun or pronoun in a sentence.	**aposición** sustantivo o pronombre que especifica o explica a otro sustantivo o pronombre en una oración.
audience person or persons who will read your work or hear your speech.	**público** persona o personas que leerán tu trabajo o escucharán tu discurso.

B

bandwagon statement appeal that leads the reader to believe that everyone is using a certain product.	**enunciado de arrastre** enunciado apelativo que lleva al lector a creer que todos usan cierto producto.
bibliographic information information about a source, such as author, title, publisher, date of publication, and Internet address.	**información bibliográfica** datos sobre una fuente: autor, título, editorial, fecha de publicación, dirección de Internet, etc.
body one or more paragraphs composed of details, facts, and examples that support the main idea.	**cuerpo** uno o más párrafos compuestos de detalles, hechos y ejemplos que apoyan la idea principal.

English	Español
brackets punctuation marks [ ] used to enclose information added to text or to indicate new text replacing the original quoted text; always used in pairs.	**corchetes** signos de puntuación [ ] utilizados para encerrar la información añadida al texto o para indicar el texto nuevo que reemplaza al texto original citado; siempre se usan en parejas.
brainstorming prewriting technique of writing down ideas that come to mind about a given subject.	**intercambio de ideas** técnica de preparación para la escritura que consiste en anotar las ideas que surgen sobre un tema.
business letter formal letter that asks for action on the part of the receiver and includes an inside address, heading, salutation, body, closing, and signature.	**carta de negocios** carta formal que solicita al destinatario que realice una acción e incluye dirección del destinatario, membrete, saludo, cuerpo, despedida y firma.

C

English	Español
case form of a pronoun that indicates its use in a sentence. In English there are three cases: the nominative case, the objective case, and the possessive case.	**caso** forma de un pronombre que indica su uso en una oración. En inglés hay tres casos: nominativo, objetivo y posesivo.
chronological order the order in which events occur.	**orden cronológico** orden en el que ocurren los sucesos.
citation note that gives credit to the source of another person's paraphrased or quoted ideas.	**cita** nota que menciona la fuente de donde se extrajeron las ideas, parafraseadas o textuales, de otra persona.
clarity the quality of being clear.	**claridad** cualidad de un texto de ser claro.
clause group of words that has a subject and verb.	**cláusula** grupo de palabras que tiene sujeto y verbo y se utiliza como parte de una oración.
close reading reading carefully to locate specific information, follow an argument's logic, or comprehend the meaning of information.	**lectura atenta** lectura minuciosa para identificar información específica, seguir un argumento lógico o comprender el significado de la información.

English	Español

clustering visual strategy a writer uses to organize ideas and details connected to the subject.

agrupación estrategia visual que emplea un escritor para organizar las ideas y los detalles relacionados con el tema.

coherence logical and smooth flow of ideas connected with clear transitions.

coherencia flujo lógico de ideas que discurren conectadas con transiciones claras.

collaboration in writing, the working together of several individuals on one piece of writing, usually done during prewriting, including brainstorming, and revising.

colaboración en el ámbito de la escritura, el trabajo en común de varios individuos en un texto, usualmente durante la etapa de preparación para la escritura, incluida la técnica de intercambio de ideas y la tarea de revisión.

collective noun noun that names a group of people or things.

sustantivo colectivo sustantivo que designa un grupo de personas o cosas.

colloquialism informal expression considered to be Nonstandard English.

coloquialismo frase informal o expresión pintoresca que no debe tomarse literalmente, pues tiene un significado figurado específico.

complement word or group of words used to complete a predicate.

complemento palabra o grupo de palabras utilizadas para completar un predicado.

complete predicate all the words that tell what the subject is doing or that tell something about the subject.

predicado completo todas las palabras que expresan qué hace el sujeto o dicen algo acerca del sujeto.

complete subject all the words used to identify the person, place, thing, or idea that the sentence is about.

sujeto completo todas las palabras utilizadas para identificar la persona, el lugar, la cosa o la idea de la que trata la oración.

complex sentence sentence that consists of a dependent and an independent clause.

oración compleja oración que consiste de una cláusula dependiente y una independiente.

composition writing form that presents and develops one main idea.

composición tipo de texto que presenta y desarrolla una idea principal.

English	Español
compound noun a single noun comprised of several words.	**sustantivo compuesto** sustantivo individual formado por varias palabras.
compound sentence consists of two simple sentences, usually joined by a comma and the coordinating conjunction *and, but, or,* or *yet.*	**oración compuesta** consiste de dos oraciones simples, unidas generalmente por una coma y la conjunción coordinante and (y), but (pero), or (o) y yet (sin embargo).
compound subject two or more subjects in a sentence that have the same verb and are joined by a conjunction.	**sujeto compuesto** dos o más sujetos en una oración que tienen el mismo verbo y están unidos por una conjunción.
compound verb two or more verbs in one sentence that have the same subject and are joined by a conjunction.	**verbo compuesto** dos o más verbos en una oración que tienen el mismo sujeto y están unidos por una conjunción.
concluding sentence a strong ending added to a paragraph that summarizes the major points, refers to the main idea, or adds an insight.	**oración conclusiva** un final que se añade a un párrafo y que resume los puntos principales, se refiere a la idea principal o añade una reflexión.
conclusion a strong ending added to a paragraph or composition that summarizes the major points, refers to the main idea, or adds an insight.	**conclusión** un final fuerte que se añade a un párrafo o a una composición y que resume los puntos principales, se refiere a la idea principal o añade una reflexión.
concrete noun noun naming something that can be seen or touched.	**sustantivo concreto** sustantivo que puede verse o tocarse.
conjunction word that joins together sentences, clauses, phrases, or other words.	**conjunción** palabra que une dos oraciones, cláusulas, frases u otras palabras.
conjunctive adverb an adverb used to connect two clauses.	**adverbio conjuntivo** adverbio utilizado para conectar dos cláusulas.
connotation meaning that comes from attitudes attached to a word.	**connotación** significado que proviene de los valores vinculados a una palabra.

English	Español
contraction word that combines two words into one and uses an apostrophe to replace one or more missing letters.	**contracción** palabra que combina dos palabras en una y utiliza un apóstrofo en lugar de la(s) letra(s) faltante(s).
coordinating conjunction single connecting word used to join words or groups of words.	**conjunción coordinante** palabra de conexión usada para unir palabras o grupos de palabras.
count noun a noun that names an object that can be counted (grains of rice, storms, songs).	**sustantivo contable** sustantivo que designa un objeto que se puede contar (granos de arroz, tormentas, canciones).
counter-argument argument offered to address opposing views in a persuasive composition.	**contraargumento** argumento que se ofrece para tratar las opiniones contrarias en una composición persuasiva.
creative writing writing style in which the writer creates characters, events, and images within stories, plays, or poems to express feelings, perceptions, and points of view.	**escritura creativa** estilo de escritura en cual el escritor crea los personajes, los sucesos y las imágenes de cuentos, obras de teatro o poemas para expresar sentimientos, percepciones y puntos de vista.

D

declarative sentence a statement or expression of an opinion. It ends with a period.	**oración enunciativa** enunciado o expresión de una opinión. Termina en punto.
demonstrative pronoun word that substitutes for a noun and points out a person or thing.	**pronombre demostrativo** palabra que está en lugar de un sustantivo y señala una persona o cosa.
denotation literal meaning of a word.	**denotación** significado literal de una palabra.
descriptive writing writing that creates a vivid picture of a person, an object, or a scene by stimulating the reader's senses.	**texto descriptivo** texto que crea una imagen vívida de una persona, un objeto o una escena estimulando los sentidos del lector.

English	Español
dialogue conversation between two or more people in a story or play.	**diálogo** conversación entre dos o más personas en un cuento o en una obra de teatro.
direct object noun or pronoun that answers the question *What?* or *Whom?* after an action verb.	**objeto directo** sustantivo o pronombre que responde la pregunta ¿Qué? *(What?)* o ¿Quién? *(Whom?)* después de un verbo de acción.
direct quotation passage, sentence, or words stated exactly as the person wrote or said them.	**cita directa** pasaje, oración o palabras enunciadas exactamente como la persona las escribió o las dijo.
documentary images, interviews, and narration put together to create a powerful report.	**documental** imágenes, entrevistas y narración que se combinan para crear un informe poderoso.
double negative use of two negative words to express an idea when only one is needed.	**negación doble** uso de dos palabras negativas para expresar una idea cuando sólo una es necesaria.
drafting stage of the writing process in which the writer expresses ideas in sentences, forming a beginning, a middle, and an ending in a composition.	**borrador** etapa del proceso de escritura en la cual el escritor expresa sus ideas en oraciones que forman el principio, el medio y el final de una composición.

E

English	Español
editing stage of the writing process in which the writer polishes his or her work by correcting errors in grammar, usage, mechanics, and spelling.	**edición** etapa del proceso de escritura en la cual el escritor mejora su trabajo y corrige los errores de gramática, uso del lenguaje, aspectos prácticos y ortografía.
elaboration addition of explanatory or descriptive information to a piece of writing, such as supporting details, examples, facts, and descriptions.	**explicación** agregar información explicativa o descriptiva a un texto, como detalles de apoyo, ejemplos, hechos y descripciones.

English

electronic publishing various ways to present information through the use of technology. It includes desktop publishing (creating printed documents on a computer), audio and video recordings, and online publishing (creating a Web site).

ellipses punctuation marks (. . .) used to indicate where text has been removed from quoted material or to indicate a pause or interruption in speech.

e-mail electronic mail that can be sent all over the world from one computer to another.

essay composition of three or more paragraphs that presents and develops one main idea.

exclamatory sentence expression of strong feeling that ends with an exclamation point.

external coherence organization of the major components of a written piece (introduction, body, conclusion) in a logical sequence and flow, progressing from one paragraph to another while holding true to the central idea of the composition.

Español

publicación electrónica o Ciberedición varias maneras de presentar la información por el uso de la tecnología. Incluye la autoedición (crear documentos impresos en una computadora), las grabaciones de audio y video y la publicación en línea (crear un sitio web).

puntos suspensivos signos de puntuación (. . .) utilizados para indicar dónde se ha quitado parte del texto de una cita o para indicar una pausa o una interrupción en el discurso.

correo electrónico mensaje electrónico que puede enviarse a cualquier lugar del mundo desde una computadora a otra.

ensayo composición de tres o más párrafos que presenta y desarrolla una idea principal.

oración exclamativa expresión de sentimiento intenso que termina con signo de exclamación.

coherencia externa organización de las partes principales de un trabajo escrito (introducción, cuerpo, conclusión) en una secuencia lógica que presenta fluidez y avanza de una idea a otra, pero sustentando la idea central de la composición.

English	Español

F

fable story in which animal characters act like people to teach a lesson or moral.

fact statement that can be proven.

fiction prose works of literature, such as short stories and novels, which are partly or totally imaginary.

figurative language language that uses such devices as imagery, metaphor, simile, hyperbole, personification, or analogy to convey a sense beyond the literal meaning of the words.

folktale story that was told aloud long before it was written.

fragment group of words that does not express a complete thought.

freewriting prewriting technique of writing freely without concern for mistakes made.

friendly letter writing form that may use informal language and includes a heading, greeting (salutation), body, closing, and signature.

fábula relato en cual los personajes son animales que actúan como personas para enseñar una lección o una moraleja.

hecho enunciado que puede probarse.

ficción obras literarias en prosa, como cuentos y novelas, que son parcial o totalmente imaginarias.

lenguaje figurado lenguaje que emplea recursos tales como imágenes, metáforas, símiles, hipérboles, personificación o analogía para transmitir un sentido que va más allá del sentido literal de las palabras.

cuento folclórico relato que se contaba en voz alta mucho antes de que fuera puesto por escrito.

fragmento grupo de palabras que no expresa un pensamiento completo.

escritura libre técnica de preparación para la escritura que consiste en escribir libremente sin preocuparse por los errores cometidos.

carta amistosa tipo de texto que puede usar un lenguaje informal e incluye membrete, saludo, cuerpo, despedida y firma.

G

generalization a conclusion based on facts, examples, or instances.

generalización conclusión basada en hechos, ejemplos o casos.

English	Español
generalizing forming an overall idea that explains something specific.	**generalizando** formar una idea general que explica algo específico.
genre a distinctive type or category of text, such as personal narrative, expository essay, or short story.	**género** tipo distintivo o categoría de texto, como la narración personal, el ensayo expositivo o el cuento.
gerund verb form ending in –ing that is used as a noun.	**gerundio** forma verbal que termina en –ing y puede usarse como sustantivo.
glittering generality word or phrase that most people associate with virtue and goodness that is used to trick people into feeling positively about a subject.	**generalidad entusiasta** palabra o frase que la mayoría de la gente asocia con la virtud y la bondad, y que se utiliza con el fin de engañar a las personas para que tengan una reacción positiva respecto de cierto tema.
graphic elements (in poetry) in poetry, use of word position, line length, and overall text layout to express or reflect meaning.	**elementos gráficos (en la poesía)** en poesía, el uso de la ubicación de las palabras, la extensión de los versos y la disposición general del texto para expresar o mostrar el significado.

H

helping verb auxiliary verb that combines with the main verb to make up a verb phrase.	**verbo auxiliar** verbo que se emplea junto con el verbo principal para formar una frase verbal.
homographs words that are spelled alike but have different meanings and pronunciations.	**homógrafos** palabras que se escriben de igual manera, pero tienen significados y pronunciaciones diferentes
homophones words that sound alike but have different meanings and spellings.	**homófonos** palabras que suenan de igual manera, pero tienen significados diferentes y se escriben de manera distinta.

English	Español
imperative sentence a request or command that ends with either a period or an exclamation point.	**oración imperativa** pedido u orden que termina en punto con signo de exclamación.
indefinite pronoun word that substitutes for a noun and refers to unnamed persons or things.	**pronombre indefinido** palabra que sustituye a un sustantivo y alude a personas o cosas que no han sido identificadas.
independent clause group of words that can stand alone as a sentence because it expresses a complete thought.	**cláusula independiente** grupo de palabras que pueden formar por sí solas una oración porque expresan un pensamiento completo.
indirect object noun or pronoun that answers the question *To or for whom?* or *To or for what?* after an action verb.	**objeto indirecto** nombre o pronombre que responde la pregunta ¿A quién o para quién? (*To or for whom?*) o ¿A qué o para qué? (*To or for what?*) después de una palabra de acción.
infinitive verb form that usually begins with *to* and can be used as a noun, adjective, or adverb.	**infinitivo** forma verbal que generalmente empieza con *to* y se puede usar como sustantivo, adjetivo o adverbio.
informative writing writing that explains with facts and examples, gives directions, or lists steps in a process.	**texto informativo** texto que explica algo con hechos y ejemplos, da instrucciones o enumera los pasos de un proceso.
interjection word that expresses strong feeling.	**interjección** palabra que expresa un sentimiento intenso.
internal coherence in a written piece, organization of sentences in a logical sequence and with a fluid progression.	**coherencia interna** en un texto escrito, la organización de las ideas y/o de las oraciones en una secuencia lógica y con un desarrollo fluido.
Internet global network of computers that are connected to one another with high speed data lines and telephone lines.	**internet** red mundial de computadoras que están conectadas entre sí con líneas de datos y líneas telefónicas de alta velocidad.

English	Español
interrogative pronoun pronoun used to ask a question.	**pronombre interrogativo** pronombre utilizado para hacer una pregunta.
interrogative sentence a question. It ends with a question mark.	**oración interrogativa** pregunta. Empieza y termina con signos de interrogación en español y termina con signo de interrogación en inglés.
intransitive verb action verb that does not pass the action from a doer to a receiver.	**verbo intransitivo** verbo de acción que no transfiere la acción del agente a un receptor.
introduction first paragraph of a composition that catches the reader's attention and states the main idea.	**introducción** primer párrafo de una composición que capta la atención del lector y enuncia la idea principal.
irregular verb verb that does not form its past and past participle by adding –ed or –d to the present tense.	**verbo irregular** verbo que no forma el pasado o el participio pasado al agregar –ed o –d al tiempo presente.

jargon specialized vocabulary used by a particular group of people.	**jerga** vocabulario especializado usado por un grupo específico de personas.

linking verb verb that links the subject with another word that renames or describes the subject.	**verbo copulativo** verbo que conecta al sujeto con otra palabra que vuelve a nombrar o describe al sujeto.
literary analysis interpretation of a work of literature supported with appropriate details and quotations from the work.	**análisis literario** interpretación de una obra literaria fundamentada con detalles apropiados y citas de la obra.

English	Español
loaded words words carefully chosen to appeal to one's hopes or fears rather than to reason or logic.	**palabras tendenciosas** palabras escogidas cuidadosamente para apelar a las esperanzas o los temores del destinatario, en lugar de la razón o la lógica.

M

modifier word that makes the meaning of another word more precise.	**modificador** palabra que hace más preciso el significado de otra palabra.

N

narrative writing writing that tells a real or an imaginary story with a clear beginning, middle, and ending.	**texto narrativo** texto que relata una historia real o imaginaria con un principio, un medio y un final.
network a system of interconnected computers.	**red** sistema de computadoras interconectadas.
noncount noun a noun that names something that cannot be counted (*health, weather, music*).	**sustantivo no contable** sustantivo que designa algo que no se puede contar (la salud, el clima, la música).
nonessential phrase phrase or clause that can be removed from a sentence without changing the meaning of the sentence.	**frase accesoria** frase o cláusula que puede eliminarse de una oración sin cambiar el significado de la oración.
nonfiction prose writing that contains facts about real people and real events.	**no ficción** texto en prosa que contiene hechos sobre gente real y sucesos reales.
nonstandard English less formal language used by people of varying regions and dialects; not appropriate for use in writing.	**inglés no estándar** lenguaje menos formal utilizado por personas de diversas regiones y dialectos; inapropiado para usarlo en la escritura.

English	Español
noun a word that names a person, place, thing, or idea. A common noun gives a general name. A proper noun names a specific person, place, or thing and always begins with a capital letter. Concrete nouns name things that can be seen or touched; abstract nouns do not.	**sustantivo** palabra que designa una persona, un lugar, una cosa o una idea. Un sustantivo común expresa un nombre general. Un sustantivo propio nombra una persona, un lugar o una cosa específica y siempre comienza con mayúscula. Los sustantivos concretos designan cosas que pueden verse o tocarse, mientras que los sustantivos abstractos no lo hacen.
noun clause a subordinate clause used as a noun.	**cláusula nominal** cláusula subordinada usada como sustantivo.

O

English	Español
object word that answers the question *What?* or *Whom?*	**objeto** palabra que responde la pregunta ¿Qué? *(What?)* o ¿Quién? *(Whom?)*.
object pronoun type of pronoun used for direct objects, indirect objects, and objects of prepositions.	**pronombre objeto** tipo de pronombre utilizado para los objetos directos, objetos indirectos y objetos de preposiciones.
occasion motivation for composing; the factor that prompts communication.	**ocasión** motivación para componer; factor que da lugar a la comunicación.
online connected to the Internet via a line modem connection.	**en línea** conectado a la Internet a través de una conexión de módem.
opinion a judgment or belief that cannot be absolutely proven.	**opinión** juicio o creencia que no se puede probar completamente.
order of importance or size way of organizing information by arranging details in the order of least to most (or most to least) pertinent.	**orden de importancia o tamaño** manera de organizar la información poniendo los detalles en orden de menor a mayor (o de mayor a menor) pertinencia.

English	Español
outline information about a subject organized into main topics and subtopics.	**esquema** información sobre un tema organizada en temas principales y subtemas.

P

English	Español
paragraph group of related sentences that present and develop one main idea.	**párrafo** grupo de oraciones relacionadas que presentan y desarrollan una idea principal.
parallelism using similar words, phrases, or clauses, grammatically speaking, creating emphasis in a piece of writing and easing its readability.	**paralelismo** repetición de dos o más palabras, frases o cláusulas similares que crea énfasis en un texto escrito y facilita su lectura.
parentheses punctuation marks ( ) used to enclose supplementary information not essential to the meaning of the sentence; always used in pairs.	**paréntesis** signos de puntuación ( ) utilizados para encerrar información adicional que no es esencial para el significado de la oración; se usan siempre en parejas.
parody humorous imitation of a serious work.	**parodia** imitación humorística de una obra seria.
participial phrase participle that works together with its modifier and complement as an adjective.	**frase participial** participio que funciona junto con su modificador y su complemento como adjetivo.
participle verb form that is used as an adjective.	**participio** forma verbal que se utiliza como adjetivo.
parts of speech eight categories into which all words can be placed: noun, pronoun, verb, adjective, adverb, preposition, conjunction, and interjection.	**categorías gramaticales** ocho categorías en las que pueden clasificarse todas las palabras: sustantivo, pronombre, verbo, adjetivo, adverbio, preposición, conjunción e interjección.
passive voice the voice a verb is in when it expresses that the action of the verb is being performed upon the subject.	**voz pasiva** voz en que está el verbo cuando expresa que la acción del verbo se realiza sobre el sujeto.

English	Español

personal narrative narrative that tells a real or imaginary story from the writer's point of view.

personal pronoun type of pronoun that renames a particular person or group of people. Pronouns can be categorized into one of three groups, dependent on the speaker's position: first person *(I)*, second person *(you)*, and third person *(she/he/it)*.

personal writing writing that tells a real or imaginary story from the writer's point of view.

personification giving human qualities to nonhuman subjects.

persuasive writing writing that expresses an opinion and uses facts, examples, and reasons in order to convince the reader of the writer's viewpoint.

play a piece of writing to be performed on a stage by actors.

plot sequence of events leading to the outcome or point of the story; contains a climax or high point, a resolution, and an outcome or ending.

plural form of a noun used to indicate two or more.

poetry form of writing that uses rhythm, rhyme, and vivid imagery to express feelings and ideas.

---

narración personal narración que cuenta una historia real o imaginaria desde el punto de vista del escritor.

pronombre personal tipo de pronombre que vuelve a nombrar a una persona o grupo de personas en particular. Los pronombres se pueden clasificar en tres grupos, según la posición del hablante: primera persona *(I [yo])*, segunda persona *(you [tú])* y tercera persona *(she/he/it [ella/él])*.

narración personal texto que cuenta una historia real o imaginaria desde el punto de vista del escritor.

personificación atribuir cualidades humanas a sujetos no humanos.

texto persuasivo texto que expresa una opinión y emplea hechos, ejemplos y razones con el fin de convencer al lector del punto de vista del escritor.

obra de teatro texto escrito para que los actores lo representen en un escenario.

argumento secuencia de sucesos que lleva a la resolución del relato o propósito del mismo; contiene un clímax o momento culminante y una resolución o final.

plural forma del sustantivo utilizada para indicar dos o más personas o cosas.

poesía tipo de texto que utiliza ritmo, rima e imágenes vívidas para expresar sentimientos e ideas.

English	Español
possessive pronoun a pronoun used to show ownership or possession.	**pronombre posesivo** pronombre utilizado para indicar propiedad o posesión.
predicate part of a sentence that tells what a subject is or does.	**predicado** parte de la oración que indica qué es o qué hace el sujeto.
predicate adjective adjective that follows a linking verb and modifies, or describes, the subject.	**adjetivo predicativo** adjetivo que sigue a un verbo copulativo y modifica, o describe, al sujeto.
predicate nominative noun or a pronoun that follows a linking verb and identifies, renames, or explains the subject.	**predicado nominal** sustantivo o pronombre que sigue a un verbo copulativo e identifica, vuelve a nombrar o explica al sujeto.
prefix one or more syllables placed in front of a base word to form a new word.	**prefijo** una o más sílabas colocadas adelante de la raíz de una palabra para formar una palabra nueva.
preposition word that shows the relationship between a noun or a pronoun and another word in the sentence.	**preposición** palabra que muestra la relación entre un sustantivo o un pronombre y otra palabra de la oración.
prepositional phrase a group of words made up of a preposition, its object, and any words that describe the object (modifiers).	**frase preposicional** grupo de palabras formado por una preposición, su objeto y todas las palabras que describan al objeto (modificadores).
prewriting invention stage of the writing process in which the writer plans for drafting based on the subject, occasion, audience, and purpose for writing.	**preescritura** etapa de invención del proceso de escritura en la cual el escritor planea un borrador basándose en el tema, la ocasión, el público y el propósito para escribir.
principal parts of a verb the present, the past, and the past participle. The principal parts help form the tenses of verbs.	**partes principales de un verbo** presente, pasado y participio pasado. Las partes principales ayudan a formar los tiempos verbales.
pronoun word that takes the place of one or more nouns. Three types of pronouns are personal, reflexive, and intensive.	**pronombre** palabra que está en lugar de uno o más sustantivos. Entre los tipos de pronombres están los pronombres personales, reflexivos y enfáticos.

English

proofreading carefully rereading and making corrections in grammar, usage, spelling, and mechanics in a piece of writing.

publishing stage of the writing process in which the writer may choose to share the work with an audience.

purpose reason for writing or speaking on a given subject.

R

reader-friendly formatting page elements such as fonts, bullet points, line length, and heads adding to the ease of reading.

reflexive pronoun pronoun formed by adding *–self* or *–selves* to a personal pronoun; it is used to refer to or emphasize a noun or pronoun.

regular verb verb that forms its past and past participle by adding *–ed* or *–d* to the present.

relative pronoun pronoun that begins most adjective clauses and relates the adjective clause to the noun or pronoun it describes.

report a composition of three or more paragraphs that uses specific information from books, magazines, and other sources.

Español

corregir relectura atenta de un texto y corrección de la gramática, del uso del lenguaje, de la ortografía y de los aspectos prácticos de la escritura.

publicar etapa del proceso de escritura en la cual el escritor puede escoger dar a conocer su trabajo a un público.

propósito razón para escribir o hablar sobre un tema dado.

formato de fácil lectura elementos que se agregan a la página escrita, como tipo de letra, viñetas, extensión de los renglones y encabezados para facilitar la lectura.

pronombre reflexivo pronombre que se forma al agregar *–self* o *–selves* al pronombre personal; se usa para aludir a un sustantivo o a un pronombre o enfatizarlos.

verbo regular verbo que forma el pasado o participio pasado al agregar *–ed* o *–d* al tiempo presente.

pronombre relativo pronombre con el que comienza la mayoría de las cláusulas adjetivas y que relaciona la cláusula adjetiva con el sustantivo o pronombre que describe.

informe composición de tres o más párrafos que emplea información específica extraída de libros, revistas y otras fuentes.

English	Español
revising stage of the writing process in which the writer rethinks what is written and reworks it to increase its clarity, smoothness, and power.	**revisar** etapa del proceso de escritura en la cual el escritor vuelve a pensar en lo que ha escrito y lo adapta para mejorar su claridad, fluidez y contundencia.
rhetorical device a writing technique, often employing metaphor and analogy, designed to enhance the writer's message.	**recurso retórico** técnica de escritura, que suele emplear metáforas y analogías, destinada a realzar el mensaje del escritor.
root the part of a word that carries its basic meaning.	**raíz** parte de una palabra que lleva en sí lo esencial del significado de la palabra.
run-on sentence two or more sentences that are written as one sentence and are separated by a comma or have no mark of punctuation at all.	**oración sin final** dos o más oraciones escritas como una sola oración y separadas por una coma o escritas sin ningún signo de puntación.

S

English	Español
sensory details details that appeal to one of the five senses: seeing, hearing, touching, tasting, and smelling.	**detalles sensoriales** detalles que apelan a uno de los cinco sentidos: vista, oído, tacto, gusto y olfato.
sentence group of words that expresses a complete thought.	**oración** grupo de palabras que expresa un pensamiento completo.
sentence fragment group of words that does not express a complete thought.	**fragmento de oración** grupo de palabras que no expresa un pensamiento completo.
sequential order the order in which details are arranged according to when they take place or when they are done.	**orden secuencial** orden en que están organizados los detalles de acuerdo con el momento en que tienen lugar o cuándo se realizan.
setting the place and time of a story.	**ambiente** lugar y tiempo de un relato.

English	Español
short story well-developed story about characters facing a conflict or problem.	**relato corto** relato bien desarrollado sobre personajes que se enfrentan a un conflicto o problema.
simple predicate the main word or phrase in the complete predicate.	**predicado simple** la palabra o la frase principal en el predicado completo.
simple sentence a sentence that has one subject and one verb.	**oración simple** oración que tiene un sujeto y un verbo.
simple subject the main word in a complete subject.	**sujeto simple** la palabra principal en un sujeto completo.
slang nonstandard English expressions that are developed and used by particular groups.	**argot** expresiones propias del inglés no estándar desarrolladas y usadas por grupos específicos.
spatial order the order in which details are arranged according to their physical location.	**orden espacial** orden en el cual los detalles se organizan de acuerdo con su ubicación física.
speaker tag in dialogue, text that indicates who is speaking; frequently includes a brief description of the manner of speaking.	**identificador del interlocutor** en un diálogo, el texto que indica quién habla; suele incluir una breve descripción de la manera de hablar.
Standard English proper form of the language that follows a set pattern of rules and conventions.	**Inglés estándar** forma correcta del lenguaje que sigue un patrón establecido de reglas y convenciones.
style visual or verbal expression that is distinctive to an artist or writer.	**estilo** expresión visual o verbal que es propia de un artista o escritor.
subject (composition) topic of a composition or essay.	**tema** idea principal de una composición o ensayo.
subject (grammar) word or group of words that names the person, place, thing, or idea that the sentence is about.	**sujeto** palabra o grupo de palabras que nombran la persona, el lugar, la cosa o la idea de la que trata la oración

English	Español
subordinate clause group of words that cannot stand alone as a sentence because it does not express a complete thought.	**cláusula subordinada** grupo de palabras que no puede funcionar por sí solo como una oración porque no expresa un pensamiento completo.
subordinating conjunction single connecting word used in a sentence to introduce a dependent clause.	**conjunción subordinante** palabra de conexión usada en una oración para introducir una cláusula dependiente que expresa una idea de menor importancia que la idea principal.
suffix one or more syllables placed after a base word to create a new word that is a different part of speech.	**sufijo** una o más sílabas colocadas después de la raíz de una palabra para modificar su categoría gramatical y, posiblemente, su significado.
supporting sentence sentence that explains or proves the topic sentence with specific details, facts, examples, or reasons.	**oración de apoyo** oración que explica o prueba la oración principal con detalles específicos, hechos, ejemplos o razones.
synonym word that has nearly the same meaning as another word.	**sinónimo** palabra que significa casi lo mismo que otra palabra.

T

English	Español
tense the form a verb takes to show time. The six tenses are the present, past, future, present perfect, past perfect, and future perfect.	**tiempo verbal** forma que toma un verbo para expresar el tiempo en que ocurre la acción. Los seis tiempos verbales son: presente, pasado, futuro, presente perfecto, pretérito perfecto y futuro perfecto.
testimonial persuasive strategy in which a famous person encourages the purchase of a certain product.	**testimonial** estrategia persuasiva en cual una persona famosa alienta a comprar un cierto producto.
thesaurus online or print reference that gives synonyms for words.	**tesauro** (Diccionario de sinónimos) material de referencia en línea o impreso que ofrece alternativas para las palabras.

English	Español
topic sentence a sentence that states the main idea of the paragraph.	**oración principal** oración que enuncia la idea principal del párrafo.
transitions words and phrases that show how ideas are related.	**elementos de transición** palabras y frases que muestran las ideas cómo están relacionadas.

U

understood subject a subject of a sentence that is not stated.	**sujeto tácito** sujeto de una oración que no está explícito.
unity combination or ordering of parts in a composition so that all the sentences or paragraphs work together as a whole to support one main idea.	**unidad** combinación u ordenamiento de las partes de una composición de tal manera que todas las oraciones o párrafos funcionen juntos como un todo para fundamentar una idea principal.

V

verb word used to express an action or state of being.	**verbo** palabra usada para expresar una acción o un estado del ser.
verb phrase main verb plus one or more helping verbs.	**frase verbal** verbo principal más uno o más verbos auxiliares.
verbal verb form that acts like another part of speech, such as an adjective or noun.	**verbal** forma del verbo que funciona como otra categoría gramatical, tal como un adjetivo o un sustantivo.
voice the particular sound and rhythm of the language the writer uses (closely related to tone).	**voz** sonido y ritmo particular del lenguaje que usa un escritor (estrechamente vinculado al tono).

English	Español

W

World Wide Web network of computers within the Internet capable of delivering multimedia content and text over communication lines into personal computers all over the globe.

writing process recursive stages that a writer proceeds through in his or her own way when developing ideas and discovering the best way to express them.

red mundial de comunicación red de computadoras dentro de la Internet capaz de transmitir contenido multimedia y textos, a través de líneas de comunicación, a las computadoras personales de todas partes del mundo.

proceso de escritura etapas recurrentes que un escritor sigue a su manera cuando desarrolla ideas y descubre la mejor manera de expresarlas.

Index

A

A, an, 541, 786
Abbreviations
　common, 832
　end marks, 954
　in dictionary, 405
　punctuation of, 831-833
　for states, 833
　without periods, 832-833
A lot, 787
Abstract noun, defined, 504, 941
Accent mark, 409
Accept, except, 786
Action verbs, 482, 522-525, 529-530, 942
Address, Internet terminology, 466
Addressing
　envelopes, 421, 426-427
　letters, 420-421
Adjectival clause, 643-646
　defined, 643, 946
　misplaced, 646, 946
Adjectival phrase
　defined, 601, 944
　diagraming, 609
　identifying, 602, 603
　misplaced, 603
Adjective, 278, 536-546, 570, 766-784, 837
　articles, 541, 943
　commas that separate, 954
　comparison of, 768-773, 951
　　comparative, 768-771, 951
　　double comparisons, 774, 776-777, 951-952
　　positive, 768-771, 951
　　superlative, 768-771, 951
　compound predicate, 586, 592
　defined, 538, 943
　diagramed, 551-552
　distinguished from nouns, *543*
　distinguished from pronouns, *544*
　exercises, *278, 536-537, 539, 541-543, 545-546, 552-555, 571-572, 574, 766-773, 775-777, 779-783, 838-839*
　nouns used as, 543
　placement of, 278
　predicate, 584, 586-587, 591-594
　pronoun used as, 544
　proper, capitalizing, 541-542, 816-817, 943
　punctuation with, 540
　using, 768-785, 951
Adverb, 51, 138, 547-557
　comparison of, 768-773, 951
　　comparative, 768-771, 951
　　double comparisons, 774, 776-778, 951-952
　　positive, 768-771, 951
　　superlative, 768-771, 951
　conjunctive, 567, 943
　defined, 547, 943
　diagramed, 551-552
　distinguished from preposition, *563*
　double negatives, 777-778, 951-952
　exercises, *51, 138, 536-537, 548-550, 552-555, 563-565, 574, 766-773, 775-783*
　fine points, 138, 939
　list of, 547
　modifying adjectives, 549
　modifying other adverbs, 549
　modifying verbs, 548
　using, 547-557, 768-785, 951
　and varying sentence beginnings, 73
Adverbial clause, 640-642, 946
Adverbial phrase
　defined, 604, 945
　diagraming, 609
　identifying, 605
　punctuation with, 605
Affect, effect, 786

Agreement, pronoun-antecedent
　confusing, 732
　defined, 509, 726
　gender and, 726-727
　identifying, 510, 515, 730-732
　indefinite pronoun and, 728-729
　missing, 731
　number and, 726-727
　unclear, 730-731
Agreement, subject-verb, 738-765, 935, 950
　collective noun, 754-755, 950-951
　common problems with, 745-760, 950
　　contraction, 746-747, 950
　　helping verb, 745, 950
　　interrupting words, 748-749, 950
　　inverted sentence, 749-750, 760, 950
　　problems with pronouns, 756, 951
　compound subject, 69, 752-753
　contractions, 746-747
　indefinite pronoun, 758-759
　interrupted subject, 748-749
　inverted order, 749-750
　number, 740-741
　with *you* and *I,* 756-757
All ready, already, 787
Alliteration, 205
Almanac, 334
Alphabetizing, of names, 322
American English, 39-40
Among, between, 787
Amount, number, 787
Analogies, 375-377
Animated graphics, on Web site, 462
Antecedent. *See also* Agreement, pronoun-antecedent.
　defined, 509, 726, 942, 950
　exercises, *510-517, 727-735*
　unclear, missing, or confusing, 730-732, 950

Note: Italic locators (page numbers) indicate skill sets

Antonyms, 373-374, 416-417
Anywhere, everywhere, nowhere, somewhere, 787
Apostrophe, 956
    contractions and, 886-887
    plural possessive and, 881-883
    plurals and, 888-889
    possessive pronoun and, 721, 883-887
    singular possessive and, 880-881
Appendix, of a book, 328
Apply and Assess, 59, 81, 99, 123, 149, 209, 235, 261, 299, 321
Appositive
    comma with, 608, 954
    defined, 67, 607, 945
    diagraming, 609
    identifying, 608, 611
    punctuation with, 608
    who or *what?*, 67, 938
Appositive phrase
    commas that enclose, 954
    defined, 607, 945
    diagraming, 609
    identifying, 608, 611
    punctuation with, 608
Arrangement of library/media center, 322
Arranging ideas/information
    classifying information, 343
    order, choosing type of, 5
Articles, 541, 943
Artistic elements within texts, 121, 206-207, 454-455
Assemble editing, of video, 461
Assonance, 205
At, 788
Atlas, 332-333
Attribution. *See* Speaker tag.
Audience, 16, 104, 131, 167
    style, 38
    voice, 6, 38
Audiovisual aids, 437-439
Author/Selection
    Alan, Jack, from *The Chosen*, 86
    Alvarez, Julia, from *Learning English: My New Found Land*, 35

Anonymous
    "Stately Verse," 204
    "The Flea and the Fly," 205
Avi, from "Who Was That Masked Man, Anyway?," 699
Bradbury, Ray
    "The Drummer Boy of Shiloh," 267
    from *The Martian Chronicles*, 523
"Carved in Stone," from *The Austin American-Statesman*, 211
Cummings, E. E., from "who knows if the moon's," 805
De Veaux, Alexis, "I am the creativity," 441
DeWitt, William A., "Cleopatra," from *Illustrated Minute Biographies*, 101
Dickinson, Emily, from "Because I Could Not Stop for Death," 207
Eckroad, Reanna, from creative writing project, 247
Eigeland, Tor, "The Santa Elena Canyon," from *America's Majestic Canyons*, 159
Eliot, T. S., from "Preludes," 207
Ferlinghetti, Lawrence, from "Don't Let That Horse . . . ," 206
Foote, Horton, from *The Dancers*, 196
Frost, Robert, from "Ghost House," 804
Fuller, Millard, from "A Simple, Decent Place to Live," 871
George, Jean Craighead, from *Julie of the Wolves*, 151
Henry, O., from "The Ransom of Red Chief," 756
Hughes, Langston, from "A Dream Deferred," 207
Kennedy, John F., from "Address at Rice University on the Nation's Space Effort," 241
London, Jack, from *The Call of the Wild*, 792
Meltzer, Milton, "Which Li Wei?," from *A Book about Names*, 219
Myers, Walter Dean, from *The Mouse Rap*, 666
Paulsen, Gary, from *Hatchet*, 61

Ramirez, Victor, excerpt from creative writing project, 60
Rossetti, Christina, from "Flint," 207
Rylant, Cynthia, from *Stray*, 175
Salisbury, Graham, "Not Your Normal Beast," from *Speaking of Dreams*, 127
Santiago, Esmeralda, from *When I Was Puerto Rican*, 83
Seuss, Dr., from *Green Eggs and Ham*, 702
Soto, Gary, from *Taking Sides*, 650
Steinbeck, John, from *The Red Pony*, 489
Stevenson, Robert Louis, from "Rain," 205
Stolz, Mary, "The Old Barn," from *The Edge of Next Year*, 157
Taylor, Mildred, from *Roll of Thunder, Hear My Cry*, 538
Volpe, Natalie, excerpt from creative writing project, 185
White, E. B., from *Charlotte's Web*, 50
Whitecloud, Thomas S., from "Blue Winds Dancing," 34
Autobiography, arrangement of in library, 324
Auxiliary verb. *See* Helping verb.

B

Bad, badly, 789
Bake, principal parts, 681
Bandwagon statements, 444-445
Be, 484, 528, 584, 700
Because, 357, 641
Begin, principal parts, 686
Bibliography. *See also* Works cited.
    defined, 354
    as research tool, 328
Biographical sketch, 100-103, 112
    model, 101-102
Biography, arrangement of in library, 324
Block style, modified, for business letters, 425
Blogs, 463
Blow, principal parts, 684

Note: Italic locators (page numbers) indicate skill sets

Body. *See also* Order of ideas.
　business letter, 425
　composition, 113, 115
　drafting, 115, 349
　friendly letter, 420
　model, 115, 349
　narrative, 129
　persuasive writing, 247-248
　research report, 308
　speech, 438
　supporting paragraphs, 220, 247
　thesis statement, 220-221
　transitions, 115, 349
Book, parts of, 328. *See also* Library/media center.
Book report
　body, 294
　conclusion, 294
　introduction, 294
　model, 296
　structure, 294
Bookmark, on Internet, 339, 466
Brainstorming, 18, 130, 309, 395
Break, principal parts, 684
Brief, for audiovisual production, 456
Bring, principal parts, 682
Bring, take, 689, 789
Browser, defined, 465-466
Burst, principal parts, 682
Business forms, 430-431
Business letters, 424-429
Buy, principal parts, 682

C

Call number, 323, 326-327
Can, may, 789
Capitalization, 408, 507, 541-542, 802-827, 953
　exercises, *802-803, 805-817, 819-825*
Captions, 455
Carry, principal parts, 681
Case forms, of pronouns, 710-723
　nominative, 711-715
　objective, 716-720
　possessive, 720-723

Catch, principal parts, 682
Cause-and-effect reasoning, 285, 364, 391, 569
Character, 181-183, 185-186, 200, 272, 277, 279-288, 290-293
Character development, 173, 180-183, 185, 200
Chat, Internet, 466
Choose, principal parts, 684
Chronological order, 133, 188, 285
Citations
　parenthetical, 349, 353-355
　works-cited page, 354-355
Clarity, revising for, 22, 142-143
Classification
　of ideas, 343
Clause, 636-659. *See also* Independent clause; Subordinate clause.
　adjectival, 643-646, 655, 850-851
　adverbial, 640-642, 655, 842
　defined, 638, 945
　dependent, 638, 945
　essential (restrictive), 644, 851
　fragment, 666-667, 947
　independent, 638-639, 649-650, 653-654, 945
　main, 638, 651-652, 945
　nonessential (nonrestrictive), 644, 850-851
　punctuating, 641-642, 644-645, 647, 649-651, 956
　subordinate, 638-646, 650-652, 654-655, 945
Climax, as literary element, 181
Closing, in a letter, 420-422, 425-427, 954
Clustering, 18-19, 160
Colloquialisms, defined, 40
Colon, 375, 894-896, 957
　exercises, *895-896, 900-902*
Combining sentences, 64-65, 68-72
Come, principal parts, 686
Comma, 540, 605, 608, 621, *624*, 641, 644-647, 649-651, 668-670, 835-857, 867, *872*, 890-891, 894, 954
　using, 836-854, 867, 869, 872, 891

Common noun
　defined, 507, 941
Comparative degree, 768-772
Comparison and contrast, 285
Comparison, of adjectives and adverbs
　comparative degree, 768-772, 951
　double comparisons, 774, 776-777
　irregular, 771
　positive degree, 768-771, 951
　regular, 769
　superlative degree, 768-772, 951
Complement, 578-597, 944
Complete predicate, 481-483, 940
Complete subject, 479-480, 940
Complex sentence, 650-653, 669, 946
Composition, 100-123
　body, 115
　conclusion, 116
　defined, 100
　details, arranging, 109-111
　drafting, 113-116
　editing, 120
　exercises, *100, 102-103, 105-106, 108, 111-112, 114-116, 119-123*
　focus points, 104
　introduction, 114
　main idea, 107-108, 114
　model, 113
　prewriting, 104-112
　publishing, 121
　revising, 118-119
　subject, 104-105
　supporting details, 106
Compound direct object, 581, 590
Compound noun, 506-507, 899, 918, 941
Compound predicate nominative, 584, 713
Compound sentence
　conjunctive adverb, 567
　coordinating conjunction, 566
　defined, 70, 647, 946
　diagramed, 653
　distinguished from simple sentence with compound elements, 648

Note: Italic locators (page numbers) indicate skill sets

Compound sentence (*continued*)
   identifying, 648-649
   punctuation with, 70-71, 649-650, 956
   revising run-on sentences, 55, 669-670, 672
Compound subject, 68-69, 490, *492*, 496, 712, 752-753, 941
Compound verb, 68, 491-492, 496, 648, 840, 941
Computers. *See also* Internet; World Wide Web.
   Autoformat command, 452-453
   desktop publishing, 449-456
   fonts, 450-451
   formatting type, 451-454
   Header and Footer function, 454
   interface, 462
   layout, 452-453
   mailing lists, 469, 471
   online catalog, 326-327
   Page Setup function, 452
   search engine, 337-338, 467
   thesaurus
      Roget's Thesaurus online, 335
      using, 46
   video editing program, 461
   Web site software programs, 463
   word-processing program, 449
Concept outline, for audiovisual production, 456
Concluding sentence, 86, 94-96, 219, 231
Conclusion
   book report, 294
   composition, 116
   defined, 116
   drafting, 116
   expository writing, 220
   literary analysis, 273
   model, 116, 351
   narrative, 140
   paragraph, 116
   personal writing, 140
   persuasive writing, 247
   research report, 308, 351
   speech, 438
Concrete noun, 504, 941

Conferencing
   defined, 24
   group discussion, 434-435
   guidelines, 24
   for revision, 24, 172-173, 263-265
Conflict
   in play, 200
   in short story, 181-182, 184
Conjugation, 694, 949
Conjunctions, 70, 490-491, 566-568, *571-572*, 573-574, 640-641, 890, 937, 943
   identifying, 571-574
   using, 10, 70-71, 500, 641
Conjunctive adverb, 567-569, 571, 943
Connotation, defined, 42
Consonance, 205
Context, reading, 411
Contractions, 722-724, 746-747, 777, 886-887, 937, 950
Controlling idea, 107
Cookies, on Internet, 466
Coordinating conjunction, 70-72, 566, 954, 956
Copyright page, as research tool, 328
Correlative conjunction, 566
Creative thinking, 12
Creative writing, 174-209. *See also* Play; Poetry; Short story.
   character sketch, 185
   dialogue, 190-192, 201
   editing, 194-195
   exercises, *174, 179-180, 183-188, 191-193, 195, 200-201, 203, 205-209*
   play, 196-203
   plot, 181, 184, 192
   poetry, 204-207
   prewriting, 183-188
   publishing, 194-195
   revising, 193
   setting, 182, 187, 200
   short story, 175, 181-188, 190-195
   sound devices, 205
   stage directions, 201
Critical analysis. *See* Literary analysis.
Critical thinking. *See* Think Critically.
Cut, principal parts, 682

Cutaway shot, in video production, 460
Cyberbullying, 473
Cyberspace, defined, 466

D

Database
   CD-ROM, 336
   online, 329-332
Dates, 843, 888, 954
Declarative sentence, 493, 941
Definition, 410. *See also* Meaning of a word.
   from context, 411
   in dictionary, 407
Degrees of comparison, 768-771
   exercises, *768-773*
Demonstrative pronoun, 512-513, 544, 942
Denotation, defined, 42
Dependent clause. *See* Subordinate clause.
Derived words, in dictionary, 408
Descriptive words, 65
Descriptive writing, 150-173, 392-393
   exercises, *150, 155, 170-173*
Desktop publishing, 449-456
Details
   brainstorming, 18, 106-107, 395
   in characterization, 185
   clustering, 18-19
   in a composition, 106
   in descriptive writing, 157-161
   elaborating, 54
   5W-How? questions, 19
   inquiring, 19
   main idea, 86, 87, 88, 90, 107
   model, 159
   observation, 172
   organizing, 20, 110, 227, 229, 285
   in a paragraph, 84-85, 91
   personal writing, 135-136, 139, 141
   recalling, 134
   sensory, 47-53, 139, 160, 187, 392-393
   with sentences, 64-65

Note: Italic locators (page numbers) indicate skill sets

Details (continued)
    supporting, 19, 92, 106, 141, 157, 223, 380, 442
    visualizing, 161
Development
    of ideas, 141
    methods of, 223
    of a paragraph, 86-96
Dewey decimal classification system, 323-325
Diacritical marks, 409
Diagraming
    adjectival clause, 654
    adjectival phrase, 609
    adjective, 551-552
    adverb, 551-552
    adverbial clause, 653
    adverbial phrase, 609
    appositive, appositive phrase, 609-610
    complements, 590-592
    complex sentence, 653-654
    compound sentence, 653
    conjunction, 496, 590-592, 653
    direct object, 590
    independent clause, 653-654
    indirect object, 590-591
    infinitive phrase, 629-630
    participial phrase, 629
    phrases, 609-610
    predicate adjective, 591
    predicate nominative, 591
    prepositional phrase, 609-610
    question, 495
    relative pronoun, 654
    sentence, 495-496, 653-654
    subject, 495-496
    subordinating conjunction, 653
    understood subject, 495-496
    verb, 495-496
    verbal, verbal phrase, 629-630
Dialects, 39
Dialogue
    capitalization, 191, 866
    defined, 190
    paragraphing, 191, 870
    play, 196, 201
    punctuating, 191, 864-870, 872
    and quotation marks, 191, 864-865, 870, 955
    short story, 182, 188, 190-191
    writing, 191, 201, 870
Diary writing, 728
Dictionaries
    accent mark, 409
    as aid to spelling, 29, 681, 769, 832, 897, 899, 909, 916-917, 922
    alphabetical order, 405
    antonyms, 416
    capitalization, 408
    definitions, 407, 410
    denotative meaning, 42
    derived words, 408
    diacritical marks, 409
    entry information, 407-408
    entry word, 407-408
    finding principal parts in, 687
    guide words, 405
    meaning, 405
    parts of speech, 410, 570
    phonetic spelling, 409
    preferred spelling, 407
    pronunciation, 407, 409
    related forms, 408
    sample entry, 407
    specialized, 334
    spelling, 407
    syllable division, 408
    synonyms, 410, 415
    variant spelling, 407
    word location, 405
    word origin, 407, 410
Direct address
    capitalization, 818
    punctuation with, 846-847, 954
Direct object, 580-583, 590, 710, 716-717, 944
    identifying, 581-583, 593
    using, 581-583, 594
Direct quotations
    capitalization of, 191, 866
    commas with, 191, 867
    end marks with, 191, 868-869
    punctuating, 191, 864-872
    quotation marks with, 191, 864-865, 955
    speaker tags with, 191, 864
Directions
    giving, 220, 223, 229, 239, 433-434
    specific, 433
    stage, 201
Discussion, 360, 434-435. *See also* Group discussion.
    making relevant contributions to, 434
Dissolve, in video production, 461
Do, 484, 526, 745
    principal parts, 686
Documentary, 314
Documenting sources in a research report. *See* Citations; Research report.
Doesn't, don't, 746-747, 790
Double comparisons, 776-777, 951-952
Double negatives, 258, 556, 777-778, 790, 935, 951-952
Download, Internet technology, 466
Drafting
    body, 115, 349-350
    book report, 294
    character sketch, 286-288
    citations, 354-355
    composition writing, 113-116
    conclusion, 94-95, 116, 140, 351
    descriptive writing, 172, 173
    essay, 236, 239
    essay test, 396
    exercises, *90, 92, 96, 114-116, 136, 137, 140, 172, 173, 192, 236, 262, 264, 265, 288, 348, 350, 351, 352, 355*
    expository writing, 236
    first draft, 21, 135, 173, 286, 347, 356
    introduction, 114, 135-136, 347-348
    journal entry, 13
    literary analysis, 286-288
    model, 21
    from outline, 349-350

Note: Italic locators (page numbers) indicate skill sets

Drafting (continued)
  personal narrative writing, 135-140
  persuasive writing, 247-248, 262, 264, 265
  research report, 347-355
  short story, 190-192
  strategies, 21
  supporting sentences, 91-92
  thesis statement, 281, 395-396
  title, 116, 352
  topic sentence, 87-88, 90, 220
  transitions, 115, 137, 162, 227-231, 254-255
works cited, 354-355
Drag and drop, on Web site, 463
Drama. *See* Creative writing; Play.
Draw conclusions, 341, 365
Drink, principal parts, 686
Drive, principal parts, 684

E

Eat, principal parts, 686
Editing
  checklist, 28, 29, 397, 501, 519, 535, 557, 577, 597, 615, 635, 659, 675, 737, 785, 827, 857, 877, 905, 933
  composition, 120
  descriptive writing, 172, 173
  essay tests, 393, 397
  exercises, *507, 542, 603, 605, 608, 624, 642, 645, 650, 651, 683, 685, 688, 691, 715, 719, 727, 729, 743, 746, 747, 750, 753, 755, 757, 759, 773, 775, 777, 779, 789, 791, 795, 798, 807, 811, 813, 815, 817, 820, 821, 831, 834, 837, 838, 840, 847, 848, 852, 862, 867, 869, 891, 898, 913, 915, 917, 919, 920, 924, 927*
  expository writing, 232, 238, 239
  literary analysis, 291, 292
  for mainstream conventions, 8-11
  personal narrative, 145
  personalized editing checklist, 29
  persuasive writing, 258, 263, 264
  research report, 357

short story, 194, 195
video production, 461
for wordiness, 28
writing process, 28-30
Editorials, writing, 815
Ei, ie, spelling rule for, 911
Elaborating, 22, 54
Electronic publishing, 449-463. *See also* Publishing.
E-mail
  attachments, 470
  business, 427
  defined, 466
  following up on, 470
  guidelines, 470
  instructions, 469
  mailing lists, 471
  netiquette, 472
  options, 470-471
  style, 469
  using, 469-471
Emotional appeals
  loaded words, 445
  persuasive essay, 251
Emphasis, transitional words, 254
Emphatic forms of verbs, 702
Empty expressions, 77-78
Encyclopedias
  citing, 354, 355
  model, 318, 438
  online, 329, 331-332
  as research tool, 312, 313, 318, 331-332
  specialized, 331-332
End marks, 493-494, 828-834, 953-954
  with direct quotations, 868-869
  exercises, *494, 670, 828-829, 830-831, 834, 853-855, 868-869*
Ending. *See* Conclusion.
English language
  antonym, 373-374, 416
  colloquialisms, 40
  connotation, 42
  denotation, 42
  dialects of, 39
  dictionaries, 405-410

figures of speech, 207
formal compared with informal, 39-41
history, 402-405
idioms, 40
loaded words, 445
meaning of a word, 404
nonstandard English, 40
slang, 40
standard English, 39
synonym, 46, 373-374, 415-416
thesaurus, 46
tired words, 56
Entry word, 407-408
Envelopes
  addressing, 421
  business, 426-427
Error recognition, 384-385
Essay tests, 391-399
Essential clause or phrase, 644, 850-851, 954
Establishing shot, in video production, 459, 460
Evaluating. *See also* Revising.
  composition writing, 118, 119
  counter-arguments, 253
  creative writing, 195, 203
  defined, 253
  descriptive writing, 158, 160, 163, 165, 167
  and drawing conclusions, 365
  expository writing, 232
  language choice, 45
  listening to, 445-446
  literary analysis, 273, 292
  personal narrative writing, 136, 146
  persuasive writing, 253, 259
  research report, 358
  reasons and consequences, 69
  sentence structure, 73
  sources, 315
    online, 315-317
    print, 315

Note: Italic locators (page numbers) indicate skill sets

Evaluating (continued)
　using rubrics
　　fluency, 79
　　organization, 119
　　six-trait, 23, 146, 167, 195, 232, 259, 292, 358
　　voice rubric, 38
　word choice, 57
Evaluation checklist, 24
　composition, 118
　descriptive writing, 168
　expository writing, 237
　literary analysis, 290
　personal writing, 142
　persuasive writing, 257
　research report, 356
　short story, 193
Exclamation point, 493, 569, 830, 841, 868, 954
Exclamatory sentence, 493, 941
Explanatory writing. See Informative writing.
Exposition. See Literary analysis; Informative writing; Research report.
Expository writing, 210-239. See also Informative writing.

F

Fact, 114, 219, 249-251, 253, 302-305, 444
　defined, 249, 444
　exercises, *250, 251, 253, 444*
Fade, in video recording, 461
FAQs, Internet technology
　defined, 466
　netiquette, 473
Favorites, Internet terminology, 339
Feedback
　giving, 82, 169
　from peers, 25, 42, 69, 76, 96, 114, 120, 131, 141, 143, 158, 160, 163, 169, 183, 185, 193, 203, 205, 206, 248, 252, 258, 280, 281, 314, 356, 423, 424, 439, 440, 445
　responding to, 119
　from teacher, 27, 160, 195, 232

Fewer, less, 790
Fiction. See also Short story.
　arrangement of in library, 322-323
　defined, 322
　elements of, 276
　finding meaning in, 277
　historical, 267-272, 298
　model, 61-62
Figurative language
　defined, 207
　imagery, 207
　metaphor, 207
　personification, 207
　simile, 207
Figures of speech, 207. See Figurative language.
Final cut, in video production, 461
First-person point of view
　as literary element, 132, 276
　in narrative, 127, 132
　in short story, 182
5W-How? questions, 19
Flaming, Internet terminology
　defined, 466
　netiquette, 472
Fluency, 939, *943*
Focus, 142-143. See also Unity.
Fonts, 233, 450-451. See also Type fonts.
Formal English, 786
Formal outline, 344-345. See also Outline.
Formal speaking. 435-440. See also Speech preparation.
Forms
　business, 430-431
　of writing, 15
Fragment. See Sentence fragment.
Freewriting
　as personal response strategy, 275
　as prewriting strategy, 20, 106, 130, 277, 280, 436
Freeze, principal parts, 684
FTP, defined, 466
Future perfect tense, 694, *949*
Future tense, 694, *948*

G

Gathering evidence, 282-284
Gathering information
　for research report, 312-339
　for speech, 437-438
Gender
　agreement of pronoun and antecedent, 726-727
　defined, 726
Generalization, 89, *957*
Gestures, 256, 400, 439, 440, 446
Give, principal parts, 684
Glossary, 328
Glossary of Usage, 786-799
Go, principal parts, 686
Good, well, 779-780, 790
Grammar QuickGuide, 940-947
Graphic elements, 206
Graphic organizer, 85, 272, 273, 284, 306, 345, 369, 370, 395, 780
　defined, 369
Graphics
　charts and graphs, 455
　clip art, 454-455
　in compositions, 121
　digital images, 454-456
　drawings, 454
　photographs, 455
　stand-alone, 456
　for Web site, 462-463
Group discussion, 434-435
　guidelines for participating in, 434-435
Grow, principal parts, 684

H

Handbooks, list of, 29
Hasn't, haven't, 747
Have, as helping verb, 484, 526-527, 745
Have, of, 790

Note: Italic locators (page numbers) indicate skill sets

Heading
- in a business letter, 425, 426
- in a friendly letter, 420, 421
- in an informational letter, 422
- on a note card, 318, 333, 342

Helping verb, 484, 526-527, 548, 620, 680, 682, 693, 694, 745-746, 942, 950

Home page, 463
- defined, 466HTML, 463, 467

http, 467

Hyphen, 897-900, 922, 957

I

Ideas for writing. *See also* Arranging ideas/information; Main idea; Order of ideas.
- brainstorming, 18, 106, 130, 395
- clustering, 18-19, 130, 160
- 5W-How? questions, 19
- freewriting, 130
- personal experience, 22, 126, 274, 341
- for play, 196-203
- for poetry, 204-207
- prewriting techniques, 13-20, 130-134, 279-285
- recalling, 134, 295
- thinking, 13-14, 54, 72, 89, 134, 295, 343

Idioms, defined, 40

Ie, ei, spelling rule for, 911-912

Illustrations. *See* Graphics.

Imagining, 186

Imperative sentence, 493, 941

Implied main idea, 87

Impression
- overall, 158, 167-168, 282

In, into, 791

In the Media
- Across the Media: Magazines, Internet, Newspapers, 97
- Across the Media: News Styles, 117
- Advertising, 43
- Classified Advertisement, 166
- Documentary, 314
- Evaluating Performances, 289
- Movies and Plays, 202
- News Lead-ins, 222
- Opinions and Advertising, 251
- Television Nightly News, 74
- Television Talk Shows, 144

In-camera editing, of video, 461

Indefinite pronoun,
- agreement problems and, 758, 759, 951
- defined, 512, 758, 942
- gender and, 728
- plural, 728-729, 758, 883
- possessive, 883-884
- singular, 728, 758, 883

Independent clause, 638, 649-650, 653-654, 890, 945

Index, as research tool, 29, 328, 331, 336

Indirect object
- complement, 580, 584
- compound, 582
- defined, 581, 944
- diagraming, 590-592
- identifying, 581, 582, 583
- pronoun and, 710, 716, 717

Indirect quotation, 864-865

Infinitive, 618, 626-630

Inflected form, in dictionary, 407-408

Informal English, 786

Information. *See also* Details.
- arrangement of, in library/media center, 322-327
- evaluating, 315-317

Information sources
- almanacs, 329, 334
- atlases, 329, 332-333
- audiovisual, 437
- biographical references, 332, 335
- CD-ROMS, 336
- database, 312, 315, 329-332
- encyclopedia, 329, 331-332
- evaluating, 315-317
- handbooks, 29
- library, 29, 322-339
- library catalog, 312, 315, 326-327, 329
- newspapers, 97, 251, 315, 329-331
- nonprint resources, 314, 329-339, 462
- online, 312, 315-317, 326-327, 463
- *Readers' Guide to Periodical Literature*, 336
- reference books, 324, 329
- research report, 302
- specialized, 331-332, 334-335
- thesaurus, 46, 335, 367
- traditional card catalog, 326
- vertical file, 335
- World Wide Web and online services, 312, 315-317, 326-327, 463, 465, 468

Informative messages
- organizing, 437-438
- preparing, 435-438
- presenting, 439-440

Informative presentations
- evaluating presentations of peers, public figures, and media, 443-446

Informative Writing, 210, 219-233 *See also* Expository writing; Literary analysis; Research report
- audience, 221
- Apply and Assess, 235
- body, 219-221
- cause-and-effect writing, 569
- checklist, 237
- coherence, 227-228, 232
- conclusion, 219, 221
- details, arranging in logical order, 227-231
- drafting, 219-232
- editing, 232
- exercises, *220, 223, 225, 228, 230-231*
- facts and examples, 223
- feature story, 211-217
- 5W-How? questions, 19
- giving directions, 220, 229
- how-to writing, 210, 219-220, 225
- introduction, 220-221
- letters, 422-423
- logical order, 227-231
- model, 211, 219-220, 227, 229
- news story, 211-217

Note: Italic locators (page numbers) indicate skill sets

Informative writing (continued)
  organizing, 219-221, 225-231
  paragraph and essay structure, 219-221
  presentations, 233
  prewriting, 236
  publishing, 233, 238-239
  revising, 231-232
  sequential order, 229
  steps in the process, 225
  supporting points, 219, 221, 223
  thesis statement, 219-221, 223, 225
  transitions, 227, 229, 231
  uses, 219-220, 225, 227, 229, 236-239
Inquiring, 19
Insert editing, of video, 461
Inside address, business letter, 425-426
Intensive pronoun, 511, 942
Interest inventory, 13
Interfaces, on Web site, 462
Interjection
  common, 569
  defined, 569, 571, 943-944
  identifying, 571-572
  review, 571-572
Internet. *See also* Electronic publishing.
  access to, 462, 464-465
  attachments, 470
  blogs, 463
  browser, 337, 463, 465-466
  chat, 466, 472
  chat rooms, 471-472
  cyberspace, 464-466
  e-mail, 418-419, 427, 466, 469-472
  graphics, 462
  guidelines, 472-473
  HyperText Markup Language (HTML), 463, 467
  HyperText Transfer Protocol (HTTP), 465, 467
  Information Super Highway, 337, 465
  Internet Relay Chat, 471

Internet Service Provider (ISP), 464, 467
keyword searches, 337, 467
links, 316, 337-338, 463, 467
mailing lists, 471-472
netiquette, 467, 472-473
newsgroups, 471-473
research guidelines, 338
research source, 337-339
search engine, 312, 329, 337-338, 467
study tool, 326-327, 331-339, 367, 401
terminology, 466-468
Uniform Research Locator (URL), 462, 465, 468
usage, 464-473
visuals, 462, 470
vocabulary, 465-468
Web sites, 465, 468
World Wide Web, 465, 468
Internet Guide, 464-473
Interrogative pronoun, 512-513, 544, 724, 942
Interrogative sentence, 493, 941
Interrupting words, subject-verb agreement, 745, 748-749, 758, 764, 950
Intransitive verb, 524, 942
Introduction
  composition, 113-114
  and conclusion, 116, 135, 221, 247, 273, 308, 351, 396, 438
  descriptive writing, 158
  functions, 273
  model, 21, 113-114, 135, 220, 247, 347-348, 351, 396
  paragraph, 114, 247, 273, 288, 308, 347-348, 396
  persuasive writing, 247
  readers' attention, 21, 114, 135, 247, 308, 347, 438
  research report, 294, 308, 347
  setting a scene, 136
  short story, 190-192
  speech, 438
  techniques for writing, 21, 114, 135, 220-221, 247, 273, 288, 308, 347-348, 396, 438

thesis statement, 220, 247, 273, 288, 396
tone, 136, 158
Introductory elements, commas and, 841-843, 954
Inverted order, agreement, subject-verb, 745, 749-751, 764
Inverted order of sentence, 487, 489, 795, 950
IRC, defined, 471
Irregular comparison of modifiers, 771-773
Irregular verbs, 8, 194, 238, 682-706, 935
  defined, 682
  principal parts, 682, 684, 686
ISP, 464, 467, 470
Italicizing titles, 291, 860
Italics (underlining), 291, 860-862, 888, 918, 955
  exercises, *861-862*
Items in a series, 278, 835-837, 856, 892, 894, 954, 956
Its, it's, 791

J

Journal
  composition, 104
  editing tool, 29
  keeping, 12-13, 29, 463, 909
  learning log, 14, 259
  Personalized Editing Checklist, 29
  persuasive writing, 259
  prewriting tool, 13-14
  vocabulary, 909
  writing
    compositions, 104
    descriptive, 82
    personal, 13, 14, 29, 82, 104, 130, 463
Juxtaposition, 192

K

Keyword, in online search, 312, 316, 337-338, 467
Know, principal parts, 684

Note: Italic locators (page numbers) indicate skill sets

L

Language, 7-11, 34, 39-56, 207, 432
Language of Power
   Agreement, 69
   Fragments, 357
   Negatives, 258
   Of v. *Have*, 291
   Past Tense, 194, 238
   Possessive Nouns, 120
   Pronouns, 145
   Run-on Sentences, 55
   Sound-Alikes, 96
   Verb Tense, 169
Lay, Lie, 792
Layout
   captions and titles, 455
   charts and graphs, 455
   clip art, 454
   drawings, 454
   font selection, 450-451
   icons, 454-455
   photographs, 455
   planning, 456, 457
   preset page layouts, 452-453
Learn, principal parts, 690
Learn, teach, 792
Learning log, as prewriting strategy, 14
Leave, let, 691
Leave, principal parts, 682, 691
Less, fewer, 790
Let, principal parts, 682, 691
Letter of request, 426-428
Letters. *See* Business letters; Personal letters.
Library/media center
   arrangement of fiction, 322
   arrangement of nonfiction, 323-324
   autobiographies, 324
   biographies, 324
   call number, 323, 324, 326
   Dewey decimal classification system, 323-324
   non-print sources, 329
   online catalog, 326
   reference materials, 329-339
Limiting a subject (of a composition), 14-15, 131, 280, 309
Link, on Internet, 337, 467
Linking verb, 528-532, 584, 943
List. *See* Items in a series.
Listening and viewing
   active, 401
   appreciative listening, 440-441
   asking relevant questions, 442
   critical listening, 443-445
   evaluate 445-446
   exercises, *440, 441, 443, 444, 446*
   focusing attention on speaker's message, 442
   for information, 441
   interpret visual information, 289
   monitoring for understanding, 442
   note-taking, 441, 442-443
   observing changes in language, 440
   to performances, 202
   to presentations, 440-442
   recognizing propaganda, 443-445
   reflective listening, 289
   responding to performances, 289
   responding to presentations, 441
   to speaker's purpose, 441, 444-445
   strategies for, 440
Literary analysis, 266-299
   body, 273
   conclusion, 273
   defined, 266
   details
      gathering, 282
      organizing, 285
   editing, 291
   exploring meaning, 277
   gathering evidence, 282, 283
   introduction, 273
   literary elements, 276
   prewriting, 281-285
   publishing, 293
   response, 274-277
   revising, 290
   structure, 273
   subject, choosing, 279-280
   thesis statement, 281
   titles, 273
   uses of, 266, 272
Literary elements
   character, 181, 185, 186, 279, 293
   contributing to meaning, 187
   dialogue, 191, 201
   figures of speech, 207
   list of, 181, 182
   meter, 276
   mood, 47, 182
   narrator, 182
   persona, 276
   plot, 181, 184, 192, 276, 277
   point of view, 132, 151, 276
   rhyme scheme, 206, 276
   setting, 182, 187, 200, 276, 277
   shape, 39, 276
   sound devices, 205
   theme, 182, 276, 277
   tone, 182, 187, 276
Literary present tense, 294, 693
Literary references, 858
   citing, 353
Literary writing. *See* Play; Poetry; Short story.
Literature. *See also* Literary analysis; Short story.
   analysis, 181-183
   characteristics, 181, 187
   evaluating, 182-183, 193
   reference books, 329, 331
Loaded words, defined, 445
Logical order, 5, 109, 113, 162, 165, 227
-ly, -ness, spelling rule for, 414

M

Mailing lists, 471, 472
Main clause. *See* Independent clause.
Main idea
   developing, 107
   implied, 87
   in outline, 443
   of a paragraph, 82

Note: Italic locators (page numbers) indicate skill sets

in personal writing, 135
in short story, 157, 182
stated, 441
thesis statement, 223, 281
Make, principal parts, 682
Manual of style, 29
Manuscript form, 31
Meaning of a word
  antonyms, 373, 416
  colloquialisms, 40
  connotation, 42
  context, 411
  denotation, 42
  dictionary definition, 42, 407
  idioms, 40
  loaded word, 445
  slang, 40
  synonyms, 46, 410, 415
Mechanics QuickGuide, 953-959
Media
  advertisements, 97, 166, 251, 444
  analyzing, 74, 144
  comparing and contrasting coverage of same event, 74, 117
  creating a media text, 117, 122, 222
  creating a project, 97, 122
  critiquing various coverage of same event, 74, 117
  cultures, 12, 97, 260, 402, 403
  distinguishing purpose of, 251, 249
  documentary, 314
  engaging specific audiences, 15, 104, 117
  entertaining texts, 15, 243
  evaluating elements of design, 117, 121
  evaluating persuasive techniques of, 240-246, 257, 259
  evaluating sources, 315-317, 447
  examining effect of media on perception of reality, 251
  genres, 15, 16, 104, 117
  ideas, 97, 233
  identifying properties of, 253
  informative texts, 38, 219
  planning media text, 314, 456-457
  presenting a project, 233
  relationships, 401
  response, 43
  revise a project, 461
  sound techniques, 461, 457
  symbols, 454, 456
  using various forms, 401
  using various technologies, 447-473
  visual techniques, 454-461
Media activity
  Across the Media: Magazines, Internet, Newspapers, 97
  Across the Media: News Styles, 117
  Advertising, 43
  Classified Advertisement, 166
  Documentary, 314
  Evaluating Performances, 289
  Movies and Plays, 202
  News Lead-ins, 222
  Opinions and Advertising, 251
  Television Nightly News, 74
  Television Talk Shows, 144
Memoir, 35-37, 82-85, 98
  model, 35-37, 83-84
Metaphor, 207
Meter. *See* Rhythm.
Middle. *See* Body.
Misplaced modifiers, 603, 624
MLA format for source credit, 355
MLA Handbook for Writers of Research Papers, 29, 355
Mnemonic device, 909, 912, 925
Modern English, 404
Modifiers. *See also* Adjective; Adverb.
  bad, badly, 413, 789
  clause, 640-646
  comparative degree, 768-770, 776
  comparison of, 769-777, 782
  distinguishing adjective and adverb, 601, 604
  exercises, *539, 542, 543, 548-555*
  irregular comparison, 771
  and linking verbs, 528-530
  misplaced, 603, 624
  placement of, 189, 278, 538, 588, 603
  positive degree, 768
  problems with
    double comparisons, 951-952
    double negatives, 951-952
  regular comparison, 769
  superlative degree, 768-770, 776
Mood, 47, 182, 190, 457
Multimedia, 208, 233, 314, 360, 456-461
Multiple-choice questions, in tests, 373-390

N

Narrative writing, 126-149
  concluding sentence, 140
  defined, 126
  drafting, 135-140
  editing, 145
  evaluating, 142
  exercises, *129, 131*
  model, 127
  practice, 139, 140, 143
  prewriting, 130-134
  purpose, 131, 135
  revising, 141-143
  structure, 129, 133
  supporting sentences, 139, 143
  topic sentence, 135
Narrator, 132, 182
Natural order of sentences, 487
Net, defined, 467
Netiquette, 467, 472
Network, on Internet, 464-473
Newsgroups, 469, 471, 472
Newspaper
  online, 329
  as research tool, 329
Nominative case, 711, 949. *See also* Predicate nominative; Pronoun; Subject of a sentence.
  exercises, *712, 714-715*
Nonessential clause or phrase, 621, 644, 850, 954

Nonfiction
    arrangement of in library, 323-324
    defined, 323
Nonrestrictive clause or phrase. *See* Nonessential clause or phrase.
Nonverbal communication, 400
Note cards, 282-283, 319, 438
Note-taking
    graphic organizer, 369
    model, 370
    note cards, 282-283
Note-taking (continued)
    in presentations, 438, 441, 442
    for research report, 342
    strategies, 369-371
    as study skill, 369
    summary, 369, 371
Noun, 502-519
    abstract, 504, 941
    antecedent, 509, 942
    collective, 752, 950
    common, 507, 807, 941
    compound, 506, 507, 897, 899, 918, 941
    concrete, 504, 505, 941
    defined, 504, 941
    exercises, *505, 515-517, 543, 882-884*
    plurals, forming, 740, 956-957
    possessive case, 710, 956
    proper, 507, 807-815, 941
Nowhere, nowheres, 787
Number. *See also* Plurals.
    agreement of pronoun and antecedent, 726-729
    agreement of subject and verb, 740
    defined, 740
    plural, 726, 740, 741
    singular, 726,
Numbers
    in dates, 843
    fractions, 897, 899
    with hyphens, 897, 898
    plural, 888
    words or numerals, 899

O

Object of preposition, 561, 562, 716, 797
Object of verb. *See* Direct object; Indirect object.
Objective case, 716, 718, 724, 949
Occasion
    defined, 15
    writing process, 15, 16
Online catalog
    explained, 326
    limiting search, 338
    search by keyword, 329, 337, 338
    search by subject, 329, 338
    search by title, 329,
    strategies for use, 327, 338
Online database. *See* Online catalog.
Online, defined, 467
Onomatopoeia, 205
Opinion
    defined, 249, 444
    exercises, *250, 444*
    expert, 253
    statement of, 241, 247
    support of, in persuasive writing, 106, 240, 250
    words, 444
Oral language
    audience, 15
    contributing to discussions, 275, 432, 436
    eye contact, 439
    formal speech, 435
    giving directions, 433
    informal speech, 432
    listening, 440-446
    nonverbal guidelines, 439
    pitch of voice, 440, 834
    purpose, 436, 434
    verbal guidelines, 433
    volume of voice, 440
Order of ideas
    chronological order, 5, 105, 133, 188, 285
    classification, 343
    logical order, 109, 113, 133, 162, 165
    order of importance, 5, 227, 254, 285, 393
    sequential order, 229-230
    spatial (space) order, 5, 162, 165
Order of importance
    arranging ideas, 227-231
    defined, 227, 254
    model, 227
    in persuasive writing, 254-257
    transitions, 227, 254-257
Organization
    of argument/counter-argument, 247, 252, 254
    of details, 110, 285
    of ideas, 20, 110, 342, 343
    of notes, 342
Out-of-sequence filming, 458
Outline
    capitalization, 345, 805
    concept, in audiovisual production, 456
    defined, 344
    guidelines, 345, 805, 833
    informal, 369, 370, 395
    main idea, 344, 345, 369, 395
    model, 344, 443
    punctuation, 345, 833, 954
    research report, 344-346
    speech preparation, 442, 443

P

Panning, in video production, 459
Paragraph
    body, 91-92, 115, 248, 273, 349-350
    composition writing, 113-116
    conclusion, 94-95, 116, 140, 247-248, 273, 308
    defined, 82
    descriptive writing, 157
    details, listing, 92, 106, 139
    expository writing, 219-221
    introduction, 114, 135-136, 247, 273, 308
    literary analysis, 273

Note: Italic locators (page numbers) indicate skill sets

Paragraph (continued)
  main idea, 86-87, 107, 114, 135, 281
  model, 86
  narrative, 135-140
  persuasive writing, 247-248
  sensory details, 47-53, 160
  sequence of events, 133
  structure, 86-95
  supporting sentences, 86, 91-92, 219-220
  topic sentence, 86-90, 219-220
  transitional words, 137, 162, 165, 227, 254-255
Parallelism, 164, 836,
  with conjunctions, 568
  with verbals, 628
Paraphrasing, 319, 349
Parenthetical citations, 349, 353-354
Parenthetical expressions, 847-848, 954
Participial phrase, 189, 525, 621-625, 664, 954
  commas with, 842, 850-851
Participle, 618-620
  defined, 525, 618
  past participle, 680-691
  present participle, 680-691
  as principal part of verb, 680-681
Part-of-Speech labels, in dictionary, 410
Parts of speech, 44, 504, 570-572
Passed, past, 793
Past perfect tense, 694, 949
Past tense, 169, 194, 238, 693-694, 706, 948
Peer conferencing
  group discussion, 434-435
  guidelines, 434
Peer evaluation, 358, 446
Performances, 202
  evaluating, 289
Period
  after abbreviation, 831-832
  as end mark, 493, 830-831, 954
  exercises, *828-829, 834, 853-855*
  inside quotation marks, 191, 868-869

  with outlines, 344-345, 833
Periodicals, 329
Personal experiences
  as prewriting strategy, 13
  and response to literature, 274-275
Personal letters, 419-424
Personal pronoun, 510-511, 710-723, 883, 942, 950. *See also* Pronoun.
  as object, 716-720
  plural, 710
  possessive, 710, 720-723
  as predicate nominative, 710, 711, 713-714
  singular, 710
  as subject, 712
Personal writing, 15, 126-149. *See also* Narrative writing.
Personalized editing checklist, 29
Personification, 207
Persuasive techniques
  bandwagon appeals, 444
  counter arguments, , 252-253
  emotional appeal, 251
  expert opinion, 247, 253
  loaded words, 445
  repetition, 256
  testimonial, 445
Persuasive writing, 240-265
  argument, developing, 247
  audience, 246
  body, 247-248, 257
  conclusion, 245, 247-248
  counter-argument, developing, 252-253
  defined, 240
  drafting, 262, 264, 265
  editing, 258, 263, 264
  evidence
    evaluating, 253
    organizing, 254-255
  examples, using, 249-250, 262-263
  exercises, *262-265*
  fact, 249-250, 264, 444
  introduction, 247
  language, emotional, 251
  model, 241-245, 247-248, 254, 255

  opinion
    defined, 249, 444
    expert, 247, 253
  order of importance, 254-255
  prewriting, 262, 264, 265
  publishing, 263, 264
  purpose, 240
  readers' attention, 247
  reasoning, 246, 265, 364
  repetition, 256
  revising, 250, 252, 255, 257, 258, 263, 264, 265
  structure, 247-248
  supporting claims and arguments, 249-250
  supporting sentences and paragraphs, 254
  thesis statement, 247, 262
  topic sentence, 254
  transitions, 254-255
Phonetic spelling, 409
Photo essay, 234
Photograph, 454-455
  describing, 47
Phrase, 112, 598-615
  adjectival, 601-603, 778, 944
  adverbial, 604-606, 945
  appositive, 607-608, 751, 945
  comma with, 841-843, 850-851
  defined, 600
  exercises, *598-599, 611-613*
  fragment, 664-665, 946
  infinitive, 627
  participial, 189, 525, 621-625, 938
  prepositional, 51, 561-562, 600-601, 943-945
  and varying sentence beginnings, 73
  verb, 484-486, 526-527, 745-746
  verbal, 616-635
Plagiarism, 319, 353
Play, 148, 196-203
  conflict, 200
  defined, 196
  dialogue, 201
  model, 196-200
  playwright, 196

Play (continued)
  setting, 200
  sketching characters, 200
  stage directions, 201
Plot
  building an engaging, 184
  climax, 180, 181, 182
  conflict, 180, 181, 182, 184, 200
  defined, 181, 276
  enhancing, 192
  as literary element, 276
  order of events, 188
  for plays, 201
  triggering event, 182, 190
Plug-in, defined, 467
Plural possessive, 881-882
Plurals, 740-744, 914-921, 957-958
  irregular, 919
  letters, 918
  noun
    regular, 914
    ending in *f* or *fe*, 916
    ending in *o*, 915
    ending in *y*, 914
  numerals, 918
  symbols, 918
  words as words, 918
Podcast, defined, 455
Poetry, 204-209
  capitalization of, 804-805
  defined, 204
  figurative language
    imagery, 207
    metaphor, 207
    personification, 207
    simile, 207
  finding ideas for, 204
  graphic elements, 206
  model, 204, 205, 206
  pun, 204
  rhyme schemes, 206
  techniques
    alliteration, 205
    assonance, 205
    consonance, 205
    onomatopoeia, 205
    repetition, 205

rhyme, 205
rhythm, 205
Point of view
  checking online, 316
  defined, 132, 276
  first-person, 132
  as literary element, 276
  model, 132
  narrator, 182
  third-person, 132
Portfolio, 31-32
Positive degree, 768
Possessive case
  and apostrophe, 120, 518, 721, 880-883
  nouns, 120, 518
  personal pronouns, 883, 949
  plural nouns, 881-883, 936
  pronouns, 710, 720-721, 883-885
  pronouns, distinguished from contractions, 722-723, 886-887
  singular nouns, 880-881, 936
Post-production, 461
Posttests
  adjectives and adverbs, 555
  capital letters, 825
  clauses, 657
  complements, 595
  end marks and commas, 855
  italics and quotation marks, 875
  nouns and pronouns, 517
  other parts of speech and review, 575
  other punctuation, 903
  phrases, 613
  sentence fragments and run-ons, 673
  sentence, the, 499
  spelling correctly, 931
  subject and verb agreement, 763
  using adjectives and adverbs, 783
  using pronouns, 735
  using verbs, 705
  verbals and verbal phrases, 633
  verbs, 533

Power of Language
  Adjectives: Modifiers Come Lately, 278
  Adverbs and Prepositional Phrases: Scene Setters, 51
  Adverbs: Fine Points, 138
  Appositives: *Who* or *What*?, 67
  Fluency: Let it Flow, 346
  Parallelism: The Power of Threes, 164
  Participial Phrases: Getting into the Action, 189
  Phrases: Scene Setters, 112
  Say It Again: Using Repetition, 256
  Semicolons: Catch and Release, 93
  Strong Verbs: In Living Color, 224
Power Rules, 8
  Language of Power
    Agreement, 69
    Fragments, 357
    Negatives, 258
    Of v. *Have*, 291
    Past Tense, 194, 238
    Possessive Nouns, 120
    Pronouns, 145
    Run-on Sentences, 55
    Sound-Alikes, 96
    Verb Tense, 169
    Writer's Corner, 500-501, 518-519, 534-535, 556-557, 576-577, 596-597, 614-615, 634-635, 658-659, 674-675, 706-707, 736-737, 764-765, 784-785, 826-827, 856-857, 876-877, 904-905, 932-933
Predicate, 481-486. *See also* Verb.
  complete, 481, 940
  defined, 481, 940
  simple, 482-483, 940
Predicate adjective, 580, 584-587, 944
Predicate nominative, 584-585, 944, 949
  exercises, *585*
Prefixes, 412-413, 922, 958-959

Note: Italic locators (page numbers) indicate skill sets

Preposition. *See also* Prepositional phrase.
  compound, 600
  defined, 560, 943
  distinguished from an adverb, 563-564
  exercises, *558-559, 561, 563-564*
  identifying, 560
  list of, 560, 600
  object of, 716-719
Prepositional phrase, 600-606. *See also* Preposition.
  compound object of, 561
  defined, 561, 600
  distinguishing from infinitive, 626-627
  identifying, 561-562
  scene setters, 51, 938
  as a sentence beginning, 73
Pre-production, audiovisual, 456-458
Present participle, 618, 680-691
Present perfect tense, 694, 949
Present tense, 693, 948
Presentations, 359, 432-446
  audience feedback, 440, 445
  evaluating, 445-446
  expository, 233
  eye contact, 439, 446
  improving for future presentations, 440
  informative, 436
  listening to, 440-446
  media presentations, 233, 456-463
  persuasive, 436
  pitch of voice, 439-440, 446
  posture, 439, 446
  self-evaluating, 440
  tone of voice, 439-440, 446
  verbal strategies, 439-440, 446
  volume of voice, 439-440, 446
Pretests
  adjectives and adverbs, 536-537
  capital letters, 802-803
  clauses, 636-637
  complements, 578-579
  end marks and commas, 828-829
  italics and quotation marks, 858-859

  nouns and pronouns, 502-503
  other parts of speech and review, 558-559
  other punctuation, 878-879
  phrases, 598-599
  sentence fragments and run-ons, 660-661
  sentence, the, 476-477
  spelling correctly, 906-907
  subject and verb agreement, 738-739
  using adjectives and adverbs, 766-767
  using pronouns, 708-709
  using verbs, 678-679
  verbals and verbal phrases, 616-617
  verbs, 520-521
Prewriting
  audience, 15-16, 39, 104-105, 131
  brainstorming, 18, 20, 106, 173, 395
  clustering, 18-19
  compositions, 104-112
  creative writing, 184-189
  defined, 13
  descriptive writing, 157-160, 172, 173
  essay test, 395
  expository writing, 219-221, 236, 239
  genre, 16
  inquiring, 19
  journal, 13
  learning log, 14
  note cards, 283-284, 319, 342, 438
  observing, 172
  occasion, 15
  outlining, 344-345
  organize, 20
  personal narrative, 130-134
  persuasive writing, 247-250, 262, 264, 265
  plays, 200-201
  poems, 204
  purpose, 15
  short story, 184-189
  strategies, 13-20

  subject, choosing and limiting, 14-15
  thesis statement, 281, 395
  writing a research report, 308-319, 341, 342
  writing about literature, 279-285
  writing process, 13-20
Prewriting strategies
  to generate ideas
    background reading, 13-14
    brainstorming, 18
    choosing and limiting a subject, 14-15
    clustering, 18-19
    discussing, 13-14
    freewriting, 20
    inquiring, 19
    interviewing, 13-14
    journal, 13
    learning log, 14
    observing, 172
    personal interests, 13
    recalling, 134
  to plan
    organize details, 18-20
Principal parts of verbs, 680-692
Problem-solving, 365
Proceed, precede, 912
Progressive forms of verbs, 700-701, 949
Pronoun, 145, 509-514, 708-737
  as adjective, 544-545
  agreement with antecedents, 509-510, 726-732, 950
  antecedent, 509, 942,
  as appositive, 67, 607-608
  defined, 509, 942
  demonstrative, 512-513, 942
  exercises, *502-503, 515-517, 708-709, 733-735*
  first-person, 510
  gender, 726, 728
  indefinite, 512, 728-729, 758-760, 883-884, 942, 951
  intensive, 510-511, 942
  interrogative, 513, 724-725, 942
  nominative case, 710-715, 949
  number, 726, 740-742

Note: Italic locators (page numbers) indicate skill sets

Pronoun (continued)
  as object, 936
  objective case, 710, 716-720, 949
  personal, 510, 710-723, 942, 956
  plurals, 510-511, 726, 728-729
  possessive case, 710, 720-723, 883-884, 949, 956
  possessive, confused with contractions, 722-723, 886
  as predicate nominative, 713-715, 949
  reflexive, 510-511, 942
  relative, 513-514, 643, 942
  second-person, 510, 710, 711, 716
  as subject, 712, 936
  third-person, 510, 710, 711, 716
  using, 949
  who, whom, 724-725, 797
Pronunciation
  and dictionaries, 404, 407-409
  as spelling strategy, 926
Proofreading, 29
  description, 29
  model, 30
  for spelling, 909
  symbols, 11
  techniques, 29
  writing process, 29
Proper adjective, 541-542, 816-817, 943, 953
Proper noun, 507-508, 541, 807-815, 941, 953
Public speaking, 435-440. *See also* Speaking.
Publishing, 30-31, 121
  audiovisual, 461
  character analysis, 293
  composition, 121
  creative writing, 194-195
  descriptive writing, 169, 172, 173
  desktop publishing, 449-456
  electronic, 449-463
  exercises, *121, 147, 169, 172, 173, 195, 233, 238, 239, 263, 264, 293, 359*
  expository writing, 233, 238, 239
  graphics, 454-456
  layout, 452-454

options, 30
personal narrative, 147
persuasive writing, 263, 264
research report, 359
for specific audiences, 16
standard manuscript form, 31
story, 194-195
on the Web, 462-463
writer's portfolio, 31-32
Punctuation, 828-905
  with adjectival clauses, 644
  with adverbial clauses, 641
  with adverbial phrases, 605
  apostrophes, 880-889, 956
  colons, 894-896
  commas, 835-852
  with compound sentences, 649, 937
  of direct quotations, 191, 864-865
  end marks, 493-494, 830-834, 868-869
  exclamation points, 493, 569, 830, 841
  exercises, *494, 828-829, 853-855, 858-859, 873-875, 878-888, 901-903*
  hyphens, 897-900
  italics, 201, 291, 860-862
  parentheses, 349, 353
  with participial phrases, 621
  periods, 493, 830, 831-834
  question marks, 493, 830
  quotation marks, 319, 863-872
  semicolons, 93, 567, 669, 890-893, 956
  of titles, 291, 860-864
Purpose, 5, 15, 131
  adjust reading rate to, 367-369
  audiovisual production, 456
  for communicating, 400, 419
  composition, 104-106
  creative writing, 174
  describe, 157, 167
  explain, 219, 220
  express, 15, 131
  inform, 219
  letters, 419-429
  list of, 5, 6, 15

narrative, 131
persuade, 240
reflect, 15, 130
self-expressive, 15
speeches, 436-437
story, 174
style, 38, 117, 142-143
voice, 6, 38
Web site, 462
of writing, 5-6, 15, 38, 124-299
Put, principal parts, 682

Q

Question mark, 493, 830, 868, 954
Questions. *See also* Interrogative sentence; Tests.
  essay tests, 391-399
  5W-How?, 19
  inverted order, 749-750
  inquiring, 19
  punctuation, 493, 830, 868
  research, 311
  standardized tests, 372-390
Quotation marks, 191, 291, 858-877, 955
  and citations, 354-355
  and commas, 191, 867
  credit for, 319
  for dialogue, 191, 870
  for direct quotations, 191, 864-865
  and end marks, 868-869
  and exclamation points, 868
  long passages, 871
  and periods, 191, 868
  and question marks, 868
  for titles, 291, 863-864
  using, 291, 858-877, 955
Quotations
  capitalizing, 866
  direct, 191, 864-869
  and quotation marks, 864-865
  taking notes, 319, 353

Note: Italic locators (page numbers) indicate skill sets

R

Raise, rise, 793
Reaction shot, in video production, 460
Reading comprehension, 380-384, 387
Reading skills
    relationships among details, 5, 162
Real time, defined, 467
Reasoning
    analogy, 375-377
    cause-and-effect, 364
    counter-argument, 252
    critical thinking, 364-366
    developing solutions, 365
    fact, 444
    generalization, 89
    opinion, 249, 444
    sound, 365
Recalling, as prewriting strategy, 134
Reference materials. *See* Information sources.
Reflecting, 130
Reflexive pronouns, 510-511, *942*
Regional dialects, 39
Regular comparison of modifiers, 769
Regular verbs, 680-681, *935*
Relative pronouns, 513-514, 643-644, 654, 794, *942*, *946*
Repetition as sound device, 205, *939*
Request letter, 418, 424-427
Research report, 302-361
    accuracy, 317
    audience, 307, 556
    body, 308, 344, 349
    conclusion, 351
    defined, 302
    drafting, 347-355
    editing, 357-358
    exercises, *313, 314, 320, 321, 323, 325, 327, 328, 330, 332, 334, 335, 346, 360*
    gathering information, 312-339
    introduction, 347
    model, 303, 305, 344, 347, 348, 349, 351, 354
    prewriting, 312-339
    publishing, 359
    quoting and paraphrasing, 319
    research questions, 311
    revising, 356
    sources, 315-317, 353-355
    structure, 308
    subject, choosing and limiting, 309
    taking notes, 318, 319, 333, 342, 343
    title, 352
    visuals, 334, 352
    works cited, 354, 355
Research skills, 311-317, 327-335
Restrictive clause or phrase. *See* Essential clause or phrase.
Revising, 22-28, 119
    adding, 22, 54, 139, 231
    for audience, 22, 142
    checklist, 24, 118, 168, 193, 237, 257, 290, 356
    for focus, clarity, and style, 142, 143
    composition, 118, 119
    through conferencing, 24, 172, 173, 236, 239, 263, 264, 265
    creative writing, 193
    descriptive writing, 172, 173
    essay tests, 397
    expository writing, 225, 231
    literary analysis, 290
    personal narrative, 141
    persuasive writing, 250, 252, 255, 257-258, 263, 264, 265
    research report, 356
    sentences, 71, 76, 78
    specific nouns, 505-506
    specific verbs, 523
    strategies, 22, 141
    for style, 142-143
    for unity, 142-143
    verbs, 488, 491, 523, 701
Rhyme, 205-207, 276
Rhythm, 205
Ride, principal parts, 686
Ring, principal parts, 686
RSS, defined, 455
Rubrics, 23
    expository writing, 232
    fluency, 79
    idea, 108
    interpretive response, 292
    organization, 119
    persuasive writing, 259
    play, 203
    research reports, 358
    six-trait, 23, 146, 167, 195, 232, 259, 292, 358
    stories, 195
    voice, 38
    word choice, 57
Run, principal parts, 686
Run-on sentence, 55, 388, 660, 661, 668-675, 856, *937*, *947*

S

Salutation, in a letter, 420-422, 425-427, 844, 894, *954*
Say, principal parts, 682
Script, 13, 174, 201-203, 457-458
Search engine, defined, 337, 467
See, principal parts, 684
Semicolon, 890-893, *956*
    catch and release, 93, 893, *939*
    combining sentences, 93, 567, 649, 669, 890
    compound sentences, 649, 890
    conjunctive adverb, 567, 669
    exercises, *93, 567, 649-650, 669, 891, 893, 896, 900*
    instead of a comma, 892
    usage, 93
Sensory details, 47-53
    description, 155, 187
    model, 160
    words, 155, 187
    in writing process, 53, 141, 155, 157, 187, 190, 392-393
Sentence, *See also* Run-on sentence; Sentence fragment; Sentence parts.
    beginnings, varying, 73
    capitalization, 804
    combining, 64-72, 93
        with adjective and adverb, 65, 73

Note: Italic locators (page numbers) indicate skill sets

Sentence (continued)
  with *and*, *but*, or *or*, 68, 839
  with prepositional phrases, 73, 841
  with specific details, 64-65
  complement, 580-581, 584-587, 596
  complete, 93, 281, 357, 478, 662-663
  complex, 6, 115, 346, 638, 647, 650-653, 669, 946
  compound, 6, 70-71, 115, 647-650, 653, 890, 946
  concluding, 86, 94-95, 116, 140, 219-220, 231
  correcting, 386-389
  declarative, 493-494, 941
  defined, 478, 940
  diagraming, 495-496, 590-592, 653-654
  end marks, 830, 868-869
  exclamatory, 493-494, 941
  fluency, 6, 64-79, 346, 489
  fragment, 9, 357, 478, 662-663, 674, 826, 856, 936, 940, 946
  imperative, 493-494, 941
  interrogative, 493-494, 745, 749, 941
  inverted order, 487, 489, 749, 950
  kinds of sentences, 86, 493-494, 638, 647-652, 941, 946
  natural order, 487, 489, 749
  patterns, 38, 588-589
  punctuating, 51, 55, 67, 112, 138, 164, 189, 278, 386, 605, 644, 649, 668-669, 828-905
  rambling, 75-76
  run-on, 10, 55, 668-670, 674, 826, 856, 937
  semicolon in, 93, 567, 649, 669, 890-894
  simple, 70, 647, 892, 946
  structure, 64-74, 489, 493, 628, 647-652
  supporting, 86, 91-92, 219
  topic, 86-87, 89-90, 219
  variety, 6, 51, 60-79 346, 939
write in complete, 93, 281, 357, 478, 662

Sentence fragment, 9, 357, 478, 662- 664, 666, 674, 826, 856
  appositive phrase, 67, 607-608, 664, 751, 848
  clause fragment, 666
  correcting, 662, 664, 666, 674, 826, 856
  defined, 478, 662, 674
  exercises, *662-663, 665, 667*
  prepositional phrase, 51, 73, 561-563, 600-606, 664, 718, 748, 841
  subordinate clause fragment, 666-667
  used for emphasis, 357
Sentence parts
  complement, 578-597
  predicate, 481-483, 584-587, 713
  subject, 479-480, 487-492
Sentence style
  concise sentences, 64-65, 75-79
  varying beginnings, 51, 73, 346
  varying length, 75-79, 346
Sequential order, 109, 229, 458
Series of items. *See* Items in a series.
Server, defined, 467
Set, principal parts, 682
Setting
  creating, 187, 200-201
  defined, 182, 276
  as literary element
    of drama, 277
    of fiction, 276
    of a short story, 182
  model, 187
  play, 200-201
  prewriting, 187
  short story, 182
Shall, will, 694, 793
Short story
  beginning, 181
  characters, 181, 182, 185-186
  checklist, 193
  climax, 181, 182
  conflict, 181, 182, 184
  defined, 181
  description, 182, 185
  details, 181, 184, 187

  dialogue, 182, 190-191
  elements of, 181-182
  ending, 181
  events, 188
  fable, 45
  middle, 181
  model, 175-179
  narrator, 182
  outcome, 182
  plot, 181
    building an engaging, 184
    enhancing, 192
  point of view, 182
  resolution, 181
  setting, 182, 187
  structure, 181
  theme, 182
  tone, 182, 187
  triggering event, 182
  writing an outstanding, 183
Sight words, 47
Signature, in a letter, 420, 421, 422, 425, 426
Simile, 207
Simple predicate, 482-483, 940
Simple sentence
  defined, 70, 647, 946
  distinguished from compound sentence, 70, 647-648
  identifying, 647-648
Simple subject, 480, 940
Sing, principal parts, 686
Singular possessive, 880-881
Sit, set, 793
Site map, for Web site, 463
Site, on Internet, 467. *See also* Web site.
Six traits of writing
  conventions, 6
  ideas, 5
  organization, 5
  rubric, 23, 146, 167, 195, 232, 259, 292, 358
  sentence fluency, 6
  voice, 6
  word choice, 6
Slang, 40-41
Social network, on Internet, 12, 467

Note: Italic locators (page numbers) indicate skill sets

Sound devices
  alliteration, 205, 276
  assonance, 205
  consonance, 205
  defined, 276
  onomatopoeia, 205, 276
  repetition, 205
  rhyme, 205
  rhythm, 205
Source credit
  citations, 353
  MLA format, 353, 355
  parenthetical citations, 349-350, 353-354
  visuals, 352
  works cited, 354
Sources
  evaluating, 315-317, 356
  quoting and paraphrasing, 319, 353
Spam
  defined, 468
  netiquette, 472
Spatial order
  arranging details, 5, 109-110, 162
  defined, 109, 162
  model, 162
  transitions, 162
Speak, principal parts, 684
Speaker tag
  capitalization with, 866
  placement of, 191, 864-865
  punctuation with, 191, 864-865, 867-868
Speaking, 432-440. See also Speech preparation.
  delivery strategies, 439
  entertaining message, 436
  group discussions, 434
  informative message, 436
  language strategies, 432, 439
  nonverbal communication, 439
  persuasive message, 436
  speech preparation, 435-439
Speech preparation
  audience, 432, 435, 438
  audiovisual aids, 437, 439
  body, 438
  conclusion, 438
  formal, 435
  gathering information, 437
  giving directions, 433
  ideas, supporting with evidence, elaborations, examples, 437-438
  index cards, gathering information with, 437
  informal, 432
  introduction, 438
  limiting a subject, 104-105, 309, 435
  logical order, 438
  opportunity for, 435
  organizing notes and materials, 437-438
  outline, 438
  practicing strategies, 439
  preparing a speech, 435-439
  presenting, (delivering), 439
  purpose of, 436
  rate of speaking, 439
  selecting a subject, 435
  speaking expressively, 439
  voice, volume, tone, and pitch, 439
Spelling, 906-933
  -cede, -ceed, -sede, 912
  exercises, *910, 912-913, 915, 917, 919-921, 924, 927-928*
  generalizations, 911-913, 932, 957
  homophones, 932
  ie, ei, 911
  -ness, -ly, 922
  patterns, 911-913, 932, 957
  plurals, 914-921, 932, 957
    compound words, 918
    nouns ending in *f* or *fe*, 916-917
    nouns ending in *o*, 915-916
    nouns ending in *y*, 914-915
    numerals, letters, symbols, and words as words, 918
    other, 919-920
    regular nouns, 914
  prefixes, 922-928, 932
  suffixes, 922-928, 932
    doubling the final consonant, 926
    words ending in *e*, 923
    words ending in *y*, 925
  strategies, 908-910
    auditory, 908
    dictionary, 909
    journal, 909
    mnemonic devices, 909, 933
    proofread, 909
    visual/kinesthetic, 908
  words to master, 929
Spine, of a book, 324
SQ3R study method, 368
Standard English, 8, 39, 786
Standard manuscript form, 31
Standardized tests, 372-390
  strategies for taking, 372-390
    analogies, 375-376
    reading comprehension, 380-382
    sentence-completion, 378
    tests of standard written English, 384-387
    vocabulary tests, 373
Steal, principal parts, 684
Stop, principal parts, 681
Story. See Short story.
Storyboard, for audiovisual production, 457
Study skills, 366-371. See also Reading skills.
  close reading, 368
  note-taking, 369, 371
  organizing information visually, 369
  outlining, 369
  reading and understanding, 368
  reading rate, 367-368
  scanning, 367
  skimming, 367
  SQ3R method, 368
  strategies, 367
  summarizing, 369

Note: Italic locators (page numbers) indicate skill sets

Index **1001**

Style, 38
    analyzing, 38
    and reader, 38
    defined, 38
    developing your own, 38
    voice, 38
Style guide. *See* Manual of style.
Subject complement, 578-597
Subject of a composition
    choosing, 104-105,
    focusing, 104
    limiting, 104-105
    agreement with verb, 738-765, 935, 950
    complete, 479, 940
    compound, 490, 941, 950-951
    defined, 479, 940
    diagramed, 495-496
    identifying, 479-480, 487-490
    inverted order, 487, 941
    natural order, 487, 940
    nominative case, 711
    plural, 69
    position in sentence, 487, 940-941
    pronouns used as, 712
    simple, 480, 940
    singular, 69
    understood, 488, 941
    and varying sentence beginnings, 73
Subject-verb agreement. *See* Agreement, subject-verb.
Subordinate clause, 638-646, 650, 666, 669, 842, 945-946
Subordinating conjunction
    identifying, 640, 643
    listed, 641
    as preposition, 640
Suffixes
    defined, 414, 922, 932
    doubling final consonant, 926
    exercises, *414, 924, 927-928*
    list of, 414
    -ness, -ly, 414, 922
    spelling rules for, 922-928, 958-959
    as word parts, 414
    for words ending in *e*, 923
    for words ending in *y*, 925
Summarizing
    defined, 295
    how to, 295, 318
    model, 295, 371
    for note-taking, 318, 369
Summary
    in conclusion, 116, 247
    as note-taking skill, 318, 369
Superlative degree of comparison, 408, 768-773, 776
Supporting information, 342-345
    organization of, 342
Supporting paragraphs, defined, 220, 247
Supporting sentences
    defined, 86, 91
    in descriptive writing, 157-158
    in informative writing, 219
    model, 86-87, 91, 219-220
    and paragraph unity, 86, 91
    in persuasive writing, 254
    writing, 86, 91, 157, 219, 254
Surf, defined, 405, 468
Swim, principal parts, 686
Syllable
    count in poetry, 205, 276
    word division, 408-409, 412, 414, 769-770, 909, 926
Symbols
    accent marks, 409
    diacritical marks, 409
    graphic, 456
    phonetic, 409
    for revising and proofreading, 11, 30
    visual, 456
Synonyms
    defined, 46, 373, 405, 410, 415
    in dictionaries, 334, 405, 415
    and meaning of a word, 46, 410, 415
    recognizing, 374
    reference books, 46, 334, 405, 415
    in thesaurus, 46
Syntax. *See* Clause; Complement; Phrase; Predicate; Sentence; Subject of a sentence.
Synthesize, 341

T

Table of contents, as research tool, 315, 328, 367
Take, bring, 689
Take, principal parts, 684
Taking notes. *See* Note-taking.
Talk, principal parts, 681
Teach, learn, 690
Teach, principal parts, 682, 690
Technical terms, 814
Technology
    creating texts, 449-456
    editing texts, 450
    revising texts, 449
Ten Tools for Powerful Writing, 938-939
Tense, 693-707
    defined, 693
    emphatic form, 702
    exercises, *697, 699-705*
    future, 694
    future perfect, 694
    past, 693-694
    past perfect, 694
    present, 693
    present perfect, 694
    progressive form, 700
    shifts in, 698
Testimonial, 445
Tests
    analogy questions, 375-377
    error-recognition questions, 384-385
    essay questions, 391-399
    multiple-choice questions, 373-390
    reading, 380-384
    revision-in-context, 387-388
    sentence-completion questions, 386-387
    standard written English, 384-386
    standardized, 372-390
    strategies for, 372-373

Note: Italic locators (page numbers) indicate skill sets

Tests (continued)
    vocabulary, 373
That there, this here, 796
That, which, who, 794
Their, there, they're, 795
Theirs, there's, 795
Them, those, 796
Theme, as literary element, 182
Thesaurus
    defined, 46
    online, *46*, 335
    print, 46, 335
Thesis statement
    and conclusion, 231, 273
    defined, 281
    developed in body, 223, 281
    drafting, 262
    in essay test, 395
    exercises, *223, 225, 231, 281, 288, 348*
    expository essay, 223,
    in introduction, 247, 273
    and limited topic, 280, 281
    in literary analysis, 273, 281
    and main idea, 286, 395
    model, 247, 280, 281, 286, 287, 303, 344, 348, 396
Think Critically
    Analyzing, 226
    Classifying, 343
    Elaborating, 54
    Evaluating Counter-Arguments, 253
    Generalizing, 89
    Imagining, 186
    Ordering, 110
    Recalling, 134
    Seeing Relationships, 72
    Summarizing, 295
    Visualizing, 161
Third-person point of view, 132
Throw, principal parts, 684
Time order. *See* Chronological order.
Tired words, defined, 56
Title page, as research tool, 328
Titles
    capital letters, 817-822, 953
    of composition or story, 273, 308

writing, 116
italics (underlining), 291, 860-861, 955
quotation marks, 291, 863, 955
To, too, two, 796
Tone
    humorous, 100, 174, 209
    identifying, 241, 383-384
    introduction, 182
    as literary element, 182
    model, 127, 175
    personal writing, 127
    in short story, 187
Topic. *See* Subject of a composition.
Topic sentence
    defined, 87
    in descriptive writing, 158
    drafting, 114
    location of, 88
    model, 86-87, 113, 219-220, 254
    in narrative writing, 135-136
    in persuasive writing, 254, 257
Tracking, in video production, 459
Transitional words
    list of, 137, 229, 254
    and logical order, 165
    and order of importance, 227, 254-255
    and paragraph coherence, 137, 162, 254-255
    and spatial order, 162
    showing contrast, 72, 254
    showing relationship, 162-163, 568, 944
    and time order, 137
Transitive verb, 524-525, 942
Treatment for audiovisual production, 456-457
Triggering event, in plot, 182
Type fonts, 233, 450-452

U

Underlining (italics). *See* Italics (underlining).
Understood subject, 488-489, 495
Unity, *See also* Focus.
    checklist, 142

defined, 142
revising for, 142-143
Upload, defined, 468
URL, 316, 355, 462, 465, 468
Usage. *See also* Agreement, pronoun-antecedent; Agreement, subject-verb; Modifiers; Pronoun; Verb.
    glossary of similar words, 786-799
Usage QuickGuide, 948-952
Use to, used to, 796

V

Variety in sentences
    varying sentence beginnings, 73
    varying sentence length, 60, 64, 79, 346
    varying sentence structure, 346, 650
Verb, 520-535, 678-707, 738-765
    action, 482, 522-524, 529, 581, 716, 942
    agreement with subject, 9, 69, 534, 738-765
    auxiliary, 484, 526-527, 534, 942
    common helping, 484, 526
    common linking, 528, 584
    complete predicate, 481-483
    compound, 68, 491, 840, 941
    conjugation, 694-697
    defined, 504, 522, 534
    diagramed, 495-496, 590-592, 609-610, 653-654
    emphatic form, 702, 949
    exercises, *523, 525, 527-530, 681, 683-692, 697, 700-702*
    helping, 484, 526-527, 534, 942
    identifying, 520-535, 678-702,
    intransitive, 524, 534, 942
    irregular, 8, 194, 238, 682-688, 706, 948
    linking, 528-530, 534-535, 540, 580, 584, 713, 943
    number, 740-742, 764
    position in sentence, 487, 749-751

Note: Italic locators (page numbers) indicate skill sets

Verb (continued)
  principal parts, 408, 680-692, 706, 948
    irregular verb, 682-688, 706, 948
    regular verb, 680-681, 706, 948
  problem verbs, 689-692
  progressive form, 700-701
  regular, 8, 194, 238, 680-681, 706
  review, 570-572
  simple predicate, 482
  specific, 35, 44, 224, 523
  state-of-being, 534
  strong verbs, 224, 938
  suffixes, 414
  tense, 9, 169, 194, 238, 693-701, 706, 936, 938, 948-949. *See also* Tense.
  transitive, 524, 534, 942
  types of, 520-535
  use appropriately, 9, 69, 487, 534, 738-760, 764, 948-949
  use consistently, 9, 169
  used as adjective, 570
  verb phrase, 484-485, 526, 745-746, 942
  vivid, 35, 44, 224, 523, 865
Verb phrase
  defined, 484, 526, 745
  identifying, 484-485, 745
  order, 484-485, 526, 745
  in questions, 485, 526
  using, 484-485, 526, 745
Verb tense
  consistent, 9, 169
  future, 693-696
  future perfect, 693-696
  future perfect progressive, 700
  future progressive, 700
  inconsistent, 9, 169
  irregular verb, 194, 238
  past, 8, 194, 238, 693, 696, 741
  past emphatic, 702
  past perfect, 693-696
  past perfect progressive, 700
  past progressive, 700
  present, 693, 695-696, 741
  present emphatic, 702

  present perfect, 693-696
  present perfect progressive, 700
  present progressive, 700
  principal parts, 408, 680-692
  progressive form, 700-701
  regular verb, 194, 238
  shifts in, 294, 698-699
  uses of, 693-694
Verb-subject agreement. *See* Agreement, subject-verb.
Verbal phrase, 621-627, 945
  and combining sentences, 622
  and comma, 621
  defined, 618
  identifying, 621, 624, 626-627
  infinitive phrase, 627, 945
  participial phrase, 621-625, 945
Verbals, 616-635, 945
  defined, 618
  infinitive, 626, 945
  participle, 618-620, 945
  parallelism, 628, 945
Vertical file, 335
Video files, on Web site, 462
Video production, 456-461
  assemble editing, 461
  background music, 461
  camera techniques, 458-460
  computer editing, 461
  cutaway shot, 460
  dissolve, 461
  editing, 461
  establishing shot, 460
  fade, 461
  final cut, 461
  in-camera editing, 461
  insert editing, 461
  panning, 459
  post-production, 461
  production, 458-460
  reaction shot, 460
  schedule, 458
  special effects, 460
  tracking, 569
  voiceover narration, 461
  zooming, 459
Viewing. *See* Listening and viewing.

Visual representations
  charts, 121, 221, 328, 333, 352, 368, 454-455
  creating a project, 359, 435-438
  presenting a project, 439, 462-463
  using a variety of forms, 359
  using a variety of technologies, 359
Visualizing, 161
Visuals
  assess how medium of contributes to meaning, 314, 352, 437,
  assess how presentation of contributes to meaning, 352
  evaluate meaning, purposes, effects, 352
  produce to complement and extend meaning, 314, 352
Vocabulary, 39, 373-374, 402-417. *See also* Word parts.
  American dialects, 39, 786
  analogies, 375-377
  antonyms, 373, 416
  base words, 412-414
  borrowed words, 403
  colloquialisms, 40, 57
  compound words, 403, 405, 918
  connotations, 42, 57
  context, 387-390, 410-412
  context clues, 411-412
  denotations, 42
  dialects, identifying, 39, 786
  exact words, importance of, 191, 353, 863-864
  expanding, 411-417
  growth of English language, 402-405
  informal language, 41, 478
  meaning, from context, 387-390, 410-412
  news story, 74
  nonstandard American English, 40, 786
  prefixes, 412-413, 922

  slang, 40, 478, 786
  standard American English, 39, 786
  suffixes, 414, 922-928

Note: Italic locators (page numbers) indicate skill sets

synonyms, 46, 373, 405, 410, 415-416
tests, 373-374
thesaurus, 46
thinking practice, 54, 72, 89, 134, 343
tired words, 56-57
word origins, 402-404, 407, 410
words from names, 403-404

Voice
analyzing, 38
developing your writing voice, 6, 38, 132
identifying, 6
narrative, 132, 146
purpose, 6, 38
use of, 6, 38, 132, 440
volume, tone, and pitch, 38, 200, 440, 804, 834

W

Wasn't, weren't, 747
Wear, principal parts, 686
Web 2.0, defined, 468
Web site. *See also* Internet; World Wide Web.
blogs, 463
drag and drop, 463
HyperText Markup Language (HTML), 463, 467
Internet terminology, 466-468
link, 467
navigation, 463
planning, 462
site map, 463
software, 463
WYSIWYG, 463
Who, whom, 724-725, 797
Who's, whose, 724-725, 797
Wiki, defined, 468
Word origins, 407
Word parts. *See also* Vocabulary.
prefixes, 412, 922
suffixes, 414, 922
Word-processing tools, in writing process, 449, 450, 452. *See also* Computers.

Wordiness, 28
Words. *See also* Prefixes; Suffixes; Vocabulary.
meaning, 411-417
often confused, 689-692
sensory, 47-53, 159-161
specific, 44-45
tired, 56
vivid, 34, 42-55
vocabulary, 402-417
Workplace skills
addressing an envelope, 424-427
business letters, 424-429
completing business forms, 430-431
group discussions, 434-435
making speeches, 432, 435-440
Works cited, 353-355
World Wide Web. *See also* Internet.
browser, 466
defined, 468
graphics, 462
hyperlink, 467
HyperText Markup Language (HTML), 463, 467
HyperText Transfer Protocol (http), 465, 467
Internet Service Provider (ISP), 464-467
publishing, 462-463
for research, 337-339
search engine, 467
terminology, 466-468
Uniform Research Locator (URL), 468
World Wide Web research, 337-339
bookmark, 339, 466
search engine, 467
Write, principal parts, 686
Writer's Corner, 500-501, 518-519, 534-535, 556-557, 576-577, 596-597, 614-615, 634-635, 658-659, 674-675, 706-707, 736-737, 764-765, 784-785, 826-827, 856-857, 876-877, 904-905, 932-933
Writing across the curriculum
business, 424-431
about literature, 266-296

Writing forms
business communication, 424-431
creative, 174-209
descriptive, 150-173
expository, 210-239
literary, 266-297
literary analysis, 266, 273-274
narrative, 126-149
personal, 126-149
persuasive, 240-265
plays, 196-203
poetry, 204-209
public speaking and presentation, 435-440
research reports, 302-339
short stories, 181-195
Writing Labs, 58, 80, 98, 122, 148, 170, 208, 234, 260, 298, 320, 360
Writing process, 13-33. *See also* Audience; Drafting; Editing; Prewriting; Proofreading; Publishing; Revising.
analyzing, 129
audience, 15-16, 18, 104-105, 131
checklist, 28-29, 118, 130, 142, 168, 193, 237, 257, 290, 356
descriptive, 150-173
developing style, 38
drafting, 21, 113-116, 135-140, 190-192, 347-355
editing, 28-30, 120, 145, 291, 357
expository, 210-239
gathering information, 282-284, 312-317
literary analysis, 266, 273-274
narrative, 126-149
occasion, 15
organizing ideas, 20, 109
outlining, 344
personal writing, 126-149
persuasive, 240-265
play, 196-203
poetry, 204-209
prewriting, 13-16, 18-20
proofreading, 11, 29
publishing, 28-31, 121, 147
purpose, 5, 6, 15

Note: Italic locators (page numbers) indicate skill sets

Writing process (continued)
    research reports, 302-339
    revising, 22-27
    short story, 181-195
    stages, 13-32
    technology, 447-448
    voice, 6, 38,
Writing projects
    Biographical Sketch
        Lives Worth Remembering, 100
    Description
        The Comfort of the Ordinary, 150
    Expository
        Welcome to My World, 210
    Imaginative
        The Way I See It, 34
    Imaginative Story
        Wishes Denied, 174
    Interpretive Response
        Character Analysis, 266
    Memoir
        Powerful Memories, 82
    Personal Narrative
        Facing Fear, 60
        Small Acts, 126
    Persuasive
        Words into Deeds, 240
    Research Report
        Don't Let Me Be Misunderstood, 302, 340
WWW, defined, 465, 468

You as understood subject, 488, 495
Your, you're, 797

Zooming, in video production, 459

Note: *Italic locators (page numbers) indicate skill sets*

Image Credits

Art Resource: p458 © The Museum of Modern Art/ Licensed by SCALA / Art Resource, NY; p506 © The Metropolitan Museum of Art / Art Resource, NY; p544 © Albright-Knox Art Gallery / Art Resource, NY; Bridgeman Art: p522 © Boltin Picture Library © Henry Moore Foundation / The Bridgeman Art Library; p734   View of the Pond at Charleston, c. 1919 (oil on canvas), Bell, Vanessa (1879-1961) / Sheffield Galleries and Museums Trust, UK / © Museums Sheffield / The Bridgeman Art Library; Corbis: p115 © Kennan Ward / Corbis; p602 © Pierre Vauthey / CORBIS SYGMA, p654 © Eadweard Muybridge / CORBIS; p672 © Ali Meyer / CORBIS; p762 © The Gallery Collection / Corbis; p796 © PHILIPPE WOJAZER / Reuters / Corbis; Dreamstime: pp. 3, 16, 28, 32, 34, 41,72, 77, 80, 96, 106, 109, 127, 137, 142, 158, 161, 164, 176, 180, 188, 196, 197, 198, 201, 202, 207, 213, 214, 217, 224, 230, 244, 271, 274, 276, 284, 287, 295, 296, 301, 317, 326, 331, 339, 359, 372, 382, 384, 389, 397, 413, 424, 450, 457, 543, 551, 569, 570, 608, 659, 671, 677, 678, 679, 680, 737, 761, 767, 776, 795, 819, 823, 834, 851, 866, 870, 876, 917, 929, 955, 962; Fotolia: p70; Fotosearch Stock Photo: p486; Getty: p104 © Frank Micelotta / Getty Images Entertainment / Getty Images for Fox; iStockphoto: pp. 21, 25, 26, 42, 50, 59, 62, 71, 89, 103, 116, 128, 131, 135, 138, 146, 149, 169, 214, 221, 222, 224, 233, 256, 322, 324, 336, 392, 491, 534, 554, 559, 562, 567, 588, 611, 622, 627, 641, 650, 653, 684, 697, 714, 719, 722, 726, 745, 756, 865, 895, 897, 899, 900, 932, 943; Jupiter Images: pp. 4, 7, 46, 56, 64, 91, 94, 179, 185, 188, 223, 279, 390, 430, 442, 482, 505, 564, 581, 601, 646, 686, 728, 769, 951; Library of Congress: pp.366, 492, 852; MC Escher: p628 All M.C. Escher works © Cordon Art B.V., Baarn Holland. All rights reserved.; National Gallery of Art: p582 The Tragedy, Pablo Picasso, 1963, courtesy of the Board of Trustees, National Gallery of Art, Washington DC; p704 Matisse, Heri, Pianist and Checker Players, National Gallery of Art; NOAA: p191; The Philips Collection: p560 Pippin, Horace, Domino Players, 1943, Oil on composition board, The Phillips Collection, Washington, DC; Time: pp.192-193 © Time 1999; VAGA: p910 Janet Fish. Yellow Pad, 1997. Oil on canvas, 36 by 50 inches. The Columbus Museum, Columbus, GA. © Janet Fish / Licensed by VAGA, New York, NY.; Wikipedia Commons: p820 Elizabeth Catlett

pages 212–217

Graphics by Linda Scott/AA-S

Photos by Tom Lankes, Deborah Cannon/AA-S

Topographic map by UT Bureau of Economic Geology

Sources: UT Bureau of Economic Geology, Geological Society of America Bulletin, Down to Earth at McKinney Falls State Park, Texas, Oxford Planet Earth, Rand McNally Picture Atlas of Prehistoric Life

Every reasonable effort has been made to contact all copyright holders. If we have omitted anyone, please let us know and we will include a suitable acknowledgement in subsequent editions.

Text Credits

Excerpt from THE DANCERS by Horton Foote. Reprinted by permission of International Creative Management, Inc. Copyright © 1955, 1983 by Horton Foote.

Excerpt from EVERY LIVING THING by Cynthia Rylant. Reprinted with the permission of Atheneum Books for Young Readers, an imprint of Simon & Schuster Children's Publishing Division. Text copyright © 1985 Cynthia Rylant.

Excerpt from HATCHET by Gary Paulsen. Reprinted with the permission of Atheneum Books for Young Readers, an imprint of Simon & Schuster Children's Publishing Division. Copyright © 1987 by Gary Paulsen.

Excerpt from JULIE OF THE WOLVES by Jean Craighead George. Copyright © 1972 by Jean Craighead George. Used by permission of HarperCollins Publishers.

LEARNING ENGLISH: MY NEW FOUND LAND by Julia Alvarez. Copyright © 1993 by Julia Alvarez. Published in Newsday, February 1993. By permission of Susan Bergholz Literary Services, New York, NY and Lamy, NM. All rights reserved.

"The Siren Who Won Anthony and Caesar: Cleopatra" from ILLUSTRATED MINUTE BIOGRAPHIES by William A. DeWitt, copyright © 1949, 1953 renewed © 1977 by Samuel Nisenson, renewed © 1981 by Rebecca Nisenson. Used by permission of Grosset & Dunlap, a Division of Penguin Young Readers Group, a Member of Penguin Group (USA) Inc., 345 Hudson Street, New York, NY 10014. All rights reserved.

Excerpt from SPEAKING OF JOURNALS by Paula W. Graham. Copyright © 1999 by Paula W. Graham. Published by Boyds Mills Press. Reprinted with permission.